Legal Foundations of Environmental Planning

Legal Foundations of Environmental Planning

Textbook–Casebook and Materials on Environmental Law

Volume I

Written and Edited by

Jerome G. Rose

Center for Urban Policy Research
Rutgers, The State University of New Jersey

About the Author

Jerome G. Rose has a J.D. degree from Harvard Law School and is a member of the New York Bar. He is Professor of Urban Planning, School of Urban and Regional Policy, Rutgers University and Editor-in-Chief, *Real Estate Law Journal.* He is author of *The Legal Advisor on Home Ownership* (1967); *Landlords and Tenants: A Complete Guide to the Residential Rental Relationship* (1973); *New Approaches to State Land Use Policies*, with Melvin R. Levin and Joseph S. Slavett (1974); *The Transfer of Development Rights* (1977); *After Mount Laurel: The New Suburban Zoning*, with Robert E. Rothman (1977); *Legal Foundations of Land Use Planning* (1979); and *Tax and Expenditure Limitations* (1982).

Published in the United States by the
Center for Urban Policy Research
New Brunswick, New Jersey

Library of Congress Cataloging in Publication Data

Rose, Jerome G.
Legal foundations of environmental planning.

Includes index.
1. Environmental law—United States—Cases.
I. Title.
KF3775.A7R67 1983 344.731046 82.23533
ISBN 0-88285-090-3 (v. 1) 347.30446

This book is dedicated to my children:

Patty, Ellie, Teddy and *Luther*

and to everyone's children:

Who Will Live in the Environment We Leave to Them

Acknowledgments

This book was written with the assistance of many students. The material was collected over a period of years during which many students, in several seminars, and several research assistants proposed, edited and analyzed the cases and other material to find the right combination to explain and illustrate the environmental and legal concepts involved. The students came from the Rutgers Department of Urban Planning, the Rutgers School of Law and the Syracuse University School of Law. Among the students who were especially helpful are (in alphabetical order) Carole W. Baker, Christine Brothers, Darrell L. Bowen, Virginia Calvert, Nathan Edelstein, David L. Evans, Alan Fintz, Susan Kaplan, Jerrold Malkin and John McDonnell.

Vera Lee, the extraordinary secretary–administrator of the Rutgers Department of Urban Planning, managed to find time among her many other duties to type and retype the manuscript with her usual good cheer and constructive suggestions. Judith Hancock prepared the index. Barry Jones edited the material and skillfully guided the work through the publishing process.

I am especially grateful to Dr. George Sternlieb, Director of the Center for Urban Policy Research, Rutgers University, who encouraged me to undertake this work and made it possible by making available to me the talent and resources of the Center.

J.G.R.

Contents

Part Two — AIR POLLUTION

Part Three — WATER POLLUTION

Part Four — CONTROL OF POPULATION GROWTH AND DISTRIBUTION

Table of Cases

A Glossary of Environmental Terms

New Jersey Department of Environmental Protection

Biodegradable. Eutrophication. Biosphere. Ambient air. Food chain. Symbiosis. Heat Island effect. Phytotoxic.

Those are typical of words which have crept into everyday language recently because of growing public concern about environmental problems.

The problems are complicated enough without the extra burden of having them come equipped with a strange new environmental vocabulary.

The New Jersey Department of Environmental Protection believes that greater understanding of environmental problems will hasten their solutions. But first must come understanding of the words describing the problems.

The glossary of environmental words and terms is a step toward that goal. Most definitions have been extracted from "Common Environmental Terms," a booklet published by the U.S. Environmental Protection Agency. The following list is not intended as a substitute for a dictionary. In fact, some of the word usages it contains can be classified as slang. But it should help the interested layman or environmental commissioner to better understand words and references pertaining to environmental conditions.

A

ABATEMENT: The method of reducing the degree or intensity of pollution, also the use of such a method.

ABSORPTION: The penetration of a substance into or through another. For example, in air pollution control, absorption is the dissolving of a soluble gas, present in an emission, in a liquid which can be extracted.

ACCELERATOR: In radiology, a device for imparting high velocity to charged particles such as electrons or protons. These fast particles can penetrate matter and are known as radiation.

ACCLIMATION: The physiological and behavioral adjustments of an organism to changes in its immediate environment.

ACCLIMATIZATION: The acclimation or adaptation of a particular species over several generations to a marked change in the environment.

ACTIVATED CARBON: A highly absorbent form of carbon, used to remove odors and toxic substances from gaseous emissions. In advanced waste treatment, activated carbon is used to remove dissolved organic matter from waste water.

ACTIVATED SLUDGE: Sludge that has been aerated and subjected to bacterial action, used to remove organic matter from sewage.

ACTIVATED SLUDGE PROCESS: The process of using biologically active sewage sludge to hasten breakdown of organic matter in raw sewage during secondary waste treatment.

ACUTE TOXICITY: Any poisonous effect produced within a short period of time, usually up to 24–96 hours, resulting in severe biological harm and often death.

ADAPTATION: A change in structure or habit of an organism that produces better adjustment to the environment.

ADSORPTION: The adhesion of a substance to the surface of a solid or liquid. Adsorption is often used to extract pollutants by causing them to be attached to such adsorbents as activated carbon or silica gel. Hydrophobic, or water-repulsing adsorbents, are used to extract oil from waterways in oil spills.

ADULTERANTS: Chemicals or substances that by law do not belong in a food, plant, animal or pesticide formulation. Adulterated products are subject to seizure by the Food and Drug Administration.

ADVANCED WASTE TREATMENT: Waste water treatment beyond the secondary or biological stage that includes removal of nutrients such as phosphorus and nitrogen and a high percentage of suspended solids. Advanced waste treatment, known as tertiary treatment, is the "polishing stage" of waste water treatment and produces a high quality effluent.

AERATION: The process of being supplied or impregnated with air. Aeration is used in waste water treatment to foster biological and chemical purification.

AEROBIC: This refers to life or processes that can occur only in the presence of oxygen.

AEROSOL: A suspension of liquid or solid particles in the air.

AFTERBURNER: An air pollution abatement device that removes undesirable organic gases through incineration.

AGRICULTURAL POLLUTION: The liquid and solid wastes from all types of farming, including runoff from pesticides, fertilizers and feedlots; erosion and dust from plowing, animal manure and carcasses and crop residues and debris. It has been estimated that agricultural pollution in the U.S. has amounted to more than 2½ billion tons per year.

AIR: A mixture of gases. Contains about 78 per cent nitrogen, 21 per cent oxygen, less than 1 per cent of carbon dioxide, argon and other gases, and varying amounts of water vapor.

AIR CURTAIN: A method for mechanical containment of oil spills. Air is bubbled through a perforated pipe causing an upward water flow that retards the spreading of oil. Air curtains are also used as barriers to prevent fish from entering a polluted body of water.

AIR MASS: A widespread body of air with properties that were established while the air was situated over a particular region of the earth's surface and that undergoes specific modifications while in transit away from that region.

AIR MONITORING: See monitoring.

AIR POLLUTION: The presence of contaminants in the air in concentrations that prevent the normal dispersive ability of the air and that interfere directly or indirectly with man's health, safety or comfort or with the full use and enjoyment of his property.

AIR POLLUTION EPISODE: The occurrence of abnormally high concentrations of air pollutants usually due to low winds and temperature inversion and accompanied by an increase in illness and death. See inversion.

AIR QUALITY CONTROL REGION: An area designated by the Federal government where two or more communities—either in the same or different states—share a common air pollution problem.

AIR QUALITY CRITERIA: The levels of pollution and lengths of exposure at which adverse effects on health and welfare occur.

AIR QUALITY STANDARDS: The prescribed level of pollutants in the outside air that cannot be exceeded legally during a specified time in a specified geographical area.

AIRSHED: The air overlying any arbitrary geographical region, frequently lumping together adjacent cities or areas which share intermixed air pollution problems.

ALGAL BLOOM: A proliferation of living algae on the surface of lakes, streams or ponds. Algal blooms are stimulated by phosphate enrichment.

ALPHA PARTICLE: A positively charged particle emitted by certain radioactive materials. It is the least penetrating of the three common types of radiation (alpha, beta and gamma) and usually not dangerous to plants, animals or man.

AMBIENT AIR: Any unconfined portion of the atmosphere: the outside air.

ANADROMOUS: Type of fish that ascend rivers from the sea to spawn.

ANAEROBIC: Refers to life or processes that occur in the absence of oxygen.

ANTICOAGULANT: A chemical that interferes with blood clotting, often used as a rodenticide.

ANTI-DEGRADATION CLAUSE: A provision in air quality and water quality laws that prohibits deterioration of air or water quality in areas where the pollution levels are presently below those allowed.

AQUIFER: An underground bed or stratum of earth, gravel or porous stone that contains water.

AQUATIC PLANTS: Plants that grow in water either floating on the surface, growing up from the bottom of the body of water or growing under the surface of the water.

AREA SOURCE: In air pollution, any small individual fuel combustion source, including any transportation sources. This is a general definition; area source is legally and precisely defined in Federal regulations. See point source.

ASBESTOS: A mineral fiber with countless industrial uses; a hazardous air pollutant when inhaled.

A-SCALE SOUND LEVEL: The measurement of sound approximating the auditory sensitivity of the human ear. The A-Scale sound level is used to measure the relative noisiness or annoyance of common sounds.

ASSIMILATION: Conversion or incorporation of absorbed nutrients into protoplasm. Also refers to the ability of a body of water to purify itself of organic pollution.

ATMOSPHERE: The layer of air surrounding the earth.

ATOMIC PILE: A nuclear reactor.

ATTRACTANT: A chemical or agent that lures insects or other pests by olfactory stimulation.

ATTRITION: Wearing or grinding down by friction. One of three basic contributing processes of air pollution, the others are vaporization and combustion.

AUDIOMETER: An instrument for measuring hearing sensitivity.

AUTOTROPHIC: Self-nourishing; denoting those oganisms capable of constructing organic matter from inorganic substances.

B

BACKFILL: The material used to refill a ditch or other excavation, or the process of doing so.

BACKGROUND LEVEL: With respect to air pollution, amounts of pollutants present in the ambient air due to natural sources.

BACKGROUND RADIATION: Normal radiation present in the lower atmosphere from cosmic rays and from earth sources.

BACTERIA: Single-celled microorganisms that lack chlorophyll. Some bacteria are capable of causing human, animal or plant diseases, others are essential in pollution control because they break down organic matter in the air and in the water.

BAFFLE: Any deflector device used to change the direction of flow or the velocity of water, sewage or products of combustion such as fly ash or coarse particulate matter. Also used in deadening sound.

BAGHOUSE: An air pollution abatement device used to trap particulates by filtering gas streams through large fabric bags, usually made of glass fibers.

BALING: A means of reducing the volume of solid waste by compaction.

BALLISTIC SEPARATOR: A machine that separates inorganic from organic matter in a composting process.

BAND APPLICATION: With respect to pesticides, the application of the chemical over or next to each row of plants in a field.

BAR SCREEN: In waste water treatment, a screen that removes large floating and suspended solids.

BASAL APPLICATION: With respect to pesticides, the application of the pesticide formulation on stems or trunks of plants just above the soil line.

BASIN: See river basin.

BENTHIC REGION: The bottom of a body of water. This region supports the benthos, a type of life that not only lives upon, but contributes to the character of the bottom.

BENTHOS: The plant and animal life whose habitat is the bottom of a sea, lake or river.

BERYLLIUM: A metal that when airborne has adverse effects on human health; it has been declared a hazardous air pollutant. It is primarily discharged by operations such as machine shops, ceramic and propellant plants and foundries.

BETA PARTICLE: An elementary particle emitted by radioactive decay that may cause skin burns. It is easily stopped by a thin sheet of metal.

BIOASSAY: The employment of living organisms to determine the biological effect of some substance, factor or condition.

BIOCHEMICAL OXYGEN DEMAND (BOD): A measure of the amount of oxygen consumed in the biological processes that break down organic matter in water. Large amounts of organic waste use up large amounts of dissolved oxygen, thus the greater the degree of pollution, the greater the BOD.

BIODEGRADABLE: The process of decomposing quickly as a result of the action of microorganisms.

BIOLOGICAL CONTROL: A method of controlling pests by means of introduced or naturally occurring predatory organsims, sterilization or the use of inhibiting hormones, etc., rather than by mechanical or chemical means.

BIOLOGICAL MAGNIFICATION: a process through which an organism can concentrate within itself vastly greater amounts of a substance than is found in its environment. Oysters or clams, for instance, can draw DDT or organic mercury from water along with their usual nutrients, and concentrate them in their bodies. Also, when a larger species of fish, bird or animal devours smaller organisms which contain such concentrations, the larger species builds up a much higher concentration than in any of the smaller ones which it ate.

BIOLOGICAL OXIDATION: The process by which bacterial and other microorganisms feed on complex organic materials and decompose them. Self-purification of waterways and activated sludge and trickling filter waste water treatment processes depend on this principle. The process is also called biochemical oxidation.

BIOMONITORING: The use of living organisms to test the suitability of effluent for discharge into receiving waters and to test the quality of such waters downstream from a discharge.

BIOSPHERE: The total environment of our planet; atmosphere, land and water in which man and all other organisms live. The ecosphere.

BIOSTABILIZER: A machine used to convert solid waste into compost by grinding and aeration.

BIOTA: All the species of plants and animals occuring within a certain area.

BLOOM: A proliferation of living algae and/or other aquatic plants on the surface of lakes or ponds. Blooms are frequently stimulated by phosphate enrichment.

BOD_5: The amount of dissolved oxygen consumed in five days by biological processes breaking down organic matter in an effluent. See biochemical oxygen demand.

BOG: Wet, spongy land usually poorly drained, highly acid and rich in plant residue.

BOOM: A floating device that is used to contain oil on a body of water.

BOTANICAL PESTICIDE: A plant-produced chemical used to control pests; for example, nicotine, strychnine or pyrethrum.

BRACKISH WATER: A mixture of fresh and salt water.

BREEDER: A nuclear reactor that produces more fuel than it consumes.

BTU: "British thermal unit." The amount of heat required to raise the temperature of one pound of water one degree fahrenheit at its point of maximum density.

BROADCAST APPLICATION: With respect to pesticides, the application of a chemical over an entire field, lawn or other area.

BURIAL GROUND (GRAVEYARD): A place for burying unwanted radioactive material to prevent radiation escape, the earth or water acting as a shield. Such materials must be placed in watertight, noncorrodible containers so the radioactive material cannot leach out and invade underground water supplies.

C

CADMIUM: See heavy metals.

CARBON DIOXIDE (CO_2): A colorless, odorless, nonpoisonous gas that is a normal part of the ambient air. CO_2 is a product of fossil fuel combustion, and some researchers have theorized that excess CO_2 raises atmospheric temperatures.

CARBON MONOXIDE (CO): A colorless, odorless, highly toxic gas that is a normal byproduct of incomplete fossil fuel combustion. CO, one of the major air pollutants, can be harmful in small amounts if breathed over a certain period of time.

CARCINOGENIC: Cancer producing.

CATALYTIC CONVERTER: An air pollution abatement device that removes organic contaminants by oxidizing them into carbon dioxide and water through chemical reaction. Can be used to reduce nitrogen oxide emissions from motor vehicles.

CAUSTIC SODA: Sodium hydroxide (NaOH), a strongly alkaline, caustic substance used as the cleaning agent in some detergents.

CELLS: With respect to solid waste disposal, earthen compartments in which solid wastes are dumped, compacted and covered over daily with layers of earth.

CENTRIFUGAL COLLECTOR: Any of several mechnical systems using centrifugal force to remove aerosols from a gas stream.

CFS: Cubic feet per second, a measure of the amount of water passing a given point.

CHANNELIZATION: The straightening and deepening of streams to permit water to move faster, to reduce flooding or to drain marshy acreage for farming. However, channelization reduces the organic waste assimilation capacity of the stream and may disturb fish breeding and destroy the stream's natural beauty, flood retention capability and ability to recharge aquifers.

CHEMICAL OXYGEN DEMAND (COD): A measure of the amount of oxygen required to oxidize organic and oxidizable inorganic compounds in water. The COD test, like the BOD test, is used to determine the degree of pollution in an effluent.

CHEMOSTERILANT: A pesticide chemical that controls pests by destroying their ability to reproduce.

CHILLING EFFECT: The lowering of the earth's temperature due to the increase of atmospheric particulates that inhibit penetration of the sun's energy.

CHLORINATED HYRODCARBONS: A class of generally long-lasting, broad-spectrum insecticides of which the best known is DDT, first used for insect control during World War II. Other similar compounds include aldrin, dieldrin, heptachlor, chlordane, lindane, endrin, mirex, benzene hexachloride (BHC), and toxaphene. The qualities of persistence and effectivess against a wide variety of insect pests were long regarded as highly desirable in agriculture, public health and home uses. But later research has revealed that these same qualities may represent a potential hazard through accumulation in the food chain and persistence in the environment.

CHLORINATION: The application of chlorine to drinking water, sewage or industrial waste for disinfection or oxidation of undesirable compounds.

CHLORINATOR: A device for adding a chlorine-containing gas or liquid to drinking or waste water.

CHLORINE-CONTACT CHAMBER: In a waste treatment plant, a chamber in which effluent is disinfected by chlorine before it is discharged to the receiving waters.

CHLOROSIS: Yellowing or whitening of normally green plant parts. It can be caused by disease organisms, lack of oxygen or nutrients in the soil or by various air pollutants.

CHROMIUM: See heavy metals.

CHRONIC: Marked by long duration or frequent recurrence, as a disease.

CLARIFICATION: In waste water treatment, the removal of turbidity and suspended solids by settling, often aided by centrifugal action and chemically induced coagulation.

CLARIFIER: In waste water treatment, a settling tank which mechanically removes settleable solids from wastes.

CLUSTER: A design technique which permits the grouping of structures into clusters while permitting remaining areas to be preserved in their natural state.

COAGULATION: The clumping of particles in order to settle out impurities; often induced by chemicals such as lime or alum.

COASTAL ZONE: Coastal waters and adjacent lands that exert a measurable influence on the uses of the sea and its ecology.

COD: See chemical oxygen demand.

COEFFICIENT OF HAZE (COH): A measurement of visibility interference in the atmosphere.

COFFIN: A thick-walled container (usually lead) used for transporting radioactive materials.

COH: See coefficient of haze.

COLIFORM BACTERIA: Microscopic one-celled bacteria always, but not exclusively, present in human intestines.

COLIFORM INDEX: An index of the purity of water based on a count of its coliform bacteria.

COLIFORM ORGANISM: Any of a number of organisms common to the intestinal tract of man and animals whose presence in waste water is an indicator of pollution and of potentially dangerous bacterial contamination.

COMBINED SEWERS: A sewage system that carries both sanitary sewage and storm water runoff. During dry weather, combined sewers carry all waste water to the treatment plant. During a storm, only part of the flow is intercepted because of plant overloading; the remainder goes untreated to the receiving stream.

COMBUSTION: Burning. Technically, a rapid oxidation accompanied by the release of energy in the form of heat and light. It is one of the three basic contributing factors causing air pollution, the others are attrition and vaporization.

COMMINUTION: Mechanical shredding or pulverizing of waste, a process that converts it into a homogeneous and more manageable material. Used in solid waste management and in the primary stage of waste water treatment.

COMMINUTOR: A device that grinds solids to make them easier to treat.

COMPACTION: Reducing the bulk of solid waste by rolling and tamping.

COMPOST: Relatively stable decomposed organic material.

COMPOSTING: A controlled process of degrading organic matter by microorganisms. (1) mechnical—a method in which the compost in continuously and mechanically mixed and aerated. (2) ventilated cell—compost is mixed and aerated by being dropped through a vertical series of ventilated cells. (3) windrow—an open-air method in which compostable material is placed in windrows, piles or ventilated bins or pits and occasionally turned or mixed. The process may be anaerobic or aerobic.

CONDOMINIUM: Ownership in common with others of a parcel of land and certain parts of a building thereon which would normally be used by all the occupants, together with individual ownership in fee of a particular unit or apartment in such building.

CONTACT PESTICIDE. A chemical that kills pests on contact with the body, rather than by ingestion (stomach poison).

CONTRAILS: Long narrow clouds caused by the disturbance of the atmosphere during passage of high-flying jets. Proliferation of contrails may cause changes in the weather.

COOLANT: A substance, usually liquid or gas, used for cooling any part of a reactor in which heat is generated, including the core, the reflector, shield and other elements that may be heated by absorption of radiation.

COOLING TOWER: A device to remove excess heat from water used in industrial operations, notably in electric power generation.

CORE: The heart of a nuclear reactor where energy is released.

COVER MATERIAL: Soil that is used to cover compacted solid waste in a sanitary landfill.

CULTURAL EUTROPHICATION: Acceleration by man of the natural aging process of bodies of water.

CURIE: A measure of radioactivity.

CUTIE-PIE: A portable instrument equipped with a direct reading meter used to determine the level of radiation in an area.

CYCLONE COLLECTOR: A device used to collect large-size particulates from polluted air by centrifugal force.

D

DDT: The first of the modern chlorinated hydrocarbon insecticides whose chemical name is 1,1,1-tricholoro-2,2-bis (p-chloriphenyl)-ethane. It has a half-life of 15 years, and its residues can become concentrated in the fatty tissues of certain organisms, especially fish. Because of its persistence in the environment and its ability to accumulate and magnify in the food chain, EPA has banned the registration and interstate sale of DDT for nearly all uses in the United States effective December 31, 1972.

DECIBEL: The unit of measurement of the intensity of sound. Zero on the scale is the tiniest sound detectable by humans: rustling leaves or breathing. The scale: 140 decibels—eardrum ruptures (jet taking off). 100 decibels—deafening (thunder, car horn at three feet, loud motorcyle or power mower). 80 decibels—very loud (portable sander, food blender; continued exposure impairs hearing, impossible to use telephone). 60 decibels—loud (city playground, average restaurant or living room). 20 decibels—faint (classroom, private office, a whisper at five feet).

DECOMPOSERS: Living plants and animals, chiefly fungi and bacteria, that live by extracting nutrients from the tissues of dead plants and animals. Vital to the life cycle.

DECOMPOSITION: Reduction of the net energy level and change in chemical composition of organic matter because of the actions of aerobic or anaerobic microorganisms.

DEMOGRAPHY: The statistical study of population growth and migrations, including births, deaths, marriages, etc.

DERMAL TOXICITY: The ability of a pesticide chemical to poison an animal or human by skin absorption.

DESALINIZATION: Salt removal from sea or brackish water.

DESICCANT: A chemical agent that may be used to remove moisture from plants or insects causing them to wither and die.

DETERGENT: Synthetic washing agent that, like soap, lowers the surface tension of water, emulsifies oils and holds dirt in suspension. Environmentalists have criticized detergents because most contain large amounts of phosphorus-containing compounds that contribute to the eutrophication of waterways.

DEVELOPMENT RIGHT: One of the bundle of rights vested in property ownership which may be acquired for, among other things, the preservation of open space or agricultural utilization while the property owner maintains ownership of the land; or an agreement sometimes defined as a "conservation easement."

DEW POINT: The temperature at which a given percentage of moisture in the air condenses into droplets of water.

DIATOMACEOUS EARTH (DIATOMITE): A fine siliceous material resembling chalk used in waste water treatment plants to filter sewage effluent to remove solids. May also be used as inactive ingredients in pesticide formulations applied as dust or powder.

DIFFUSED AIR: A type of sewage aeration. Air is pumped into the sewage through a perforated pipe.

DIGESTER: In a waste water treatment plant, a closed tank that decreases the volume of solids and stabilizes raw sludge by bacterial action.

DIGESTION: The biochemical decomposition of organic matter. Digestion of sewage sludge takes place in tanks where the sludge decomposes, resulting in partial gasification, liquefaction and mineralization of pollutants.

DILUTION RATIO: The ratio of the volume of water of a stream to the volume of incoming waste. The capacity of a stream to assimilate waste is partially dependent upon the dilution ratio.

DISINFECTION: Effective killing by chemical or physical processes of all organisms capable of causing infectious disease. Chlorination is the disinfection method commonly employed in sewage treatment processes.

DISPERSANT: A chemical agent used to break up concentrations of organic material. In cleaning oil spills, dispersants are used to disperse oil from the water surface.

DISSOLVED OXYGEN: Oxygen suspended in water in the form of microscopic bubbles. Not to be confused with the oxygen which is combined with hydrogen to form the water itself. Fish "breathe" dissolved oxygen and it is essential for many kinds of bacteria to be able to destroy pollution. The amount of dissolved oxygen in water is a guide to the "health" of a stream or lake. It naturally enters water from the atmosphere, and does so at a much greater rate when the water is turbulent, as from rainfall, rapids or waterfalls. Low dissolved oxygen concentrations generally are due to discharge of excessive organic solids having high BOD, the result of inadequate waste treatment.

DISSOLVED SOLIDS: The total amount of dissolved material, organic and inorganic, contained in water or wastes. Excessive dissolved solids make water unpalatable for drinking and unsuitable for industrial uses.

DISTILLATION: The removal of impurities from liquids by boiling. The steam, condensed back into liquid, is almost pure water; the pollutants remain in the concentrated residue.

DOSE: In radiology, the quantity of energy or radiation absorbed.

DOSIMETER (DOSEMETER): An instrument used to measure the amount of radiation a person has received.

DREDGING: A method for deepening streams, swamps or coastal waters by scraping and removing solids from the bottom. The resulting mud is usually deposited in marshes in a process called filling. Dredging and filling can disturb natural ecological cycles. For example, dredging can destroy oyster beds and other aquatic life; filling can destroy the feeding and breeding grounds for many fish species.

DRY LIMESTONE PROCESS: A method of controlling air pollution caused by sulfur oxides. The polluted gases are exposed to limestone which combines with oxides of sulfur to form manageable residues.

DUMP: A land site where solid waste is disposed of in a manner that does not protect the environment.

DUST: Any solid particle over 1 micron (one millionth of a meter) in size, capable of being suspended in air.

DUSTFALL JAR: An open-mouthed container used to collect large particles that fall out of the air. The particles are measured and analyzed.

DYSTROPHIC LAKES: Lakes between eutrophic and swamp stages of aging. Such lakes are shallow and have high humus content, high organic matter content, low nutrient availability and high BOD.

E

ECOCIDE: Killing an entire system, whether the system is a single living organism, a forest, a lake or a human community. Also the substance which can accomplish this, such as a poison.

ECOLOGICAL IMPACT: The total of an environmental change, either natural or man-made, on the ecology of the area.

ECOLOGY: The interrelationships of living things to one another and to their environment or the study of such interrelationships.

ECONOMIC POISONS: Those chemicals used to control insects, rodents, plant diseases, weeds and other pests, and also to defoliate economic crops such as cotton.

ECOSYSTEM: An integrated unit or "system" in nature, sufficient unto itself with a balanced assortment of life forms, to be studied as a separate entity. Examples might be a rotting log in a forest, a pond, a coral atoll, a continent or the earth itself.

EFFLUENT: A discharge from an exit that is relatively self-contained such as an industrial smokestack, nuclear power plant thermal plume or a sewage treatment plant. In common usage, referred to as a source of pollution, or as the pollution itself. Generally used in regard to discharges into waters.

ELECTRODIALYSIS: A process that uses electrical current and an arrangement of permeable membranes to separate soluble minerals from water. Often used to desalinize salt or brackish water.

ELECTROSTATIC PRECIPITATOR: An air pollution control device that removes particulate matter by imparting an electrical charge to particles in a gas stream for mechanical collection on an electrode.

EMERGENCY EPISODE: See air pollution episode.

EMISSION: See effluent. (Generally used in regard to discharges into air.)

EMISSION FACTOR: The average amount of a pollutant emitted from each type of polluting source in relation to a specific amount of material processed. For example, an emission factor for a blast furnace (used to make iron) would be a number of pounds of particulates per ton of raw materials.

EMISSION INVENTORY: A list of air pollutants emitted into a community's atmosphere, in amounts (usually tons) per day, by type of source. The emission inventory is basic to the establishment of emission standards.

EMISSION STANDARD: The maximum amount of a pollutant legally permitted to be discharged from a single source, either mobile or stationary.

EMULSIFY: To blend different materials, especially oils and water, into a smooth mixture, usually by reducing them to tiny droplets or particles. To homogenize.

ENERGY CYCLE: The process by which the energy of the sun is passed from one living organism to another or is stored, as in coal or oil. The life cycle.

ENVIRONMENT: The combination of all external influences and conditions affecting the life, development and ultimate survival of an organism, including man.

ENVIRONMENTAL IMPACT STATEMENT: A document prepared by a Federal agency on the environmental impact of its proposals for legislation and other major actions significantly affecting the quality of the human environment. Environmental impact statements are used as tools for decision making and are required by the National Environmental Policy Act, as well as lower levels of government.

EPIDEMIOLOGY: The study of diseases as they affect populations.

EROSION: The wearing away of the land surface by wind or water. Erosion occurs naturally from weather or runoff but is often intensified by man's land-clearing practices.

ESTUARY: A coastal area of high marine productivity where fresh and salt waters mingle, including the associated tidal rivers, marshes, flats, lagoons, bays and shallow sounds. The source of nutrients and shelter during infancy for a high percentage of the food and game fish caught in the oceans, as well as the home of shellfish and many kinds of birds and animals. A delicate ecosystem.

EUTROPHICATION: The natural aging process that occurs in aquatic ecosystems, such as lakes, over a long period of time. Nutrients in the water feed aquatic vegetation which dies and gradually builds a layer of decayed matter on the bottom. In time a body of water progresses from lake or pond to swamp, marsh and finally meadow. Eutrophication can be greatly speeded up by excess nutrients such as fertilizers, detergents and human or animal wastes. Dissolved oxygen in water can be exhausted by bacterial action in decomposing vegetation, thus making the water unable to support fish life or bacteria which would normally clean up pollution.

EUTROPHIC LAKES: Shallow lakes, weedchoked at the edges and very rich in nutrients. The water is characterized by large amounts of algae, low water transparency, low dissolved oxygen and high BOD.

EVAPORATION PONDS: Shallow, artificial ponds where sewage sludge is pumped, permitted to dry and either removed or buried by more sludge.

F

FABRIC FILTER: A device for removing dust and particulate matter from industrial emissions much like a home vacuum cleaner filter.

FECAL COLIFORM BACTERIA: A group of organisms common to the intestinal tracts of man and of animals. The presence of fecal coliform bacteria in water is an indicator of pollution and of potentially dangerous bacterial contamination.

FEEDLOT: A relatively small, confined land area for raising cattle. Although an economical method of fattening beef, feedlots concentrate a large amount of animal wastes in a small area. This excrement cannot be handled by the soil as it could be if the cattle were scattered on open range. In addition, runoff from feedlots contributes excessive quantities of nitrogen, phosphorous and potassium to nearby waterways, thus contributing to eutrophication.

FEN: A low-lying land area partly covered by water.

FILLING: The process of depositing dirt and mud in marshy areas to create more land for real estate development. Filling can disturb natural ecological cycles. See dredging.

FILM BADGE: A piece of masked photographic film worn like a badge by nuclear workers to monitor an exposure to radiation. Nuclear radiation darkens the film.

FILTRATION: In waste water treatment, the mechanical process that removes particulate matter by separating water from solid material usually by passing it through sand.

FLOC: A clump of solids formed in sewage by biological or chemical action.

FLOCCULATION: In waste water treatment, the process of separating suspended solids by chemical creation of clumps or flocs.

FLOWMETER: In waste water treatment, a meter that indicates the rate at which waste water flows through the plant.

FLUE GAS: A mixture of gases resulting from combustion and emerging from a chimney. Flue gas includes nitrogen oxides, carbon oxides, water vapor and often sulfur oxides or particulates.

FLUORIDES: Gaseous, solid or dissolved compounds containing fluorine, emitted into the air or water from a number of industrial processes. Fluorides in the air are a cause of vegetation damage and, indirectly, of livestock damage.

FLUME: A channel, either natural or man-made, which carries water.

FLY ASH: All solids, including ash, charred paper, cinders, dust, soot or other partially incinerated matter, that are carried in a gas stream.

FOG: Condensation of water vapor in the air. Combines with smoke or other air pollutants to form smog.

FOGGING: The application of a pesticide by rapidly heating the liquid chemical, thus forming very fine droplets with the appearance of smoke. Fogging is often used to destroy mosquitoes and blackflies.

FOOD CHAIN: The process in which one species is devoured by a bigger one, starting with one-celled organisms called plankton in the marine environment and running up through various species to the biggest fish, fish-eating birds, mammals and man. On land the food chain can begin with vegetation and include insects and various birds and animals. Man is considered the top of the food chain, as are eagles, hawks and various carnivorous animals.

FOOD WASTE: Animal and vegetable waste resulting from the handling, storage, sale, preparation, cooking and serving of foods; commonly called garbage.

FOSSIL FUELS: Coal, oil and natural gas; so-called because they are derived from the remains of ancient plant and animal life.

FUME: Tiny solid particles commonly formed by the condensation of vapors of solid matter.

FUMIGANT: A pesticide that is burned or evaporated to form a gas or vapor that destroys pests. Fumigants are often used in buildings or greenhouses.

FUNGI: Small, often microscopic plants without chlorophyll. Some fungi infect and cause disease in plants or animals; other fungi are useful in stabilizing sewage or in breaking down wastes for compost.

FUNGICIDE: A pesticide chemical that kills fungi or prevents them from causing diseases, usually on plants of economic importance. See pesticide.

G

GAME FISH: Those species of fish sought by sports fishermen; for example, salmon, trout, black bass, striped bass, etc. Game fish are usually more sensitive to environmental changes and water quality degradation than "rough" fish.

GAMMA RAY: Waves of radiant nuclear energy. Gamma rays are the most penetrating of the three types of radiation and are best stopped by dense materials such as lead.

GARBAGE: See food waste.

GARBAGE GRINDING: A method of grinding food waste by a household disposal, for example, and washing it into the sewer system. Ground garbage then must be disposed of as sewage sludge.

GEIGER COUNTER: An electrical device that detects the presence of radioactivity.

GENERATOR: A device that converts mechanical energy into electrical energy.

GERMICIDE: A chemical or agent that kills microorganisms such as bacteria and prevents them from causing disease. Such compounds must be registered as pesticides with EPA.

GRAIN: A unit of weight equivalent to 65 milligrams or 2/1,000 of an ounce.

GRAIN LOADING: The rate of emission of particulate matter from a polluting source. Measurement is made in grains of particulate matter per cubic foot of gas emitted.

GREEN BELTS: Certain areas restricted from being used for buildings and houses; they often serve as separating buffers between pollution sources and concentrations of population.

GREENHOUSE EFFECT: The heating effect of the atmosphere upon the earth. Light waves from the sun pass through the air and are absorbed by the earth. The earth then reradiates this energy as heat waves that are absorbed by the air, specifically by carbon dioxide. The air thus behaves like glass in a greenhouse, allowing the passage of light but not of heat. Thus many scientists theorize that an increase in the atmospheric concentration of CO_2 can eventually cause an increase in the earth's surface temperature. Others argue that this effect might be offset by particulate pollution which could keep heat from entering the atmosphere; an effect that might lower temperatures around the world.

GROUND COVER: Grasses or other plants grown to keep soil from being blown or washed away.

GROUNDWATER: The supply of freshwater under the earth's surface in an aquifer or soil that forms the natural reservoir for man's use.

GROUNDWATER RUNOFF: Groundwater that is discharged into a stream channel as spring or seepage water.

H

HABITAT: The sum total of environmental conditions of a specific place that is occupied by an organism, a population or a community.

HALF-LIFE: The time it takes certain materials, such as persistent pesticides or radioactive isotopes, to lose half their strength. For example, the half-life of DDT is 15 years; the half-life of radium is 1,580 years.

HAMMERMILL: A broad category of high-speed equipment that uses pivoted or fixed hammers or cutters to crush, grind, chip or shred solid wastes.

HARD WATER: Water containing dissolved mineral such as calcium, iron and magnesium. The most notable characteristic of hard water is its inability to lather soap. Some pesticide chemicals will curdle or settle out when added to hard water.

HAZARDOUS AIR POLLUTANT: According to law, a pollutant to which no ambient air quality standard is applicable and that may cause or contribute to an increase in mortality or in serious illness. For example, asbestos, beryllium and mercury have been declared hazardous air pollutants.

HEAT ISLAND EFFECT: An air circulation problem peculiar to cities. Tall buildings, heat from pavements and concentrations of pollutants create a haze dome that prevents rising hot air from being cooled at its normal rate. A self-contained circulation system is put in motion that can be broken by relatively strong winds. If such winds are absent, the heat island can trap high concentrations of pollutants and present a serious health problem.

HEATING SEASON: The coldest months of the year when pollution emissions are higher in some areas because of increased fossil-fuel consumption.

HEAVY METALS: Metallic elements with high molecular weights, generally toxic in low concentrations to plant and animal life. Such metals are often residual in the environment and exhibit biological accumulation. Examples include mercury, chromium, cadmium, arsenic and lead.

HERBICIDE: A pesticide chemical used to destroy or control the growth of weeds, bush and other undesirable plants. See pesticide.

HERBIVORE: An organism that feeds on vegetation.

HETEROTROPHIC ORGANISM: Organisms dependent on organic matter for food.

HIGH DENSITY POLYETHYLENE: A material often used in the manufacture of plastic bottles that produces toxic fumes if incinerated.

HI-VOLUME SAMPLER: A device used in the measurement and analysis of suspended particulate pollution. Also called a Hi-Vol.

HOT: A colloquial term meaning highly radioactive.

HUMUS: Decomposed organic material.

HYDROCARBONS: A vast family of compounds containing carbon and hydrogen in various combinations, found especially in fossil fuels. Some hydrocarbons are major air pollutants, some may be carcinogenic and others contribute to photochemical smog.

HYDROGEN SULFIDE (H_2S): A malodorous gas made up of hydrogen and sulfur with the characteristic odor of rotten eggs. It is emitted in the natural decomposition of organic matter and is also the natural accompaniment of advanced stages of eutrophication. H_2S is also a byproduct of refinery activity and the combustion of oil during power plant operations. In heavy concentrations, it can cause illness.

HYDROLOGY: The science dealing with the properties, distribution and circulation of water and snow.

I

IMPEDANCE: The rate at which a substance can absorb and transmit sound.

IMPLEMENTATION PLAN: A document of the steps to be taken to ensure attainment of environmental quality standards within a specified time period. Implementation plans are required by various laws.

IMPOUNDMENT: A body of water, such as a pond, confined by a dam, dike, floodgate or other barrier.

INCINERATION: The controlled process by which solid, liquid or gaseous combustible wastes are burned and changed into gases; the residue produced contains little or no combustible material.

INCINERATOR: An engineered apparatus used to burn waste substances and in which all the combustion factors—temperature, retention time, turbulence and combustion air—can be controlled.

INERT GAS: A gas that does not react with other substances under ordinary conditions.

INERTIAL SEPARATOR: An air pollution control device that uses the principle of inertia to remove particulate matter from a stream of air or gas.

INFILTRATION: The flow of a fluid into a substance through pores or small openings. Commonly used in hydrology to denote the flow of water into soil material.

INOCULUM: Material such as bacteria placed in compost or other medium to initiate biological action.

INTEGRATED PEST CONTROL: A system of managing pests by using biological, cultural and chemical means.

INTERCEPTOR SEWERS: Sewers used to collect the flows from main and trunk sewers and carry them to a central point for treatment and discharge. In a combined sewer system, where street run-off from rains is allowed to enter the system along with sewage, interceptor sewers allow some of the sewage to flow untreated directly into the receiving stream, to prevent the plant from being overloaded.

INTERSTATE CARRIER WATER SUPPLY: A water supply whose water may be used for drinking or cooking purposes, aboard common carriers (planes, trains, buses and ships) operating interstate. Interstate carrier water supplies are regulated by the Federal government.

INTERSTATE WATERS: According to law, waters defined as: (1) rivers, lakes and other waters that flow across or form a part of State or international boundaries; (2) waters of the Great Lakes; (3) coastal waters—whose scope has been defined to include ocean waters seaward to the territorial limits and waters along the coastline (including inland streams) influenced by the tide.

INVERSION: An atmospheric condition where a layer of cool air is trapped by a layer of warm air so that it cannot rise. Inversions spread polluted air horizontally rather than vertically so that contaminating substances cannot be widely dispersed. An inversion of several days can cause an air pollution episode.

IONIZATION CHAMBER: A device roughly similar to a Geiger counter that reveals the presence of ionizing radiation.

ISOTOPE: A variation of an element having the same atomic number as the element itself, but having a different atomic weight because of a different number of neutrons. Different isotopes of the same element have different radioactive behavior.

J, K, L

LAGOON: In waste water treatment, a shallow pond usually man-made where sunlight, bacterial action and oxygen interact to restore waste water to a reasonable state of purity.

LATERAL SEWERS: Pipes running underneath city streets that collect sewage from homes or businesses.

LC_{50}: Median lethal concentration, a standard measure of toxicity. LC_{50} indicates the concentration of a substance that will kill 50 percent of a group of experimental insects or animals.

LEACHATE: Liquid that has percolated through solid waste or other mediums and has extracted dissolved or suspended materials from it.

LEACHING: The process by which soluble materials in the soil, such as nutrients, pesticide chemicals or contaminants, are washed into a lower layer of soil or are dissolved and carried away by water.

LEAD: A heavy metal that may be hazardous to human health if breathed or ingested.

LIFE CYCLE: The phases, changes or stages an organism passes through during its lifetime.

LIFT: In a sanitary landfill, a compacted layer of solid waste and the top layer of cover material.

LIMNOLOGY: The study of the physical, chemical, meteorological and biological aspects of fresh waters.

M

MARSH: A low-lying tract of soft, wet land that provides an important ecosystem for a variety of plant and animal life but often is destroyed by dredging and filling.

MASKING: Covering over of one sound or element by another. Quantitatively, masking is the amount the audibility threshold of one sound is raised by the presence of a second masking sound. Also used in regard to odors.

MECHANICAL TURBULENCE: The erratic movement of air caused by local obstructions such as buildings.

MERCURY: A heavy metal, highly toxic if breathed or ingested. Mercury is residual in the environment, showing biological accumulation in all aquatic organisms, especially fish and shell fish. Chronic exposure to airborne mercury can have serious effects on the central nervous system.

METHANE: Colorless, nonpoisonous and flammable gaseous hydrocarbon. Methane, (CA_4), is emitted by marshes and by dumps undergoing anaerobic decomposition.

MGD: Millions of gallons per day. Mgd is commonly used to express rate of flow.

MICROBES: Minute plant or animal life. Some disease-causing microbes exist in sewage.

MIST: Liquid particles in air formed by condensation of vaporized liquids. Mist particles vary from 500 to 40 microns in size. By comparison, fog particles are smaller than 40 microns in size.

MIXED LIQUOR: A mixture of activated sludge and water containing organic matter undergoing activated sludge treatment in the aeration tank.

MOBILE SOURCE: A moving source of air pollution such as an automobile.

MOLECULE: The smallest part of a substance that can exist separately and still retain its chemical properties and characteristic composition; the smallest combination of atoms that will form a specific chemical compound.

MONITORING: Periodic or continuous determination of the amount of pollutants or radioactive contamination present in the environment.

MUCK SOILS: Soils made from decaying plant materials.

MULCH: A layer of wood chips, dry leaves, straw, hay, plastic strips or other material placed on the soil around plants to retain moisture, to prevent weeds from growing and to enrich soil.

MUTAGENIC: The ability of certain substances to cause changes in an organism's genetic material. Capable of causing a "mutation," or abnormal form of a living organism.

MUTATION: An organism which is basically unlike its parents, and which may or may not be able to reproduce itself.

N

NATURAL GAS: A fuel gas occurring naturally in certain geologic formations. Natural gas is usually a combustible mixture of methane and hydrocarbons.

NATURAL SELECTION: The natural process by which the organisms best adapted to their environment survive and those less well adapted are eliminated.

NECROSIS: Death of plant cells resulting in a discolored, sunken area or death of the entire plant.

NEW TOWN: Any new, large-scale development planned to provide housing, work places, and related facilities within a more or less self-contained environment.

NITRIC OXIDE (NO): A gas formed in great part from atmospheric nitrogen and oxygen when combustion takes place under high temperature and high pressure, as in internal combustion engines. NO is not itself a pollutant; however, in the ambient air, it converts to nitrogen dioxide, a major contributor to photochemical smog.

NITROGEN DIOXIDE (NO_2): A compound produced by the oxidation of nitric oxide in the atmosphere; a major contributor to photochemical smog.

NITROGEN FIXATION: The process in which bacteria and other soil organisms convert atmospheric nitrogen into nitrates, which then become available to feed growing plants.

NITROGENOUS WASTES: Wastes of animal or plant origin that contain a significant concentration of nitrogen.

NO: A notation meaning oxides of nitrogen. See nitric oxide.

NOISE: Any undesired audible signal. Thus, in acoustics, noise is any undesired sound.

NON-RENEWABLE RESOURCES: Resources which, once used or misused, cannot replenish themselves. Examples are coal, petroleum and natural gas.

NTA: Nitrilotriacetic acid, a compound once used to replace phosphates in detergents.

NUCLEAR POWER PLANT: Any device, machine or assembly that converts nuclear energy into some form of useful power, such as mechanical or electrical power. In a nuclear electric power plant, heat produced by a reactor is generally used to make steam to drive a turbine that in turn drives an electric generator.

NUTRIENTS: Elements or compounds essential as raw materials for organism growth and development; for example, carbon, oxygen, nitrogen and phosphorus.

O

OIL SPILL: The accidental discharge of oil into oceans, bays or inland waterways. Methods of oil spill control include chemical dispersion, combustion, mechanical containment and absorption.

OLIGOTROPHIC LAKES: Deep lakes that have a low supply of nutrients and thus contain little organic matter. Such lakes are characterized by high water transparency and high dissolved oxygen.

OPACITY: Degree of obscuration of light. For example, a window has zero opacity; a wall is 100 percent opaque. The Ringelmann system of evaluating smoke density is based on opacity.

OPEN BURNING: Uncontrolled burning of wastes in an open dump.

OPEN DUMP: See dump.

ORGANIC: Referring to or derived from living organisms. In chemistry, any compound containing carbon.

ORGANISM: Any living human, plant or animal.

ORGANOPHOSPHATES: A group of pesticide chemicals containing phosphorus, such as malathion and parathion, intended to control insects. These compounds are short-lived and, therefore, do not normally contaminate the environment. However, some organophosphates, such as parathion, are extremely toxic when initially applied and exposure to them can interfere with the normal processes of the nervous system, causing convulsions and eventually death. Malathion, on the other hand, is low in toxicity and relatively safe for humans and animals; it is a common ingredient in household insecticide products.

OUTFALL: The mouth of a sewer, drain or conduit where an effluent is discharged into the receiving waters.

OVERFIRE AIR: Air forced into the top of an incinerator to fan the flame.

OXIDANT: Any oxygen-containing substance that reacts chemically in the air to produce new substances. Oxidants are the primary contributors to photochemical smog.

OXIDATION: A chemical reaction in which oxygen unites or combines with other elements. Organic matter is oxidized by the action of aerobic bacteria; thus oxidation is used in waste water treatment to break down organic wastes.

OXIDATION POND: A man-made lake or pond in which organic wastes are reduced by bacterial action. Often oxygen is bubbled through the pond to speed the process.

OZONE (O_3): A pungent, colorless, toxic gas. Ozone is one component of photochemical smog and is considered a major air pollutant.

P

PACKAGE PLANT: A prefabricated or prebuilt waste water treatment plant.

PACKED TOWER: An air pollution control device in which polluted air is forced upward through a tower packed with crushed rock or wood chips while a liquid is sprayed downward on the packing material. The pollutants in the air stream either dissolve or chemically react with the liquid.

PAN: Peroxyacetyl nitrate, a pollutant created by the action of sunlight on hydrocarbons and nitrogen oxides in the air. PANs are an integral part of photochemical smog.

PARTICULATES: Finely divided solid or liquid particles in the air or in an emission. Particulates include dust, smoke, fumes, mist, spray and fog.

PARTICULATE LOADING: The introduction of particulates into the ambient air.

PATHOGENIC: Causing or capable of causing disease.

PCBs: Polychlorinated biphenyls, a group of organic compounds used in the manufacture of plastics. In the environment, PCBs exhibit many of the same characteristics as DDT and may, therefore, be confused with that pesticide. PCBs are highly toxic to aquatic life, they persist in the environment for long periods of time, and they are biologically accumulative.

PEAT: Partially decomposed organic material.

PERCOLATION: Downward flow of infiltration of water through the pores or spaces of a rock or soil.

PERSISTENT PESTICIDES: Pesticides that will be present in the environment for longer than one growing season or one year after application.

PESTICIDE: An agent used to control pests. This includes insecticides for use against harmful insects; herbicides for weed control; fungicides for control of plant diseases; rodenticides for killing rats, mice, etc.; and germicides used in disinfectant products, algaecides, slimicides, etc. Some pesticides can contaminate water, air, or soil and accumulate in man, animals and the environment. Certain of these chemicals have been shown to interfere with the reproductive processes of predatory birds and possibly other animals.

PESTICIDE TOLERANCE: A scientifically and legally established limit for the amount of chemical residue that can be permitted to remain in or on a harvested food or feed crop as a result of the application of a chemical for pest-control purposes. Such tolerances or safety levels, established federally by EPA, are set well below the point at which residues might be harmful to consumers.

pH: A measure of the acidity or alkalinity of material, liquid or solid. pH is represented on a scale of 0 to 14 with 7 representing a neutral state, 0 representing the most acid and 14, the most alkaline.

PHENOLS: A group of organic compounds that in very low concentrations produce a taste and odor problem in water. In higher concentrations, they are toxic to aquatic life. Phenols are by-products of petroleum refining, tanning and textile, dye and resin manufacture.

PHOSPHATE: A salt or ester of phosphoric acid. Examples are calcium phosphate, a compound derived from phosphoric acid and often used in fertilizer and medicine, and sodium tripolyphosphate (STPP) additive, commonly used in detergents. Found also in human and animal wastes and blamed for contributing to eutrophication, or accelerated growth and decay of aquatic vegetation.

PHOTOCHEMICAL OXIDANTS: Secondary pollutants formed by the action of sunlight on the oxides of nitrogen and hydrocarbons in the air; they are the primary contributors to photochemical smog.

PHOTOCHEMICAL SMOG: Air pollution associated with oxidants rather than with sulfur oxides, particulates, etc. Produces necrosis, chlorosis and growth alterations in plants and is an eye and respiratory irritant in humans.

PHOTOSYNTHESIS: The process through which sunlight, acting in the presence of the green plant pigment chlorophyl, converts atmospheric carbon dioxide, water and inorganic salts into living tissue. The fundamental food-making process in green plants, upon which all life on earth directly or indirectly depends.

PHYTOPLANKTON: The plant portion of plankton.

PHYTOTOXIC: Injurious to plants.

PIG: A container usually made of lead used to ship or store radioactive materials.

PILE: A nuclear reactor.

PLANKTON: The floating or weakly swimming plant and animal life in a body of water, often microscopic in size.

PLUME: The visible emission from a flue or chimney.

POINT SOURCE: In air pollution, a stationary source of a large individual emission, generally of an industrial nature. This is a general definition; point source is legally and precisely defined in Federal regulations. See area source.

POLLEN: A fine dust produced by plants; a natural or background air pollutant.

POLLUTANT: Any introduced gas, liquid or solid that makes a resource unfit for a specific purpose.

POLLUTION: The presence of matter or energy whose nature, location or quantity produces undesired environmental effects.

POLYELECTROLYTES: Synthetic chemicals used to speed flocculation of solids in sewage.

POTABLE WATER: Water suitable for drinking or cooking purposes from both health and aesthetic considerations.

PPM: Parts per million. The unit commonly used to represent the degree of pollutant concentration where the concentrations are small. Larger concentrations are given in percentages. Thus BOD is represented in ppm while suspended solids in water are expressed in percentages. In air, ppm is usually a volume/volume ratio; in water, a weight/volume ratio.

PRECIPITATE: A solid that separates from a solution because of some chemical or physical change or the formation of such a solid.

PRECIPITATORS: In pollution control work, any of a number of air pollution control devices usually using mechanical/electrical means to collect particulates from an emission.

PRETREATMENT: In waste water treatment, any process used to reduce pollution load before the waste water is introduced into a main sewer system or delivered to a treatment plant for substantial reduction of the pollution load.

PRIMARY TREATMENT: The first stage in waste water treatment in which substantially all floating or settleable solids are mechanically removed by screening and sedimentation.

PROCESS WEIGHT: The total weight of all materials, including fuels, introduced into a manufacturing process. The process weight is used to calculate the allowable rate of emission of pollutant matter from the process.

PRODUCERS: Green plants upon which all other life ultimately depends.

P.U.D.: Planned Unit Development, or a form of land development which increases the carrying capacity of the land, utilizing common open space, cluster development, and a variety of both housing types and land uses.

PULVERIZATION: The crushing or grinding of material into small pieces.

PUMPED STORAGE: A method of generating electricity. Favored by utility companies because surplus electricity produced by steam generators in a power system during hours of low customer consumption of electricity may be stored for partial recovery when demand is high. Surplus electricity is used to pump water to an elevated reservoir. During hours of high electrical demand, water runs downhill to generators which produce electricity. About three kilowatts of electricity are spent in pumping enough water uphill to produce two kilowatts during its downward flow.

PUMPING STATION: A station at which sewage is pumped to a higher level. In most sewer systems pumping is unnecessary; waste water flows by gravity to the treatment plant.

PUTRESCIBLE: Capable of being decomposed by microorganisms with sufficient rapidity to cause nuisances from odors, gases, etc. For example, kitchen wastes or dead animals.

Q

QUENCH TANK: A water-filled tank used to cool incinerator residues.

R

RAD: A unit of measurement of any kind of radiation absorbed by man.

RADIATION: The emission of fast atomic particles or rays by the nucleus of an atom. Some elements are naturally radioactive while others become radioactive after bombardment with neutrons or other particles. The three major forms of radiation are alpha, beta and gamma.

RADIATION STANDARDS: Regulations that include exposure standards, permissible concentrations and regulations for transportation.

RADIOBIOLOGY: The study of the principles, mechanisms and effects of radiation on living matter.

RADIOECOLOGY: The study of the effects of radiation on species of plants and animals in natural communities.

RADIOISOTOPES: Radioactive isotopes. Radioisotopes such as cobalt-60 are used in the treatment of disease.

RASP: A device used to grate solid waste into a more manageable material, ridding it of much of its odor.

RAW SEWAGE: Untreated domestic or commercial waste water.

RECEIVING WATERS: Rivers, lakes, oceans or other bodies that receive treated or untreated waste waters.

RECYCLING: The reuse of natural resources and manmade products. Examples are making new paper out of old, melting down bottles to make new ones, melting aluminum or steel to use it again. Valuable in protecting vanishing natural resources, as well as reducing the problems of solid waste disposal and land pollution by junk and debris.

RED TIDE: A proliferation or bloom of a certain type of plankton with red-to-orange coloration, that often causes massive fish kills. Though they are a natural phenomenon, blooms are believed to be stimulated by phosphorus and other nutrients discharged into waterways by man.

REFUSE: See solid waste.

REFUSE RECLAMATION: The process of converting solid waste to saleable products. For example, the composting of organic solid waste yields a saleable soil conditioner.

REM: A measurement of radiation dose to the internal tissues of man.

RENEWABLE RESOURCES: Biological resources which renew themselves by growth and reproduction.

REP: A unit of measurement of any kind of radiation absorbed by man.

RESERVOIR: A pond, lake, tank or basin, natural or man-made, used for the storage, regulation and control of water.

RESOURCE RECOVERY: The process of obtaining materials or energy, particularly from solid waste.

REVERBERATION: The persistence of sound in an enclosed space after the sound source has stopped.

RINGELMANN CHART: A series of illustrations ranging from light grey to black used to measure the opacity of smoke emitted from stacks and other sources. The shades of grey simulate various smoke densities and are assigned numbers ranging from one to five. Ringelmann No. 1 is equivalent to 20 percent dense; No. 5 is 100 percent dense. Ringelmann charts are used in the setting and enforcement of emission standards.

RIPARIAN RIGHTS: Rights of a land owner to the water on or bordering his property, including the right to prevent diversion or misuse of upstream water.

RIVER BASIN: The total area drained by a river and its tributaries.

RODENTICIDE: A chemical or agent used to destroy or prevent damage by rats or other rodent pests. See pesticide.

ROUGH FISH: Those fish species considered to be of poor fighting quality when taken on tackle or of poor eating quality; for example, gar, suckers, etc. Most rough fish are more tolerant of widely changing environmental conditions than are game fish.

RUBBISH: A general term for solid waste—excluding food waste and ashes—taken from residences, commercial establishments and institutions.

RUNOFF: The portion of rainfall, melted snow or irrigation water that flows across ground surface and eventually is returned to streams. Runoff can pick up pollutants from the air or the land and carry them to the receiving waters.

S

SALINITY: The degree of salt in water.

SALT WATER INTRUSION: The invasion of salt water into a body of fresh water, occurring in either surface or groundwater bodies. When this invasion is caused by oceanic waters, it is called sea water intrusion.

SALVAGE: The utilization of waste materials.

SANITATION: The control of all the factors in man's physical environment that exercise or can exercise a deleterious effect on his physical development, health and survival.

SANITARY LANDFILL: A site for solid waste disposal using sanitary landfilling techniques.

SANITARY LANDFILLING: An engineered method of solid waste disposal on land in a manner that protects the environment; waste is spread in thin layers, compacted to the smallest practical volume and covered with soil at the end of each working day.

SANITARY SEWERS: Sewers that carry only domestic or commercial sewage. Storm water runoff is carried in a separate system. See sewer.

SCRAP: Discarded or rejected materials that result from manufacturing or fabricating operations and are suitable for reprocessing.

SCREENING: The removal of relatively coarse floating and suspended solids by straining through racks or screens.

SCRUBBER: An air pollution control device that uses a liquid spray to remove pollutants from a gas stream by absorption or chemical reaction. Scrubbers also reduce the temperature of the emission.

SECONDARY TREATMENT: Waste water treatment, beyond the primary stage, in which bacteria consume the organic parts of the wastes. This biochemical action is accomplished by use of trickling filters or the activated sludge process. Effective secondary treatment removes virtually all floating and settleable solids and approximately 90 percent of both BOD_5 and suspended solids. Customarily, disinfection by chlorination is the final stage of the secondary treatment process.

SEDIMENTATION: In waste water treatment, the settling out of solids by gravity.

SEDIMENTATION TANKS: In waste water treatment, tanks where the solids are allowed to settle or to float as scum. Scum is skimmed off; settled solids are pumped to incinerators, digesters, filters or other means of disposal.

SEEPAGE: Water that flows through the soil.

SELECTIVE HERBICIDE: A pesticide intended to kill only certain types of plants, especially broad-leafed weeds, and not harm other plants such as farm crops or lawn grasses. The leading herbicide in the United States is 2, 4-D. A related but stronger chemical used mostly for brush control on range, pasture, and forest lands and on utility or highway rights-of-way is 2, 4, 5-T. Uses of the latter chemical have been somewhat restricted because of laboratory evidence that it or a dioxin contaminant in 2, 4, 5-T can cause birth defects in test animals.

SENESCENCE: The process of growing old. Sometimes used to refer to lakes nearing extinction.

SEPTIC TANK: An underground tank used for the deposition of domestic wastes. Bacteria in the wastes decompose the organic matter, and the sludge settles to the bottom. The effluent flows through drains into the ground. Sludge is pumped out at regular intervals.

SETTLEABLE SOLIDS: Bits of debris and fine matter heavy enough to settle out of waste water.

SETTLING CHAMBER: In air pollution control, a low-cost device used to reduce the velocity of flue gases usually by means of baffles, promoting the settling of fly ash.

SETTLING TANK: In waste water treatment, a tank or basin in which settleable solids are removed by gravity.

SEWAGE: The total of organic waste and waste water generated by residential and commercial establishments.

SEWAGE LAGOON: See lagoon.

SEWER: Any pipe or conduit used to collect and carry away sewage or stormwater runoff from the generating source to treatment plants or receiving streams. A sewer that conveys household and commercial sewage is called a sanitary sewer. If it transports runoff from rain or snow, it is called a storm sewer. Often storm water runoff and sewage are transported in the same system or combined sewers.

SEWERAGE: The entire system of sewage collection, treatment and disposal. Also applies to all effluent carried by sewers whether it is sanitary sewage, industrial wastes or storm water runoff.

SHIELD: A wall that protects workers from harmful radiation released by radioactive materials.

SILT: Finely divided particles of soil or rock. Often carried in cloudy suspension in water and eventually deposited as sediment.

SINKING: A method of controlling oil spills that employs an agent to entrap oil droplets and sink them to the bottom of the body of water. The oil and sinking agent are eventually biologically degraded.

SKIMMING: The mechanical removal of oil or scum from the surface of water.

SLUDGE: The construction of solids removed from sewage during waste water treatment. Sludge disposal is then handled by incineration, dumping or burial.

SMOG: Originally a combination of smoke and fog. It now means air that is heavily contaminated with particulates, nitrogen oxides and waste hydrocarbons, often aggravated by ozone resulting from the photochemical process caused by sunlight. Generally used as an equivalent of air pollution.

SMOKE: Solid particles generated as a result of the incomplete combustion of materials containing carbon.

SOx: A symbol meaning oxides of sulfur.

SOFT DETERGENTS: Biodegradable detergents.

SOIL CONDITIONER: A biologically stable organic material such as humus or compost that makes soil more amenable to the passage of water and to the distribution of fertilizing material, providing a better medium for necessary soil bacteria growth.

SOLID WASTE: Useless, unwanted or discarded material with insufficient liquid content to be free flowing. Also see waste. (1) agricultural—solid waste that results from the raising and slaughtering of animals, and the processing of animal products and orchard and field crops. (2) commercial—waste generated by stores, offices and other activities that do not actually turn out a product. (3) industrial—waste that results from industrial processes and manufacturing. (4) institutional—waste originating from educational, health care and research facilities (5) municipal—residential and commercial solid waste generated within a community. (6) pesticide—the residue from the manufacturing, handling or use of chemicals intended for killing plant and animal pests. (7) residential—waste that normally originates in a residential environment. Sometimes called domestic solid waste.

SOLID WASTE DISPOSAL: The ultimate disposition of refuse that cannot be salvaged or recycled.

SOLID WASTE MANAGEMENT: The purposeful, systematic control of the generation, storage, collection, transport, separation, processing, recycling, recovery and disposal of solid wastes.

SONIC BOOM: The tremendous booming sound produced as a vehicle, usually a supersonic jet airplane, exceeds the speed of sound, and the shock wave reaches the ground.

SOOT: Agglomerations of tar-impregnated carbon particles that form when carbonaceous material does not undergo complete combustion.

SORPTION: A term including both adsorption and absorption. Sorption is basic to many processes used to remove gaseous and particulate pollutants from an emission and to clean up oil spills.

SPOIL: Dirt or rock that has been removed from its original location, specifically materials that have been dredged from the bottoms of waterways.

STABILITY: An atmospheric condition which exists when the temperature of the air rises rather than falls with increasing altitude. It allows for little or no vertical air movement.

STABILIZATION: The process of converting active organic matter in sewage sludge or solid wastes into inert, harmless material.

STABILIZATION PONDS: See lagoon, oxidation pond.

STABLE AIR: An air mass that remains in the same position rather than moving in its normal horizontal and vertical directions. Stable air does not disperse pollutants and can lead to high build-ups of air pollution.

STACK: A smokestack; a vertical pipe or flue designed to exhaust gases and suspended particulate matter.

STACK EFFECT: The upward movement of hot gases in a stack due to the temperature difference between the gases and the atmosphere.

STAGNATION: Lack of wind in an air mass or lack of motion in water. Both cases tend to entrap and concentrate pollutants.

STATIONARY SOURCE: A pollution emitter that is fixed rather than moving as an automobile.

STORM SEWER: A conduit that collects and transports rain and snow runoff back to the ground water. In a separate sewerage system, storm sewers are entirely separate from those carrying domestic and commercial waste water.

STRATIFICATION: Separating into layers.

STRIP MINING: A process in which rock and top soil strata overlying ore or fuel deposits are scraped away by mechanical shovels. Also known as surface mining.

SULFUR DIOXIDE (SO_2): A heavy, pungent, colorless gas formed primarily by the combustion of fossil fuels. SO_2 damages the respiratory tract as well as vegetation and materials and is considered a major air pollutant.

SUMP: A depression or tank that serves as a drain or receptacle for liquids for salvage or disposal.

SURFACTANT: An agent used in detergents to cause lathering. Composed of several phosphate compounds, surfactants are a source of external enrichment thought to speed the eutrophication of our lakes.

SURVEILLANCE SYSTEM: A monitoring system to determine environmental quality. Surveillance systems should be established to monitor all aspects of progress toward attainment of environmental standards and to identify potential episodes of high pollutant concentrations in time to take preventive action.

SUSPENDED SOLIDS (SS): Small particles of solid pollutants in sewage that contribute to turbidity and that resist separation by conventional means. The examination of suspended solids and the BOD test constitute the two main determinations for water quality performed at waste water treatment facilities.

SYMBIOSIS: The association of two or more kinds of organism for mutual benefit.

SYNERGISM: The cooperative action of separate substances so that the total effect is greater than the sum of the effects of the substances acting independently. An effect which may be environmentally important because of mixtures of various pollutants.

SYSTEMIC PESTICIDE: A pesticide chemical that is carried to other parts of a plant or animal after it is injected or taken up from the soil or body surface.

T

TAILINGS: Second grade or waste material derived when raw material is screened or processed.

TERATOGENIC: The ability of a substance to cause birth defects, especially when the mother is exposed to it during pregnancy.

TERTIARY TREATMENT: Waste water treatment beyond the secondary, or biological stage that includes removal of nutrients such as phosphorus and nitrogen, and a high percentage of suspended solids. Tertiary treatment, also known as advanced waste treatment, produces a high quality effluent.

THERMAL POLLUTION: Degradation of water quality by the introduction of a heated effluent. Primarily a result of the discharge of cooling waters from industrial processes, particularly from electrical power generation. Even small deviations from normal water temperatures can affect aquatic life. Thermal pollution usually can be controlled by cooling towers.

THRESHOLD DOSE: The minimum dose of a given substance necessary to produce a measurable physiological or psychological effect.

TOLERANCE: The relative capability of an organism to endure an unfavorable environmental factor. The amount of a chemical considered safe on any food to be eaten by man or animals. Also see pesticide tolerance.

TOPOGRAPHY: The configuration of a surface area including its relief, or relative elevations, and the position of its natural and man-made features.

TOXICANT: A substance that kills or injures an organism through its chemical or physical action or by altering its environment; for example, cyanides, phenols, pesticides or heavy metals. Especially used for insect control.

TOXICITY: The quality or degree of being poisonous or harmful to plant or animal life.

TRICKLING FILTER: A device for the biological or secondary treatment of waste water consisting of a bed of rocks or stones that support bacterial growth. Sewage is trickled over the bed enabling the bacteria to break down organic wastes.

TROPHIC LEVEL: The energy level at which an organism sustains itself.

TROPOSPHERE: The layer of the atmosphere extending seven to ten miles above the earth. Vital to life on earth, it contains clouds and moisture that reach earth as rain or snow.

TURBIDIMETER: A device used to measure the amount of suspended solids in a liquid.

TURBIDITY: A thick, hazy condition of air due to the presence of particulates or other pollutants or the similar cloudy condition in water due to the suspension of silt or finely divided organic matter.

U

URBAN RUNOFF: Storm water from city streets and gutters that usually contains a great deal of litter and organic and bacterial wastes.

V

VAPOR: The gaseous phase of substances that normally are either liquids or solids at atmospheric temperature and pressure; for example, steam and phenolic compounds.

VAPOR PLUME: The stack effluent consisting of flue gas made visible by condensed water droplets or mist.

VAPORIZATION: The change of a substance from the liquid to the gaseous state. One of three basic contributing factors to air pollution, the others are attrition and combustion.

VARIANCE: Sanction granted by a governing body for delay or exception in the application of a given law, ordinance or regulation.

VECTOR: Disease vector—a carrier, usually an arthropod, that is capable of transmitting a pathogen from one organism to another.

VOLATILE: Evaporating readily at a relatively low temperature.

W

WASTE: Also see solid waste. (1) bulky waste—items whose large size precludes or complicates their handling by normal collection, processing or disposal methods. (2) construction and demolition waste—building materials and rubble resulting from construction, remodeling, repair and demolition operations. (3) hazardous waste—wastes that require special handling to avoid illness or injury to persons or damage to property. (4) special waste—those wastes that require extraordinary management. (5) wood pulp waste—wood or paper fiber residue resulting from a manufacturing process. (6) yard waste—plant clippings, prunings and other discarded material from yards and gardens. Also known as yard rubbish.

WASTE WATER: Water carrying wastes from homes, businesses and industries that is a mixture of water and dissolved or suspended solids.

WATER POLLUTION: The addition of sewage, industrial wastes or other harmful or objectionable material to water in concentration or in sufficient quantities to result in measurable degradation of water quality.

WATER QUALITY CRITERIA: The levels of pollutants that affect the suitability of water for a given use. Generally, water use classification includes: Public water supply; recreation; propagation of fish and other aquatic life; agricultural use and industrial use.

WATER QUALITY STANDARD: A plan for water quality management containing four major elements: The use (recreation, drinking water, fish and wildlife propagation, industrial or agricultural) to be made of the water; criteria to protect those uses; implementation plans (for needed industrial-municipal waste treatment improvements) and enforcement plans, and an anti-degradation statement to protect existing high quality waters.

WATERSHED: The area drained by a given stream.

WATER SUPPLY SYSTEM: The system for the collection, treatment, storage and distribution of potable water from the sources of supply to the consumer.

WATER TABLE: The upper level of underground water.

WETLAND: Inland—land that is often wet or flooded because the water table rises to or above the surface. Coastal—land types such as salt marshes or tidal marshes subject to regular tidal action or occasional flooding by storms or abnormally high tides.

X, Y, Z

ZOOPLANKTON: Planktonic animals that supply food for fish.

Part One

Legal Theories and Procedures

Part One

Legal Theories and Procedures

A. Legal Theories on Which Suits May Be Based

Planners and lawyers engaged in the formulation and implementation of plans affecting the environment would be aided by a good working knowledge of the legal principles affecting those plans. More particularly, they should be familiar with the principles of environmental law. However, environmental law has not been a traditional part of the curriculum of law schools. In fact, many lawyers practicing today have never taken a course in environmental law; nor have many of the judges charged with deciding cases whose outcome may have serious consequences for the environment.

Environmental law has developed as a composite subject, drawing on the traditional subjects of the law, to derive those components that have implications for the environment. For example, **property law** is concerned with the rights associated with the ownership of title to the land. Among those rights are certain obligations relating to the environment. It is these environmental implications of property law that are properly included in the study of environmental law. Similarly, a **tort** is a legal wrong for which a legal remedy may be sought. Legal wrongs relating to the environment are also considered part of environmental law. Other components of environmental law include **administrative law**, which deals with the rights and obligations of government officials in the performance of their duties; **procedure**, which deals with the process by which a person who believes he has a legal right may seek a judicial response; **constitutional law**, which deals with the principles and values that are the foundations of our legal system and may impose limitations on actions; and the interpretation and writing of **legislation**.

Legal scholars have long recognized that there is a relationship between justice and certainty in the law. When law is definite and certain, freedom may be enhanced within the precise boundaries created by the law. Legal theories have been created to make the law more definite and certain by delineating areas of conduct that are permissible and prescribing the consequences if the principles are violated. By this system, individual rights may be protected and society may develop an understanding of what it may do. Thus, if the quality of the environment is threatened, it is useful to have general legal theories on which a law suit may be brought. However, protection of the environment often comes into conflict with the rights of individuals. The legal theories on which environmental law suits are based seek to balance the interests of society in preserving the environment and the private rights of individuals.

1. NUISANCE

Nuisance is a common law principle that is defined as an unreasonable and substantial interference with the use or enjoyment of one's property without an actual physical trespass or unauthorized physical entry. It is an important concept of both the law of property and the law of torts.

The nuisance doctrine is an important legal theory on which environmental law suits are based because it can be used when one person causes annoyance, inconvenience, discomfort or damage to another without ever crossing the boundary line of the property owner. For example, if someone creates noises or smells or carries on any activity that is offensive or dangerous and thereby deprives the owner of reasonable use and enjoyment of his property that activity may be characterized as a nuisance for which the law provides a remedy.

In determining whether a particular activity constitutes a nuisance, it is difficult to define just how much annoyance or inconvenience is necessary to make it objectionable. It is always a question of degree, depending on the circumstances. In every case the right of one landowner to use his property must be balanced against the right of the other landowner to enjoy his own property without unreasonable interference and annoyance by his neighbor. Each case also involves a balancing of the usefulness and social need of the activity against the amount of harm which it inflicts. This process of balancing the competing interests is one of the central themes of environmental law.

One of the traditional common law distinctions of the nuisance doctrine is the comparison of the **private nuisance** and the **public nuisance**. A private nuisance involves the interference with the use and enjoyment of the property of one or a limited number of persons. A public nuisance involves the interference with the enjoyment, comfort, standards of health, safety and convenience of the **community at large**. For example, if an electric generating plant causes air pollution by the use of high sulfur coal as fuel, the act would constitute a public nuisance because of the large numbers of persons affected. The distinction between the public and private nuisance is important because if a person seeks to enjoin a public nuisance he must be able to prove "special damages," that is, damages that are peculiar to him and greater than the damages to the general public. Thus, it would be difficult for a private person to bring a suit to enjoin an electric generating plant from causing air pollution unless the plaintiff could show "special damages." For additional information see Prosser, *Private Action for Public Nuisance*, 52 VA. L. REV. 997 (1966) and Trumbull, *Private Environmental Legal Action*, 7 U. SAN FRANCISCO L. REV. 27 (1972).

HULBERT v. CALIFORNIA PORTLAND CEMENT CO.

161 Cal. 239, 118 P. 928 (1911)

MELVIN, J. Petitioner has made an original application to this court to suspend the operation of a certain injunction until the decision of the appeals in two cases, in each of which the California Portland Cement Company, a corporation, is the defendant, on the ground that the property of the corporation would be so greatly damaged by the operation of the injunction pending the appeals that a judgment in defendant's favor would be almost fruitless; while it is contended the damage to plaintiffs is easily susceptible of satisfaction by a payment of money. Petitioner offers to furnish any bond this court may require, if the order which is prayed for shall be granted. As this was the first case in America, so far as this court knew, in which the operation of a cement plant had been enjoined because of the dust produced in the processes of manufacture, and as the showing which was made indicated that petitioner's loss would be very great if the injunction were enforced at once, an order was entered, temporarily staying its operation until both sides to the controversy could be heard. The court was moved somewhat to such action also because the trial court had made an order staying the operation of the injunction for 60 days, so that this court might have the opportunity of passing upon this application. Two principal questions are presented: (1) Has the Supreme Court the authority in aid of its appellate jurisdiction, under section 4 of article 6 of the Constitution, to suspend the operation of an injuction pending appeal? (2) If it have such power, is this a proper case for the exercise thereof? Owing to the conclusion which we have reached, it is unnecessary to answer the first question authoritatively, because, assuming a reply to it in the affirmative, we cannot say that the facts of this case warrant any other response to the second inquiry than a negative one.

The salient facts shown by the petitioner are that the California Portland Cement Company is engaged in the manufacture of cement on property situated nearly two miles from the center of the city of Colton, in the county of San Bernardino, but not within the limits of said city; that said manufactory is located at Slover mountain, where the substances necessary to the production of Portland cement are quarried; that long before the surrounding country had been generally devoted to the production of citrus fruits Slover mountain had been known as a place where limestone was produced; that quarries of marble and limestone had been established there; that lime kilns had been operated upon said mountain for many years; that in 1891 the petitioner obtained title to said premises, and commenced thereon the manufacture of Portland cement; that the said corporation has expended upon said property more than $800,000; that at the time when petitioner began the erection of the cement plant the land surrounding the plant was vacant and unimproved, except some land lying to the north which had been planted to young citrus trees; that these trees were first planted about a year before the erection of the cement plant was commenced (but long after the lime kilns and the marble quarries had been operated) that subsequently other orange groves had been planted in the neighborhood; that the petitioner's plant on Slover mountain has a capacity of 3,000 barrels of cement per day; but that by the judgment of the superior court in two certain actions against petitioner, entitled Lillie A. Hulbert, Administratrix, etc., v. California Portland Cement Company, a Corporation, and Spencer E. Gilbert, plaintiff, v. Same Defendant, the corporation aforesaid was enjoined from operating its plant in such manner as to produce an excess of 88,706 barrels of finished cement per annum; that the regular pay roll of the company includes the names of about 500 men, who are paid about $35,000 a month; that the fixed, constant monthly expenses for supplies and materials amount to $35,000; that the California Portland Cement Company employs the best, most modern methods in its processes of manufacture, but that nevertheless there is an unavoidable escape into the air of certain dust and smoke; that petitioner has no other location for the conduct of its business at a profit; that the land of the Hulbert estate is located from 1,500 to 2,500 feet from petitioner's cement works, and that Spencer E. Gilbert's land is all within 1,000 feet therefrom; that petitioner has diligently sought some means of preventing the escape of dust from its factories; that it has consulted the best experts and sought the best information obtainable, and that it is now and has been for a long time conducting experiments along the lines suggested by the most eminent engineering authorities upon this subject, and that as soon as any process can be evolved for preventing the escape of the dust, the petitioner will adopt such process in its works, and it is believed that a process now constructing with all diligence by petitioner will effectually prevent the escape of dust. Petitioner also alleges that it is easily possible to estimate the damages of the plaintiffs in money, while it is utterly impracticable to estimate the damage in money which will be caused to the petitioner by the closing of the plant, and that stopping the plant pending the appeals will cause financial ruin to the chief stockholders of the petitioner, and that the elements of loss averred are irreparable on account of the disorganization of petitioner's working force, loss of market, and deterioration of machinery.

The learned judge of the superior court, in deciding the cases in which petitioner here was defendant, described the method of manufacturing cement and the injury to the trees. He said, in part: "The output from these two mills at the present time is about 2,500 barrels of cement every 24 hours, and to produce this there is fed into the various kilns of the defendant, during the time mentioned, about 1,500,000 pounds of raw mix, composed of limestone and clay, ground as fine as flour and thoroughly mixed. This raw mix is fed into the tops of kilns, wherein the temperature varies from 1,800 to 3,000 degrees Fahrenheit, and through which kilns the heated air and combustion gases pass at the rate of many thousands of feet per minute. The result of this almost inconceivable draft is to carry out, in addition to the usual products of combustion, particles of the raw mix, to the extent of probably 20 tons per day or more, the greater part of which, without question, is carried up into the air by the rising gases, and thereafter, through the action of the winds and force of gravity, distributed over the surrounding territory." Speaking of the premises of the plaintiffs, he said that, because of prevailing westerly winds and on account of the proximity of the mills, said lands were almost continually subject to the deposit of dust. In this regard he said: "It is the fact incontrovertibly established by both the testimony of witnesses and personal inspections made by the court that a well-nigh continuous shower of cement dust, emanating from defendant's cement mills and caused by their operation, is, and for some years past has been, falling upon the properties of the plaintiffs, covering and coating the ground, filtering through their homes, into all parts thereof, forming an opaque semi-cemented incrustation upon the upper sides of all exposed flowers and foliage, particularly leaves of citrus trees, and leaving ineradicable, yet withal plainly discernable, marks and evidence of dust, dusty deposits, and grayish colorings resulting therefrom, upon the citrus fruits. The incrustations above mentioned, unlike the deposits occasionally occurring on leaves because of the presence of undue amounts of road dust or field dust, are not dissipated by the strongest winds, nor washed off through the action of the most protracted rains. Their presence, from repeated observations, seems to be as continuous as their hold upon the leaves seems tenacious." The court further found that the deposit of dust on the fruit decreased its value; that the constant presence of dust on the limbs and leaves of the trees rendered the cultivation of the ground and the harvesting of the crop more costly than it would have been under ordinary conditions; and that said dust added to the usual and ordinary discomforts of life by its presence in the homes of the plaintiffs. The court also found that the operation of the old mill of the defendant corporation had occurred with the acquiescence of the plaintiffs, and that the defendant had acquired a prescriptive right to manufacture the maximum quantity of cement produced annually by that factory.

In view of such facts solemnly found by the court after trial, we cannot say that there is reason for a suspension by this court of the injunction, even conceding that we have power under proper circumstances thus to prevent a disturbance of existing conditions, pending an appeal. We are not insensible to the fact that petitioner's business is a very important enterprise; that its location is peculiarly adapted for the manufacture of cement; and that great loss may result to the corporation by the enforcement of the injunction. Even if the officers of the corporation are willing to furnish a bond in a sum equal to the value of the properties of Gilbert and of the Hulbert estate here involved, we cannot, under plain principles of equity, compel these plaintiffs to have recourse to their action at law only, and take from them the benefit of the injunctive relief accorded them by the chancellor below. To permit the cement company to continue its operations, even to the extent of destroying the property of the two plaintiffs and requiring payment of the full value thereof, would be, in effect, allowing the seizure of private property for a use other than a public one—something unheard of and totally unauthorized in the law. Nor may we say, as petitioner urges us to declare, that cement dust is not a nuisance, and therefore that the restraint imposed is illegal, even though this is one of the first cases, if not the very first, of its kind, in which the emission of cement dust from a factory has been enjoined, for we are bound by the findings of the court in this proceeding, and may not consider their sufficiency or lack of it until we take up the appeals on their merits. The court has found that the plaintiffs in the actions tried were specially damaged by a nuisance maintained by the cement company. This entitles the plaintiffs, not only to damages, but to such relief as the facts warrant, and the chancellor has determined that limiting the production in the manner selected is a proper form of protection to their rights. It is well settled in California that a nuisance which consists in pouring soot or the like upon the property of a neighbor in such manner as to interfere with the comfortable enjoyment of the premises is a private nuisance, which may be enjoined or abated, and for which, likewise, the persons specially injured may recover pecuniary damages. . . . The last-named case was one in which the operation of a gas factory had been enjoined, and the following language was used: "A gas factory does not constitute a nuisance per se. The manufacture in or near a great city of gas for illuminating and heating is not only legitimate, but is very necessary to the comfort of the people. But in this, as in any other sort of lawful business, the person conducting it is subject to the rule, "Sic utere tuo ut alienum non laedas," even when operating under municipal permission, or under public obligation to furnish a commodity. Nor will the adoption of the most approved appliances and methods of production justify the continuance of that which, in spite of them, remains a nuisance.

Petitioner contends for the rule that the resulting injuries must be balanced by the court, and that, where the hardship inflicted upon one party by the granting of an injunction would be very much greater than that which would be suffered by the other party if the nuisance were permitted to continue, injunctive relief should be denied. This doctrine of "the balance of hardship" and the associated rule that "an injunction is not of right but of grace" are the bases of petitioner's argument, and many authorities in support of them have been called to our attention. In petitioner's behalf are cited such cases as Richards' Appeal, where an injunction which had been sought to restrain defendant from using large quantities of bituminous coal to plaintiff's damage was refused, and the plaintiff was remitted to his action at law; the court saying, among other things: "Whatever of injury may have or shall result to his (the plaintiff's) property from the defendant's works, by reason of a nuisance complained of, is only such as is incident to a lawful business conducted in the ordinary way, and by no unusual means. Still, there may be injury to the plaintiff, but this of itself may not entitle him to the remedy he seeks. It may not, if ever so clearly established, be a cause in which equity ought to enjoin the defendant in the use of a material necessary to the successful production of an article of such prime necessity as good iron, especially if it be very certain that a greater injury would ensue by enjoining than would result by refusal to enjoin." The same rule was announced in Dilworth's Appeal, a case involving the building of a powder house near plaintiff, and in Huckenstine's Appeal. Petitioner admits that in the later case of Sullivan v. Jones & Laughlin Steel Co., supra, the Supreme Court of Pennsylvania reached a different conclusion, but contends that the opinion in that case merely defines the word "grace" as a used in Huckenstine's Appeal: the real meaning of the expression "an injunction is a matter of grace" being that a high degree of discretion is exercised by a chancellor in awarding or denying an injunction. An examination of the case, however, shows that the court went very much further than a mere definition of the phrase "of grace." In that case the defendant had erected a large factory for the manufacture of steel on land purchased from one of the plaintiffs, but after many years defendant had commenced the use of "Mesaba" ore, which caused the emission of great quantities of fine dust upon the property of plaintiffs. The Supreme Court of Pennsylvania, in reversing the decree of the lower court, dismissing the bill, went into the matter of "balancing injuries" and "injuctions of grace" very thoroughly, and we may with propriety, I think, quote and adopt some of its language upon these subjects as follows:

"It is urged that, as an injuction is a matter of grace, and not of right, and more injury would result in awarding than refusing it, it ought not to go out in this case. A chancellor does act as of grace, but that grace sometimes becomes a matter of right to the suitor in its court, and, when it is clear that the law cannot give protection and relief—to which the complainant in equity is admittedly entitled—the chancellor can no more withhold his grace than the law can deny protection and relief, if able to give them. This is too often overlooked when it is said that in equity a decree is of grace, and not of right, as a judgment at law. In Walters v. McElroy et al. the defendants gave as one of the reasons why the plaintiff's bill should be dismissed that his land was worth but little, while they were engaged in a great mining industry, which would be paralyzed if they should be enjoined from a continuance of the acts complained of; and the principle was invoked that, as a decree in equity is of grace, a chancellor will never enjoin an act where, by so doing, greater injury will result than from a refusal to enjoin. To this we said: The phrase "of grace," predicated of a decree in equity, had its origin in an age when kings dispensed their royal favors by the hands of their chancellors; but, although it continues to be repeated occasionally, it has no rightful place in the jurisprudence of a free commonwealth, and ought to be relegated to the age in which it was appropriate. It has been somewhere said that equity has its laws, as law has its equity. This is but another form of saying that equitable remedies are administered in accordance with rules as certain as human wisdom can devise, leaving their application only in doubtful cases to the discretion, not the unmerited favor or grace, of the chancellor. Certainly no chancellor in any English-speaking country will at this day admit that he dispenses favors or refuses rightful demands, or deny that, when a suitor has brought his case clearly within the rules of equity jurisprudence the relief he asks is demandable ex debito justitiae, and needs not to be implored ex gratia. And as to the principle invoked, that a chancellor will refuse to enjoin when greater injury will result from granting than from refusing an injunction, it is enough to observe that it has no application where the act complained of is in itself, as well as in its incidents, tortious. In such case it cannot be said that injury would result from an injunction, for no man can complain that he is injured by being prevented from doing to the hurt of another that which he has no right to do. Nor can it make the slightest difference that the plaintiff's property is of insignificant value to him, as compared with the advantages that would accrue to the defendants from its occupation.' There can be no balancing of conveniences when such balancing involves the preservation of an established right, though possessed by a peasant only to a cottage as his home, and which will be extinguished if relief is not granted against one who would destroy it in artificially using his own land. Though it is said a chancellor will consider whether he would not do a greater injury by enjoining than would result from refusal, and leaving the part to his redress at the hands of a court and jury, and if, in conscience, the former should appear, he will refuse to enjoin (Richard's Appeal, supra), that 'it often becomes a grave question whether so great an injury would not be done to the community by enjoining the business that the complaining party should be left to his remedy at law' (Dilworth's Appeal, supra), and similar expressions are to be found in other cases, 'none of them, nor all of them, can be authority for the proposition that equity, a case for its cognizance being otherwise made out, will refuse to protect a man in the possession and enjoyment of his property, because that right is less valuable to him than the power to destroy it may be to his neighbor or to the public.' The right of a man to use and enjoy his property is as supreme as his neighbor's, and no artificial use of it by either can be permitted to destroy that of the other." * * *

Let the temporary order staying the operation of the injunction be dismissed, and the petition be denied.

BOOMER v. ATLANTIC CEMENT CO.

26 N.Y.2d 219, 309 N.Y. S.2d 312 (1970)

BERGAN, Judge.

Defendant operates a large cement plant near Albany. These are actions for injunction and damages by neighboring land owners alleging injury to property from dirt, smoke and vibration emanating from the plant. A nuisance has been found after trial, temporary damages have been allowed; but an injunction has been denied.

Public concern with air pollution arising from many sources in industry and in transportation is currently accorded ever wider recognition accompanied by a growing sense of responsibility in State and Federal Governments to control it. Cement plants are obvious sources of air pollution in the neighborhoods where they operate.

But there is now before the court private litigation in which individual property owners have sought specific relief from a single plant operation. The threshold question raised by the division of view on this appeal is whether the court should resolve the litigation between the parties now before it as equitably as seems possible; or whether, seeking promotion of the general public welfare, it should channel private litigation into broad public objectives. * * *

It is a rare exercise of judicial power to use a decision in private litigation as a purposeful mechanism to achieve direct public objectives greatly beyond the rights and interests before the court.

Effective control of air pollution is a problem presently far from solution even with the full public and financial powers of government. In large measure adequate technical procedures are yet to be developed and some that appear possible may be economically impracticable.

It seems apparent that the amelioration of air pollution will depend on technical research in great depth; on a carefully balanced consideration of the economic impact of close regulation; and of the actual effect on public health. It is likely to require massive public expenditure and to demand more than any local community can accomplish and to depend on regional and interstate controls.

A court should not try to do this on its own as a by-product of private litigation and it seems manifest that the judicial establishment is neither equipped in the limited nature of any judgment it can pronounce nor prepared to lay down and implement an effective policy for the elimination of air pollution. This is an area beyond the circumference of one private lawsuit. It is a direct responsibility for government and should not thus be undertaken as an incident to solving a dispute between property owners and a single cement plant—one of many—in the Hudson River valley.

The cement making operations of defendant have been found by the court at Special Term to have damaged the nearby properties of plaintiffs in these two actions. That court, as it has been noted, accordingly found defendant maintained a nuisance and this has been affirmed at the Appellate Division. * * *

The rule in New York has been that such a nuisance will be enjoined although marked disparity be shown in economic consequence between the effect of the injunction and the effect of the nuisance. * * *

Thus the unconditional injunction granted at Special Term was reinstated. The rule laid down in that case, then, is that whenever the damage resulting from a nuisance is found not "unsubstantial," viz., $100 a year, injunction would follow. * * *

Although the court at Special Term and the Appellate Division held that injunction should be denied, it was found that plaintiffs had been damaged in various specific amounts up to the time of the trial and damages to the respective plaintiffs were awarded for those amounts.

* * *

This result at Special Term and at the Appellate Division is a departure from a rule that has become settled; but to follow the rule literally in these cases would be to close down the plant at once. This court is fully agreed to avoid that immediately drastic remedy; the difference in view is how best to avoid it.[†]

One alternative is to grant the injunction but postpone its effect to a specified future date to give opportunity for technical advances to permit defendant to eliminate the nuisance; another is to grant the injunction conditioned on the payment of permanent damages to plaintiffs which would compensate them for the total economic loss to their property present and future caused by defendant's operations. For reasons which will be developed the court chooses the latter alternative.

If the injunction were to be granted unless within a short period—e.g., 18 months—the nuisance be abated by improved methods, there would be no assurance that any significant technical improvement would occur.

The parties could settle this private litigation at any time if defendant paid enough money and the imminent threat of closing the plant would build up the pressure on defendant. If there were no improved techniques found, there would inevitably be applications to the court at Special Term for extensions of time to perform on showing of good faith efforts to find such techniques.

Moreover, techniques to eliminate dust and other annoying by-products of cement making are unlikely to be developed by any research the defendant can undertake within any short period, but will depend on the total resources of the cement industry nationwide and throughout the world. The problem is universal wherever cement is made.

For obvious reasons the rate of the research is beyond control of defendant. If at the end of 18 months the whole industry has not found a technical solution a court would be hard put to close down this one cement plant if due regard be given to equitable principles.

On the other hand, to grant the injunction unless defendant pays plaintiffs such permanent damages as may be fixed by the court seems to do justice between the contending parties. All of the attributions of economic loss to the properties on which plaintiffs' complaints are based will have been redressed.

The nuisance complained of by these plaintiffs may have other public or private consequences, but these particular parties are the only ones who have sought remedies and the judgment proposed will fully redress them. The limitation of relief granted is a limitation only within the four corners of these actions and does not foreclose public health or other public agencies from seeking proper relief in a proper court.

It seems reasonable to think that the risk of being required to pay permanent damages to injured property owners by cement plant owners would itself be a reasonable effective spur to research for improved techniques to minimize nuisance. * * *

[†]Respondent's investment in the plant is in excess of $45,000,000. There are over 300 people employed there.

The present cases and the remedy here proposed are in a number of other respects rather similar to Northern Indiana Public Service Co. v. W. J. & M. S. Vesey, 210 Ind. 338, 200 N.E. 620 decided by the Supreme Court of Indiana. The gases, odors, ammonia and smoke from the Northern Indiana company's gas plant damaged the nearby Vesey greenhouse operation. An injunction and damages were sought, but an injunction was denied and the relief granted was limited to permanent damages "present, past, and future" (p. 371, 200 N.E. 620).

Denial of injunction was grounded on a public interest in the operation of the gas plant and on the court's conclusion "that less injury would be occasioned by requiring the appellant [Public Service] to pay the appellee [Vesey] all damages suffered by it * * * than by enjoining the operation of the gas plant; and that the maintenance and operation of the gas plant should not be enjoined." * * *

Thus it seems fair to both sides to grant permanent damages to plaintiffs which will terminate this private litigation. The theory of damage is the "servitude on land" of plaintiffs imposed by defendant's nuisance. (See United States v. Causby, 328 U.S. 256, 261, 262, 267, 66 S.Ct. 1062, 90 L.Ed. 1206, where the term "servitude" addressed to the land was used by Justice Douglas relating to the effect of airplane noise on property near an airport.) * * *

The orders should be reversed, without costs, and the cases remitted to Supreme Court, Albany County to grant an injunction which shall be vacated upon payment by defendant of such amounts of permanent damage to the respective plaintiffs as shall for this purpose be determined by the court.

JASEN Judge (dissenting).

It has long been the rule in this State, as the majority acknowledges, that a nuisance which results in substantial continuing damage to neighbors must be enjoined. (Whalen v. Union Bag & Paper Co., 208 N.Y. 1, 101 N.E. 805; Campbell v. Seaman, 63 N.Y. 568; see, also, Kennedy v. Moog Servocontrols, 21 N.Y.2d 966, 290 N.Y.S.2d 193, 237 N. E.2d 356.) To now change the rule to permit the cement company to continue polluting the air indefinitely upon the payment of permanent damages is, in my opinion, compounding the magnitude of a very serious problem in our State and Nation today.

In recognition of this problem, the Legislature of this State has enacted the Air Pollution Control Act (Public Health Law, Consol.Laws, c. 45, §§ 1264 to 1299–m) declaring that it is the State policy to require the use of all available and reasonable methods to prevent and control air pollution (Public Health Law § 1265).

The harmful nature and widespread occurrence of air pollution have been extensively documented. Congressional hearings have revealed that air pollution causes substantial property damage, as well as being a contributing factor to a rising incidence of lung cancer, emphysema, bronchitis and asthma.

The specific problem faced here is known as particulate contamination because of the fine dust particles emanating from defendant's cement plant. The particular type of nuisance is not new, having appeared in many cases for at least the past 60 years. (See Hulbert v. California Portland Cement Co., 161 Cal. 239, 118 P. 928 [1911].) It is interesting to note that cement production has recently been identified as a significant source of particulate contamination in the Hudson Valley. This type of pollution, wherein very small particles escape and stay in the atmosphere, has been denominated as the type of air pollution which produces the greatest hazard to human health. We have thus a nuisance which not only is damaging to the plaintiffs, but also is decidedly harmful to the general public.

I see grave dangers in overruling our long-established rule of granting an injunction where a nuisance results in substantial continuing damage. In permitting the injunction to become inoperative upon the payment of permanent damages, the majority is, in effect, licensing a continuing wrong. It is the same as saying to the cement company, you may continue to do harm to your neighbors so long as you pay a fee for it. Furthermore, once such permanent damages are assessed and paid, the incentive to alleviate the wrong would be eliminated, thereby continuing air pollution of an area without abatement.

It is true that some courts have sanctioned the remedy here proposed by the majority in a number of cases, but none of the authorities relied upon by the majority are analogous to the situation before us. In those cases, the courts, in denying an injunction and awarding money damages, grounded their decision on a showing that the use to which the property was intended to be put was primarily for the public benefit. Here, on the other hand, it is clearly established that the cement company is creating a continuing air pollution nuisance primarily for its own private interest with no public benefit.

This kind of inverse condemnation (Ferguson v. Village of Hamburg, 272 N.Y. 234, 5 N.E.2d 801) may not be invoked by a private person or corporation for private gain or advantage. Inverse condemnation should only be permitted when the public is primarily served in the taking or impairment of property. (Matter of New York City Housing Auth. v. Muller, 270 N.Y. 333, 343, 1 N.E.2d 153, 156; Pocantico Water Works Co. v. Bird, 130 N.Y. 249, 258, 29 N.E. 246, 248.) The promotion of the interests of the polluting cement company has, in my opinion, no public use or benefit. * * *

I would enjoin the defendant cement company from continuing the discharge of dust particles upon its neighbors' properties unless, within 18 months, the cement company abated this nuisance.

It is not my intention to cause the removal of the cement plant from the Albany area, but to recognize the urgency of the problem stemming from this stationary source of air pollution, and to allow the company a specified period of time to develop a means to alleviate this nuisance.

* * *

In a day when there is a growing concern for clean air, highly developed industry should not expect acquiescence by the courts, but should, instead, plan its operations to eliminate contamination of our air and damage to its neighbors.

---

2. NEGLIGENCE

Negligence is a legal theory that is part of the subject of **torts**, or legal wrongs. To bring a lawsuit on the basis of this theory the plaintiff must be able to allege and prove the following:

Negligence of the defendant. The plaintiff must allege and prove that the defendant's conduct was "negligent"; i.e., that it was not reasonable, or the kind of conduct that a prudent person would have adopted under the circumstances. The standard that is applied in trying to determine what constitutes negligence is known as "the prudent person principle."

Proximate cause. The plaintiff must allege and prove that it was the negligence of the defendant that caused the injury.

Freedom from **contributory negligence** of the plaintiff. The plaintiff must allege and prove that he or she was not also negligent.

Damages. The plaintiff must allege and prove that he or she has in fact been hurt, either by damage to his property or by some personal injury.

When using negligence as a legal theory on which to bring suit in environmental cases, there are two major problems:

Proof of negligence; i.e., imprudent conduct. Such proof is difficult to obtain in environmental cases because it may be practically impossible for the plaintiff to obtain sufficient information about the details of a manufacturing process to allege and prove negligence. For example, under what circumstances is it negligent for a manufacturer to discharge a pollutant into the air or a stream? If imprudent conduct cannot be proved, the defendant will not be liable under the theory of negligence. In meeting the burden of proof, the plaintiff will try to persuade the court to adopt the principle of **res ipsa loquitur,** meaning, "the thing speaks for itself." The theory of *res ipsa loquitur* enables the plaintiff to allege that the defendant has exclusive control over an instrumentality or process capable of producing injury. This principle creates an inference of negligence that causes the burden of proof to shift to the defendant. Not all states have adopted this principle but, in states which have, it is very much easier to bring a law suit to protect the environment against an industrial defendant. When the burden of proof is shifted to the defendant he must show that his conduct was prudent and, therefore, not negligent.

Proof of causation. The issue of causation is one that must be faced consistently in environmental cases. It is not enough to qualify for a private cause of action to allege that somebody is engaged in an activity that causes pollution. It is also necessary to show a relationship between the alleged wrongful act and an injury suffered. When the injuries sustained are the result of the long-term cumulative effect of pollution, for example, this relationship becomes very difficult to prove.

The varying attitude of the courts on the subject of *res ipsa loquitur* and the problem of proof of causation are illustrated in *Kelley v. National Lead Co.* and *Reynolds Metals Co. v. Yturbide.*

KELLEY v. NATIONAL LEAD COMPANY

210 S.W.2d 728 (Mo. 1948)

BENNICK, Commissioner.

This is an action to recover compensation for personal injuries and property damage allegedly sustained by plaintiffs, Harry Kelley and Florence L. Kelley, his wife, as a consequence of the negligence of defendant, National Lead Company, in causing and permitting gases, fumes, and chemical particles to be emitted from its chemical plant and discharged over the neighborhood where plaintiffs resided.

The action was brought pursuant to the authority of the new code, which permits all persons to join in one action as plaintiffs if they assert any right to relief jointly or severally in respect to or arising out of the same transaction or occurrence, and if any question of law or fact common to all of them will arise in the action.

* * *

Upon a trial to a jury, a verdict was returned awarding plaintiff Harry Kelley the sum of $500 for personal injuries, and awarding both plaintiffs the sum of $500 for damage to their property, but denying plaintiff Florence L. Kelley a recovery on her claim for personal injuries.

Judgment was entered in accordance with the verdict; and following an unavailing motion for a new trial, defendant gave notice of appeal, and by subsequent steps has caused the case to be transferred to this court for our review.

Defendant's plant is located in St. Louis County just south of the city limits of the City of St. Louis at the point where the River Des Peres flows into the Mississippi River. The surrounding territory is utilized for both industrial and residential purposes.

The plant was originally operated by the Titanium Pigment Company, but was taken over as a division of defendant company around 1935. The plant was constructed for the manufacture of titanium pigments, which are chiefly consumed in the making of paints.

An essential ingredient in the process of making pigments out of titanium ore is sulphuric acid, which, prior to 1934, had been purchased on the open market. However in that year the original company decided to begin the manufacture of its own sulphuric acid; and in the period from 1934 to 1941 four separate units were designed and constructed under contracts with reputable, established firms with experience throughout the country in that particular undertaking. As a matter of fact, there is no suggestion in the record of any defect or insufficiency in the construction or installation of the plant.

The four units were designed to manufacture 93% sulphuric acid, and in the course of the process of operating the units certain fumes and mists escaped through stacks and were discharged into the surrounding atmosphere. There was some dispute regarding the density of such fumes and mists during the time before the war that defendant was merely engaged in the manufacture of 93% sulphuric acid. Defendant admitted that a few complaints were received during that period, but offered the explanation that the situation in those instances was usually found to be due to some particular set of circumstances occurring in connection with atmospheric conditions that would bring the fumes to the ground in the surrounding residential area. Indeed, defendant's evidence showed that prior to the outbreak of war, it was not unusual to delay operations, sometimes for several days, until the atmospheric conditions and wind direction would be such that if any undue amount of fumes and gases should be emitted from the stacks, they would not be carried into a residential area. On the other hand, plaintiffs' evidence disclosed that between 1939 and 1941, the Smoke Commissioner of the City of St. Louis, because of complaints received in his office, was prompted to conduct an investigation in the neighborhood, and not only detected the presence of sulphur fumes in the air as well as a white mist or vapor which reduced visibility to a matter of feet, but also traced such fumes and mist to their point of origin, which he found to be defendant's plant.

But whatever may have been the difficulty encountered during the period before the war when defendant was merely engaged in the manufacture of 93% sulphuric acid in connection with its regular peacetime activities, the situation was in any event greatly aggravated and intensified in the latter part of 1941 when one of the units was converted to the manufacture of 40% oleum at the direction of the Ordnance Department of the United States Army.

* * *

The direction for the conversion of defendant's plant was made under the authority of an act for the conscription of industry, which was enacted by the Congress in 1940. 50 U.S.C.A.Appendix, § 309.

Suffice to say that by the provisions of such act, the President was empowered, through the War and Navy Departments, to place an order with any manufacturer for such product or material as might be required, and which was of the nature and kind usually produced or capable of being produced by such manufacturer. Compliance with all such orders for products or material was made obligatory upon the manufacturer, and the orders were required to be given precedence over all other orders and contracts theretofore placed with the manufacturer. In the event of the refusal of any manufacturer to comply with any such order, the President, through the War and Navy Departments, was authorized to take over the operation of the plant for the Government; and it was further provided that any corporation or its responsible officers who should fail to comply with the provisions of the act should be deemed guilty of a felony, and upon conviction should be punished by imprisonment for not more than three years and a fine not exceeding $50,000.

Oleum, which is sometimes referred to as fuming sulphuric acid, is made by dissolving sulphur trioxide in concentrated sulphuric acid. * * *

Before the war emergency it had only been manufactured in very limited quantities; and in undertaking to carry out the direction of the Ordnance Department, not only had defendant never made oleum at any time, but it had no experience to guide it derived from any prior instance where a plant constructed for the manufacture of sulphuric acid was converted into a plant for the manufacture of oleum. As might have been expected, serious difficulties were encountered from the very outset. Moreover there was no opportunity for shutting down the plant while awaiting favorable atmospheric conditions and wind direction as in the case of the manufacture of sulphuric acid during peacetime. The amount of oleum furnished the Weldon Springs Ordnance Works determined how much T.N.T. could be made available for the progress of the war, and all during the duration of the war defendant was under constant pressure from the Ordnance Department to increase its output. The result of all this was that the discharge of fumes was greatly intensified over what had been the situation before the manufacture of oleum was begun. * * *

The gist of plaintiffs' cause of action was embodied in paragraph 4 of their petition, in which they charged that defendant then and for some years past had "negligently and carelessly" caused large quantities of poisonous and deleterious gases, fumes, and chemical particles, including concentrated sulphuric acid and oleum, to be discharged from a number of very tall stacks at its plant, and that whenever the wind blew from the direction of the stacks towards plaintiffs' home, it caused such gases, fumes, and chemical particles to be deposited in plaintiffs' neighborhood, resulting in injury to their persons and damage to their property. * * *

Throughout the trial counsel emphasized on repeated occasions that the issue was one of negligence; and in the submission of the case both sides requested and received instructions upon such theory. There can be no doubt that the parties themselves, as well as the lower court, construed the pleadings as putting negligence in issue, and they will therefore be given the same construction in disposing of the case on this appeal.

By the time of the submission of the case, this issue had been reduced to the question of whether defendant could have remedied or prevented the escape of fumes and gases from its plant, but negligently failed to do so.

The question involved the use of a device or principle known as the Cottrell Precipitator. * * *

It seems to be unquestioned that owing to the higher strength of the materials employed as well as the difference in temperature at which the process is required to be carried on, the manufacture of oleum results in the giving off of far larger amounts of fumes and gases than in the case of the manufacture of sulphuric acid. Not only is the production of fumes and gases inherent in the very nature of the process, but there is no known way of preventing it.

When defendant converted its plant to the manufacture of oleum, it did not know what to expect in the way of fumes and gases, but the result was beyond its worst foreboding. Immediate efforts were made by defendant's own officials to study the problem and find its reason and solution, * * * and while their recommendations may have helped the condition to some extent, they did not succeed in eliminating the fumes.

Early in 1942 the question of the application of the Cottrell process was taken up with the Research Corporation of America. It was known that Cottrell Precipitators had been used successfully in other classes of sulphuric acid plants for various purposes, and it was thought that the process was worthy of a trial, though the same had never before been employed in a plant converted to the manufacture of oleum.

* * *

On the contrary, all the evidence, including that for plaintiffs, disclosed that the application of the Cottrell principle to any particular situation requires testing and experimentation, and that in each and every instance it has to be what some of the witnesses referred to as a tailor-made job.

In the summer of 1943 a test plant was constructed upon defendant's premises according to specifications furnished by the Research Corporation of America. The evidence showed that the test plant was required because of the fact that the Research Corporation of America had had no previous experience in designing equipment for a plant of the type and nature of defendant's plant. * * *

On January 14, 1944, defendant was instructed by the Ordnance Department to discontinue the manufacture of oleum, and negotiations with the Research Corporation of America for the installation of a Cottrell Precipitator were thereupon abandoned. However in October, 1944, defendant was directed to resume the manufacture of oleum, and negotiations for the installation of a Cottrell Precipitator were once again begun. On V-J Day, which was August 15, 1945, the manufacture of oleum was finally terminated. Some time later a Cottrell Precipitator was completed and installed; and while defendant's assistant superintendent testified in his direct examination that it had accomplished the desired purpose of eliminating the fumes in the manufacture of sulphuric acid, it was brought out in his cross-examination that there was still a certain amount of gas and mist coming out of the stacks at the time of the trial in May, 1946. * * *

Plaintiffs' petition charged mere general negligence, that is, that defendant carelessly and negligently caused gases, fumes, and chemical particles to be emitted from its plant and deposited in plaintiffs' neighborhood. * * *

But while referring to the case as one of res ipsa loquitur, what plaintiffs doubtless mean to urge is that it comes within the principle of Fletcher v. Rylands, L.R. 1 Exch. 265, L.R. 3 H.L. 330, which is that one, who for his own purposes collects and keeps anything upon his land which is likely to do mischief if it escapes, must keep it at his peril, and if he does not do so is prima facie actionable for all the damage which is the natural consequence of its escape. In any event, the petition was drawn upon this theory. It is enough to say, however, that such principle has been seriously questioned in practically all jurisdictions, and at any rate is not the law in our own jurisdiction, where it is held that liability cannot be imposed upon the owner or occupant for damage caused by the escape of substances from his premises except upon proof of some fault or negligence on his part. Murphy v. Gillum, 73 Mo.App. 487; Greene v. Spinning, Mo.App., 48 S.W.2d

* * *

It is interesting to note that while plaintiffs drew their peitition upon the principle announced in Fletcher v. Rylands, and while they presented their evidence upon that theory, when they came to the submission of the case they abandoned their reliance upon the mere fact of the escape of the fumes and gases, and included the element of whether defendant had permitted such fumes and gases to escape, when, in the exercise of ordinary care, it could have remedied or prevented said condition, but failed to do so. Such specific element of liability was undoubtedly suggested by the evidence regarding the eventual designing and installation of a Cottrell Precipitator; and the obvious purpose of the instruction was to submit the question of whether defendant had been guilty of negligence in failing to prevent the escape of fumes and gases by at all times making use of such a device.

Having due regard for the fundamental concepts of the law of negligence, we cannot escape the conclusion that plaintiffs failed to make a case for the jury upon this issue. * * *

There is a distinction to be drawn between negligence and actionable negligence. Hight v. American Bakery Co., 168 Mo.App. 431, 151 S.W. 776. Even though a given act or omission might be thought to indicate a lack of care and thus to constitute negligence from the viewpoint of the ordinary layman, it does not follow that a cause of action will inevitably arise therefrom. On the contrary, in order to impose liability there must not only be a lack of care, but such lack of care must involve a breach of some duty owed to another under the particular circumstances existing at the time of the act or omission complained of, which act or omission must have proximately resulted in such other person's injury. * * *

It may be that defendant was in one sense negligent in so long delaying its experimentation with the Cottrell principle, but such negligence, if any, lacked the essential elements to make it actionable in this character of proceeding. If a Cottrell Precipitator had been readily procurable on the market, defendant would no doubt have owed plaintiffs the duty of promptly installing one, but since such a device was not available on the market, defendant was not guilty of any breach of duty so as to have afforded plaintiffs a remedy by an action for negligence.

The whole trouble is that while plaintiffs may have a cause of action, they have mistaken the remedy to be pursued for its enforcement. If they are to obtain redress for whatever injury and damage they have sustained, it seems clear that it must be upon the theory of nuisance. It is well recognized that for one to permit fumes and gases to escape from his premises and be deposited on the premises of another to his injury and damage may constitute an actionable wrong in the maintenance of a nuisance. * * *

What is of course meant is that such a condition may constitute a nuisance in fact, depending on the circumstances of the particular case, such as the location and character of the neighborhood; the nature of the use to which the property is put; the extent and frequency of the injury; and the effect upon the enjoyment of life, health, property, and the like. * * *

The doctrine is not limited to any particular character of industry, and it has been expressly held that the emission of fumes and gases from a sulphuric acid plant may constitute a nuisance, although the business itself is not unlawful, nor is the plant a nuisance per se. * * *

But notwithstanding the relevancy of any of the evidence to the questions that would arise in the case of nuisance, plaintiffs appreciate that a petition based on the theory of negligence will not sustain a recovery on the theory of nuisance. * * *

It has been repeatedly held that where it appears from the record that the plaintiff has rights growing out of an occurrence but has misconceived his remedy, it is within the province of an appellate court to remand the case to permit the petition to be amended, if the plaintiff is so advised, and the case retried upon the cause of action disclosed. * * *

It follows from what has been said that the judgment of the circuit court should be reversed and the case remanded for a new trial.

REYNOLDS METALS CO. v. YTURBIDE

258 F.2d 321 (9th Cir.)
cert. den., 358 U.S. 840 (1958)

POPE, Circuit Judge.

In July, 1946, Reynolds Metals Company, a Delaware corporation, acquired through lease, an aluminum plant belonging to the Government and located at Troutdale, Oregon. It commenced operation of its first potline for the production of aluminum in September of that year. In the operation of the plant chemical compounds containing aluminum were collected in the reduction cells of the so-called "pots" and were reduced or separated by the process of electrolysis or passage of current through the cell. In the process, temperatures up to 1775° F. were developed. As the compounds with which the cells were charged, (cryolite or sodium fluoride or calcium fluoride and aluminum fluoride) contain large percentages of fluorine ranging around 50 percent, a considerable portion of fluoride material was volatized in the process and reached the atmosphere.

Shortly after the operation of the plan began, and in December, 1946, the appellees in these three appeals, Paul Martin, his wife, Verla Martin, and his daughter, Paula Martin (now Mrs. Yturbide), moved to their cattle farm or ranch near Troutdale located about a mile to a mile and one-half from the aluminum plant, and they resided there until November, 1950. The law suits out of which these appeals grew were based upon claims that during the period of their residence on the farm they were poisoned by fluorides which originated at the appellant's plant and were borne on the air to the farm where they breathed these fluoride effluents claimed to be highly toxic and also ate vegetables growing in their garden which also had been absorbing the same toxic elements.

The principal question presented here is whether the evidence adduced at the trial below, (the three cases were tried together and upon the same evidence) was sufficient to permit the case to go to the jury. Upon the part of the appellant it is contended, (1) that there was insufficient proof to demonstrate that the damage to the persons of the plaintiffs, of which they complain, was caused by the fluorides escaping from defendant's plant; and (2), that there was no evidence of any negligence, or any other breach of duty, on the part of the defendant.

With respect to the question of causation:—whether the escaping fluorides did in fact cause plaintiffs' injuries,—the evidence was sufficient to warrant the jury's conclusion that the escaping fluorides were the cause of the injuries.

* * *

A horticulturist from the Oregon State College, in the years 1948, 1949 and 1950 made test samples of plants grown on selected plots in the vicinity of the Martin property, for the purpose of determining the fluoride content of such plants.* * *

The plants tested on plots which were farther away from the plant showed a substantially decreasing fluorine content, thus indicating that relatively speaking the nearer the aluminum plant the greater the concentration of the gases, fumes and particulates, (i. e. fine solids).* * *

In general there was an absence of proof as to just what quantities of fluorides contained in these gases, fumes, and particulates, passed over the Martin land or were inhaled by them or ingested from the garden vegetables eaten by them. There was, however, proof that these fluorides were toxic.* * *

That very large quantities of these gases, fumes, and particulates, did leave the plant and were diffused into the air, was unquestioned. Appellant's own exhibits disclose that with the equipment which was used to control the escape of gases during the period that the Martins lived on their farm, hundreds of pounds of these effluents escaped each day. Thus in the year 1947, the amount of fluorine alone escaping per day from the plant averaged 2845 pounds. Comparable amounts escaped in the years 1948–1949 and throughout the first half of 1950, after which time the appellant began the installation of a new control system which was much more efficient in arresting the escape and fall-out.

There is no showing as to where these large quantities of effluents finally settled. The experiments mentioned above would indicate that the greater portion settled on those areas nearest the plant, and those areas included the Martin farm. That the effluents did have some degree of toxic or harmful effect was indicated by proof that cattle upon the Martin place showed damage from fluorosis. Generally with respect to cattle it does not appear to have been controverted that cattle damage from an aluminum plant is a fairly common phenomenon.

Of course it does not follow from mere proof of some damage to cattle on the Martin place that the plaintiffs' physical injuries were due to excessive amounts of fluorides from the plant.

* * *

A significant bit of testimony adduced was proof that glass in the Martin home became etched by acid, probably hydrofluoric acid which was one of the effluents from the aluminum plant. One of the expert witnesses, the British doctor who had some prior experience with similar etching of glass located near industrial plants abroad, testified that the glass from the Martin window which he was shown during the testimony was an indication of excessive quantities of fluoride contamination in the atmosphere.

Although the cases of the Martins are unique in that they were unable to produce either from medical literature or expert witnesses histories of persons situated as they were, namely, persons not working in the plant but simply living outside and near the plant, who developed symptoms similar to theirs in consequence of the fall-out of emanations from an aluminum plant, (see footnote 5a infra) nevertheless they did produce substantial medical testimony which did connect their disabilities and physical injuries with the fluorides escaping from the plant. Of course there was also testimony to the contrary, but the evidence adduced on their behalf, principally from the British medical expert referred to in footnote 3, supra, and from a Dr. Capps, a Chicago specialist on diseases of the liver, was substantial, and in our view, fully worthy of credit.* * *

The medical witnesses expressed confidence in their conclusions because of the fact that they found substantially the same symptoms in the three individuals, thus lessening the possibility that the symptoms were attributable to individual idiosyncracies. Neither one was able to testify as to the degree of concentration,—how many parts per million of fluorides,—would be required to bring about the injuries found, but both attached some significance to the fact that the window in the house was etched by acid. As stated by Dr. Capps, "I think that if there is enough fluorine to etch a window, it should be able to etch a lung." Dr. Hunter related his own experience in finding in England a family with the same symptoms as the Martins who lived in a house near an industrial plant whose windows were similarly etched and said that the etching he observed in the glass taken from the Martin home was an indication of excessive quantities of fluorine in the atmosphere. He referred to studies made in 1946 warning the industrial world "against throwing into the atmosphere an effluent which would etch glass."

A further circumstance which the medical witnesses emphasized was that in the case of the Martins their abnormal symptoms were reduced and lessened after they had moved away from the vicinity of the plant. We are thus led to the conclusion that the jury was warranted in finding, as they did, that physical injuries to the Martins were caused by the fluoride emanations from the plant which found their way to the Martin place.

On behalf of the defendant evidence was adduced to show that only a very small concentration of fluorides could have reached the Martin home. We think the jury were warranted in accepting plaintiffs' testimony, and the inferences therefrom, that excessive amounts of fluorides reached them, for they actually suffered fluoride poisoning. There was no proof on the part of plaintiffs as to what particular percentage or concentration of fluorides was necessary to produce such results. Plaintiffs were obliged to accept in that respect the concession made by the defendant to the effect that such fluorides are "poisonous in excessive amounts." The only possible conclusion is that because the damage was actually caused by the fluorides, they somehow managed to

The important question is whether there was proof of any negligence or other breach of duty on the part of the defendant which brought about these injuries as its proximate result.* * *

Appellant argues that there is a complete absence of proof of any want of care on its part in the operation of the aluminum plant. In this respect its contention is that before the plant was put in operation it equipped it with facilities for minimizing the amount of effluents that escaped from the plant.* * * The result of this spray system was that it removed some 60 percent of the fluorides from the air coming through the roof so that only 40 percent of these compounds actually escaped from the plant.

Defendant's Assistant Vice-President testified that during this period from 1946 to

1950, when the spray system of fluorides elimination was in use, the company was carrying on experiments to devise and find better ways of making a more efficient capture of the effluents.

* * *

The result of the use of this improved system was to eliminate 90 percent of the fluoride compounds from the air which escaped from the plant.* * *

In short, by this improved method, the portion of the emanating fluorides which reached the air was 10 percent of the total as against 40 percent under the earlier system.

In determining the duty of care the law imposed upon the defendant, it is to be borne in mind that the ordinary care which the law requires of such a defendant is measured in part by the defendant's knowledge of potential dangers.* * *

We think we must accept this as a permissible finding of the jury.

As stated in the Restatement of Torts, § 289, in determining the standard of reasonable conduct, "the actor should recognize that his conduct involves a risk of causing an invasion of another's interest, if a person, possessing* * *such superior perception as the actor himself has* * *would infer that the act creates an appreciable chance of causing such invasion." Comment (n) under this section headed "Superior knowledge" recites: "If the actor has a wider knowledge, whether gained from personal experience or otherwise, the propriety of his judgment as to the risk involved in his conduct is determined by what a reasonable man having such knowledge would regard as probable."

* * *

Not only that, but it was the duty of one in the position of the defendant to know of the dangers incident to the aluminum reduction process. As the last named authors point out in § 16.5, "The manufacturer must learn of dangers that lurk in his processes and his products."

The record here amply demonstrates that the defendant was fully aware of the potential dangers in the escape of fluorides. It is not questioned that numerous claims of injury to cattle from the operation of such plants had been presented to this and other manufacturers. The defendant's senior chemist at the Troutdale laboratory testified that he was familiar with the literature upon the toxic qualities of these fluorides; that he knew that in quantities they were toxic; that some of these were heavier than air and would reach the earth after being air-borne; that quantities of them would drift in the direction of the Martin land and that there were publications which dealt with dangers to human beings from fluorides.

The quesiton is whether in view of the knowledge which the company was reasonably required to have as a manufacturer in this field, and the knowledge which it actually did have of the potential dangers of these escaping fluorides there was evidence of a failure to use reasonable care for the protection of persons in the situation of the Martins.

On behalf of the defendant it was testified that at all these times defendant was utilizing and had installed the latest and best known means of protecting against the escape of the flourides; that the company, continually studying the problem, installed an experimental pilot plant to develop a new process and then changed over to the improved process as soon as its feasibility was developed.

On behalf of plaintiffs it was urged that the evidence warranted a conclusion that the company did not excerise the care in this direction which it might have done in that it allowed the plant to be operated with the less efficient elimination system from 1946 until 1950 whereas proper care required an earlier use of the better devices.* * *

We are of the opinion that the trial court properly submitted to the jury the question of negligence on the part of the defendant on the theory that this was a case correctly permitting the application of the doctrine of res ipsa loquitur.

The court instructed the jury as follows: "Under the law and the facts of these actions, the defendant was the sole operator and in exclusive possession and direct control of the aluminum plant involved during the time involved, namely, between on or about September 23, 1946, and November 30, 1950. Further, that under the ordinary course of events, it is unexpected that persons being in the vicinity of such a plant would be injured or harmed by fluorine compounds emanating therefrom, and that such a mishap would not occur." The statement in the first of these two sentences is unquestionable; the second sentence is in conformity with defendant's theory and much of the evidence adduced by it at the trial. The instruction was consistent with the testimony that the plant as equipped and operated, would not cause fluorosis to persons who had not been employed in the plant itself. The court noted that there was no evidence as to the amount or concentration of fluorides that would bring about fluorosis in the case of such persons. While during the critical period here 40 percent of the gases, fumes and particulates got by the sprinkler system and escaped into the air, the fluorine contents aggregating hundreds of pounds all told, the tests made at various localities near the plant and on every side thereof, according to defendant's witnesses, produced no significant concentration of fluorides at the time the tests were made. Hence, the court, accepting this proof, told the jury that, "under the ordinary course of events, it is unexpected that persons being in the vicinity of such a plant would be injured or harmed by fluorine compounds emanating therefrom."

In so ruling the court in effect determined that the accident was of a kind which ordinarily does not occur in the absence of someone's negligence. That is a prime condition for the application of the so-called rule of res ipsa loquitur. Said the court (135 F.Supp. at page 381): "Here was an instrumentality that was in the exclusive possession and control of the defendant. Something that ordinarily we would not expect to happen did happen and damage resulted. This is the pure and simple test as the Court sees it, of res ipsa loquitur."* * *

Viewing plaintiffs' case in the most favorable light, as we are required to do, we have the following: (1), Damage to persons in the position of the Martins was possible from "excessive amounts" of fluorides; (2), the Martins were poisoned and from this plant and by these fluorides; (3), from this it is permissible to infer that "excessive amounts" reached them,—that there were such excessive amounts; (4), the emission of excessive amounts from the plant was circumstantial evidence of negligence. Res ipsa loquitur.

Appellant says that the res ipsa rule was misapplied here.* * *"Defendant in a res ipsa case may show by evidence how the accident happened, but ordinarily this does not entitle him to a directed verdict. The jury may still reject the evidence or find that the explanation does not preclude the likelihood of negligence.* * * In most res ipsa loquitur cases defendant cannot definitely explain the accident. His usual defense consists of proof of the precautions he did take in constructing, maintaining, and operating the injuring instrumentality. Once in a great while such proof may conclusively show that the accident did not in fact happen, or that it was not caused by defendant. But this is seldom the outcome. And where it is not, defendant is in this dilemma: the less effective his precautions to prevent the occurrence the more apt they are to appear negligent; the more effective the precautions testified to, the less likely they are to have [been] taken in this case since the accident *did happen*."* * *

When res ipsa loquitur is applied the facts of the occurrence warrant the inference of negligence. They furnish substantial evidence of negligence where the direct evidence of it may be lacking, but they make a case to be decided by the jury. In finding itself in the dilemma mentioned by Harper & James in the language quoted above, appellant is in no different situation than any other defendant who finds itself in a res ipsa case and before a jury. It is not, as appellant asserts, the victim of the application of a rule of absolute liability.* * *

The judgments are affirmed.

---

3. TRESPASS

Trespass is a traditional common law theory that is used frequently today to protect the environment. Trespass may be defined as an intentional invasion of someone's property. Unlike negligence, allegation and proof of injury and damages are not required to bring suit under this legal theory, which is a part of **property law**, as distinguished from **tort law**, and is designed to protect the exclusive possession of real estate. Trespass is a good example of a legal theory that was intended for another purpose but has been adapted successfully by environmental lawyers for the protection of the environment. The concept of **physical invasion** has been enlarged to include action not only by a person but also by his agent or instrumentality. For instance, if a person steps on his neighbor's lawn, that is clearly trespass; but the same is true if the person's dog steps on the neighbor's lawn or if a rock is thrown on his property. The dog and the rock are agents or instrumentalities constituting a physical invasion that undermines the exclusive right of the owner. What was originally a principle designed to protect a person's property from intrusion by people has been extended to form the basis of suits to stop intrusions by air and water pollution.

The decision in *Reynolds Metals Co. v. Martin* illustrates some of the issues that may arise when the legal theory of trespass is used for environmental protection. One of the complicating factors in this case is the applicability of the **statute of limitations**, a state statute that imposes a limitation on the time during which a law suit must be started. A second complication in this decision involves an alleged violation of an administrative procedure prescribed by the state legislature. Proponents of environmental protection may point to this case as an example of astute judicial reasoning designed to protect the environment. What is the underlying weakness in the court's reasoning?

REYNOLDS METALS CO. v. MARTIN

337 F.2d 780 (9th Cir. 1964)

The action was commenced on December 18, 1961, in the Circuit Court of the State of Oregon for the County of Multnomah. The plaintiffs, Paul Martin and Verla Martin, his wife, were citizens and residents of Oregon, and defendant, Reynolds Metals Company, is a Delaware corporation.

The original purpose of the action was to recover actual damages in the sum of three hundred thousand dollars and punitive damages in the sum of one hundred thousand dollars, by reason of the alleged contamination of plaintiff's fifteen-hundred acre cattle ranch. Such contamination, it was asserted, was caused by the emanation of fluoride fumes and particulates from defendant's nearby aluminum reduction plant at Troutdale, Oregon, during the years 1956 to 1961.

* * *

After pretrial proceedings had been in progress for some time the plaintiffs, on October 28, 1963, filed their second amended complaint. By that time plaintiffs were seeking actual damages in the sum of $1,428,342 and punitive damages in the sum of one million dollars. Injunctive relief against continued operation of the Troutdale plant was also sought, unless adequate controls were installed to eliminate the emanation of fluorides.

Defendants thereupon moved to dismiss the action for lack of jurisdiction over the subject matter and for failure to state a claim upon which relief can be granted. Both grounds for the motion were premised on the assertion that primary administrative jurisdiction rests with the Sanitary Authority of the State of Oregon, which has certain functions and duties with respect to air pollution pursuant to ORS 449.760 to 449.830. Because of the primary jurisdiction of that agency, defendant contended, the exercise of jurisdiction by the district court must be suspended pending administrative determination of the matters involved in the suit.

The district court denied the motion and this appeal followed.

The doctrine of primary administrative jurisdiction, unlike the rule requiring exhaustion of administrative remedies, applies where a claim is originally cognizable in the courts. It comes into play, as the Supreme Court said in United States v. Western Pac. R. Co., 352 U. S. 59, 64, 77 S.Ct. 161, 165, 1 L.Ed.2d 126,

> "* * * whenever enforcement of the claim requires the resolution of issues which, under a regulatory scheme, have been placed within the special competence of an administrative body; in such a case the judicial process is suspended pending referral of such issues to the administrative body for its views."

Appellant concedes that since this is a diversity action the law of Oregon governs in determining whether the doctrine of primary administrative jurisdiction should be applied in this case. It urges that the courts of Oregon will apply the doctrine in a proper case, and that this is such a case.

While the doctrine may not have been mentioned by name in the decisions of the Supreme Court of Oregon, it appears to have been applied in at least one case. See

Valley & Siletz R. R. Co. v. Flagg, 195 Or. 683, 247 P.2d 639, 654, which involved the railroad rate-making function of the Oregon Public Utilities Commissioner. We can therefore assume, and appellee does not argue to the contrary, that cases can arise in which the courts of Oregon, applying the doctrine of primary administrative jurisdiction, would suspend judicial proceedings pending referral of the issues to a state administrative body for its views.

The precise question presented, therefore, is whether the courts of Oregon would hold that effectuation of the purpose of the legislature in enacting ORS 449.760 to 449.830, requires that the Sanitary Authority should first pass on some or all of the matters in dispute.

One section of the statutes in question, namely ORS 449.820, gives the Sanitary Authority power to institute suits for injunction to compel compliance with the agency's rules, regulations and orders pertaining to air pollution. The last sentence of subsection (1) of ORS 449.820 reads:

> "The provisions of this section shall not prevent the maintenance of actions or suits relating to private or public nuisances brought by any other person, or by the state on relation of any person without prior order of the Sanitary Authority."

The question of whether this statutory language evidenced a legislative purpose that the doctrine of primary administrative purpose should not apply with regard to the air pollution statutes, ORS 449.760 to 449.830, was before the Supreme Court of Oregon in the recent case of Diercks v. Hodgdon, Or., 390 P.2d 935. On review in that case was a decree enjoining the operator of a shingle mill from permitting smoke, cinders and ashes to invade the plaintiff's residential property, and awarding damages in the sum of three hundred dollars.

On the basis of the quoted provision of ORS 449.820(1), the court rejected the argument that the plaintiff should have instituted administrative proceedings under ORS 449.760 to 449.830, before resorting to a suit in equity. The court said (at page 936):

> "ORS 449.820 specifically provides that resort to administrative abatement proceedings is not a condition precedent to relief in law or equity from public or private nuisance."

The company argues, however, that the Diercks decision is not controlling here because that case sounded in nuisance, and the provision of ORS 449.820(1) on which the court relied in Diercks refers to the maintenance of actions or suits relating to "private or public nuisances." Our case, it is contended, does not sound in nuisance, but in trespass.

The complaint in Diercks made no mention of either nuisance or trespass, but the decree which was entered referred to the grievance as a "nuisance." Likewise the Oregon Supreme Court regarded the condition caused by the invasion of the plaintiff's property by smoke, cinders and ashes emanating from the defendant's shingle mill as a "nuisance." In our case, on the other hand, the complaint refers to the contamination of the plaintiff's ranch by reason of fluorides emanating from the Troutdale plant as a "trespass" upon the lands of the plaintiff, the term "nuisance" not being used.

The distinction between trespass and nuisance in the law of Oregon is dealt with at length in Martin v. Reynolds Metals Co., 221 Or. 86, 342 P.2d 790, involving these same parties and the identical kind of grievance, but for an earlier period of time. In that suit, as here, the complaint made reference to "trespass" and not to "nuisance," but the company contended that, in actuality, only a cause of action in nuisance was stated. In taking this position the company sought to apply the two-year statute of limitations applicable to nuisance actions (ORS 12.110), instead of the six-year statute applicable to actions sounding in trespass (ORS 12.080).

Upholding a trial court determination that the suit sounded in trespass, the Supreme Court (342 P.2d at page 794) defined trespass as:

> "* * * any intrusion which invades the possessor's protected interest in exclusive possession, whether that intrusion is by visible or invisible pieces of matter or by energy whch can be measured only by the mathematical language of the physicist."

Measured by this definition, and especially in view of the fact that this case involves precisely the same kind of grievance between the same parties, the conduct complained of in the case before us constituted a trespass, as alleged in the complaint.

In the course of its opinion in the Oregon Martin case, however, the court defined trespass and nuisance in a way which indicates that they overlap. Citing 4 Restatement, Torts 224, Intro. Note Chapter 40, the court defined a trespass as "* * * an actionable invasion of a possessor's interest in the exclusive possession of land * * *" and a nuisance as "* * * an actionable invasion of a possessor's interest in the use and enjoyment of his land.* * *." 342 P.2d at 792. The Supreme Court of Oregon itself recognized this overlap, saying:

> "The same conduct on the part of a defendant may and often does result in the actionable invasion of both of these interests, in which case the choice between the two remedies is, in most cases, a matter of little consequence.* * *" *Ibid.*

At least where a trespass, consisting of an interference with the possessor's interest in the exclusive possession of land, is of a continuing nature, it would seem also to interfere with that possessor's interest in the use and enjoyment of his land, and thus be a nuisance. Such is the kind of interference complained of in our case, for it has assertedly continued over a long period of time.

We are therefore of the opinion that, under Oregon law, the conduct complained of is both a trespass and nuisance but that the trespass aspect of the case will govern in determining which statute of limitations is to be applied.

We see no reason why the trespass aspect of the case should govern in determining whether the quoted provision of ORS 449.820(1) stands in the way of applying the doctrine of primary administrative jurisdiction. That provision speaks of actions or suits "relating" to private or public nuisances. For the reasons indicated above we think this suit relates to a private nuisance even though it sounds in trespass for purposes of the statute of limitations.

Under the company's interpretation of this statutory provision, the doctrine of primary administrative jurisdiction will or will not apply, depending upon whether the plaintiff calls the same conduct, warranting the same relief, a trespass or a nuisance. Such a demarcation between cases in which the doctrine would or would not apply borders on the capricious and could serve no perceivable purpose relevant to the air pollution statutes of Oregon. We do not believe that in ORS 449.820(1), the legislature used the term "nuisance" in a restricted sense that would produce such an arbitrary result.

In our opinion the quoted provision in ORS 449.820 renders inapplicable, under the circumstances of this case, the doctrine of primary administrative jurisdiction. It is unnecessary to consider the other reasons advanced by appellee why the doctrine is inapplicable.

Affirmed.

4. ULTRA-HAZARDOUS ACTIVITIES

The legal theory of **ultra-hazardous activities** permits an action to be brought in cases where it can be alleged and proved that a person was engaged in an activity that was so inherently dangerous per se that he should be held liable without any additional evidence of wrongdoing. An activity that is not of common usage, i.e., one which is not customarily carried out by the community at large, becomes suspect and may very well be the subject of an allegation that it is an ultra-hazardous activity. Negligence does not have to be proved, nor does it matter if the defendant had the best of intentions. This theory reflects the notion that a person should be held responsible for damages when he engages in ultra-hazardous activities, because of the unreasonable risk he imposes on the public at large. This may be expressed in the caveat, "If the lion gets away, the keeper has to pay!" It should be evident that the theory of ultra-hazardous activities can be particularly relevant and applied to such issues as chemical manufacturing, nuclear power plants and similar activities that create serious threats to the environment.

Luthringer v. Moore involves a somewhat prosaic application of the theory to the use of hydrocyanic acid to exterminate vermin. In *Chapman Chemical Co. v. Taylor* the court applied the theory to the spraying of 2-4-D on rice crops. Do you think that the court should have treated the farmer any differently than the chemical company that manufactured the chemical dust?

LUTHRINGER v. MOORE

31 Cal.2d 489, 190 P.2d 1 (1948)

CARTER, Justice.

Plaintiff recovered a judgment on a verdict for damages for personal injuries against defendant, R. L. Moore. Plaintiff stated his action in two counts, the first predicated upon an absolute liability or liability without fault, and the second, alleged negligence of defendants. The defendants are Bedell, the tenant of the restaurant building hereafter mentioned and the operator of the restaurant therein, Sacramento Medico-Dental Building Company, a corporation, the owner of the office and restaurant buildings, and Moore, an individual engaged in the pest eradication business. A nonsuit was granted as to all defendants as to the second count in the complaint. Bedell and Medico-Dental Building Company were exonerated. Plaintiff appeals from the unfavorable result as to those defendants but advises this court that he urges that appeal only in the event the judgment is reversed as to Moore who is the only appealing defendant. In view of the result (affirmance of the judgment) reached herein we will treat plaintiff's position as an abandonment of his appeal, and accordingly, it is dismissed.

From the foregoing it is apparent that we have presented, the question of whether Moore was absolutely liable for the injury—was liable without fault—whether the doctrine of strict liability is applicable.

The locale of the accident giving rise to the action is commercial buildings in the business district of the City of Sacramento. Defendant, Sacramento Medico-Dental Building Company, is the owner of two contiguous buildings, one a ten story concrete office building and the other a restaurant building. Tenants of that defendant occupy the buildings. Beneath the first floor of both buildings are basement rooms. They are connected by passageways. A room on the street level floor of the office building was occupied by a tenant Flynn in which he conducted a pharmacy. There was also a dress shop on that floor. A restaurant occupied the restaurant building. Flynn's store was adjacent to the main entrance lobby of the office building.

Defendant Moore was engaged to exterminate cockroaches and other vermin in the basement under the restaurant and that part under the dress shop. He made his preparations and released hydrocyanic acid gas in those rooms about midnight on November 16, 1943. Plaintiff, an employee of Flynn in the latter's pharmacy, in the course of his employment, arrived at the pharmacy about 8:45 a.m. on November 17, 1943, with the purpose of opening the store. Although there is a conflict in the evidence, there is testimony that none of the three entrances to the drug store bore any signs or notices warning of the presence or danger of the above mentioned gas. The evidence is clear that there was none on the door used by plaintiff. He entered by a door from the office building lobby. He was suffering from a cold. After entering the store he proceeded to a small mezzanine floor to put on his working clothes. Feeling ill he returned to the main floor and lost consciousness. He was discovered in that condition by Flynn's bookkeeper who arrived at the pharmacy between 9:15 and 9:30 a.m. Plaintiff was removed from the store, treated by the firemen of the city with a resuscitator and taken to the hospital where he received medical attention. He was found suffering from hydrocyanic acid gas poisoning and his injuries are from that source.

Counsel for defendant Moore contends that the evidence is insufficient to justify the verdict in favor of plaintiff. He asserts that there is no evidence of the escape of hydrocyanic acid gas from the basement to the pharmacy or the presence of such gas when plaintiff was there; that there is no evidence that plaintiff suffered from such gas poisoning on the morning in question or that his condition since was due to such poisoning.

It is beyond dispute that Moore released the gas in the basement of the building the night preceding the morning of plaintiff's injury. It is unlikely that such lethal gas was present and released at any other place in the vicinity. The evidence shows the gas is lighter than air, readily diffuses in air, is very penetrating and in the language of witness Bell: "It will penetrate behind baseboards, cracks and crevices that we couldn't get at with any type of liquid insecticide. It will go through mattresses, chesterfields, furniture, some types of porous walls.

"Q. It does a good job of fumigating? A. That's right.

"Q. Because it can get into small cracks and apertures? A. That's right."

* * *

The foregoing evidence points unerringly to the conclusion that there was cyanide gas in the pharmacy; that it came from the fumigation operation in the basement; and that plaintiff was poisoned by such gas. Moore's arguments with reference to the care used to confine the gas, the failure of some persons to detect any gas odor, the possibility that the presence of gas in the lobby of the office building and elsewhere was due to the gas being blown from the restaurant by Moore and the like, pose nothing more than conflicts in the evidence.

Moore alleges error in the giving of the instruction reading: "I instruct you that any person engaging in an ultra-hazardous activity, who knew, or in the exercise of reasonable care, should have known its ultra-hazardous character, and thereby proximately causes injury to another by a miscarriage of such activity, is liable to the person harmed, unless the latter knew or in the exercise of reasonable care should have known its ultra-hazardous nature and failed to exercise reasonable care for his own safety, or unless he knowingly and voluntarily invited the injury, and brought it upon himself.

"Likewise, any person, firm or corporation who brings, or permits to be brought upon its premises that which is of an ultra-hazardous nature, and who knew, or in the exercise of reasonable care should have known its ultra-hazardous nature, is liable for any injury proximately caused another, by its miscarriage, unless the person so harmed knew, or in the exercise of reasonable care should have known of its ultra-hazardous nature and failed to exercise reasonable care for his own safety or unless he knowingly and voluntarily invited the injury, and brought it upon himself.

"This principal of law does not require a finding of negligence upon those so engaging in such activity, or upon those bringing or permitting it to be brought upon the premises.

"I instruct you as a matter of law that under all the facts and circumstances of this case, the use and release of hydrocyanic acid gas by the defendant Moore, in the premises of defendants Bedell and Sacramento Medico-Dental Building, a corporation, all as appears in the evidence, constituted an ultra-hazardous activity." He asserts that it advised the jury on questions of fact, such as that gas did escape from the basement to the pharmacy which was present when plaintiff entered the pharmacy, and such condition was unknown to plaintiff; that plaintiff came in contact with the gas and became ill therefrom, and that plaintiff was acting in the course of his employment when he entered the pharmacy. Suffice it to say, a mere reading of the instruction refutes Moore's argument. In any event, the jury were fully instructed on proximate cause and fully informed with relation to ultra-hazardous activities (later discussed) as follows: "You are instructed that defendant R. L. Moore, doing business as 'Orchard Supply Company,' was engaged under all the facts and circumstances of this case in what the law considers to be an ultra-hazardous activity when he used hydrocyanic acid gas to fumigate the connected basement rooms which have been referred to as Bedell's storeroom and the Superintendent's office, the latter being located in the basement of the Medico-Dental Office Building. A person who carries on an ultra-hazardous activity is liable to another whom the actor should recognize as likely to be harmed by the miscarriage of the acitvity for harm resulting to said person from that which makes the activity ultra-hazardous, although the utmost care is exercised to prevent the harm, unless the person injured knew or in the exercise of reasonable care should have known its ultra-hazardous nature and fails to exercise reasonable care to avoid the harm threatened thereby after acquiring knowledge that the ultra-hazardous activity is being carried on and after it has miscarried or is about to miscarry. In the present case, if you find from a preponderance of the evidence that defendant R. L. Moore, doing business as 'Orchard Supply Company,' should have recognized that persons in nearby parts of the Medico-Dental Office Building were likely to be harmed if hydrocyanic acid gas escaped from the rooms being fumigated and that hydrocyanic acid gas did in fact escape and find its way to the Medico-Dental Pharmacy premises thereby coming in contact with and causing harm to the plaintiff Albert L. Luthringer, unless you also find from a preponderance of the evidence that plaintiff Albert L. Luthringer knew or in the exercise of reasonable care should have known that fumigation with hydrocyanic acid gas was being carried on and that the gas had escaped or was about to escape to the pharmacy premises and then failed to exercise reasonable care to avoid the harm threatened, or unless he knowingly and voluntarily invited the injury and brought it upon himself, your verdict must be for the plaintiff Albert L. Luthringer and against defendant R. L. Moore, doing business as 'Orchard Supply Company.' "

In connection with the foregoing it is urged that the instructions declare as a matter of law that the release of such gas on the premises constitutes an ultra-hazardous activity. It appears to be settled that the question of whether the case is a proper one for imposing absolute or strict liability is one of law for the court. See, Green v. General Petroleum Corp., 205 Cal. 328, 270 P. 952, 60 A.L.R. 475; Munro v. Pacific Coast Dredging, etc., Co., 84 Cal. 515, 24 P. 303, 18 Am.St.Rep. 248; Rest.,Torts, sec. 520, Com.h.

Turning to the question of whether absolute or strict liability is appropriate in the instant case, we find that according to witness Bell (a man engaged in the pest control business), there are only three operators licensed to use lethal gas in pest control in Sacramento. And in regard to the nature of hydrocyanic acid gas he testified: * * * A. The operator going into a building isn't too familiar with the construction of the building. There might be a hidden flue and cracks some place you might miss. If you did miss that, the people above the area would be fumigated. That gas might leak up there. They would be subject to being gassed that way. The safest way is to vacate the building, no matter how careful you are to always be careful of every piece of construction of the building." Hydrocyanic acid gas is defined as a "dangerous or lethal chemical" in the statutes dealing with licensing of those engaged in the pest control business (Business & Professions Code, sec. 8513.) Bell testified on cross examination that the gas was generally used in the community, and that it is used for fumigating railroad cars, homes, apartments, and fruit trees, but as seen there are only three licensed operators in Sacramento.

Defendant Moore introduced a written notice which he claims was attached to the door of the pharmacy directing that he be contacted before entering the building because of possible gas leakage, indicating that he believed a leakage possible although he testified that he took every precaution to seal the basement before he released the gas. This evidence, as above discussed, clearly points to the conclusion that the gas escaped from the basement into the pharmacy although great care to prevent it was exercised by Moore. As before seen, the activity in releasing the gas was carried on in the basement of commercial buildings where there are a great many tenants. Under these circumstances we have a case which calls for liability without fault—a case falling within the category of what has been defined as the miscarriage of an ultra-hazardous activity. It has been said: "One who carries on an ultra-hazardous activity is liable to another whose person, land or chattels the actor should recognize as likely to be harmed by the unpreventable miscarriage of the activity for harm resulting thereto from that which makes the activity ultra-hazardous, although the utmost care is exercised to prevent the harm. * * * An activity is ultra-hazardous if it (a) necessarily involves a risk of serious harm to the person, land or chattels of others which cannot be eliminated by the exercise of the utmost care, and (b) is not a matter of common usage. * * * An activity is a matter of common usage if it is customarily carried on by the great mass of mankind or by many people in the community. It does not cease to be so because it is carried on for a purpose peculiar to the individual who carries it on. Certain activities may be so generally carried on as to be regarded as customary. Thus, automobiles have come into such general use that their operation is a matter of common usage. This, together with the fact that the risk involved in the careful operation of a carefully maintained automobile is slight, is sufficient to prevent their operation from being an ultrahazardous activity. However,

the use of an automotive vehicle of such size and weight as to be incapable of safe control and to be likely to crush water and gas mains under the surface of the highway is not as yet a usual means of transportation and, therefore, the use of such an automobile is ultrahazardous. * * *
* * The rule stated * * * does not apply if the activity is carried on in pursuance of a public duty imposed upon the actor as a public officer or employee or as a common carrier. * * * The rule stated * * * does not apply where the person harmed by the unpreventable miscarriage of an ultra-hazardous activity has reason to know of the risk which makes the activity ultrahazardous and (a) takes part in it, or (b) brings himself within the area which will be endangered by its miscarriage, (i) without a privilege, or (ii) in the exercise of a privilege derived from the consent of the person carrying on the activity, or (iii) as a member of the public entitled to the services of a public utility carrying on the activity. * * * (1) A plaintiff is not barred from recovery for harm done by the miscarriage of an ultrahazardous activity caused by his failure to exercise reasonable care to observe the fact that the activity is being carried on or by intentionally coming into the area which would be endangered by its miscarriage. (2) A plaintiff is barred from recovery for harm caused by the miscarriage of an ultrahazardous activity if, but only if, (a) he intentionally or negligently causes the activity to miscarry, or (b) after knowledge that it has miscarried or is about to miscarry, he fails to exercise reasonable care to avoid harm threatened thereby." Rest., Torts, secs. 519, 520, 521, 523. In the case of Green v. General Petroleum Corporation, supra, an oil well had "blown out" due to natural gas pressure while in the process of being drilled, and plaintiff's property was damaged by debris being cast thereon. The court declared the driller of the well to be liable although he had used all care possible to avoid the accident, and announced the rule that: "Where one, in the conduct and maintenance of an enterprise lawful and proper in itself, deliberately does an act under known conditions, and, with knowledge that injury may result to another, proceeds, and injury is done to the other as the direct and proximate consequence of the act, however carefully done, the one who does the act and causes the injury should, in all fairness, be required to compensate the other for the damage done." Page 333 of 205 Cal., page 955 of 270. P. * * *

Whatever the situation may be in that regard, there can be no doubt that the case of Green v. General Petroleum Corporation, supra, enunciated a principle of absolute liability which is applicable to the instant case. It is not significant that a property damage, as distinguished from a personal injury, was there involved. The important factor is that certain activities under certain conditions may be so hazardous to the public generally, and of such relative infrequent occurrence, that it may well call for strict liability as the best public policy.

The above quoted evidence shows that the use of gas under the circumstances presented is a hazardous activity; that it is perilous and likely to cause injury even though the utmost care is used; that defendant Moore knew or should have known that injury might result; and that the use of it under these circumstances is not a matter of "common usage" within the meaning of the term. In regard to the last feature it may be used commonly by fumigators, but they are relatively few in number and are engaged in a specialized activity. It is not carried on generally by the public, especially under circumstances where many people are present, thus enhancing the hazard, nor is its use a common everyday practice. It is not a common usage within the definition: "An activity may be ultra-hazardous because of the instrumentality which is used in carrying it on, the nature of the subject matter with which it deals or the condition which it creates." Rest., Torts, sec. 520 (b), com. Cl. (b). And in this connection the instruction advising the jury that the usage was not common, was proper.

Moore claims error in respect to the refusing of instructions offered by him dealing with inevitable accident, negligence on his part and refuting the rule of strict liability. Manifestly such instructions are not appropriate in a case of strict liability.

Moore complains that the modification of an instruction offered by him was error. The instruction was: "The court instructs the jury that it was plaintiff's duty to exercise his faculties of sight and smell to apprise himself of danger and to use ordinary care at all times in exercising such senses. (To look in a careless manner, or to exercise his sense of smell in a careless manner, is not to look or smell at all.)" The court did not give the portion in parenthesis. Assuming the instruction was applicable, it is clear the part given was sufficient.

Complaint is made of the refusal to give an instruction reading: "The court instructs you that no man is responsible for that which no man can control." Such an instruction would only lead to confusion in the type of case under consideration and is based on cases where there was common usage in the sense used in the Restatement.

Error is urged in the refusal to give Moore's instructions on contributory negligence of plaintiff phrased in the language used in an ordinary negligence case. Such an instruction was improper as seen from the foregoing discussion of what conduct on part of plaintiff bars his recovery, and was correctly covered by plaintiff's instruction No. 10 heretofore quoted.

* * *

The judgment against defendant Moore is affirmed. Plaintiff's appeal is dismissed.

CHAPMAN CHEMICAL CO. v. TAYLOR

215 Ark. 630, 222 S.W.2d 820 (1949)

FRANK G. SMITH, Justice.

Mrs. Virginia C. Wilson owns a farm in Jefferson County, which she rented in the year 1947 to G. E. Taylor for an agreed share of the crops grown on the land, the principal crop being cotton. She and her tenant filed this suit against Elms Planting Co., a corporation, to recover damages to their crop occasioned by the use of a chemical dust by the Elms Co. called 2-4-D, in spraying a rice crop on land owned by the Elms Co. which was three-fourths of a mile from plaintiffs' crop.

The testimony shows that within very recent years there has been developed a powerful chemical referred to as 2-4-D, which is very damaging to any broad leaved plant with which it has contact, but which does no harm to grasses and plants which are not broad leaved. The Elms Co. used this chemical in spraying its rice crop and particles thereof drifted and settled on plaintiffs' cotton crop, greatly reducing the yield thereof and this suit was brought to recover compensation for this damage.

The Elms Co. filed an answer in which liability was denied. In addition it filed a cross-complaint against Chapman Chemical Co. and others who have passed out of the case. * * *

These contentions of the Elms Co. and of the Chemical Co. bring us to a consideration of the case on its merits, and we shall treat the two contentions together, as they are inseparately connected. * * *

It is undisputed that 2-4-D powder will answer the purpose for which it was designed, that is of killing plants with large leaves which appear in fields of rice. The most noxious of those weeds is the coffee bean plant which matures about the same time the rice does, and if allowed to mature its seed will mix with the rice when threshed and will destroy or greatly lessen the marketability of the rice, unless separated from the rice at great expense and trouble, usually by hand.

The chief objection to the use of the powder is that it is very dangerous to such plants as cotton, potatoes, vegetables, etc., when it comes in contact with them. This characteristic of the powder was well known, in fact the literature which the Chemical Co. published and circulated gave warning of that fact. The plaintiffs, or cross-appellants, insist therefore that both the Chemical Co. and the Elms Co. are liable to them for the damage to their cotton crop caused by the use of this powder. It is undisputed that the use of the powder caused the damage for which plaintiff sued.

It was shown by testimony, which is undisputed, that the practice of dusting agricultural crops, as well as truck farms, etc., has prevailed for a number of years and is becoming a common practice. Some of these chemicals are dangerous to live stock and others to plants of certain kinds and they are used for various purposes. Extensive and experienced planters who have used chemical dust for a number of years for different purposes, testified that when the areas to be treated are sufficiently large, aeroplanes are used in scattering the dust or chemical, and that if properly applied even by planes, the dust does not float or extend more than fifty or one hundred fifty feet beyond the area intended to be treated, and that no damage results beyond that distance to plants which would be damaged if touched by the dust.

The testimony developed the fact of which the Elms Co. was unaware and it was not shown that the Chemical Co. was aware, and that is that the 2-4-D dust possessed the quality of floating for great distances when cast in the air, even for miles. None of the experienced farmers who dusted their crops for various purposes had ever known any other dust, when properly applied, to float for a greater distance than from fifty to one hundred fifty feet. As has been said, cross-appellants' cotton crop was three-fourths of a mile from the Elms Co. rice field at the nearest point.

The testimony shows that the Elms Co. used the dust on a morning when no wind was blowing and that it was distributed over the rice field by an aviator whose regular business it was to dust crops with the use of his plane, and who testified that but little of the dust was cast upon any land except the rice crop as he was careful to shut off the distribution of the dust when making the necessary turns of his plane.

The operator supervising the dusting process testified that he had been engaged in the crop dusting business for 22 years, operating from California to Florida and from Mexico to Canada and that when properly distributed the dust did not extend more than 40 to 50 feet beyond the area treated, but this testimony did not relate to 2-4-D.

The question of foreseeability of probable injury from the use of 2-4-D was submitted to the jury in instructions given at the request of cross appellants over the objections of both Elms Co. and the Chemical Co.

The jury might well have found, and evidently did find, that there was no previous experience in the use of agricultural chemicals which gave any indication of the danger of using 2-4-D to a crop three-fourths of a mile away, or that its use was "a cause from which a person of ordinary experience and sagacity could foresee that the result might probably ensue."

The testimony shows that before buying or applying the 2-4-D chemical the manager of the Elms Co. consulted one L. C. Carter of Ark. Rice Growers Assn. regarding the use of 2-4-D. Carter had been and was a manager of the Rice

Experimental Station near Stuttgart, 7 or 8 years, and was at that time manager of the Rice Growers Coop. Assn. and the Elms Co. manager was informed by Carter that he, Carter, thought its use would be all right. In other words, there is no evidence upon which to predicate liability against the Elms Co. except the fact alone that the Elms Co. did use a dangerous chemical, and we conclude that the verdict of the jury in favor of the Elms Co. was not unsupported by the testimony and should be affirmed.

As to the Chemical Co. a different test as to liability must be applied. The three chemical companies operated under a single officer, Chapman being the president of all three and the owner of practically all of the stock of all the corporations. The Illinois company did not manufacture the 2-4-D chemical dust, but its Memphis affiliate did. Appellant Chemical Co. was the distributor and sole agent for the Tennessee company in this State, and the testimony shows that it was selling an extremely hazardous product and was selling it as its own product. Indeed the testimony shows that the Tennessee Co. was in effect and in fact the agent of the Chemical Co. in manufacturing the dust, as all sales thereof here involved were made by the appellant Chemical Co. The testimony shows that the Chemical Co. was selling the dust as its own product. It controlled and distributed all advertising material which recommended its use and gave directions therefor. At Sec. 400 of the Chapter on Torts, Restatement of the Law, it is said that one who puts out as his own product a chattel manufactured by another is subject to the same liability as though he were its manufacturer.

It is said there was no privity of contract between the Chemical Co. and cross appellants. This showing was at one time, and for some time considered necessary to occasion liability, the line of decisions to that effect going back to the early English case of Winterbottom v. Wright, 10 Mees. & W. 109, 152 Eng. Reprint 402, decided in 1842. But the courts have been getting away from that doctrine and many have entirely repudiated it and discarded it. The opinion of Justice Cardozo, then a member of the Court of Appeals of New York, and later an Associate Justice of the United States Supreme Court in the case of MacPherson v. Buick Motor Co., 217 N.Y. 382, 111 N.E. 1050, L.R.A.1916F, 696, Ann.Cas. 1916C, 446, is credited with the inception of the modern doctrine of manufacturer's liability based upon foreseeability rather than privity of contract. * * *

"The question in each case was whether the danger was sufficient to require the manufacturer to guard against it." In other words, that foreseeability and not privity was the proper test. See also Sec. 824, Chapter on Sales, Sec. 824, 46 Am. Jur. page 946.

Now this 2-4-D powder is highly efficient for its intended purposes, that is to kill broad leaved plants, but its very efficiency for that purpose makes its use extremely hazardous to other plant life.

An article appeared in the Ark. State Plant Board News in July, 1948, which began, "Effective June 24th the U.S. Civil Aeronautics Administration prohibits the use of 2-4-D dust by aeroplanes. This action was taken at the request of the U.S. Dept. of Agriculture following many complaints that drifting dust had injured cotton and other broad leaved crops."

This was subsequent to the spraying of the Elms rice crop which damaged appellants cotton crop and in the law of negligence it is generally true that foresight and not retrospect is the standard of negligence. But here we are dealing with an extra hazardous chemical known to be highly dangerous.

The essence of this case is contained in instruction number 10-A given over the objection of the Chemical Co., which reads as follows: "It was the duty of the defendant Chapman Chemical Company before putting an inherently dangerous product on the market to make tests to determine whether or not it would damage crops of others; if you believe from a preponderance of the evidence in this case that the 2-4-D dust applied on July 1, 1947, by the Elms Planting Company was an inherently dangerous product liable to damage the property of others, and that such tests were not made, then you are told that the defendant Chapman Chemical Company is negligent."

If this instruction is correct, the judgment against the Chemical Co. should be affirmed, if it is not it should be reversed. Now a test was made but its purpose was to ascertain whether or not 2-4-D could be distributed by aeroplane as other dusts could be. It was found that it could be, but no test was made as to the floating quality of the dust, and it is this characteristic or quality of 2-4-D which makes its use extra hazardous. In other words, was the Chemical Co. under the duty of testing and knowing that 2-4-D dust, unlike other chemical dusts, would float for great distances. The undisputed testimony is that this 2-4-D, unlike other dusts, does not immediately or soon settle, but on the contrary floats in the air for long periods of time and for great distances, as much as 10, 15 or 20 miles, and one witness placed the distance at 35 miles.

That peril attended the use of the dust is undisputed. Indeed the literature circulated by the Chemical Co. contained this caution, "Chapman 2-4-D weed killer should be applied in such a manner as to avoid contacting crop plants such as cotton, sweet potatoes, vegetables, ornamental trees, etc." With this knowledge the Chemical Co. sold the dust, knowing that it would in its ordinary use be distributed from an aeroplane and it did this without making any test to determine what the effect thereof would be. Its literature referred to the dust as a proved weed killer and recommended the application of it by means of an aeroplane.

The undisputed testimony is that the Elms Co. bought the dust from the Chemical Co. and applied it in the manner directed for the known purpose for which it was sold and that this use thereof resulted in serious damage to cross appellants. We think this testimony presents the question whether absolute or strict liability should apply.

In the case of Luthringer v. Moore, 31 Cal.2d 489, 190 P.2d 1, 5, it was said by the Supreme Court of California that, "It appears to be settled that the question of whether the case is a proper one for imposing absolute or strict liability is one of law for the court." Among other authorities cited to support this statement is the restatement of the Law of Torts, Section 520, Com. H.

If one casts into the air a substance which he knows may do damage to others, and in some circumstances will certainly do so, principles of elementary justice, as well as the best public policy require that he know how far the substance will carry or be conveyed through the air and what damage it will do in the path of its journey, and if he releases such a substance either from ignorance of, or in indifference to the damage that may be done, the rule of strict liability should be applied.

* * *

We do not think the Chemical Company excused itself from liability by the mere showing that it was unaware of the peculiar carrying quality of the dust it was selling. Ordinary care required that it should know in view of the dangerous nature of the product it was selling, and it was charged with the knowledge which tests would have revealed. The case is therefore one in which the rule of strict liability should be applied. * * *

Justices Holt and McFaddin are of the opinion that the judgment for the Elms Co. should be reversed. Other members of the court are of the opinion that the judgment in favor of that Company should be affirmed. Justice George Rose Smith is of the opinion that Instruction No. 10-A above copied, which we said was of the essence of the case was erroneous and that the judgment against the Chemical Co. should be reversed for that reason. The result of these views is that the judgment for the Elms Co. should be affirmed and that the judgment against the Chemical Co. should also be affirmed. It is therefore so ordered.

GEORGE ROSE SMITH, Justice (dissenting in part).

I agree that the standard of ordinary care is applicable in the case of the Elms Company, but I am unable to concur in the rule of absolute liability on the part of the Chemical Company. Instruction 10-A in effect told the jury that the latter company was negligent if it failed to discover by tests any possible harm that might result from the use of 2-4-D. Similarly, the majority hold that the manufacturer who puts a dangerous commodity on the market is responsible for the consequences of its use, no matter how unexpected or unforeseeable they may be.

I think the manufacturer's duty should be that of making such tests as are reasonably necessary in the circumstances—it being understood, of course, that the duty to take precautions increases proportionately with the degree of danger inherent in the commodity. It is shown that 2-4-D is harmless to narrow-leaved plants, but suppose for argument's sake that there is in the world one narrow-leaved plant that the dust will injure. Upon the majority's reasoning the Chemical Company would be liable for failing to test the dust on that particular plant, even though it may have made experiments with ten thousand other species. So as to the drifting quality of the chemical. The proof shows that many agricultural dusts have been widely used during a quarter of a century, yet none has ever before been known to drift more than a few rods. I think the jury should have had the opportunity to decide whether the Chemical Company acted with ordinary prudence in assuming that 2-4-D would float in the same way as other dusts. * * *

I find no reason for bringing into our law the principle of absolute liability. Experience elsewhere has shown that this doctine is hard to confine once its existence has been recognized. We shall be asked to extend the scope of this case in the future, and I can hardly see the point at which its application may logically be said to end.

---

5. THE PUBLIC TRUST DOCTRINE

The **public trust doctrine** is a legal theory based on the principle that property owned by government is held in trust for the public. As such, government cannot just give it away for private benefit but must use it and dispose of it in a way that serves the public interest rather than a private interest. When government disposes of land it may either sell the land for funds which will in turn be used for some public purpose or it may dispose of the land to be used for a public use. Environmentalists contend that the public trust doctrine applies to all land owned by the government and to lands privately owned but currently or previously covered by water. The argument for including these privately owned lands is based on the common law principle dating from the feudal period in England that the sovereign—i.e., the state—held prior right to all public lands and waterways, including that land partially or temporarily submerged under water. Thus, several issues may arise in determining whether privately owned lands are held in the public trust. First, does the right of the sovereign power extend to the high or the low water mark? This can become an issue in determining the public's right to access and use of our beaches: In some states there has been a statutory response to this issue, with some states taking title to the high water mark and others taking title to the low water mark. A second issue that may arise is whether the public trust doctrine should apply to land that is currently dry but was under water at the time of the grant of the charter from the king of England. Another argument frequently raised by environmentalists is that the land in question is vested in the public trust and cannot be conveyed or used in any way or for any purpose not related to the public trust. This is the argument with which the court was faced in *New Jersey Sports and Exposition Authority v. McCrane*, which involved the validity of a New Jersey statute establishing a sports complex on a vast swampland known as the Hackensack Meadows and creating a sports authority to which part of the swampland was conveyed. An action was brought to declare the statute invalid for many different reasons, one of which was that the meadowlands are held in a public trust and cannot be conveyed in any way not related to the public trust. Excerpts from that decision dealing with the public trust issue are set forth below.

NEW JERSEY SPORTS AND EXPOSITION AUTHORITY v. McCrane

119 N.J. Super. 457, 292 A.2d 580 (1971)

VI
The Public Trust

(A) *Tidelands*

Section 6 of the act authorizes the Authority to "effectuate a project to be located in the Hackensack meadowlands upon a site not to exceed 750 acres* * *." The Authority has stipulated that the project site will include substantial acreage designated by the State to be tideland. Cheval and the Audubon Society contend that this property is vested in the public trust and cannot be conveyed, leased or utilized in any way by the State for any purpose not related to the public trust. Specifically, Cheval and Audubon make a two-pronged attack. First, they urge that the proposed racetrack usage is in violation of the public trust. Secondly, they argue that section 17 of the act permits the granting, leasing or conveying of "meadowlands, riparian lands or lands under water and similar lands" without compensation.

The New Jersey Const. (1947), Art. VIII, § IV, par. 1, concerns itself with the perpetual fund for the support of free public schools. By statute, N.J.S.A. 18A:56–5 provides:

> All lands belonging to this state now or formerly lying under water are dedicated to the support of public schools. All moneys hereafter received from the sales of such lands shall be paid to the board of trustees, and shall constitute a part of the permanent school fund of the state.

N.J.S.A. 18A:56–6 provides similarly for income arising from leases of such lands.* * *

The following statutory authorities are relevant to the contemplated conveyance. N.J.S.A. 13:1B–13.7(b) provides that an "instrumentality of the State * * * may apply to the [Natural Resource Council] for a conveyance * * * of the State's interest in the meadowlands * * *." N.J.S.A. 13:1B–13.8(c) states that the Hackensack Meadowland Negotiation Board shall fix the consideration for the conveyance. Pursuant to N.J.S.A. 13:1B–13.9, the Natural Resource Council "shall approve an application for conveyance, if * * * it is satisfied that the conveyance will be in the public interest." N.J.S.A. 12:3–7 declares that riparian lands may be conveyed for a reasonable compensation, which shall be fixed by the Natural Resource Council, the Governor and the Attorney General.

N.J.S.A. 13:1B–13:13 is addressed to the aforementioned constitutional provision:

> The net proceeds for the sale, lease or transfer of the State's interest in the meadowlands shall be paid to the Fund for the Support of Free Public Schools established by the Constitution, Article VIII, Section IV, after deducting from the net proceeds any expenditures of the Hackensack Meadowlands Development Commission for reclaiming land within the district. The amount of said deduction for reclamation shall be paid to the Hackensack Meadowland Development Commission.

Clearly, the statutes cited provide for compensation to be paid to the Fund for the Support of Free Public Schools. This is in exact accord with the New Jersey Constitution. The deduction of costs of reclamation from the proceeds is no argument for ambiguity. There is no confusion as to the meaning of this portion of the legislative enactment.* * *

The argument raised in regard to the tidelands, however, goes much deeper than the just compensation claim. It goes to the very core of the act, for Cheval and Audubon vigorously submit that no conveyance can be permitted in view of the proposed use by the Authority. They opt for a re-examination of the means utilized for protection of the tidelands and seek to revisit the proposition that the tidelands belong to the sovereign in trust for the people, *i. e.*, a public trust. As they view it, the trust will be violated *per se* by a conveyance of the type proposed and will be further breached by the destruction of the ecological balance of the area. More broadly, East Rutherford and public counsel strongly urge that the proposed complex will have a deleterious effect, not solely on the tidelands but on the surrounding area as well. It can be seen, then, that while counsel focus on different areas, the trust is essentially the same, to wit, the abrogation by the Legislature of its duties as trustee of the tidelands and as overseer of the people's right to a clean and healthy environment. This latter position will be included in the discussion under (B) of this section, captioned "Environment and Ecology."

As stated previously, the parties have stipulated that "the projected site includes substantial acreage designated by the State to be state-owned tideland." In O'Neill v. State Highway Dept., 50 N.J. 307, 235 A.2d 1 (1967), Chief Justice Weintraub defined these lands as follows:

> The State owns in fee simple all lands that are flowed up to the high-water line or mark. The high-water line or mark is the line formed by the intersection of the tidal plane of mean high tide with the shore. The mean (sometimes called "ordinary") high tide is defined as the medium between the spring and the neap tides. [at 323] 235 A.2d at 9.

The genesis of the public trust doctrine can be gleaned from the opinion by Chief Justice Kirkpatrick in Arnold v. Mundy, 6 N.J.L. 1, 69–78 (Sup.Ct.1821). There are two types of public property, one "reserved for the necessities of the state, and * * * used for the public benefit" (at 71), the other "common to all the citizens, who take of them and use them, each according to his necessities, and according to the laws which regulate their use, and are called common property." *Id.* This common property consisted of navigable rivers, ports, bays, sea coasts, including the land under the water which could be utilized for "navigation, fishing, fowling, sustenance, and all the other uses of the water and its products (a few things excepted * * *)." *Id.* at 77. Since by its nature common property did not permit title to vest in the people, the common law "placed it in the hands of the sovereign power, to be held, protected, and regulated for the common use and benefit." *Id.* at 71. Subsequent to the American Revolution, the sovereign's power vested in the people of each State, to be exercised through their representatives, the Legislature. *Id.* at 78.

Arnold was cited favorably in the landmark decision of the United States Supreme Court in Illinois Central Railroad Co. v. Illinois, 146 U.S. 387, 13 S.Ct. 110, 36 L.Ed. 1018 (1892). In discussing the duties incumbent upon the State in carrying out its fiduciary duty, the court declared that there could be no abdication of the trust. However, this statement was not without qualification:

> The control of the State for the purposes of the trust can never be lost, *except as to such parcels as are used in promoting the interests of the public therein, or can be disposed of without any substantial impairment of the public interest in the lands and waters remaining.* [13 S.Ct. at 118; emphasis added]

It can be seen, then, that subject to the aforementioned qualifications, there is nothing that prevents the alienability of the trust lands. The New Jersey Legislature has recognized this in its enactment of N.J.S.A. 18A:56–5 and N.J.S.A. 13:1B–13.13.

The conveyance of land envisioned in the act clearly meets the trust qualifications. As previously indicated, just compensation has been safeguarded and the proceeds will be applied to the support of free public schools. Most importantly, the conveyance will promote a purpose which has been deemed beneficial to the public. The inclusion of a racetrack in no way detracts from the public purpose character of the project. Accordingly, the conveyance of the tidelands will not violate the public trust.

I will now consider the argument raised in regard to the tidelands in its broadest and perhaps most serious impact, that is, the ecological or environmental controversy.

(B) *Environment and Ecology*

In fashioning their arguments, Cheval, Audubon, East Rutherford and public counsel all concede, as they must, that they are required to exhibit a right to relief. Two approaches are taken, one via the Ninth Amendment, to the United States Constitution, the other via the Fourteenth.

The Ninth Amendment states:

> The enumeration in the Constitution, of certain rights, shall not be construed to deny or disparage others retained by the people.

In Griswold v. Connecticut, 381 U.S. 479, 85 S.Ct. 1678, 14 L.Ed.2d 510 (1965), the majority and concurring opinions concerned themselves with this amendment and both spoke of "penumbral rights" as rights guaranteed in addition to those specifically enumerated in the first eight amendments. One commentator has constructed the following theory:

> The rule of construction embodied in the Ninth Amendment could be the foundation for a declaration by the Supreme Court of a constitutional right to an

uncontaminated environment. Perhaps no principle is as fundamental as the preciousness of every human life. The Fifth and Fourteenth Amendments offer no less protection to "life" than to "liberty." Surely liberty and the various rights specifically enumerated in the Constitution are meaningless abstractions if life itself is ended through pollution's often invisible but unrelenting and imminently cataclismic environmental assault on the human body. [Esposito, "Air and water pollution: What to do while waiting for Washington," 5 Harv.Civ.Lib.—Civ. Rights L.Rev. 32, 47–48 (1970)].

Another commentator would combine the "public trust concept with the constitutional basis given by the Ninth Amendment" as a weapon in the battle against the defiling of our environment. Cohen, "The Constitution, The Public Trust Doctrine and The Environment," 1970 Utah L.Rev. 388, 399 (1970).

The theory based upon the Fourteenth Amendment is that certain civil rights, *i. e.*, environmental rights, are being abridged by state action, in contravention of 42 U.S.C.A. § 1983.* * *

The challengers come armed with more than theory. They point to case law which they believe supports their environmental and ecological claims.* * *

In the landmark case of Scenic Hudson Preservation Conference v. FPC, 354 F.2d 608 (2 Cir. 1965), cert. den. 384 U.S. 941, 86 S.Ct. 1462, 16 L.Ed.2d 540 (1966), various conservation groups were successful in setting aside action taken by the Federal Power Commission (FPC). This case involved the controversial "Storm King Project" wherein Consolidated Edison sought to construct a pumped storage hydroelectric project adjacent to the Hudson River. The Second Circuit, in remanding, held that the FPC failed to follow its statutory mandate, which required it to consider the conservation aspects of the project. It was noted that the FPC had refused to receive certain testimony, including some pertaining to fish protection devices.* * *

In Citizens Committee for Hudson Valley v. Volpe, 425 F.2d 97 (2 Cir. 1970), plaintiffs challenged the issuance of a permit to allow dredging and filling for the construction of the Hudson River Expressway. In anwer to defendant's claim that one of the plaintiffs lacked standing, the court noted (at 105) that unless that plaintiff had standing at that stage of the project, it would be in a very difficult position "at some later date to overbalance the equities in favor of the State such a large commitment of public funds would engender and its legitimate concern could be irretrievably subverted even though the permit was issued unlawfully."

These decisions hold that the courts will intervene to prevent agency action in contravention of a statutory mandate to consider a project's environmental and ecological ramifiations.

The Authority, for the purposes of this motion, has stipulated an assumption that a "factual issue exists with respect to the impact of a major project such as the sports complex upon the environment of the meadowlands district." However the Authority claims that the issue is premature in view of the fact that no decisions have been made and no action has been taken which will affect the environment or ecology. Cheval, Audubon, East Rutherford and public counsel submit that the issue should be considered now, since a considerable investment is contemplated. The challengers rely upon the foregoing federal court decisions in support of their argument that irreparable damage will result if they are foreclosed from a hearing at this time.

I fail to discern the parallel in the case at hand. The foregoing cases and other authorities are clearly based upon statutory mandates which require the particular agency or commission to consider the conservation aspects of the project. These federal mandates support the legal holding that the applicable agency explore all issues relevant to the "public interest" before any action is taken. Each agency is required to make factual findings concerning the environmental and ecological ramifications. But, I repeat, this is the result of a statutory directive—not a constitutional mandate. All parties agree that the United States Supreme Court has not spoken on the constitutional right to a clean environment to the exclusion of various other rights. This does not mean that any one is opposed to wholesome ecology.

This court is most alert to the changing attitudes of society. I understand fully the prevailing reform in the manner we look at our problems and even in the fashion that we make decisions. I am unequivocally sensitive to the fact that we should view the law in the light of what it good for the people. There must be an awareness of the necessity for environmental balance.

The tempo of the times is such that the Ninth Amendment may carry such a constitutional interpretation. And even if this comes to pass, in the absence of statute, there is no bar to a declaration of constitutionality of this act and then the necessity for the administrative hearings as to the environmental balance. If the act is unconstitutional, there is no need for environmental hearings. Such determinations are to be made only by virtue of a constitutional act. The case cited by counsel in support of a statement that it may be too late to wait do not involve the determination of the constitutionality of a statute.

No case has been cited to demonstrate that the time is ripe at this stage of the proceedings to consider the environmental impact of the act. Public counsel points to the alleged legislative failure during the one-day hearing to consider any of the environmental repercussions. But an examination of the hearing shows this to be inaccurate.* * *

The act itself addresses the issue. The Legislature specifically provided in section 23 that the Authority

> * * * shall consult with the Meadowlands Commission and the Department of Environmental Protection with respect to the ecological factors constituting the environment of the Hackensack meadowlands to the end that the delicate environmental balance of the Hackensack meadowlands may be maintained and preserved.* * *

Thus, the Legislature was aware of N.J.S.A. 13:17–1 et seq., wherein it declared that the meadowlands area

> * * * is a land resource of incalculable opportunity for new jobs, homes and recreational sites, which may be lost to the State through piecemeal reclamation and unplanned development; that much of this acreage may be subject to redevelopment under section 3, Article VIII, of the State Constitution; that the orderly, comprehensive development of these areas due to their strategic location in the heart of a vast metropolitan area with urgent needs for more space for industrial, commercial, residential, and *public recreational* and other uses, can no longer be deferred. * * * [N.J.S.A. 13:17–1; emphasis added]

This section goes on to state that the area needs "special protection from air and water pollution" and that "the necessity to consider the ecological factors constituting the environment of the meadowlands and the need to preserve the delicate balance of nature must be recognized to avoid any artificially imposed development that would adversely affect not only the area but the entire State. * * *" *Id.*

It is from this vantage point that the act in its entirety, and section 23 in particular, must be viewed. It cannot be assumed that the Legislature, on the one hand, carefully drafted an act for the development of the area and then, on the other hand, in callous and utter disregard thereof, passed a further enactment which would frustrate the former's purpose. To opt for this result is to read the enactments in a vacuum, in utter disregard of the historical background and policy considerations.* * *

A further observation is proper. The executive and legislative branches of the State Government have clearly made known their awareness to environmental problems by the passage of such acts as the Clean Ocean Act, Pesticide Control Act, Green Acres Act, Air Pollution Control Act, etc. And it must be emphasized that N.J.S.A. 13:1D established the Department of Environmental Protection in 1970. This Department, referred to in section 23 of the act, was established and is empowered to initiate complaints, to hold hearings and institute legal proceedings, etc. N.J.S.A. 13:1D–9. Thus, the executive and legislative branches have brought the problem of environment and pollution to the door of every citizen and industry. If these are the facts, it cannot be argued that section 23 is not meaningful and not responsive to the need.* * *

I am satisfied that the Legislature has given much consideration to the environmental and ecological issues. In any case, the issue is not relevant at this time. The day may come when a decision or act by the Authority will affect the environment. At that time judicial and/or administrative relief, if necessary, will undoubtedly be available. For example, if after consultation with the Authority, the Department of Environmental Protection claims the project will have ill effects, it has the machinery necessary to pursue the matter further. The court must presume that the Department will serve vigorously. And when building is undertaken one day, all legal requirements outlined in anti-pollution legislation, in upgrading waste treatment facilities and in maintaining an ecological balance will be enforced. I cannot agree with public counsel that the State will stand committed in the absence of an immediate environmental hearing.

I fully agree that the public should be and is entitled to a further opportunity to be heard on the environmental and ecological overtones of the legislation. Although the court may not have the facilities or power to be able to police the ecological factors, it may perhaps oversee the actions of the administrative agencies in this vital area. It is before these agencies that experts may appear if the Authority is violating any provision of environmental law. But to determine that this is not the juncture for such a hearing is not to deny the right. Every piece of legislation carries its advantages and disadvantages. The mere passage of the act is not enough to bring about judicial intervention. And this is as it should be, because in the final analysis government by judges is inferior to government by legislators.

The environmental issue is ripe for summary judgment under existing law. The judgment of the court declares that the arguments as to the trusteeship of the tidelands and the legal objections surrounding the environmental and ecological factors do not affect the constitutionality of this act.

For additional information about the public trust doctine, see:

1. Sax, *The Public Trust Doctrine in Natural Resource Law: Effective Judicial Intervention*, 86 MICH. L. REV. 471 (1970).
2. Cohen, *The Constitution, Public Trust Doctrine, and the Environment*, 1970 UTAH L. REV. 388.
3. Note, *The Public Trust in Tidal Areas: A Sometime Submerged Traditional Doctrine*, 79 YALE L. J. 762 (1970).

---

6. The Ninth Amendment

The **Ninth Amendment** to the United States Constitution provides: "The enumeration in the Constitution, of certain rights, shall not be construed to deny or disparage others retained by the people."

The purpose of this provision was to make it clear that the first eight amendments were not intended to exhaust the basic and fundamental rights protected by the Constitution. This provision has been used by environmentalists, with only limited success, to argue that the right to a clean and healthy environment is one of the fundamental rights protected by the Constitution. One of the most explicit descriptions of the nature of the protection offered by the Ninth Amendment is contained in a concurring opinion in *Griswold v. Connecticut*, written by Mr. Justice Goldberg. That case involved a challenge to the validity of a Connecticut anticontraception law. The majority of the court held the law invalid. The following paragraph is the most frequently cited excerpt from that opinion:

> "The foregoing cases suggest that specific guarantees in the Bill of Rights have penumbras, formed by emanations from those guarantees that help give them life and substance. . . . Various guarantees create zones of privacy. The right of association contained in the penumbra of the First Amendment is one, as we have seen. The Third Amendment in its prohibition against the quartering of soldiers "in any house" in time of peace without the consent of the owner is another facet of that privacy. The Fourth Amendment explicitly affirms the "right of the people to be secure in their persons, houses, papers, and effects, against unreasonable searches and seizures." The Fifth Amendment in its Self-Incrimination Clause enables the citizen to create a zone of privacy which government may not force him to surrender to his detriment. The Ninth Amendment provides: "The enumeration in the Constitution, of certain rights, shall not be construed to deny or disparage others retained by the people. . . ."

The following are excerpts from the concurring opinion in the *Griswold* decision.

GRISWOLD v. CONNECTICUT

381 U.S. 479 (1965)

* * *

MR. JUSTICE GOLDBERG, whom THE CHIEF JUSTICE and MR. JUSTICE BRENNAN join, concurring.

I agree with the Court that Connecticut's birth-control law unconstitutionally intrudes upon the right of marital privacy, and I join in its opinion and judgment.* * *

I do agree that the concept of liberty protects those personal rights that are fundamental, and is not confined to the specific terms of the Bill of Rights. My conclusion that the concept of liberty is not so restricted and that it embraces the right of marital privacy though that right is not mentioned explicitly in the Constitution is supported both by numerous decisions of this Court, referred to in the Court's opinion, and by the language and history of the Ninth Amendment. In reaching the conclusion that the right of marital privacy is protected, as being within the protected penumbra of specific guarantees of the Bill of Rights, the Court refers to the Ninth Amendment, *ante*, at 484. I add these words to emphasize the relevance of that Amendment to the Court's holding.

The Court stated many years ago that the Due Process Clause protects those liberties that are "so rooted in the traditions and conscience of our people as to be ranked as fundamental." *Snyder* v. *Massachusetts*, 291 U. S. 97, 105.* * *

This Court, in a series of decisions, has held that the Fourteenth Amendment absorbs and applies to the States those specifics of the first eight amendments which express fundamental personal rights. The language and history of the Ninth Amendment reveal that the Framers of the Constitution believed that there are additional fundamental rights, protected from governmental infringement, which exist alongside those fundamental rights specifically mentioned in the first eight constitutional amendments.

The Ninth Amendment reads, "The enumeration in the Constitution, of certain rights, shall not be construed to deny or disparage others retained by the people." The Amendment is almost entirely the work of James Madison. It was introduced in Congress by him and passed the House and Senate with little or no debate and virtually no change in language. It was proffered to quiet expressed fears that a bill of specifically enumerated rights could not be sufficiently broad to cover all essential rights and that the specific mention of certain rights would be interpreted as a denial that others were protected. * * *

The Framers did not intend that the first eight amendments be construed to exhaust the basic and fundamental rights which the Constitution guaranteed to the people. * * * This Court has had little occasion to interpret the Ninth Amendment.* * *

The Ninth Amendment to the Constitution may be regarded by some as a recent discovery and may be forgotten by others, but since 1791 it has been a basic part of the Constitution which we are sworn to uphold. To hold that a right so basic and fundamental and so deep-rooted in our society as the right of privacy in marriage may be infringed because that right is not guaranteed in so many words by the first eight amendments to the Constitution is to ignore the Ninth Amendment and to give it no effect whatsoever. Moreover, a judicial construction that this fundamental right is not protected by the Constitution because it is not mentioned in explicit terms by one of the first eight amendments or elsewhere in the Constitution would violate the Ninth Amendment, which specifically states that "[t]he enumeration in the Constitution, of certain rights, shall not be *construed* to deny or disparage others retained by the people." (Emphasis added.)

A dissenting opinion suggests that my interpretation of the Ninth Amendment somehow "broaden[s] the powers of this Court." *Post*, at 520. With all due respect, I believe that it misses the import of what I am saying. I do not take the position of my Brother BLACK in his dissent in *Adamson* v. *California*, 332 U. S. 46, 68, that the entire Bill of Rights is incorporated in the Fourteenth Amendment, and I do not mean to imply that the Ninth Amendment is applied against the States by the Fourteenth. Nor do I mean to state that the Ninth Amendment constitutes an independent source of rights protected from infringement by either the States or the Federal Government. Rather, the Ninth Amendment shows a belief of the Constitution's authors that fundamental rights exist that are not expressly enumerated in the first eight amendments and an intent that the list of rights included there not be deemed exhaustive.* * *

The Ninth Amendment simply shows the intent of the Constitution's authors that other fundamental personal rights should not be denied such protection or disparaged in any other way simply because they are not specifically listed in the first eight constitutional amendments. I do not see how this broadens the authority of the Court; rather it serves to support what this Court has been doing in protecting fundamental rights.* * *

I agree fully with the Court that * * * the right of privacy is a fundamental personal right, emanating "from the totality of the constitutional scheme under which we live."* * *

The entire fabric of the Constitution and the purposes that clearly underlie its specific guarantees demonstrate that the rights to marital privacy and to marry and raise a family are of similar order and magnitude as the fundamental rights specifically protected.

Although the Constitution does not speak in so many words of the right of privacy in marriage, I cannot believe that it offers these fundamental rights no protection. The fact that no particular provision of the Constitution explicitly forbids the State from disrupting the traditional relation of the family—a relation as old and as fundamental as our entire civilization—surely does not show that the Government was meant to have the power to do so. Rather, as the Ninth Amendment expressly recognizes, there are fundamental personal rights such as this one, which are protected from abridgment by the Government though not specifically mentioned in the Constitution.* * *

In sum, I believe that the right of privacy in the marital relation is fundamental and basic—a personal right "retained by the people" within the meaning of the Ninth Amendment. Connecticut cannot constitutionally abridge this fundamental right, which is protected by the Fourteenth Amendment from infringement by the States. I agree with the Court that petitioners' convictions must therefore be reversed.

7. INVERSE CONDEMNATION

The theory of **inverse condemnation** is a controversial basis for environmental law suits. This theory is based on the power of **eminent domain**, or the power of government to take private property without the consent of the owner for a public purpose on the payment of just compensation. Inverse condemnation may be used where the government engages in an activity resulting in a deprivation of someone's property but does not enter into the prescribed procedure for making just compensation. The owner of the property will start the action, giving rise to the word "inverse" and will allege that the government has *in fact* taken his property and therefore he is entitled to just compensation. The difficult issue for the court to decide is whether the governmental regulation, activity or course of conduct, under the circumstnaces, did in fact deprive the owner of his property.

The *City of Walla Walla v. Conkey* provides a good illustration of the use of the inverse condemnation theory to protect the environment. The plaintiff-owner of property downstream from a municipal water treatment sewage plant alleged that the pollution of the stream by the municipal treatment plant deprived him of his riparian property right to use and enjoy the stream. One of the issues to be decided was whether this action by a governmental agency did in fact "take" the "property" of the downstream owner as those words are used in the constitution. A second issue that arose in this case is whether the continuing pollution of the stream for a period longer than prescribed by the statute of limitations gives rise to a prescriptive right to continue to pollute. A **prescriptive right** is a right similar to the right of **adverse possession** that gives an individual, who uses someone's property for a specified period of time, the right to continue to use that property in that manner if the owner fails to protect his exclusive property right within the specified period.

In a one-year period between 1980 and 1981 the United States Supreme Court decided two cases dealing with inverse condemnation. In 1980 in *Agins v. Tiburon*, the court held that an ordinance that was designed to discourage the "premature and unnecessary conversion of open space to urban uses" and to protect the residents from the ill effects of urbanization and to achieve those purposes limited the use of plaintiff's five-acre tract to five residential units did not constitute a "taking" and consequently the court did not have to decide whether inverse condemnation was a proper remedy.

In 1981, the Supreme Court decided *San Diego Gas and Electric Co. v. City of San Diego* involving the validity of San Diego's open space plan that included 230 acres of the plaintiff-utility's land. The utility claimed that the city adopted a policy of refusing to approve any development of its land that was inconsistent with the open space plan and that the only beneficial use of its land was an industrial park. Plaintiff sought damages for inverse condemnation but never applied for permission to develop the land. The court once again avoided the issue by deciding that there had been no final judgment rendered in the trial court and consequently it did not have jurisdiction to hear the case. In the court's 5 to 4 decision the majority held that no final judgment had been rendered. In a concurring opinion Justice Rehnquist said that if there had been a final judgment he would have had little difficulty in agreeing with much of what was said in the dissenting opinion of Justice Brennan, written on behalf of the four dissenting justices. Thus, the dissenting opinion of Justice Brennan takes on a significance greater than the usual minority opinion.

The article that follows, entitled "When Are Environmental Restrictions on Land Use Compensable?", provides an analysis of the test used by many courts to determine whether restrictions on the use of land for environmental purposes constitute a taking of property for which just compensation is required or a valid exercise of the police power, for which no compensation is required.

CITY OF WALLA WALLA v. CONKEY

6 Wash.App. 300, 492 P.2d 589 (1971)

PEARSON, Judge.

The respondent, City of Walla Walla, commenced a declaratory judgment action, naming as defendants the numerous appellants and others who own property near Mill Creek, some 3 miles west of Walla Walla, and whose property is in close proximity to respondent's sewage treatment plants. Many of the appellants use the waters from Mill Creek and an irrigation ditch known as "Gose Ditch" for farm irrigation purposes. The city has for years been depositing sewage from its treatment plants into Mill Creek and Gose Ditch.

The properties of appellants were benefited by a 1927 decree of the Superior Court for Walla Walla county, which required the city to:

> [D]ischarge, deliver, and return into the bed of the natural channel of Mill Creek . . . all of the sewage water and other waters accumulating from time to time in the sewer system of the . . . City of Walla Walla, and when the said City of Walla Walla shall treat, purify or otherwise sterilize the sewage of the City of Walla Walla, to then return the purified or sterilized product to said point . . . to the end that each of the plaintiffs . . . may use the same for irrigation purposes. . .

The decree also provided that the appellants whose property was served for irrigation by Gose Ditch were entitled to a prior right to 1.77 cubic feet of water per second of time at all seasons of the year.

The city alleged in its complaint that because of increased population and industrial expansion it was now using 6 wells in addition to the Mill Creek water and that it was now treating sewage waters from various institutions which had not existed in 1927 and which institutions had their own water supply systems. Accordingly, the city claimed that sewage and industrial waste was being created far in excess of the amounts the city could treat and purify, despite the addition of an industrial sewage treatment facility.

The city sought to have the 1927 decree modified, so as to obligate the city to supply the appellants

> only an amount of treated sewage waste that bears the same proportion to the total sewage effluent as plantiff's [the city's] water right of 22 cubic feet per second of water from Mill Creek bears to the total water supplies available to plaintiff which contribute to the production of sewage waters.

The appellants filed counterclaims, alleging that their property rights had been unconstitutionally taken through the operation of the city's sewer plants because of noxious odors emanating from the discharge of polluted water into Gose Ditch and Mill Creek. There was testimony at trial that the pollution also caused the appellants' sprinkling systems to become plugged, and covered the creek and ditch beds with a slimy material.

The declaratory judgment action was tried separately to the court and the disposition of that action is not before us. The counterclaims were tried to a jury. At the conclusion of appellants' case, the court granted respondent's motion challenging the sufficiency of the evidence and entered judgments of dismissal from which this appeal is taken.

The dismissal of the counterclaims was granted on two grounds. First, the trial court believed that appellants had not established when the unconstitutional "taking" had occurred. Accordingly, there was insufficient evidence to allow the jury to apply the proper measure of damages, namely, the value of the property immediately before and after the taking. Secondly, the trial court believed that appellants' claims were barred because of more than 10 years of adverse use of or interference with appellants' property rights by the city.* * *

The questions raised on appeal are these. (1) Have respondent's actions in dumping raw and partially treated waste matter into Mill Creek and Gose Ditch, causing noxious odors, clogging irrigation sprinklers, and so forth, constituted a constitutional taking of appellants' property, requiring constitutional compensation? (2) Was it necessary for appellants to prove the exact time of "taking" so as to permit a factual determination of damages, and if so, was the offered evidence sufficient to make a prima facie case? (3) Does the statute of limitations applicable to adverse prescription apply to the type of constitutional taking or damaging which occurred in this case?

There is no question that pollution of a stream by a municipality in carrying out its sewage disposal functions constitutes a constitutional taking, where the disposal results in pollution of the stream on such a scale as to create a public nuisance. Snavely v. Goldendale, 10 Wash.2d 453, 117 P.2d 221 (1941).

2 J. Sackman, Nichols on Eminent Domain § 5.795(2) (3d ed. 1970) states at page 5–383:

> When a city or town gathers the sewage of its inhabitants and pours it into a private watercourse there is a serious impairment of the enjoyment of riparian rights and the injury resulting therefrom undoubtedly constitutes a "damage," but whether

> such injury is of such a character as to constitute a "taking" is not entirely clear. In a few states it is held that a lower riparian owner upon a private watercourse is not entitled to compensation for the pollution of the water by a municipal sewer system. But the weight of authority favors the principle that the court cannot balance the public convenience and inconvenience; that the pollution of a stream by sewage or for any other public purpose is a taking of property in the constitutional sense and that it cannot be effected without compensation.

We thus conclude that there was clearly established a prima facie case of an inverse condemnation in the nature of a taking, which occurred as a result of the city's sewage disposal activities.* * *

We now turn to the question of whether appellants established a prima facie case of damages which are not barred by the applicable statute of limitations.* * *

Respondent city also argues persuasively and the trial court ruled that the evidence showed a long history of pollution dating back to the 1920's, with gradual aggravations in the 1930's and 1940's when vegetable processing plant residue was added to the city sewage disposal system. Respondent urges that the prescriptive use period had long since established the city's rights to interfere with the use and enjoyment of appellants' property. This argument would persuade us were it not for the undisputed fact that it was not until the 1960's that the city started accepting large quantities of industrial waste which its plants could not properly treat, to the end that sewage and industrial waste were deposited into Mill Creek and Gose Ditch with no treatment at all.* * *

The unique problems presented in the inverse condemnation situation are exemplified by the two rulings made by the learned trial judge in dismissing the cross-complaints. They are these. When did the interference with the use and enjoyment of appellants' property reach the proportions where the law recognizes that a "taking" in the constitutional sense has occurred? It is necessary to answer that question because when an inverse condemnation has occurred, the right to claim compensation must be asserted within 10 years of the "taking." In Ackerman v. Port of Seattle, 55 Wash.2d 400, 405, 348 P.2d 664, 667 (1960), the rule was aptly stated:

> We have held that an action for constitutional taking is not barred by any statute of limitations and may be brought at any time before title to the property taken is acquired by prescription. The prescriptive period in this state has been held to be ten years. [Citing cases.]

It is also necessary to ascertain the time the taking has occurred because the measure of compensation is usually determined at that time. Again, in Ackerman v. Port of Seattle, *supra*, at page 413, 348 P.2d at page 371, the rule was announced that damages for an inverse condemnation would be "the difference between the value of their property before the airport was *extensively used* and the value thereafter, plus interest from that date."* * *

We view the policies and problems of the interference with the use and enjoyment of property by noxious odors and water pollution caused by the municipality's sewage disposal system, strikingly similar to the airport cases. Remedies of trespass or nuisance are largely inappropriate. Martin v. Port of Seattle, *supra*. There is no less reason to allow the property owners in this case the decline in market value of their property than in the airport noise cases. The harm is only different in kind. However, there is one marked distinction in the two types of cases and we must determine whether that distinction is sufficient to call for a different application of the rules cited above. That difference has to do with the permanence of the damages caused by the acts of municipality.

In the airport cases, there is little likelihood that the airplane noise will ever be abated, unless, of course, the genius of American technology develops the noiseless aircraft. However, when it comes to sewage pollution of air and water, there is a compelling and urgent necessity for municipal governments to solve that problem; and in fact, the City of Walla Walla has been required by court order to deliver effluent from its treatment facilities, meeting purity standards set by either the state or federal government. In the event such order is complied with, appellants' market value decline may be minimized. Therefore, to assess damages, as is done in the airport case, at the time *extensive* use has been established, would be unfair to the public who in all likelihood will also bear the cost, as it ultimately must, of treatment facilities sufficient to reduce or eliminate the air and water pollution. Such a result could also be grossly unfair to the property owner in cases where the pollution is allowed to worsen as the city grows and develops industrially.

We also point out that where inverse condemnation by air and water pollution has taken place, the degree of harm, as demonstrated by the facts of this case, is seasonable and subject to wide variations from month to month or from year to year. The variations are affected by (1) the weather, (2) the amount of industrial wastes or sewage discharged, and (3) the effectiveness of the treatment facilities. Accordingly, a determination of damages at some unpredictable time in the past will neither accurately measure the loss to a particular property owner, nor will it enable him to guess with any degree of accuracy *when* the jury will determine that his property rights have been taken. This will make it necessary for him to place before the jury numerous obsolete evaluations of the decline in market value, to the confusion of the jury, when the interests of justice would best be served by determination of the current effect the pollution has on the market value of the land involved.

Accordingly, it is our view that in this unique type of inverse condemnation, damages should be measured as the decline in market value at the time of trial.* * *

In Wilshire v. Seattle, 154 Wash. 1, 6, 280 P. 65, 67 (1929) the court stated:

> This court has held that in case possession of land is taken prior to the initiation of condemnation proceedings the compensation to the owner, based upon the market value of the land, is to be determined as of the date of trial, and not as of the date possession was taken.

We are of the opinion that such rule is workable and fair when applied to inverse condemnation by air and water pollution. Since appellants' evidence showed the decline in market value as of the time of trial, we conclude that a prima facie case was made on the issue of damages.

However, because of the city's claim of adverse prescription, we do think it was necessary for appellants to establish a prima facie case that substantial or extensive pollution occurred within 10 years prior to the commencement of the actions, which was different in kind or substantially greater in degree than that which existed before that period commenced. Cheskov v. Port of Seattle, *supra*.

We think there was sufficient evidence from appellants' witnesses and from respondent's plant supervisor to create an issue of fact for the jury. The pollution worsened in the early 1960's and became severe in the mid-1960's when sewage without treatment was deposited in Mill Creek in great quantities.

Consequently, the jury should have been allowed to make that factual determination under instructions to the effect that, to recover, appellants must establish by a preponderance of the evidence that the damage to their property had, within 10 years prior to the commencement of the action, differed substantially in kind or was substantially greater in degree than it had been prior to the commencement of that period. *See* Ackerman v. Port of Seattle, *supra*; Cheskov v. Port of Seattle, *supra*; Anderson v. Port of Seattle, 66 Wash.2d 457, 403 P.2d 368 (1965).

We think the trial court should also submit to the jury the question of which of the appellants, if any, acquired his property *after* the time of "taking." No damages should be allowed any appellant found to have acquired his property for a price commensurate with its diminished value. Such parties should not be entitled to recover damages which they did not, in fact, sustain, even though the current market value of their land may be less than it would be without the pollution.

Reversed and remanded.

AGINS v. CITY OF TIBURON

447 U.S. 255 (1980)

Mr. Justice Powell delivered the opinion of the Court.

The question in this case is whether a municipal zoning ordinance took appellants' property without just compensation in violation of the Fifth and Fourteenth Amendments.

I

After the appellants acquired five acres of unimproved land in the city of Tiburon, Cal., for residential development, the city was required by state law to prepare a general plan governing both land use and the development of open-space land. Cal. Govt. Code Ann. §§ 65302 (a) and (e) (West Supp. 1979); see § 65563. In response, the city adopted two ordinances that modified existing zoning requirements. Tiburon, Cal., Ordinances Nos. 123 N. S. and 124 N. S. (June 28, 1973). The zoning ordinances placed the appellants' property in "RPD–1," a Residential Planned Development and Open Space Zone. RPD–1 property may be devoted to one-family dwellings, accessory buildings, and open-space uses. Density restrictions permit the appellants to build between one and five single-family residences on their 5-acre tract. The appellants never have sought approval for development of their land under the zoning ordinances.

The appellants filed a two-part complaint against the city in State Superior Court. The first cause of action sought $2 million in damages for inverse condemnation.[2] The second cause of action requested a declaration that the zoning ordinances were facially unconstitutional. The gravamen of both claims was the appellants' assertion that the city had taken their property without just compensation in violation of the Fifth and Fourteenth Amendments. The complaint alleged that land in Tiburon has greater value than any other suburban property in the State of California. App. 3.

[2]Inverse condemnation should be distinguished from eminent domain. Eminent domain refers to a legal proceeding in which a government asserts its authority to condemn property. *United States* v. *Clarke*, 445 U. S. 253, 255–258 (1980). Inverse condemnation is "a shorthand description of the manner in which a landowner recovers just compensation for a taking of his property when condemnation proceedings have not been instituted." *Id.*, at 257.

The ridgelands that appellants own "possess magnificent views of San Francisco Bay and the scenic surrounding areas [and] have the highest market values of all lands" in Tiburon. *Id.*, at 4. Rezoning of the land "forever prevented [its] development for residential use. . . ." *Id.*, at 5. Therefore, the appellants contended, the city had "completely destroyed the value of [appellants'] property for any purpose or use whatsoever. . . ." *Id.*, at 7.

The city demurred, claiming that the complaint failed to state a cause of action. The Superior Court sustained the demurrer, and the California Supreme Court affirmed. 24 Cal. 3d 266, 598 P. 2d 25 (1979). The State Supreme Court first considered the inverse condemnation claim. It held that a landowner who challenges the constitutionality of a zoning ordinance may not "sue in inverse condemnation and thereby transmute an excessive use of the police power into a lawful taking for which compensation in eminent domain must be paid." *Id.*, at 273, 598 P. 2d, at 28. The sole remedies for such a taking, the court concluded, are mandamus and declaratory judgment. Turning therefore to the appellants' claim for declaratory relief, the California Supreme Court held that the zoning ordinances had not deprived the appellants of their property without compensation in violation of the Fifth Amendment.

We noted probable jurisdiction. 444 U. S. 1011 (1980). We now affirm the holding that the zoning ordinance on its face does not take the appellants' property without just compensation.

II

The Fifth Amendment guarantees that private property shall not "be taken for public use, without just compensation." The appellants' complaint framed the question as whether a zoning ordinance that prohibits all development of their land effects a taking under the Fifth and Fourteenth Amendments. The California Supreme Court rejected the appellants' characterization of the issue by holding, as a matter of state law, that the terms of the challenged ordinance allow the appellants to construct between one and five residences on their property. The court did not consider whether the zoning ordinance would be unconstitutional if applied to prevent appellants from building five homes. Because the appellants have not submitted a plan for development of their property as the ordinances permit, there is as yet no concrete controversy regarding the application of the specific zoning provisions. See *Socialist Labor Party* v. *Gilligan*, 406 U. S. 583, 588 (1972). See also *Goldwater* v. *Carter*, 444 U. S. 996, 997 (1979) (POWELL, J., concurring). Thus, the only question properly before us is whether the mere enactment of the zoning ordinances constitutes a taking.

The application of a general zoning law to particular property effects a taking if the ordinance does not substantially advance legitimate state interests, see *Nectow* v. *Cambridge*, 277 U. S. 183, 188 (1928), or denies an owner economically viable use of his land, see *Penn Central Transp. Co.* v. *New York City*, 438 U. S. 104, 138, n. 36 (1978). The determination that governmental action constitutes a taking is, in essence, a determination that the public at large, rather than a single owner, must bear the burden of an exercise of state power in the public interest. Although no precise rule determines when property has been taken, see *Kaiser Aetna* v. *United States*, 444 U. S. 164 (1979), the question necessarily requires a weighing of private and public interests. The seminal decision in *Euclid* v. *Ambler Co.,* 272 U.S. 365 (1926), is illustrative. In that case, the landowner challenged the constitutionality of a municipal ordinance that restricted commercial development of his property. Despite alleged diminution in value of the owner's land, the Court held that the zoning laws were facially constitutional. They bore a substantial relationship to public welfare, and their enactment inflicted no irreparable injury upon the landowner. *Id.*, at 395–397.

In this case, the zoning ordinances substantially advance legitimate governmental goals. The State of California has determined that the development of local open-space plans will discourage the "premature and unnecessary conversion of open-space land to urban uses." Cal. Govt. Code Ann. § 65561 (b) (West. Supp. 1979).[7] The specific zoning regulations at issue are exercises of the city's police power to protect the residents of Tiburon from the ill effects of urbanization.[8] Such governmental purposes long have been recognized as legitimate. See *Penn Central Transp. Co.* v. *New York City, supra*, at 129; *Village of Belle Terre* v. *Boraas*, 416 U. S. 1, 9 (1974); *Euclid* v. *Ambler Co., supra*, at 394–395.

The ordinances place appellants' land in a zone limited to single-family dwellings, accessory buildings, and open-space uses. Construction is not permitted until the builder submits a plan compatible with "adjoining patterns of development and open space." Tiburon, Cal., Ordinance No. 123 N. S. § 2 (F). In passing upon a plan, the city also will consider how well the proposed development would preserve the surrounding environment and whether the density of new construction will be offset by adjoining open spaces. *Ibid.* The zoning ordinances benefit the appellants as well as the public by serving the city's interest in assuring careful and orderly development of residential property with provision for open-space areas. There is no indication that the appellants' 5-acre tract is the only property affected by the ordinances. Appellants therefore will share with other owners the benefits and burdens of the city's exercise of its police power. In assessing the fairness of the zoning ordinance, these benefits must be considered along with any diminution in market value that the appellants might suffer.

Although the ordinances limit development, they neither prevent the best use of appellants' land, see *United States* v. *Causby*, 328 U. S. 256, 262, and n. 7 (1946), nor extinguish a fundamental attribute of ownership, see *Kaiser Aetna* v. *United States, supra*, at 179–180. The appellants have alleged that they wish to develop the land for residential purposes, that the land is the most expensive suburban property in the State, and that the best possible use of the land is residential. App. 3–4. The California Supreme Court has decided, as a matter of state law, that appellants may be permitted to build as many as five houses on their five acres of prime residential property. At this juncture, the appellants are free to pursue their reasonable investment expectations by submitting a development plan to local officials. Thus, it cannot be said that the impact of general land-use regulations has denied appellants the "justice and fairness" guaranteed by the Fifth and Fourteenth Amendments. See *Penn Central Transp. Co.* v. *New York City*, 438 U. S., at 124.[9]

[7]The State also recognizes that the preservation of open space is necessary "for the assurance of the continued availability of land for the production of food and fiber, for the enjoyment of scenic beauty, for recreation and for the use of natural resources." Cal. Govt. Code Ann. § 65561 (a) (West. Supp. 1979); see Tiburon, Cal., Ordinance No. 124 N. S. §§ 1 (f) and (h).

[8]The City Council of Tiburon found that

> "[i]t is in the public interest to avoid unnecessary conversion of open space land to strictly urban uses, thereby protecting against the resultant adverse impacts, such as air, noise and water pollution, traffic congestion, destruction of scenic beauty, disturbance of the ecology and environment, hazards related to geology, fire and flood, and other demonstrated consequences of urban sprawl." Ordinance No. 124 N. S. § 1 (c).

[9]Appellants also claim that the city's precondemnation activities constitute a taking. . . . The State Supreme Court correctly rejected the contention that the municipality's good-faith planning activities, which did not result in successful prosecution of an eminent domain claim, so burdened the appellants' enjoyment of their property as to constitute a taking. See also *City of Walnut Creek* v. *Leadership Housing Systems, Inc.*, 73 Cal. App. 3d 611, 620–624, 140 Cal.

III

The State Supreme Court determined that the appellants could not recover damages for inverse condemnation even if the zoning ordinances constituted a taking. The court stated that only mandamus and declaratory judgment are remedies available to such a landowner. Because no taking has occurred, we need not consider whether a State may limit the remedies available to a person whose land has been taken without just compensation.

The judgment of the Supreme Court of California is

Affirmed.

SAN DIEGO GAS & ELECTRIC CO.
v.
CITY OF SAN DIEGO

450 U.S. 621 (1981)

JUSTICE BLACKMAN delivered the opinion of the Court.

Appellant San Diego Gas & Electric Company, a California corporation, asks this Court to rule that a State must provide a monetary remedy to a landowner whose property allegedly has been "taken" by a regulatory ordinance claimed to violate the Just Compensation Clause of the Fifth Adendment. This question was left open last Term in *Agins* v. *City of Tiburon*, 447 U. S. 225, 263 (1980). Because we conclude that we lack jurisdiction in this case, we again must leave the issue undecided.

I

Appellant owns a 412-acre parcel of land in Sorrento Valley, an area in the northwest part of the city of San Diego, Cal. It assembled and acquired the acreage in 1966, at a cost of about $1,770,000, as a possible site for a nuclear power plant to be constructed in the 1980's. Approximately 214 acres of the parcel lie within or near an estuary known as the Los Penasquitos Lagoon. These acres are low-lying land which serves as a drainage basin for three river systems. About a third of the land is subject

---

Rptr. 690, 695–697 (1977). Even if the appellants' ability to sell their property was limited during the pendency of the condemnation proceeding, the appellants were free to sell or develop their property when the proceedings ended. Mere fluctuations in value during the process of governmental decisionmaking, absent extraordinary delay, are "incidents of ownership. They cannot be considered as a 'taking' in the constitutional sense." *Danforth* v. *United States*, 308 U. S. 271, 285 (1939). See *Thomas W. Garland, Inc.* v. *City of St. Louis*, 596 F. 2d 784, 787 (CA8), cert. denied, 444 U. S. 899 (1979); *Reservation Eleven Associates* v. *District of Columbia*, 136 U. S. App. D. C. 311, 315–316, 420 F. 2d 153, 157–158 (1969); *Virgin Islands* v. *50.05 Acres of Land*, 185 F. Supp. 495, 498 (V. I. 1960); 2 J. Sackman & P. Rohan, Nichols' Law of Eminent Domain § 6.13 [3] (3d ed. 1979).

to tidal action from the nearby Pacific Ocean. The 214 acres are unimproved, except for sewer and utility lines.

When appellant acquired the 214 acres, most of the land was zoned either for industrial use or in an agricultural "holding" category. The city's master plan, adopted in 1967, designated nearly all the area for industrial use.

Several events that occurred in 1973 gave rise to this litigation. First, the San Diego City Council rezoned parts of the property. It changed 39 acres from industrial to agricultural, and increased the minimum lot size in some of the agricultural areas from 1 acre to 10 acres. The Council recommended, however, that 50 acres of the agricultural land be considered for industrial development upon the submission of specific development plans.

Second, the city, pursuant to Cal. Govt. Code Ann. § 65563 (West) (Supp. 1979), established an open-space plan. This statute required each California city and county to adopt a plan "for the comprehensive and long-range preservation and conservation of open-space land within its jurisdiction." The plan adopted by the city of San Diego placed appellant's property among the city's open-space areas, which it defined as "any urban land or water surface that is essentially open or natural in character, and which has appreciable utility for park and recreation purposes, conservation of land, water or other natural resources or historic or scenic purposes." App. 159. The plan acknowledged appellant's intention to construct a nuclear power plant on the property, stating that such a plant would not necessarily be incompatible with the open-space designation. The plan proposed, however, that the city acquire the property to preserve it as parkland.

Third, the City Council proposed a bond issue in order to obtain funds to acquire open-space lands. The council identified appellant's land as among those properties to be acquired with the proceeds of the bond issue. The proposition, however, failed to win the voters' approval. The open-space plan has remained in effect, but the city has made no attempt to acquire appellant's property.

On August 15, 1974, appellant instituted this action in the Superior Court for the County of San Diego against the city and a number of its officials. It alleged that the city had taken its property without just compensation, in violation of the Constitutions of the United States and California. Appellant's theory was that the city had deprived it of the entire beneficial use of the property through the rezoning and the adoption of the open-space plan. It alleged that the city followed a policy of refusing to approve any development that was inconsistent with the plan, and that the only beneficial use of the property was as an industrial park, a use that would be inconsistent with the open-space designation. The city disputed this allegation, arguing that appellant had never asked its approval for any development plan for the property. It also contended that, as a charter city, it was not bound by the open-space plan, even if appellant's proposed development would be inconsistent with the plan, citing Cal. Govt. Code Ann., §§ 65700, 65803 (West) (1966 and Supp. 1979).

Appellant sought damages of $6,150,000 in inverse condemnation, as well as mandamus and declaratory relief. Prior to trial, the court dismissed the mandamus claim, holding that "mandamus is not the proper remedy to challenge the validity of a legislative act." Clerk's Tr. 42. After a nonjury trial on the issue of liability, the court granted judgment for appellant, finding that:

> "29. [Due to the] continuing course of conduct of the defendant City culminating in June of 1973, and, in particular, the designation of substantially all of the subject property as open space . . . , plaintiff has been deprived of all practical, beneficial or economic use of the property designated as open space, and has further suffered severance damage with respect to the balance of the subject property.
>
> "30. No development could proceed on the property designated as open space unless it was consistent with open space. In light of the particular characteristics of

the said property, there exists no practical, beneficial or economic use of the said property designated as open space which is consistent with open space.

"31. Since June 19, 1973, the property designated as open space has been devoted to use by the public as open space.

"32. Following the actions of the defendant City in June of 1973, it would have been totally impractical and futile for plaintiff to have applied to defendant City for the approval of any development of the property designated as open space or the remainder of the subject property.

"33. Since the actions of the defendant City of June of 1973, the property designated as open space and the remainder of the larger parcel is unmarketable in that no other person would be willing to purchase the property, and the property has at most a nominal fair market value." App. 41–42.

The court concluded that these findings established that the city had taken the property and that just compensation was required by the Constitutions of both the United States and California. A subsequent jury trial on the question of damages resulted in a judgment for appellant for over $3 million.

On appeal, the California Court of Appeal, Fourth District, affirmed. App. to Juris. Statement B–1; see 146 Cal. Rptr. 103 (1978). It held that neither a change in zoning nor the adoption of an open-space plan automatically entitled a property owner to compensation for any resulting diminution in the value of the property. In this case, however, the record revealed that the city followed the policy of enacting and enforcing zoning ordinances that were consistent with its open-space plan. The Court of Appeal also found that the evidence supported the conclusion that industrial use was the only feasible use for the property and that the city would have denied any application for the industrial development because it would be incompatible with the open-space designation. Appellant's failure to present a plan for developing the property therefore did not preclude an award of damages in its favor. The Court of Appeal, with one judge dissenting, denied the city's petition for rehearing. See 146 Cal. Rptr., at 118.

The Supreme Court of California, however, on July 13, 1978, granted the city's petition for a hearing. This action automatically vacated the Court of Appeal's decision depriving it of all effect. *Knouse* v. *Nimocks*, 8 Cal. 2d 482, 483–484, 66 P. 2d 438 (1937). See also Cal. Rules of Court 976 (d) and 977. Before the hearing, the Supreme Court in June 1979 retransferred the case to the Court of Appeal for reconsideration in light of the intervening decision in *Agins* v. *City of Tiburon*, 24 Cal. 3d 366, 598 P. 2d 25 (1979), aff'd, 447 U. S. 255 (1980). The California court in *Agins* held that an owner who is deprived of substantially all beneficial use of his land by a zoning regulation is not entitled to an award of damages in an inverse condemnation proceeding. Rather, his exclusive remedy is invalidation of the regulation in an action for mandamus or declaratory relief. *Agins* also held that the plaintiffs in that case were not entitled to such relief because the zoning ordinance at issue permitted the building of up to five residences on their property. Therefore, the court held, it did not deprive those plaintiffs of substantially all reasonable use of their land.

When the present case was retransferred, the Court of Appeal, in an unpublished opinion, reversed the judgment of the Superior Court. App. 63. It relied upon the California decision in *Agins* and held that appellant could not recover compensation through inverse condemnation. It, however, did not invalidate either the zoning ordinance or the open-space plan. Instead, it held that factual disputes precluded such relief on the present state of the record:

"[Appellant] complains it has been denied all use of its land which is zoned for agriculture and manufacturing but lies within the open space area of the general plan. It has not made application to use or improve the property nor has it asked [the] City what development might be permitted. Even assuming no use is acceptable to the City, [appellant's] complaint deals with the alleged overzealous use of the police power by [the] City. Its remedy is mandamus or declaratory relief, not inverse condemnation. [Appellant] did in its complaint seek these remedies asserting that [the] City had arbitrarily exercised its police power by enacting an unconstitutional zoning law and general plan element or by applying the zoning and general plan unconstitutionally. However, on the present record these are disputed fact issues not covered by the trial court in its findings and conclusions. They can be dealt with anew should [appellant] elect to retry the case." App. 66.

The Supreme Court of California denied further review. App. to Juris. Statement I-1. Appellant appealed to this Court, arguing that the Fifth and Fourteenth Amendments require that compensation be paid whenever private property is taken for public use. Appellant takes issue with the California Supreme Court's holding in *Agins* that its remedy is limited to invalidation of the ordinance in a proceeding for mandamus or declaratory relief. We postponed consideration of our jurisdiction until the hearing on the merits.—U. S.—(1980). We now conclude that the appeal must be dismissed because of the absence of a final judgment.

II

In *Agins*, the California Supreme Court held that mandamus or declaratory relief is available whenever a zoning regulation is claimed to effect an uncompensated taking in violation of the Fifth and Fourteenth Amendments. The Court of Appeal's failure, therefore, to award such relief in this case clearly indicates its conclusion that the record does not support appellant's claim that an uncompensated taking has occurred. Because the court found that the record presented "disputed fact issues not covered by the trial court in its findings and conclusions," App. 66, it held that mandamus and declaratory relief would be available "should [appellant] elect to retry the case." *Ibid.* While this phrase appears to us to be somewhat ambiguous, we read it as meaning that appellant is to have an opportunity on remand to convince the trial court to resolve the disputed issues in its favor. We do not believe that the Court of Appeal was holding that judgment *must* be entered for the city. It certainly did not so direct. This indicates that appellant is free to pursue its quest for relief in the Superior Court. The logical course of action for an appellate court that finds unresolved factual disputes in the record is to remand the case for the resolution of those disputes. We therefore conclude that the Court of Appeal's decision contemplates further proceedings in the trial court.

III

Ever since this Court's decision in *Grays Harbor Co.* v. *Coats-Fordney Co.*, 243 U. S. 251 (1917), a state court's holding that private property has been taken in violation of the Fifth and Fourteenth Amendments and that further proceedings are necessary to determine the compensation that must be paid has been regarded as a classic example of a decision not reviewable in this Court because it is not "final." In such a case, "the remaining litigation may raise other federal questions that may later come here." *Radio Station WOW, Inc.* v. *Johnson*, 326 U. S. 120, 127 (1945). This is because "the federal constitutional question embraces not only a taking, but a taking on payment of just compensation. A state judgment is not final unless it covers both aspects of that integral problem." *North Dakota Board of Pharmacy* v. *Snyder's Drug Stores, Inc.*, 414 U. S. 156, 163 (1973).

This case presents the reverse aspect of that situation. The Court of Appeal has decided that monetary compensation is not an appropriate remedy for any taking of appellant's property that may have occurred, but it has not decided whether any other remedy is available because it has not decided whether any taking in fact has occurred. Thus, however we might rule with respect to the Court of Appeal's decision that appellant is not entitled to a monetary remedy—and we are frank to say that the federal constitutional aspects of that issue are not to be cast aside lightly—further proceedings are necessary to resolve the federal question whether there has been a taking at all. The court's decision, therefore, is not final, and we are without jurisdiction to review it.

Because § 1257 permits us to review only "[f]inal judgments or decrees" of a state court, the appeal must be, and is, dismissed.

It is so ordered.

JUSTICE REHNQUIST, concurring.

If I were satisfied that this appeal was from a "final judgment or decree" of the California Court of Appeal, as that term is used in 28 U. S. C. § 1257, I would have little difficulty in agreeing with much of what is said in the dissenting opinion of JUSTICE BRENNAN. Indeed, the Court's opinion notes "that the federal constitutional aspects of that issue are not to be cast aside lightly. . . ." *Ante*, p. 11.

But "the judicial Power of the United States" which is vested in this Court by Art. III of the Constitution is divided by that article into original jurisdiction and appellate jurisdiction. With respect to appellate jurisdiction, Art. III provides:

> "In all the other Cases before mentioned, the Supreme Court shall have appellate Jurisdiction, both as to Law and Fact, with such Exceptions, and under such Regulations as the Congress shall make."

The particular "regulation" of our appellate jurisdiction here relevant is found in § 1257 of Title 28 U. S. C. which provides:

> "Final judgments or decrees rendered by the highest court of a State in which a decision could be had, may be reviewed by the Supreme Court as follows:
>
> "(2) By appeal, where it is drawn in question the validity of a statute of any state on the ground of its being repugnant to the Constitution, treaties or laws of the United States, and the decision is in favor of its validity."

The principal case construing § 1257 is *Cox Broadcasting Corp.* v. *Cohn*, 420 U. S. 469 (1975), from which I dissented on the issue of finality. In *Cox*, the Court said:

> "The Court has noted that '[c]onsiderations of English usage as well as those of judicial policy' would justify an interpretation of the final-judgment rule to preclude review 'where anything further remains to be determined by a State court, no matter how dissociated from the only federal issue that has finally been adjudicated by the highest court of the State.' *Radio Station WOW, Inc.* v. *Johnson*, 326 U. S. 120, 124 (1945). But the Court there observed that the rule had not been administered in such a mechanical fashion and that there were circumstances in which there had been 'a departure from this requirement of finality for federal appellate jurisdiction.' *Ibid.*
>
> "These circumstances were said to be 'very few,' *ibid.*; but as the cases have unfolded, the Court has recurringly encountered situations in which the highest court of a State has finally determined the federal issue present in a particular case, but in which there are further proceedings in the lower state courts to come. There are now at least four categories of such cases in which the Court has treated the decision of the federal issue as a final judgment for the purposes of 28 U. S. C. § 1257 and has taken jurisdication without awaiting the completion of the additional proceedings anticipated in the lower state courts." 420 U. S. 469, 477 (1979).

In *Cox*, the Court stated that the fourth category of cases which fell within the ambit of § 1257 finality were "those situations where the federal issue has been finally decided in the state courts with further proceedings pending in which the party seeking review here might prevail on the merits on nonfederal grounds, thus rendering unnecessary review of the federal issue by this Court, and where reversal of the state court on the federal issue would be preclusive of any further litigation on the relevant cause of action rather than merely controlling the nature and character of, or determining the admissibility of evidence in, the state proceedings still to come. In these circumstances, if a refusal to immediately review the state-court decision might seriously erode federal policy, the Court has entertained and decided the federal issue, which itself has been finally determined by the state courts for purposes of the state litigation." 420 U. S. 469, 482–483.

I am not sure under how many of the four exceptions of *Cox* JUSTICE BRENNAN may view this case as falling, but it seems to me that this case illustrates the problems which arise from a less than literal reading of the language "final judgment or decree." The procedural history of this case in the state courts is anomalous, to say the least, and it has resulted in a majority of this Court concluding that the California courts have not decided whether any taking in fact has occurred, *ante*, p. 9, n. 11, and JUSTICE BRENNAN concluding that the Court of Appeal has held that the city of San Diego's course of conduct could not effect a "taking" of appellant's property. (BRENNAN, J., dissenting, *post*, p. 25, n. 25). Having read the characterization of the California court proceedings in the opinion of this Court and in the opinion of JUSTICE BRENNAN as carefully as I can, I can only conclude that they disagree as to what issues remain open on remand from the state Court of Appeal to the Superior Court, but agree that such proceedings may occur.

Under these circumstances, it seems to me to be entirely in accord with the language of 28 U. S. C. § 1257, though perhaps not entirely in accord with the above-quoted portion of the opinion in *Cox Broadcasting Corp.* v. *Cohn, supra*, to conclude that this appeal is not from a "final judgment or decree." I would feel much better able to formulate federal constitutional principles of damages for land use regulation which amounts to a taking of land under the eminent domain clause of the Fifth Amendment if I knew what disposition the California courts finally made of this case. Because I do not, and cannot at this stage of the litigation, know that, I join the opinion of the Court today in which the appeal is dismissed for want of a final judgment.

JUSTICE BRENNAN, with whom JUSTICE STEWART, JUSTICE MARSHALL, and JUSTICE POWELL join, dissenting.

Title 28 U. S. C. § 1257 limits this Court's jurisdiction to review judgments of state courts to "[f]inal judgments or decrees rendered by the highest court of a State in which a decision could be had." The Court today dismisses this appeal on the ground that the Court of Appeal of California, Fourth District, failed to decide the federal question whether a "taking" of appellant's property had occurred, and therefore had not entered a final judgment or decree on that question appealable under § 1257. Because the Court's conclusion fundamentally mischaracterizes the holding and judgment of the Court of Appeal, I respectfully dissent from the Court's dismissal and reach the merits of appellant's claim.

I

In 1966, appellant assembled a 412-acre parcel of land as a potential site for a nuclear power plant. At that time, approximately 116 acres of the property were zoned for industrial use, with most of the balance zoned in an agricultural holding category. In 1967, appellee adopted its General Plan for San Diego, designating most of appellant's property for industrial use. In 1973, the city took three critical actions which together form the predicate of the instant litigation: it down-zoned some of appellant's property from industrial to agricultural; it incorporated a new open space element in its Plan that designated about 233 acres of appellant's land for open space use;[1] and it prepared a report mapping appellant's property for purchase by the city for open space use, contingent on passage of a bond issue. Joint App. 49.

Appellant filed suit in California Superior Court alleging, *inter alia*, a "taking" of its property by "inverse condemnation" in violation of the United States and California Constitutions,[2] and seeking compensation of over $6 million. After a nonjury trial on liability, the Court held that appellee had taken a portion of appellant's property without just compensation, thereby violating the United States and California Constitutions. *Id.*, at 42–43. A subsequent jury trial on damages resulted in a judgment of over $3 million, plus interest as of the date of the "taking," and appraisal, engineering, and attorneys' fees. *Id.*, at 46.

The California Court of Appeal, Fourth District, affirmed, holding that there was "substantial evidence to support the court's conclusion [that] there was inverse condemnation." *Id.*, at 54. The California Supreme Court granted the city's petition for a hearing, App. to Juris. Statement D–1, but later transferred the case back to the Court of Appeal for reconsideration in light of *Agins* v. *City of Tiburon*, 24 Cal. 3d 266, 598 P. 2d 25 (1979), aff'd, ___ U. S. ___ (1980). App. to Juris. Statement E–1. Expressly relying on *Agins*, the Court of Appeal this time reversed the Superior Court, holding that:

> "Unlike the person whose property is taken in eminent domain, the individual who is deprived of his property due to the state's exercise of its police power is not entitled to compensation. . . . A local entity's arbitrary unconstitutional exercise of the police power which deprives the owner of the beneficial use of his land does not require compensation; rather the party's remedy is administrative mandamus. . . ." Joint App. 65–66.

The California Supreme Court denied further review. App. to Juris. Statement I-1.

[1]The City's Plan defined "open space" as "any urban land or water surface that is essentially open or natural in character, and which has appreciable utility for park and recreation purposes, conservation of land, water or other natural resources or historic or scenic purposes." Joint App. 52, n. 3.

[2]The phrase "inverse condemnation" generally describes a cause of action against a government defendant in which a landowner may recover just compensation for a "taking" of his property under the Fifth Amendment, even though formal condemnation proceedings in exercise of the sovereign's power of eminent domain have not been instituted by the government entity. *Agins* v. *City of Tiburon*, ___ U. S. ___, ___, n. 2 (1980); *United States* v. *Clarke*, 445 U. S. 253, 257 (1980). See, *e. g.*, Cal. Code Civ. Proc. Ann. § 1245.260 (Supp. 1980). In the typical condemnation proceeding, the government brings a judicial or administrative action against the property owner to "take" the fee simple or an interest in his property; the judicial or administrative body enters a decree of condemnation and just compensation is awarded. See *ibid*. See generally P. Nichols, 6 Eminent Domain § 24.1 (3d rev. ed. 1980). In an "inverse condemnation" action, the condemnation is "inverse" because it is the landowner, not the government entity, who institutes the proceeding.

"Eminent domain" is the "power of the sovereign to take property for public use without the owner's consent." *Id.*, § 1.11, at 1–7. Formal proceedings initiated by the government are loosely referred to as either "eminent domain" or "condemnation" proceedings. See *Agins* v. *City of Tiburon, supra*, ___ U. S., at ___, n. 2.

II

The Court today holds that the judgment below is not "final" within the meaning of 28 U. S. C. § 1257 because, although the California Court of Appeal "has decided that monetary compensation is not an appropriate remedy for any taking of appellant's property that may have occurred, . . . it has not decided whether any other remedy is available because *it has not decided whether any taking in fact has occurred.*" *Ante*, at 9 (emphasis added). With all due respect, this conclusion misreads the holding of the Court of Appeal. In faithful compliance with the instructions of the California Supreme Court's opinion in *Agins* v. *City of Tiburon, supra*, the Court of Appeal held that the city's exercise of its police power, however arbitrary or excessive, could not *as a matter of federal constitutional law* constitute a "taking" under the Fifth and Fourteenth Amendments, and therefore that there was no "taking" without just compensation in the instant case.

Examination of the Court of Appeal's opinion and the California Supreme Court's *Agins* opinion confirms this reading. The Court of Appeal noted that, "[u]nlike the person whose property is *taken* in eminent domain, the individual who is *deprived* of his property due to the state's exercise of its police power is not entitled to compensation." Joint App. 65–66 (emphasis added). Under the Court of Appeal's view, there can be no Fifth Amendment "taking" outside of the eminent domain context. Thus, a "local entity's arbitrary unconstitutional exercise of the police power which *deprives* the owner of the beneficial use of his land does not require compensation; rather the party's remedy is administrative mandamus." *Id.*, at 66 (emphasis added).

The Court of Appeal's analysis was required by the California Supreme Court's opinion in *Agins* v. *City of Tiburon, supra.* There the Court stated:

> "Plaintiffs contend that the limitations on the use of their land imposed by the ordinance constitute an unconstitutional 'taking of [plaintiff's] property without payment of just compensation' for which an action in inverse condemnation will lie. *Inherent in the contention is the argument that a local entity's exercise of its police power which, in a given case, may exceed constitutional limits is equivalent to the lawful taking of property by eminent domain thereby necessitating the payment of compensation. We are unable to accept this argument* believing the preferable view to be that, while such governmental action is invalid because of its excess, remedy by way of damages in eminent domain is not thereby made available. 24 Cal. 3d, at 272, 598 P. 2d, at 28 (brackets in original) (emphasis added).

A landowner may not "elect to sue in inverse condemnation and thereby *transmute an excessive use of the police power into a lawful taking* for which compensation in eminent domain must be paid." *Id.*, at 273, 598 P. 2d, at 28 (emphasis added).

This Court therefore errs, I respectfully submit, when it concludes that the Court of Appeal "has not decided whether any taking in fact has occurred." *Ante*, at 9. For whatever the merits of the California courts' substantive rulings on the federal constitutional issue, see *infra*, it is clear that the California Supreme Court has held that California courts in a challenge, as here, to a police power regulation, are barred from holding that a Fifth Amendment "*taking*" requiring just compensation has occurred. No set of factual circumstances, no matter how severe, can "transmute" an arbitrary exercise of the city's police power into a Fifth Amendment "taking." *Agins* v. *City of Tiburon, supra*, 24 Cal. 3d, at 273, 598 P. 2d, at 28. This Court's focus on the last full paragraph of the Court of Appeal decision, *ante*, at 7, to support its conclusion is misplaced, because that paragraph merely raises the possibility that appellant may "elect to retry the case" on a different constitutional theory—an allegation of "overzealous use of the police power," Joint App. 66. Whatever factual findings of the trial court might be relevant to that inquiry, they would have no bearing on a Fifth Amendment "taking" claim. Therefore, the Court's suggestion that "further proceedings are necessary to resolve the federal question whether there has been a taking at all," is plainly wrong. *Ante*, at 9.

The trial court has held expressly that the "actions of defendant City . . . taken as a whole, constitute a *taking* of the portion of plaintiff's property designated as open space without due process of law and just compensation within the meaning of the California and United States constitutions." Joint App. 42–43 (emphasis added). The Court of Appeal reversed this holding and concluded as a matter of law that no Fifth Amendment "taking" had occurred. This is indistinguishable, then, from a dismissal of appellant's case for legal insufficiency. In any such dismissal, factual questions are necessarily left unresolved. But when a litigant is denied relief as a matter of law, the judgment is necessarily final within the meaning of § 1257. See, *e. g., Allenberg Cotton Co.* v. *Pittman*, 419 U. S. 20, 24–25 (1974); *Windward Shipping (London) Ltd.* v. *American Radio Association*, 415 U. S. 104, 108 (1974).

Since the Court of Appeal held that no Fifth Amendment "taking" had occurred, no just compensation was required. This is a classic final judgment. See *North Dakota State Board of Pharmacy* v. *Snyder's Drug Stores, Inc.*, 414 U. S. 156, 163 (1973); *Grays Harbor Logging Co.* v. *Coats-Fordney Logging Co.*, 243 U. S. 251, 256 (1917). I therefore dissent from the dismissal of this appeal, and address the merits of the question presented.

III

The Just Compensation Clause of the Fifth Amendment, made applicable to the States through the Fourteenth Amendment, *Webb's Fabulous Pharmacies, Inc.* v. *Beckwith*, ___ U. S. ___, ___ (1980); see *Chicago, B. & Q. R. Co.* v. *Chicago*, 166 U. S. 226, 239, 241 (1897), states in clear and unequivocal terms: "[N]or shall private property be taken for public use, without just compensation." The question presented on the merits in this case is whether a government entity must pay just compensation when a police power regulation has effected a "taking" of "private property" for "public use" within the meaning of that constitutional provision. Implicit in this question is the corollary issue whether a government entity's exercise of its regulatory police power can ever effect a "taking" within the meaning of the Just Compensation Clause.

A

As explained in Part II, *supra*, the California courts have held that a city's exercise of its police power, however arbitrary or excessive, cannot as a matter of federal constitutional law constitute a "taking" within the meaning of the Fifth Amendment. This holding flatly contradicts clear precedents of this Court. For example, in last Term's *Agins* v. *City of Tiburon*, ___ U. S. ___, ___ (1980), the Court noted that "[t]he application of a general zoning law to particular property effects a taking if the ordinance does not substantially advance legitimate state interests . . . or [if it] denies an owner economically viable use of his land." Applying that principle, the Court examined whether the Tiburon zoning ordinance effected a "taking" of the Agins' property, concluding that it did not have such an effect. *Id.*, at ___.

In *Penn Central Transportation Co.* v. *New York City*, 438 U. S. 104 (1978), the Court analyzed "whether the restrictions imposed by New York City's [Landmark Preservation] law upon appellants' exploitation of the [Grand Central] Terminal site effect a 'taking' of appellants' property within the meaning of the Fifth Amendment." *Id.*, at 122. Canvassing the appropriate inquiries necessary to determine whether a particular restriction effected a "taking," the Court identified the "economic impact of the regulation on the claimant" and the "character of the governmental action" as particularly relevant considerations, *Id.*, at 124; see, *id.*, at 130–131. Although the Court ultimately concluded that application of New York's

Landmark law did not effect a "taking" of the railroad property, it did so only after deciding that "[t]he restrictions imposed are substantially related to the promotion of the general welfare and not only permit reasonable beneficial use of the landmark site but also afford appellants opportunities further to enhance not only the Terminal site proper but also other properties." *Id.*, at 138 (footnote omitted).

The constitutionality of a local ordinance regulating dredging and pit excavating on a property was addressed in *Goldblatt* v. *Town of Hempstead*, 369 U. S. 590 (1962). After observing that an otherwise valid zoning ordinance that deprives the owner of the most beneficial use of his property would not be unconstitutional, *id.*, at 592, the Court cautioned: "That is not to say, however, that governmental action in the form of regulation cannot be so onerous as to constitute a taking which constitutionally requires compensation," *id.*, at 594. On many other occasions, the Court has recognized in passing the vitality of the general principle that a regulation can effect a Fifth Amendment "taking." See, *e. g., Prune Yard Shopping Center* v. *Robins*, ___ U. S. ___, ___ (1980); *Kaiser Aetna* v. *United States*, 444 U. S. 164, 174 (1979); *Andrus* v. *Allard*, 444 U. S. 51, 65–66 (1979); *United States* v. *Central Eureka Mining Co.*, 357 U. S. 155, 168 (1958).

The principle applied in all these cases has its source in Justice Holmes' opinion for the Court in *Pennsylvania Coal Co.* v. *Mahon*, 260 U. S. 393, 415 (1922), in which he stated: "The general rule at least is, that while property may be regulated to a certain extent, if regulation goes too far it will be recognized as a taking." The determination of a "taking" is "a question of degree—and therefore cannot be disposed of by general propositions." *Id.*, at 416. While acknowledging that "[g]overnment hardly could go on if to some extent values incident to property could not be diminished without paying for every such change in the general law," *id.*, at 413, the Court rejected the proposition that police power restrictions could never be recognized as a Fifth Amendment "taking." Indeed, the Court concluded that the Pennsylvania statute forbidding the mining of coal that would cause the subsidence of any house effected a "taking." *Id.*, at 414–416.

B

Not only does the holding of the California Court of Appeal contradict precedents of this Court, but it also fails to recognize the essential similarity of regulatory "takings" and other "takings." The typical "taking" occurs when a government entity formally condemns a landowner's property and obtains the fee simple pursuant to its sovereign power of eminent domain. See, *e. g., Berman* v. *Parker*, 348 U. S. 26, 33 (1954). However, a "taking" may also occur without a formal condemnation proceeding or transfer of fee simple. This Court long ago recognized that

> "[i]t would be a very curious and unsatisfactory result, if in construing [the Just Compensation Clause] . . . it shall be held that if the government refrains from the absolute conversion of real property to the uses of the public it can destroy its value entirely, can inflict irreparable and permanent injury to any extent, can, in effect, subject it to total destruction without making any compensation, because in the narrowest sence of that word, it is not *taken* for the public use." *Pumpelly* v. *Green Bay Co.*, 80 U. S. (13 Wall.) 166, 177–178 (1872) (emphasis in original).

See *Chicago, R. I. & P. R. Co.* v. *United States*, 284 U.S. 80, 96 (1931).

In service of this principle, the Court frequently has found "takings" outside the context of the formal condemnation proceedings or transfer of fee simple, in cases where government action benefiting the public resulted in destruction of the use and enjoyment of private property. *E. g., Kaiser Aetna* v. *United States, supra*, 444 U. S., at 178–180 (navigational servitude allowing public right of access); *United States* v. *Dickinson*, 331 U. S. 745, 750–751 (1947) (property flooded because of government dam project); *United States* v. *Causby*, 328 U. S. 256, 261–262 (1946) (frequent low altitude flights of Army and Navy aircraft over property); *Pennsylvania Coal Co.* v. *Mahon, supra*, 260 U. S., at 414–416 (state regulation forbidding mining of coal).

Police power regulations such as zoning ordinances and other land-use restrictions can destroy the use and enjoyment of property in order to promote the public good just as effectively as formal condemnation or physical invasion of property. From the property owner's point of view, it may matter little whether his land is condemned or flooded, or whether it is restricted by regulation to use in its natural state, if the effect in both cases is to deprive him of all beneficial use of it. From the government's point of view, the benefits flowing to the public from preservation of open space through regulation may be equally great as from creating a wildlife refuge through formal condemnation or increasing electricity production through a dam project that floods private property. Appellee implicitly posits the distinction that the government *intends* to take property through condemnation or physical invasion whereas it does not through police power regulations. See Brief for Appellee, at 43. But "the Constitution measures a taking of property not by what a State says, or by what it intends, but by what it *does*." *Hughes* v. *Washington*, 389 U. S. 290, 298 (1967) (Stewart, J., concurring) (emphasis in original); see *Davis* v. *Newton Coal Co.*, 267 U. S. 292, 301 (1925). It is only logical, then, that government action other than acquisition of title, occupancy, or physical invasion can be a "taking," and therefore a *de facto* exercise of the power of eminent domain, where the effects completely deprive the owner of all or most of his interest in the property. *United States* v. *Dickinson, supra*, 331 U. S., at 748; *United States* v. *General Motors Corp.*, 323 U. S. 373, 378 (1945).

IV

Having determined that property may be "taken for public use" by police power regulation within the meaning of the Just Compensation Clause of the Fifth Amendment, the question remains whether a government entity may constitutionally deny payment of just compensation to the property owner and limit his remedy to mere invalidation of the regulation instead. Appellant argues that it is entitled to the full fair market value of the property. Appellee argues that invalidation of the regulation is sufficient without payment of monetary compensation. In my view, once a court establishes that there was a regulatory "taking," the Constitution demands that the government entity pay just compensation for the period commencing on the date the regulation first effected the "taking," and ending on the date the government entity chooses to rescind or otherwise amend the regulation. This interpretation, I believe, is supported by the express words and purpose of the Just Compensation Clause, as well as by cases of this Court construing it.

The language of the Fifth Amendment prohibits the "tak[ing]" of private property for "public use" without payment of "just compensation." As soon as private property has been taken, whether through formal condemnation proceedings, occupancy, physical invasion, or regulation, the landowner has *already* suffered a constitutional violation, and "'the self-executing character of the constitutional provision with respect to compensation,'" *United States* v. *Clarke*, 445 U. S. 253, 257 (1980), quoting 6 P. Nichols, Eminent Domain § 25.41 (3d rev. ed. 1972), is triggered. This Court has consistently recognized that the just compensation requirement in the Fifth Amendment is not precatory: once there is a "taking," compensation *must* be awarded. In *Jacobs* v. *United States*, 290 U. S. 13 (1933), for example, a government dam project creating intermittent overflows onto petitioners' property resulted in the "taking" of a servitude. Petitioners brought suit against the government to recover just compensation for the partial "taking." Commenting on the nature of the landowners' action, the Court observed:

> "The suits were based on the right to recover just compensation for property taken by the United States for public use in the exercise of its power of eminent domain. That right was guaranteed by the Constitution. The fact that condemnation proceedings were not instituted and that the right was asserted in suits by the owners did not change the essential nature of the claim. The form of the remedy did not qualify the right. It rested upon the Fifth Amendment. Statutory recognition was not necessary. A promise to pay was not necessary. Such a promise was implied because of the duty to pay imposed by the Amendment." *Id.*, at 16.

See also *Griggs* v. *Allegheny County*, 369 U. S. 84, 84–85, 88–90 (1962); *United States* v. *Causby, supra*, 328 U. S., at 268. Invalidation unaccompanied by payment of damages would hardly compensate the landowner for any economic loss suffered during the time his property was taken.

Moreover, mere invalidation would fall far short of fulfilling the fundamental purpose of the Just Compensation Clause. That guarantee was designed to bar the government from forcing some individuals to bear burdens which, in all fairness, should be borne by the public as a whole. *Armstrong* v. *United States*, 364 U. S. 40, 49 (1960). See *Agins* v. *City of Tiburon, supra*, ___ U. S., at ___; *Andrus* v. *Allard, supra*, 444 U. S., at 65. When one person is asked to assume more than a fair share of the public burden, the payment of just compensation operates to redistribute that economic cost from the individual to the public at large. See *United States* v. *Willow River Power Co.*, 324 U. S. 499, 502 (1945); *Monongahela Navigation Co.* v. *United States*, 148 U. S. 312, 325 (1893). Because police power regulations must be substantially related to the advancement of the public health, safety, morals, or general welfare, see *Village of Euclid* v. *Ambler Realty Co.*, 272 U. S. 365, 395 (1926), it is axiomatic that the public receives a benefit while the offending regulation is in effect. If the regulation denies the private property owner the use and enjoyment of his land and is found to effect a "taking," it is only fair that the public bear the cost of benefits received during the interim period between application of the regulation and the government entity's rescission of it. The payment of just compensation serves to place the landowner in the same position monetarily as he would have occupied if his property had not been taken. *Almota Farmers Elevator & Warehouse Co.* v. *United States*, 409 U. S. 470, 473–474 (1973); *United States* v. *Reynolds*, 397 U. S. 14, 16 (1970).

The fact that a regulatory "taking" may be temporary, by virtue of the government's power to rescind or amend the regulation, does not make it any less of a constitutional "taking." Nothing in the Just Compensation Clause suggests that "takings" must be permanent and irrevocable. Nor does the temporary reversible quality of a regulatory "taking" render compensation for the time of the "taking" any less obligatory. This Court more than once has recognized that temporary reversible "takings" should be analyzed according to the same constitutional framework applied to permanent irreversible "takings." For example, in *United States* v. *Causby, supra*, 328 U. S., at 258–259, the United States had executed a lease to use an airport for a one-year term "ending June 30, 1942, with a provision for renewals through June 30, 1967, or six months after the end of the national emergency, whichever [was] the earlier." The Court held that the frequent low-level flights of Army and Navy airplanes over respondent's chicken farm, located near the airport, effected a "taking" of an easement on respondents' property. *Id.*, at 266, 267. However, because the flights could be discontinued by the government at any time, the Court remanded the case to the Court of Claims: "Since on this record *it is not clear whether the easement taken is a permanent or a temporary one*, it would be premature for us to consider whether the amount of the award made by the Court of Claims was proper." *Id.*, at 268 (emphasis added). In other cases where the government has taken only temporary use of a building, land, or equipment, the Court has not hesitated to determine the appropriate measure of just compensation. See *Kimball Laundry Co.* v. *United States*, 338 U. S. 1, 6 (1949); *United States* v. *Petty Motor Co.*, 327 U. S. 372, 374–375 (1946); *United States* v. *General Motors Corp., supra*, 323 U. S., at 374–375.

But contrary to appellant's claim that San Diego must formally condemn its property and pay full fair market value, nothing in the Just Compensation Clause empowers a court to order a government entity to condemn the property and pay its full fair market value, where the "taking" already effected is temporary and reversible and the government wants to halt the "taking." Just as the government may cancel condemnation proceedings before passage of title, see P. Nichols, 6 Eminent Domain § 24.113, at 24–21 (3d rev. ed. 1980), or abandon property it has temporarily occupied or invaded, see *United States* v. *Dow*, 357 U. S. 17, 26 (1958), it must have the same power to recind a regulatory "taking." As the Court has noted, "an abandonment does not prejudice the property owner. It merely results in an alteration of the property interest taken—from full ownership to one of temporary use and occupation. . . . In such cases compensation would be measured by the principles normally governing the taking of a right to use property temporarily." *Id.*; see *Danforth* v. *United States*, 308 U. S. 271, 284 (1939).

The constitutional rule I propose requires that, once a court finds that a police power regulation has effected a "taking," the government entity must pay just compensation for the period commencing on the date the regulation first effected the "taking," and ending on the date the government entity chooses to rescind or otherwise amend the regulation. Ordinary principles determining the proper measure of just compensation, regularly applied in cases of permanent and temporary "takings" involving formal condemnation proceedings, occupations, and physical invasions, should provide guidance to the courts in the award of compensation for a regulatory "taking." As a starting point, the value of the property taken may be ascertained as of the date of the "taking." *United States* v. *Clarke, supra*, 445 U. S., at 258; *Almota Farmers Elevators & Warehouse Co.* v. *United States, supra*, 409 U. S., at 474; *United States* v. *Miller*, 317 U. S. 369, 374 (1943); *Olson* v. *United States*; 292 U. S. 246, 255 (1934). The government must inform the court of its intentions vis-à-vis the regulation with sufficient clarity to guarantee a correct assessment of the just compensation award. Should the government decide immediately to revoke or otherwise amend the regulation, it would be liable for payment of compensation only for the interim during which the regulation effected a "taking." Rules of valuation already developed for temporary "takings" may be particularly useful to the courts in their quest for assessing the proper measure of monetary relief in cases of revocation or amendment, see generally *Kimball Laundry Co.* v. *United States, supra*; *United States* v. *Petty Motor Co., supra; United States* v. *General Motors Corp., supra*, although additional rules may need to be developed, see *Kimball Laundry Co.* v. *United States, supra*, 338 U. S., at 21–22 (Rutledge, J., concurring); *United States* v. *Miller, supra*, 317 U. S., at 373–374. Alternatively the government may choose formally to condemn the property, or otherwise to continue the offending regulation: in either case the action must be sustained by proper measures of just compensation. See generally *United States* v. *Fuller*, 409 U. S. 488, 490–492 (1973); *United States ex rel. Tennessee Valley Authority* v. *Powelson*, 319 U. S. 266, 281–285 (1942).

It should be noted that the Constitution does not embody any specific procedure or form of remedy that the States must adopt: "[t]he Fifth Amendment expresses a principle of fairness and not a technical rule of procedure enshrining old or new niceties regarding 'causes of action'—when they are born, whether they proliferate, and when they die." *United States* v. *Dickinson, supra*, 331 U. S., at 748. Cf. *United States* v. *Memphis Cotton Oil Co.*, 288 U. S. 62, 67–69 (1933). The States should be free to experiment in the implementation of this rule, provided that their chosen procedures and remedies comport with the fundamental constitutional command. See generally Hill, The Bill of Rights and the Supervisory Power, 69 Colum. L. Rev. 181, 191–193 (1969). The only constitutional requirement is that the landowner must be able meaningfully to challenge a regulation that allegedly effects a "taking," and recover just compensation if it does so. He may not be forced to resort to piecemeal litigation or otherwise unfair procedures in order to receive his due. See *United States* v. *Dickinson, supra*, 331 U. S., at 749.

IV

In *Agins* v. *City of Tiburon, supra*, 24 Cal. 3d, at 275, 598 P. 2d, at 29, the California Supreme Court was "persuaded by various policy considerations to the view that inverse condemnation is an inappropriate and undesirable remedy in cases in which unconstitutional regulation is alleged." In particular, the Court cited "the need for preserving a degree of freedom in land-use planning function, and the inhibiting financial force which inheres in the inverse condemnation remedy," in reaching its conclusion. *Id.*, at 276, 598 P. 2d, at 31. But the applicability of express constitutional guarantees is not a matter to be determined on the basis of policy judgments made by the legislative, executive, or judicial branches. Nor can the vindication of those rights depend on the expense in doing so. See *Watson* v. *City of Memphis*, 373 U. S. 526, 537–538 (1963).

Because I believe that the Just Compensation Clause requires the constitutional rule outlined, *supra*, I would vacate the judgment of the California Court of Appeal, Fourth District, and remand for further proceedings not inconsistent with this opinion.

When Are Environmental Restrictions on Land Use Compensable?

JEROME G. ROSE
9 *Real Est. L. J.* 233 (1981)

Two recent decisions have redirected attention to the recurring question facing courts in many states where the validity of environmental protection legislation is challenged. More specifically, the questions raised are: At what point do restrictions on the use of land imposed by environmental regulation constitute a taking of property for which just compensation is required and/or when is the environmental regulation a valid police power regulation for which no compensation is required?

Public Benefit vs. Private Deprivation

In *Agins v. City of Tiburon*[1] the U.S. Supreme Court was faced with the question whether a muncipal zoning ordinance, designed to discourage premature and unnecessary conversion of open-space land to urban use, constituted a taking of the owners' property without just compensation. The ordinance limited development on

[1]Agins v. City of Tiburon, 100 S. Ct. 2138, 65 L. Ed. 2d 106, 48 U.S.L.W. 4700 (1980).

the plaintiffs' land to five houses on five acres on scenic highlands with a magnificent view of San Francisco Bay. The plaintiffs sought $2 million in damages for inverse condemnation and also requested a declaration that the zoning ordinance was unconstitutional.

In *Usdin v. Department of Environmental Protection*,[2] a New Jersey Superior Court was called on to decide whether the restriction of use of the plaintiff's land, because of its temporary designation as a "floodway" within the meaning of the state flood control legislation,[3] is a "taking" of property that requires just compensation. The plaintiff's land had been designated as a "floodway" in which no construction was permitted. The "floodway" designation and use restriction had been attached to the plaintiff's land for a period of four years. The plaintiff's land was subsequently redesignated from a "floodway" to "flood fringe" classification in which construction was permitted. The plaintiff sought money damages for the temporary "taking" of his property during the period of time that the property was designated as a "floodway" and construction thereon was prohibited.

In both cases the courts upheld the validity of the regulations. In *Agins*, the Supreme Court determined that as long as the landowners may be permitted to build as many as five houses on their five acres of land, they had not been denied a reasonable use of their property in violation of the due process clause. Based on this determination, it was not necessary for the Court to determine whether a landowner may recover damages for inverse condemnation when the zoning ordinance constitutes a taking of property. In *Usdin*, the New Jersey court determined that the flood control legislation is a valid exercise of the police power rather than a taking of property, and, therefore, the availability of inverse condemnation as the appropriate remedy became moot.

The two cases, considered together, make an interesting subject for analysis because each focuses on one of the two countervailing factors considered by a court in determining the validity of any police power regulation; that is, a balancing of the importance of the public benefit against the extent of the deprivation of use and value imposed by that regulation upon the property owner.

In *Agins*, the Supreme Court adopted, without much discussion, the finding that the prevention of "premature and unnecessary conversion of open-space land to urban uses" is a legitimate purpose of police power regulation. In the other half of the balancing process, the court determined that the plaintiff could fulfill reasonable investment expectations by development pursuant to the zoning ordinance. The *Usdin* decision contained an extensive and scholarly analysis of the public purpose half of the equation.

The New Jersey Superior Court in *Usdin* characterized the legal issue to be decided as a "classic constitutional confrontation" between the governmental exercise of the police power to provide for the general welfare on one hand, and the right of citizens to privately own property and receive just compensation when such property is taken by government. When government exercises the police power, such as environmental or zoning regulations, the property owner may suffer a loss of value and not be entitled to compensation. When the power of eminent domain is "taken," the owner is entitled to compensation.

The issue before the court was: Is the restriction of the use of land under a flood control regulation a valid exercise of the police power without compensation to the landowner, or is such governmental action a "taking" of property that requires just compensation to be paid? The importance of the *Usdin* case arises from the criteria adopted by the court to answer this question.

[2]Usdin v. Department of Environmental Protection, 173 N.J. Super. 311, 414 A.2d 280 (1980).

[3]N.J. Stat. Ann. §§ 58:16A et seq.

The Usdin *Criterion: The "Legislative Purpose" Test*

The criterion selected by the court was the classic basis for resolution of this issue used since the U.S. Supreme Court decision in *Mugler v. Kansas*[4] in 1887, namely the *purpose* of the Legislative action; that is, if the *purpose* of the restriction is to prevent harm or abuse, and the restrictions are reasonably related to that end, the restriction is a valid exercise of the police power. On the other hand, if the *purpose* of the restriction is to impart a public benefit, then the restricted owner is entitled to compensation.

The "legislative purpose" criterion adopted by the court is well established by precedent of the highest courts of the nation and many states. In the landmark U.S. Supreme Court decision, *Pennsylvania Coal Co. v. Mahon*,[5] this issue was debated in the majority opinion of the court written by Justice Holmes and a dissenting opinion written by Justice Brandeis. That case involved the validity of legislation restricting mining in a way that undermined structures used for habitation. Justice Brandeis concluded that legislation designed to protect the public safety or health, rather than intended to devote the property to a public use, is a valid exercise of the police power. He based this distinction in part on the reasoning in *Mugler v. Kansas*, as follows:

> A prohibition simply upon the use of property for *purposes* that are declared, by valid legislation, to be injurious to the health, morals or safety of the community, cannot, in any just sense, be deemed a taking or an appropriation of property for the public benefit. Such legislation does not disturb the owner in the control or use of his property for lawful purposes, nor restrict his right to dispose of it, but it is only a declaration by the State that its use by any one, for certain forbidden purposes, is prejudicial to the public interests. . . . The power which the States have prohibiting such use . . . cannot be burdened with the condition that the State must compensate such individual owners for pecuniary losses they may sustain, by reason of their not being permitted, by a noxious use of their property, to inflict injury upon their community. *Mugler* v. *Kansas*, 123 U.S. 623, 668-669 (1887). [Emphasis added.]

The landmark decision on this issue in New Jersey is *Morris County Land v. Parsippany-Troy Hills Township*,[6] where a zoning ordinance prohibited the development of privately owned swampland. The New Jersey Supreme Court held the ordinance to be an unconstitutional taking of property because the *purpose* of the regulation was to preserve the property in its natural state for the public benefit resulting from its function as a sponge for run-off water in aid of flood control and by preserving a natural wildlife refuse.

The legislative purpose test was subsequently adopted in California in *Candlestick Properties Inc. v. San Francisco Bay Conservation and Development Corp.*,[7] where a landowner was denied permission to fill land that was submerged at high tide by San Francisco Bay. The court described the issue to be decided as a question whether the police power or the power of eminent domain was being exercised. In making this determination, the court considered the *purpose* of the law as the primary consideration. The court concluded that there were sufficient planning reasons to control deleterious development of the area to justify the exercise of the police power.

[4]Mugler v. Kansas, 123 U.S. 623 (1887).

[5]Pennsylvania Coal Co. v. Mahon, 270 U.W. 383 (1922).

[6]Morris County Land v. Parsippany-Troy Hills Township, 40 N.J. 539, 193 A.2d 232 (1963).

[7]Candlestick Properties Inc. v. San Francisco Bay Conservation & Dev. Corp. 11 Cal. App. 3d 557, 89 Cal. Rptr. 897 (1st Dist. 1970).

The distinction between governmental action adopted for the purpose of *preventing public harm as* compared to *creating a public benefit* was also discussed by the Wisconsin court in *Just v. Marionette County*,[8] involving the validity of a shoreline development ordinance that prohibited plaintiff landowner from depositing fill on his shoreline land without a permit. In upholding the validity of the ordinance the Wisconsin Court said:

> This case causes us to reexamine the concepts of *public benefit* in contrast to *public harm* and the scope of an owner's right to use his property. In the instant case we have a restriction on the use of a citizen's property, not to secure a benefit for the public, but to prevent a harm from the change in the natural character of a citizen's property. . . .[9]

Is the "Legislative Purpose" Test Valid?

It may be interesting to note that both the New Jersey Court in the *Morris County Land* case, and the Wisconsin Court in the *Just* case have adopted the legislative purpose test. However, the New Jersey court held the environmental legislation *invalid* because of its finding that the legislative purpose was the preservation of the property in its natural state for a *public* benefit; the Wisconsin court upheld the environmental legislation because of its finding that the purpose of the legislation was the preservation of the property in its natural state to *prevent the public harm* of pollution. The ability of two courts to come to the contrary decisions on similar facts using the same test raises the question of the adequacy of the test.

It is well established that a governmental "taking" of property must be compensated under the federal and most state constitutions. It is also clear that, within limits, the use of private property may be restricted by police power regulations without the payment of compensation. The unresolved question is how to distinguish the two situations. The legislative *purpose* test has been used by the courts cited above. It would be useful to examine whether the legislative *purpose* test is the best or even a satisfactory basis for resolving this issue.

What's the Difference between the Creation of a Public Benefit and the Prevention of Public Harm?

The judicial test of the validity of environmental restrictions on the use of property is based upon a judicial characterization of the legislative purpose of the restrictions. If the purpose is characterized as "creation of a public benefit," the failure to compensate the owner makes the law invalid. If the purpose is characterized as "prevention of public harm" the regulation is valid without compensation. However, there may be some question whether the two classes of characterization are, in fact, different in kind or whether they are merely two different facets of the same entity (i.e., two sides of the same coin).

For example, what is "the purpose" of legislation that prohibits the filling of swampland? The court in the *Morris County Land* case held that the purpose of the legislation was the preservation of the land as a sponge to absorb run-off water in aid of down-stream land and also as a wildlife refuge. By characterizing "the purpose" in this manner, a public benefit is created for which compensation is required. But would it not have been equally fair and reasonable to characterize "the purpose" of the legislation as a restriction of the use of property to limit the harm of flooding of

[8]Just v. Marionette County, 56 Wis. 2d 7, 201 N.W.2d 760 (1972).
[9]*Id.* at 767-768 (emphasis added).

downstream land as well as avoidance of the problems of flooding of basements in the area resulting for the raising of the water table? In short, is it not possible to describe both the positive benefits and the avoidance of negative impact involved in every police power regulation?

For example, in the *Agins* case what was the purpose of the municipal zoning ordinance? Was the purpose of the law to preserve the beautiful open space on the high lands overlooking San Francisco Bay for all to enjoy? Was the purpose to preserve the benefit of low-density population within a metropolitan area? Or, was the purpose of the law to avoid the dangers and ill effects of urbanization?[10] If the reasoning of the *Usdin* case were accepted by the U.S. Supreme Court, the *Agins* decision could have gone the other way if the court determined that the purpose of the zoning ordinance was to preserve a public benefit rather than to avoid the ill effects of urbanization. Consider the following illustrations of other environmental regulations with dual public purposes:

- Floor area ratio (FAR) limitations on density in commercial zones avoid the danger of air pollution from traffic generated by development and at the same time preserve the property in its natural state for the public benefit of clean air.
- An ordinance that prohibits construction in a floodway avoids the danger of damage to structures and injury to the occupants of structures built in the floodway and preserves the property in its natural state for the public benefit of upstream water storage for avoidance of downstream flooding.
- An air contaminant emission limitation avoids the danger of air pollution from the emission of specified pollutants and at the same time preserves the quality of air in the area for the public benefit of the residents.

Should Evidence of Legislative Intent Determine the Existence of a Constitutional Right?

If the validity of legislation restricting the use of property depends upon the *purpose* of the law, its validity may very well depend upon direct evidence of legislative purpose set forth in the legislation. For example, suppose the statute contains a statement of legislative intent that expressly declares the purpose to be a police power regulation to prevent public harm. Is the court bound by an express declaration of legislative purpose? Should a constitutional protection against a government taking a private property without just compensation be avoidable by a simple declaration of legislative purpose?

It is clear that the adoption of the legislative purpose test of distinguishing a compensable taking of property from an uncompensated police power regulation involves the recurring issue of the need for judicial deference to the legislative prerogative to make public policy, subject to a restrained intervention of the courts when the limits of reasonableness have been transcended by the legislature. It may be significant to take note of the fact that in both the *Agins* and *Usdin* decisions, the courts deferred to the legislative policy of environmental protection and upheld the restriction on land use.

[10]The City Council of Tiburon found that:

> It is in the public interest to avoid unnecessary conversion of open space land to strictly urban uses, thereby protecting against the resultant adverse impacts, such as air, noise and water pollution, traffic congestion, destruction of scenic beauty, disturbance of the ecology and the environment, hazards related to ecology, fire and flood, and other demonstrated consequences of urban sprawl.

Ord. No. 124 N.S. § 1(c) as set forth in Agins v. City of Tiburon, note 1 *supra*.

8. Statutory Basis of Action

Under the common law there is a distinction between a **public nuisance** and a **private nuisance**. To enjoin a public nuisance plaintiff must allege and prove **special damages**. This distinction makes it difficult for a private individual to bring suit against a polluter unless he can show that he was particularly damaged in some special way greater than the public at large. The justification for this principle was that where there is a nuisance that has a detrimental impact on the public at large, a public official, rather than a private individual, ought to bring the suit on behalf of the public. It was feared that the public interest might be compromised in a suit brought by an individual. As a result of this rule it has been difficult for private individuals to bring suit to protect the environment. State and federal statutes were necessary to overcome this obstacle.

a. *State Citizen Suit Legislation*

During the 1970s, when the environmental movement had an initial spurt of public support, several state legislatures adopted statutes designed to overcome the common law limitation on the ability of private individuals to bring suits to enjoin a public nuisance. One of the first and best known citizens' statutes was drafted by Professor Joseph L. Sax and adopted by the state of Michigan.

MICHIGAN ENVIRONMENTAL PROTECTION ACT

(1970) Mich. Stats Ann. 14.528(201)-14.528(207).

14.528(202) Action in circuit court; granting of relief.) Sec. 2 (1) The attorney general, any political subdivision of the state, any instrumentality or agency of the state or of a political subdivision thereof, any person, partnership, corporation, association, organization or other legal entity may maintain an action in the circuit court having jurisdiction where the alleged violation occurred or is likely to occur for declaratory and equitable relief against the state, any political subdivision thereof, any person, partnership, corporation, association, organization or other legal entity for the protection of the air, water and other natural resources and the public trust therein from pollution, impairment or destruction.

(2) In granting relief provided by subsection (1) where there is involved a standard for pollution or for an antipollution device or procedure, fixed by rule or otherwise, by an instrumentality or agency of the state or a political subdivision thereof, the court may:

(a) Determine the validity, applicability and reasonableness of the standard.

(b) When a court finds a standard to be deficient, direct the adoption of a standard approved and specified by the court.

(CL'48, 691.1202.)

14.528(202a) Posting of bond or cash.) Sec. 2a. If the court has reasonable ground to doubt the solvency of the plaintiff or the plaintiff's ability to pay any cost or judgment which might be rendered againt him in an action brought under this act the court may order the plaintiff to post a surety bond or cash not to exceed $500.00.

14.528(203) Evidentiary showing; principles applicable; master or referee; costs.) Sec. 3. (1) When the plaintiff in the action has made a prima facie showing that the conduct of the defendant has, or is likely to pollute, impair or destroy the air, water or other natural resources or the public trust therein, the defendant may rebut the prima facie showing by the submission of evidence to the contrary. The defendant may also show, by way of an affirmative defense, that there is no feasible and prudent alternative to defendant's conduct and that such conduct is consistent with the promotion of the public health, safety and welfare in light of the state's paramount concern for the protection of its natural resources from pollution, impairment or destruction. Except as to the affirmative defense, the principles of burden of proof and weight of the evidence generally applicable in the civil actions in the circuit courts shall apply to actions brought under this act.

(2) The court may appoint a master or referee, who shall be a disinterested person and technically qualified, to take testimony and make a record and a report of his findings to the court in the action.

(3) Costs may be apportioned to the parties if the interests of justice require.

(CL'48, 691.1203.)

Similar **citizen suit legislation** has been adopted in Florida, Minnesota, Connecticut, Ohio, Illinois and New Jersey, among others. For additional information see J. Sax, *Defending the Environment* (1971); Mannino, *Citizen Suits to Protect the Environment: An Introduction to Some "New Remedies,"* PENN. BAR ASSOC. Q. 181 (Jan. 1973); Trumbull, *Private Environmental Legal Action*, 7 U. SAN FRANCISCO L. REV. 27 (1972).

---

b. *Federal Citizen Suit Provisions*

During the 1970s Congress adopted comprehensive environmental legislation addressed to the problems of air pollution, water pollution and noise pollution, among others. Most of these statutes contain provisions authorizing citizen suits. The Clean Air Act of 1970, 42 U.S.C. 1857h-2, authorizes an action to be brought by "any person" or "any citizen" against any person who is alleged to be in violation of an emission standard or governmental order relating thereto. Under this provision it is not necessary for the plaintiff to allege or prove special damages.

However, under the terms of the citizen suit provision of the Federal Water Pollution Control Act, 33 U.S.C. 1365(d), now known as the Clean Water Act, a suit may be brought only by a "citizen" defined as "a person

. . . having an interest which is adversely affected." Thus the Clean Water Act citizen-suit provision is much more restrictive than the provision in the Clean Air Act. The authorization in the Noise Control Act of 1972 is similar to that in the Clean Air Act.

In all of the above citizen-suit provisions Congress has authorized the court to award the costs of litigation, including reasonable attorney and expert witness fees, to any party whenever the court determines that such award is appropriate. This provision provides a double-edged sword. It may be used by plaintiffs to help pay for the very high costs of environmental litigation. But it may also be used by the defendant as a threat to potential plaintiffs. Congress apparently adopted this language to discourage frivolous or harassing environmental litigation.

The federal citizen-suit provisions require plaintiff to give 60 days notice to the EPA, the state government and to the alleged violators. The United States Supreme Court has made it clear in *Middlesex County Sewer Authority v. Sea Clammers* that the failure to comply with the notice provision can be fatal to a citizen suit.

MIDDLESEX COUNTY SEWERAGE AUTHORITY v. NATIONAL SEA CLAMMERS ASSN

453 U.S. 1 (1981)

JUSTICE POWELL delivered the opinion of the Court.

In this case, involving alleged damage to fishing grounds caused by discharges and ocean dumping of sewage and other waste, we are faced with questions concerning the availability of a damages remedy, based either on federal common law or on the provisions of two Acts—the Federal Water Pollution Control Act (FWPCA), as amended, 33 U. S. C. § 1251 *et seq.*, and the Marine Protection, Research, and Sanctuaries Act of 1972 (MPRSA), 33 U. S. C. § 1401 *et seq.*

I

Respondents are an organization whose members harvest fish and shellfish off the coast of New York and New Jersey, and one individual member of that organization. In 1977, they brought suit in the United States District Court for the District of New Jersey against petitioners—various governmental entities and officials from New York, New Jersey and the Federal Government. Their complaint alleged that sewage, sewage "sludge," and other waste materials were being discharged into New

York Harbor and the Hudson River by some of the respondents. In addition it complained of the dumping of such materials directly into the ocean from maritime vessels. The complaint alleged that, as a result of these activities, the Atlantic Ocean was becoming polluted, and it made special reference to a massive growth of algae said to have appeared offshore in 1976. It then stated that this pollution was causing the "collapse of the fishing, clamming and lobster industries which operate in the waters of the Atlantic Ocean."

Invoking a wide variety of legal theories, respondents sought injunctive relief, $250 million in compensatory damages, and $250 million in punitive damages. The District Court granted summary judgment to petitioners on all counts of the complaint.

In holdings relevant here, the District Court rejected respondents' nuisance claim under federal common law, see *Illinois* v. *Milwaukee*, 406 U.S. 91 (1972), on the ground that such a cause of action is not available to private parties. With respect to the claims based on alleged violations of the FWPCA, the court noted that respondents had failed to comply with the 60-day notice requirement of the "citizen suit" provision in § 505 of the Act, 33 U. S. C. § 1365 (b)(1)(A). This provision allows suits under the Act by private citizens, but authorizes only prospective relief, and the citizen plaintiffs first must give notice to the EPA, the State, and any alleged violator. *Ibid.*[9] Because respondents did not give the requisite notice, the court refused to

[9]Section 505 provides, in part:

"(a) Except as provided in subsection (b) of this section, any citizen may commence a civil action on his own behalf—

"(1) against any person (including (i) the United States, and (ii) any other governmental instrumentality or agency to the extent permitted by the eleventh amendment to the Constitution) who is alleged to be in violation of (A) an effluent standard or limitation under this chapter or (B) an order issued by the Administrator or a State with respect to such a standard or limitation, or

"(2) against the Administrator where there is alleged a failure of the Administrator to perform any act or duty under this chapter which is not discretionary with the Administrator.

> "The district courts shall have jurisdiction, without regard to the amount in controversy or the citizenship of the parties, to enforce such an effluent standard or limitation, or such an order, or to order the Administrator to perform such act or duty, as the case may be, and to apply any appropriate civil penalties under section 1319 (d) of this title.

"(b) No action may be commenced—

"(1) under subsection (a)(1) of this section—

"(A) prior to sixty days after the plaintiff has given notice of the alleged violation (i) to the Administrator, (ii) to the State in which the alleged violation occurs, and (iii) to any alleged violator of the standard, limitation, or order, or

"(B) if the Administrator or State has commenced and is diligently prosecuting a civil or criminal action in a court of the United States, or a State to require compliance with the standard, limitation, or order, but in any such action in a court of the United States any citizen may intervene as a matter of right.

"(2) under subsection (a)(2) of this section prior to sixty days after the plaintiff has given notice of such action to the Administrator, except that such action may be brought immediately after such notification in the case of an action under this section respecting a violation of sections 1316 and 1317 (a) of this title. Notice under this subsection shall be given in such a manner as the Administrator shall prescribe by regulation." § 505 (a), (b), 33 U. S. C. § 1365 (a), (b).

The Administrator may intervene in any citizen suit. *Id.*, § 505 (c)(2), 33 U. S. C. § 1365 (c), (2).

allow them to proceed with a claim under the Act independent of the citizen-suit provision and based on the general jurisdictional grant in 28 U. S. C. § 1331.[10] The court applied the same analysis to respondents' claims under the MPRSA, which contains similar citizen-suit and notice provisions. 33 U. S. C. §1415 (g).[11] Finally, the court rejected a possible claim of maritime tort, both because respondents had failed to plead such claim explicitly and because they had failed to comply with the procedural requirements of the federal and state tort claims acts.

The United States Court of Appeals for the Third Circuit reversed as to the claims based on the FWPCA, the MPRSA, the federal common law of nuisance, and maritime tort. 616 F. 2d 1222 (1980). With respect to the FWPCA, the court held that failure to comply with the 60-day notice provision in § 505 (b)(1)(A), 33 U. S. C. § 1365 (b)(1)(A), does not preclude suits under the Act in addition to the specific "citizen suits" authorized in § 505. It based this conclusion on the savings clause in § 505 (e), 33 U. S. C. § 1365 (e), preserving "any right which any person (or class of

---

See n. 27, *infra* (legislative history emphasizing the limited forms of relief available under the Act).

In this opinion we refer to sections of the original FWPCA, added in the 1972 Amendments, with parallel citations to the United States Code.

[10]In so holding the court rejected an argument that the notice requirement is inapplicable because of the "savings clause" in § 505 (e), which states:

> "Nothing in this section shall restrict any right which any person (or class of persons) may have under any statute or common law to seek enforcement of any effluent standard or limitation or to seek any other relief (including relief against the Administrator or a State agency)." 33 U. S. C. § 1365 (e).

[11]The citizen-suit provision in the MPRSA provides in part:

"(g)(1) Except as provided in paragraph (2) of this subsection any person may commence a civil suit on his own behalf to enjoin any person, including the United States and any other governmental instrumentality or agency (to the extent permitted by the eleventh amendment to the Constitution), who is alleged to be in violation of any prohibition, limitation, criterion, or permit established or issued by or under this subchapter. The district courts shall have jurisdiction, without regard to the amount in controversy or the citizenship of the parties, to enforce such prohibition, limitation, criterion, or permit, as the case may be.

"(2) No action may be commenced—

"(A) prior to sixty days after notice of the violation has been given to the Administrator or to the Secretary, and to any alleged violator of the prohibition, limitation, criterion, or permit; or

"(B) if the Attorney General has commenced and is diligently prosecuting a civil action in a court of the United States to require compliance with the prohibition, limitation, criterion, or permit; or

"(C) if the Administrator has commenced action to impose a penalty pursuant to subsection (a) of this section, or if the Administrator, or the Secretary, has initiated permit revocation or suspension proceedings under subsection (f) of this section; or

"(D) if the United States has commenced and is diligently prosecuting a criminal action in a court of the United States or a State to redress a violation of this subchapter." 33 U. S. C. § 1415 (g)(1), (2).

The United States may intervene in any citizen suit brought under the Act. 33 U. S. C. § 1415 (g)(3)(b).

Like the FWPCA, the MPRSA contains a "savings clause," which states:

> "The injunctive relief provided by this subsection shall not restrict any right which any person (or class of persons) may have under any statute or common law to seek enforcement of any standard or limitation or to seek any other relief (including relief against the Administrator, the Secretary, or a State agency)." *Id.*, at § 1415 (g)(5).

persons) may have under any statute or common law to seek enforcement of any effluent standard or limitation or to seek any other relief." 616 F. 2d, at 1226–1228; see n. 10, *supra*. The Court of Appeals then went on to apply our precedents in the area of implied statutory rights of action, and concluded that "Congress intended to permit the federal courts to entertain a private cause of action implied from the terms of the [FWPCA], preserved by the savings clause of the Act, on behalf of individuals or groups of individuals who have been or will be injured by pollution in violation of its terms." 616 F. 2d, at 1230–1231.

The court then applied this same analysis to the MPRSA, concluding again that the District Court had erred in dismissing respondents' claims under this Act. Although the court was not explicit on this question, it apparently concluded that suits for *damages*, as well as for injunctive relief, could be brought under the FWPCA and the MPRSA.

With respect to the federal common law nuisance claims, the Court of Appeals rejected the District Court's conclusion that private parties may not bring such claims. It also held, applying common law principles, that respondents "alleged sufficient individual damage to permit them to recover damages for this essentially public nuisance." 616 F.2d, at 1234. It thus went considerably beyond *Illinois* v. *Milwaukee*, *supra*, which involved purely prospective relief sought by the state plaintiff.

Petitions for a writ of certiorari raising a variety of arguments were filed in this Court by a group of New Jersey sewerage authorities (No. 79–1711), by the Joint Meeting of Essex and Union Counties in New Jersey (No. 79–1754), by the City and Mayor of New York (No. 79–1760), and by all of the federal defendants named in this suit (No. 80–12). We granted these petitions, limiting review to three questions: (i) whether FWPCA and MPRSA imply a private right of action independent of their citizen-suit provisions, (ii) whether all federal common law nuisance actions concerning ocean pollution now are pre-empted by the legislative scheme contained in the FWPCA and the MPRSA, and (iii) if not, whether a private citizen has standing to sue for damages under the federal common law of nuisance. We hold that there is no implied right of action under these statutes and that the federal common law of nuisance has been fully pre-empted in the area of ocean pollution.

II

The Federal Water Pollution Control Act was first enacted in 1948. Act of June 30, 1948, 62 Stat. 1155. It emphasized state enforcement of water quality standards. When this legislation proved ineffective, Congress passed the Federal Water Pollution Control Act Amendments of 1972, Pub. L. 92–500, 33 U. S. C. § 1251 *et seq*. The Amendments shifted the emphasis to "direct restrictions on discharges," *EPA* v. *California ex rel. State Water Resource Control Board*, 426 U. S. 200, 204 (1976), and made it "unlawful for any person to discharge a pollutant without obtaining a permit and complying with its terms," *id*., at 205. While still allowing for state administration and enforcement under federally approved state plans, §§ 402 (b), (c), 33 U. S. C. §§ 1342 (b), (c), the Amendments created various federal minimum effluent standards, *id*., §§ 301–307, 33 U. S. C. §§ 1311–1317.

The Marine Protection, Research, and Sanctuaries Act of 1972, Pub. L. 92–532, 86 Stat. 1052, sought to create comprehensive federal regulation of the dumping of materials into ocean waters near the United States coastline. Section 101 of the Act requires a permit for any dumping into ocean waters, when the material is transported from the United States or on an American vessel or aircraft. 33 U. S. C. § 1411 (a). In addition, it requires a permit for the dumping of material transported from outside the United States into the territorial seas or in the zone extending 12 miles from the coastline, "to the extent that it may affect the territorial sea or the territory of the United States." *Id*., § 1411 (b).

The exact nature of respondents' claims under these two Acts is not clear, but the claims appear to fall into two categories. The main contention is that the EPA and the Army Corps of Engineers have permitted the New Jersey and New York defendants to discharge and dump pollutants in amounts that are not permitted by the Acts. In addition, they seem to allege that the New York and New Jersey defendants have violated the terms of their permits. The question before us is whether respondents may raise either of these claims in a private suit for injunctive and monetary relief, where such a suit is not expressly authorized by either of these Acts.

A

It is unnecessary to discuss at length the principles set out in recent decisions concerning the recurring question whether Congress intended to create a private right of action under a federal statute without saying so explicitly. The key to the inquiry is the intent of the legislature. *Texas Industries, Inc.* v. *Radcliff Materials, Inc.*, ___ U. S. ___, ___ (1981); *California* v. *Sierra Club*, ___ U. S. ___, ___ (1981); *Universities Research Assn.* v. *Coutu*, ___ U. S. ___, ___ (1981); *Transamerica Mortgage Advisors, Inc.* v. *Lewis*, 444 U. S. 11, 15 (1979); *Touche Ross & Co.* v. *Redington*, 442 U. S. 560, 568 (1979). We look first, of course, to the statutory language, particularly to the provisions made therein for enforcement and relief. Then we review the legislative history and other traditional aids of statutory interpretation to determine congressional intent.

These Acts contain unusually elaborate enforcement provisions, conferring authority to sue for this purpose both on government officials and private citizens. The FWPCA, for example, authorizes the EPA Administrator to respond to violations of the Act with compliance orders and civil suits. § 309, 33 U. S. C. § 1319. He may seek a civil penalty of up to $10,000 per day, *id.*, § 309 (d), 33 U. S. C. § 1319 (d), and criminal penalties also are available, *id.*, at § 309 (c), 33 U. S. C. § 1319 (c). States desiring to administer their own permit programs must demonstrate that state officials possess adequate authority to abate violations through civil or criminal penalties or other means of enforcement. *Id.*, § 402, 33 U. S. C. § 1342 (b)(7). In addition, under § 509 (b), 33 U. S. C. § 1369 (b) "any interested person" may seek judicial review in the United States Courts of Appeals of various particular actions by the Administrator, including establishment of effluent standards and issuance of permits for discharge of pollutants. Where review could have been obtained under this provision, the action at issue may not be challenged in any subsequent civil or criminal proceeding for enforcement. *Id.*, at § 1369 (b)(2).

These enforcement mechanisms, most of which have their counterpart under the MPRSA, are supplemented by the express citizen-suit provisions in § 505 (a) of the FWPCA, 33 U. S. C. § 1365 (a), and § 105 (g) of the MPRSA, 33 U. S. C. § 1415 (g). See nn. 9, 11, *supra*. These citizen-suit provisions authorize private persons to sue for injunctions to enforce these statutes. Plaintiffs invoking these provisions first must comply with specified procedures—which respondents here ignored—including in most cases 60 days' prior notice to potential defendants.

In view of these elaborate enforcement provisions it cannot be assumed that Congress intended to authorize by implication additional judicial remedies for private citizens suing under MPRSA and FWPCA. As we stated in *Transamerica Mortgage Advisers, supra*, "it is an elemental canon of statutory construction that where a statute expressly provides a particular remedy or remedies, a court must be chary of reading others into it." 444 U. S., at 19. See also *Touche Ross & Co.* v. *Redington, supra*, 442 U. S., at 571–574. In the absence of strong indicia of a contrary congressional intent, we are compelled to conclude that Congress provided precisely the remedies it considered appropriate.

As noted above, the Court of Appeals avoided this inference. Discussing the

FWPCA, it held that the existence of a citizen-suit provision in § 505 (a) does not rule out implied forms of private enforcement of the Act. It arrived at this conclusion by asserting that Congress intended in § 505 (a) to create a limited cause of action for "private attorneys general"—"non-injured member[s] of the public" suing to promote the general welfare rather than to redress an injury to their own welfare. 616 F. 2d, at 1227. It went on to conclude:

> "A private party who is *injured* by the alleged violation, as these plaintiffs allege they were, has an alternate basis for suit under section 505 (e), 33 U. S. C. § 1365 (e), and the general federal question jurisdiction of the Judicial Code, 28 U. S. C. § 1331 (1976). Section 505 (e) is a savings clause that preserves all rights to enforce the Act or seek relief against the Administrator. Coupled with the general federal question jurisdiction it permits this suit to be brought by these parties." 616 F. 2d, at 1227 (footnotes omitted) (emphasis added).

There are at least three problems with this reasoning. First, the language of the savings clause on which the Court of Appeals relied, see n. 10, *supra*, is quite ambiguous concerning the intent of Congress to "preserve" remedies under the FWPCA itself. It merely states that nothing in the citizen-suit provision "shall restrict any right which any person . . . may have under any statute or common law to seek enforcement of any effluent standard or limitation or to seek any other relief." It is doubtful that the phrase "any statute" includes the very statute in which this statement was contained.

Moreover, the reasoning on which the Court of Appeals relied is flawed for another reason. It draws a distinction between "non-injured" plaintiffs who may bring citizen suits to enforce provisions of these Acts, and the "injured" plaintiffs in this case who claim a right to sue under the Acts, not by virtue of the citizen-suit provisions, but rather under the language of the savings clauses. In fact, it is clear that the citizen-suit provisions apply only to persons who can claim some sort of injury and there is, therefore, no reason to infer the existence of a separate right of action for "injured" plaintiffs. "Citizen" is defined in the citizen-suit section of the FWPCA as "a person or persons having an interest which is or may be adversely affected." § 505 (g), 33 U. S. C. § 1316 (g). It is clear from the Senate Conference Report that this phrase was intended by Congress to allow suits by all persons possessing standing under this Court's decision in *Sierra Club* v. *Morton*, 405 U. S. 727 (1972). See S. Conf. Rep. No. 92–1236, p. 146 (1972). This broad category of potential plaintiffs necessarily includes both plaintiffs seeking to enforce these statutes as private attorneys general, whose injuries are "non-economic" and probably noncompensable, and persons like respondents who assert that they have suffered tangible economic injuries because of statutory violations.

Finally, the Court of Appeals failed to take account of the rest of the enforcement scheme expressly provided by Congress—including the opportunity for "any interested person" to seek judicial review of a number of EPA actions within 90 days, § 509 (b), 33 U. S. C. § 1369 (b). See pp. 11–12, *supra*.

The Court of Appeals also applied its reasoning to the MPRSA. But here again we are persuaded that Congress evidenced no intent to authorize by implication private remedies under these Acts apart from the expressly authorized citizens suits. The relevant provisions in the MPRSA are in many respects almost identical to those of the FWPCA. 33 U. S. C. § 1415 (g). Although they do not expressly limit citizen suits to those who have suffered some injury from a violation of the Act, we are not persuaded by this fact alone that Congress affirmatively intended to imply the existence of a parallel private remedy, after setting out expressly the manner in which private citizens can seek to enjoin violations.

In *Cort* v. *Ash*, 422 U. S. 66, 78 (1975), the Court identified several factors that are relevant to the question of implied private remedies. These include the legislative history. See *ibid.* ("Second is there any indication of legislative intent, explicit or implicit, either to create such a remedy or to deny one?"). This history does not lead to a contrary conclusion with respect to implied remedies under either Act. Indeed, the reports and debates provide affirmative support for the view that Congress intended the limitations imposed on citizen suits to apply to all private suits under these acts. Thus, the structure of the Acts and their legislative history both lead us to conclude that Congress intended that private remedies in addition to those expressly provided should not be implied. Where, as here, Congress has made clear that implied private actions are not contemplated, the courts are not authorized to ignore this legislative judgment.

B

Although the parties have not suggested it, there remains a possible alternative source of *express* congressional authorization of private suits under these Acts. Last Term, in *Maine* v. *Thiboutot*, 448 U. S. ___ (1980), the Court construed 42 U. S. C. § 1983 as authorizing suits to redress violations by state officials of rights created by federal statutes. Accordingly, it could be argued that respondents may sue the municipalities and sewage boards among the petitioners under the FWPCA and MPRSA by virtue of a right of action created by § 1983.

It is appropriate to reach the question of the applicability of *Maine* v. *Thiboutot* to this setting, despite the failure of respondents to raise it here or below. This case began long before that decision. Moreover, if controlling, this argument would obviate the need to consider whether Congress intended to authorize private suits to enforce these particular federal statutes. The claim brought here arguably falls within the scope of *Maine* v. *Thiboutot* because it involves a suit by a private party claiming that a federal statute has been violated under color of state law, causing an injury. The Court, however, has recognized two exceptions to the application of § 1983 to statutory violations. In *Pennhurst State School and Hospital* v. *Halderman*, ___ U. S. ___ (1981), we remanded certain claims for determination (i) whether Congress had foreclosed private enforcement of that statute in the enactment itself, and (ii) whether the statute at issue there was the kind that created enforceable "rights" under § 1983. *Id.*, at ___. In the present case, because we find that Congress foreclosed a § 1983 remedy under these Acts, we need not reach the second question whether these Acts created "rights, privileges, or immunities" with the meaning of § 1983.

When the remedial devices provided in a particular act are sufficiently comprehensive, they may suffice to demonstrate congressional intent to preclude the remedy of suits under § 1983. As Justice Stewart, who later joined the majority in *Maine* v. *Thiboutot*, stated in *Chapman* v. *Houston Welfare Rights Organization*, 441 U. S. 600, 673, n. 2 (1979) (dissenting opinion), when "a state official is alleged to have violated a federal statute which provides its own comprehensive enforcement scheme, the requirements of that enforcement procedure may not be bypassed by bringing suit directly under § 1983. As discussed above, the FWPCA and MPRSA do provide quite comprehensive enforcement mechanisms. It is hard to believe that Congress intended to preserve the § 1983 right of action when it created so many specific statutory remedies including the two citizen-suit provisions. See *Chesapeake Bay Foundation* v. *Virginia State Water Control Board*, 501 F. Supp. 821 (ED Va. 1980) (rejecting a § 1983 action under the FWPCA against the Chairman of a State Water Board, with reasoning based on the comprehensiveness of the remedies provided and the federalism concerns raised). We therefore conclude that the existence of these express remedies demonstrates not only that Congress intended to foreclose implied private actions but also that it intended to supplant any remedy that otherwise would be available under § 1983. Cf. *Carlson* v. *Green*, 446 U. S. 14, 23 (1980).

III

The remaining two issues on which we granted certiorari relate to respondents' federal claims based on the federal common law of nuisance. The principal precedent on which these claims were based is *Illinois* v. *Milwaukee*, 406 U. S. 91 (1972), where the Court found that the federal courts have jurisdiction to consider the federal common law issues raised by a suit for injunctive relief by the State of Illinois against various Wisconsin municipalities and public sewerage commissions, involving the discharge of sewage into Lake Michigan. In this case, we need not decide whether a cause of action may be brought under federal common law by a private plaintiff, seeking damages. This Court has now held that the federal common law of nuisance in the area of water pollution is entirely pre-empted by the more comprehensive scope of the FWPCA, which was completely revised soon after the decision in *Illinois* v. *Milwaukee*. See *Milwaukee* v. *Illinois*, ___ U. S. ___ (1981).

This decision disposes entirely of respondents' federal common law claims, since there is no reason to suppose that the pre-emptive effect of the FWPCA is any less when pollution of coastal waters is at issue. To the extent that this case involves ocean waters not covered by the FWPCA, and regulated under the MPRSA, we see no cause for different treatment of the pre-emption question. The regulatory scheme of the MPRSA is no less comprehensive, with respect to ocean dumping, than are analogous provisions of the FWPCA.

We therefore must dismiss the federal common law claims because their underlying legal basis is now pre-empted by statute. As discussed above, we also dismiss the claims under the MPRSA and the FWPCA because respondents lack a right of action under those statutes. We vacate the judgment below with respect to these two claims, and remand for further proceedings.

It is so ordered.

---

9. The Environmental Impact Statement (EIS) Requirement of the National Environmental Policy Act (NEPA)

When it was enacted by Congress in 1969 the National Environmental Policy Act (NEPA) was intended to be a means of requiring federal agencies to consider the environmental consequences of their actions. NEPA was not intended to provide a statutory basis for private law suits. The most important provision of NEPA is the requirement for the preparation of an **environmental impact statement (EIS)**. This provision has become the statutory basis for a private law suit designed to hold up governmental action that may have a detrimental environmental impact.

Section 102(2)(c) of the Act provides that "all agencies of the Federal government shall . . .

> (C) include in every recommendation or report on proposals for legislation and other major Federal actions significantly affecting the quality of the human environment, a detailed statement by a responsible official on—
> (i) the environmental impact of the proposed action,
> (ii) any adverse environmental effects which cannot be avoided should the proposal be implemented,

(iii) alternatives to the proposed action,
(iv) the relationships between local short-term uses of man's environment and the maintenance and enhancement of long-term productivity, and
(v) any irreversible and irretrievable commitments of resources which would be involved in the proposed action should it be implemented."

NEPA also creates a Council on Environmental Quality (CEQ), as part of the Office of the President, that is given the responsibility of developing national environmental policies and reviewing the environmental consequences of federal programs. Under Presidential Executive Order No. 11,514, CEQ was authorized to promulgate guidelines for the preparation of environmental impact statements. For additional information, see Lynch, *The 1973 CEQ Guidelines: Cautious Updating of the Environmental Impact Statement Process*, 11 CALIF. WESTERN L. REV. 297 (1975).

The EIS was intended to accomplish two purposes. It provides a disclosure statement of the environmental consequences of proposed federal action and it forces the federal decision maker to consider the environmental issues rather than ignore environmental consequences of a difficult decision. The EIS provision has provided the basis for law suits against federal agencies by private persons who seek to enjoin the proposed action by arguing that an EIS should have been, but was not, prepared, or that the decision to proceed with the project is unreasonable in view of the information brought forth in the EIS. The legal issues that arise in such a law suit are (*1*) Is the preparation of an EIS required under the facts of the case?, and (*2*) To what extent will a court overturn an administrative decision to proceed with action that has detrimental environmental consequences as disclosed by the EIS?

The answer to the first question, whether an EIS is required under the facts of the case, depends on a series of sub-issues, such as (*1*) Is there a *federal* action involved? (*2*) Is that action a *major* one? and (*3*) Does that action "significantly" affect the environment? For a discussion of these issues see, Shea, *The Judicial Standard for Review of Environmental Impact Statement Threshold Decisions*," 9 ENVIRONMENTAL AFFAIRS 63 (1980). The second question, of the extent to which a court will overturn an administrative decision that appears to be made in disregard of detrimental environmental consequences, has brought a wide variety of decisions in the Circuit Courts of the United States Court of Appeals. For a review of these decisions, see the Shea article at pages 88 to 99.

The question of how much weight must be given to "environmental" factors is a continuing troublesome issue. In *Strycker's Bay Neighborhood Council v. Karlen*, the Second Circuit Court of Appeals held that it was an error for a federal agency not to give "determinative weight" to environmental factors." In the decision that follows the United States Supreme

Court overturned the Second Circuit Court and reaffirmed its statement in *Vermont Yankee Nuclear Power Corp. v. NRDC*, 435 U.S. 519 (1978) that NEPA was designed to ensure a fully informed and well-considered decision but not necessarily a decision that members of a court would have made had they been decision makers of the administrative agency.

STRYKER'S BAY NEIGHBORHOOD COUNCIL v. KARLEN

444 U.S. 1307 (1980)

PER CURIAM.

The protracted nature of this litigation is perhaps best illustrated by the identity of the original federal defendant, "George Romney, Secretary of the Department of Housing and Urban Development." At the center of this dispute is the site of a proposed low-income housing project to be constructed on Manhattan's Upper West Side. In 1962 the New York City Planning Commission (the Commission), acting in conjunction with the United States Department of Housing and Urban Development (HUD), began formulating a plan for the renewal of 20 square blocks known as the "West Side Urban Renewal Area" (WSURA) through a joint effort on the part of private parties and various government agencies. As originally written, the plan called for a mix of 70% middle-income housing and 30% low-income housing and designated the site at issue here as the location of one of the middle-income projects. In 1969, after substantial progress toward completion of the plan, local agencies in New York determined that the number of low-income units proposed for WSURA would be insufficient to satisfy an increased need for such units. In response to this shortage the Commission amended the plan to designate the site as the future location of a high-rise building containing 160 units of low-income housing. HUD approved this amendment in December 1972.

Meanwhile, in October 1971 the Trinity Episcopal School Corp. (Trinity), which had participated in the plan by building a combination school and middle-income housing development at a nearby location, sued in the United States District Court for the Southern District of New York to enjoin the Commission and HUD from constructing low-income housing on the site. The present respondents, Roland N. Karlen, Alvin C. Hudgins, and the Committee of Neighbors to Insure a Normal Urban Environment (CONTINUE), intervened as plaintiffs, while petitioner Strycker's Bay Neighborhood Council, Inc., intervened as a defendant.

The District Court entered judgment in favor of petitioners. See *Trinity Episcopal School Corp. v. Romney*, 387 F.Supp. 1044 (SDNY 1974). It concluded, *inter alia*, that petitioners had not violated the National Environmental Protection Act of 1969 (NEPA), 83 Stat. 852, 42 U.S.C. § 4321 *et seq*.

On respondents' appeal, the Second Circuit affirmed all but the District Court's treatment of the NEPA claim. See *Trinity Episcopal School Corp. v. Romney*, 523 F.2d 88 (CA2 1975). While the Court of Appeals agreed with the District Court that HUD was not required to prepare a full-scale environmental impact statement under § 102(2)(c) of NEPA, 42 U.S.C. § 4332(2)(C), it held that HUD had not complied with § 102(2)(E), which requires an agency to "study, develop, and describe appropriate alternatives to recommended courses of action in any proposal which involves unresolved conflicts concerning alternative uses of available resources." 42 U.S.C. § 102(2)(E). See 523 F.2d., at 92–95. According to the Court of Appeals, any consideration by HUD of alternatives to placing low-income housing on the site "was either highly limited or non-existent." *Id.*, at 94. Citing the "background of urban environmental factors" behind HUD's decision, the Court of Appeals remanded the case, requiring HUD to prepare "[a] statement of possible alternatives, the consequences thereof and the facts and reasons for and against. . . ." *Ibid.* The statement was not to reflect "HUD's concept or the Housing Authority's views as to how these agencies would choose to resolve the city's low income group housing situation," but rather was to explain "how within the framework of the Plan its objective of economic integration can best be achieved with a minimum of adverse environmental impact." *Ibid.* The Court of Appeals believed that, given such an assessment of alternatives, "the agencies with the cooperation of interested parties should be able to arrive at an equitable solution." *Id.*, at 95.

On remand, HUD prepared a lengthy report entitled "Special Environmental Clearance." After marshaling the data, the report asserted that, "while the choice of site 30 for development as a 100 percent low-income project has raised valid questions about the potential social environmental impacts involved, the problems associated with the impact on social fabric and community structures are not considered so serious as to require that this component be rated as unacceptable." Special Environmental Clearance, at 42. The last portion of the report incorporated a study wherein the Commission evaluated nine alternative locations for the project and found none of them acceptable. While HUD's report conceded that this study may not have considered all possible alternatives, it credited the Commission's conclusion that any relocation of the units would entail an unacceptable delay of two years or more. According to HUD, "[m]easured against the environmental costs associated with the minimum two-year delay, the benefits seem insufficient to justify a mandated substitution of sites." *Id.*, at 54.

After soliciting the parties' comments on HUD's report, the District Court again entered judgment in favor of petitioners. See *Trinity Episcopal School Corp. v. Harris*, 445 F.Supp. 204 (SDNY 1978). The court was "impressed with [HUD's analysis] as being thorough and exhaustive," 445 F.Supp. at 209–210, and found that "HUD's consideration of the alternatives was neither arbitrary nor capricious"; on the contrary, "[i]t was done in good faith and in full accordance with the law." *Id.*, at 220.

On appeal, the Second Circuit vacated and remanded again. The appellate court focused upon that part of HUD's report where the agency considered and rejected alternative sites, and in particular upon HUD's reliance on the delay such a relocation would entail. The Court of Appeals purported to recognize that its role in reviewing HUD's decision was defined by the Administrative Procedure Act (APA), 5 U.S.C. § 706(2)(A), which provides that agency actions should be set aside if found to be "arbitrary, capricious, an abuse of discretion or otherwise not in accordance with law. . . ." *Ibid.* Additionally, however, the Court of Appeals looked to "[t]he provisions of NEPA" for "the substantive standards necessary to review the merits of agency decisions. . . ." 590 F.2d, at 43. The Court of Appeals conceded that HUD had "given 'consideration' to alternatives" to redesignating the site. 590 F.2d, at 44. Nevertheless, the court believed that "'consideration' is not an end in itself." *Ibid.* Concentrating on HUD's finding that development of an alternative location would entail an unacceptable delay, the appellate court held that such delay could not be "an overriding factor" in HUD's decision to proceed with the development. *Ibid.* According to the court, when HUD considers such projects, "environmental factors, such as crowding low-income housing into a concentrated area, should be given determinative weight." *Ibid.* The Court of Appeals therefore remanded the case to the District Court, instructing HUD to attack the shortage of low-income housing in a manner that would avoid the "concentration" of such housing on Site 30. *Id.*, at 45.

In *Vermont Yankee Nuclear Power Corp. v. NRDC*, 435 U.S. 519, 558, 98 S.Ct. 1197, 1219, 55 L.Ed.2d 460 (1978), we stated that NEPA, while establishing "significant substantive goals for the Nation," imposes upon agencies duties that are "essentially procedural." As we stressed in that case, NEPA was designed "to insure a fully-informed and well-considered decision," but not necessarily "a decision the judges of the Court of Appeals or of this Court would have reached had they been members of the decisionmaking unit of the agency." *Vermont Yankee* cuts sharply against the Court of Appeals' conclusion that an agency, in selecting a course of action, must elevate environmental concerns over other appropriate considerations. On the contrary, once an agency has made a decision subject to NEPA's procedural requirements, the only role for a court is to insure that the agency has considered the environmental consequences; it cannot "interject itself within the area of discretion of the executive as to the choice of the action to be taken." *Kleppe v. Sierra Club*, 427 U.S. 390, 410, n. 21, 96 S.Ct. 2718, 2730, n. 21, 49 L.Ed.2d 576 (1976). See also *FPC v. Transcontinental Gas Pipeline Corp.*, 423 U.S. 326, 96 S.Ct. 579, 46 L.Ed.2d 533 (1976).

In the present case there is no doubt that HUD considered the environmental consequences of its decision to redesignate the proposed site for low-income housing. NEPA requires no more. The judgment of the Court of Appeals is therefore

Reversed.

The value of an EIS will depend upon its accuracy, completeness and the care and skill with which it was prepared. The kinds of information it may reveal should be apparent from an analysis of the following "Guidelines for the Preparation of an Environmental Impact Statement" issued by the New Jersey Department of Environmental Protection.

GUIDELINES FOR THE PREPARATION OF AN ENVIRONMENTAL IMPACT STATEMENT

The environmental impact statement shall provide all the necessary information needed to evaluate the effects of the proposed project on the environment. The statement shall be prepared in accordance with the format of the guidelines hereinafter set forth.

The environmental impact statement shall be prepared by the project sponsor or consultant or consultants as may be deemed qualified by virtue of their systematic interdisciplinary approach which will ensure the integrated use of the natural and social sciences and the environmental design arts. The information provided in the statement should clearly indicate the authors, their qualifications, how the investigations were conducted, and a complete bibliography of the sources consulted.

A DESCRIPTION OF THE PROPOSED PROJECT

Included in this section will be a comprehensive description of the project as outlined in the following categories:

A. Identify the project sponsor.
B. Explain the purpose of the proposed project—include a description of the products and services being provided and the extent of benefits being realized by the owner, the community within which the project is located, and the area being served.
C. Locate the project in a regional, municipal, and neighborhood setting.
D. Describe the project design and operational features:
   1. Include a site plan of the project.
   2. Describe the construction phase:
      a. Identify development schedule and construction phasing;
      b. Work force required;
      c. Construction traffic;
      d. Site preparation, including clearing, excavating, filling and cutting, burning and blasting;
      e. Precautions taken (noise control, dust control, erosion and sedimentation control, temporary sanitation);
      f. Materials required (general).
   3. Describe the operational phase:
      a. Output and capacity;
      b. Work force;
      c. Discharges and emissions (both point sources and nonpoint sources);
      d. Traffic and access;
      e. Use of resources.
E. Include a listing of all licenses, permits and certifications necessary for approval of the project—include status of each.

DESCRIPTION OF THE ENVIRONMENT PRIOR TO THE IMPLEMENTATION OF THE PROJECT

Include a comprehensive description of existing environmental conditions in each of the following areas:

A. Natural Resources of the Site and Surrounding Area:
   Describe geological character, soil characteristics, land form, hydrological features (surface and subsurface), climate, terrestrial plants and animals, aquatic plants and animals (include species diversity & frequency).

B. Man-made Resources:
   Present site land use, adjacent land use, access and transportation patterns, zoning, community facilities (sewer, water, waste removal), population density and distribution.

C. Human Resources:
   Cultural and social factors, aesthetic features, historical, archeological and architectural aspects of the environment.

D. Economic Resources:
   Local tax base, levels of economic development within the municipality and the region.

E. Identification of All Pollution Problems Existing in the Area:
   Provide an analysis of existing environmental problems, including water and air quality, as a basis to assess any cumulative problems that may result from the project.

THE PROBABLE ENVIRONMENTAL IMPACT OF THE PROJECT IF IMPLEMENTED

Identify and describe both primary and secondary environmental impacts, beneficial and adverse, anticipated from the proposed project by components on all natural, manmade, human and economic resources during all aspects of site preparation, construction and operation.

Using the existing environment without the project as a basis for analysis, provide the following information:

A. Land:
   1. Discuss the consistency of the proposed action with accepted federal, state, regional and local plans in progress. Identify instances where land use practices, even though accepted, would pose an environmental problem.
   2. Discuss how the areas are currently zoned, and the relationship to the proposed action.
   3. Discuss how the proposed action will encourage or discourage population or industrial growth to the extent that it will change the character and economy of the area.
   4. Discuss whether the proposed action will result in the loss or alteration of any ecologically sensitive lands such as flood plains, steep slopes and wetlands.

B. Water:
   1. Identify and discuss all instances of noncompliance between proposed action and approved state water quality standards, with particular attention to low flow periods.
   2. Discuss whether or not the proposed action will result in increased pollution or turbidity levels within the receiving waterway and, if so, what the effects downstream and upstream will be.
   3. Discuss the beneficial and adverse effects of the proposed action on aquatic biota and habitats.

4. Discuss the effects that the proposed action will have on ground water quality and quantity and the basis of the determination.
5. Discuss whether or not there will be any depletive loss of water as a result of the proposed action. Include decreases in infiltration capacity.
6. Discuss whether or not the proposed action will have any effect on natural salinity in tidal waters.
7. Discuss whether or not there will be any increased incidents of flooding caused by structural obstructions or increased flow due to the proposed project. Include the probable effects in terms of flood levels, channel erosion, velocity and siltation of stream channels.
8. Discuss any cumulative effects, e.g. coupling thermal discharges from other existing facilities with the proposed project for analysis of cumulative impact on the receiving water body.

C. Air:
1. Provide all data necessary to permit the state to perform diffusion modeling on the effect of the proposed action on the air quality of the area surrounding the project. All the aspects of the project should be given consideration in terms of possible receptor sites of air pollutants directly or indirectly generated from the proposed project. Include a discussion of the cumulative aspects.
   Discuss ambient air quality data present and projected so that direct comparisons may be made between present air quality, projected air quality, and air quality standards.
2. Discuss if the project will meet applicable emission standards and regulations contained in the state implementation plan.
3. Discuss precautions taken to prevent odor problems from becoming a public nuisance and/or being in violation of the State Air Pollution Control Act.
4. Discuss long-term consideration given to the relationship between nearby residences and businesses, the project and prevailing wind patterns on the seasonal and annual air quality in the area (give meteorological patterns macro and micro where possible).
5. Discuss precautions taken to prevent the airborne transmission of pathogenic organisms, if applicable.
6. Discuss the possible influence of the proposed action on immediate area local receptors.
7. Base the evaluation of air quality on complete diffusion climatology providing adequate references.

D. Aquatic and Terrestrial Wildlife:
1. Discuss the gain/loss of their habitat and its effect.
2. Discuss the gain/loss of food chain on the aquatic and terrestrial wildlife.
3. Discuss the effect of noise, dust, lighting, turbidity and siltation from construction and after completion on aquatic and terrestrial wildlife.
4. Discuss any recreation gain/loss with regard to hunting and fishing.

E. Social and Economic:
1. Discuss the socioeconomic effects on the community due to any induced development attributable to the proposed action. Will adequate public services be available to serve this development such as schools, parks, fire, and police protection? Include a discussion of local controls on development.
2. How will noise levels due to operation of facilities affect humans and wildlife? Describe these potential problems in terms of decibels, time of noise, duration, and types and discuss any noise control methods to be used.
3. Describe how the action will affect recreation capabilities of the area.
4. Discuss how the project will affect historical, archaeological, or cultural values.

F. Solid Wastes:
   1. Discuss methods of solid waste handling both during construction and subsequent operation.

G. Aesthetics:
   1. Discuss how the natural or present character of the area will be changed as a result of the proposed action.
   2. Graphically describe the shadow cast by any structures.

ABNORMAL ENVIRONMENTAL IMPACTS

Discuss the potential of man-made accidents and natural catstrophes, their probabilities and risks, with regard to the proposed project.

METHODS OF MITIGATING ADVERSE ENVIRONMENTAL IMPACTS

A. Discuss the remedial, protective and mitigative measures to be taken as part of the proposed project in response to the adverse environmental impact. Mitigating measures should discuss the methods to be used for the project to be brought into compliance with all applicable air and water quality standards plus noise, solid waste, radiation, and land-use regulations. Mitigation of adverse environmental effects should reflect latest state-of-the-art technology. Included, but not limited to, in the discussion of mitigating measures may be the following design considerations and operational strategies:
   1. Site location;
   2. Air quality through control apparatus and/or controlled combustion process;
   3. Water quality through treatment of domestic and industrial wastewater, thermal cooling, eutrophication control;
   4. Erosion and sedimentation control measures, storm water runoff control measures from paved areas;
   5. Dust control measures;
   6. Noise control measures;
   7. Traffic control measures;
   8. Solid waste reuse and resource recovery;
   9. Establishment of buffer zones, selective clearing and/or landscaping;
   10. Protective measures for aquatic and terrestrial plants and animals;
   11. Architectural techniques to blend structures with the surrounding area;
   12. Continuous and systematic monitoring of all emissions and discharges;
   13. Contingency plans and emergency procedures in the event of an accident or natural catastrophe;
   14. Employee education and on-going inspection program;
   15. Containment areas, floating booms, check valves or nonpermeable barriers to control accidental spills or leaks.

ANY ADVERSE ENVIRONMENTAL IMPACTS WHICH CANNOT BE AVOIDED SHOULD THE PROJECT BE IMPLEMENTED

This section should provide a discussion of the kinds and magnitude of adverse impacts which cannot be reduced in severity or reduced to an acceptable level.

A. For those impacts which cannot be reduced, their implications and the reasons why the action being proposed notwithstanding their effect should be described in detail.

B. Where abatement measures can reduce adverse impacts to acceptable levels, discuss the effectiveness, costs of the abatement measures and the basis for considering the adequacy of the determination.

ALTERNATIVES TO THE PROPOSED PROJECT

The analysis of alternatives should be sufficiently detailed and rigorous to permit independent and comparative evaluation of the benefits, costs and environmental risks of the proposed project and each reasonable alternative.

A. Include the alternative of taking no action. Other alternatives include other sites, designs, processes and operations considered and rejected.
B. Include alternatives capable of substantially reducing or eliminating any adverse impacts, even at the expense of reducing project objectives.
C. For each alternative discussed include reasons why each was not as acceptable as the proposed action.

ANY IRREVERSIBLE AND IRRETRIEVABLE COMMITMENT OF RESOURCES SHOULD THE PROJECT BE IMPLEMENTED

This section should identify the extent to which the proposed action curtails the diversity and range of beneficial uses of the environment.

A. Use of renewable and nonrenewable resources during construction and continued operation should be outlined.
B. Consideration should be given to irreversible damage which may result from accidents.
C. Energy consumption of the project during both the construction and operational phases should be described and analyzed. Alternative energy sources should be presented and compared with the one selected. The reasons for the selection should be stated.

AN EVALUATION OF THE ACTION IN RELATION TO SHORT-TERM USE OF MAN'S ENVIRONMENT AND THE MAINTENANCE AND ENHANCEMENT OF LONG-TERM PRODUCTIVITY

Short-term refers to the period of time during which the proposed action takes place (including the lifespan of operation). Long-term refers to the time period extending beyond the life of the proposed action.

Describe those cumulative and long-term effects of the proposed action which either significantly reduce or enhance the state of the environment for future generations. This analysis should include the cumulative effects of all actions or activities in the vicinity with similar environmental impacts as the proposed action.

---

10. State Environmental Protection Acts

Shortly after the adoption of NEPA at the federal level, several states, including California, Minnesota, Washington, Maine and Wisconsin, adopted NEPA-like statutes, sometimes called "baby NEPAs" or "**state NEPAs**." The primary purpose of these statutes is to require the preparation of an EIS for state actions. The cases that have arisen under these statutes usually involve the question whether the action of the state involved is the kind of state activity for which an EIS is required under the statute. This was the issue involved in the landmark decision of *Friends of Mammoth v. Board of Supervisors*, 8 Cal. 3d 1, 502 P.2d 1360, 104 Cal. Rptr. 16 (1972), *modified on denial of rehearing*, 8 Cal. 3d 247, 502 P.2d 1049, 104 Cal. Rptr. 761 (1972), interpreting the California Environmental

Quality Act (CEQA). That statute requires governmental agencies to file an EIS upon a finding that "any project they intend to carry out . . . may have a significant impact upon the environment." A private developer applied to the planning board for a conditional use permit for a mixed use development of condominiums and commercial uses. The issue was whether it was necessary for the municipal planning board to submit an EIS under the CEQA. The answer to this question depends on whether the word "project" as used in the statute includes *private* activities for which a government permit is necessary. The California Supreme Court held that such action is a "project" within the meaning of CEQA and that an EIS must be prepared by the planning board before granting a conditional use permit. The dissenting opinion argues that the majority opinion disregards the legislative history and well-established principles of statutory construction.

For additional information about state NEPAs, see Hagman, *NEPA's Progeny Inhabit the States—Were the Genes Defective?* 7 URBAN L. ANN. 3 (1974); Note, *State Environmental Impact Statements*, 15 WASHBURN L.J. (1976).

B. Who May Sue?

To the nonlawyer, the technical rules that permit some people to bring suit but deny access to the courts to others may seem unnecessary and unduly harsh. This feeling is particularly strong when a law suit is brought to protect the environment. Because of the large quantities of scientific and technical information required, it is very expensive to bring environmental protection law suits. The question is frequently asked, "If someone is willing to incur these substantial expenses to protect the environment on behalf of the public why shouldn't he be permitted to do so?" The answer to this question is not an easy one. The underlying response is based on the **principle of separation of powers**, by which governmental functions are allocated to the legislative, executive and judicial branches of government. The function of the legislature is to enact laws that incorporate basic policy decisions. The function of the courts is to adjudicate controversies that arise between individuals relating to those laws. It is not the function of the courts to establish public policy except when necessary in the adjudication of a law suit properly brought before it. Therefore, it is argued, only when a bona fide law suit, brought by parties involved in a real controversy, is brought before it should a court engage in the judicial process. Thus it becomes necessary to determine when there is a bona fide law suit and a real controversy. To answer these questions the courts and the legislatures have established rules relating to standing to sue, class actions, intervention and circumstances under which a government may be a plaintiff.

1. STANDING TO SUE

The concept of **standing to sue** is based on principles of constitutional and statutory law and judicial policy. Arguments based on any one, or all, of these principles may be used to deny a plaintiff access to the courts on the grounds that he does not have standing to sue.

a. *Constitutional Law*

This principle arises from the provision in the United States Constitution, Article 3, Section 2, that the "judicial power shall extend to all cases . . . and to controversies . . ." The phrase "cases and controversies" has been interpreted to mean matters brought before the court involving parties who allege that they are injured or aggrieved or who seek the protection of a legal right. Thus, if an environmental organization becomes a plaintiff in a law suit seeking protection of the environment in a federal court a constitutional issue arises whether the plaintiff is "injured or aggrieved" in a way that provides the court with jurisdiction to hear the case.

b. *Statutory Law*

The Administrative Procedure Act (APA) adopted by Congress in 1967 prescribes the procedural rights and responsibilities of federal administrative agencies. The act also prescribes the rights of the public when dealing with those agencies. Section 702 of the APA provides: "A person suffering legal wrong because of agency action, or adversely affected or aggrieved by agency action within the meaning of a relevant statute, is entitled to judicial review thereof." This provision gives a person the right to bring suit in a federal court against a federal agency. However, to do so the plaintiff must allege and prove that he is "adversely affected or aggrieved" by agency action. Without such allegations the court will find that the plaintiff "does not have standing to sue."

c. *Judicial policy*

Most courts have recognized that there may be sound judicial policy reasons for the courts not to get involved in certain kinds of controversies for which a judicial remedy would not be appropriate. An illustration of this type of controversy, sometimes called "nonjusticiable," would include actions that put the court in conflict with the president of the United States or the Congress. In addition there are good judicial policy reasons, or "prudential reasons" to avoid issues that are more hypothetical than real, such as "nice" legal questions that legal scholars may want to pose and have resolved by the courts. There are also good policy reasons for the courts to avoid deciding issues that have become moot because they are no longer in controversy.

The standing-to-sue issue has evolved over a period of time in the federal courts. In 1923, the United States Supreme Court held in *Frothingham v. Mellon*, 262 U.S. 447, that for a plaintiff to have standing to sue he must be able to show that he has sustained, or is in danger of sustaining, some direct injury. In 1923 the Court held, in *Tennessee Electric Power Co. v. TVA*, 306 U.S. 118, that a plaintiff must allege that some **legal interest** or legal right has been invaded. In 1962 in *Baker v. Carr*, 369 U.S. 186, the court said that a plaintiff must allege "sufficient harm to support a personal stake."

Then, starting in 1968, the United States Supreme Court began to adopt a more permissive attitude on standing to sue. In *Flast v. Cohen*, 392 U.S. 83 (1968) the court held that a taxpayer could have standing based on a personal stake in the outcome of the litigation that would cause him to prosecute the matter in an adversarial context. But it was not until 1970 that the Supreme Court reconsidered the standing-to-sue question, rejected the "legally protected interest" criterion and established a two-part test in *Association of Data Processing Service Organizations v. Camp*, 397 U.S. 150. Under the standards set forth in this decision a plaintiff must show:

(*1*) *Injury in fact*; i.e., he must show that he has suffered some injury in fact, economic or otherwise. The type of injury may be aesthetic, conservational or recreational.

(*2*) *Zone of interest*; i.e., the issue litigated must be within the zone of interests sought to be protected by the pertinent statute or constitutional guarantee.

It is in the context of the above historical development of the tests for standing to sue that *Sierra Club v. Morton* arises, involving the standing of the Sierra Club to sue to prevent the development of a ski resort in Sequoia National Park.

SIERRA CLUB v. MORTON

405 U.S. 727 (1972)

MR. JUSTICE STEWART delivered the opinion of the Court.

The Mineral King Valley is an area of great natural beauty nestled in the Sierra Nevada Mountains in Tulare County, California, adjacent to Sequoia National Park. It has been part of the Sequoia National Forest since 1926, and is designated as a national game refuge by special Act of Congress. Though once the site of extensive mining activity, Mineral King is now used almost exclusively for recreational purposes. Its relative inaccessibility and lack of development have limited the number of visitors each year, and at the same time have preserved the valley's quality as a quasi-wilderness area largely uncluttered by the products of civilization.

The United States Forest Service, which is entrusted with the maintenance and administration of national forests, began in the late 1940's to give consideration to Mineral King as a potential site for recreational development. Prodded by a rapidly increasing demand for skiing facilities, the Forest Service published a prospectus in 1965, inviting bids from private developers for the construction and operation of a ski resort that would also serve as a summer recreation area.

* * *

The final Disney plan, approved by the Forest Service in January 1969, outlines a $35 million complex of motels, restaurants, swimming pools, parking lots, and other structures designed to accommodate 14,000 visitors daily. This complex is to be constructed on 80 acres of the valley floor under a 30-year use permit from the Forest Service. * * *

To provide access to the resort, the State of California proposes to construct a highway 20 miles in length. A section of this road would traverse Sequoia National Park, as would a proposed high-voltage power line needed to provide electricity for the resort. Both the highway and the power line require the approval of the Department of the Interior, which is entrusted with the preservation and maintenance of the national parks.

Representatives of the Sierra Club, who favor maintaining Mineral King largely in its present state, followed the progress of recreational planning for the valley with close attention and increasing dismay. * * *

In June 1969 the Club filed the present suit in the United States District Court for the Northern District of California, * * *

The petitioner Sierra Club sued as a membership corporation with "a special interest in the conservation and the sound maintenance of the national parks, game refuges and forests of the country," and invoked the judicial-review provisions of the Administrative Procedure Act, 5 U. S. C. § 701 *et seq.*

After two days of hearings, the District Court * * * rejected the respondents' challenge to the Sierra Club's standing to sue. * * *

The respondents appealed, and the Court of Appeals for the Ninth Circuit reversed. 433 F. 2d 24. With respect to the petitioner's standing, the court noted that there was "no allegation in the complaint that members of the Sierra Club would be affected by the actions of [the respondents] other than the fact that the actions are personally displeasing or distasteful to them," *id.*, at 33, and concluded:

> "We do not believe such club concern without a showing of more direct interest can constitute standing in the legal sense sufficient to challenge the exercise of responsibilities on behalf of all the citizens by two cabinet level officials of the government acting under Congressional and Constitutional authority."

Alternatively, the Court of Appeals held that the Sierra Club had not made an adequate showing of irreparable injury and likelihood of success on the merits to justify issuance of a preliminary injunction. The court thus vacated the injunction. The Sierra Club filed a petition for a writ of certiorari which we granted, 401 U. S. 907, to review the questions of federal law presented.

The first question presented is whether the Sierra Club has alleged facts that entitle it to obtain judicial review of the challenged action. Whether a party has a sufficient stake in an otherwise justiciable controversy to obtain judicial resolution of that controversy is what has traditionally been referred to as the question of standing to sue. Where the party does not rely on any specific statute authorizing invocation of the judicial process, the question of standing depends upon whether the party has alleged such a "personal stake in the outcome of the controversy," *Baker* v. *Carr*, 369 U. S. 186, 204, as to ensure that "the dispute sought to be adjudicated will be presented in an adversary context and in a form historically viewed as capable of judicial resolution." *Flast* v. *Cohen*, 392 U. S. 83, 101. Where, however, Congress has authorized public officials to perform certain functions according to law, and has provided by statute for judicial review of those actions under certain circumstances, the inquiry as to standing must begin with a determination of whether the statute in question authorizes review at the behest of the plaintiff.

The Sierra Club relies upon § 10 of the Administrative Procedure Act (APA), 5 U. S. C. § 702, which provides:

> "A person suffering legal wrong because of agency action, or adversely affected or aggrieved by agency action within the meaning of a relevant statute, is entitled to judicial review thereof."

Early decisions under this statute interpreted the language as adopting the various formulations of "legal interest" and "legal wrong" then prevailing as constitutional requirements of standing. But, in *Data Processing Service* v. *Camp*, 397 U. S. 150, and *Barlow* v. *Collins*, 397 U. S. 159, decided the same day, we held more broadly that persons had standing to obtain judicial review of federal agency action under § 10 of the APA where they had alleged that the challenged action had caused them "injury in fact," and where the alleged injury was to an interest "arguably within the zone of interests to be protected or regulated" by the statutes that the agencies were claimed to have violated.

In *Data Processing*, the injury claimed by the petitioners consisted of harm to their competitive position in the computer-servicing market * * *

In *Barlow*, the petitioners were tenant farmers who claimed that certain regulations of the Secretary of Agriculture adversely affected their economic position *vis-à-vis* their landlords. * * *

Thus, neither *Data Processing* nor *Barlow* addressed itself to the question, which has arisen with increasing frequency in federal courts in recent years, as to what must be alleged by persons who claim injury of a noneconomic nature to interests that are widely shared. That question is presented in this case.

The injury alleged by the Sierra Club will be incurred entirely by reason of the change in the uses to which Mineral King will be put, and the attendant change in the aesthetics and ecology of the area. Thus, in referring to the road to be built through Sequoia National Park, the complaint alleged that the development "would destroy or otherwise adversely affect the scenery, natural and historic objects and wildlife of the park and would impair the enjoyment of the park for future generations." We do not question that this type of harm may amount to an "injury in fact" sufficient to lay the basis for standing under § 10 of the APA. Aesthetic and environmental well-being, like economic well-being, are important ingredients of the quality of life in our society, and the fact that particular environmental interests are shared by the many rather than the few does not make them less deserving of legal protection through the judicial process. But the "injury in fact" test requires more than an injury to a cognizable interest. It requires that the party seeking review be himself among the injured.

The impact of the proposed changes in the environment of Mineral King will not fall indiscriminately upon every citizen. The alleged injury will be felt directly only by those who use Mineral King and Sequoia National park, and for whom the aesthetic and recreational values of the area will be lessened by the highway and ski resort. The Sierra Club failed to allege that it or its members would be affected in any of their activities or pastimes by the Disney development. Nowhere in the pleadings or affidavits did the Club state that its members use Mineral King for any purpose, much less that they use it in any way that would be significantly affected by the proposed actions of the respondents.

The Club apparently regarded any allegations of individualized injury as superfluous, on the theory that this was a "public" action involving questions as to the use of natural resources, and that the Club's longstanding concern with and expertise in such matters were sufficient to give it standing as a "representative of the public." This theory reflects a misunderstanding of our cases involving so-called "public actions" in the area of administrative law.

The origin of the theory advanced by the Sierra Club may be traced to a dictum in *Scripps-Howard Radio* v. *FCC*, 316 U. S. 4. * * *

Taken together, *Sanders* and *Scripps-Howard* thus established a dual proposition: the fact of economic injury is what gives a person standing to seek judicial review under the statute, but once review is properly invoked, that person may argue the public interest in support of his claim that the agency has failed to comply with its statutory mandate. It was in the latter sense that the "standing" of the appellant in *Scripps-Howard* existed only as a "representative of the public interest." It is in a similar sense that we have used the phrase "private attorney general" to describe the function performed by persons upon whom Congress has conferred the right to seek judicial review of agency action. * * *

The trend of cases arising under the APA and other statutes authorizing judicial review of federal agency action has been toward recognizing that injuries other than economic harm are sufficient to bring a person within the meaning of the statutory language, and toward discarding the notion that an injury that is widely shared is *ipso facto* not an injury sufficient to provide the basis for judicial review. We noted this development with approval in *Data Processing*, 397 U. S., at 154, in saying that the interest alleged to have been injured "may reflect 'aesthetic, conservational, and recreational' as well as economic values." But broadening the categories of injury that may be alleged in support of standing is a different matter from abandoning the requirement that the party seeking review must himself have suffered an injury.

Some courts have indicated a willingness to take this latter step by conferring standing upon organizations that have demonstrated "an organizational interest in the problem" of environmental or consumer protection. *Environmental Defense Fund* v. *Hardin*, 138 U. S. App. D. C. 391, 395, 428 F. 2d 1093, 1097. It is clear that an organization whose members are injured may represent those members in a proceeding for judicial review. See, *e. g., NAACP* v. *Button*, 371 U. S. 415, 428. But a mere "interest in a problem" no matter how longstanding the interest and no matter how qualified the organization is in evaluating the problem, is not sufficient by itself to render the organization "adversely affected" or "aggrieved" within the meaning of the APA. The Sierra Club is a large and long-established organization, with a historic commitment to the cause of protecting our Nation's natural heritage from man's depredations. But if a "special interest" in this subject were enough to entitle the Sierra Club to commence this litigation, there would appear to be no objective basis upon which to disallow a suit by any other bona fide "special interest" organization, however small or short-lived. And if any group with a bona fide "special interest" could initiate such litigation, it is difficult to perceive why any individual citizen with the same bona fide special interest would not also be entitled to do so.

The requirement that a party seeking review must allege facts showing that he is himself adversely affected does not insulate executive action from judicial review, nor does it prevent any public interests from being protected through the judicial process. It does serve as at least a rough attempt to put the decision as to whether review will be sought in the hands of those who have a direct stake in the outcome. That goal would be undermined were we to construe the APA to authorize judicial review at the behest of organizations or individuals who seek to do no more than vindicate their own value preferences through the judicial process. The principle that the Sierra Club would have us establish in this case would do just that.

As we conclude that the Court of Appeals was correct in its holding that the Sierra Club lacked standing to maintain this action, we do not reach any other questions presented in the petition, and we intimate no view on the merits of the complaint. The judgment is

Affirmed.

MR. JUSTICE DOUGLAS, dissenting.

I share the views of my Brother BLACKMUN and would reverse the judgment below.

The critical question of "standing" would be simplified and also put neatly in focus if we fashioned a federal rule that allowed environmental issues to be litigated before federal agencies or federal courts in the name of the inanimate object about to be despoiled, defaced, or invaded by roads and bulldozers and where injury is the subject of public outrage. Contemporary public concern for protecting nature's ecological equilibrium should lead to the conferral of standing upon environmental objects to sue for their own preservation. * * *

This suit would therefore be more properly labeled as *Mineral King* v. *Morton*.

Inanimate objects are sometimes parties in litigation. A ship has a legal personality, a fiction found useful for maritime purposes. The corporation sole—a creature of ecclesiastical law—is an acceptable adversary and large fortunes ride on its cases. The ordinary corporation is a "person" for purposes of the adjudicatory processes, whether it represents proprietary, spiritual, aesthetic, or charitable causes.

So it should be as respects valleys, alpine meadows, rivers, lakes, estuaries, beaches, ridges, groves of trees, swampland, or even air that feels the destructive pressures of modern technology and modern life. The river, for example, is the living symbol of all the life it sustains or nourishes—fish, aquatic insects, water ouzels, otter, fisher, deer, elk, bear, and all other animals, including man, who are dependent on it or who enjoy it for its sight, its sound, or its life. The river as plaintiff speaks for the ecological unit of life that is part of it. Those people who have a meaningful relation to that body of water—whether it be a fisherman, a canoeist, a zoologist, or a logger—must be able to speak for the values which the river represents and which are threatened with destruction. * * *

Perhaps the bulldozers of "progress" will plow under all the aesthetic wonders of this beautiful land. That is not the present question. The sole question is, who has standing to be heard?

Those who hike the Appalachian Trail into Sunfish Pond, New Jersey, and camp or sleep there, or run the Allagash in Maine, or climb the Guadalupes in West Texas, or who canoe and portage the Quetico Superior in Minnesota, certainly should have standing to defend those natural wonders before courts or agencies, though they live 3,000 miles away. Those who merely are caught up in environmental news or propaganda and flock to defend these waters or areas may be treated differently. That is why these environmental issues should be tendered by the inanimate object itself. Then there will be assurances that all of the forms of life which it represents will stand before the court—the pileated woodpecker as well as the coyote and bear, the lemmings as well as the trout in the streams. Those inarticulate members of the ecological group cannot speak. But those people who have so frequented the place as to know its values and wonders will be able to speak for the entire ecological community.

Ecology reflects the land ethic; and Aldo Leopold wrote in A Sand County Almanac 204 (1949), "The land ethic simply enlarges the boundaries of the community to include soils, waters, plants, and animals, or collectively: the land."

That, as I see it, is the issue of "standing" in the present case and controversy.

MR. JUSTICE BRENNAN, dissenting.

I agree that the Sierra Club has standing for the reasons stated by my Brother BLACKMUN in Alternative No. 2 of his dissent. I therefore would reach the merits.

Since the Court does not do so, however, I simply note agreement with my Brother Blackmun that the merits are substantial.

Mr. Justice Blackmun, dissenting.

The Court's opinion is a practical one espousing and adhering to traditional notions of standing as somewhat modernized by *Data Processing Service* v. *Camp*, 397 U. S. 150 (1970); *Barlow* v. *Collins*, 397 U. S. 159 (1970); and *Flast* v. *Cohen*, 392 U. S. 83 (1968). If this were an ordinary case, I would join the opinion and the Court's judgment and be quite content.

But this is not ordinary, run-of-the-mill litigation. The case poses—if only we choose to acknowledge and reach them—significant aspects of a wide, growing, and disturbing problem, that is, the Nation's and the world's deteriorating environment with its resulting ecological disturbances. Must our law be so rigid and our procedural concepts so inflexible that we render ourselves helpless when the existing methods and the traditional concepts do not quite fit and do not prove to be entirely adequate for new issues? * * *

Rather than pursue the course the Court has chosen to take by its affirmance of the judgment of the Court of Appeals, I would adopt one of two alternatives:

1. I would reverse that judgment and, instead, approve the judgment of the District Court which recognized standing in the Sierra Club and granted preliminary relief. I would be willing to do this on condition that the Sierra Club forthwith amend its complaint to meet the specifications the Court prescribes for standing. If Sierra Club fails or refuses to take that step, so be it: the case will then collapse. * * *

2. Alternatively, I would permit an imaginative expansion of our traditional concepts of standing in order to enable an organization such as the Sierra Club, possessed, as it is, of pertinent, bona fide, and well-recognized attributes and purposes in the area of environment, to litigate environmental issues. * * *

For additional information on standing to sue, see:

1. Davis, *The Liberalized Law of Standing*, 37 U. Chi. L. Rev. 450 (1970).
2. Sax, *Standing to Sue: A Critical Review of the Mineral King Decision*, 13 Nat. Resources J. 77 (1973).
3. Note, *Environmental Lawsuits—What Must Organizations Allege to Have Standing to Sue?* 38 Mo. L. Rev. 292 (1973).

---

2. Class Actions

The definition of "environment" includes the aggregate of all of the external conditions and influences that affect the life and development of organisms. Consequently, environmental law is concerned with the rights and liabilities of large numbers of persons who may be affected by such external conditions and influences. It is not surprising, therefore, that there are many occasions when environmental law suits are brought on behalf of a large number, or a class, of persons. **Class actions**, or lawsuits brought on behalf of a group of persons alleged to be injured by the defendant's actions, can be a useful legal procedure. By combining the causes of action of many persons into a single suit it is possible to resolve the issue in one action rather than a multiplicity of suits. A class action may also provide the mechanism by which a few persons can arrange to pay the many costs of an expensive lawsuit on behalf of others who may not be willing to undertake the costs and obligations of a suit.

There are rules regulating the procedure in the federal and state courts that authorize class actions under prescribed circumstances. In federal courts, Rule 23 governs prerequisites and procedure for class actions. Under Section 23 (C) (1) the court must decide as soon as practical after a suit is started whether the action may be maintained as a class action. This may be a difficult decision to make because under Rule 23 (and similar provisions in the state courts) a judgment in a class action binds all members of the class. Thus, if a class action is brought on behalf of all riparian homeowners adjoining a lake against a polluter of the lake and the defendant wins, all the members of the class will be bound by that judgment, unless they were previously excluded from the class by the court. Where damages are sought and the plaintiff wins, the proceeds of the judgment, less all costs, including a reasonable attorney's fee, will be distributed among the members of the class. For these reasons a court will usually require adequate notice to inform the members of the proposed class. The costs of such notice will usually have to be paid initially by the plaintiff who seeks to bring the class action.

Biechele v. *Norfolk & Western Railway Co.* illustrates the kind of notice and procedure a court may impose as a condition for a class action. *Zahn* v. *International Paper Co.* deals with an interpretation of the statute that prescribes the minimum amount of monetary damages for class actions brought in the federal courts.

RULE 23, FEDERAL RULES OF CIVIL PROCEDURE

Rule 23. Class Actions

(a) Prerequisites to a Class Action. One or more members of a class may sue or be sued as representative parties on behalf of all only if (1) the class is so numerous that joinder of all members is impracticable, (2) there are questions of law or fact common to the class, (3) the claims or defenses of the representative parties are typical of the claims or defenses of the class, and (4) the representative parties will fairly and adequately protect the interests of the class.

(b) Class Actions Maintainable. An action may be maintained as a class action if the prerequisites of subdivision (a) are satisfied, and in addition:

(1) the prosecution of separate actions by or against individual members of the class would create a risk of

(A) inconsistent or varying adjudications with respect to individual members of the class which would establish incompatible standards of conduct for the party opposing the class, or

(B) adjudications with respect to individual members of the class which would as a practice matter be dispositive of the interests of the other members not parties to the adjudications or substantially impair or impede their ability to protect their interests; or

(2) the party opposing the class has acted or refused to act on grounds generally applicable to the class, thereby making appropriate final injunctive relief or corresponding declaratory relief with respect to the class as a whole; or

(3) the court finds that the questions of law or fact common to the members of the class predominate over any questions affecting only individual members, and that a class action is superior to other available methods for the fair and efficient adjudication of the controversy. The matters pertinent to the findings include: (A) the interest of members of the class in individually controlling the prosecution or defense of separate actions; (B) the extent and nature of any litigation concerning the controversy already commenced by or against members of the class; (C) the desirability or undesirability of concentrating the litigation of the claims in the particular forum; (D) the difficulties likely to be encountered in the management of a class action.

BIECHELE v. NORFOLK & WESTERN RAILWAY CO.

309 F. Supp. 345 (D.C. Ohio 1969)

DON J. YOUNG, District Judge.

This action was originally commenced in the Court of Common Pleas of Erie County, Ohio, and was removed to this Court by defendant on the ground of diversity of citizenship. The action was intended as a class action, and seeks damages and an injunction because of an alleged nuisance created by defendant in the operation of its coal storage and shipping facilities in Sandusky.

After some preliminary skirmishing the Court concluded that this was properly maintainable as a class action and that a representative class was present. Federal Rules of Civil Procedure 23(a). Actually, there are two separate and distinct class actions involved. The first and principal action is that for injunctive relief. The action is founded upon Rule 23(b) (1) and (2) of the Federal Rules of Civil Procedure. Jurisdiction for this action is based upon diversity, 28 U.S.C. § 1332, the amount in controversy being the value of the right involved.* * * It appears to the Court that the right of each member of the class to live in an environment free from excessive coal dust and conversely, the right of defendant to operate its coal loading facility are both in excess of $10,000.00.

The second action is one for damages resulting from the action of defendant. This action has predominating factual questions in common with the injunctive action and requiring the same evidence as presented in that action. The damage action is properly maintainable as a class action under Rule 23(b)(3) of the Federal Rules of Civil Procedure, common questions of fact predominating. Although diversity of citizenship exists between the parties, the Court does not believe that any of the claims exceed $10,000.00. These claims cannot be aggregated to achieve the jurisdictional amount.

Jurisdiction properly lies in this Court under 28 U.S.C. § 1441(c). The claims are sufficiently separate to allow removal of the injunctive action alone. Therefore this Court, in the interest of judicial efficiency, will assume jurisdiction over the entire controversy.

Delineation of the class in the damage action through the establishment of geographical boundries was undertaken. Evidence taken at a hearing for a temporary restraining order before Senior District Judge Kloeb as to the extent and locations of the complaints together with a knowledge of the prevailing winds was employed in ascertaining the geographical boundries to be employed. Without such geographical delineation any person who felt that he had been aggrieved by defendant's operation of its coal dock, regardless of the geographical remoteness of his claim, would have had the right to gain redress in this Court. Through this limitation the Court is able to give attention to the vast body of claims for which a reasonably plausible geographical basis can be determined, avoid placing great strain on its docket with numerous actions with only nuisance value, and preserve to the truly aggrieved individual whose claim is geographically remote his right of action (since he, not being a member of the class, is not bound by the judgment).

In furtherance of the policy of the 1966 amendment to Rule 23 to prevent one way intervention and to prevent as much as possible the solicitation of claims as well as to provide the court and the parties with some idea of the real magnitude of the controversy, the Court entered an order requiring all those desiring to present damage claims to enter an appearance in the case on or before November 8, 1968. * * *

No list of the potential members of the class in the damage suit was available nor could one have been compiled. Therefore the Court determined that the best possible service would be by publication of its orders delineating the class and requiring the presentation of claims together with the notice required by Rule 23(c)(2) of the Federal Rules of Civil Procedure. It was, however, determined that the publication in the Sandusky Register would not be a standard legal notice, but would be prominently placed so that the class members would better have the attention drawn to it. See, Booth v. General Dynamics Corp., 264 F.Supp. 465 (N.D.Ill.1965). As a result of this notice, seven hundred thirty-one (731) persons joined the damage action as plaintiffs, five hundred thirty-two (532) filed declinations to participate and several thousand others took no action.

Promptly thereafter, by agreement of the parties, the case was submitted to the Court upon evidence and written argument for a determination of the question of whether or not there was an actionable nuisance, and, if there was, whether plaintiffs were entitled to an injunction, to damages, or to both. The agreement provides that if the Court finds there is an actionable nuisance entitling plaintiffs to damages, a special master will be appointed to hear the evidence as to the amount of damages suffered by each of the seven hundred thirty-one individual parties plaintiff.

Several days were required to present the evidence, and very extensive briefs were filed by the parties, as a result of which the Court has come to the findings of fact and conclusions of law that are expressed in this opinion. * * *

Defendant determined to modernize the facilities to use them for the loading and storage of industrial coals, which are much smaller in size than heating coals, and include large quantities of "fines," which are actually coal dust.

* * *

These operations commenced in earnest about in September of 1967. As the time passed, and the amount of coal in storage on the defendant's pier increased, the citizens of Sandusky, particularly those near the pier, began to be troubled by black dust accumulating on their houses and furniture. By March of 1968, the situation was causing a great deal of difficulty, which continued through the summer into the early fall. It was obvious to the casual observer that coal dust was blowing off defendant's storage piles, and the black dust observed by the irate citizenry was assumed to be coal dust. The evidence in the case leaves no doubt whatever of the correctness of this assumption.* * *

At the trial of the case, the overwhelming weight of the evidence showed that persons who lived in various parts of Sandusky, and had had no more problem with dust and dirt than is common in cities, started to have serious problems when the defendant began to stockpile coal. Black, greasy, dirt, which was difficult to wash or clean off, accumulated on their sidewalks, porches, outdoor furniture, and automobiles.* * *

The factual conclusion is inescapable that the plaintiffs were injured in various respects, and to various extents, in their real estate, their personal property and effects, and in their persons by large quantities of coal dust blown from the shipping and storage facilities of the defendant.

As is frequently the case when the factual situation is clear and simple, the legal issues are of some complexity, and the defendant has used great technical skill in taking advantage of the tendency of the courts to use loose, ambiguous, and confusing language in discussing legal problems in this area. The problems arise because there is no sharp line of demarcation between the fields of negligence and nuisance, and in cases in the borderline area, the courts will use expressions relating to both fields interchangeably and imprecisely.

It is not this Court's intention to write a learned treatise on the law of nuisance. The facts of the present case bring it squarely within the following statement of the law of nuisance:

> "Strict or absolute liability is always applied where one does anything, or permits anything under his control or direction, to be done, without just cause or excuse, the necessary consequence of which interferes with or annoys another in the enjoyment of his legal rights. In such case the actor commits an intentional act involving a culpable wrong. Where the harm and resulting damage are the necessary consequences of just what the defendant is doing, or is incident to the activity itself or the manner in which it is conducted, the law of negligence has no application and the rule of absolute liability applies." Taylor v. Cincinnati, 143 Ohio St. 426, 432, 433, 55 N.E. 2d 724, 727, 155 A.L.R. 44 (1944).

The *Taylor* case, of course, bears not the remotest resemblance to the present case upon its facts, but it contains an elaborate treatise upon the law of nuisance generally which, while it might arguably be dictum, is generally followed as summarizing and expressing the law of Ohio upon the subject, and hence is binding upon this Court in this case.

The defendant makes much point in argument that it is and has been doing everything possible to prevent the difficulty, and was not negligent in its operation of coal storage and loading, and hence is not liable to the plaintiffs. Assuming this to be true, which plaintiffs strenuously deny, this argument may be answered by reference to an old case, citation unknown, dealing with the action of a man whose house was being shaken to pieces by blasting in a neighbor's quarry. The court held that it was no comfort to the plaintiff to know that his house was being demolished by the defendant in the most careful manner possible.

We are, happily, departing from the era in which it was considered proper for any commercial enterprise, in the name of those profits which are not a dirty word in Ohio, to pollute the atmosphere, earth, and water beyond the endurance of the general public. The defendant may or may not have succeeded to some of Commodore Vanderbilt's enterprises, but his attitude is an impermissible anachronism, and ill becomes defendant.

It is possible that this Court has the burden of deciding whether the plaintiffs must continue to suffer in defendant's filth, or become citizens of a ghost town on an abandoned railway line and a silted-up harbor. If so, the latter seems the lesser of two evils, especially in view of the maxim "Sufficient unto the day is the evil thereof." The present difficulty is certain, but the future disasters are uncertain. It may well be that the citizens of Sandusky can jump out of the frying pan and still avoid falling into the fire.

Plaintiffs are entitled to judgment in this case, but the form that the judgment should take presents serious questions. Certainly each of the individual plaintiffs is entitled to a judgment for the damages that he can show he has suffered as a result of defendant's activities. Necessarily, this means that if the amounts of damages to each of the seven hundred thirty-one plaintiffs cannot be stipulated, the evidence will have to be heard in order to establish them.

The only practical means of working out the damage matters appears to be to refer the matter to a special master, who should be a resident of the Sandusky area. The special master should fix a deadline to file a written statement of claim, either personally or by counsel, before the deadline. All counsel should consult with the special master to work out the forms and procedures for filing and processing the damage claims, with the objective of reducing to a minimum the number of claims which will have to be heard upon the evidence. With respect to claims which cannot be stipulated as to amount, those claimants whose recovery does not exceed the sum of one hundred dollars shall have to pay the fees of the special master for conducting the hearing upon their claims, together with the other costs of the hearing.

* * *

The question of whether the award of damages up to the time of commencement of the action, with the right to bring successive actions if the nuisance continues, affords an adequate remedy at law, is not a simple one. The weight of authority appears to be that since the nuisance is a continuing one, actions at law for damages are not an adequate remedy since a multiplicity of damage suits for each individual plaintiff would result. Hence equitable relief by way of injunction is permissible. However, just as the defendant has no right to destroy the property of the plaintiffs by its operations, it is questionable whether plaintiffs have a right to relief which would destroy the legitimate activities of defendant.

Under the principles of equity, the Court has broad powers to fashion effective relief, even though it may have to retain a continuing jurisdiction to modify or change orders granted.

A mandatory order of injunction must issue, requiring defendant to continue the various methods of dust control it has been employing on the coal docks, until further order of the Court.

* * *

From the evidence, it appears to the Court that it should be possible to work out economically feasible methods of controlling the emission of coal dust without inhibiting the operations of defendant's facilities, and even permitting defendant to expand the operations should it desire to do so.

Counsel should, within ten days, endeavor to agree upon an order, or should submit to the Court their separate forms of order, if they cannot agree, which will embody the foregoing conclusions, and vest in this Court a continuing jurisdiction until the coal dust problems are resolved.

APPENDIX

LEGAL NOTICE

TO ALL PERSONS CLAIMING TO BE AFFECTED BY COAL DUST FROM THE LOWER LAKE DOCKS OF THE NORFOLK & WESTERN RAILWAY COMPANY

IN THE UNITED STATES DISTRICT COURT FOR THE NORTHERN DISTRICT OF OHIO WESTERN DIVISION

Dallas Biechele, et al., Plaintiffs, vs. Norfolk & Western Railway Company, Defendant.	No. C 68-139

TO ALL PERSONS LIVING OR OWNING REAL ESTATE WITHIN THE AREA OUTLINED ON THE MAP BELOW, AND THE BOUNDARIES SET FORTH IN THE BODY OF THIS NOTICE:

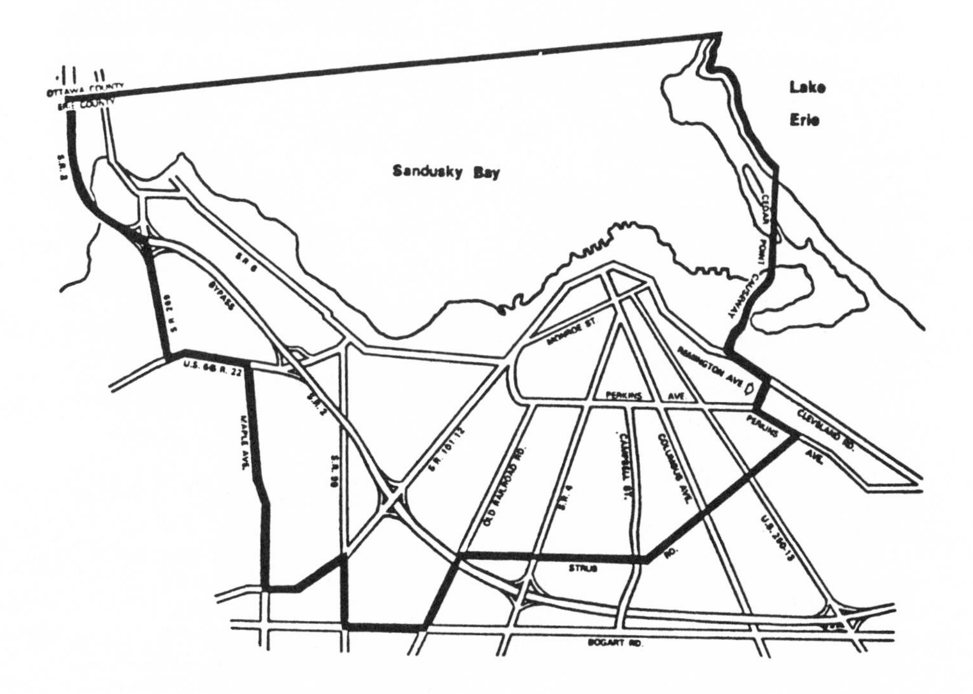

You are hereby notified that the District Court of the United States for the Northern District of Ohio, Western Division, has ordered that this action proceed as a class action, wherein all persons living or owning property within the following described boundaries are members of the class:

Commencing on the shore of Lake Erie at the northernmost point of Cedar Point; thence southeasterly along the shore of Lake Erie to the beginning of the Cedar Point Causeway; thence southerly along the center of the Cedar Point Causeway and Causeway Drive to the center of Cleveland Road; thence easterly along the center of Cleveland Road to Remington Avenue; thence southerly along the center of Remington Avenue to Perkins Avenue; thence easterly along the center of Perkins Avenue to Strub Road; thence southwesterly and westerly along the center of Strub Road to Old Railroad Road; thence southwesterly along the center of Old Railroad Road to Bogart Road; thence westerly along the center of Bogart road to State Route 99; thence northerly along the center of State Route 99 to State Routes 12 and 101; thence westerly along the center of State Routes 12 and 101 to Maple Avenue; thence northerly along the center of Maple Avenue to U.S. Route 6 and State Route 22; thence westerly along the center of U.S. Route 6 and State Route 22 to State Route 269; thence northerly along the center of State Route 269 to State Route 2; thence northerly along the center line of State Route 2 to its point of intersection with the Erie-Ottawa County Line; thence easterly across Sandusky Bay to the place of beginning.

IF YOU LIVE OR OWN REAL ESTATE WITHIN THOSE BOUNDARIES, you are a member of the class, and unless you make a written request to be excluded. YOU WILL BE INCLUDED IN AND BOUND BY THE JUDGMENT RENDERED BY THE COURT, whether it is favorable or unfavorable to you.

IF YOU WANT TO BE EXCLUDED from membership in the class, you must complete and sign the form headed REQUEST FOR EXCLUSION at the bottom of this notice or write a letter requesting exclusion, and mail it to the Clerk of the United States District Court, 1716 Spielbusch Avenue, Toledo, Ohio, 43624, or have your lawyer do this for you.

IF YOU DO NOT WANT TO BE EXCLUDED, but want to have your own lawyer represent you, you should instruct him to enter your appearance.

This action involves two matters, a claim for an order of injunction restraining the defendant Norfolk & Western Railway Company from continuing the activities alleged to cause coal dust to be blown about, and claims for damages to person and property alleged to have been caused by coal dust.

As to the claim for injunction, all persons living or owning real estate within the boundaries described above will be bound by the judgment in this action whether it is favorable or unfavorable, unless they request exclusion. They need take no action of any kind to be assured of the protection of an order of injunction if one is ultimately issued.

As to claims for damages to person or property, regardless of the outcome of this lawsuit, all such claims will be barred unless the person asserting such claim enters his appearance in this action on or before November 8, 1968.

IF YOU WANT TO MAKE A CLAIM FOR DAMAGES, you may preserve your right to do so by completeing the form headed ENTRY OF APPEARANCE at the bottom of this notice, or by writing a letter saying that you enter your appearance in this lawsuit, and mailing the notice or letter to the Clerk of the United States District Court, 1716 Spielbusch Avenue, Toledo, Ohio, 43624, or by having your lawyer do this for you.

ALL REQUESTS FOR EXCLUSION OR ENTRIES OR APPEARANCE MUST BE FILED WITH THE CLERK OR POSTMARKED NO LATER THAN MIDNIGHT ON FRIDAY, NOVEMBER 8, 1968, OR THEY WILL BE INEFFECTUAL.

This action is presently at issue, and may be called for hearing by the Court at any time after November 8, 1968.

THE COURT'S ORDER THAT THIS ACTION SHALL PROCEED AS A CLASS ACTION IS NOT A DETERMINATION OF THE MERITS OF THE CLAIMS ASSERTED, AND IS ONLY A PRELIMINARY PROCEDURAL DETERMINATION AS TO THE POTENTIAL PARTIES INVOLVED. THE DECISION AS TO WHETHER ANY INJUNCTIVE RELIEF WILL BE GRANTED OR ANY DAMAGES AWARDED WILL FOLLOW A TRIAL ON THE MERITS OF THE ACTION.

DON J. YOUNG
United States District Judge

REQUEST FOR EXCLUSION

Dallas Biechele, et al.,
Plaintiffs,
v. No. C 68-139
Norfolk & Western Railway Company,
Defendant.

The undersigned requests to be excluded from the class of parties plaintiff to the above captioned action.

Name ....
Address ....
....

ENTRY OF APPEARANCE

Dallas Biechele, et al.,
Plaintiffs,
v. No. C 68-139
Norfolk & Western Railway Company.
Defendant.

I hereby enter my appearance as a member of the class of parties plaintiff to the above action.

Name ....
Address ....
....

ZAHN v. INTERNATIONAL PAPER CO.

414 U.S. 291 (1973)

MR. JUSTICE WHITE delivered the opinion of the Court.

Petitioners, asserting that they were owners of property fronting on Lake Champlain in Orwell, Vermont, brought this action in the District Court on behalf of a class consisting of themselves and 200 lakefront property owners and lessees. They sought damages from International Paper Co., a New York corporation, for allegedly having permitted discharges from its pulp and paper-making plant, located in New York, to flow into Ticonderoga Creek and to be carried by that stream into Lake Champlain, thereby polluting the waters of the lake and damaging the value and utility of the surrounding properties. The suit was brought as a diversity action, jurisdiction assertedly resting on 28 U.S.C. § 1332 (a)(1). The claim of each of the named plaintiffs was found to satisfy the $10,000 jurisdictional amount, but the District Court was convinced "to a legal certainty" that not every individual owner in the class had suffered pollution damages in excess of $10,000. Reading *Snyder* v. *Harris*, 394 U. S. 332 (1969), as precluding maintenance of the action by any member of the class whose separate and distinct claim did not individually satisfy the jurisdictional amount and concluding that it would not be feasible to define a class of property owners each of whom had more than a $10,000 claim, the District Court then refused to permit the suit to proceed as a class action. 53 F. R. D. 430 (Vt. 1971). A divided Court of Appeals affirmed, 469 F. 2d 1033 (CA2 1972), principally on the authority of *Snyder* v. *Harris, supra*. We granted the petition for writ of certiorari, 410 U. S. 925 (1973).

The Court of Appeals correctly held that this case is governed by the rationale of this Court's prior cases construing the statutes defining the jurisdiction of the District Court. We therefore affirm its judgment.

From the outset, Congress has provided that suits between citizens of different States are maintainable in the district courts only if the "matter in controversy" exceeds the statutory minimum, now set at $10,000. 28 U. S. C. § 1332 (a).* * *

The meaning of the "matter in controversy" language of § 1332 as it applied to class actions under Rule 23 reached this Court in *Snyder* v. *Harris, supra*, the occasion being a division of opinion in the courts of appeals as to whether the 1966 amendments to Rule 23 had changed the jurisdictional-amount requirement of § 1332 as applied to class actions involving separate and distinct claims. None of the named plaintiffs and none of the unnamed members of the class before the Court alleged claims in excess of the requisite amount. It was nevertheless urged that in class action situations, particularly in light of the 1966 amendments to the rule, aggregation of separate and distinct claims should be permitted. The Court was of a contrary view, holding that class actions involving plaintiffs with separate and distinct claims were subject to the usual rule that a federal district court can assume jurisdiction over only those plaintiffs presenting claims exceeding the $10,000 minimum specified in §1332. Aggregation of claims was impermissible, and the federal court was without jurisdiction where none of the plaintiffs presented a claim of the requisite size. The Court unmistakably rejected the notion that the 1966 amendments to Rule 23 were intended to effect, or effected, any change in the meaning and application of the jurisdictional-amount requirement insofar as class actions are concerned.

> "The doctrine that separate and distinct claims could not be aggregated was never, and is not now, based upon the categories of old Rule 23 or of any rule of procedure. That doctrine is based rather upon this Court's interpretation of the statutory phrase 'matter in controversy.' The interpretation of this phrase as precluding aggregation substantially predates the 1938 Federal Rules of Civil Procedure. . . . Nothing in the amended Rule 23 changes this doctrine. . . . The fact that judgments under class actions formerly classified as spurious may now have the same effect as claims brought under the joinder provisions is certainly no reason to treat them *differently* from joined actions for purposes of aggregation." 394 U. S., at 336–337.

The Court also refused to reconsider its prior constructions of the "matter in controversy" phrase, concluding that it should not do so where Congress, with complete understanding of how the courts had construed the statute, had not changed the governing language and down through the years had continued to specify and had progressively increased the jurisdictional amount necessary for instituting suit in the federal courts.

None of the plaintiffs in *Snyder* v. *Harris* alleged a claim exceeding $10,000, but there is no doubt that the rationale of that case controls this one. As previously indicated, *Snyder* invoked the well-established rule that each of several plaintiffs asserting separate and distinct claims must satisfy the jurisdictional-amount requirement if his claim is to survive a motion to dismiss. This rule plainly mandates not only that there may be no aggregation and that the entire case must be dismissed where none of the plaintiffs claims more than $10,000 but also requires that any plaintiff without the jurisdictional amount must be dismissed from the case, even though others allege jurisdictionally sufficient claims.

This follows inescapably from the Court's heavy reliance on *Clark* v. *Paul Gray, Inc., supra*, where only one of several plaintiffs had a sufficiently large claim and all other plaintiffs were dismissed from the suit. Moreover, the Court cited with approval the decision in *Alvarez* v. *Pan American Life Insurance Co.*, 375 F. 2d 992 (CA5), cert. denied, 389 U. S. 827 (1967), which was decided after the 1966 amendments to Rule 23 and which involved a class action with only one member of the class having a claim sufficient to satisfy § 1332. Only that claim was held within the jurisdiction of the District Court.

We conclude, as we must, that the Court of Appeals in the case before us accurately read and applied *Snyder* v. *Harris*: Each plaintiff in a Rule 23 (b)(3) class action must satisfy the jurisdictional amount, and any plaintiff who does not must be dismissed from the case—"one plaintiff may not ride in on another's coattails." 469 F. 2d, at 1035.

Neither are we inclined to overrule *Snyder* v. *Harris* nor to change the Court's longstanding construction of the "matter in controversy" requirement of § 1332. The Court declined a like invitation in *Snyder* v. *Harris* after surveying all relevant considerations and concluding that to do so would undermine the purpose and intent of Congress in providing that plaintiffs in diversity cases must present claims in excess of the specified jurisdictional amount. At this time, we have no good reason to disagree with *Snyder* v. *Harris* or with the historic construction of the jurisdictional statutes, left undisturbed by Congress over these many years.

It also seems to us that the application of the jurisdictional-amount requirement to class actions was so plainly etched in the federal courts prior to 1966 that had there been any thought of departing from these decisions and, in so doing, of calling into question the accepted approach to cases involving ordinary joinder of plaintiffs with separate and distinct claims, some express statement of that intention would surely have appeared, either in the amendments themselves or in the official commentaries. But we find not a trace to this effect. As the Court thought in *Snyder* v. *Harris*, the matter must rest there, absent further congressional action.

Affirmed.

MR. JUSTICE BRENNAN, with whom MR. JUSTICE DOUGLAS and MR. JUSTICE MARSHALL join, dissenting.

The Court holds that, in a diversity suit, a class action under Fed. Rule Civ. Proc. 23 (b)(3) is maintainable only when every member of the class, whether an appearing party or not, meets the $10,000 jurisdictional-amount requirement of 28 U.S.C. § 1332 (a). It finds this ruling compelled by the "rationale of this Court's prior cases construing the statutes defining the jurisdiction of the District Court." I disagree and respectfully dissent.* * *

For additional information on class actions see:

1. Note, *Rule 23 Class Action Enforcement of the Clean Air Act of 1970*, 7 U. RICH. L. R. 549 (1973).
2. Lamm & Davison, *Environmental Class Actions for Damages*, 16 ROCKY M. MIN. LAW. INST. 59 (1971).

---

3. INTERVENTION

Intervention is a procedure under which a person may present his position before an agency or a court even though he was not a party to the action originally. In the early history of real property law, intervention was useful where someone brought suit against another person in a dispute over legal title to property. A third party claiming he, rather then the parties in the suit, has legal title to the property would want to introduce himself into, or **to intervene**, in the legal proceeding. Thus, when the court hears the evidence relating to ownership of the property, it would also hear evidence from the third party which it will take into consideration in making its determination.

Intervention can be useful in environmental matters. For example, in a hearing for granting a license to establish a nuclear plant, a power company would appear before the appropriate governmental entity. However, there may very well be an individual or a class living in the area and affected by the action who would like to participate in the proceeding. Building a nuclear plant could result in the degradation of the environment. By the use of this procedural device, it may be possible under some circumstances for a third party to participate in some proceedings, or to intervene.

In federal courts, Rule 24 of the Federal Rules of Civil Procedure describes the circumstances under which intervention may take place. There may be intervention as of right where it is so provided by statute and where the applicant has an interest in the subject matter and it is alleged that the ongoing suit may impair the applicants' rights; or there may be permissive intervention where the court may in its discretion permit intervention. Most states have similar rules describing the circumstances under which a person may intervene.

In general, intervention may be a useful device in proceedings involving an applicant and a governmental entity in which it would be advantageous for some representative of the public at large to be heard.

The brief excerpt from *Ladue v. Goodhead* contains some general principles relating to intervention under a state procedure.

RULE 24, FEDERAL RULES OF CIVIL PROCEDURE

Rule 24. Intervention

(a) Intervention of Right. Upon timely application anyone shall be permitted to intervene in an action: (1) when a statute of the United States confers an unconditional right to intervene; or (2) when the applicant claims an interest relating to the property or transaction which is the subject of the action and he is so situated that the disposition of the action may as a practical matter impair or impede his ability to protect that interest, unless the applicant's interest is adequately represented by existing parties.

(b) Permissive Intervention. Upon timely application anyone may be permitted to intervene in an action: (1) when a statute of the United States confers a conditional right to intervene; or (2) when an applicant's claim or defense and the main action have a question of law or fact in common. When a party to an action relies for ground of claim or defense upon any statute or executive order administered by a federal or state governmental officer or agency or upon any regulation, order, requirement, or agreement issued or made pursuant to the statute or executive order, the officer or agency upon timely application may be permitted to intervene in the action. In exercising its discretion the court shall consider whether the intervention will unduly delay or prejudice the adjudication of the rights of the original parties.

(c) Procedure. A person desiring to intervene shall serve a motion to intervene upon the parties as provided in Rule 5. The motion shall state the grounds therefor and shall be accompanied by a pleading setting forth the claim or defense for which intervention is sought. The same procedure shall be followed when a statute of the United States gives a right to intervene. When the constitutionality of an act of Congress affecting the public interest is drawn in question in any action to which the United States or an officer, agency, or employee thereof is not a party, the court shall notify the Attorney General of the United States as provided in Title 28, U.S.C. § 2403.

LADUE v. GOODHEAD

44 N.Y.S. 2d 783
181 Misc. 807 (Erie County Ct., 1943).

WARD, Judge

The law of this forum for the intervention of a third person into a pending action as a party is set forth in Section 193 of the Civil Practice Act, which provides, in part:

"1. The court may determine the controversy as between the parties before it where it can do so without prejudice to the rights of others or by saving their rights; but where a complete determination of the controversy cannot be had without the presence of other parties the court must direct them to be brought in."

"3. Where a person not a party to the action has an interest in the subject thereof, * * * and makes application to the court to be made a party, it must direct him to be brought in by the proper amendment."

Generally, it is the duty of the court to direct that necessary parties be brought in, and to refuse the determination of the controversy affecting their rights, until they are all made parties to the action. Mahr v. Nowich Union Fire Ins. Soc., 127 N.Y. 452, 459, 28 N.E. 391. The purpose of Section 193, Civil Practice Act, is to avoid circuity and multiplicity of suits and to encourage and authorize the determination of damage and liability in one suit, in the sound, judicial discretion of the court. Mirsky v. Seaich Realty Co., 256 App.Div. 658. 11 N.Y.S.2d 191, 194; Lepel High Frequency Laboratories, Inc., v. Capita, 168 Misc. 583, 6 N.Y.S.2d 171,172, affirmed 256 App.Div. 804, 9 N.Y.S.2d 896. The words "the interest in the subject" of the action mean a direct interest in the cause of action pleaded, which would allow the intervener to litigate a material fact in the complaint. Bulova v. E. L. Barnett, Inc., 194 App.Div. 418, 185 N.Y.S. 424, 426. "This interest must be individual and not public, direct and not indirect, present and not remote. Interest in the result or outcome of the action will not suffice." Town of Irondequoit v. Monroe County, 171 Misc. 125, 11 N.Y.S.2d 933, 939, and see cited cases. Where the plaintiff seeks a money judgment merely, he cannot be compelled under this Section 193 to bring a third person into the action as a party upon the stranger's application. Brooklyn Cooperage Co. v. A. Sherman Lumber Co., 220 N.Y. 642, 643, 115 N.E. 715. In order to bring in a new party, the application must be based upon a moving affidavit or affidavits containing sufficient probative facts. George A. Moore & Co. v. Heymann, 207 App.Div. 416, 202 N.Y.S. 99, 101. * * *

"An intervener is a person who voluntarily interposes in an action or other proceeding with the leave of the court." (Black's Dictionary) Intervention in practice may be defined as: "A proceeding in a suit or action by which a third person is permitted by the court to make himself a party, either joining the plaintiff in claiming what is sought by the complaint, or uniting with the defendant in resisting the claims of the plaintiff, or demanding something adversely to both of them." Black's Dictionary. * * *

---

4. THE GOVERNMENT AS PLAINTIFF

Under some circumstances a governmental agency may seek to bring an action against an individual to enforce a regulation pursuant to the authority given to it by the statute creating the agency. An issue may arise whether the agency has the statutory authority to do so. Governmental agencies exist by virtue of having been created by a legislative body and their authority is determined by the statute that created them. Some governmental agencies have the authority to bring law suits; some do not. For those that do, their power is usually limited to specific circumstances.

The second limitation on governmental agencies to bring a lawsuit is procedural. The statute will ordinarily set forth the kind of notice to be given and certain prior activities required before bringing suit, such as negotiation of the claim. Where such a prescribed procedure exists, if the governmental agency brings suit without following it, the defendant will claim that the suit is premature or unauthorized.

In addition to the statutory limitations on the ability of a governmental entity to bring a law suit, there is the constitutional limitation imposed by the due process clause. Even if the agency follows the letter of the law, if the procedure as applied to the circumstances does not provide the defendant with a fair opportunity to be heard, there is a basis for an argument that procedural due process has been violated.

United States v. Bishop Processing Co. illustrates the consequence of an agency failure to comply with the prescribed procedure before bringing suit. *Huron Cement Company v. Detroit* involves a challenge to a municipal attempt to enforce an ordinance relating to a subject concurrently regulated by the federal government.

UNITED STATES
v.
BISHOP PROCESSING COMPANY

287 F. Supp. 624 (D. Md. 1968)

THOMSEN, Chief Judge.

This action has been brought by the United States under the Clean Air Act (the Act), 42 U.S.C. § 1857 et seq., particularly section 108(g) (1) of the Act, as amended November 21, 1967, 81 Stat. 496, 507, now codified as 42 U.S.C. § 1857d(g) (1). The government seeks to enjoin Bishop Processing Company (the defendant), the operator of a rendering and animal reduction plant near Bishop, Worcester County, Maryland, from discharging malodorous air pollutants, which it is alleged, move across the state line and pollute the air in and around Selbyville, Delaware. Defendant has filed a motion to dismiss the complaint on four grounds, namely:* * * (III) that the requisite administrative steps have not been adequately defined or properly concluded as required by law; and (IV) that remedial action concerning defendant's alleged pollution was and is currently pending in a state court in Maryland, and that this Court cannot take jurisdiction under the Act while such an action is pending.

* * *

The administrative proceeding which led to this suit was initiated by a request from the Delaware State Air Pollution Authority under section 1857d(d) (1) (A). In response to that request the Secretary called a conference, which was held in Selbyville, Delaware, on November 9 and 10, 1965. The statute specified the parties who should be invited to participate in such a conference, namely, representatives of the air pollution control agencies of the states and municipalities concerned, and provided that the agencies called to attend such conference might bring such persons as they desired to the conference. Bishop was not invited to the conference and did not request an opportunity to participate.

Pursuant to section 1857d(e) the Secretary forwarded to the participants a summary of the conference discussions and recommendations for remedial action. Those recommendations called upon the Maryland authorities to require Bishop to complete certain remedial action on or before September 1, 1966. The recommended remedial action was not taken.

Under section 1857d(f) (1) the Secretary is authorized to call a public hearing if "at the conclusion of the period so allowed, such remedial action or other action which in the judgment of the Secretary is reasonably calculated to secure abatement of such pollution has not been taken."

Appropriate findings to that effect were included in a Notice of Public Hearing Concerning Interstate Air Pollution in the Selbyville, Delaware-Bishop, Maryland area, which the Secretary issued on April 21, 1967.* * *

The composition of the Board and the hearing procedures were in accordance with Part 81 of Title 42, C.F.R., set out in the Notice of Proposed Rule Making, dated March 28, 1967, published in the Federal Register on April 3, 1967.

The Hearing Board met on May 17 and May 18, 1967, heard testimony and received other evidence. Bishop was represented by counsel, who made and raised

38 objections to evidence and other points, challenging inter alia the authority and composition of the Hearing Board.

The Hearing Board made findings and recommendations and forwarded them to the Secretary, as required by section 1857d(f) (2). Such a Board is not authorized to issue any order, but its recommendations are not subject to review or modification by the Secretary, who is required by law to forward the findings and recommendations of the Board to the polluter, together with a notice specifying a reasonable time (not less than six months) to secure abatement of the pollution. See section 1857d(f) (3). Accordingly, on May 25, 1967, the Secretary sent the following notice to Bishop:

"THE SECRETARY OF HEALTH, EDUCATION, AND WELFARE WASHINGTON

In the Matter of

INTERSTATE AIR POLLUTION IN SELBYVILLE, DELAWARE-BISHOP, MARYLAND, AREA

NOTICE

"There are attached hereto, and made a part hereof, the Findings, Conclusions, and Recommendations, dated May 19, 1967, of the Hearing Board convened pursuant to the provisions of section 105(e) (1) of the Clean Air Act [42 U.S.C. 1857d(e) (1)] which held a public hearing in the matter of the interstate air pollution in the Selbyville, Delaware-Bishop, Maryland area.

"In accordance with section 105(e) (3) of the Clean Air Act [42 U.S.C. 1857d(e) (3)] the Bishop Processing Company, Bishop, Maryland is hereby notified and directed to cease and desist from discharging malodorous air pollutants and to abate such air pollution not later than December 1, 1967, by the installation, completion and placing into operation adequate and effective control systems and devices, as recommended by the Hearing Board.

"Dated: May 25, 1967.

(S) John W. Gardner

Secretary"

The Secretary is not authorized to impose any sanctions for failure to comply with such a "notice" and what is "directed" therein. What the Secretary may do is set out in section 1857d(g) (1), which provides in pertinent part:

> "If action reasonably calculated to secure abatement of the pollution within the time specified in the notice following the public hearing is not taken, the Secretary—
>
> "(1) in the case of the pollution of air which is endangering the health or welfare of persons (A) in a State other than that in which the discharge or discharges (causing or contributing to such pollution) originate, * * * may request the Attorney General to bring a suit on behalf of the United States in the appropriate United States district court to secure abatement of the pollution."

Section 1857d(h) provides:

> "The court shall receive in evidence in any suit brought in a United States court under subsection (g) of this section a transcript of the proceedings before the board and a copy of the board's recommendations and shall receive such further evidence as the court in its discretion deems proper. The court, giving due consideration to the practicability of complying with such standards as may be applicable and to the physical and economic feasibility of securing abatement of any pollution proved, shall have jurisdiction to enter such judgment, and orders

enforcing such judgment, as the public interest and the equities of the case may require.* * *

To support its contention that the requisite administrative steps have not been adequately defined nor properly concluded as required by law, defendant argues several points, which will be considered below. Preliminarily, however, the nature of the administrative proceedings and of the present suit should be reviewed. The history of those proceedings has been outlined above.

The *conference*, which was held in 1965, was a conference between representatives of public agencies to consider the problem. Due process did not require that the alleged polluter be invited to that conference, which was neither a rule-making nor an adjudicative hearing. The 1967 amendments do require that in the future, thirty days notice of such a conference be given by publication, and that "interested parties" be given an opportunity to present their views. Section 1857d(d) (2). The Report of the House Committee indicates that the purpose of this amendment was to provide the conferees with the broadest review of the pollution problems in a given area. The amendment was not required by due process or by any provisions of the APA.

The *hearing* in May 1967, some eighteen months after the conference, was held in strict accordance with the provisions of the Act. Section 1857d(f) provides, with minor amendments made in November 1967:

"(1) If, at the conclusion of the period so allowed, such remedial action or other action which in the judgment of the Secretary is reasonably calculated to secure abatement of such pollution has not been taken, the Secretary shall call a public hearing, to be held in or near one or more of the places where the discharge or discharges causing or contributing to such pollution originated, before a hearing board of five or more persons appointed by the Secretary. Each State in which any discharge causing or contributing to such pollution originates and each State claiming to be adversely affected by such pollution shall be given an opportunity to select one member of such hearing board and each Federal department, agency, or instrumentality having a substantial interest in the subject matter as determined by the Secretary shall be given an opportunity to select one member of such hearing board, and one member shall be a representative of the appropriate interstate air pollution agency if one exists, and not less than a majority of such hearing board shall be persons other than officers or employees of the Department of Health, Education, and Welfare. At least three weeks' prior notice of such hearing shall be given to the State, interstate, and municipal air pollution control agencies called to attend such hearing and to the alleged polluter or polluters. All interested parties shall be given a reasonable opportunity to present evidence to such hearing board.

"(2) On the basis of evidence presented at such hearing, the hearing board shall make findings as to whether pollution referred to in subsection (a) of this section is occurring and whether effective progress toward abatement thereof is being made. If the hearing board finds such pollution is occurring and effective progress toward abatement thereof is not being made it shall make recommendations to the Secretary concerning the measures, if any, which it finds to be reasonable and suitable to secure abatement of such pollution.

"(3) The Secretary shall send such findings and recommendations to the person or persons discharging any matter causing or contributing to such pollution; to air pollution control agencies of the State or States and of the municipality or municipalities where such discharge or discharges originate; and to any interstate air pollution control agency whose jurisdictional area includes any such municipality, together with a notice specifying a reasonable time (not less than six months) to secure abatement of such pollution."

The Secretary was not authorized before the 1967 amendments and is not now authorized to impose any sanctions for failure to comply with such a "notice" and what is "directed" therein. What the Secretary *may* do is set out in section 1857d(g), quoted in the first part of this opinion, namely, ask the Attorney General to bring such an action as the present suit.

The *hearing*, therefore, is not an adjudicative hearing. It is not subject to the provisions of the APA dealing with adjudicative hearings, 5 U.S.C.A. § 555. The conference and the hearing were merely the statutory prerequisites to the bringing of the lawsuit.* * *

(a)Defendant complains because no procedural rules for hearings called for by section 1857d(f) (1) were adopted by the Secretary before the hearing in defendant's case. Defendant's case was the first case which had ever proceeded to hearing under the Act, and this suit is the first suit ever filed by the government under the Act.* * *

Since that was the first hearing to be held under the Act, and since the procedures established for that hearing were appropriate therefor, the Court finds no violation of due process by reason of the fact that similar procedures for future hearings had not been adopted. The equal protection argument made by defendant is not supported by the present record, since it does not appear that any other hearings have ever been held, or that any different hearing procedures have ever been adopted.

(b)Defendant argues that the issuance of air quality criteria and control emission standards are a prerequisite to an administrative hearing under section 1857d(f) (1) and such an action as this under section 1857d(g). There is no merit in this contention. Courts of equity have always had the power to abate nuisances. Section 1857d gives the district courts jurisdiction to abate "pollution of the air in any State or States which endangers the health and welfare of any persons", subject to other provisions in the Act which limit the jurisdiction of the federal courts under section 1857d(g) (1) to cases which properly come within the commerce power.

* * *

* * *Under section 1857d(c) (4), the Secretary may now, when an air quality standard is violated, request that suit be instituted without invoking the conference-hearing procedure. Separate provisions are made in that subsection for judicial action in such a case.

* * *

Defendant's final challenge to the complaint is that this Court cannot take jurisdiction under the Act because of a suit pending in the Circuit Court for Worcester County, Maryland, filed against defendant on February 2, 1967, by the State of Maryland on the relation of the Maryland State Board of Health and Mental Hygiene, the Maryland State Department of Health, and the Maryland Department of Water Resources, raising similar issues, inter alia. It is true that the philosophy of the Act is not to displace but to encourage state, local and interstate action to abate air pollution. But a pending suit in a state court does not oust the jurisdiction of a district court over such a suit as this. The action in this Court arises out of proceedings instituted under the federal Act a year and a half before the filing of the state court suit, which has not proceeded to judgment. Moreover, it appears that the state court suit is addressed primarily to defendant's water pollution. Comity does not require this Court to abstain from proceeding with the present action instituted by the United States.

Defendant's motion to dismiss must be and it is hereby denied.

HURON CEMENT COMPANY v. DETROIT

362 U.S. 440 (1960)

MR. JUSTICE STEWART delivered the opinion of the Court.

This appeal from a judgment of the Supreme Court of Michigan draws in question the constitutional validity of certain provisions of Detroit's Smoke Abatement Code as applied to ships owned by the appellant and operated in interstate commerce.

The appellant is a Michigan corporation, engaged in the manufacture and sale of cement. It maintains a fleet of five vessels which it uses to transport cement from its mill in Alpena, Michigan, to distributing plants located in various states bordering the Great Lakes. Two of the ships, the S. S. *Crapo* and the S. S. *Boardman*, are equipped with hand-fired Scotch marine boilers. While these vessels are docked for loading and unloading it is necessary, in order to operate deck machinery, to keep the boilers fired and to clean the fires periodically. When the fires are cleaned, the ship's boiler stacks emit smoke which in density and duration exceeds the maximum standards allowable under the Detroit Smoke Abatement Code. Structural alterations would be required in order to insure compliance with the Code.

Criminal proceedings were instituted in the Detroit Recorder's Court against the appellant and its agents for violations of the city law during periods when the vessels were docked at the Port of Detroit. The appellant brought an action in the State Circuit Court to enjoin the city from further prosecuting the pending litigation in the Recorder's Court, and from otherwise enforcing the smoke ordinance against its vessels, "except where the emission of smoke is caused by the improper firing or the improper use of the equipment upon said vessels." The Circuit Court refused to grant relief and the Supreme Court of Michigan affirmed, 355 Mich. 227, 93 N. W. 2d 888. An appeal was lodged here, and we noted probable jurisdiction, 361 U. S. 806.

In support of the claim that the ordinance cannot constitutionally be applied to appellant's ships, two basic arguments are advanced. First, it is asserted that since the vessels and their equipment, including their boilers, have been inspected, approved and licensed to operate in interstate commerce in accordance with a comprehensive system of regulation enacted by Congress, the City of Detroit may not legislate in such a way as, in effect, to impose additional or inconsistent standards. Secondly, the argument is made that even if Congress has not expressly pre-empted the field, the municipal ordinance "materially affects interstate commerce in matters where uniformity is necessary." We have concluded that neither of these contentions can prevail, and that the Federal Constitution does not prohibit application to the appellant's vessels of the criminal provisions of the Detroit ordinance.

The ordinance was enacted for the manifest purpose of promoting the health and welfare of the city's inhabitants. Legislation designed to free from pollution the very air that people breathe clearly falls within the exercise of even the most traditional concept of what is compendiously known as the police power. In the exercise of that power, the states and their instrumentalities may act, in many areas of interstate commerce and maritime activities, concurrently with the federal government.

* * *

The basic limitations upon local legislative power in this area are clear enough. The controlling principles have been reiterated over the years in a host of this Court's decisions. Evenhanded local regulation to effectuate a legitimate local public interest is valid unless pre-empted by federal action. *Erie R. Co.* v. *New York*, 233 U. S. 671; *Oregon-Washington Co.* v. *Washington*, 270 U. S. 87; *Napier* v. *Atlantic Coast Line*, 272 U. S. 605; *Missouri Pacific Co.* v. *Porter*, 273 U. S. 341; *Service Transfer Co.* v. *Virginia*, 359 U. S. 171, or unduly burdensome on maritime activities or interstate commerce. *Minnesota* v. *Barber*, 136 U. S. 313; *Morgan* v. *Virginia*, 328 U. S. 373; *Bibb* v. *Navajo Freight Lines*, 359 U. S. 520.

In determining whether state regulation has been pre-empted by federal action, "the intent to supersede the exercise by the State of its police power as to matters not covered by the Federal legislation is not to be inferred from the mere fact that Congress has seen fit to circumscribe its regulation and to occupy a limited field. In other words, such intent is not to be implied unless the act of Congress fairly interpreted is in actual conflict with the law of the State."* * *

In determining whether the state has imposed an undue burden on interstate commerce, it must be borne in mind that the Constitution when "conferring upon Congress the regulation of commerce, . . . never intended to cut the States off from legislating on all subjects relating to the health, life, and safety of their citizens, though the legislation might indirectly affect the commerce of the country. Legislation, in a great variety of ways, may affect commerce and persons engaged in it without constituting a regulation of it, within the meaning of the Constitution." *Sherlock* v. *Alling*, 93 U. S. 99, 103; *Austin* v. *Tennessee*, 179 U. S. 343; *Louisville & Nashville R. Co.* v. *Kentucky*, 183 U. S. 503; *The Minnesota Rate Cases*, 230 U. S. 352; *Boston & Maine R. Co.* v. *Armburg*, 285 U. S. 234; *Collins* v. *American Buslines, Inc.*, 350 U. S. 528. But a state may not impose a burden which materially affects interstate commerce in an area where uniformity of regulation is necessary.* * *

As is apparent on the face of the legislation, however, the purpose of the federal inspection statutes is to insure the seagoing safety of vessels subject to inspection. Thus 46 U. S. C. § 392 (c) makes clear that inspection of boilers and related equipment is for the purpose of seeing to it that the equipment "may be safely employed in the service proposed." The safety of passengers, 46 U. S. C. § 391 (a), and of the crew, 46 U. S. C. § 391 (b), is the criterion. The thrust of the federal inspecton laws is clearly limited to affording protection from the perils of maritime navigation. Cf. *Ace Waterways* v. *Fleming*, 98 F. Supp. 666. See also *Steamship Co.* v. *Joliffe*, 2 Wall. 450.

By contrast, the sole aim of the Detroit ordinance is the elimination of air pollution to protect the health and enhance the cleanliness of the local community. Congress recently recognized the importance and legitimacy of such a purpose, when in 1955 it provided:

> "[I]n recognition of the dangers to the public health and welfare, injury to agricultural crops and livestock, damage to and deterioration of property, and hazards to air and ground transportation, from air pollution, it is hereby declared to be the policy of Congress to preserve and protect the primary responsibilities and rights of the States and local governments in controlling air pollution,* * *

Congressional recognition that the problem of air pollution is peculiarly a matter of state and local concern is manifest in this legislation. Such recognition is underlined in the Senate Committee Report:

> "The committee recognizes that it is the primary responsibility of State and local governments to prevent air pollution. The bill does not propose any exercise of police power by the Federal Government and no provision in it invades the sovereignty of States, counties or cities." S. Rep. No. 389, 84th Cong., 1st Sess. 3.

We conclude that there is no overlap between the scope of the federal ship inspection laws and that of the municipal ordinance here involved. For this reason we cannot find that the federal inspection legislation has pre-empted local action. To hold otherwise would be to ignore the teaching of this Court's decisions which enjoin seeking out conflicts between state and federal regulation where none clearly exists. *Savage* v. *Jones*, 225 U. S. 501; *Welch Co.* v. *New Hampshire*, 306 U. S. 79; *Maurer* v. *Hamilton*, 309 U. S. 598.

An additional argument is advanced, however, based not upon the mere existence of the federal inspection standards, but upon the fact that the appellant's vessels were actually licensed, 46 U. S. C. § 263, and enrolled, 46 U. S. C. §§ 259–260, by the national government. It is asserted that the vessels have thus been given a dominant federal right to the use of the navigable waters of the United States, free from the local impediment that would be imposed by the Detroit ordinance.

The scope of the privilege granted by the federal licensing scheme has been well delineated. A state may not exclude from its waters a ship operating under a federal license. *Gibbons* v. *Ogden*, 9 Wheat. 1. A state may not require a local occupation license, in addition to that federally granted, as a condition precedent to the use of its waters.* * *

The mere possession of a federal license, however, does not immunize a ship from the operation of the normal incidents of local police power, not constituting a direct regulation of commerce. Thus, a federally licensed vessel is not, as such, exempt from local pilotage laws,* * *

Indeed this Court has gone so far as to hold that a state, in the exercise of its police power, may actually seize and pronounce the forfeiture of a vessel "licensed for the coasting trade, under the laws of the United States, while engaged in that trade." *Smith* v. *Maryland*, 18 How. 71, 74. The present case obviously does not even approach such an extreme, for the Detroit ordinance requires no more than compliance with an orderly and reasonable scheme of community regulation. The ordinance does not exclude a licensed vessel from the Port of Detroit, nor does it destroy the right of free passage. We cannot hold that the local regulation so burdens the federal license as to be constitutionally invalid.* * *

The claim that the Detroit ordinance, quite apart from the effect of federal legislation, imposes as to the appellant's ships an undue burden on interstate commerce needs no extended discussion. State regulation, based on the police power, which does not discriminate against interstate commerce or operate to disrupt its required uniformity, may constitutionally stand.* * *

It is a regulation of general application, designed to better the health and welfare of the community. And while the appellant argues that other local governments might impose differing requirements as to air pollution, it has pointed to none. The record contains nothing to suggest the existence of any such competing or conflicting local regulations. Cf. *Bibb* v. *Navajo Freight Lines*, 359 U. S. 520. We conclude that no impermissible burden on commerce has been shown.

The judgment is affirmed.

MR. JUSTICE DOUGLAS, with whom MR. JUSTICE FRANKFURTER concurs, dissenting.

The Court treats this controversy as if it were merely an inspection case with the City of Detroit supplementing a federal inspection system as the State of Washington did in *Kelly* v. *Washington*, 302 U. S. 1. There a state inspection system touched matters "which the federal laws and regulations" left "untouched." *Id.*, at 13. This is not that type of case. Nor is this the rare case where state law adopts the standards and requirements of federal law and is allowed to exact a permit in addition to the one demanded by federal law. *California* v. *Zook*, 336 U. S. 725, 735. Here we have a criminal prosecution against a shipowner and officers of two of its vessels for using the very equipment on these vessels which the Federal Government says may be used. At stake are a possible fine of $100 on the owner and both a fine and a 30-day jail sentence on the officers.* * *

Appellant, operating the vessel in waters at the Detroit dock, is about to be fined criminally for using the precise equipment covered by the federal certificate because, it is said, the use of that equipment will violate a smoke ordinance of the City of Detroit.* * *

The requirements of the Detroit smoke ordinance are squarely in conflict with the federal statute.* * *

The fact that the Federal Government in certifying equipment applies standards of safety for seagoing vessels, while Detroit applies standards of air pollution seems immaterial. Federal pre-emption occurs when the boilers and fuel to be used in the vessels are specified in the certificate. No state authority can, in my view, change those specifications. Yet that is in effect what is allowed here.* * *

By what authority can a local government fine poeple or send them to jail for using in interstate commerce the precise equipment which the federal regulatory agency has certified and approved?

* * *The variety of requirements for equipment which the States may provide in order to meet their air pollution needs underlines the importance of letting the Coast Guard license serve as authority for the vessel to use, in all our ports, the equipment which it certifies.

C. Who May Be Sued—The Doctrine of Sovereign Immunity

When an action is brought against a government agency or official the defendant may have a defense that is unique to government, namely, that the defendant may not be sued without its consent. This defense raises the issue of **sovereign immunity**, or the immunity of the state from lawsuits against it. The doctrine of sovereign immunity is an archaic principle arising out of the concepts of "the divine right of kings" and the "king can do no wrong." Under these concepts the king, or state, is "subject to no power other than God." Consequently the state may not be called upon to account to anyone for its actions. Under modern principles of democracy, the doctrine of sovereign immunity is somewhat of an embarrassment. Nevertheless the defense is raised in actions against the federal, state and local governments.

1. THE FEDERAL GOVERNMENT

The principle of sovereign immunity was adopted into American jurisprudence by Chief Justice Marshall in 1821 in *Cohens v. Virginia*, 19 U.S. 264, in which the court declared that no suit could be brought against the United States without its consent. A few years later the Supreme Court confirmed this principle in *Osborn v. Bank of United States* 22 U.S. 738 (1824), where it held that the United States government could not be sued without its consent.

Congress has given its consent to be sued under prescribed circumstances. For example, actions for negligence and other wrongful acts may be brought under the Federal Tort Claims Act of 1946, 28 U.S.C. 1346; actions for breach of contract may be brought under the Tucker Act, 28 U.S.C. 1346, 1481; actions against administrative agencies may be brought under the Administrative Procedure Act, 5 U.S.C. 701; and as we have seen in an earlier discussion above, consent to be sued is provided in the Clean Air Act, the Clean Water Act and several other environmental protection statutes.

In *Larson v. Domestic and Foreign Commerce Corp.* set forth below, the United States Supreme Court faced the troublesome question involved when a law suit seeks to enjoin a federal agency from action it is alleged is illegal or wrongful.

LARSON
v.
DOMESTIC AND FOREIGN COMMERCE CORP.

337 U.S. 682 (1949)

MR. CHIEF JUSTICE VINSON delivered the opinion of the Court.

This suit was brought in the United States District Court for the District of Columbia by the Domestic & Foreign Commerce Corporation against . . . the . . . head of the War Assets Administration. The complaint alleged that the Administration had sold certain surplus coal to the plaintiff; that the Administrator refused to deliver the coal but, on the contrary, had entered into a new contract to sell it to others. The prayer was for an injunction prohibiting the Administrator from selling or delivering the coal to anyone other than the plaintiff and for a declaration that the sale to the plaintiff was valid and the sale to the second purchaser invalid.

A temporary restraining order was issued *ex parte*. At the subsequent hearing on the issuance of a preliminary injunction, the defendant moved to dismiss the complaint on the ground, among others, that the court did not have jurisdiction because the suit was one against the United States. The motion was granted. The Court of Appeals reversed, holding that the jurisdictional capacity of the court depended on whether or not title to the coal had passed. Since this was also one of the questions on the merits, it remanded the case for trial. We granted certiorari.

The controversy on the merits concerns the interpretation to be given to the contract of sale. The War Assets Administration construed the contract as requiring the plaintiff to deposit funds to pay for the coal in advance and, when an unsatisfactory letter of credit was offered in place of a deposit, it considered that the contract was breached. The respondent, on the other hand, construed the contract as requiring payment only on delivery of the documents covering the coal shipment. In its view, it was not obliged to deposit any funds in advance of shipment and, therefore, had not breached the contract by failing to do so.

A second question, related to but different from the question of breach, was whether legal title to the coal had passed to the respondent when the contract was made. If the contract required the deposit of funds then, of course, title could not pass until the contract terms were complied with. If, on the other hand, the contract required payment only on the delivery of documents, a question remained as to whether title nevertheless passed at the time the contract was made.

Since these questions were not decided by the courts below we do not pass on them here. They are important only insofar as they illuminate the basis on which it was claimed that the district court had jurisdiction over the suit. It was not alleged that the contract for the sale of the coal was a contract with the officer personally. The basis of the action, on the contrary, was that a contract had been entered into with the United States. Nor was it claimed that the Administrator had any personal interest in this coal or, indeed, that he himself had taken any wrongful action. The complaint was directed against him because of his official function as chief of the War Assets Administration. It asked for an injunction against him in that capacity, and against "his agents, assistants, deputies and employees and all persons acting or assuming to act under their direction." The relief sought was, in short, relief against the Administration for wrongs allegedly committed by subordinate officials in that Administration. The question presented to the courts below was whether such an injunction was barred by the sovereign's immunity from suit.

Before answering that question it is perhaps advisable to state clearly what is and what is not involved. There is not involved any question of the immunization of Government officers against responsibility for their wrongful actions. If those actions are such as to create a personal liability, whether sounding in tort or in contract, the fact that the officer is an instrumentality of the sovereign does not, of course, forbid a court from taking jurisdiction over a suit against him. Sloan Shipyards Corp. v. United States Shipping Bd. Emergency Fleet Corp., 258 U.S. 549, 567, 66 L.Ed. 762, 768, 42 S.Ct. 386, 48 Am Bankr 249 (1922). As was said in Brady v. Roosevelt S.S. Co. 317, U.S. 575, 580, 87 L.Ed. 471, 476, 63 S.Ct. 425 (1943), the principle that an agent is liable for his own torts "is an ancient one and applies even to certain acts of public officers or public instrumentalities." But the existence of a right to sue the officer is not the issue in this case. The issue here is whether this particular suit is not also, in effect, a suit against the sovereign. If it is, it must fail, whether or not the officer might otherwise be suable.

If the denomination of the party defendant by the plaintiff were the sole test of whether a suit was against the officer individually or against his principal, the sovereign, our task would be easy. Our decision then would be that the United States is not being sued here because it is not named as a party. This would be simple and would not leave room for controversy. But controversy there has been, in this field above all others, because it has long been established that the crucial question is whether the relief sought in a suit nominally addressed to the officer is relief against the sovereign. In a suit against the officer to recover damages for the agent's personal actions that question is easily answered. The judgment sought will not require action by the sovereign or disturb the sovereign's property. There is, therefore, no jurisdictional difficulty. The question becomes difficult and the area of controversy is entered when the suit is not one for damages but for specific relief: i.e., the recovery of specific property or monies, ejectment from land, or injunction either directing or restraining the defendant officer's actions. In each such case the question is directly posed as to whether, by obtaining relief against the officer, relief will not, in effect, be obtained against the sovereign. For the sovereign can act only through agents and, when an agent's actions are restrained, the sovereign itself may, through him, be restrained. As indicated, this question does not arise because of any distinction between law and equity. It arises whenever suit is brought against an officer of the sovereign in which the relief sought from him is not compensation for an alleged wrong but, rather, the prevention or discontinuance, *in rem*, of the wrong. In each such case the compulsion, which the court is asked to impose, may be compulsion against the sovereign, although nominally directed against the individual officer. If it is, then the suit is barred, not because it is a suit against an officer of the Government, but because it is, in substance, a suit against the Government over which the court, in the absence of consent, has no jurisdiction.

The relief sought in this case was not the payment of damages by the individual defendant. To the contrary, it was asked that the court order the War Assets Administrator, his agents, assistants, deputies and employees and all persons acting under their direction, not to sell the coal involved and not to deliver it to anyone other than the respondent. The district court held that this was relief against the sovereign and therefore dismissed the suit. We agree.

There may be, of course, suits for specific relief against officers of the sovereign which are not suits against the sovereign. If the officer purports to act as an individual and not as an official, a suit directed against that action is not a suit against the sovereign. If the War Assets Administrator had completed a sale of his personal home, he presumably could be enjoined from later conveying it to a third person. On a similar theory, where the officer's powers are limited by statute, his actions beyond those limitations are considered individual and not sovereign actions. The officer is not doing the business which the sovereign has empowered him to do or he is doing it in a way which the sovereign has forbidden. His actions are *ultra vires* his authority and therefore may be made the object of specific relief. It is important to note that in such cases the relief can be granted, without impleading the sovereign, only because of the officer's lack of delegated power. A claim of error in the exercise of that power is therefore not sufficient. And, since the jurisdiction of the court to hear the case may depend, as we have recently recognized, upon the decision which it ultimately reaches on the merits, it is necessary that the plaintiff set out in his complaint the statutory limitation on which he relies.

A second type of case is that in which the statute or order conferring power upon the officer to take action in the sovereign's name is claimed to be unconstitutional. Actions for habeas corpus against a warden and injunctions against the threatened enforcement of unconstitutional statutes are familiar examples of this type. Here, too, the conduct against which specific relief is sought is beyond the officer's powers and is, therefore, not the conduct of the sovereign. The only difference is that in this case the power has been conferred in form but the grant is lacking in substance because of its constitutional invalidity.

These two types have frequently been recognized by this Court as the only ones in which a restraint may be obtained against the conduct of Government officials. The rule was stated by Mr. Justice Hughes in Philadelphia Co. v. Stimson, 223 U.S. 605, 620, 56 L.Ed. 570, 576, 32 S.Ct. 340 (1912), where he said, ". . . in case of an injury threatened by his illegal action, the officer cannot claim immunity from injunction process. The principle has frequently been applied with respect to state officers seeking to enforce unconstitutional enactments. [Citing cases.] And it is equally applicable to a Federal officer acting in excess of his authority or under an authority not validly conferred.

It is not contended by the respondent that the present case falls within either of these catgegories. There was no claim made that the Administrator and his agents, etc., were acting unconstitutionally or pursuant to an unconstitutional grant of power. Nor was there any allegation of a limitation on the Administrator's delegated power to refuse shipment in cases in which he believed the United States was not obliged to deliver. There was, it is true, an allegation that the Administrator was acting "illegally," and that the refusal to deliver was "unauthorized." But these allegations were not based and did not purport to be based upon any lack of delegated power. Nor could they be, since the Administrator was empowered by the sovereign to administer a general sales program encompassing the negotiation of contracts, the shipment of goods and the receipt of payment. A normal concomitant of such powers, as a matter of general agency law, is the power to refuse delivery when, in the agent's view, delivery is not called for under a contract and the power to sell goods which the agent believes are still his principal's to sell.

The respondent's contention, which the Court of Appeals sustained, was that there exists a third category of cases in which the action of a Government official may be restrained or direct. If, says the respondent, an officer of the Government wrongly takes or holds specific property to which the plaintiff has title then his taking or holding is a tort, and "illegal" as a matter of general law, whether or not it be within his delegated powers. He may therefore be sued individually to prevent the "illegal" taking or to recover the property "illegally" held.

If this is an adequate theory on which to rest the conclusion that the relief asked is not relief against the sovereign, then the respondent's complaint made out a sufficient basis for jurisdiction.

* * *

We therefore reject the contention here. We hold that if the actions of an officer do not conflict with the terms of his valid statutory authority, then they are the actions of the sovereign, whether or not they are tortious under general law, if they would be regarded as the actions of a private principal under the normal rules of agency. A Government officer is not thereby necessarily immunized from liability, if his action is such that a liability would be imposed by the general law of torts. But the astion itself cannot be enjoined or directed, since it is also the action of the sovereign.

* * *

. . . [W]e adhere to . . . the principle which has been frequently repeated by this Court. . . : the action of an officer of the sovereign (be it holding, taking or otherwise legally affecting the plaintiff's property) can be regarded as so "illegal" as to permit a suit for specific relief against the officer as an individual only if it is not within the officer's statutory powers or, if within those powers, only if the powers, or their exercise in the particular case, are constitutionally void.

The application of this principle to the present case is clear. The very basis of the respondent's action is that the Administrator was an officer of the Government, validly appointed to administer its sales program and therefore authorized to enter, through his subordinates, into a binding contract concerning the sale of the Government's coal. There is no allegation of any statutory limitation on his powers as a sales agent. In the absence of such a limitation he, like any other sales agent, had the power and the duty to construe such contracts and to refuse delivery in cases in which he believed that the contract terms had not been complied with. His action in so doing in this case was, therefore, within his authority even if, for purposes of decision here, we assume that his construction was wrong and that title to the coal had, in fact, passed to the respondent under the contract. There is no claim that his action constituted an unconstitutional taking. It was, therefore, inescapably the action of the United States and the effort to enjoin it must fail as an effort to enjoin the United States.

It is argued that the principle of sovereign immunity is an archaic hangover not consonant with modern morality and that it should therefore be limited wherever possible. There may be substance in such a viewpoint as applied to suits for damages. The Congress has increasingly permitted such suits to be maintained against the sovereign and we should give hospitable scope to that trend. But the reasoning is not applicable to suits for specific relief. For, it is one thing to provide a method by which a citizen may be compensated for a wrong done to him by the Government. It is a far different matter to permit a court to exercise its compulsive powers to restrain the

Government from acting, or to compel it to act. There are the strongest reasons of public policy for the rule that such relief cannot be had against the sovereign. The Government, as representative of the community as a whole, cannot be stopped in its tracks by any plaintiff who presents a disputed question of property or contract right. As was early recognized, "the interference of the Courts with the performance of the ordinary duties of the executive departments of the government, would be productive of nothing but mischief. . . ."

There are limits, of course. Under our constitutional system, certain rights are protected against governmental action and, if such rights are infringed by the actions of officers of the Government, it is proper that the courts have the power to grant relief against those actions. But in the absence of a claim of constitutional limitation, the necessity of permitting the Government to carry out its functions unhampered by direct judicial intervention outweighs the possible disadvantage to the citizen in being relegated to the recovery of money damages after the event.

It is argued that a sales agency, such as the War Assets Administration, is not the type of agency which requires the protection from direct judicial interference which the doctrine of sovereign immunity confers. We do not doubt that there may be some activities of the Government which do not require such protection. There are others in which the necessity of immunity is apparent. But it is not for this Court to examine the necessity in each case. That is a function of the Congress. The Congress has, in many cases, entrusted the business of the Government to agencies which may contract in their own names and which are subject to suit in their own names. In other cases it has permitted suits for damages, but, significantly, not for specific relief, in the Court of Claims. The differentiations as to remedy which the Congress has erected would be rendered nugatory if the basis on which they rest—the assumed immunity of the sovereign from suit in the absence of consent—were undermined by an unwarranted extension of the Lee doctrine.

The cause is reversed with directions that the complaint be dismissed.

It is so ordered.

---

2. STATE GOVERNMENTS

After the adoption of the United States Constitution in 1789 many state officials became concerned with the possibility that private citizens in one state might bring suit against another state in a federal court. To overcome this fear the **Eleventh Amendment** was adopted, providing as follows:

> "The Judicial power of the United States shall not be construed to extend to any suit in law or equity, commenced or prosecuted against one of the United States by Citizens of another State, or by Citizens or Subjects of any Foreign State."

The Eleventh Amendment prohibits suits by citizens of other states and foreign states. This prohibition was expanded to include suits against a state by its own citizens in a federal court. *Hans v. Louisiana*, 134 U.S. 1 (1890). The jurisdiction of state courts to hear suits by private persons against the state is determined by the state constitution and legislation. All states have adopted statutes that waive their immunity to private suits under prescribed circumstances. The following excerpts from the New

Jersey Tort Claims Act illustrate such state legislation. This is followed by *Ward v. Ackroyd* that deals with the issue of the circumstances under which there may be implied waiver of sovereign immunity arising from a state's actions.

NEW JERSEY TORT CLAIMS ACT

N.J.S.A. 59:1-1 to 14-4

59:1-2. Legislative declaration

The Legislature recognizes the inherently unfair and inequitable results which occur in the strict application of the traditional doctrine of sovereign immunity. On the other hand the Legislature recognizes that while a private entrepreneur may readily be held liable for negligence within the chosen ambit of his activity, the area within which government has the power to act for the public good is almost without limit and therefore government should not have the duty to do everything that might be done. Consequently, it is hereby declared to be the public policy of this State that public entities shall only be liable for their negligence within the limitations of this act and in accordance with the fair and uniform principles established herein. All of the provisions of this act should be construed with a view to carry out the above legislative declaration.
L.1972, c. 45, § 59:1-2.* * *

59:2-1. Immunity of public entity generally

a. Except as otherwise provided by this act, a public entity is not liable for an injury, whether such injury arises out of an act or omission of the public entity or a public employee or any other person.

b. Any liability of a public entity established by this act is subject to any immunity of the public entity and is subject to any defenses that would be available to the public entity if it were a private person.
L.1972, c. 45, § 59:2-1.* * *

59:2-2. Liability of public entity

a. A public entity is liable for injury proximately caused by an act or omission of a public employee within the scope of his employment in the same manner and to the same extent as a private individual under like circumstances.

b. A public entity is not liable for an injury resulting from an act or omission of a public employee where the public employee is not liable.
L.1972, c. 45, § 59:2-2.* * *

59:2-3. Discretionary activities

a. A public entity is not liable for an injury resulting from the exercise of judgment or discretion vested in the entity;

b. A public entity is not liable for legislative or judicial action or inaction, or administrative action or inaction of a legislative or judicial nature;

c. A public entity is not liable for the exercise of discretion in determining whether or to seek or whether to provide the resources necessary for the purchase of equipment, the construction or maintenance of facilities, the hiring of personnel and, in general, the provision of adequate governmental services;

d. A public entity is not liable for the exercise of discretion when, in the face of competing demands, it determines whether and how to utilize or apply existing resources, including those allocated for equipment, facilities and personnel unless a court concludes that the determination of the public entity was palpably unreasonable. Nothing in this section shall exonerate a public entity for negligence arising out of acts or omissions of its employees in carrying out their ministerial functions.

L.1972, c. 45 § 59:2-3.* * *

59:2-4. Adoption or failure to adopt or enforce a law

A public entity is not liable for an injury caused by adopting or failing to adopt a law or by failing to enforce any law.

L.1972, c. 45, § 59:2-4.

Effective date, see § 59:14-4.

59:2-5. Issuance, denial, suspension or revocation of permit, license, etc.

A public entity is not liable for an injury caused by the issuance, denial, suspension or revocation of, or by the failure or refusal to issue, deny, suspend or revoke, any permit, license, certificate, approval, order, or similar authorization where the public entity or public employee is authorized by law to determine whether or not such authorization should be issued, denied, suspended or revoked.* * *

L.1972, c. 45, § 59:2-5.

59:2-6. Failure to inspect, or negligent inspection of, property

A public entity is not liable for injury caused by its failure to make an inspection, or by reason of making an inadequate or negligent inspection of any property; provided, however, that nothing in this section shall exonerate a public entity from liability for negligence during the course of, but outside the scope of, any inspection conducted by it, nor shall this section exonerate a public entity from liability for failure to protect against a dangerous condition as provided in chapter 4.

L.1972, c. 45, § 59:2-6.* * *

59:2-7. Recreational facilities

A public entity is not liable for failure to provide supervision of public recreational facilities: provided, however, that nothing in this section shall exonerate a public entity from liability for failure to protect against a dangerous condition as provided in chapter 4.

L. 1972, c. 45, § 59:2-7.* * *

59:2-8. Public assistance programs—termination of benefits

A public entity is not liable for injuries caused by the termination or reduction of benefits under a public assistance program.

L.1972, c. 45, § 59:2-8.* * *

59:2-9. Slander of title

A public entity is not liable for its acts or omissions resulting in a slander on the title of any property.
L.1972, c. 45, § 52:2-9.* * *

59:2-10. Public employee conduct—limitation on entity liability

A public entity is not liable for the acts or omissions of a public employee constituting a crime, actual fraud, actual malice, or willful misconduct.
L.1972, c. 45, § 52:2-10.

* * *

WARD v. ACKROYD

344 F.Supp. 1202 (D.Md. 1972)

MILLER, District Judge:

* * *

III. *Sovereign Immunity*

Plaintiffs have asked this court to issue a permanent injunction in this action against the state defendants restraining and enjoining them, *inter alia*, ". . . from taking or continuing any action on behalf of the State of Maryland . . . in furtherance of the proposed construction of Segment 9 of I-70N, including without limitation, the solicitation of or advertising for bids from any person, corporation or other entity and the awarding or execution of contracts for construction of Segment 9 of I-70N or portions thereof. . . ." The state defendants have raised the defense of sovereign immunity as an absolute bar to this action. Thus the issue arises whether a state that applies for federal highway aid, and is accepted for and participates in the federal highway aid program, pursuant to 23 U.S.C. § 101 *et seq.*, may successfully plead sovereign immunity in a federal court suit brought against it and the federal government for alleged noncompliance with various federal enactments setting conditions on the availability of that federal aid.

The Eleventh Amendment provides:

> "The judicial power of the United States shall not be construed to extend to any suit in law or equity, commenced or prosecuted against one of the United States by Citizens of another State, or by Citizens who are Subjects of any Foreign State."

This has been interpreted to mean that an unconsenting state is immune from federal court suits brought by its own citizens as well as citizens from another state. *Hans v. Louisiana*, 134 U.S. 1 (1890). Under this amendment, a state is not divested of its immunity "on the mere ground that the case is one arising under the Constitution or laws of the United States." *Parden v. Terminal R.R.*, 377 U.S. 184, 186 (1964). But the immunity may be waived; the state's freedom from suit without its consent does not protect it from a suit to which it has consented.* * * The "conclusion that there has been a waiver of immunity will not be lightly inferred."* * *

At the outset, this court concluded that since the action against the state defendants here is in fact and in law one against the state, the defense of sovereign immunity can be raised by these defendants as a defense to the action.* * * The only question before this court is whether immunity has been waived.

It is true in suits for damages, such as in the *Petty* and *Parden* cases, waiver of immunity will not be found unless there is clear and explicit language to that effect. In suits for damages where a state has entered into an area regulated by federal statutes, such as the field of navigation in the *Lauritzen* case, a waiver may be implied when the claimant is a member of the class intended to be protected by the statute and when that statute gives him a cause of action.* * * Such situations have generally been held to be the only instances when a state will be found to waive its immunity.

However, in determining whether or not a state has waived its immunity I believe that a distinction should be made between suits for damages, where one seeks an affirmative judgment against the state, and suits for injunctive relief or similar relief, where one seeks to restrain the state from doing or performing a particular action. In the latter case I believe that the defense of immunity should yield more readily where the issue sought to be litigated is the compliance or noncompliance by the state with the preconditions set forth in a federal statute or regulation for the enjoyment by the state of federal aid for the specific project for which the state has applied for the aid. In seeking the federal aid the state has necessarily agreed to be bound by the terms of the federal statutes and regulations which govern the availability and disposition of the federal aid. Where there is proper standing, it is beyond cavil that a citizen generally may sue federal agencies in the federal courts when administrative decisions have been made by federal officials in violation of federal law.* * * In a case of this type, involving as it does the question of compliance by state and federal officials with the federal law regulating the eligibility of the state for federal financial aid on a specific highway project, the federal government and the state and city governments are inextricably connected together in the building of the highway. It would seem futile to allow relief against the federal defendants and, on the other hand, preclude the plaintiffs, if relief is otherwise appropriate, from obtaining relief against the state defendants when the ultimate object is to insure that federal money is paid to and utilized by the state in accordance with the federal law regulating such payment and use.

Recently, in *Arlington Coalition v. Volpe, supra*, the Fourth Circuit dealt with the question of whether or not the Commissioner of the Virginia Department of Highways was subject to federal jurisdiction since the challenged activities of his department—condemnation of right of way and eviction of the landowners—are authorized by state law and could be carried out independently of the highway project under consideration. Rejecting these contentions of Virginia, the court stressed the close relationship between the state and the federal government in constructing the road and the undesirable effect the state's independent action could have on any future judicial or administrative decisions. Judge Craven for the court said:

> ". . .these activities [state activities] would not in fact be independent of this project.* * * Appellee Fugate does not suggest that the Commonwealth of Virginia no longer seeks to build this highway with federal funds. If we were to find—as we do—that federal law requires that the proposed route . . . be reconsidered, acquisition by the state of right of way along the proposed route during the reconsideration would make proceeding with the proposed route increasingly easier and, therefore, a decision to alter or abandon the route increasingly undesirable. Thus the challenged activities of the state highway department would make a sham of the reconsideration required by federal law. Action of a state highway department, challenged because furthering a project that under federal

law allegedly must be reconsidered, is a matter in controversy arising under the laws of the United States. Federal jurisdiction over such state action is essential to preserve federal question jurisdiction in the application of federal statutes. It is a form of pendant jurisdiction, but based upon necessity rather than convenience and limited to preventing emasculation of remedy clearly available against the federal respondents." [footnote omitted]. Slip opinion, pp. 10–11.

Although the issue of sovereign immunity was not specifically raised in *Arlington Coalition*, I believe that the rationale of that decision is essentially the same as that applicable to the defense of sovereign immunity in this case. This court holds that when a state applies for and accepts federal aid highway funds, it can be deemed to have waived its immunity from suit under the Eleventh Amendment, at least as to a suit for injunctive or other relief designed to enforce the provisions of federal law which establish the conditions under which the federal aid can be distributed to or obtained by the state.

* * *

---

3. Municipal Governments

The immunity of municipal government from lawsuits is based on a distinction as archaic as the concept of sovereign immunity on which it is based. As a general rule, a municipality may rely on the defense of sovereign immunity where the issue involves a **governmental function** such as the police, fire, sanitation or educational departments but not where it exercises the so called **proprietary functions**, such as a municipal garage, public housing, public markets, airport or ferries. Of course there are many modern municipal functions that do not fall clearly in either category. In *State v. City of Bowling Green*, below, the interesting question was presented whether a city may interpose the defense of sovereign immunity when sued by the state of which it is a part.

STATE v. CITY OF BOWLING GREEN

38 Ohio St.2d 281, 313 N.E.2d 409 (1974)

PAUL W. BROWN, Justice.

This action for money damages for a fish-kill was brought by the state against the city of Bowling Green. The damage is alleged to have arisen from the negligent operation by the defendant municipal corporation of its sewage treatment plant which resulted in the introduction of pollutants into the north branch of the Portage River.

The Court of Common Pleas sustained the defendant's motion, which alleged that its operation of the sewage treatment plant was a governmental function in the conduct of which it was clothed with sovereign immunity, and dismissed the action.

The Court of Appeals held the operation of a sewage treatment plant by a municipal corporation to be a proprietary function and reversed the judgment of the Court of Common Pleas.

Each party proposes that the proper characterization of the municipal operation of a sewage treatment plant as governmental or proprietary should resolve the appellate dispute.

Appellant, city of Bowling Green, additionally contends that, apart from any issue of sovereign immunity, the failure of the General Assembly to include municipal corporations within the purview of the definition of the word "persons" in R.C. 1531.-01(a) bars the state from seeking a damage award against it.* * *

The controlling question in this case is whether a municipality may impose the defense of sovereign immunity in an action brought against it by the state, based upon the negligent performance of a municipal function by the municipality. This question is one of first impression in this court.

Neither the parties' nor this court's exhaustive research have produced any case which has squarely confronted the questions; all prior cases involved a suit by a *private party* against a municipality. None involved a suit by the *state* against a municipality. For this reason, none of this court's past cases on municipal tort immunity are directly controlling in the present case.

The issue of governmental immunity was discussed in Wooster v. Arbenz (1927), 116 Ohio St. 281, 283, 156 N.E. 210, 211, wherein this court said:

"* * * The nonliability for governmental functions is placed upon the ground that the *state* is sovereign, that the sovereign cannot be sued without its consent, and that the *municipality* is the mere agent of the *state* and therefore cannot be sued unless the state gives its consent by legislation." (Emphasis added.) This language was favorably cited in Williams v. Columbus (1973), 33 Ohio St.2d 75, 294 N.E.2d 891, the most recent municipal immunity case decided by this court. In discussing the proprietary-governmental dichotomy, Wooster v. Arbenz, *supra*, 116 Ohio St. at page 284, 156 N.E. at page 211, further illuminates the source of a municipality's immunity:

"* * * In performing those duties which are imposed upon the state as obligations of sovereignty, such as protection from crime, or fires, or contagion, or preserving the peace and health of citizens and protecting their property, it is settled that the function is governmental, and if the municipality undertakes the performance of those functions, whether voluntarily or by legislative imposition, the municipality becomes an arm of sovereignty and a governmental agency and is entitled to that immunity from liability which is enjoyed by the state itself.* * *"

It is thus clear that a municipality in Ohio is not inherently immune from liability in tort. Unlike the state, whose historic sovereign immunity is controlled by the provisions of Section 16, Article I of the Ohio Constitution (Krause v. State [1972], 31 Ohio St.2d 132, 285 N.E.2d 736), a municipality is not directly clothed with or relieved from immunity from liability in tort by any constitutional provision. Its immunity is derivative; it arises because the municipality, when performing a governmental function, is acting as an arm or agent of the state.

Where a municipality negligently performs a governmental function, and as a proximate result thereof a private injury is caused, the injured party cannot maintain a damage suit against the municipality because the city is clothed with the state's immunity. In such a situation the state is analogous to a principal with immunity, and the municipality to an agent, and the injured party to a third person. The immunity of the principal filters down to the agent. However, where the injured party is the state itself, this analogy disintegrates. Instead, the situation resembles a suit by a principal against an agent whose negligence has resulted in damage to the principal. In such a situation it would be illogical to allow the municipality to assert its general tort immunity against the very source of that immunity.

We are not called upon to decide the effect of state statutes, such as those in R.C. Chapter 6111, which authorize the Water Pollution Control Board to issue permits for the discharge of sewage into the waters of the state, for it is not maintained that any such permit was in effect at the time of the acts complained of.

The judgment of the Court of Appeals, reversing and remanding this cause to the Court of Common Pleas, is affirmed.

Judgment affirmed.

---

4. PUBLIC OFFICIALS AS INDIVIDUALS

Many sovereign immunity cases involve suits against public officials. The issue arises whether the defense of sovereign immunity may be used by individual public officials. Several general rules have evolved. For example, it is well established that sovereign immunity may not be used where it is alleged that the official acted outside the scope of his statutory authority or pursuant to an unconstitutional grant of authority.

A somewhat different but related issue arises in suits against public officials where the plaintiff seeks to compel the public official to perform a ***discretionary***, as distinguished from a ***ministerial*, act**. *Roy v. Farr*, below, illustrates the dilemma that can arise in such cases.

ROY v. FARR

258 A.2d 799 (Vt. 1969)

KEYSER, Justice.

This is a petition for a writ of mandamus by which the petitioner seeks to compel the board of health of the town of Richmond to abate an unhealthful condition existing on land adjacent to the residential property of both the petitioner and other persons as provided by 18 V.S.A. § 609.

The petition was brought on February 28, 1969. At that time defendants Farr, Conant and Palermo were the selectmen of the town of Richmond. Selectman Farr was the appointed health officer of the town. 18 V.S.A. § 601. The selectmen, together with the health officer, constitute the local board of health. 18 V.S.A. § 604.

The record shows that defendant Farr's term of office expired on town meeting day, March 4, 1969. At that time one Gordon B. Stensrud was elected selectman to fill this vacancy.* * *

In order to have the proper and necessary parties before the court, an interlocutory order and summons was issued and served on the present members of the Richmond Board of Health not named in the original petition shown by the public records to be Dr. John Lantman, Health Officer, and Selectmen Willard Conant and Gordon Stensrud.* * *

The board of health resists the petition on two grounds—(1) it claims the removal of the unhealthful condition by the board under 18 V.S.A. § 609 is not mandatory duty for the reason that such action requires the exercise of its judgment and discretion and is not a ministerial act, and (2) it contends that the petitioner has an adequate remedy by an action for abatement of a public nuisance against the offending landowner.

The following facts which appear in the petition and answer are undisputed. The petitioner is a resident and owner of certain real estate located on Lemroy Court in the town of Richmond. In 1966 an unhealthful condition existed on land adjacent to petitioner's residential property on Lemroy Court and to other lands which he had developed into residential properties. This condition resulted from the discharge of raw sewage by one George Dutil into an open gully southeast of petitioner's residence. The defendants were notified of this unhealthful condition by the Vermont Department of Health in March 1967, and were advised that the discharge of the sewage was considered to be a public health hazard. On June 27, 1967, defendant Farr, as the town health officer, notified the offending property owner, George Dutil, that the unhealthful condition was due to the discharge of raw sewage from his disposal facilities and that in the event he, Dutil, failed to comply with the order of the defendants requiring him to remove the unhealthful condition within thirty days, the defendant would order the removal of the condition pursuant to 18 V.S.A. § 609 and charge him, Dutil, with the expense of the same. Dutil failed to comply with the order and the unhealthful condition still exists.

The critical question to be first decided is whether mandamus will lie on the facts shown in this case.

The duties of the health officer regarding sanitary inspections are prescribed by 18 V.S.A. § 606 as follows:

> The health officer shall make sanitary inspections when and where he has reason to suspect that anything exists which may be detrimental to the public health. He may enter any house or other building or place for the purpose of making such inspections. By written order he shall direct the destruction or removal within a specified time of unhealthful conditions or causes of sickness; and shall in all things conform to the rules and regulations of the board.

The facts show a compliance with the mandate of this statute. The inspection was made and a written order was given to the offending party, George Dutil. He was directed by said order to remove the condition, failing which the board of health would do so at his expense.* * *

The local board took no remedial steps to enforce its order by having the condition prevented or removed. The petitioner claims that since Dutil did not comply with the order, the board, under Section 609, supra, must take action to have the condition eliminated. The defendant contends that its duty under the statute is discretionary and requires the exercise of its judgment which, if true, will supersede mandamus since the writ does not lie to enforce the performance of judicial or quasi-judicial acts. Under such circumstances, this Court will not order the board to act.

* * *

On the other hand, mandamus will lie to compel a public officer to perform an official act which is merely ministerial. Town of Bennington v. Booth, 101 Vt. 24, 27, 140 A. 157, 57 A.L.R. 156; Town of Glover v. Anderson, 120 Vt. 153, 155, 134 A.2d 612. So here, in order to justify the issuance of a writ of mandamus, it must be made to appear that the duty of the local board of health to remove the public health hazard is a ministerial one. Barber v. Chase, 101 Vt. 343, 351, 143 A. 302, and that the right sought to be enforced is certain and clear. Glover v. Anderson, supra.

However, there is a well-recognized exception to these general propositions depending upon whether the facts make it a proper case to come within the exception. Where such facts show, in some manner, an arbitrary abuse of the power vested by law in an administrative officer or board which amounts to a virtual refusal to act or to perform a duty imposed by law, mandamus may be resorted to in the absence of other adequate legal remedy.* * *

The petitioner has a clear right not to be subjected to the unhealthful condition determined by the State Department of Health to be a public health hazard. The defendant admits that the discharge of raw sewage as shown is a condition which has existed for many years. The situation ostensibly developed to such a serious and hazardous unhealthful condition that the State health authorities acted in 1967. It is evident that the local health officer likewise determined that such condition existed or else the order of removal would not have been issued. The right which the petitioner seeks to be enforced is adequately shown to be certain and clear.

The defendant argues that the action of the board of health is the performance of a discretionary act and involves an inquiry of fact.

The general supervision of the public health of the town is committed to the local health officer and board of health. Their authority to act in such matters is expressly granted by 18 V.S.A., Chapter 11. The state board of health and commissioner in their discretion may exercise similar powers. 18 V.S.A. § 109.

The health officer chose to act by making an inspection of the situation after which the removal order was given Dutil. This required a determination based on his inquiry that the condition was detrimental to public health and created an unhealthful condition. It was at this point that the judgment and discretionary action came into play and was exercised. After the decision was made to issue the order of removal there remained only the action of the board to have the condition removed upon non-compliance with the order. This required neither an inquiry of fact nor exercise of judgment or discretion. Each had already been exercised.

We think the dangerous public health hazard was a compelling reason for the board to exercise its powers under the statute and required it to cause the condition to be eliminated or removed in accordance with the order to Dutil and the applicable statute. The failure and neglect of the board to take such action amounted to an arbitrary abuse of its lawful authority.

We turn to the remaining question of whether a writ of mandamus is the only fully adequate and complete remedy available to the petitioner.

While it is true that the writ will not issue where the right is doubtful, it will not be refused because of the existence of another remedy unless that remedy is clear and adequate. Town of Bennington v. Booth, supra. The remedy here suggested by the defendants is an action by the petitioner for the abatement of a public nuisance.

Mandamus affords a plain, speedy and adequate remedy. It is practical, efficient and prompt in its administration toward the result sought to be accomplished. In order to supersede mandamus, the other remedy must be competent to afford relief on the very subject matter in question, and be equally convenient, beneficial and effective. Glover v. Anderson, supra, 120 Vt. at page 160, 134 A.2d 612.

It is well settled that a person who suffers special damage from the erection and maintenance of a public nuisance is entitled to relief in his own right; but, it must appear that the injury is distinct from that suffered by the general public.

* * *

It is manifestly clear from the facts before us that the injury is not a personal one peculiar only to the petitioner but is one suffered by the public as well. To require the petitioner to bring a petition to abate a nuisance which affects the public health would cause him to bear all of the expense and delay which are involved in personal litigation. We are persuaded by the facts in the case that an action by the petitioner to abate a public nuisance does not meet the test laid down by this Court in Glover v. Anderson, supra, and would not afford him such a clear, speedy and fully adequate remedy as the law provides. Town of Bennington v. Booth, supra.

Judgment that the prayer of the petition is granted, and that a mandamus issue directing the Board of Health of the Town of Richmond, namely, Dr. John Lantman, Vincent Palermo, Willard Conant and Gordon Stensrud, to forthwith remove, or cause to be removed, the health hazard resulting from the open discharge of raw sewage by one George Dutil on land adjacent to the residential property of the petitioner, Louis G. Roy, all in accordance with the order given to said Dutil and the statutes in such case made and provided, with actual costs of this proceeding to the petitioner.

D. Defenses to Environmental Law Suits

Only the most idealistic and naive environmentalist would argue that it is necessary only to allege facts indicating that the defendant is polluting or degrading the environment for a court to order the defendant to stop the pollution or pay for the damages he has inflicted, or both. Environmental lawsuits are no different from any other judicial proceeding in that the defendant has the legal right to deny the truth of the allegations and to show that even if those facts are true his actions are not wrongful or illegal under the circumstances. The defenses available to such defendants may be based on arguments that seek to show that the alleged activities are not wrongful; they may be based on technical legal reasons why no remedy is available even if their acts are technically "wrongful"; they may include policy reasons why the judiciary is an inappropriate forum to resolve the complex issues involved.

1. Balancing of Equities

A defendant in an environmental law suit may have a valid defense even under circumstances where he admits that his actions result in the degradation of the environment. For example, in an action brought by riparian homeowners whose use of the adjoining lake is impaired by pollution caused by a farmer who uses fertilizers and pesticides that are washed into the lake by rainfall, the farmer's defense will be based on the argument that those chemicals are necessary to produce a crop in sufficient quantity to make farming economical. An issue of fact may be litigated relating to the amounts and concentrations of chemicals used and the feasibility of alternative methods, but ultimately it may be necessary for a court to decide whether the farmer is to be allowed to continue to use some measure of chemicals in spite of the degradation of the quality of the water in the adjoining lake. It will be necessary to **balance the equities**, i.e., make a comparative evaluation of the competing values involved. *People ex rel Stream Control Commission v. City of Port Huron* illustrates the kind of policy problem a court faces when it is called on to enjoin an otherwise useful and necessary activity that pollutes the environment.

PEOPLE EX REL. STREAM CONTROL COMMISSION v. CITY OF PORT HURON

305 Mich. 153, 9 N.W.2d 41 (1943)

BUSHNELL, J. The stream control commission, created by Act No. 245, Pub. Acts 1929 (1 Comp. Laws 1929 § 278 *et seq.* [Stat. Ann. § 3.521 *et seq.*]), issued an order on February 11, 1936, requiring the city of Port Huron to "proceed to the construction of a sewage treatment plant, and the necessary collecting and intercepting sewers, pumping stations, force mains and other appurtenances, in connection therewith, all when and as approved by the Michigan department of health, to permit treatment for the sewage of the city before its discharge to State waters." The city having failed to comply with this order, the commission filed a bill of complaint on December 9, 1939, for the purpose of enforcing its order and restraining the city from discharging untreated sewage into the Black or St. Clair rivers.

The trial judge held that the grounds of public necessity as disclosed by the testimony were insufficient to warrant "the present interference" by the court. He denied the relief sought, until further order, on the principle that:

> "A court of equity will refuse to grant an injunction when it appears that greater injury and inconvenience will be caused to the defendant by granting the injunction than will be caused to the complainant by refusing it."

An appeal was taken by the State from a decree in favor of the city.* * *

The city of Port Huron takes its water from the St. Clair river near Lake Huron, which is connected with Lake St. Clair by the St. Clair river, and discharges its raw sewage into the St. Clair river, which borders it on the east, and into the Black river, a tributary of the St. Clair, which runs through the city. The city of Sarnia and the village of Point Edward, which are situated almost directly opposite the city of Port Huron on the east bank of the St. Clair river in the Province of Ontario, also discharge raw sewage into this river, as does a large oil refinery. During the years 1937, 1938 and 1939, a total of 45,168 vessels passed Port Huron, which added to the pollution of these waters.

The city argues that the construction of a sewage disposal plant will not materially reduce the pollution in the rivers, and insists that its present method of sewage disposal does not create a health hazard amounting to a public nuisance to the people residing along the river and those in the cities of Marysville, St. Clair, Marine City and Algonac, located within 30 miles below Port Huron.

The record contains sufficient testimony to substantiate the State's contention that the present raw sewage disposal method is a constant menace to the health and well-being of the downriver communities, as well as to tourists. This evidence clearly justifies the commission's order. Under the authority of the *City of Niles Case, supra,* where similar arguments were advanced, it is no defense to a statutory charge of river-water pollution that others have or are contributing to that condition. This court said:

> "In order to stop pollution of the river it was necessary for the commission to take action against the city of Niles inasmuch as it was the first city in the State, on the course of the river, below the Indiana cities and thus open the way for suit to compel the Indiana cities to stop pollution of the waters of the river. It is an instance where the State must clean up its own dooryard before being in a position to ask or seek to compel its neighbor to clean up. This was not an arbitrary exercise of power by the commission but a practical movement toward accomplishment of a most desirable end."

Even if we should concur with the trial judge in his conclusion that "a balancing of equities" favors the city, this is not a proper case for the application of that doctrine. The doctrine of "comparative injury" should be confined to those situations where the plaintiff can be substantially compensated. This principle is distinguished in *City of Harrisonville* v. *W. S. Dickey Clay Manfg. Co.,* 289 U. S. 334, 337 (53 Sup. Ct. 602, 77 L. Ed. 1208), where Mr. Justice Brandeis said:

> "The discharge of the effluent into the creek is a tort; and the nuisance, being continuous or recurrent, is an injury for which an injunction may be granted. Thus, the question here is not one of equitable jurisdiction. The question is whether, upon the facts found, an injunction is the appropriate remedy. For an injunction is not a remedy which issues as of course. Where substantial redress can

be afforded by the payment of money and issuance of an injunction would subject the defendant to grossly disproportionate hardship, equitable relief may be denied although the nuisance is indisputable. This is true even if the conflict is between interests which are primarily private."* * *

The doctrine of "comparative injury" should not be invoked to justify the continuance of an act that tends to impair public health. In *Board of Commissioners of the County of Ohio* v. *Elm Grove Mining Co.*, 122 W. Va. 442, 451 (9 S.E. [2d] 813), the court said:

> "Notwithstanding a business be conducted in the regular manner, yet if in the operation thereof, it is shown by facts and circumstances to constitute a nuisance affecting public health 'no measure of necessity, usefulness or public benefit will protect it from the unflinching condemnation of the law.' 1 Wood on Nuisances (3d Ed.), § 19.* * * There is extremely narrow basis for undertaking to balance conveniences where people's health is involved."* * *

The act creating the commission was under the police power vested in the State, and the order in question was not arbitrary or unreasonable but became necessary by reason of the previous refusal of the city of Port Huron to stop pollution of the St. Clair and Black rivers. The evidence justified the order of the commission, and the decree entered below must be vacated.* * *

The decree is vacated and one will be entered here in conformity with this opinion. A public question being involved, no costs will be allowed. It is so ordered.

For additional discussion of the balancing of equities as a defense in environmental suits see Coase, *The Problem of Social Cost*, 3 J. LAW & ECON. 1 (1960).

---

2. STATE OF THE ART: I DID ALL THAT COULD BE DONE

In a complex, industrialized, densely populated civilization the preservation of pristine air, pure water and other environmental resources may be too much to ask of the producers of the products necessary for the continuation of our industrial economy and society. For example, until satisfactory alternative sources of energy are found, fossil fuels will continue to be used as a source of energy; food processing will result in biochemical wastes; and refining of metals will result in tailings, toxic salts and the residues of combustion. The producers of energy and manufactured products and the processors of organic materials cannot be required to terminate their activities.

Should the obligation of the defendant be limited to a requirement that he utilize the best available techniques economically feasible to minimize the damage to the environment? Should a defendant be permitted to argue that he is currently doing all that can be done and that he therefore should not be enjoined or subjected to monetary damages? *Renken v. Harvey Aluminum* and *McElwain v. Georgia-Pacific Corp.* deal with these questions.

RENKEN v. HARVEY ALUMINUM

226 F. Supp. 169 (D. Ore. 1963)

KILKENNY, District Judge.

Each of the plaintiffs, since 1958, and in many instances prior to that year, has been in continuous possession of land in Wasco County, Oregon, which land was and is used principally for agricultural and horticultural purposes, in growing and production, for home and commercial purposes, of certain fruit consisting of cherries, prunes, peaches and apricots.

Plaintiffs seek to enjoin the defendant from operating its plant in such a manner as to permit the escape therefrom of excessive quantities of the element, fluorine, which is carried by air currents to plaintiffs' lands. Defendant is a corporation, incorporated under the laws of the State of California.* * *

Defendant's plant was constructed, and is being operated, pursuant to the Defense Production Act of 1950, as amended. Its original cost, and subsequent additions, is in excess of $40,000,000.00. The plant annually produces approximately 80,000 tons of aluminum, which is used by the defendant, and others, throughout the United States for industrial and National Defense purposes. Approximately 550 persons, living in the area of The Dalles, are employed in said plant. It has a gross annual payroll of $3,500,000.00.

The plant produces primary aluminum, by the use of what is known as the vertical stud soderberg electrolytic cells. At present 300 cells are in operation. The basic process employed at the plant is the same as that employed the world over in making aluminum, the process being precisely described by Judge East in his opinion in Fairview Farms, Inc. v. Reynolds Metals Company, 176 F.Supp. 178 (D.C.Or.1959). The vertical stud soderberg cells employed by Harvey were not used in the Reynolds plant. The essential difference between the cells, or pots, used in the Reynolds plant is, insofar as the escape of particulates and gasses is concerned, that Reynolds uses a hood, with a controlling air system, which captures most of the stray gasses, effluents and particulates which might escape into the open area around the pots. The vertical type, employed by Harvey, has an apron which collects approximately 80% of these gasses and particulates, but the remaining 20% escapes from the area where the hoods would be located, mixes with other air in the building and then drifts upward into the water spray controls in the roof. It is conceded that in the production of aluminum there is inevitably a release, from the cells, of some gasses and particulates, including fluorides.

The initial fume control apparatus at the Harvey plant consisted of a cast iron skirt surrounding the anode, which collected a portion of the fumes at the source and directed them to burners mounted at both ends of each anode. To these burners were connected fume exhaust ducts which led the fumes to a main collector pipe carrying them to the dust collector and a fan. The fan created a suction which pulled the fumes from the cells and the burners, through the ducts. From the fans the fumes are directed to a humidifying and bubbling chamber before entering the scrubber tower.

The fumes are washed in the tower by multiple layers of water sprayers placed 10 feet apart. At the top of the towers is a mist eliminator.

Tests made, from time to time, indicate that the fume control system, thus described, operated at 95% efficiency, or better, during the test periods on the portion of the fumes caught and delivered to the system. The amount of equivalent fluoride ion leaving the scrubbing towers into the atmosphere from this control apparatus is calculated at 800 pounds per day. This system treats approximately 80% of the fumes released from the cells. The remaining 20% of the fumes escape into the open building, and rise to the top where they pass into roof monitors located at the top of each of the buildings housing the cells. In the spring of 1962, a system of sprayers and screens [was] installed in the roof monitor and this system has been operating at full capacity since the beginning of 1963. These sprayers and screens collect a portion of the fluorides reaching the roof monitor. Since this latest installation the roof monitor sprays and screens have been between 67 and 70% effective in collecting the fluorides reaching the roof monitors. The amount of equivalent fluoride ion leaving the roof monitors into the atmosphere is calculated at 1,000 pounds per day. Overall, the combination of the original fume control system, as it has been added to and improved from time to time, and the roof monitor sprays and screens has achieved approximately 90% effectiveness with respect to collecting the fluorides released from the aluminum cells.

The record is undisputed that approximately 1,300 pounds of fluoride ion escape from the roof monitors and scrubbing towers into the atmosphere each day. Although the prevailing wind is southwesterly, the record clearly shows that on numerous days each month and on many hours of each day, the area is without measurable wind. At such times, a blanket of smoke from defendant's plant covers the area, including plaintiffs' lands and orchards. This blanket was observed by the Court, not only on the day of inspection of the plant, but also on many occasions since that time. There is no doubt in my mind but that better controls can be exercised over the escape of the material in question. No sound reason has been advanced by defendant why hoods, similar to those employed by Reynolds, should not be installed. While it is true that a substantial portion of the gasses and particulates escape at the time when the new aluminum ore is being introduced into the pot or the liquid metal is removed, I am convinced that such an escape could be prevented by a properly designed hood over the open area. I agree with the expert, that after the installation of the hood, the small amount of gasses which might escape on the introduction of ore or the removal of liquid metal would be inconsequential.

Likewise, the record convinces me of the feasability of the introduction of electrostatic precipitators for the removal of the minute or small particulates which are not removed by the other processes. The multi-cyclone dust collector now used in the plant at The Dalles is efficient in collecting the large or heavy particulates, but is of little value in removing the smaller variety. All of the experts agree that this is the field in which the electrostatic precipitators are at their best. The great weight of the evidence points to the conclusion that the installation of the cell hoods and the employment of electrostatic precipitators would greatly reduce, if not entirely eliminate, the escape of the excessive material now damaging the orchards of the plaintiffs.

While the cost of the installations of these additional controls will be a substantial sum, the fact remains that effective controls must be exercised over the escape of these noxious fumes. Such expenditures would not be so great as to substantially deprive defendant of the use of its property. While we are not dealing with the public as such, we must recognize that air pollution is one of the great problems now facing the American public. If necessary, the cost of installing adequate controls must be passed on to the ultimate consumer. The heavy cost of corrective devices is no reason why plaintiffs should stand by and suffer substantial damage.* * *

Defendant concedes that plaintiffs repeatedly warned it of the emissions, damages to and alleged trespasses on plaintiffs' property. The evidence supports, and I find, that the emissions from defendant's plant continued to settle on plaintiffs' land and orchards to and including the time of the trial. That the continued settling of the fluorides from defendant's plant on plaintiffs' property constituted a continuing trespass, as a matter of law, is beyond question.* * *

That equity will intervene to prevent a continuing trespass is well recognized.* * *

Plaintiffs rely on Fairview Farms, Inc. v. Reynolds Metal Co., supra, and in particular on that portion of the opinion in which it is indicated that an award of compensatory damages for past trespasses and future trespasses would adequately compensate the plaintiffs. The basic reason the Court did not grant an injunction in the Fairview case was that there was no evidence the acts or conduct of Reynolds were reasonably certain to be repeated in the future. Here, of course, the evidence is entirely to the contrary. Here, Harvey has taken the position that it has done everything possible to eliminate the problem, and that it must continue to operate with its present control system. The 1962–1963 improvement by Harvey was of no particular significance.

* * *

Frankly stated, there is no good reason why the defendant company, like other companies similarly situated, should not make a reasonable expenditure in the erection of hoods, or like devices, over or around its pots or cells. To require less would be placing a premium on air pollution. What's good for Reynolds should be good for Harvey, even though the cost of the new system might exceed $2,000,000.00, as it did in the case of Reynolds.* * *

The defendant will be required to install proper hoods around the cells and electrostatic precipitators in usual, advantageous and proper places in the plant, within one year of the date of the decree. Otherwise, an injunction will issue as prayed for by plaintiffs.

There is no room for application of the doctrine of balancing of the equities at this time. The required improvements should entirely eliminate the problem.

McELWAIN v. GEORGIA-PACIFIC

245 Ore. 247, 421 P.2d 957 (1967)

McALLISTER, Chief Justice.

This is an action brought by the plaintiffs, Ross and Edith McElwain, against the defendant, Georgia-Pacific Corporation, to recover both compensatory and punitive damages for injury to plaintiffs' real property caused by the operation of defendant's paper mill in Toledo.

Plaintiffs own two and one-half acres of land, improved with a dwelling house and garage, located directly east of defendant's mill. The complaint alleged that since defendant commenced operation of its plant on or about January 1, 1958, plaintiffs' property was damaged by "certain noxious and toxic gases, fumes and smoke and particles" blown and deposited thereon by defendant's mill. It is further alleged that the effluents from defendant's mill killed the trees and vegetation on plaintiffs' property and otherwise depreciated the value of the property. Plaintiffs prayed for $35,000 in compensatory damages and $20,000 in punitive damages. The court withdrew the issue of punitive damages, and the jury returned a verdict of $2,000, compensatory damages. The plaintiffs appeal.

Plaintiffs assign as error the withdrawal by the trial court of plaintiffs' claim for punitive damages.

Although this court has on occasion indulged in the dictum that punitive damages are not "favored in the law," it has, nevertheless, uniformly sanctioned the recovery of punitive damages whenever there was evidence of a wrongful act done intentionally, with knowledge that it would cause harm to a particular person or persons. Hodel, The Doctrine of Exemplary Damages in Oregon, 44 Or.L.Rev. 175 (1965). Malice is the term most frequently used in our decisions to define a state of mind that will justify the imposition of punitive damages. Malice, as a basis for punitive damages, signifies nothing more than a wrongful act done intentionally, without just cause or excuse.* * *

The intentional disregard of the interest of another is the equivalent of legal malice, and justifies punitive damages for trespass. Allison v. Hodo, 84 Ga.App. 790, 67 S.E.2d 606, 608 (1951). Where there is proof of an intentional, unjustifiable infliction of harm with deliberate disregard of the social consequences, the question of award of punitive damages is for the jury.

* * *

It is abundantly clear from the record that defendant knew when it decided to construct its kraft mill in Toledo, that there was danger, if not a probability, that the mill would cause damage to adjoining property. This is disclosed by defendant's evidence that the plans for the mill included, as an integral part thereof, certain air pollution control devices designed to minimize the damage caused by the mill to surrounding property.

The record is equally clear that, almost from the day it began to operate, the effluents from defendant's mill were a source of concern to the State Board of Health, and its successor, the State Sanitary Authority, and to the owners of the adjacent property. Although the trial judge excluded most of the relevant evidence offered by plaintiffs to show the extent and nature of the effluents deposited on their property, the defendant's evidence discloses that it was required to keep and furnish records to the state regulating authorities concerning the fallout of effluents on the neighboring properties.* * *

When defendant's mill was constructed the following air control equipment was installed therein:

Date	Equipment	Function
12/57	No. 1 Electrostatic Precipitator	Remove dust from Recovery furnace gases
12/57	No. 1 Peabody Scrubber	Remove dust from kiln gases
12/57	No. 1 Black Liquor Oxidation Tower	Stabilize liquor and minimize release odors
12/57	Blow Heat Accumulator	Condense all digester gases so that non-condensables can be vented to oxidation tower for re-absorption

In about June, 1960 the capacity of defendant's mill was increased from about 240 tons to 600 tons of paper per day. In connection with that expansion program two additional pieces of pollution control equipment were installed, as follows:

3/60	No. 2 Peabody Scrubber	Remove dust from kiln
5/60	No. 2 Electrostatic Precipitator	Remove dust from Recovery furnace gases

In 1961 a Turpentine Recovery System was installed "to remove turpentine vapors," and in 1962 two Lagoon Surface Aerators and other oxidation equipment was installed to "reduce odor release from liquid streams." According to defendant the equipment described above is all the pollution control equipment which had been installed prior to the filing of the complaint in this action. There is no contention by defendant that the fallout of effluents on plaintiffs' property was eliminated or even alleviated by its efforts at control.

Defendant contends that it should not be liable for punitive damages if it did everything reasonably possible to eliminate or minimize the damage caused by its mill to the neighboring properties. We need not pause to determine whether there is merit in defendant's contention. It is sufficient to call attention to the substantial evidence from which the jury could have found that during the period involved in this action the defendant had not done everything reasonably possible to eliminate or minimize the damage to adjoining properties by its mill. That evidence was introduced by defendant itself. Its expert in charge of its pollution control program, Dr. Taylor, testified that between the filing of plaintiffs' complaint and the time of the trial the defendant had installed or was in process of installing the following additional pollution control equipment:

4/63	Rebuild #1 Precipitator	Replace internal units and increase electrical capacity
11/63	No. 2 Black Liquor Oxidation System	Stabilize liquor and minimize release of odors
3/64	#3 Electrostatic Precipitator	Remove dust from Recovery furnace gases (Expansion)
3/64	#3 Peabody Scrubber	Remove dust from kiln gases (Expansion)
3/64	290-ft Stack	High level discharge of all three recovery furnace gases
4 to 6/64	Three wet scrubber systems for three Recovery Furnaces	Wash residual salt from recovery furnace gases and reduce odor
5/64	Relocated #2 stack at kilns	High level discharge of kiln gases

Dr. Taylor testified that the increase in the height of the stack and the other controls were designed to minimize particulate fallout.* * *

Except as to the three "wet scrubbers" installed from April to June, 1964, there is no contention that the additional controls could not have been installed either (a) when the mill was built, or (b) as soon as it became apparent that the mill pollution was damaging the adjoining properties. It was admitted that the increase of the stack height to 290 feet would decrease the fallout on plaintiffs' property. The failure to increase the stack height earlier is not explained.

The evidence also discloses that the defendant's efforts to control pollution were influenced by the cost factor.* * *

There was an abundance of evidence sufficient by any standard to support an award of punitive damages. We conclude that the trial court erred in withdrawing the issue of punitive damages from the jury.

The case is remanded for a new trial.

DENECKE, Justice (dissenting).

The majority holds that the fact the defendant did not install all the possible air pollution controls at the beginning of the plant's operation is evidence defendant did not do everything reasonably possible to eliminate or minimize the damage to plaintiffs and, therefore, the jury may punish the defendant by awarding plaintiffs punitive damages. I disagree that the facts permit this inference.* * *

There was no witness who expressed an opinion that a reasonably prudent mill operator would have proceeded any differently than did the defendant. It appears from the testimony of both parties that the control of air pollution from a Kraft mill is as difficult for lay understanding as some portions of the practice of medicine. As in medical malpractice cases, it is appropriate to require opinion testimony whether the defendant has or has not observed the applicable standard of care. As in a medical malpractice case, I do not believe it is evidence of negligence merely to show that the defendant used procedures later which he could have used initially. The question is, did reasonable prudence require that such procedures be used initially? There was no testimony that it did.

My principal difference with the majority, however, is concerning the legal basis for permitting the jury, in its discretion, to award punitive damages.

The majority bases its decisions upon the state of mind of the defendant at the time the tortious acts were committed. This is an accepted thesis. They apparently have selected alternate states of mind, proof of which would permit a jury to award punitive damages. According to the majority, punitive damages are awardable "whenever there was evidence of a wrongful act done intentionally, with knowledge that it would cause harm to a particular person or persons" and punitive damages are awardable in this case because there is "substantial evidence from which the jury could have found that during the period involved in this action the defendant had not done everything reasonably possible to eliminate or minimize the damage to adjoining properties by its mill."

I construe the first basis, stripped to its essentials, to state the principle that punitive damages are awardable for all intentional torts. I do not interpret our past decisions to so hold.

We have previously decided that punitive damages could not be awarded in cases in which there was an intentional trespass to land, but the trespasser's motive was deemed not "malicious." * * *

The other ground upon which the majority rests its decision that punitive damages are awardable is upon the proposition that defendant has not done everything reasonably possible to prevent or minimize damage to plaintiffs, i.e., on the state-of-mind scale,—negligence.

In certain malpractice cases we have permitted the award of punitive damages although the defendant was at most guilty of a high degree of negligence. However, we have regarded these cases as a separate category.* * *

Reynolds Metals Company v. Lampert, 316 F.2d 272; 324 F.2d 465 (9th Cir. 1963), relied upon by plaintiffs, does not hold, in my opinion, that punitive damages can be assessed against an industrial concern that a jury finds did not do everything reasonably possible to prevent damage by air pollution. I base this particularly on the evidence in that case that the defendant had conscious knowledge that it could do more to prevent or reduce pollution than it was doing, but it continued to pollute at the same or greater rate because it was cheaper to continue to damage plaintiffs' property and pay compensatory damages than to install available and feasible air pollution equipment. There was no such evidence or inference in the present case. The State Sanitary Authority Director of Air Pollution testified that Georgia-Pacific was proceeding in the only feasible manner,—trial and error—trying, testing, revising, reversing and repeating the sequence.

In my opinion a negligent state of mind should not be sufficient to enable the jury to award punitive damages.* * *

Many times this court has stated: "[P]unitive damages are not favored in the law."* * *

The purpose of punitive damages is to deter the defendant and others in like circumstances from committing the intentional act which has injured the plaintiffs.* * * It is not to provide additional compensation to damaged parties.* * *

Punitive damages is an oddity in the law of damages. An award of punitive damages is not to compensate for injury, but to penalize, with the object of deterring. To deter by means of punitive damages was an integral part of the ancient English tort law when public purpose and private compensation were intermingled. When a clear division was made between criminal law, with the object of protection to the public at large, and civil tort law, with the object of compensating injured persons, punishment as a deterrent was left to the state acting through the criminal law. Today, the sole remaining vestige in civil law which provides for punishment is the awarding of punitive damages.

We have never sought to deter defendants from future negligent conduct by awarding of punitive damages, with the exceptions stated above. Negligent vehicle drivers are a much more serious menace than negligent papermill operators; however, we have never intimated we would permit a jury to assess punitive damages against a negligent motorist to deter negligent driving. Permitting a jury to award punitive damages to deter a negligent industry is a change in direction in the law of punitive damages.

Turning to the other bases for the majority opinion, I am also of the opinion that granting the jury the power of deterrence to prevent an intentional trespass is not warranted.

The witnesses called by both parties agree that with the present state of knowledge the defendant cannot prevent its plant from polluting the air in some degree and damaging plaintiffs' property. Therefore, the only way in which an award of punitive damages can deter defendant from intentionally operating its plant knowing it will cause a trespass or continue a nuisance to plaintiffs' damage is if the award is large enough to amount so that the defendant cannot continue profitably to operate its plant. Any lesser award would be only for the private profit of the parties plaintiff and would not accomplish the public purpose.

In my opinion the granting to a jury of the power to award punitive damages is not a suitable vehicle to decide whether or not an industry should continue to operate.

The jury in the award of punitive damages "acts something like a judge in passing sentence on the defendant in a criminal case."* * *

It also seems anomalous to me that we would permit juries to close down industries by punitive damage awards when there may be factors present which would cause an equity court to refuse to close down the same industry when asked to issue an injunction.* * *

We are committed to the doctrine in considering injunctions that an industry will not be closed down if it is merely proven that the operator is knowingly and continuously committing a trespass or nuisance to the damage of the adjoining landowner; the equities must be "balanced." I cannot understand why we should adopt a contrary view by permitting a jury to award punitive damages in order to accomplish the same end, closing down the operation.* * *

If a court sitting in equity would not shut down the defendant's operation, a jury should not be given the discretion to bring about a contrary result.

O'CONNELL, Justice (dissenting).

The only justification for the imposition of punitive damages is to deter wrongful conduct in those circumstances where other legal sanctions are not available to effect deterrence.* * *

PERRY, J., joins in this dissent.

---

3. Government Approval of the Activity

Many businesses are subject to federal, state or local regulation. These regulations create the possibility of a defense in an environmental action where the defendant may argue that he is not liable because he performed his activity in accordance with the rules of the government agency. This defense raises several issues. One of these issues was raised in *Huron Cement Company v. Detroit*, 362 U.S. 400 (1960) *supra*, where the defendant argued that he complied with federal regulations relating to the operation of vessels in interstate waters and therefore could not be prosecuted by a city for violation of city regulation of emission of smoke from these vessels. Where there is a conflict between the regulations of two levels of government the issue becomes one of deciding which system of regulation will prevail. The *Huron Cement* case deals with that question.

The second issue is a more fundamental one, namely, is the defendant's action wrongful so as to impose liability, although the activities comply with standards imposed by a government-sanctioned system of regulation. This was one of the questions raised in *Costas v. City of Fond du Lac*, 24 Wis. 2d 409, 129 N.W. 2d 217 (1964) *infra*, involving an action to enjoin a nuisance created by the operation of a sewage disposal plant. The defendant argued that there should be no liability for a nuisance because the operation of the sewage plant was approved by a state agency. The judicial response to this question will depend on such circumstances as the nature of the damage, the type and extent of the regulation and the willingness of the court to interpose the judicial process into the administrative process.

4. Compliance with Requirements of Administrative Law

Administrative law is a subject that deals with the rules relating to the procedures and obligations of administrative agencies and the rights of individuals subject to their jurisdiction, including the rights of persons to seek judicial redress from administrative actions. When a person seeks judicial review of administrative action the agency may defend on any of several procedural grounds: (*1*) ***Primary jurisdiction*** is a defense based on the argument that the issue should *first* be resolved by the administrative agency and only after such administrative action may it be reviewed by a court based on the record made by the agency. (*2*) **Ripeness** is an issue related to the question whether there is a "case or controversy." A court should avoid issuing "advisory opinions" and should reserve its power to situations where there is a real controversy. Consequently courts should wait until the administrative agency has made its decision before reviewing administrative actions. For an interesting case involving an allegation that the failure of an administrator to take action promptly is tantamount to an order denying relief and therefore "ripe" for judicial action, see *Environmental Defense Fund v. U.S. Department of H.E.W.*, 428 F.2d 1083 (D.C. Cir. 1970). (*3*) **Exhaustion of remedies** may be a defense based on the argument that the plaintiff had not utilized, i.e., "exhausted," all of the opportunities for administrative remedies before a judicial remedy was sought. (*4*) **Scope of review** raises the issue of the extent to which the court will review the evidence on which the administrative decision was based and examines the criteria to be used in deciding whether an agency's action should be set aside.

The Federal Administrative Procedures Act., 5 U.S.C. 701–706, prescribes the rules for judicial review of administrative acts in the federal courts. Each state has its own rules for judicial review of action of state agencies. *Nor-Am Agricultural Products, Inc., v. Hardin* illustrates the kind of problem that may arise when deciding whether an administrative decision should be reviewed by the court.

NOR-AM AGRICULTURAL PRODUCTS, INC.
v.
HARDIN

435 F.2d 1151 (7th Cir. 1970)

CUMMINGS, Circuit Judge.

This is an appeal from a preliminary injunction granted by the district court which effectually restrains the Secretary of Agriculture and other personnel of the Department of Agriculture from continuing the suspension of the registration of 17 Panogenic compounds as "economic poisons" under the Federal Insecticide, Fungicide and Rodenticide Act. 7 U.S.C. § 135 et seq. A three-judge panel of this Court, one judge dissenting, upheld the preliminary injunction. 435 F.2d 1133. Subsequently,the Government's petition for a rehearing *en banc* was granted.

Plaintiff Morton International, Inc. manufactures seventeen types of cyano (methylmercuri) guanidine known as Panogens. Plaintiff Nor-Am Agricultural Products, Inc. distributes Morton's Panogens. These mercury compounds are used as fungicides in treating seeds intended for planting. They were duly registered as "economic poisons" with the Secretary of Agriculture, as required by Section 4(a) of the Federal Insecticide, Fungicide and Rodenticide Act. 7 U.S.C. § 135b(a).

Pursuant to Section 4(c) of the Act (7 U.S.C. § 135b(c)), on February 18, 1970, the Department of Agriculture telegraphed plaintiff Nor-Am that its Panogen registrations had been suspended "in view of the recent accident involving the ingestion of pork from hog feed seed treated with cyano (methylmercuri) guanidine." * * *

On March 9, 1970, the registrations of similar products of other manufacturers were suspended. The suspensions prevent the shipment of these products until their registration is again permitted. Plaintiffs and the other distributors and manufacturers were not, however, required to recall existing stocks from their customers.

Administrative review of the Secretary's order was initiated on March 27, 1970, when Non-Am requested an expedited administrative hearing as provided by Section 4(c) of the Act. Instead of awaiting such a hearing, however, plaintiffs filed this suit on April 9, 1970, and quickly sought a preliminary injunction. Thereupon defendants moved to dismiss the proceeding. They claimed that the district court lacked jurisdiction to review the suspension order in advance of the hearing established by the statute; that plaintiffs had not exhausted the administrative procedures established by the Act; that the Secretary's order was a non-reviewable, discretionary act; and that the Secretary had not acted arbitrarily or capriciously.* * *

At the hearing on the motion for the preliminary injunction, two Nor-Am employees and the general manager of a seed improvement association testified that Panogen products had been marketed for 20 years as a very useful fungicide seed treatment.* * *

After the hearing, the district judge found that the court had jurisdiction over the subject matter of the dispute pursuant to the provisions of 28 U.S.C. § 1331, 28 U.S.C. § 1337, 28 U.S.C. §§ 2201–2202, Section 10 of the Administrative Procedure Act, 5 U.S.C. §§701–706, and the "general equity powers of this Court." The district judge also determined that unless preliminary injunctive relief were granted, plaintiffs would suffer irreparable harm for which they had no adequate administrative or legal remedy, although they were "likely to prevail on the merits." The judge further concluded that preliminary relief was "consistent with the public interest." Accordingly, he held the suspension of the Panogen registrations to have been arbitrary, capricious, and contrary to law, and defendants were enjoined from taking action against plaintiffs or the Panogens in reliance on the suspension order. Defendants were also ordered to give notice that the Panogens may again be distributed and sold in interstate commerce. Finally, the preliminary injunction permitted defendants to issue notices of cancellation of the registrations of these "economic poisons" effective only after the public hearing permitted by Section 4(c) of the Act. Upon consideration of this cause by the entire court, we are of the opinion that the district court lacked power to grant this relief because the plaintiffs have not exhausted their administrative remedy.

The fundamental provisions regulating judicial review of administrative actions are contained in the 1946 Administrative Procedure Act. 5 U.S.C. § 701 et seq. Section 10(c) of that Act governs which agency actions shall be reviewable:

> "Agency action made reviewable by statute and final agency action for which there is no other adequate remedy in a court are subject to judicial review. A preliminary, procedural, or intermediate agency action or ruling not directly reviewable is subject to review on the review of the final agency action.* * *" 5 U.S.C. § 704.* * *

In determining the status of the instant suspension in the light of the Administrative Procedure Act, we must turn first to the pertinent provisions of the Federal

Insecticide, Fungicide and Rodenticide Act. 7 U.S.C. § 135 et seq. The 1964 amendments to Section 4 of that Act (Pub.L. 88–305, 88th Cong., 2nd Sess.) greatly strengthened the ability of the Secretary of Agriculture to take affirmative action protecting the public from hazardous and mislabeled commodities. Congress enacted new powers to deny, suspend, and cancel registrations where the Secretary had previously been compelled to accede to registration under protest should he be faced with an adamant demand. In Section 4(c), Congress also added hearing procedures guiding the exercise of these new powers.* * *

These statutory provisions do not expressly or impliedly contemplate immediate review of emergency suspensions by either district or appellate courts.* * *

Equally unacceptable is the contention that an emergency suspension order is a "final order" of the Secretary made reviewable by Section 4(c). That limitation on judicial review serves to avoid delay and interference with agency proceedings by confining review to orders effectively terminating administrative adjudication.* * *

We conclude that Congress intended to confine judicial review of registration disputes under Section 4(c) of the Act to final orders of the Secretary culminating administrative adjudication. Under this Act, the emergency suspension of registration preceding such adjudication does not constitute such a final order and is therefore not "reviewable by statute" within Section 10(c) of the Administrative Procedure Act, *supra*, p. 1155.* * *

Plaintiffs contend that this order should nevertheless entitle them to review under the "final agency action" provision of Section 10(c) of the Administrative Procedure Act. They argue that suspension of registration by the Secretary possesses sufficient "finality" as an administrative action to warrant immediate recourse to the courts despite its status as a preliminary act within the framework of Section 4(c) of the Federal Insecticide, Fungicide and Rodenticide Act. Suspension, they urge, immediately and drastically affects their rights and interests as greatly as formally finalized cancellation. They suggest that neither subsequent agency proceedings nor judicial review established by Section 4(d) adequately test the Secretary's determination of "imminent hazard to the public." Unless they are permitted this exceptional remedy, they claim that the Secretary's findings amount to autonomous discretion.

Under Section 10(c) of the Administrative Procedure Act, the concept of finality of administrative action encompasses a complex array of considerations which may vary in accordance with the character and activities of the administrative agency, and with the nature and role of the agency action from which judicial review is sought. See Abbott Laboratories v. Gardner, 387 U.S. 136, 148–156, 87 S.Ct. 1507, 18 L.Ed.2d 681. The flexibility of the finality concept does not, however, permit facile disregard of the purposes of congressional delegation of power and of the clear procedural scheme delineated in this particular statute.* * *

The function of the Secretary's emergency power, as well as the practical exigencies of coordinating administrative and judicial machinery, militates against avoiding the prescribed procedures. The emergency suspension of registration of an economic poison under Section 4(c) involves highly discretionary administrative action with deeply rooted antecedents in the realm of public health and safety. In subtle areas of regulation, summary emergency action frequently precedes formal administrative or judicial adjudication.* * * Where, as here, Congress follows discretionary preliminary or interlocutory agency action with specially fashioned adjudication machinery, strict observance of the prescribed procedure prior to judicial intervention is compellingly indicated.

Precipitous judicial review of this tentative judgment would at best be a difficult matter of dubious social benefit. Moreover, it strains administrative resources at a stage in the process which is most delicate and to a degree which may ultimately be rendered unnecessary by ordinary agency operations, both formal and informal.

Even the limited review here contemplated nullifies the need or utility of the further agency action desired by Congress. The administrative process is interrupted before issues have been crystalized and narrowed and without affording opportunity for application of technical expertise and informed judgment. As this record demonstrates, judicial review at this stage requires factual elaboration by the district court. Such bifurcation and duplication of governmental resources and efforts demonstrates the wisdom of judicial restraint, since once the district court has inserted itself into the process, it becomes wasteful or pointless to return the matter to the agency.* * *

Judicial review of the Secretary's suspension order is inconsistent with the procedural remedies created by Congress for such an occasion. It is also at odds with the restraint courts have long exercised in dealing with preventive measures available to agencies charged with protecting such sensitive areas of public welfare. Here the plaintiffs have not yet exhausted their statutorily prescribed administrative remedies and there has as yet been no "final agency action" within Section 10(c) of the Administrative Procedure Act.* * *

In addition to the statutory avenues of review, plaintiffs urge that the equity powers of the court have been properly invoked to prevent irreparable injury caused by the suspension order.

The circumvention of clearly prescribed administrative procedures by awarding equitable relief is an exceptional practice. As explained in Aircraft & Diesel Equipment Corp. v. Hirsch, 331 U.S. 752, 773–774, 67 S.Ct. 1493, 1503–1504, 91 L.Ed. 1796, the rule that administrative remedies may occasionally be by-passed to protect strong private interests from irreparable harm

> "is not one of mere convenience or ready application. Where the intent of Congress is clear to require administrative determination, either to the exclusion of judicial action or in advance of it, a strong showing is required, both of inadequacy of the prescribed procedure and of impending harm, to permit short-circuiting the administrative process. Congress' commands for judicial restraint in this respect are not lightly to be disregarded."

Plaintiffs have failed to establish such an irremediable threat to sufficiently strong interests to warrant equitable intercession at this juncture.

We cannot accept the verdict of the judge below that the administrative remedies are inadequate.* * *

The primary interests threatened in this case are not public but private. They are interests of property rather than of life or liberty. Although plaintiffs claim danger to farmers and consumers from removal of their products, their direct and immediate concern is the impact of suspensions upon their business.* * *

We do not demean plaintiffs' possible losses when noting, moreover, that the temporary suspension affects business profits, not the very existence of the commodities plaintiffs seek to purvey. Where public health and safety demand emergency removal of a commodity from the market, even unrecoverable financial losses incurred *pendente lite* must be deemed an expense of the litigation itself.* * *

Congress was not bound to supply the optimal protection to registrants affected by emergency suspensions. Congress balanced the public and private interests when it fashioned not only the Secretary's discretionary power but also the administrative procedures to follow exercise of that power.* * *

If this preliminary injunction were approved, other litigants could obtain district court threshold review by parroting plaintiffs' claim that the Secretary had acted arbitrarily and capriciously in suspending their registrations, even though Sections 4(c) and 4(d) specify that review shall only be in the courts of appeals after action by the advisory committee and then by the Secretary. We should not countenance such an evasion of the review procedure provided by Congress in this statute. In reaching this conclusion, we express no opinion on the merits of the controversy between these parties concerning the registration of Panogens.

The preliminary injunction is dissolved and the case is remanded to the district court with instructions to dismiss the complaint.

Reversed.

PELL, Circuit Judge (dissenting).

See *Reynolds Metals Company v. Martin, supra*, in which the court held that a nuisance action is an exception to the requirement of review by the state sanitary authority before a court action may be brought.

---

5. Contributory Negligence

Contributory negligence is the most common defense to an action based on the defendant's negligence. **Contributory negligence** is conduct on the part of the plaintiff, contributing as a legal cause of the harm he has suffered, that falls below the standard that a reasonable person would have adopted for his own protection. Various theories have been offered to explain the existence of this defense, such as the attempt to punish plaintiffs for their own misconduct, the desire not to let courts reward wrongdoers, the theory that plaintiff's negligence is an intervening cause between defendant's negligence and the damages and as a judicial means of countermanding a plaintiff-biased jury.

Whatever the reasons for the creation of the defense at common law it may be argued that contributory negligence should not be a defense in actions that affect the environment. *High Voltage Engineering Corp. v. Pierce* illustrates the general rule that the characterization of contributory negligence is a question of fact to be submitted to the jury.

HIGH VOLTAGE ENGINEERING CORP.
v.
PIERCE

359 F.2d 33 (10th Cir. 1966)

MURRAH, Chief Judge.

This appeal is from a judgment on a jury verdict in an action by appellee Pierce against appellant High Voltage for personal injuries caused by a radioactive beam from an electron accelerator manufactured and supplied by High Voltage to the intervenor Sandia Corporation, Pierce's employer.

The Van deGraaff two million volt accelerator was designed and used to propel electron beams at target material for nuclear experimental purposes. This is accomplished by spraying electrons on a moving belt for transmission to a high voltage terminal. From the terminal they flow to a cathode for emission into the accelerator tube and propulsion to the experiment target at the end of the tube. Four switches control the accelerator's operation. One switch turns on the power and another controls the belt and its drive motor. A third switch determines the amount of voltage on the terminal. Another, the beam switch, allows the electrons to be emittted as a beam from the cathode into the accelerator tube. The electron beam causes radiation and potential human danger in the target area.

The accelerator is housed in a concrete chamber or "target room." On the date of the accident, a Sandia Corporation employee, trained by appellant, was operating the drive motor and belt to dispel a 1,700,000 volt "self-charge" on the voltage terminal. The beam switch was off. The appellee-Pierce asked the operator if it was safe to enter the accelerator chamber to set up an experiment. After being told it was safe because the beam switch was off, Pierce entered the chamber despite the blinking of warning lights and a sounding horn indicating that the drive motor was operating. Two minutes later he left the room and discovered the injuries complained of.

The theory of appellees' case as correctly submitted to the jury is that a radioactive beam referred to as "dark current phenomenon" was emitted from the accelerator tube while the beam switch was off and the accelerator was in a condition of self-charge at high voltage. The court defined the issues by telling the jury that the accelerator was a dangerous instrumentality when emitting an electron beam; that it could and did emit an electron beam under the conditions prevailing at the time the appellee was injured; and that High Voltage knew that this phenomenon could occur. The issues were further sharpened by stating the contention of appellees to the effect that they did not know of the phenomenon and High Voltage was, therefore, under a duty to give adequate warning of the attendant danger. The trial court then succinctly stated the appellant's contention to the effect that it was under no duty to warn the appellees of the particular danger because as scientists they knew or should have known of it. Moreover, if they did not know, they had been given adequate warning of the particular hazard, and entry into the chamber under the prevailing circumstances was contributorily negligent.

The trial court then proceeded to state the applicable law of the case to the effect that as the supplier of a dangerous instrumentality the appellant was under a legal duty to warn prospective users of dangers which it knew or should know, and that such warning should be commensurate with the degree of danger involved, i. e., the warning must be directed to the specific danger and sufficient to cause a reasonable man acting under similar circumstances with the same knowledge and background to know the potential danger involved in the exercise of reasonable care.

The appellant makes no objection to the statement of the issues or the law of the case as stated in the trial court's instructions. It takes the position, however, that the trial court should have followed the law and the ruling in Marker v. Universal Oil Products Co., 10 Cir., 250 F.2d 603, and directed a verdict on the grounds that the evidence conclusively shows that the peculiar danger causing the injury was equally within the knowledge of the parties and the appellant was, therefore, under no duty to warn or inform. Alternatively, it contends that as a matter of law its legal duty was fulfilled by complete and adequate instructions to any user of the accelerator and that the harm in this case resulted from an unanticipated misuse by an adequately informed user.

The directed verdict in Marker was sustained on the conclusiveness of the proof that the dangerous condition was equally within the technical knowledge of both parties and that the harm, therefore, resulted from an unanticipated misuse. If the appellee had equal knowledge of the danger involved, or if he was adequately informed of it, his subsequent entry into the chamber would constitute unanticipated misuse or contributory negligence, both barring recovery. See Marker v. Universal Oil Products Co., supra; Parkinson v. California Co., 10 Cir., 255 F.2d 265.

The court in our case gave no equal knowledge instruction, and the appellant does not complain of its failure to do so. But, if, as in Marker, the evidence conclusively shows equal technical knowledge of the danger, High Voltage was entitled to a directed verdict under applicable law. Unlike Marker, however, we do not think the proof in our case conclusively shows equal technical knowledge of the dark current phenomenon which admittedly caused the danger and consequent harm.* * *

The Director of Physical Research at Sandia, who was completely familiar with accelerators, testified that he was aware of the principle of dark current phenomenon, but that he was not aware of the scientific fact that it could occur in this particular accelerator. Appellee Pierce testified he did not know about it; the operator denied he knew of it; another scientist who had been similarly injured testified that he did not know of it or of anyone who did. The issue of equal scientific knowledge was well within the realm of fact.

Alternatively, High Voltage cites seven specific instances of unanticipated gross misuse of the accelerator based upon adequate notice, any one of which would bar recovery. Five of the cited instances are based upon failure to heed specific warnings contained in the manual of instructions accompanying delivery of the accelerator.* * *

The fifth asserted warning contained in the manual under the heading "Radiation Hazard" stated that "The output from the high voltage accelerator tube of this apparatus can produce radiation effects with serious and possibly fatal consequences to personnel.* * *

Another misuse was claimed for failure of Pierce to take a hand survey meter (a geiger-counter) into the target room with him in accordance with the safety instructions promulgated by Sandia. The testimony was to the effect that the hand survey meter was required and that the operator of the accelerator had been instructed to always take the meter into the room when doing maintenance work on the accelerator, whether the beam switch was on or off. There was also evidence to the effect that Pierce knew of the hand meter and its purpose and that he did not take it into the target room with him and was not instructed to do so by the operator. The operator first indicated that if Pierce had taken the hand meter into the target room the accident would not have happened. Upon reflection, he indicated that because of the time it took the meter to register radiation the accident might have happened in any event. Pierce testified that if there had been any question of safety, he would not have gone into the target room or would have taken a meter with him; that he did not realize the danger under the circumstances because he knew the beam switch was off.

High Voltage takes the position that even if Pierce was not guilty of misuse or contributory negligence, Sandia was negligent and such negligence was the sole cause of the injury, first, for failure to promulgate proper safety rules for the operation of the machine and, second, failure to observe and enforce the safety rules it did promulgate, namely the proper use of both the remote metering system and the hand survey meter.

Judge Payne thought these defenses presented questions of fact under the evidence and told the jury that the warnings, if any, in the instruction manual would be binding upon Pierce only if he knew about them or should have known in the exercise of due care, but if the warnings were adequate they were binding upon Sandia in any event and it was under a duty to pass them on to its employees, including Pierce; that the jury should determine whether the instructions did contain warnings and, if so, whether they were adequate and whether Sandia passed them on to Pierce; that they should make this determination in determining whether Sandia was negligent and whether its negligence, if any, was the sole and proximate cause of the accident.

The seventh claimed misuse of the machine has to do with Dr. Pierce's entry into the target room in disregard of the door interlocks and the audible, visual warnings, i. e., flashing lights and sounding horn. The horn blows for forty-five seconds after entry into the target room when the power is on even though the beam switch is off, and the lights continue to flash as long as the drive motor is in operation. When Pierce went to the operator in the console room outside the target room, the drive motor was in operation, the beam switch was off and the lights were flashing.* * *

High Voltage contends that Pierce was negligent in entering the room in these circumstances and that in any event Sandia was solely negligent by failing to prohibit Pierce from entering the target room under prevailing conditions; that the interlocking doors, horn and flashing lights were clear warning to anyone.

Judge Payne submitted this issue to the jury instructing them to determine from all the evidence and surrounding circumstances whether these warnings were sufficient to adequately warn a reasonable man in the exercise of ordinary care. On both the motion for directed verdict and motion for judgment n. o. v. Judge Payne was deeply disturbed and perplexed concerning whether as a matter of law the warning signals were adequate in and of themselves to inform Sandia and Pierce of the peculiar danger which prevailed at the time of the accident and which caused the harm. He was impressed with the significance of the words on the console panel: "Radiation Beam" "On" "Off" and seemed to think the operator may have been lulled into the belief that with the radiation beam switch off the target chamber was safe from radiation despite the warning signals. Considered in the light of all the circumstances, the court could not say as a matter of law that the warnings were sufficient to constitute unanticipated misuse or contributory negligence.

* * *

It is, of course, the function of the trial court to analyze the evidence and appraise its sufficiency in the first instance. Judge Payne did analyze and appraise the evidence with extreme care, and we should not superimpose our judgment on that of the trial court unless we can say from our objective appraisal of all of the facts and circumstances that his judgment on the adequacy of notice was clearly wrong. When all of the evidence is considered in the light most favorable to appellees, we cannot say that the trial court erroneously submitted it to the jury.

* * *

The judgment is affirmed.

6. ASSUMPTION OF RISK

Assumption of risk is a defense that is closely related to, but nevertheless different from, **contributory negligence**. Assumption of risk may be a defense under circumstances where the plaintiff was not negligent but where he undertook a known risk of danger. The issue may arise where a visitor to a nuclear power plant claims that he has been injured by excessive radiation or where an investigator of the dangers of toxic wastes is injured during his investigations. The following excerpt from *Potter v. Brittan* illustrates the difficulty that courts continue to have with this distinction.

POTTER v. BRITTAN

286 F.2d 521 (1961)

GOODRICH, Circuit Judge

* * *

The one point left in the case on this appeal involves the plaintiffs' insistence that the trial judge incorrectly charged the jury. The defenses of assumption of risk and contibutory negligence were both made by the defendants. The trial judge charged on each and his clear statement of the rule of contributory negligence is not challenged. As to assumption of risk the judge said: "Assumption of risk is so closely identified with contributory negligence that a practical distinction is difficult when considered in relation to the facts in a particular case. * * * The tendency is to treat assumption of risk and contributory negligence as convertible terms so that they are now virtually identical concepts."

This did not satisfy plaintiffs' counsel and in colloquy on exceptions to the court's charge he said: "My request is really that they shouldn't get the impression that assumption of risk and contributory negligence are two separate defenses. * * * The pleading makes them two, but the law does not. * * * It's a contributory negligence defense which one judge will call assumption of risk and one will call contributory negligence."* * *

The position of the legal scholars on the subject is perfectly clear. At the risk of tiresome repetition a few quotations are in order because the subject seems to be one on which there is a good deal of confusion. The first quotation is from a very famous tort scholar, Francis H. Bohlen, and it was written in 1926:

> "The defense of contributory negligence is quite distinct. Negligence involves the idea of misconduct, a failure to measure up to the standard of that ideal personage, the normal social man; assumption of risk does not. A risk while

obvious may not be so imminently dangerous that a prudent man would necessarily avoid it, yet if it shall be freely encountered it will in general be held to be so far assumed that no recovery for the consequent injury is possible. Voluntary conscious action may be negligent if the known danger be great and imminent, but it is not negligent because voluntary. By contributory negligence a plaintiff is barred from recovery by his own misconduct, though the defendant has been guilty of an act admittedly wrongful as to him. Voluntary subjection to a known risk negatives the existence of any duty on the defendant's part by the breach of which he could be a wrongdoer.

"It is essential that the two ideas should be kept quite distinct. * *" (Footnotes omitted.)

The same point is made by current writers. Prosser on Torts, for example, talks about the situation where the two defenses overlap. He says:

"Ordinarily it makes little difference which the defense is called. The distinction may become important, however, under such statutes as the Federal Employers' Liability Act, which has now abrogated the defense of assumption of risk entirely, but has left contributory negligence as a partial defense reducing the amount of recovery. In working out the distinction, the courts have arrived at the conclusion that assumption of risk is a matter of knowledge of the danger and intelligent acquiescence in it, while contributory negligence is a matter of some fault or departure from the standard of reasonable conduct, however unwilling or protesting the plaintiff may be. The two may coexist, or either may exist without the other." (Footnotes omitted.)

Finally, in the last work on the subject, Harper and James on Torts, 1956, the authors say:

"*Assumption of risk.* Contributory negligence has sometimes been thought to be no more than an aspect of assumption of risk, so that plaintiff is barred from recovery under the maxim volenti non fit injuria. This explanation, too, would warrant the rule in its present form, as a complete bar to plaintiff's action. The two notions, however, do not cover the same ground and in many situations do not even overlap, though they may. Assumption of risk involves the negation of defendant's duty; contributory negligence is a defense to a breach of such duty. Assumption of risk may involve perfectly reasonable conduct on plaintiff's part; contributory negligence never does." (Footnotes omitted.)

It would be hard to find any point on which scholarly discussion is so completely unanimous.* * *

---

7. STATUTES OF LIMITATIONS

All states have **statutes of limitations**, or laws that limit the period of time during which an action may be brought. After the expiration of the prescribed period of time the defendant is no longer liable for that act. The statutory period will usually be different for different types of lawsuits, as the following excerpts from the New Jersey statutes illustrate.

---

a. Actions Against Private Persons: N.J.S.A. 2A:14–1

2A:14–1. 6 years

Every action at law for trespass to real property, for any tortious injury to real or personal property, for taking, detaining, or converting personal property, for replevin of goods or chattels, for any tortious injury to the rights of another not stated in sections 2A:14–2 and 2A:14–3 of this title, or for recovery upon a contractual claim or liability, express or implied, not under seal, or upon an account other than one which concerns the trade or merchandise between merchant and merchant, their factors, agents and servants, shall be commenced within 6 years next after the cause of any such action shall have accrued.

b. Actions Against the State: N.J.S.A. 59:13–5

* * *

In all contract claims against the State, the claimant shall be forever barred from recovering against the State if:

a. he fails to notify the appropriate contracting agency within 90 days of accrual of his claim except as otherwise provided in section 6 hereof; or

b. he fails to file suit within 2 years of accrual of his claims or within 1 year after completion of the contract giving rise to paid claim, whichever may be later; or

c. the claimant accepts personally or through his agent or legal representative any award, compromise or settlement made by the state of New Jersey.

---

8. PRESCRIPTIVE RIGHT TO CONTINUE A NUISANCE

Under the common law, and as prescribed by statute in most states, if an owner of property fails to stop someone from using his property for a prescribed period of time, the user of the property will obtain an **easement by prescription** to continue such use. The issue arises whether an easement by prescription can be established for an action that constitutes a nuisance. For example, should an upstream owner who discharges pollutants into a stream without being stopped by the downstream riparian owners be allowed to use this concept to acquire a **prescriptive right** to continue this pollution. There seems to be some ambiguity in the law, as the following two cases illustrate.

WEST KENTUCKY COAL CO. v. RUDD

328 S.W.2d 156 (Ky. 1959)

CULLEN, Commissioner.

C. B. Moore, owner of a 528-acre farm lying on Pond River, in Hopkins and Muhlenberg Counties, brought action against eight coal mining companies who operate in the Pond River drainage area, alleging that the companies were casting and discharging from their properties large quantities of coal slack, copperas waters and other deleterious substances which were carried into the waters of Pond River and were deposited on his land during overflow periods, causing damage to the productivity and fertility of his land. He sought a permanent injunction, and damages.* * *

The court entered judgment granting a permanent injunction, and an order transferring the damage phase of the case to the common law docket, for a jury trial. The coal companies have appealed from the judgment.* * *

As to one of the appellants alone, the W. G. Duncan Coal Company, it is contended that a *prescriptive* right has been acquired to discharge pollutants into Pond River, by reason of continued use of the stream for such purposes by that company for more than 15 years before commencement of the action. Reliance is placed upon W. G. Duncan Coal Company v. Jones, Ky., 254 S.W.2d 720, 721, 723, wherein such a right was recognized. The Jones case, however, limits such a right to use "for the same purpose, to the same extent, and under the same circumstances and conditions." The evidence in the instant case would warrant the conclusion that there had been a substantial change in the operations of the W. G. Duncan Coal Company in the Pond River area in recent years, in that a washing process had been instituted, and in that there had been a material increase in the quantity of coal produced. So we cannot say that the chancellor erred in determining that the present operations of the Duncan Company were not within the scope of a prescriptive right.* * *

The judgment is affirmed.

AUBELE v. A.B. GALETOVICH, INC.

83 Ohio L. Abs. 200, 165 N.E.2d 683 (1960)

HUNSICKER, Presiding Judge

On March 31, 1958, Garthe Aubele and several of his neighbors, residents of the village of Seven Hills, Cuyahoga County, Ohio, filed an action in the Common Pleas Court of Cuyahoga County against A. B. Galetovich, Inc. * * *

The petition asks that the parties defendant be enjoined from casting surface waters and effluent from septic tanks into a watercourse which passes through the property of the plaintiffs. The petition also asks that the village be enjoined from granting any further building permits to the developers, and that the village "declare to be null and void those permits already issued for the construction of dwellings on the tract of land described in the petition."

The answers of the defendants admit that a housing development along Justo Lane is being made. The answers also say that houses in this development, as in all other houses of the village, have septic tanks which discharge therefrom an effluent. The answers deny that surface water has been diverted or increased in the natural water course which drains the developed area; and further deny that such surface waters cause serious erosion on the lands of the plaintiffs, or that the effluent is a cause of any injury to the premises.

As in most cases of this type, there is a great conflict in the evidence, and the claims of the parties cannot easily be reconciled. There are, however, certain facts that cannot be disputed; among which are that there is a combination sanitary and storm sewer along Justo Lane, which crosses certain lands over which an easement has been obtained, and which sewer then empties into the small watercourse that crosses the lands of the plaintiffs. This watercourse is the natural drainage point for nearly all of the watershed area covered by the housing development.

* * *

The septic tanks of the 16 houses now found in the proposed 62-house development, and all of the septic tanks that will be constructed in the future along Justo Lane, will connect by lateral sewers to the main or combination sewer that eventually empties into the watercourse which traverses the lands of the plaintiffs (appellants in this court).* * *

Much of the argument advanced by the defendants (appellees in this court) seeks to justify all acts of the parties: first, upon the fact that everyone else in the village uses septic tanks, and the effluent therefrom is either cast upon the ground or into a watercourse; and, second, that the appellants are also contributing to the conditions about which they complain, by the use of their own septic tanks.

The village of Seven Hills could not give consent to any of its inhabitants to cast sewage upon the land of another, nor could it, as a municipal corporation, cast sewage upon the lands of another without incurring liability therefor.

As we view the matter raised by this action, we must first determine whether the appellants have established a case with that degree of proof which is required to grant the extraordinary relief sought herein.* * *

To say that an owner of land may never improve such lands or develop it to its highest and best use without being subject to a claim for damages or injunction, by reason of the resulting natural increase in the flow of water into a watercourse, such as we have herein, is to take a position that would prevent the progress that results from a growing industrial and commercial area. A lower riparian owner, along a watercourse, must expect that, as the upper lands are built up with homes and stores, much of the water which was absorbed by the land will now run off of hard-surfaced streets and the roofs of buidings, to seek its natural outlet in the channel developed with the contour of the land.* * *

The matter of the effluent which is being passed over the lands of the appellants presents a different problem than the surface waters from a natural watershed.* * *

It is clear to the members of this court that one may not obtain by prescription, or otherwise than by purchase, a right to cast sewage upon the lands of another without his consent.* * *

The difficulty we have in this case, however, is that the appellants have failed to establish their claims by that degree of proof necessary to warrant this court, in this appeal on questions of law and fact, to order the relief sought by the claimants. What may occur in the future in this development, or what proof of acts on the part of the appellees and others may warrant either an action in injunction or an action for damages, is not for this court to conjecture. The appellees are not absolved by the action we take herein, but the petition of the appellants is dismissed only because they have failed to establish their claims.

* * *

Petition dismissed at the costs of the appellants. The parties will prepare and file the necessary and proper journal entry.

Petition dismissed.

---

9. Pre-emption by the Federal Government

One of the problems of environmental regulation is that the subject is regulated by more than one government. For example, water pollution may be regulated by the federal, state and municipal governments. This multiplicity of regulatory activity often presents the question of which system of regulation will prevail when there is conflict among them. Under the federal system, established by the United States Constitution, the federal government is given certain specified powers and all remaining powers are reserved to the individual states. However, where Congress is authorized to regulate, its laws are the "supreme law of the land." Thus, when an issue arises whether a federal law will prevail over a state or municipal law, the answer is clear: the federal law will prevail if Congress so intended. The more difficult question for a Court to decide is whether Congress intended its law to **pre-empt**, or supersede the regulations of the other levels of government. As the majority and dissenting opinions in *City of Burbank v. Lockheed Air Terminal, Inc.* indicate, this decision is not always an easy one.

CITY OF BURBANK
v.
LOCKHEED AIR TERMINAL INC.

411 U.S. 624 (1973)

Mr. Justice DOUGLAS delivered the opinion of the Court.

The Court in Cooley v. Board of Wardens, 12 How. 299, 13 L.Ed. 996, first stated the rule of pre-emption which is the critical issue in the present case. Speaking through Justice Curtis, it said:

> "Now the power to regulate commerce embraces a vast field, containing not only many, but exceedingly various subjects, quite unlike in their nature; some imperatively demanding a single uniform rule, operating equally on the commerce of the United States in every port; and some, like the subject now in question, as imperatively demanding that diversity, which alone can meet the local necessities of navigation. . . . Whatever subjects of this power are in their nature national, or admit only of one uniform system, or plan of regulation, may justly be said to be of such a nature as to require exclusive legislation by Congress." *Id.*, at 319.

This suit brought by appellees asked for an injunction against the enforcement of an ordinance adopted by the City Council of Burbank, California, which made it unlawful for a so-called pure jet aircraft to take off from the Hollywood-Burbank Airport between 11 p. m. of one day and 7 a. m. the next day, and making it unlawful for the operator of that airport to allow any such aircraft to take off from that airport during such periods.* * *

The District Court found the ordinance to be unconstitutional on both Supremacy Clause and Commerce Clause grounds. 318 F.Supp. 914. The Court of Appeals affirmed on the grounds of the Supremacy Clause both as respects pre-emption and as respects conflict. 457 F.2d 667. The case is here on appeal.* * *

The Federal Aviation Act of 1958, 72 Stat. 737, 49 U.S.C. § 1301 et seq., as amended by the Noise Control Act of 1972, 86 Stat. 1234, and the regulations under it, 14 CFR Pts. 71–77, 91–97, are central to the question of pre-emption.

Section 1508 provides in part, "The United States of America is declared to possess and exercise complete and exclusive national sovereignty in the airspace of the United States. . . ." By § 1348 the Administrator of the Federal Aeronautics Act (FAA) has been given broad authority to regulate the use of the navigable airspace, "in order to insure the safety of aircraft and the efficient utilization of such airspace . . ." and "for the protection of persons and property on the ground. . . ."

The Solicitor General, though arguing against pre-emption, concedes that as respects "airspace management" there is pre-emption.* * *

Curfew, such as Burbank has imposed, would according to the testimony at the trial and the District Court's findings increase congestion, cause a loss of efficiency, and aggravate the noise problem. FAA has occasionally operated curfews. See Virginians for Dulles v. Volpe, D. C., 344 F.Supp. 573. But the record shows that FAA has consistently opposed curfews, unless managed by it, in the interests of its management of the "navigable airspace."

* * *

The Noise Control Act of 1972, 86 Stat. 1234, which was approved October 27, 1972, provides that the Administrator "after consultation with appropriate Federal, State, and local agencies and interested persons" shall conduct a study of various facets of the aircraft "noise" problems and report to the Congress within nine months, *i. e.*, by July 1973. The 1972 Act by amending § 611 of the Federal Aviation Act, also involves the Environmental Protection Agency (EPA) in the comprehensive scheme of federal control of the aircraft noise problem. Under the amended § 611(b)(1) the FAA, after consulting with EPA, shall provide "for the control and abatement of aircraft noise and sonic boom, including the application of such standards and regulations in the issuance, amendment, modification, suspension or revocation of any certificate authorized by this title." Section 611(b)(2) as amended provides that future certificates for aircraft operations shall not issue unless the new aircraft noise requirements are met. Section 611(c)(1) as amended provides that not later than July 1973 EPA shall submit to FAA proposed regulations to provide such "control and abatement of aircraft noise and sonic boom" as EPA determines is "necessary to protect the public health and welfare." The FAA is directed within 30 days to publish the proposed regulations in a notice of proposed rule making. Within 60 days after that publication FAA is directed to commence a public hearing on the proposed rules Section 611(c)(1). That subsection goes on to provide that within "a reasonable time after the conclusion of such hearing and after consultation with EPA," FAA is directed either to prescribe the regulations substantially as submitted by EPA; or prescribe them in modified form, or publish in the Federal Register a notice that it is not prescribing any regulation in response to EPA's submission together with its reasons therefor.

Section 611(c)(2) as amended also provides that if EPA believes that FAA's action with respect to a regulation proposed by EPA "does not protect the public health and welfare from aircraft noise or sonic boom," EPA shall consult with FAA and may request FAA to review and report to EPA on the advisability of prescribing the regulation orginally proposed by EPA. That request shall be published in the Federal Register; FAA shall complete the review requested and report to EPA in the time specified together with a detailed statement of FAA's findings and the reasons for its conclusion and shall identify any impact statement filed under § 102(2)(C) of the National Environmental Policy Act of 1969, 83 Stat. 853, 42 U.S.C. § 4332, with respect to FAA's action. FAA's action, if adverse to EPA's proposal, shall be published in the Federal Register.* * *

There is to be sure no express provision of pre-emption in the 1972 Act. That, however, is not decisive. As we stated in Rice v. Santa Fe Elevator Corp., 331 U.S. 218, 230, 67 S.Ct. 1146, 1152, 91 L.Ed.1447:

> "Congress legislated here in a field which the States have traditionally occupied. . . . So we start with the assumption that the historic police powers of the States were not to be superseded by the Federal Act unless that was the clear and manifest purpose of Congress. . . . Such a purpose may be evidenced in several ways. The scheme of federal regulation may be so pervasive as to make reasonable the inference that Congress left no room for the States to supplement it. . . . Or the Act of Congress may touch a field in which the federal interest is so dominant that the federal system will be assumed to preclude enforcement of state laws on the same subject. . . . Likewise, the object sought to be obtained by the federal law and the character of obligations imposed by it may reveal the same purpose. . . . Or the state policy may produce a result inconsistent with the objective of the federal statute."

It is the pervasive nature of the scheme of federal regulation of aircraft noise that leads us to conclude that there is pre-emption.* * *

"Federal control is intensive and exclusive. Planes do not wander about in the sky like vagrant clouds. They move only by federal permission, subject to federal inspection, in the hands of federally certified personnel and under an intricate system of federal commands. The moment a ship taxis onto a runway it is caught up in an elaborate and detailed system of controls."

Both the Senate and House Committees included in their Reports clear statements that the bills would not change the existing pre-emption rule.

* * *

The Senate Report stated: "States and local governments are preempted from establishing or enforcing noise emission standards for aircraft unless such standards are identical to standards prescribed under this bill.

* * *

When the blended provisions of the present Act were before the House, Congressman Staggers, Chairman of the House Commerce Committee, in urging the House to accept the amended version, said:

"I cannot say what industry's intention may be, but I can say to the gentleman what my intention is in trying to get this bill passed. We have evidence that across America some cities and States are trying to do [*sic*] pass noise regulations. Certainly we do not want that to happen. It would harass industry and progress in America. That is the reason why I want to get this bill passed during this session."

When the House approved the blended provisions of the bill, Senator Tunney moved that the Senate concur. He made clear that the regulations to be considered by EPA for recommendation to FAA would include:

". . . proposed means of reducing noise in airport environments through the application of emission controls on aircraft, the regulation of flight patterns and aircraft and airport operations, and *modifications in the number, frequency, or scheduling of flights* [as well as] . . . *the imposition of curfews on noisy airports*,

* * *

When the President signed the bill he stated that "many of the most significant sources of noise move in interstate commerce and can be effectively regulated only at the federal level."

Our prior cases on pre-emption are not precise guidelines in the present controversy, for each case turns on the peculiarities and special features of the federal regulatory scheme in question. CF. Hines v. Davidowitz, 312 U.S. 52, 61 S.Ct. 339, 85 L.Ed. 581; Huron Portland Cement Co. v. Detroit, 362 U.S. 440, 80 S.Ct. 813, 4 L.Ed. 2d 852. Control of noise is of course deep-seated in the police power of the States. Yet the pervasive control vested in EPA and in FAA under the 1972 Act seems to us to leave no room for local curfews or other local controls. What the ultimate remedy for aircraft noise which plagues many communities and tens of thousands of people is not known. The procedures under the 1972 Act are underway. In addition, the Administrator has imposed a variety of regulations relating to takeoff and landing procedures and runway preferences. The Federal Aviation Act requires a delicate balance between safety and efficiency, 49 U.S.C. § 1348(a), and, the protection of persons on the ground. 49 U.S.C. § 1348(c). Any regulations adopted by the Administrator to control noise pollution must be consistent with the "highest degree of safety." 49 U.S.C. § 1431(d)(3). The interdependence of these factors requires a uniform and exclusive system of federal regulation if the congressional objectives underlying the Federal Aviation Act are to be fulfilled.

If we were to uphold the Burbank ordinance and a significant number of municipalities followed suit, it is obvious that fractionalized control of the timing of takeoffs and landings would severely limit the flexibility of the FAA in controlling air traffic flow. The difficulties of scheduling flights to avoid congestion and the concomitant decrease in safety would be compounded.* * *

We are not at liberty to diffuse the powers given by Congress to FAA and EPA by letting the States or municipalities in on the planning. If that change is to be made, Congress alone must do it.

Affirmed.

Mr. Justice REHNQUIST, with whom Mr. Justice STEWART, Mr. Justice WHITE, and Mr. Justice MARSHALL join, dissenting.

The Court concludes that congressional legislation dealing with aircraft noise has so "pervaded" that field that Congress has *impliedly* pre-empted it, and therefore the ordinance of the city of Burbank here challenged is invalid under the Supremacy Clause of the Constitution. The Court says that the 1972 "Act reaffirms and reinforces the conclusion that FAA, now in conjunction with EPA, has full control over aircraft noise, pre-empting state and local control." *Ante* at 1859. Yet the House and Senate committee reports explicitly state that the 1972 Act to which the Court refers was *not* intended to alter the balance between state and federal regulation which had been struck by earlier congressional legislation in this area.

* * *

Appellees do not contend that the noise produced by jet engines could not reasonably be deemed to affect adversely the health and welfare of persons constantly exposed to it; control of noise, sufficiently loud to be classified as a public nuisance at common law, would be a type of regulation well within the traditional scope of the police power possessed by States and local governing bodies. Because noise regulation has traditionally been an area of local, not national, concern, in determining whether congressional legislation has, by implication, foreclosed remedial local enactments "we start with the assumption that the historic police powers of the States were not to be superseded by the Federal Act unless that was the clear and manifest purpose of Congress." Rice v. Santa Fe Elevator Corp., 331 U.S. 218, 230, 67 S.Ct. 1146, 1152, 91 L.Ed. 1447 (1947).* * *

Since Congress's intent in enacting the 1972 Act was clearly to retain the status quo between the federal regulation and local regulation, a holding of *implied* pre-emption of the field depends upon whether two earlier congressional enactments, the Federal Aviation Act of 1958, 72 Stat. 737, 49 U.S.C. § 1301 et seq., and the 1968 Noise Abatement Amendment to that Act, 49 U.S.C. § 1431, manifested the clear intent, to preclude local regulations, that our prior decisions require.* * *

Considering the language Congress enacted into law, the available legislative history, and the light shed by these on the congressional purpose, Congress did not intend either by the 1958 Act or the 1968 Amendment to oust local governments from the enactment of regulations such as that of the city of Burbank. The 1972 Act quite clearly intended to maintain the status quo between federal and local authorities. The legislative history of the 1972 Act, quite apart from its concern with avoiding additional pre-emption, discloses a primary focus on the alteration of procedures within the Federal Government for dealing with problems of aircraft noise already entrusted by Congress to federal competence. The 1972 Act set up procedures by which the Administrator of the Environmental Protection Agency would have a role to play in the formulation and review of standards promulgated by the Federal Aviation Administration dealing with noise emissions of jet aircraft.

* * *

The history of congressional action in this field demonstrates, I believe, an affirmative congressional intent to allow local regulation. But even if it did not go that far, that history surely does not reflect "the clear and manifest purpose of Congress" to prohibit the exercise of "the historic police powers of the States" which our decisions required before a conclusion of implied preemption is reached. Clearly Congress could preempt the field to local regulation if it chose.* * * But neither Congress nor the Administrator has chosen to go that route. Until they do, the ordinance of the city of Burbank is a valid exercise of its police power.

E. Judicial Remedies

After deciding that a defendant in an environmental law suit is responsible for the pollution or other environmental damage the court must decide on an appropriate judicial remedy. Where the plaintiff has suffered damages or injury that may be measured in monetary terms, **compensatory damages** may be appropriate. In many environmental law suits the plaintiff may seek an **injunction**, or court order, to stop the activity resulting in the environmental damage. Where the defendant has acted in wanton disregard of the rights of the plaintiff or there are other aggravating circumstances, **punitive damages** may be awarded. Where the defendant is a governmental official who has failed or refused to do something that he is required by law to do, the court may issue a writ of **mandamus** that orders him to perform a nondiscretionary duty. The cases that follow illustrate each of these judicial remedies.

---

1. Compensatory Damages

HARRISONVILLE
v.
DICKEY CLAY COMPANY

289 U.S. 334 (1932)

MR. JUSTICE BRANDEIS delivered the opinion of the Court.

W. S. Dickey Clay Manufacturing Company, a Delaware Corporation, owns a stock farm of 300 acres lying near the sewage disposal plant of the City of Harrisonville, Missouri. A small, meandering intermittent stream called Town Creek flows through a detached portion of the farm, consisting of 100 acres, devoted solely to pasturage. Since 1923, a drain pipe has discharged into the creek, at a point in the pasture, the effluent from the disposal plant of the City's general sewage system. In 1928, the Company brought, in the federal court for western Missouri, this suit against the City, alleging injury to the property through drainage of the effluent from the disposal plant and seeking both damages and an injunction.* * *

The District Court found that the detached portion of the Company's land use for pasturage is seriously affected by the pollution of Town Creek; that the aggregate loss in rental for the five years during which it owned the land had been $500; and that it would cost $3500 to restore the creek to the condition existing prior to the nuisance. The court, therefore, awarded damages in the sum of $4000. It held, also, that the Company was entitled to an injunction; but allowed the City six months within which to abate the nuisance by introducing some method that would prevent the discharge of putrescible sewage into the creek. Upon an appeal by the City, the Circuit Court of Appeals modified the decree by eliminating therefrom the item of $3500 damages. As so modified the decree was affirmed. 61 F. (2d) 210. The Company acquiesced in the modification; and in this Court the City did not question the propriety of the award of $500 damages. But, on the ground that the injunction should have been denied, it petitioned for a writ of certiorari, which was granted. 288 U.S. 594.* * *

The discharge of the effluent into the creek is a tort; and the nuisance, being continuous or recurrent, is an injury for which an injunction may be granted. Thus, the question here is not one of equitable jurisdiction. The question is whether, upon the facts found, an injunction is the appropriate remedy. For an injunction is not a remedy which issues as of course. Where substantial redress can be afforded by the payment of money and issuance of an injunction would subject the defendant to grossly disproportionate hardship, equitable relief may be denied although the nuisance is indisputable. This is true even if the conflict is between interests which are primarily private.* * * Where an important public interest would be prejudiced, the reasons for denying the injunction may be compelling. Such we think is the situation in the case at bar.

If an injunction is granted the courses open to the City are (a) to abandon the present sewage disposal plant, erected at a cost of $60,000, and leave the residents to the primitive methods theretofore employed, if the State authorities should permit; or (b) to erect an auxiliary plant at a cost of $25,000 or more, if it should be legally and practically possible to raise that sum. That expenditure would be for a desirable purpose; but the City feels unable to make it. On the other hand, the injury to the Company is wholly financial. The pasture land affected by the effluent would be worth, it was said, $50 or $60 an acre if the stream were freed from pollution. Denial of the injunction would subject the Company to a loss in value of the land amounting, on the basis of the trial court's findings, to approximately $100 per year. That loss can be measured by the reduction in rental or the depreciation in the market value of the farm, assuming the nuisance continues; and can be made good by the payment of money. The compensation payable would obviously be small as compared with the cost of installing an auxiliary plant, for the annual interest on its cost would be many times the annual loss resulting to the Company from the nuisance. Complete monetary redress may be given in this suit by making denial of an injunction conditional upon prompt payment as compensation of an amount equal to the depreciation in value of the farm on account of the nuisance complained of. We require this payment not on the ground that the nuisance is to be deemed a permanent one as contended, but because to oblige the Company to bring, from time to time, actions at law for its loss in rental would be so onerous as to deny to it adequate relief.

Second. By the Company it is contended that the City should be enjoined because it had the power to condemn the land or its use for sewage purposes. The City questions the existence of that power. We have no occasion to determine this issue of Missouri law. Possession of the right of condemnation would afford added reason why compensation should be substituted for an injunction.

* * *

The decree is reversed and the cause remanded to the District Court for further proceedings to determine the depreciation in value of the property on account of the nuisance, and to enter a decree withholding an injunction if such sum be paid within the time to be fixed by that court.

Reversed.

---

2. INJUNCTIONS

COSTAS v. CITY OF FOND DU LAC

24 Wis.2d 409, 129 N.W.2d 217 (1964)

HALLOWS, Justice.

The defendant claims it has not created a nuisance by the operation of its sewage disposal plant; the plaintiffs have suffered no irreparable injury; the condition of the injunction is impossible of performance; and the court may not direct the details and the manner in which a nuisance is to be abated.* * *

The city of Fond du Lac since 1913 has operated a sewage disposal plant in the north end of the city not far from Lake Winnebago. The plaintiffs are owners of valuable real estate located a short distance south and somewhat to the east of the sewage disposal plant. Plaintiffs' property consists of an outdoor-movie theater and an outdoor restaurant; a large motel with an outdoor swimming pool is in the process of being constructed. Construction of this motel was undertaken upon the assurances the offensive odors emanating from the sewage disposal plant would be corrected.

For some years and more specifically since 1956 or 1957, the problem of obnoxious and offensive odors from the sewage disposal plant has existed. It is established by the evidence that these strong and obnoxious odors, developed at the plant, were carried by the wind over the plaintiffs' premises and over a large part of the city. There is some testimony the odors were noticeable as far as two miles out in Lake Winnebago. The odors have made life extremely annoying and unbearable to people subjected to them, and particularly the evidence shows the plaintiffs' business, customers, and employees were affected by the odors. Plaintiffs' theater is subject to a lease which permits the lessee during the term of the lease to purchase the premises at its then market value.* * *

The city's contention that it is not causing a nuisance in the operation of its sewage disposal plant can hardly be taken seriously. The argument, in effect, is that the nuisance, if any, is a public nuisance and not a private one as to the plaintiffs and, therefore, the plaintiffs have no cause of action. A nuisance may be both public and private in character.* * * A public nuisance which causes a particular injury to an individual different in kind and degree from that suffered by the public constitutes a private nuisance. Such injury is usually a material and unreasonable impairment of the right of enjoyment or the individual's right to the reasonable use of his property or the impairment of its value.* * * This concept is expressed in sec. 280.01, Stats., by providing any person may maintain an action to recover damages for or to abate a private nuisance and any person, county, city, village or town, may maintain an action to recover damages or to abate a public nuisance from which injuries peculiar to the complainant are suffered.

A private nuisance to an individual may also be a private nuisance to other individuals in their capacity other than as members of the public. The test is not the number of persons injured but the character of the injury and of the right impinged upon. One may be especially affected although others are similarly affected.* * * Conversely, the fact the nuisance may or may not be enjoined as a public nuisance has no effect upon the right to abate a private nuisance.

The city contends the plaintiffs had not been injured in relation to their property because they have not lost money in their business and point to an advertisement of the outdoor restaurant in the daily paper thanking the public for a most successful season in 1963. There is no requirement the plaintiffs must go broke in their business in order to establish irreparable damages as a ground for abating a nuisance. If the damages cannot be adequately compensated in money or are impossible of determination, an injunction is the appropriate relief to abate a nuisance unless there are other intervening considerations which require the denial of the injunctional relief or at least its delay. The court's finding that the plaintiffs were substantially injured in their use and enjoyment of their property and that the value of the property was affected is not against the great weight and clear preponderance of the evidence and will not be disturbed.

Relying on Hasslinger v. Hartland (1940), 234 Wis. 201, 290 N.W. 647, the defendant contends the nuisance was caused by the operation of the plant approved by a state agency and, therefore, was not actionable. In Hasslinger it is observed but not held, "It may be that if the claim of the adjoining landowner is that the manner of operation is such as to constitute a nuisance, the fact that the plant was built according to specifications of the State Board of Health and is being operated in accordance with their orders and regulations may conclusively establish that there is no nuisance arising out of design or operation of the plant." This misleading language is overruled because of the implication that operation of the sewage disposal plant in accordance with specifications and orders and regulations of the state board of health cannot constitute a nuisance.

This court does not subscribe to the doctrine that the state board of health by virtue of sec. 144.03, Stats., is given exclusive jurisdiction over the determination of nuisance so as to foreclose a judicial determination of whether the operation of a sewage disposal plant results in creating a nuisance.* * *

In Hasslinger we held the approval by the state board of health of the plans which involved the location of the sewage disposal plant did not foreclose a judicial determination of whether the plant was a nuisance by reason of its location; the same may be said of the method of its operation.* * *

It is contended the trial court has imposed an impossible condition upon the city. This argument centers upon the fact the order enjoins the city absolutely after June 15th from permitting gases to escape from the sewage disposal plant without deodorizing and purifying them so as to avoid the creation of a nuisance.* * *

Attached to the back of the order was a memorandum in which the court stated the order contemplated the city would attempt to comply in a bona fide way with the order and take immediate steps to place the plant in a businesslike working and operating condition and to deodorize and purify gases by the use of in-plant chlorination and of deodorizing chemicals. The court stated it recognized that 100 percent success might not always be obtainable but such efforts on the part of the city would be a basis for the city temporarily being relieved from the strict compliance with the order.

By this manner of enjoining the city and although the injunction is absolute in form, the city is not required to do the impossible. The city has not shown that to maintain the plant in a businesslike working and operating condition is impossible or that the use of in-plant chlorination and the use of deodorizing chemicals is likewise impossible. The position of the defendant-city is it should not be hurried or nudged along in abating this nuisance because it has existed so long now there is no need to hurry and the city will eventually take care of the problem. Essentially, the attitude is that the city because it is a city is not subject to the law. It is quite apparent from the record and so believed by the trial court that the city was not inclined to take the nuisance seriously or to do much about it. The reasons advanced for the delay in solving this problem by the city officials did not justify, in the trial court's opinion, the city's inaction. We cannot say on the evidence presented the trial court was in error in considering the city as dragging its feet in providing new digesters and in abating the nuisance. We approve the form of the order made by the trial court. It is substantially what was approved in Briggson v. Viroqua (1953), 264 Wis. 47, 58 N.W.2d 546, and in Winchell v. City of Waukesha, supra.

The city argues the order directs the manner in which it must abate the nuisance and this a court of equity cannot do.* * *

However, there are situations in which the balancing of convenience or equities is attempted by the court and the decree does provide in detail how the nuisance shall be abated or partially controlled. It is recognized the court may require the defendant to adopt methods and appliances where their adoption will avoid the conditions complained of. 39 Am.Jur., Nuisances, p. 443, sec. 172, Form and Scope of Injunction. The issue of whether the form of the decree should be affirmative and mandatory in requiring specific acts to abate the nuisance or should be prohibitive is not a question of the court's powers but whether a need exists for the exercise of equitable power in requiring affirmative acts to reach a desired result. Many prohibitory orders require only desisting for compliance but when a nuisance results from the omission of an act the prohibitory form of the order necessarily requires the doing, in fact, of an act.* * *

Any act which will abate the nuisance will comply with the order. The memorandum is not an order requiring the performance of the acts therein contemplated by the court. The performance of such methods of abating the nuisance is a condition or as the court states a basis for relief if such methods are tried and bona fide performance does not eliminate the nuisance.

The order is not broader, and should not be, than necessary to give the plaintiffs the relief to which they are entitled. We do not condemn its manner of coercion. It is the very nature of an injunction to be coercive. While the injunction may fit the facts snuggly and be embarrassing to the city officials, no reason appears why it is unjust or how the city will be harmed or why the city should be relieved from showing good faith in respecting the private rights of its citizens.

Order affirmed.

---

3. PUNITIVE DAMAGES

REYNOLDS METALS CO. v. LAMPART

324 F.2d 465 (1963)

CROCKER, District Judge.

Appellants, Reynolds Metals Co. and Henry W. Shoemaker, petitioned for rehearing in banc, and were granted a rehearing limited to the question of punitive damages before the panel which heretofore acted in this case.

To bring this case into proper focus, it should be reiterated:

* * *

(2) That the settling of fluorides from appellants' plant on appellees' property constituted trespass as a matter of law in the State of Oregon. Martin v. Reynolds Metals Co. (1959), 221 Or. 86, 342 P.2d 790.

(3) That the Supreme Court of Oregon has said that the jury may award punitive damages if "* * *the injury was done maliciously or willfully and wantonly or committed with bad motive or recklessly so as to imply a disregard of social obligations." Fisher v. Carlin (1959), 219 Or. 159, 346 P.2d 641.

In addition, it should be noted:

(1) That in Oregon a jury may award punitive damages if there was "evidence of malice or wilfull wanton disregard of the property rights of plaintiff or other aggravating circumstances." Hall v. Work (1960), 223 Or. 347, 354, P.2d 837, 366 P.2d 533.

(2) That Alvarez v. Retail Credit Ass'n of Portland, Oregon, Inc. (1963), 76 Or.Adv.Sh. 671, 381 P.2d 499, cited by appellants, does not overrule Fisher v. Carlin. In fact, it recognizes that there may be "other improper motives" than ill will "that make the aggravated wrong one for which punitive damages may be allowed."

(3) That the Oregon legislature has not spoken on this subject.

The decision in this case is that under the law of the State of Oregon and the particular facts in this case the question of punitive damages should have been submitted to the jury, as the jury could reasonably have found that appellants had acted with wanton disregard of the property rights of appellees or other aggravating circumstances, *or* recklessly so as to imply a disregard of social obligations *or* other improper motive.

The particular facts that lead to this conclusion are,

(1) That appellants had knowledge that fluorides from their plant had caused injury every year since 1949 to gladiolus grown on appellees' property.

(2) That in 1957 appellants increased their production by putting more electricity into reduction cells, which almost doubled the amount of escaping fluorides.

(3) That Paul R. Martin testified that on April 23, 1959, Mr. Shoemaker, Manager of appellants' plant, when asked why he didn't use better fluoride controls, said: "It is cheaper to pay claims than it is to control fluorides." The trial court erroneously instructed the jury to disregard this testimony but only after withdrawing the ques-

tion of punitive damages from them. The credibility of this testimony was for the jury.

* * *

After rehearing the question of punitive damages, the original decision in this case that the judgment of the trial court be reversed and the case remanded to the District Court for retrial not inconsistent with the opinion remains the decision of this court.

---

4. MANDAMUS

SMITH v. UNITED STATES

333 F.2d 70 (1964)

BREITENSTEIN, Circuit Judge.

This action was brought by the settlers on an ill-fated federal reclamation project to recover their losses. Recovery is sought by way of mandamus and the Federal Tort Claims Act. The trial court sustained a motion to dismiss and this appeal followed.

The plaintiffs-appellants are the members of the Board of Commissioners of the Third Division Irrigation District, Riverton Project, Wyoming, who sue on their own behalf and on behalf of other individuals similarly situated. The defendants-appellees are the United States, Department of Interior, Bureau of Reclamation, Secretary of the Interior, and the Commissioner of Reclamation.

The first claim is for mandamus under 28 U.S.C. §§ 1361 and 1391(e). In substance the allegations are: In 1917 a government engineer, in reporting on the project lands, called attention to the danger of seepage and the necessity of drainage to maintain irrigability. In spite of this report the Department in 1948 published a circular and notices describing the project lands as potentially productive for agricultural purposes. Relying thereon and on representations of the Bureau of Reclamation that a living could be made on the land, the plaintiffs applied for, and each was awarded, a farm unit in the Third Division Irrigation District of the project. They entered on the land in 1950 and 1951, invested their life savings, and attempted to farm. The doubt of reasonable opportunity for success soon became apparent. A series of studies and reports began in 1952 and continued to 1961. These pointed out the drainage problems and recommended substantial and continuing reductions in the irrigable acreage. The 1961 report of a board of consultants said that "drainability of some lands in the Third Division is questionable, if not entirely lacking, and their rehabilitation in the foreseeable future seems economically unfeasible." There was no compliance with 43 U.S.C. § 412 which provides that no new project or new division of a project shall be approved for construction until the Secretary makes a finding "that it is feasible, that it is adaptable for actual settlement and farm homes, and that it will probably return the cost thereof to the United States." The plaintiffs were induced to enter the Third Division without knowledge of the conditions and in reliance upon the representations that a living could be made on the family units. Although the complete inadequacy of the project and its development had been described in various surveys, the agents of the United States induced plaintiffs to enter the lands. The plaintiffs are destitute; they have asked defendants to correct the mistakes; and they "have been advised by agents of the United States Government that the project is to be closed."

The relief, in the nature of mandamus, sought by the first claim is that (1) the defendants "provide adequate recompense for the losses sustained by the plaintiffs"; (2) the defendants make a determination of the lack of economic feasibility of the project, and (3) the defendants request Congress to give such relief "as will provide equity" to the plaintiffs.* * *

For a variety of reasons the first claim cannot be sustained. The courts have no power to control or influence the judgment of an officer or to direct the performance of a discretionary duty. Any effort by a court to compel the Secretary to find lack of feasibility would violate this established principle. The courts have no control over the decisions of the individual defendants with respect to the feasibility or lack of feasibility of a reclamation project.

The concept that the court should order the individual defendants to request Congress to give equitable relief to the plaintiffs violates the well established principle of separation of powers. We agree with the trial court that it "would thwart every constitutional canon for this court to order an arm of the Executive Department to demand action by the Legislative Department."

Plaintiffs rely on the 1962 Act relating to mandamus against federal officers and employees. Prior thereto the review of decisions of the Secretary of the Interior and similar officers was in the District of Columbia courts, in terms of mandamus to force them to perform ministerial duties. The 1962 Act provides a remedy by which the same jurisdiction can be exercised throughout the country. It did not enlarge the scope of permissible mandamus relief.

The claim that the court should order that the plaintiffs be compensated for their losses is an effort to obtain a money judgment against the United States because of the failure of a federal reclamation project. The United States has never waived sovereign immunity to permit recovery in such circumstances.

In any event Congress has acted to alleviate the plight of the plaintiffs. Since the entry of judgment in the trial court, relief has been afforded by the Act of March 10, 1964, Public Law 88–278, 78 Stat. 156. This Act authorizes the Secretary of the Interior to negotiate with the entrymen on the Third Division of the Riverton Project for the purchase of their lands at an appraised value determined without reference to deterioration in irrigability because of seepage or inadequate drainage and appropriates $2,000,000 for such acquisitions and other purposes. Water deliveries are to continue for the period 1964–1966. Before January 1, 1967, the Secretary is to determine the economic feasibility of described areas in the Third Division and report his findings to Congress.

Congress has acted, required the determination of economic feasibility, and provided for recompense. Plaintiffs say that there should be a judicial determination of value. This is no more than criticism of the Act, which in substance grants the relief sought by the first claim.

* * *

Affirmed.

Part Two

Air Pollution

Part Two

Air Pollution

A. Introduction[1]

1. What Is Air Pollution?

The air around us has never been completely pure. It has always contained some natural pollution: windblown dust, smoke from forest fires, salt particles from the oceans, gases generated by the decay of plant and animal life, and occasional torrents of gases and dust particles from volcanic eruptions.

For millions of years, scientists believe, nature's own air conditioning system kept the air fairly clean. Winds mixed and dispersed the pollutants. Rain and snow washed some of them to the ground. Plants absorbed carbon dioxide from the air and contributed fresh oxygen. The system ran itself.

With the coming of the industrial age and the vast increase in population, our ability to pollute began to overtake nature's ability to purify. The effects were first felt in areas of heavy industry, where thousands of factory smokestacks poured soot and sulfurous gases in the air. When stagnant weather conditions kept these pollutants close to the ground in one area for days on end, there were outbreaks of respiratory disease and increased deaths from lung and heart ailments. From the middle of the 19th century such episodes occurred with disturbing frequency in the industrial cities of Europe and America, accompanied each time with sharp rises in sickness and mortality.

The first air pollution control ordinance in the United States was enacted in Pittsburgh around 1815.

Other industrial cities also passed local ordinances to limit factory fumes and reduce smoke from the burning of coal and to control such smelly operations as glue factories and rendering plants. (Odor was regarded as a public nuisance rather than a health hazard.)

Smoke controls often seemed to be effective in improving the appearance and general cleanliness of cities, but much of this improvement was probably due to a widespread shift in fuels after World War II: from coal to oil and gas for electric power production, industrial and home heating; and from coal to diesel oil for

[1]The material in this section is derived from United States, Environmental Protection Agency, Office of Public Awareness, *Cleañ The Air* (A-107).

railroads. Pittsburgh and St. Louis became noticeably less smokey in the 1950s, and household cleaning and maintenance costs were reduced. In London, after soft coal heating fires were banned early in the next decade, the traditional "peasoup" fogs disappeared; landmark buildings were cleaned of centuries of grime and stayed clean.

Despite scattered successes in smoke and soot cleanup after the war, air pollution continued to increase and its nature began to change. Pollution episodes occurred in cities like Los Angeles that had little heavy industry but lots of automobiles. The smoke-and-sulfur type of pollution, though still widespread, was no longer dominant. The principal pollutant was "photochemical smog," a complex assortment of gases that were formed in the air itself. Prof. A.J. Haagen-Smit of the California Institute of Technology in Pasadena was the first to demonstrate (in 1951) that photochemical smog was a product of the action of sunlight upon automobile exhausts primarily, plus gaseous wastes from industry, refineries, and incinerators.

Today there are more than two and a half times as many motor vehicles in the country as there were when Dr. Haagen-Smit pointed the finger at them as a major source of modern air pollution.

Two-Thirds of One-Tenth of One Percent

To understand the air pollution problem, we must realize that all pollution makes up a very small fraction of the air itself. The air that is near the earth's surface is called the troposphere. It is about 30 kilometers (18 miles) thick and is kept pretty thoroughly mixed by winds and convection currents. This is the air we breathe.

What is it made up of? Seventy-eight percent is nitrogen, a gaseous element that is very hard to burn, that is, it doesn't unite readily with oxygen. Twenty-one percent is oxygen, a gaseous element whose ability to unite with other elements, like carbon, releasing energy in the form of heat, constitutes the engine that runs all animal life and almost all plant life.

These two gases make up 99 percent of the air we breathe. Only one percent is left. Nine-tenths of this one percent is argon, a very inert gas, which is simply there.

It never does anything.

Now we have only one-tenth of one percent for all the other ingredients of air and all the pollution. What's in this 1/10 of 1 percent, or 1,000 parts per million?

Carbon dioxide (CO_2) is about a third of it, 330 parts per million. This seems like a small amount for such an important constituent of the atmosphere. All green plants that make food for themselves and for animals by photosynthesis depend on this carbon dioxide. And carbon dioxide helps to keep the earth warm by being transparent to the sun's visible-light radiation and opaque to the infrared, or heat, energy radiating from the earth. Carbon dioxide is the earth's greenhouse window.

The last two-thirds of one-tenth of one percent contains all the remaining ingredients of dry air: neon, helium, and krypton (all inert gases like argon) plus all the pollutants: ozone, (a form of oxygen), carbon monoxide, hydrocarbons, and particles of solid or liquid substances so small that they float around suspended in air.

All these percentages are for "dry" air, ignoring the water vapor which is so important in Nature's weather machine. The water content can vary a thousandfold, from about half again as much as argon (9/10ths of 1 percent, 900 ppm) to 0.9 ppm. Air that is saturated with water vapor, all the water it can hold, never has much more than 1 percent water.

We are concerned, therefore, with a tiny fraction of the atmosphere, a thin, chemical soup that is constantly changing in a complex of actions and reactions, influenced by the energy of sunlight and the presence or absence of water vapor.

Sulfur oxide gases can combine with some of the water to form particles of sulfur acids and salts. Oxides of nitrogen combine with hydrocarbons to form ozone and other photochemical oxidants. Carbon monoxide seems to disappear in ways not yet understood; probably it converts to carbon dioxide. Particles are lifted into the air by the wind.

Most of the chemical reactions in the air are reversible, and Nature tends to maintain a rough balance, an equilibrium, which may vary with the hour of the day, the season of the year, and with weather conditions: air temperature, pressure, and humidity.

Small Percentages, Big Amounts

When air pollution is considered as a fraction of all the air, it seems very small, but the total *amounts* of pollution in the air over the United States at any given time add up to *hundreds of millions of tons.*

The U.S. Environmental Protection Agency (EPA) and its predecessor, the National Air Pollution Control Administration, have been keeping track of man-made pollutant emissions for more than a decade.

The total pollution figures are estimates, of course, but they are based on careful and conservative accounting of fuel consumption, records of industrial production, and similar official statistics related to pollutant emissions. . . . The five most pervasive pollutants spewed into the air each year in the United States totalled from 175 million to more than 200 million metric tons, nearly a ton for every man, woman, and child in the country. . . .

Internal combustion engines (automobiles and trucks) account for 80 percent of the carbon monoxide and 51 percent of total emissions. Stationary fuel burning produced 23 percent of total emissions, and industrial processes 16 percent.

But total emissions are of little use in planning and carrying out the reduction of emissions. Adding particulates and nitrogen oxides and carbon monoxide is a little like adding apples and newspapers and brake shoes; the total is essentially meaningless. Reducing emissions depends on actions that can be taken with each type of pollutant; each requires different methods of control. . . .

Certain types of sources predominate for different types of pollution. Stationary fuel burning and industrial processes account for 81 percent of particle emissions, fuel burning for 82 percent of sulfur oxides, transportation and fuel burning for 96 percent of nitrogen oxides, transportation and industrial processing for 72 percent of hydrocarbons, and transportation for 80 percent of carbon monoxide.

Therefore, measures taken to reduce emissions from principal sources—automobiles, for instance, or electric power plants—presumably could bring about substantial reductions in the levels in ambient air of several kinds of pollution. That's a key aspect of EPA's pollution control strategy.

Emissions are estimated by carefully noting the statistics of automotive mileage driven and fuel consumption, industrial fuel consumption and the production figures for various industries—steelmaking and other metal smelting, cement plants, petrochemical plants, etc., all the principal stationary sources of various pollutants—the numbers and output figures of incinerators, burning dumps; and records of windstorms; fires, both accidental and natural; and volcanic eruptions.

The amounts of pollution known to be emitted by such sources are not always reflected in the pollution levels found in ambient air measurements. The discrepancy is due to several factors. First, measurement methods are not perfect, either for monitoring the air or for estimating emissions. Second, changing weather conditions can vary the rates at which pollutants are transported from one area to another and dispersed. Third, certain important pollutants—ozone and other photochemical oxidants—are not emitted directly by human activities; they are formed in air when sunlight spurs chemical combinations among two kinds of emitted pollutants: hydrocarbons and nitrogen oxides.

2. PRINCIPAL AIR POLLUTANTS, THEIR SOURCES AND EFFECTS

Particulates

These are solid particles or liquid droplets small enough to remain suspended in air. They range widely in size, from particles visible as soot or smoke to those too small to detect except with an electron microscope. Smaller sizes may remain suspended for a long time and be carried great distances by winds. Particulates are produced primarily by industrial process (47 percent) and combustion (34 percent). About 7 percent come from natural, and largely uncontrollable, sources such as windblown dust, forest fires, volcanoes, etc.

The health hazard of particulates may be physical, from the clogging of the lung sacs by the particles, or chemical, from reactions of the body to very small substances that can pass through the lung membranes into the blood and thence to other body organs. Many kinds of particles are hazardous in themselves: asbestos, certain metal salts and acids, and some complex organic compounds.

Sulfur Dioxide

This is a corrosive and poisonous gas produced mainly from the burning of sulfur-containing fuel (82 percent) and from certain industrial processes (15 percent). Most sulfurous coal and oil is burned in urban areas, where population and industry are concentrated, but sources that produce several hundred tons of the gases each year may be located in rural areas also.

Sulfur dioxide affects human breathing in direct relation to the amount of the gas in the air breathed. Many types of respiratory disease, such as coughs and colds, asthma and bronchitis, are associated with sulfur pollution. Sulfur dioxide and particulates often occur together, and the two pollutants combined have a greatly increased effect on the body.

Carbon Monoxide

This is a colorless, odorless, poison gas produced by the incomplete burning of the carbon in fuels (carbon being the element supplying most of the energy from combustion). About 80 percent of the carbon monoxide put into the air is from gasoline and diesel engines, i.e., autos and trucks. It is by far the most plentiful air pollutant: more than 87 million tons per year in the United States. Fortunately it usually disperses and apparently is slowly converted or absorbed by natural processes. Its danger comes from localized concentrations, as in traffic-filled city streets.

Carbon monoxide replaces oxygen in the red blood cells, reducing the amount of oxygen that can reach the body cells and maintain life. Continued lack of oxygen affects the brain and the heart, in that order, and death can result from deep or prolonged inhalation of carbon monoxide.

Hydrocarbons

These gases, like carbon monoxide, represent unburned and wasted fuel. They come from incomplete combustion of gasoline and from evaporation of petroleum fuels, industrial solvents, painting and dry cleaning.

Although some individual hydrocarbons are poisonous, most are not. Their harm comes from the ozone and other oxidants they help to form by reacting with nitrogen oxides in sunlight.

Nitrogen Dioxide

This poisonous and highly reactive gas is produced when fuel is burned at high temperatures, about 650°C (1200°F), causing some of the abundant nitrogen in the air to burn also. Most emissions come from industries (52 percent) and autos (44 percent). Control depends on careful adjustment of the combustion process.

Nitrogen irritates and causes structural and chemical changes in the lungs. It lowers the body's resistance to respiratory infections like influenza. Its principal harm, however, comes from the ozone that it helps to form by reacting in sunlit air with hydrocarbons.

Ozone

It is the principal constituent of modern smog and serves as an indicator of all the other photochemical oxidants—peroxyacetal nitrates (PAN), formaldehydes, and other organic compounds of nitrogen. Ozone is a poisonous form of oxygen that irritates the mucous membranes of the breathing system, causing coughing, choking, and impaired lung function. It aggravates chronic respiratory diseases like asthma and bronchitis.

Ozone causes structural and chemical changes in the lungs and some alterations of blood components. PAN and other photochemical oxidants that accompany ozone are powerful eye irritants. All oxidants are formed in the air, by chemical combination of nitrogen oxides and hydrocarbons, using the energy of sunlight. They are almost never emitted by human activities and sources.

Lead

An ambient standard for lead in air was adopted by EPA in 1978, seven years after the other six. Lead is a poison when ingested or inhaled. It accumulates in the body, in bone and soft tissue, and affects the bloodforming organs, the kidneys, and the nervous system. About 90 percent of airborne lead (in particles of lead salts and other compounds, not the pure metal) comes from lead-containing anti-knock agents in gasoline. The rest comes from industries that smelt or process the metal.

3. Definitions of Air Pollution Terms

acid rain: rain containing sulfuric or nitric acid, typically resulting from the contact of sulfur oxides or nitrogen oxides with water. Acid rain has already produced a dramatic slowdown of the rate of growth in forests in Sweden and New England and may be about to reduce agricultural production in much of the U.S. by acidifying the soil. Rain clouds do not observe political boundaries so this type of pollution can be felt thousands of miles from the source of pollution.

aerosol: a mist of solid or liquid particles of microscopic size.

air quality criteria: data showing the effects of various levels of each air pollutant on animals, plants, people, buildings, of whatever else is of concern.

air quality control region: a region considered as a unit for air quality planning purposes.

Air Quality Maintenance Plan: a part of the State Implementation Plan that is designed to insure that an area does not develop new pollution problems from uncontrolled growth once it has cleared up its present problems.

air quality standard: the maximum allowable level for an air pollutant, usually expressed as the maximum amount of pollutant allowed in each cubic meter of air (micrograms per cubic meter).

attainment area: an area that meets the air quality standards for a given pollutant. The same area can be "attainment" for one pollutant and "nonattainment" for another.

Best Available Control Technology: air pollution technology required for new polluters (example: a new factory) in areas that are presently meeting air quality standards. Less stringent than Lowest Achievable Emission Rate but more stringent than Reasonably Available Control Technology.

carbon monoxide: an invisible, odorless, highly poisonous gas often produced from incomplete combustion in automobile engines. Carbon monoxide has been shown to aggravate several circulatory diseases.

catalytic converter: a device attached to the exhaust pipe of an automobile that employs platinum or certain other substances to speed up the reaction by which carbon monoxide is converted into carbon dioxide and by which hydrocarbons are converted into carbon dioxide and water.

emission control device: a device installed on an engine, factory, or power plant that reduces the amount of pollutant emitted.

emission standard: a limit set for the amount of a given pollutant a particular factory, incinerator, motor vehicle, or power plant may discharge into the atmosphere.

hydrocarbon: substances such as gasoline, paint thinner, and alcohol that are made of hydrogen and carbon. Hydrocarbons react with the air in the presence of sunlight to form photochemical oxidants.

inversion: a state in which the air temperature increases with increasing altitude, holding cooler surface air down—along with its pollutants. (Normally the air near the surface is warmer and it rises, causing pollutants to mix and disperse.)

Lowest Achievable Emission Rate: the strictest possible emission rate that can presently be met by using the most up-to-date technology. Required of all new polluters (e.g., a new factory) in areas that presently do not meet air quality standards. Stricter than both Best Available Control Technology and Reasonably Available Control Technology.

micrograms per cubic meter (mg/m^3): a measure of the amount of pollutant present. One microgram in one cubic meter is about the same as one-twentieth of one-billionth of a pound of pollutant in each cubic foot of air.

mobile source: automobiles, buses, trucks, airplanes, etc.

National Ambient Air Quality Standards: federal standards that set the maximum level for several pollutants. There are two types: "primary" standards, which are calculated to protect human health, and "secondary" standards, which are calculated to protect public welfare (plants, animals, buildings, and aesthetics in addition to humans).

National Emission Standard for Hazardous Air Pollutants: special emission limits for hazardous pollutants such as lead, asbestos, and pesticides that are not regulated by the National Ambient Air Quality Standards because they are not as widespread.

New Source Performance Standards: the level of pollution control required for new polluters such as new factories. If the new polluter is in an area with poor air quality (nonattainment area), then Lowest Achievable Emission Rate is required. If the new polluter is in an area with acceptable air quality (attainment area) then Best Available Control Technology is required.

nitrogen oxides (*NOx*): nitric oxide (NO), nitrogen dioxide (NO_2), and nitrogen trioxide (NO_3). These are gases formed by the high temperature combustion of atmospheric nitrogen, such as in the internal combustion engine. Early emission control devices often increased the emissions of nitrogen oxides in the process of reducing the emissions of carbon monoxide and hydrocarbons. Honda's stratified charge engine (CVCC) emits far fewer nitrogen oxides than conventional engines because it burns much cooler. Nitrogen oxides have been shown to aggravate several respiratory diseases.

nonattainment area: an area that violates air quality standards for a given pollutant. An area can be "nonattainment" for one pollutant and "attainment" for another.

offset (also called "tradeoff"): a procedure whereby a proposed polluter (e.g., an industry that wants to build a new factory) arranges for existing polluters to reduce their present pollution levels so that the total pollutant levels *after* the new polluter begins operation will be less than the total level before. If necessary, the new polluter is expected to pay for the cost of pollution control devices for the existing polluters. Required in "nonattainment" areas.

ozone: a pungent, highly poisonous gas that's invisible in low concentrations. Ozone is the principal photochemical oxidant.

particulates: small suspended particles. Particulates can aggravate several respiratory diseases.

parts per million (ppm): one gram of air pollutant for every million grams of air is one part per million of that pollutant. Alternatively, one part per million means that there is one pound of air pollutant for every million pounds of air—the units of measurement don't really matter as long as the same ones are used to measure both the pollutant and the air.

photochemical oxidants: the substances produced when hydrocarbons and nitrogen oxides combine with the air in the presence of sunshine (the primary photochemical oxidant is ozone). Also known as smog. Can cause eye irritation and chest discomfort.

Prevention of Significant Deterioration: a provision of the Clean Air Act as amended in 1977 that protects air that's already good (pollutant levels are below the limits) by strictly regulating the amount of additional pollution that can be emitted by new sources.

primary standards: the levels of air pollution below which there will be no adverse health effects on humans (a margin of safety is included).

Reasonably Available Control Technology: air pollution control technology required for existing polluters in areas that presently do not meet air quality standards. It takes into account the costs and problems of retrofitting pollution control devices and tries to deal with the worst excesses. Less strict than either Lowest Achievable Emission Rate or Best Available Control Technology.

secondary standards: the levels of air pollution below which there will be no adverse effects. Secondary standards protect plants, animals, buildings, aesthetics, and humans, whereas primary standards only protect humans. Thus, secondary standards are more stringent.

smog: irritating haze resulting from the sun's effect on certain pollutants, notably those from automobile exhausts (see "photochemical oxidants").

State Implementation Plan: a plan being prepared by each state for submittal to the Environmental Protection Agency that will outline the State's strategy for achieving the air quality standards and complying with the other requirements of the Clean Air Act.

stationary sources: nonmoving polluters such as industry, dirt roads, grain loading facilities, dry cleaners, fires, etc.

sulfur oxides (SO_x): sulfur dioxide (SO_2) and sulfur trioxide (SO_3). These are invisible gases having a pungent odor that result from the burning of high sulfur fuels in industry, homes and power plants. Sulfur oxides can cause eye irritation, can aggravate lung disease, and can damage plants, buildings, and metals. Sulfur oxides often react with water vapor or rain to form sulfuric acid.

threshold level: the level of a given pollutant at which specified harmful effects begin to occur.

trace elements: toxic substances such as mercury, cadmium, and beryllium found in very small quantities in fuels. Trace elements are emitted into the atmosphere as fine particulates when fuel containing them is burned. In general, clean fuels, such as natural gas contain far fewer trace elements than dirty ones such as coal. However, so-called "clean" Western coal contains far more trace elements than so-called "dirty" Eastern coal. No emission control system exists to adequately control trace elements from burning coal.

Transportation Control Plan: a plan being prepared as part of the State Implementation Plan (SIP) designed to reduce the reliance on private auto traffic in the non-attainment areas and to make certain that necessary traffic emits the least pollution possible. Elements of the plan might include an annual emission inspection program for all cars, improved mass transit, and improved traffic flow.

Total Suspended Particulates (*TSP*): particulate matter which is floating in the air. See particulates.

B. Private Law Suits

The extensive regulation of air quality under the Federal Clean Air Act has tended to divert attention from the common law theories continuing to provide a basis for legal action to prevent air pollution. Some of the cases and material set forth in the prior chapter provide good illustrations: The **nuisance** doctrine was applied in *Hulbert v. California Portland Cement, supra*, where the court enjoined the air pollution causing damage to plaintiff's orange groves. In *Boomer v. Atlantic Cement Co., supra*, the court found that emission from defendant's cement plant constituted a nuisance and proposed damages rather than a permanent injunction as a more appropriate remedy. The **negligence** theory was applied in *Reynolds Metals v. Yturbide, supra*, where Reynolds Metals was held liable for injuries resulting from its negligence in permitting fluorides to be emitted from its plant. The **trespass** theory was applied in *Reynolds Metals v. Martin, supra*, where the defendant was held to be liable for damages caused by fluoride particles emitted from its plant. The **ultrahazardous activities** theory was applied in *Luthringer v. Moore, supra*, where defendant was held liable for injuries resulting from the inhalation of hydrocyanic acid discharged into the air by defendant in the process of rodent extermination regardless of fault.

In addition to the common law theories, private law suits to protect air quality may be based on citizen suit provisions of statutes such as the Clean Air Act, 42 U.S.C. 1957h that authorizes an action to be brought by "any person" or "any citizen" against any person who is alleged to be in violation of an emission standard or governmental order relating thereto.

C. Federal Regulation: The Clean Air Act

Congress created a multifaceted system of regulation in the Clean Air Act. There are provisions dealing with both **stationary sources** (e.g. industrial plants, grain loading facilities, etc.) and **mobile sources** (e.g. cars and trucks) of air pollution. The Act assigns designated responsibilities and powers to the federal government and other responsibilities to the state governments. For example, the federal government has responsibility for (*1*) the establishment of air quality standards, (*2*) the creation of air quality control regions, (*3*) the approval of State Implementation Plans

(SIPS), (*4*) emission standards for specified new sources of air pollution and (*5*) emission standards for hazardous air pollutants. States have the responsibility for the creation and implementation of plans to maintain and improve the quality of air. The system of regulation created by the Clean Air Act will be more readily understood by analyzing each of these categories.

1. Regulation of Stationary Sources

Among the typical stationary sources of air pollution are power plant and factory smokestacks, industrial producers of gases and dusts, coke ovens, incinerators and garbage-burning dumps. The control of **existing stationary sources** under the Clean Air Act is left to state control and reviewed by the federal government as part of the state implementation plan (SIP). There is a designated group of industrial sources of pollution for which **new construction** is regulated directly by the federal government. The system of federal regulation is composed of the following components.

a. *National Air Quality Standards*

The Clean Air Act requires EPA to set standards for ambient air quality. There are two levels of standards: **Primary Air Quality Standards** set a limit for each pollutant at a level stringent enough to protect the *public health* with an adequate margin of safety. **Secondary Air Quality Standards** are a more stringent standard or limit of each pollutant necessary to protect the **public welfare** from any known or anticipated adverse effects. Both standards are expressed in terms of maximum permissible concentrations of the pollutant for specified periods of time.

The pollutants for which air quality standards have been established include particulates, sulfur dioxide, carbon monoxide, hydrocarbons, nitrogen dioxide, ozone and lead. The table set forth below indicates the primary and secondary standard for each. Lead was not included in the list of **criteria pollutants** until the decision in *National Resources Defense Council, Inc. v. Train.*

CLEAN AIR ACT

Section 108, 42 U.S.C. 7408

AIR QUALITY CRITERIA AND CONTROL TECHNIQUES

Sec. 108. (a) (1) For the purpose of establishing national primary and secondary ambient air quality standards, the Administrator shall within 30 days after the date of enactment of the Clean Air Amendments of 1970 publish, and shall from time to time thereafter revise, a list which includes each air pollutant—

(A) which in his judgment has an adverse effect on public health or welfare;
(B) the presence of which in the ambient air results from numerous or diverse mobile or stationary sources; and
(C) for which air quality criteria had not been issued before the date of enactment of the Clean Air Amendments of 1970, but for which he plans to issue air quality criteria under this section.

(2) The Administrator shall issue air quality criteria for an air pollutant within 12 months after he has included such pollutant in a list under paragraph (1). Air quality criteria for an air pollutant shall accurately reflect the latest scientific knowledge useful in indicating the kind and extent of all identifiable effects on public health or welfare which may be expected from the presence of such pollutant in the ambient air, in varying quantities. The criteria for an air pollutant, to the extent practicable, shall include information on—

(A) Those variable factors (including atmospheric conditions) which of themselves or in combination with other factors may alter the effects on public health or welfare of such air pollutant;
(B) the types of air pollutants which, when present in the atmosphere, may interact with such pollutant to produce an adverse effect on public health or welfare; and
(C) any known or anticipated adverse effects on welfare.

(b) (1) Simultaneously with the issuance of criteria under subsection (a), the Administrator shall, after consultation with appropriate advisory committees and Federal departments and agencies, issue to the States and appropriate air pollution control agencies information on air pollution control techniques, which information shall include data relating to the technology and costs of emission control. Such information shall include such data as are available on available technology and alternative methods of prevention and control of air pollution. Such information shall also include data on alternative fuels, processes, and operating methods which will result in elimination or significant reduction of emissions.
(2) In order to assist in the development of information on pollution control techniques, the Administrator may establish a standing consulting committee for each air pollutant included in a list published pursuant to subsection (a) (1). . . .

* * *

NATIONAL AMBIENT AIR QUALITY STANDARDS

Sec. 109. (a) (1) The Administrator—

(A) within 30 days after the date of enactment of the Clean Air Amendments of 1970, shall publish proposed regulations prescribing a national primary ambient air quality standard and a national secondary ambient air quality standard for each air pollutant for which air quality criteria have been issued prior to such date of enactment; and

(B) after a reasonable time for interested persons to submit written comments thereon (but no later than 90 days after the initial publication of such proposed standards) shall by regulation promulgate such proposed national primary and secondary ambient air quality standards with such modifications as he deems appropriate.

(2) With respect to any air pollutant for which air quality criteria are issued * * * Administrator shall publish, simultaneously with the issuance of such criteria and information, proposed national primary and secondary ambient air quality standards for any such pollutant.* * *

(b) (1) National primary ambient air quality standards, prescribed under subsection (a) shall be ambient air quality standards the attainment and maintenance of which in the judgment of the Administrator, based on such criteria and allowing an adequate margin of safety, are requisite to protect the public health.* * *

(2) Any national secondary ambient air quality standard prescribed under subsection (a) shall specify a level of air quality the attainment and maintenance of which in the judgment of the Administrator, based on such criteria, is requisite to protect the public welfare from any known or anticipated adverse effects associated with the presence of such air pollutant in the ambient air.* * *

NATIONAL QUALITY STANDARDS FOR AMBIENT AIR

(in micrograms or milligrams per cubic meter—ug/m^3 and mg/m^3—and in parts per million—ppm)

Pollutant	*Averaging Time*	*Primary Standards (health)*	*Secondary Standards (welfare, materials)*
Particulates	annual	75 ug/m^3	60 ug/m^3
	24-hour	260 ug/m^3	150 ug/m^3
Sulfur dioxide	annual	80 ug/m^3 (.03 ppm)	
	24-hour	365 ug/m^3 (.14 ppm)	
	3-hour		1300 ug/m^3 (.5 ppm)
Carbon monoxide	8-hour	10 mg/m^3 (9 ppm)	same as primary
	1-hour	40 mg/m^3 (35 ppm)	
Hydrocarbons (nonmethane)	3-hour (6-9 am)	160 ug/m^3 (.24 ppm)	same as primary
Nitrogen dioxide	annual	100 ug/m^3 (.05 ppm)	same as primary
Ozone	1-hour	240 ug/m^3 (.12 ppm)	same as primary
Lead	3-month	1.5 ug/m^3 (.006 ppm)	

NATURAL RESOURCES DEFENSE COUNCIL, INC.
v.
TRAIN

545 F.2d 320 (2d Cir. 1976)

Before SMITH, OAKES and MESKILL, Circuit Judges.

J. JOSEPH SMITH, Circuit Judge:

The Environmental Protection Agency, ("EPA"), and its Administrator, Russell Train, appeal from an order of the United States District Court for the Southern District of New York, Charles E. Stewart, Jr., Judge, in an action under § 304 of the Clean Air Act, as amended, 42 U.S.C. § 1857h–2(a), requiring the Administrator of the EPA, within thirty days, to place lead on a list of air pollutants under § 108(a)(1) of the Clean Air Act, as amended, 42 U.S.C. § 1857c–3(a)(1), ("the Act"). We affirm the order of the district court.

The 1970 Clean Air Act Amendments provide two different approaches for controlling pollutants in the air. One approach, incorporated in §§ 108–110, 42 U.S.C. §§ 1857c–3 to c–5, provides for the publication of a list of pollutants adverse to public health or welfare, derived from "numerous or diverse" sources, the promulgation of national ambient air quality standards for listed pollutants, and subsequent implementation of these standards by the states. The second approach of the Act provides for control of certain pollutants at the source, pursuant to §§ 111, 112, 202, 211 and 231 (42 U.S.C. §§ 1857c–6, c–7, f–1, f–6c, f–9).

The relevant part of § 108 reads as follows:

> (a)(1) For the purpose of establishing national primary and secondary ambient air quality standards, the Administrator shall within 30 days after December 31, 1970, publish, and shall from time to time thereafter revise, a list which includes each air pollutant—
>
> (A) which in his judgment has an adverse effect on public health or welfare;
>
> (B) the presence of which in the ambient air results from numerous or diverse mobile or stationary sources; and
>
> (C) for which air quality criteria had not been issued before December 31, 1970, but for which he plans to issue air quality criteria under this section.

Once a pollutant has been listed under § 108(a)(1), §§ 109 and 110 of the Act are automatically invoked.[4] These sections require that for any pollutant for which air

[4]Section 109, 42 U.S.C. § 1857c–4 provides in relevant part:

SEC. 109. (a)(1) The Administrator—

(A) within 30 days after the date of enactment of the Clean Air Amendments of 1970, shall publish proposed regulations prescribing a national primary ambient air quality standard and a national secondary ambient air quality standard for each air pollutant for which air quality criteria have been issued prior to such date of enactment; and

(B) after a reasonable time for interested persons to submit written comments thereon (but no later than 90 days after the initial publication of such proposed standards) shall by

quality criteria are issued under § 108(a)(1)(C) after the date of enactment of the Clean Air Amendments of 1970, the Administrator must simultaneously issue air quality standards.* * *

The EPA concedes that lead meets the conditions of §§ 108(a)(1)(A) and (B)—that it has an adverse effect on public health and welfare, and that the presence of lead in the ambient air results from numerous or diverse mobile or stationary

---

regulation promulgate such proposed national primary and secondary ambient air quality standards with such modifications as he deems appropriate.

(2) With respect to any air pollutant for which air quality criteria are issued after the date of enactment of the Clean Air Amendments of 1970, the Administrator shall publish, simultaneously with the issuance of such criteria and information, proposed national primary and secondary ambient air quality standards for any such pollutant. The procedure provided for in paragraph (1)(B) of this subsection shall apply to the promulgation of such standards.

(b)(1) National primary ambient air quality standards, prescribed under subsection (a) shall be ambient air quality standards the attainment and maintenance of which in the judgment of the Administrator, based on such criteria and allowing an adequate margin of safety, are requisite to protect the public health. Such primary standards may be revised in the same manner as promulgated.

Section 110, 42 U.S.C. § 1857c–5, provides in pertinent part:

SEC. 110. (a)(1) Each State shall, after reasonable notice and public hearings, adopt and submit to the Administrator, within nine months after the promulgation of a national primary ambient air quality standard (or any revision thereof) under section 109 for any air pollutant, a plan which provides for implementation, maintenance, and enforcement of such primary standard in each air quality control region (or portion thereof) within such State. In addition, such State shall adopt and submit to the Administrator (either as a part of a plan submitted under the preceding sentence or separately) within nine months after the promulgation of a national ambient air quality secondary standard (or revision thereof), a plan which provides for implementation, maintenance, and enforcement of such secondary standard in each air quality control region (or portion thereof) within such State. Unless a separate public hearing is provided, each State shall consider its plan implementing such secondary standard at the hearing required by the first sentence of this paragraph.

(2) The Administrator shall, within four months after the date required for submission of a plan under paragraph (1), approve or disapprove such plan or each portion thereof. The Administrator shall approve such plan, or any portion thereof, if he determines that it was adopted after reasonable notice and hearing and that—

(A)(i) in the case of a plan implementing a national primary ambient air quality standard, it provides for the attainment of such primary standard as expeditiously as practicable but (subject to subsection (e)) in no case later than three years from the date of approval of such plan (or any revision thereof to take account of a revised primary standard); and (ii) in the case of a plan implementing a national secondary ambient air quality standard, it specifies a reasonable time at which such secondary standard will be attained;

. . . . .

(c) The Administrator shall, after consideration of any State hearing record, promptly prepare and publish proposed regulations setting forth an implementation plan, or portion thereof, for a State if—

(1) the State fails to submit an implementation plan for any national ambient air quality primary or secondary standard within the time prescribed.

(2) the plan, or any portion thereof, submitted for such State is determined by the Administrator not to be in accordance with the requirements of this section, or

(3) the State fails within 60 days after notification by the Administrator or such longer period as he may prescribe, to revise an implementation plan as required pursuant to a provision of its plan referred to in subsection (a)(2)(H).

* * *

sources. The EPA maintains, however, that under § 108(a)(1)(C) of the Act, the Administrator retains discretion whether to list a pollutant, even though the pollutant meets the criteria of §§ 108(a)(1)(A) and (B). The EPA regards the listing of lead under § 108(a)(1) and the issuance of ambient air quality standards as one of numerous alternative control strategies for lead available to it. Listing of substances is mandatory, the EPA argues, only for those pollutants for which the Administrator "plans to issue air quality criteria." He may, it is contended, choose not to issue, *i. e., not* "plan to issue" such criteria, and decide to control lead solely by regulating emission at the source, regardless of the total concentration of lead in the ambient air. The Administrator argues that if he chooses to control lead (or other pollutants) under § 211, he is not required to list the pollutant under § 108(a)(1) or to set air quality standards.

The EPA advances three reasons for the position that the Administrator has discretion whether to list a pollutant even when the conditions of § 108 (a)(1)(A) and (B) have been met: the plain meaning of § 108(a)(1)(C); the structure of the Clean Air Act as a whole; and the legislative history of the Act.

The issue is one of statutory construction.

* * *

I

Section 108(a)(1) and the Structure of the Clean Air Act

Section 108(a)(1) contains mandatory language. It provides that "the Administrator *shall* . . . publish . . . a list . . . ." (Emphasis added.) If the EPA interpretation were accepted and listing were mandatory only for substances "for which [the Administrator] plans to issue air quality criteria . . . ", then the mandatory language of § 108(a)(1)(A) would become mere surplusage. The determination to list a pollutant and to issue air quality criteria would remain discretionary with the Administrator, and the rigid deadlines of § 108(a)(2), § 109, and § 110 for attaining air quality standards could be bypassed by him at will. If Congress had enacted § 211 as an alternative to, rather than as a supplement to, §§ 108–110, then one would expect a similar fixed timetable for implementation of the fuel control section. The absence of such a timetable for the enforcement of § 211 lends support to the view that fuel controls were intended by Congress as a means for attaining primary air quality standards rather than as an alternative to the promulgation of such standards.

The EPA Administrator himself initially interpreted § 108(a)(1) as requiring inclusion of the initial list to be issued of those pollutants for which air quality criteria had not been issued but which he had already found in his judgment to have an adverse effect on public health or welfare and to come from sources specified in § 108(a)(1)(B). 26 Fed.Reg. 1515 (1971). * * *

It is to the initial list alone that the phrase "but for which he plans to issue air quality criteria" is directed, and that the Administrator *must* list those pollutants which he has determined meet the two requisites set forth in section 108.

II

Legislative History

When a specific provision of a total statutory scheme may be construed to be in conflict with the congressional purpose expressed in an act, it becomes necessary to examine the act's legislative history to determine whether the specific provision is reconcilable with the intent of Congress.

* * *

The EPA contention that the language of § 108(a)(1)(C) "for which [the Administrator] plans to issue air quality criteria" is a separate and third criterion to be met before § 108 requires listing lead and issuing air quality standards, thereby leaving the decision to list lead within the discretion of the Administrator, finds no support in the legislative history of the 1970 Amendments to the Act.

* * *

The section-by-section analysis of the National Air Standards Act of 1970 in the Senate Report on S. 4358, 91st Cong., 2d Sess., * * * contains the following explicit language regarding §§ 108 and 109:

> Air quality criteria for five pollution agents have already been issued (sulfur oxides, particulates, carbon monoxide, hydrocarbons, and photochemical oxidants). *Other contaminants of broad national impact include fluorides, nitrogen oxides, polynuclear organic matter, lead, and odors. Others may be added to this group as knowledge increases. The bill would require that air quality criteria for these and other pollutants be issued within 13 months from enactment.* If the [Secretary] subsequently should find that there are other pollution agents for which the ambient air quality standards procedure is appropriate, he could list those agents in the Federal Register, and repeat the criteria process.
>
> Proposed national air quality standards for pollutants for which criteria would be issued subsequent to enactment would be published simultaneously with the issuance of such criteria. *These pollutants would include nitrogen oxides, lead, polynuclear organics, odors, and fluorides.*

(Emphasis added.)

Language relating to the issuance of new source performance standards makes it clear that the Senate intended these standards to be supplementary to, not in lieu of, ambient air quality standards:

> The committee recognizes that the construction of major new industrial facilities in some regions may conflict with implementation plans for national air quality standards and goals—even where such new facilities are designed, equipped, and operated so as to comply with applicable Federal standards of performance. This is most likely to occur in places where existing levels of air pollution are excessive. Accordingly, the bill would provide that new-source certification procedures must include preconstruction review of the location as well as the design of affected new facilities so that certified new sources would not hinder the implementation of air quality standards and goals.

While the literal language of § 108(a)(1)(C) is somewhat ambiguous, this ambiguity is resolved when this section is placed in the context of the Act as a whole and in its legislative history. The deliberate inclusion of a specific timetable for the attainment of ambient air quality standards incorporated by Congress in §§ 108–110 would become an exercise in futility if the Administrator could avoid listing pollutants simply by choosing not to issue air quality criteria. The discretion given to the Administrator under the Act pertains to the review of state implementation plans under § 110, and to § 211 which authorizes but does not mandate the regulation of fuel or fuel additives. It does not extend to the issuance of air quality standards for substances derived from specified sources which the Administrator had already adjudged injurious to health.

III

Judicial Interpretations

The Supreme Court in *Union Electric Co. v. Environmental Protection Agency*, 427 U.S. 246, 256, 96 S.Ct. 2518, 2525, 49 L.Ed.2d 474 (1976), referred to the 1970 Amendments of the Clean Air Act as "a drastic remedy to what was perceived as a serious and otherwise uncheckable problem of air pollution."

* * *

Previously the Court had referred to the attainment of the national air quality standards within three years from the date of approval of state implementation plans as "the heart of the 1970 Amendments." *Train v. Natural Resources Defense Council*, 421 U.S. 60, 66, 95 S.Ct. 1470, 1475, 43 L.Ed.2d 731 (1975).

* * *

The Court's language in *Train* and *Union Electric* lends no support to appellants' position that the EPA Administrator may order emission source controls instead of promulgating ambient air quality standards for substances, such as lead, which meet the criteria of §§ 108(a)(1)(A) and (B). Under the scheme of the Act, emission source control is a supplement to air quality standards, not an alternative to them.

* * *

The structure of the Clean Air Act as amended in 1970, its legislative history, and the judicial gloss placed upon the Act leave no room for an interpretation which makes the issuance of air quality standards for lead under § 108 discretionary. The Congress sought to eliminate, not perpetuate, opportunity for administrative foot-dragging. Once the conditions of §§ 108(a)(1)(A) and (B) have been met, the listing of lead and the issuance of air quality standards for lead become mandatory.

The order of the district court is affirmed.

---

b. *Air Quality Regions*

The Clean Air Act requires the EPA to establish **air quality control regions**, defined as an area with similar pollution problems, common pollution sources and characteristic weather. Under the 1977 amendments, each state is charged with the responsibility of rating each region within the state for its attainment of the air quality standard for each criteria pollutant. All regions are classified into either **nonattainment areas** or **nondeterioration** (clean air) areas. A nonattainment area is a region in which the ambient concentration of any pollutant is in excess of the national primary standard. A nondeterioration area is an area where the air is of higher quality than required by the National Air Quality Standards.

(1) **Nondeterioration Areas**. EPA has adopted regulations to protect the quality of air in nondeterioration areas. The objective of these regulations is to **prevent significant deterioration (PSD)** in areas where the air quality is better than required by the national air quality standards. The validity of the original regulations were challenged in *Sierra Club v. EPA* (1976) below. Subsequent to that decision, in the clean air amendments of 1977, Congress specifically required **State Implementation Plans (SIPS)** to contain **Prevention of Significant Deterioration (PSD)** provisions to prevent relatively clean air from deteriorating below the prescribed standards for sulfur dioxides and particulate matter.

Clean air areas, also known as **PSD areas**, are divided into three categories: Class I, where very little air pollution will be permitted. This designation includes the national parks and wilderness areas larger than 5000 acres; Class II, where moderate amounts of air quality deterioration will be permitted. Most clean air areas were put into this category initially: Class

III, where degradation of air quality is permitted up to limits of national primary standards. Procedures were adopted to redesignate land from Class II to Class III so that industrial expansion could take place.

Under the provisions of Section 165 of the Clean Air Amendments of 1977, no "major emitting facility" may be erected in a PSD area unless a permit is issued. To receive a permit the applicant must show that (*1*) the emission from the proposed operation will not violate a *prescribed maximum allowable increase for a pollutant* (*2*) will not violate a national air quality standard in any region, and (*3*) the proposed facility will use the **best available control technology (BAT)** for each pollutant. In *Alabama Power Company v. Costle*, the court reviewed several PSD regulations adopted by EPA in response to the Clean Air Amendments of 1977.

SIERRA CLUB
v.
E.P.A.

540 F.2d 1114 (D.C.Cir. 1976)

J. SKELLY WRIGHT, Circuit Judge:

I. INTRODUCTION

One of the primary purposes of the Clean Air Act, 42 U.S.C. § 1857 *et seq.* (1970), is "to protect and enhance the quality of the Nation's air resources so as to promote the public health and welfare and the productive capacity of its population * * * ." Section 101(b)(1), 42 U.S.C. § 1857 (b)(1). Pursuant to the court order in *Sierra Club v. Ruckelshaus*, 344 F.Supp. 253 (D. DC.1972), *aff'd per curiam*, 4 ERC 1815 (D.C. Cir. 1972), *aff'd by an equally divided Court, sub nom. Fri v. Sierra Club*, 412 U.S. 541, 93 S.Ct. 2770, 37 L.Ed.2d 140 (1973), the Administrator of the Environmental Protection Agency (EPA) promulgated regulations designed to prevent "significant deterioration" of air quality in those areas which have air that already is cleaner than the national ambient air quality standards.[1] The regulations employ a classification

[1]The twin objectives of the Clean Air Act are to improve air quality where pollution levels do not meet national minimum standards, and to protect the quality of air that already, as in this case, is cleaner than national standards. *See* Part V–A of this opinion *infra*. Accomplishment of those objectives is to be a joint enterprise of the federal government and the states, the former providing informed guidance to the implementation efforts of the latter. *See* §§ 101(a)(3), (4) of the Act, 42 U.S.C. §§ 1857(a)(3), (4).

Section 108 of the Act, 42 U.S.C. § 1857c–3, required the Administrator of EPA to publish a list of air pollutants which have "an adverse effect on public health or welfare." The Adminis-

scheme under which these "clean air" regions may be designated Class I, II, or III. All such areas initially are designated Class II, under which specified increments in sulfur dioxide and particulate matter pollution are considered "insignificant." A state, Indian territory, or federal land may be redesignated after hearing and by application to EPA. Designation as Class I implies a region of very clean air, in which relatively small increments in air pollution would be considered significant deterioration; Class III areas are those in which deterioration of air quality to the national ambient air quality standards would be considered insignificant.

The court has heard the regulations attacked from several perspectives. Petitioner Sierra Club contends that the regulations fail, in a variety of ways, to prevent significant deterioration of existing clean air. The States of New Mexico, Wyoming, and California agree in some respects with Sierra Club, but are concerned that the

---

trator was then to promulgate national primary and secondary ambient air quality standards for those specified pollutants. National *primary* air quality standards are those "the attainment and maintenance of which * * * are requisite to protect the public health"; national *secondary* standards are those "requisite to protect the public welfare from any known or anticipated adverse effects associated with the presence of such air pollutant in the ambient air." Section 109, 42 U.S.C. § 1857c–4. The Administrator has promulgated national primary and secondary air quality standards for six pollutants: sulfur dioxide, particulate matter, carbon monoxide, photochemical oxidants, hydrocarbons, and nitrogen dioxide. 40 C.F.R. §§ 50.4–50.11 (1975).

The states are charged with the duty to develop implementation plans designed to achieve the level of air quality prescribed by the national primary and secondary standards:

> Each State shall have the primary responsibility for assuring air quality within the entire geographic area comprising such State by submitting an implementation plan for such State which will specify the manner in which national primary and secondary ambient air quality standards will be achieved and maintained within each air quality control region in such State.

Section 107, 42 U.S.C. § 1857–2. The plans are submitted to the Administrator for approval under the provisions of § 110 of the Act, 42 U.S.C. § 1857c–5 (1970), *as amended* (Supp. IV 1974). A proposed implementation plan must satisfy the requirements of § 110(a)(2)(A)–(H), 42 U.S.C. § 1857c–5(a)(2)(A)–(H), which requirements include attainment of the national primary standards within three years after approval of the plan, and attainment of the secondary standards within a "reasonable time." Section 110(a)(2)(A), 42 U.S.C. § 1857c–5(a)(2)(A).

Section 110 also provides that the Administrator is promptly to prepare and publish his own regulations for a state if (a) it fails to submit a plan, (b) the plan "is determined by the Administrator not to be in accordance with the requirements of this section," or (c) the state fails to revise its plan pursuant to a provision required by § 110(a)(2)(H). Section 110(c)(1), 42 U.S.C. § 1857c–5(c)(1) (Supp. IV 1974). Subsection (c)(1) of § 110 also contains a conditional hearing requirement for these "replacement" implementation plans: "If such state held no public hearing associated with respect to such plan (or revision thereof), the Administrator shall provide opportunity for such hearing within such State on any proposed regulation." Subsection (a)(2)(H) requires that an implementation plan provide for revision (i) to take account of changes in either technology or the national standards and (ii) whenever the Administrator determines that the plan is inadequate to achieve the primary or secondary standards.

The basic structure described above is supplemented by § 111 of the Act, 42 U.S.C. § 1857c–6 (1970), *as amended* (Supp. IV 1974), which provides for promulgation of "standards of performance" for emission limitations of significant new sources of pollution, by categories of sources. The standards must reflect "the degree of emission limitation achievable through the application of the best system of emission reduction which (taking into account the cost of achieving such reduction) the Administrator determines has been adequately demonstrated."

regulations infringe on the general regulatory authority vested in the states by the Clean Air Act. A large number of electric power companies and industrial organizations have argued that the regulations are not authorized by the Clean Air Act, that their promulgation was procedurally defective, that the allowable increments are arbitrary and capricious, and that the regulatory structure created by the regulations is unconstitutional.

We conclude that the Administrator's action is rationally based and has not been shown to be either without his authority or unconstitutional. We therefore do not disturb the regulations as promulgated.

* * *

III. THE REGULATIONS

In promulgating final regulations EPA was concerned primarily with the meaning of "significant deterioration." As it stated in the discussion preceding the new regulations:

> Most of the comments implicitly recognized that there is a need to develop resources in presently clean areas of the country, and that significant deterioration regulations should not preclude all growth, but should ensure that growth occurs in an environmentally acceptable manner. However, there are some areas, such as national parks, where any deterioration would probably be viewed as significant. A single nationwide deterioration increment would not be able to accommodate these two situations.

39 Fed.Reg. at 42520. The solution was to prescribe, for those areas with air cleaner than the national standards, three classes of allowable total increments above the levels of particulate matter and sulfur dioxide pollution as of January 1, 1975, with the intention that each area could determine which class would prevent significant deterioration of its air in light of the area's air quality and social and economic needs and objectives:

> Class I applie[s] to areas in which practically any change in air quality would be considered significant; Class II applie[s] to areas in which deterioration normally accompanying moderate well-controlled growth would be considered insignificant; and Class III applie[s] to those areas in which deterioration up to the national standards would be considered insignificant.
>
> * * *
>
> Since the consideration of "air quality factors" alone essentially leads to an arbitrary definition of what is "significant," this term only has meaning when the economic and social implications are analyzed and considered. Therefore, the Administrator believes that it is most important to recognize and consider these implications, since the consideration of air quality factors alone provides no basis for selecting one deterioration increment over another.

Id. The regulations, 40 C.F.R. §§ 52.01(d), (f), and 52.21 (1975), were promulgated as amendments to the disapproved state implementation plans.

All areas initially are designated Class II, and may be redesignated by proposal of a state, federal land manager, or Indian governing body where the state has not assumed jurisdiction over Indian lands. Federal land may be designated only to a more restrictive classification than that provided by the state(s) in which it is located.

A state may redesignate if a hearing is held after notice to states, federal land managers, and Indian governing bodies that may be affected, and if the proposed redesignation is based on the record of the hearing,

> which must reflect the basis for the proposed redesignation, including consideration of (1) growth anticipated in the area, (2) the social, environmental, and economic effects of such redesignation upon other areas and States, and (3) any impacts of such proposed redesignation upon regional or national interests.

A redesignation is to be approved if the state has complied with the listed requirements, has not "arbitrarily and capriciously disregarded" the considerations listed in the passage quoted above, and has undertaken the new source review requirements of Sections 52.21(d) and (e), discussed below. 40 C.F.R. § 52.21(c)(3)(vi)(*a*) (1975). Federal land managers and Indian governing bodies are subject to requirements parallel to those imposed on the states, with the added requirement that they consult with the state(s) in which they are located.

If an area is designated as Class I or II, the allowable incremental pollution is measured from January 1, 1975. No increments are specified for Class III; areas so designated are required to meet only the national secondary standards.

Enforcement of the limitation on incremental pollution is accomplished partly through preconstruction review of 19 categories of stationary sources considered to be significant sources of pollution. Permission to construct or to modify significantly one of the listed stationary sources is conditioned on a showing that the source's emissions, together with all other increases or decreases in emissions in the area since January 1, 1975, will not violate the air quality increments applicable to *any* area. The source also must meet an emission limit, specified by the Administrator, "which represents that level of emission reduction which would be achieved by the application of best available control technology, as defined in § 52.01(f), for particulate matter and sulfur dioxide" Preconstruction review of new proposed sources will be conducted by the Administrator or, by delegation, by the individual states.

Last, it should be noted that the described classification scheme is no procrustean bed to which all states are to be bound. The states retain the option of proposing an alternative method of preventing significant deterioration of air quality, thereby abandoning the regulatory framework described by the regulations under review. As EPA stated in proposing regulations:

> The State plans need not be identical to the regulations proposed herein, but should be developed to accommodate more appropriately individual conditions and procedures unique to specific State and local areas. States are urged to develop and submit individual plans as revisions to State Implementation Plans as soon as possible. When individual State Implementation Plan revisions are approved as adequate to prevent significant deterioration of air quality, the applicability of the regulations proposed herein will be withdrawn for that State.

39 Fed. Reg. at 31000 (August 27, 1974).

* * *

A. Should *Sierra Club v. Ruckelshaus* be rejected on further consideration?

The question whether the Clean Air Act should be interpreted to prohibit significant deterioration of air cleaner than the national standards is necessarily the first level of analysis.

* * *

It is posited that neither the "protect and enhance" language of Section 101(b)(1) nor the legislative history of the Clean Air Act need be read to impose a requirement of nondeterioration; petitioners then point out that, to the contrary, a 1970 amendment to the Act, Section 110(a)(2), 42 U.S.C. § 1857c–5(a)(2), states that the Administration "shall approve" a state implementation plan which meets the criteria listed in that section, none of which implies a nondeterioration standard. The conclusion advanced by petitioners is that the judicially-created requirement of nondeterioration violates this plain language of the 1970 amendment.

* * *

When a specific provision of a total statutory scheme reasonably may be construed to be in conflict with the congressional purpose expressed in the act, our first task is to examine the act's legislative history to determine whether the specific provision is reconcilable and consistent with the intent of Congress. We find, in the legislative history of the Clean Air Act of 1970, a clear understanding that the Act embodied a pre-existing policy of nondeterioration of air cleaner than the national standards. Inasmuch as we find no support for the proposition that the addition of Section 110(a)(2) was intended to limit that policy in any way, we reaffirm our prior holding in *Sierra Club v. Ruckelshaus*.

B. Are the regulations invalid on the ground that only two of the six primary air pollutants are considered?

The regulations provide for control only of particulate matter and sulfur dioxide emissions, whereas the Administrator also has identified carbon monoxide, nitrogen oxides, hydrocarbons, and photochemical oxidents as air pollutants which have an adverse effect on public health or welfare. It is contended that the regulations violate the District Court's order in *Sierra Club v. Ruckelshaus* by failing to prevent significant deterioration of air quality with respect to those four pollutants.

EPA has responded that the interrelationships among those four pollutants, and the relationships between incremental increases in those pollutants and deterioration of air quality, are poorly understood and cannot be determined with any reasonable degree of accuracy:

> These [four pollutants] are commonly referred to as "automotive pollutants," because the automobile is the major source of each of them * * *. The first three (HC, NO_2, and O_x) are also known as "photochemical" or "reactive" pollutants, because under the influence of sunlight, they enter into a complex chemical reaction in the atmosphere. * * * The rate at which the reaction occurs depends on a number of variables, including temperature, humidity, solar intensity, and the concentrations of the input pollutants. * * *
>
> The chief reason for excluding photochemical pollutants from these regulations is that the relationship between the emission of HC and oxides of nitrogen, on the one hand, and the resulting ambient levels of the harmful pollutants O_x and NO_2, on the other, is very poorly understood. The only method for relating emissions to air quality for these pollutants is the "area-wide proportional model." This model assumes, as its name suggests, that ambient pollutant levels are proportional to total emissions. The model is useful only in areas where ambient pollutant levels are substantial and well-monitored, as in urban areas with smog problems. * * * But the proportional model cannot be used to regulate air quality deterioration in clean-air areas. This is because the assumptions underlying the model do not hold in clean-air areas, and also because it is not possible to make accurate measurements of ambient levels of photochemical pollutants that are substantially below the levels of the national standards.

EPA concluded that existing technology "is appropriate for analyzing the incremental impact of individual new sources" with respect to the four "automotive pollutants," and that "[a]t this time, the only practical approach for dealing with these pollutants appears to be to minimize emissions as much as possible." 39 Fed.Reg. 42511 (December 5, 1974). EPA further has contended that ongoing programs toward reduction of automotive emissions "are adequate to prevent any significant deterioration due to sources of carbon monoxide, hydrocarbons or nitrogen oxides."

* * *

This is the type of policy decision in which the Agency's developed expertise is heavily implicated, and with which the court will not tamper so long as the decision was rational and based on consideration of the relevant factors. * * *

We therefore hold that EPA did not act unlawfully in excluding from its regulations the four "automotive pollutants."

* * *

C. Are Class II and Class III invalid as permitting significant deterioration of air quality?

D. [Is it] unlawful to make determinations as to permissible air quality deterioration on the basis of considerations other than air quality?

It is argued by Sierra Club that Classes II and III, by permitting increases in sulfur dioxide and particulate matter pollution to levels which in some areas may be many times present concentrations, allow significant deterioration of air quality. The "significance" is primarily a matter of the numbers involved; although evidence has been presented that levels of polution below the national secondary standards may have adverse health effects, it is for the Administrator rather than the courts to determine that the national secondary standards no longer can be said to protect the public from "any known or anticipated adverse effects" of a pollutant. The question of significance thus leads by implication to a second line of argument—that it is unlawful to consider deterioration of air quality "insignificant" simply because it accompanies normal, controlled economic development.

* * *

EPA recognized, in developing the concept of "significant deterioration" pursuant to Judge Pratt's order that "[p]ending the development of adequate scientific data on the kind and extent of adverse effects of air pollutant levels below the secondary standards, significant deterioration must necessarily be defined without a direct quantitative relationship to specific adverse effects on public health and welfare." 39 Fed.Reg. 18987 (July 16, 1973). It therefore determined that each state must determine what level of incremental pollution, taking into account the air quality and social and economic needs and objectives of the area, would be "significant deterioration" of its air quality.

In that context, it was a rational policy decision that the significance of deterioration of air quality should be determined by a qualitative balancing of clean air considerations against the competing demands of economic growth, population expansion, and development of alternative sources of energy. The approach provides a workable definition of significant deterioration which neither stifles necessary economic development nor permits unregulated deterioration to the national standards. We therefore find that EPA acted within the discretion it is granted as to matters of policy in choosing this design to prevent significant deterioration of air quality.

We may state our belief, as a general overview at this point, that for the most part it somewhat misses the mark to raise objections to the specific emission limits of the regulations under review. EPA has emphasized that the individual states are free to conceive and adopt their own methods of preventing significant deterioration. A state may use EPA's system to classify itself as industrial-metropolitan (Class III), as anticipating normal economic growth (II), or as desirous of protecting its clean air (I). But it also may develop its own scheme, based on its own needs, so long as the regulatory structure prevents significant deterioration of air cleaner than the national standards. Given the broad power vested in the states to alter or amend these regulations, we find little merit in objections to the specifics of the classification scheme itself.

* * *

L. Are the regulations constitutional?

We find the arguments challenging the constitutionality of the nondeterioration regulations to be insubstantial. Regulation of air pollution clearly is within the power of the federal government under the commerce clause, and we can see no basis on which to distinguish deterioration of air cleaner than national standards from pollution in other contexts. Nor do we agree that the regulations bear no rational relationship to protection of public health and welfare and therefore violate the due process clause of the Fifth Amendment. There is a rational relationship between air quality deterioration and the public health and welfare, and there is a proper legislative purpose in prevention of significant deterioration of air quality. Neither can the regulations be construed as an unconstitutional "taking" under the Fifth Amendment, any more than existing emission control regulations represent such a "taking." The use of private land certainly is limited, but the limitation is not so extreme as to represent an appropriation of the land.

The Tenth Amendment is not implicated either by infringement on the reserved powers of the states, *cf. National League of Cities v. Usery*, —— U.S. ——, 96 S.Ct. 2465, 49 L.Ed.2d 245 (1976), or by any requirement of affirmative action, as in *District of Columbia v. Train*, 172 U.S.App. D.C. 311, 521 F.2d 971 (1975). The states retain broad discretion under the regulations to control the use of their land and the scope of their economic development, and are required to take no affirmative action. Preconstruction review under the regulations is conducted by the Administrator unless a state requests that responsibility be delegated to it. 40 C.F.R. § 52.21(d), (f) (1975).

* * *

VI. CONCLUSION

We find no ground on which to disturb the regulations under review, and we therefore affirm the EPA "Prevention of Significant Air Quality Deterioration" regulations. Our review of *Sierra Club v. Ruckelshaus* and subsequent events has revealed no substantial reason for rejection of that decision, and we hold that the nondeterioration regulations promulgated pursuant to that decision are both rational and in accordance with law.

Affirmed.

WILKEY, Circuit Judge, concurs in the result only.

ALABAMA POWER COMPANY
v.
COSTLE

606 F.2d 1068 (D.C.Cir. 1979)

Before LEVENTHAL, ROBINSON and WILKEY, Circuit Judges.

PER CURIAM:

This case concerns the validity of final regulations promulgated by the Environmental Protection Agency (EPA) on June 19, 1978 embracing the prevention of significant deterioration of air quality in the nation's "clean air areas."[2] These "PSD" regulations interpreted and began the implementation of title I, part C of the Clean Air Act as amended.

* * *

A. *Potential To Emit*

The definition of "major emitting facility" is of central importance to the statutory scheme and is the source of a pivotal question in this case. Only major emitting facilities are subject to the preconstruction review and permit requirements of section 165 of the Act. Such facilities are defined in section 169(1) as those stationary sources of air pollutants from among 28 listed categories which "emit, or have the potential to emit" 100 tons per year or more of any air pollutant plus any other stationary source with the "potential to emit" 250 tons per year or more of any air pollutant.

* * *

EPA has interpreted the phrase "potential to emit" as referring to the measure of a source's "uncontrolled emissions"—*i. e.*, the projected emissions of a source when operating at full capacity, with the projection increased by hypothesizing the absence of the air pollution control equipment designed into the source. We think the fairly discernible meaning of the statute, applying its text and giving consideration both to the comprehensive statutory scheme and to the legislative history, is that an emitting facility is "major" within the meaning of section 169(1), only if it either (1) actually emits the specified annual tonnage of any air pollutant, or (2) has the potential, when operating at full design capacity, to emit the statutory amount. The purpose of Congress was to require a permit before major amounts of emissions were released.

* * *

C. *Source Definition*

EPA has defined the term "source" to include "any structure, building, facility, equipment, installation or operation (or combination thereof) which is located on

[2]"Clean air areas" are those air quality control regions designated under sections 107(d)(1)(D) & (E) of the Clean Air Act as having ambient air quality better than the applicable national primary or secondary ambient air quality standard, or for which there is insufficient data to make a determination of the air quality. 42 U.S.C. §§ 7407(d)(1)(D), (E) (1978).

one or more contiguous or adjacent properties and which is owned or operated by the same person (or by persons under common control)."

1. *Constituents of "Source"*

We hold that the definition of "stationary source" provided in section 111(a)(3) of the Act controls the meaning of that term when used in the PSD part of the statute. We come to our conclusion after evaluating the interplay of various provisions of the Act in light of applicable principles of statutory construction. Section 111(a)(3) restricts the term "stationary source" to the nouns "building, structure, facility, or installation." We find that EPA exceeded its statutory authority by including within its definition of "stationary source" the terms "equipment" and "operation," though we rule that EPA has considerable latitude in defining the four remaining terms—"structure," "building," "facility" and "installation"—to include a wide range of pollution-emitting sources within the reach of the PSD provisions. To the extent EPA intended its definition of the term "stationary source" to constitute an interpretation of the four statutory terms for purposes of the PSD part, it may recast its definition in appropriate fashion.

2. *Combination of "Sources" To Comprise a Single "Stationary Source"*

The definition of "stationary source" was interpreted within the context of the section 111 new source performance standards (NSPS) in *ASARCO Inc. v. EPA*, 188 U.S. App.D.C. 77, 578 F.2d 319 (1978). In *ASARCO* we held that a "stationary source" could be comprised of only a single building, structure, facility, or installation. EPA's PSD regulations are challenged as combining numerous facilities as a single source, in contravention of *ASARCO*. EPA argues that *ASARCO*'s interpretation of the 1970 version of the Act was overruled because the 1977 Amendments, adopted prior to *ASARCO*, implicitly ratified EPA's pre-*ASARCO* interpretation. In our view, *ASARCO* defined the *initial* intent of Congress; in the 1977 Amendments, Congress made no change. Hence *ASARCO* controls our ruling.

However, EPA has flexibility to refashion its regulations so as to achieve what it presented as its objectives. In *ASARCO*, we recognized that EPA retained broad discretion to define the scope of each term—building, structure, facility, and installation. While a "stationary source," as used in the PSD provisions of the Act, may consist of only a single, *e. g.*, "facility," EPA has latitude to define the term "facility," to encompass an entire plant or other "common sense industrial grouping" appropriate to the PSD review and permit process.[13] The pertinent regulations are remanded for further consideration.

* * *

F. *Major Modification/Bubble*

1. *"Major" Modification*

The PSD provisions of the Act incorporate the definition of "modification" provided in section 111(a)(4):

> The term "modification" means any physical change in, or change in the method of operation of, a stationary source which increases the amount of any air pollutant emitted by such source or which results in the emission of any air pollutant not previously emitted.

[13]The individual terms "facility," "building," "structure" and "installation" are not defined by the Act. EPA has latitude to adopt definitions of the terms for the purposes of the PSD provisions that are different in scope from the definitions of the terms employed for the purposes of, *e. g.*, the NSPS provisions. But the definitions applicable to each set of provisions must be reasonably appropriate for the purposes of those sections.

EPA's regulations define a "modification" for the purposes of the PSD part as a "major modification," incorporating the same tonnage thresholds EPA employed in its interpretation of the term major emitting facility—*i. e.*, 100 or 250 tons per year "uncontrolled emissions."

We find no basis in the statutory language or in the legislative history for EPA's transformation of the term "modification" specified by Congress. A modification within the meaning of the PSD part is any physical change in or change in the method of operation of a stationary source that increases in *any* amount the quantity (when calculated for operation at full design capacity) of any air pollutant emitted by the source or that results in the emission of any air pollutant not previously emitted.

2. *Restriction of Offset*

Industry petitioners claim discretion to make changes in a single major emitting facility, without prior permit or authorization, provided a change in design or operation that increases emissions is offset by other contemporaneous changes that decrease emissions so that there is no net increase in the potential to emit any air pollutant. EPA's regulations restrict in certain respects the ability of the emitter to make such offsetting changes without permission. Its restrictions are beyond EPA's statutory authority.

Industry's freedom to offset properly may be circumscribed by EPA if it chooses to exercise its broad discretion to define the components of the term "stationary source" so as to provide a narrow scope. EPA's latitude in this respect is in turn confined by the condition that EPA's definition of "stationary source" for purposes of administration of the PSD provisions would govern not only the definition of "modification" but also the coverage of section 169(1). However, given a concept of "stationary source," the "modification" of the source has two components: (1) there must be a physical change in or a change in the method of operation of a stationary source; and (2) there must be a net increase in the potential to emit any air pollutant. A series of contemporaneous changes in the source does not qualify as a "Modification" within the meaning of the PSD part if it does not result in a net increase in the source's potential to emit any air pollutant. We do not begrudge what we discern as the intent of Congress because it gives freedom in the scheduling of source changes. There may be a policy basis for this in a legislative forecast that the prospect of avoiding or of deferring the regulatory cost of the PSD preconstruction review and permit process provides an incentive to upgrade the quality of air pollution control technology employed in each facility by accompanying each design change or expansion with an offsetting improvement in air pollution control. As for the possibility of abuse in a company's deliberate deferral of BACT, EPA may cope with this by adopting a narrower definition of "facility" for purpose of new source performance standards under section 111 than it has adopted for purposes of the PSD part.

* * *

H. *Sources Located in Non-Attainment Areas*

Section 165(a) provides that a PSD permit is required before a major emitting facility "may be constructed in any area to which this part applies." Industry petitioners contend that this text makes the permit requirement applicable only to sources located within "clean air areas." That term refers to those air quality control regions in which the ambient air quality does not exceed the applicable NAAQS, or for which there is insufficient data to make such a determination. In contrast are the "nonattainment areas," defined in section 171(2) as those air quality control regions designated, under sections 107(d)(1)(A)–(C), as regions that fail to meet the standards of an applicable NAAQS. EPA's regulations extend the permit requirements of section 165 to all sources, wherever located, if the emissions from the source have an impact on any clean air area. In our view, the preconstruction review and permit requirements of section 165 apply both to major emitting facilities located in clean air areas and to those major emitting facilities located in nonattainment areas that have a substantial impact on a clean air area *in another State*. However, the requirements of section 165 are not triggered by sources located in nonattainment areas simply because they have an adverse impact on a clean air area *within the same State*. We reach this conclusion after a careful analysis of the statutory scheme and the specific language of the provisions.

We do not accept the premise of industry petitioners that "any area to which this part applies" is a phrase synonymous with the term "clean air areas." The statutory scheme contemplates in section 107 that States will be divided into "air quality control regions" (not "areas"). Section 162 takes up the air quality control regions that have been designated pursuant to section 107(d)(1)(D) or (E) and breaks them down into "class I areas" and "class II areas." It is apparent that an "area" may constitute only a portion of an air quality control region, and further evident from the operation of section 162(a) that an "area" may be plucked from the midst of an air quality control region and given an individual identity on the basis of the use to which that area has been put. Section 164 controls the redesignation of areas previously classified as "class I", "II" or "III," but neither section 162 nor section 164 gives full content to the phrase "any area to which this part applies." Certainly, all class I, II, and III areas (*i. e.*, the clean air areas) are areas "to which this part applies." But the phrase has a more comprehensive aspect.

* * *

We do find in section 160(4) a statutory basis for extension of the section 165 phrase "any area to which this part applies" to an "area" that may be a part of a "nonattainment area." Section 160(4) provides as one purpose of the PSD part: "to assure that emissions from any source in any State will not interfere with any portion of the applicable implementation plan to prevent significant deterioration of air quality for any other State." The congressional intention to avoid "interference" with maintenance of allowable increment ceilings or maximum concentrations in any clean air area encompasses a sensitivity to any substantial adverse interstate impact on air quality. It embraces impact from sources in both nonattainment areas and clean air areas in another State.

* * *

Section 126 provides a mechanism for detecting interstate air pollution and for enforcing the congressional objective. It requires enforcement of the provision in section 110(a)(2)(E)(i) prohibiting "interference" with another State's pollution control efforts. The structure of the comprehensive notice provision in section 126(a) indicates that a major emitting facility located in a nonattainment area is "subject to part C"—*i. e.*, subject to the section 165 preconstruction review and permit process—if emissions from that facility would have a substantial adverse impact on air quality in a clean air area of another State.

* * *

We do not discern from the statute or from the legislative history a similar intention to subject to section 165 permit requirements major emitting facilities located within nonattainment areas that have an adverse impact on air quality in a clean air area of the same State but no such impact on a clean air area of another State. Under the statute absolute limitations are placed on air pollution in both clean air areas and nonattainment areas, but the States are given latitude to manage the pattern of their internal growth within the confines of these limitations. In effect, the Act gives to the States authority to determine as a matter of internal resolution that the sound course is to adopt a policy of growth favoring concentration of industry to nonattainment areas (with pollution perhaps spilling over into clean air areas), rather than favoring dispersal of new economic development throughout the clean air areas of the State.

However, a federalist policy of deferring to a State concerning its internal growth management is inadequate to control the problems of interstate pollution abatement. For this the statute provides special mechanisms. The statute includes: the statement of purpose in section 160(4); the requirement of section 110 that a State's plan (SIP) prohibit its sources from emitting air pollution that will substantially "interfere" with another State's PSD control measures; the enforcement mechanism of section 126 to detect and to abate such interstate interferences. These provide a statutory foundation for application of the preconstruction review and permit requirements of section 165 to certain sources in nonattainment areas with substantial interstate air pollution impacts.

J. *Best Available Control Technology (BACT)*

1. *Inclusion of Visible Emission Standard*

Section 169(3) defines the term "best available control technology."[36] EPA's regulations provide that BACT "means an emission limitation (including a visible emissions standard). . . ." The addition of the phrase within the parentheses is the only way in which the text of the pertinent regulation varies from the statutory language. It is challenged by industry petitioners as a usurpation of authority.

In our view, industry petitioners misconstrue the import of inclusion of the parenthetical phrase within the regulation's definition. BACT is defined, in general, as a level of control technology appropriate to the facts and circumstances of the particular permit applicant. EPA is correct in its view that, where appropriate, BACT may include a visible emissions standard.

2. *Scope of BACT*

Section 165(a)(4) provides a requirement that the permit applicant has employed "the best available control technology for each pollutant subject to regulation under this Act emitted from, or which results from, such facility." EPA's regulations require BACT only for those pollutants for which the applicant would qualify as a major emitting facility—*i. e.*, pollutants emitted in amounts surpassing the 100 or 250 tons-per-year thresholds of section 169(1). We agree with the petition of the District of Columbia that there is an unambiguous statutory command—BACT "for each pollutant subject to regulation under this Act emitted from, or which results from, such facility." This phrase encompasses each pollutant for which EPA has promulgated *e. g.*, an NAAQS, a new source performance standard, or a hazardous pollutant standard. Those regulations do not require or depend on emissions as large as 100 tons per year. We find no basis for circumscribing the BACT requirement as EPA has done.

* * *

[36]C.A.A. § 169(3) provides:

The term "best available control technology" means an emission limitation based on the maximum degree of reduction of each pollutant subject to regulation under this Act emitted from or which results from any major emitting facility, which the permitting authority, on a case-by-case basis, taking into account energy, environmental, and economic impacts and other costs, determines is achievable for such facility through application of production, processes and available methods, systems, and techniques, including fuel cleaning or treatment or innovative fuel combustion techniques for control of each such pollutant. In no event shall application of "best available control technology" result in emissions of any pollutants which will exceed the emissions allowed by any applicable standard established pursuant to section 111 or 112 of this Act.

L. *Monitoring*

Environmental petitioners challenge EPA's monitoring regulations as falling short of the statutory mandate in several respects. EPA argues that the Act, specifically the text of sections 165(a)(2) and (a)(7), grants broad discretion to the agency to formulate monitoring regulations.

The arguably discretionary language of section 165(a)(2) and (a)(7) is in our view restricted by the plain language of section 165(e), which provides in part:

> The review provided for in subsection (a) shall be preceded by an analysis in accordance with regulations of the Administrator *promulgated under this subsection.*

(Emphasis supplied.) Subsection (e) unambiguously provides that certain requirements must be included in the monitoring regulations.

* * *

1. *Pollutants for Which Monitoring Is Required*

Section 165(e)(1) provides that the monitoring requirement "shall" include:

> an analysis . . . of the ambient air quality at the proposed site and in areas which may be affected by emissions from such facility *for each pollutant subject to regulation under this Act which will be emitted from such facility.*

(Emphasis supplied.) The regulations require monitoring only for pollutants for which there exists an NAAQS. This falls short of the statutory requirement since the source may emit pollutants that are "subject to regulation" by virtue of *e. g.*, new source performance standards or regulation of hazardous pollutants. However, EPA has administrative discretion to dispense with monitoring for *de minimis* situations.

2. *Required Uses of Monitoring Data*

Subsection 165(e)(2) provides in part:

> Effective one year after date of enactment of this part, the analysis required by this subsection shall include continuous air quality monitoring data gathered for purposes of determining whether emissions from such facility will exceed the maximum allowable increases or the maximum allowable concentration permitted under this part.

This is a requirement for use of monitoring data to determine actual or potential violation of the allowable increments. EPA's regulations have required monitoring only to determine whether an applicable NAAQS will be exceeded. Again, the regulation falls short of statutory command.

EPA argues in justification for its restrictions both on the use of monitoring and on the number of pollutants covered that monitoring for actual air quality concentrations is technologically infeasible for all but a small number of pollutants and that current monitoring techniques are at best of questionable accuracy even for the relatively straight-forward measurement of whether an applicable NAAQS has been exceeded.

We discern from the statute a technology-forcing objective.

* * *

This objective is furthered by the development of sophisticated monitoring techniques, and the collection of the data base that would result from monitoring's widespread use. Of course even a congressional mandate, such as a technology-forcing requirement based on a congressional projection of emergence of technology for the future, is subject to a justified excuse from compliance where good-faith effort to comply has not been fruitful of results. That is far different from the exemption created by EPA on the basis of current technological infeasibility.

* * *

(*2*) **Nonattainment Areas**. Under the Clean Air Amendments of 1977 each state must submit to EPA a list identifying those areas in the state that do not meet the national primary and secondary air quality standard. On the basis of the information furnished by the states, EPA designates the regions as **attainment** or **nonattainment** areas. This designation is important because permits for *new* stationary sources of pollution will be issued only if (*1*) the net effect of the new sources is reduced emissions (i.e., existing sources are reduced so that they will more than offset new or modified sources within the area); (*2*) the sources meet **lowest achievable emission rate (LAER)** standards; and (*3*) all other facilities of the applicant within the state are in compliance.

The following three cases involve issues arising from the designation of nonattainment areas: *Republic Steel Corp. v. Costle* and *PPG Industries, Inc. v. Costle* deal with the procedure for designation of nonattainment areas; *New England Legal Foundation v. Costle* involves the obligation of EPA to require the **state implementation plans (SIPS)** of states with nonattainment areas to take such action as is required to prevent the transport of pollutants to other states, preventing those other states from attaining and maintaining national air quality standards.

REPUBLIC STEEL CORPORATION
v.
COSTLE

621 F.2d 797 (6th Cir. 1980)

Before EDWARDS, Chief Judge, and PHILLIPS and PECK, Senior Circuit Judges.

EDWARDS, Chief Judge.

In this petition for review of the actions of the Administrator of the United States Environmental Protection Agency, Republic Steel Corporation and seven other major corporations in Ohio attack the rules promulgated by the Agency under the Clean Air Act Amendments of 1977 to control sulfur dioxide (SO_2) in the ambient air of Ohio.

Each petitioner operates one or more plants in Ohio in an area which has been designated by EPA as a "nonattainment area." This term means, in the context of this case, that in the area concerned EPA had found the ambient air to contain SO_2 pollutants in excess of the National Ambient Air Quality Standards (NAAQS) set by federal law. Petitioners complained that the nonattainment designations were based upon illegal methodology which produced erroneous results. They also claim that these results will adversely affect them by making them subject to a prohibition on major new installations or additions to plants without offsetting SO_2 pollution reductions and that existing facilities would be required to make incremental reductions in SO_2 emissions yearly so as to achieve compliance with NAAQS by December 31, 1982.

The pollutant which is the subject of this litigation is sulfur dioxide emitted when industrial power plants or public utility plants burn high sulfur coal. Much prior legal history has been written in this Circuit concerning the efforts of the Congress of the United States to accomplish effective control of SO_2 pollution.

* * *

In our opinion in *Cleveland Electric Illuminating Co. v. EPA*, 572 F.2d at 1152, we gave the history of congressional action on this subject:

The United States Congress has been wrestling with the problem of pollution of the ambient air since 1955. *See* Act of July 14, 1955, Pub. L. No. 84–159, 69 Stat. 622. The original act has now been amended many times. It now is cited as the Clean Air Act and has been codified in 42 U.S.C. §§ 1857–1857*l* (1970 & Supp. V 1975).[2]

* * *

[2]The Clean Air Act was originally enacted in 1963, Pub. L. No. 88–206, 77 Stat. 392. It was amended in relatively minor ways three times during the following six years. Pub. L. No. 89–272, 79 Stat. 992 (1965); Pub. L. No. 89–675, 80 Stat. 954 (1966); Pub. L. 90–148, 81 Stat. 485 (1967).

The Act's present form, however, is derived from amendments adopted in 1970 and subsequently. Clean Air Act Amendments of 1970, Pub. L. No. 91–604, 84 Stat. 1676 *as amended*, Pub. L. No. 92–157, 85 Stat. 464 (1971); Pub. L. No. 93–319, 88 Stat. 246 (1974); Pub. L. No. 95–95, 91 Stat. 685 (1977).

The Act is being recodified as 42 U.S.C. §§ 7401–7626.

National Air Quality Standards for Sulfur Dioxide

In *Cleveland Electric Illuminating Co. v. EPA,* 572, F.2d at 1153–54, this court described the setting of national air quality standards by Congress and the congressional objectives:

> **§ 50.4 National primary ambient air-quality standards for sulfur oxides (sulfur dioxide).**
>
> The national primary ambient air quality standards for sulfur oxides measured as sulfur dioxide by the reference method described in Appendix A to this part, or by an equivalent method, are:
>
> (a) 80 micrograms per cubic meter (0.03 p.p.m.)—annual arithmetic mean.
>
> (b) 365 micrograms per cubic meter (0.14 p.p.m.)—Maximum 24-hour concentration not to be exceeded more than once per year.
>
> **§ 50.5 National secondary ambient air quality standards for sulfur oxides (sulfur dioxide).**
>
> The national secondary ambient air quality standard for sulfur oxide measured as sulfur dioxide by the reference method described in Appendix A to this part, or by any equivalent method is 1,300 micrograms per cubic meter (0.5 p.p.m.) maximum 3-hour concentration not to be exceeded more than once per year.
>
> Ambient Air Standards (Primary & Secondary), 40 C.F.R. §§ 50.4, 50.5 (1976) (Footnote omitted).
>
> The federal Clean Air Act program which produced these standards is based primarily upon the adverse effect which air pollution has upon human life and health.
>
> * * *
>
> There is a large and increasing body of evidence that significant health effects are produced by long-term exposure to air pollutants. Acute respiratory infections in children, chronic respiratory diseases in adults, and decreased levels of ventilatory lung function in both children and adults have been found to be related to concentrations of SO_2 and particulates, after apparently sufficient allowance has been made for such confounding variable as smoking and socioeconomic circumstances.
>
> * * *

We emphasize that this court is not engaged in setting air quality standards nor are they in dispute in this litigation. On April 30, 1971, acting under the 1970 amendments, the Administrator issued national primary and secondary ambient air quality standards. This court's examination of them in the preceding ambient air SO_2 cases served to convince this court that the NAAQS as set by the Agency under Congressional authorization allowed little if any margin for error without proximate damage to at least the sick, the aged and the infant population of the area affected.

* * *

The Procedural Issue

As to the first issue in this case, EPA admits that it did not give prior public notice, hold hearings or solicit public comment as normally required by rulemaking under the Administrative Procedures Act, 5 U.S.C. §§ 553(b)–553(c) (1976) before issuing the list of designations of attainment and nonattainment areas. Its reliance for these omissions is upon the good cause exception contained in the Administrative Procedures Act, 5 U.S.C. § 553(b)(B) which reads:

> "Except when notice or hearing is required by statute, this subsection does not apply—
>
> * * *

When the agency for good cause finds (and incorporates the finding and a brief statement of reasons therefor in the rules issued) that notice and public procedure thereon are impracticable, unnecessary or contrary to the public interest."

* * *

We believe the Administrator acted consistently with the good cause exception in the Administrative Procedures Act for at least the following reasons:

First, Congress had confronted him with the second of two mandatory attainment dates for national air quality standards for sulfur dioxide and it was obvious that the January 1, 1979, date could not be achieved if notice and comment procedures were allowed in advance. It would, indeed, have been "impracticable" to ignore the January 1, 1979, date.

Second, the Administrator was not dealing with the SO_2 problem in Ohio for the first time. As noted above, every EPA move toward reducing SO_2 pollution in the ambient air of Ohio has been met with immediate and repetitive protest and litigation. The Administrator had every reason to contemplate a continuation of the record already recited above.

* * *

Fourth, we agree with the Administrator that it would have been "contrary to the public interest to ignore the statutory schedule." Important as are the economic arguments against SO_2 control which are now presented for a sixth time to this court, the effect of continued lack of control of SO_2 emissions must be held, as Congress clearly intended, to outweigh them.

Fifth, this record indicates that EPA did give serious consideration to the industry comments received in the post promulgation period and made 36 changes or modifications in the previously announced designations.

* * *

The Modeling Issue

In their second issue petitioners attack the substance of the regulations designating sulfur dioxide attainment areas and make essentially two claims which are closely related. The first is that the use of modeling based upon full capacity operational data of all emissions sources in a given area on a hypothetical second worst day in the year assumption is arbitrary and capricious in itself. This same argument, applicable of course to single emission sources, was made and squarely rejected by this court in *Cleveland Electric Illuminating Co. v. EPA, supra* and our *Cincinnati Gas & Electric v. EPA, supra,* opinions. We reject this argument as a thinly disguised, belated motion for rehearing.

Additionally, petitioners assert that in all such nonattainment designations, EPA arbitrarily and capriciously paid no attention to or too little attention to actual air quality as shown on monitors. This last argument has also been made to this court in *Cleveland Electric Illuminating Co.* and *Cincinnati Gas & Electric* cases and rejected in those cases as to the monitoring systems there and then in place.

Theoretically, of course, actual air quality tests would have to be superior to modeling assumptions if there were sufficient monitors to constitute a fair test of the ambient air in a county. How many such monitors would be needed for a meaningful sample of the ambient air of a county cannot be deduced from this record.

Congress has recognized that EPA may employ either monitoring or modeling. In § 171(2) of the Act, a nonattainment area is defined as "an area which is shown by monitored data or which is calculated by air quality modeling . . . to exceed any national ambient air quality standard." § 171(2), 42 U.S.C. § 7501(2).

Where Congress has itself described two alternative methods for EPA to determine nonattainment, the decision as to which to employ is certainly not initially one for this court. Our review concerns whether there has been a violation of law and if not, whether the EPA decision can appropriately be termed arbitrary and capricious.

In *Cleveland Electric Illuminating Co. v. EPA, supra*, we described one of the two models employed by EPA:

> The RAM model is a general formula which can be applied to many individual sources of pollution to derive specific estimates of SO_2 emission rates for each. It employs a wider, more complete and more accurate data base than any prior model yet employed in devising a sulfur dioxide control strategy for a state or county. The crucial data with which the RAM model starts are the design capacity figure, plus the fuel sulfur content, from which is computed the SO_2 emission rate for each of the heating or power plants sought to be controlled. Thus at the outset the RAM model starts with ascertainable specific figures for each source where disputes can be resolved by inspection of the equipment or fuel concerned. Many of the additional components such as stack height, wind direction, physical relationship of sources to each other, and topography of the area are similarly ascertainable as matters of fact. With the enormous financial stakes involved in this litigation, every effort to avoid disputes about the accuracy of the data base should be made. This record shows that United States EPA's design of the RAM model was brought about at least in large part by Ohio industry's requests for greater specificity and hence lower costs of compliance with National Air Quality Standards.
>
> While there may yet be developed (and hopefully will be) a better method of establishing a control strategy for sulfur dioxide emissions than the RAM model, no one has yet come forward with such. Nor do petitioners point to any such.
>
> This is not to ignore that petitioners do cite Enviroplan's claims of a superior model termed Air Pollution Evaluation System. This record shows, however, that United States EPA asked for the Enviroplan model and was refused, and is now refused the operative details of that model on the grounds of proprietary interest. While such withholding may be both defensible as a matter of law and understandable as a matter of economics, this court cannot consider Enviroplan's model as available technology until and unless it is fully disclosed and evaluated by United States EPA—the agency charged by Congress with making these decisions.
>
> We recognize that this record does not present positive proofs of the accuracy of RAM's predictions. Thus far technology has not developed foolproof methods for validating predictions concerning pollution of the ambient air absent years of collection of monitoring data with far more monitors and far more personnel than have thus far been available.

572 F.2d at 1162–63.

The conclusions arrived at in *Cleveland Electric Illuminating Co. v. EPA* quoted above are generally applicable to the present cases.

We emphasize again that in these cases we are dealing only with general objections to the procedures and formulae employed by EPA in devising its Ohio SO_2 control strategy. We reserve for later decision those attacks upon specific nonattainment designations wherein petitioners assert that the agency has made specific mistakes or arrived at results claimed to be demonstrably erroneous.

For the reasons outlined above, the petitions for review described above are hereby dismissed.

PPG INDUSTRIES, INC.
v.
COSTLE

630 F.2d 462 (6th Cir. 1980)

Before EDWARDS, Chief Judge, and PHILLIPS and PECK, Senior Circuit Judges.

JOHN W. PECK, Senior Circuit Judge.

Petitioners are four companies with industrial plants in Summit County, Ohio. They challenge the United States Environmental Protection Agency's designation of part of Summit County as "nonattainment" of the national air-quality standards for the pollutant sulfur dioxide (SO_2); by this designation the EPA labeled parts of Summit County, including most notably the City of Akron, as problem areas where special air pollution abatement measures should be undertaken.[1] We find EPA's designation to be unsupported by the administrative record, and we remand the agency's rule for further consideration. We do so reluctantly, but with the observation that zeal for cleaning the air does not justify administrative caprice or complacency.

I.
THE MEANING OF "ATTAINMENT"

U.S. EPA promulgated the attainment status designation of Summit County pursuant to the legislative command of the Clean Air Act Amendments of 1977, which provided that

> (d)(1) For the purpose of transportation control planning, part D of this subchapter (relating to nonattainment), part C of this subchapter (relating to prevention of significant deterioration of air quality), and for other purposes, each State, within one hundred and twenty days after August 7, 1977, shall submit to the Administrator a list, together with a summary of the available information, identifying those air quality control regions or portions thereof, established pursuant to this section in such State which on August 7, 1977—
>
> (A) do not meet a national primary ambient air quality standard for any air pollutant other than sulfur dioxide or particulate matter;
>
> (B) do not meet, or in the judgment of the State may not in the time period required by an applicable implementation plan attain or maintain, any national primary ambient air quality standard for sulfur dioxide or particulate matter;
>
> (C) do not meet a national secondary ambient air quality standard;
>
> (D) cannot be classified under subparagraph (B) or (C) of this paragraph on the basis of available information, for ambient air quality levels for sulfur oxides or particulate matter; or

[1]The abatement measure most abhorrent to the petitioners is a more onerous permit requirement for the construction or modification of pollution sources in nonattainment areas than in attainment ones. *Compare* 42 U.S.C.A. § 7503 *with id.* § 7475.

(E) have ambient air quality levels better than any national primary or secondary air quality standard other than for sulfur dioxide or particulate matter, or for which there is not sufficient data to be classified under subparagraph (A) or (C) of this paragraph.

(2) Not later than sixty days after submittal of the list under paragraph (1) of this subsection the Administrator shall promulgate each such list with such modifications as he deems necessary. Whenever the Administrator proposes to codify a list submitted by a State, he shall notify the State and request all available data relating to such region or portion, and provide such State with an opportunity to demonstrate why any proposed modification is inappropriate.

42 U.S.C.A. § 7407(d)(1)–(2) (Supp. 1979).

At first blush this subsection appears to require an assessment of the nation's air quality as of August 7, 1977. Petitioners conclude from the statute's reference to this specific date that actual, and not predicted, air quality must be the basis for attainment designations. EPA, however, has interpreted subsection (d)(1)(B), *supra*, to mean that "projected future violations may provide the basis for a nonattainment designation in currently clean areas." 43 Fed.Reg. 45998 (1978). Our agreement with this interpretation is implicit in our decision in *Republic Steel v. Costle*, 621 F.2d 797 (6th Cir. 1980), holding that the EPA's use of computer modeling in making attainment designations was not in itself arbitrary and capricious. Even computer models of air quality incorporating "worst case" assumptions regarding weather conditions, and assuming full capacity operation of polution sources, may be used to determine "attainment" as defined by the EPA under its interpretation of the Clean Air Act Amendments. *See Republic Steel, supra*, at 804–806. We therefore reject petitioners' argument that EPA violated the Clean Air Act in basing its Summit County SO_2 designation on "hypothetical future circumstances rather than on actual August 7, 1977 air quality."

II.
THE VALIDITY OF EPA'S RELIANCE ON ITS SUMMIT COUNTY AIR-QUALITY MODEL

Our broad approval of the use of computer modeling in making attainment status designations does not mean that modeling practices in individual cases need not be supported by the administrative record. We hold that the administrative record does not support the agency's Summit County SO_2 designation, and therefore we remand to the agency for development of the record.

* * *

III.
MODELING v. MONITORING

Petitioners have argued, and may again on remand, that the EPA should base its new Summit County SO_2 designation on air-quality data produced by the extensive pollution monitoring network in Summit County. Petitioners base this argument on an interpretation of the Clean Air Act which has been outlined above: their contention is that attainment status designations must be based on "actual," and not predicted air quality. We do not find EPA's contrary interpretation of the Act to be unreasonable. We noted in *Republic Steel, supra*, that:

> Congress has recognized that EPA may employ either monitoring or modeling. In § 171(2) of the Act, a nonattainment area is defined as "an area which is shown by monitored data or which is calculated by air quality modeling . . . to exceed any national ambient air quality standard." § 171(2), 42 U.S.C. § 7501(2).
>
> Where Congress has itself described two alternative methods for EPA to

determine nonattainment, the decision as to which to employ is certainly not initially one for this court. Our review concerns whether there has been a violation of law and if not, whether the EPA decision can appropriately be termed arbitrary and capricious.

F.2d at 805.

We believe, then, that if a nonattainment designation is based on modeling, EPA need only offer record support of the accuracy of the model used. The agency is not required by the Act, nor by its own policies, to prefer monitoring to modeling in making attainment status designations. We acknowledge that "[t]heoretically, of course, actual air quality tests would have to be superior to modeling assumptions if there were sufficient monitors to constitute a fair test of the ambient air in a country." *Republic Steel, supra* at 805. If, however, EPA based a nonattainment designation on predictions of future violations, as the agency may do under the act (*see* Part I *supra*), monitored data which merely show historical attainment of air-quality standards do not undermine the agency's designation. Once EPA has chosen modeling as a basis for its designation, monitored data are relevant in a challenge to that designation only if (1) the parties proffering the data offer evidence of its reliability, and (2) the data tend to show that the agency's *predictions* were unsupportable. If these two tests are met, then at some point—the present record certainly does not indicate at what point—it could be arbitrary and capricious for the agency to rely on air-quality modeling instead of on available monitored data in making an attainment status designation.

IV.
CONCLUSION

We grant the companies' petitions and remand these causes so that an administrative record supporting an SO_2 designation for Summit County may be developed. It may be that the agency's designation will remain unchanged in light of the agency's "reanalysis" of its Summit County model; we trust, however, that the agency's future promulgation will follow the procedures prescribed by law.

NEW ENGLAND LEGAL FOUNDATION
v.
COSTLE

475 F.Supp. 425 (1979)

NEWMAN, Circuit Judge.

The plaintiffs in this action seek a declaratory judgment and injunctive relief based upon alleged violations of the Federal Clean Air Act, 42 U.S.C. § 7401 *et seq.*, of federal common law, and of various constitutional provisions. Plaintiffs include three nonprofit organizations representing the interests of the citizens, businesses, and industries of Connecticut, thirty-one municipalities of Connecticut, and individual citizens and residents of Connecticut, who are concerned with the harmful effects felt in Connecticut from air pollution allegedly generated from New York and New Jersey. Defendants Costle and Beck are, respectively, the Administrator and Region II Administrator of the Environmental Protection Agency ("EPA"), and defendant Long Island Lighting Company ("LILCO") is a New York Corporation.

This matter is before the Court on defendants' motions to dismiss and for summary judgment, and on plaintiffs' motion for summary judgment. As the complaint raises different issues with respect to the federal and corporate defendants, EPA's motions will be considered separately from LILCO's.

Background of the Suit

To prevent and control air pollution, Congress passed the 1970 Amendments to the Clean Air Act ("the Act"). The Amendments foster cooperative effort between the federal government and the states to achieve air quality standards set by EPA. EPA's Administrator is required to promulgate national air quality standards for various pollutants to protect public health and welfare from the adverse effects of pollutants for which air quality criteria are available. 42 U.S.C. § 7409. Each state must then develop a state implementation plan ("SIP"). The SIP establishes emission limitations and pollution abatement measures to ensure the attainment of air quality standards within the areas of the state that are designated by EPA as part of interstate or major intrastate air quality control regions ("control regions"). §§ 7404, 7410.

After a state adopts or revises a SIP, the plan must be approved by EPA. § 7410(a)(2). If the plan meets certain requirements, the Administrator is obligated to approve it. § 7410(a)(3). However, if the SIP is found deficient in whole or in part, and the state fails within 60 days of notification to revise the plan satisfactorily, the Administrator must promulgate and implement a plan correcting the deficiencies. § 7410(c).

Recognizing that many control regions had failed to meet national air standards because of inadequate state regulation and enforcement, and because of noncompliance by sources of pollution, Congress significantly amended the Act in 1977. The 1977 Amendments require each state to identify those areas that either do not meet national standards as of August 7, 1977, or may not meet the standards for sulfur dioxide or particulates by the applicable SIP deadline, or cannot be classified on the basis of available information for sulfur dioxide or particulate quality levels. § 7407 (d). An area not meeting one or more national standards is to be designated as "nonattainment" for each pollutant as to which the pertinent standard is violated. § 7501(3).

After the designations are approved or modified by the Administrator, § 7407(d)(2) and (5),[4] a state must revise its SIP before permitting the construction or modification after July 1, 1979, of any facility that will contribute to concentrations of any pollutant for which the area is "nonattainment." §§ 7410(a)(2)(I), 7501–7508. The revised plan must provide for attainment of national air quality standards no later than December 31, 1982, except that the deadline with respect to severe oxidant and carbon monoxide problems may be extended to as late as December 31, 1987.

[4]On March 3, 1978, the Administrator promulgated air quality designations for all areas of the country. 43 Fed.Reg. 8962 (1978). Of relevance to this case are the designations for areas in New York and New Jersey that may affect the air quality in Connecticut. The entire states of New York, New Jersey, and Connecticut were designated "nonattainment" for the national standards for photochemical oxidants. New York City was designated "unclassifiable" for sulfur oxide and particulate primary and secondary standards. Staten Island was designated "nonattainment" for secondary particulate standards, and Northern and Southern New Jersey were designated "nonattainment" for particulates.

§ 7502(a)(2). The revisions must implement all reasonably available control measures as expeditiously as practicable, require reasonable further progress toward attainment in the interim, including reductions through the use of reasonably available control technology, provide an inventory of actual emissions from all sources to assure that progress is made, and require permits for construction and operation of new or modified major pollution sources. § 7502(b).

Moreover, § 7410(a)(2)(E), as amended in 1977, requires SIP revisions that will prohibit any stationary source from interfering with another state's measures to attain national air quality standards, to prevent significant deterioration of existing air quality, and to protect visibility. Where there is an interstate control region, such as the New York–New Jersey–Connecticut region, EPA requires all of the states to revise their SIPs to account for the worst case of nonattainment among them for any national standard. * * * In this case, New York and New Jersey are required to tailor their SIP revisions to take account of Connecticut's air quality for those pollutants for which Connecticut's control attainment is poorest.

All revisions for nonattainment areas must be submitted to EPA by January 1, 1979, and are to be in effect no later than July 1, 1979.

* * *

The Suit Against EPA

The basic thrust of the plaintiffs' action against EPA is the agency's alleged failure to perform its statutory duties to revise the New York and New Jersey SIPs, in both their stationary source and transportation control aspects, in order to abate the transport of air pollutants from those states to Connecticut. Because EPA does not have a mandatory duty at this time to take any of the actions that the plaintiffs seek, the complaint fails to state valid claims against EPA.

The Clean Air Act, which provides the entire basis for this Court's jurisdiction over the subject matter of the complaint, establishes federal court jurisdiction over EPA in two ways. Section 7607(b) of Title 42 gives to the appropriate court of appeals exclusive jurisdiction to review EPA's regulations, orders, SIP approvals or disapprovals and revisions, and "any other final action of the Administrator . . . which is locally or regionally applicable" or which is not determined by the Administrator to have "nationwide scope or effect." The district courts are given jurisdiction under § 7604(a)(2) in a civil action against the Administrator only "where there is alleged a failure of the Administrator to perform any act or duty under this chapter which is not discretionary with the Administrator."

Plaintiffs bring their claims under § 7604(a)(2). Hence, to survive a motion to dismiss for failure to state a claim, the alleged actions by the Administrator must constitute a refusal to perform a non-discretionary duty imposed elsewhere in the Act, and must not be directly reviewable by the Court of Appeals for the Second Circuit under § 7607(b).

* * *

1. *Revision of the New York and New Jersey SIPs*

Plaintiffs allege that, on June 30, 1976, the Region II Administrator issued "Notices of Required Revisions" to the New York and New Jersey SIPs.[5] The New York notice presented the Administrator's findings that the SIP was inadequate to attain standards for sulfur oxides in New York City, for particulate matter in New

[5]These notices, published in the Federal Register on July 12, 1976, 41 Fed.Reg. 21618, and July 13, 1976, 41 Fed.Reg. 28842, were two of 221 such notices issued by EPA at that time. A notice was published for every air quality control region in which a national ambient air quality standard was not currently being met. For the relevant history, *see* S.Rep.No.95–127, 95th Cong., 1st Sess. 55 (May 10, 1977).

York City and portions of the Hudson Valley Region, and for photochemical oxidants throughout the New York portion of the New Jersey–New York–Connecticut Interstate Air Quality Control Region. The New Jersey notice presented the Administrator's findings that the SIP was inadequate to attain standards for photochemical oxidants and particulates in the New Jersey portion of the same control region.[6]

Plaintiffs further assert that the notices required the states to submit plan revisions by July 1, 1977, to include all readily available control measures, and by July 1, 1978, to include those necessary measures not readily available. The revisions were also to demonstrate that the proposed strategies would be adequate to attain the national air quality standards "as expeditiously as practicable." 41 Fed.Reg. 28625 (1976). If the Governors failed to send a letter of intent to comply with the notices, the EPA was to presume that the states would not prepare revisions, in which case the "EPA will begin to develop for promulgation a Federal plan to attain and maintain national standards." *Id.* at 28626.

Both New York and New Jersey have allegedly failed to revise their SIPs in accordance with the Notices of Required Revisions. Their plans, therefore, remain inadequate to attain the national standards for particulate matter, sulfur oxides, and photochemical oxidants, in violation of § 7410(a). Moreover, EPA has allegedly failed to correct the acknowledged SIP deficiencies by federal regulation as is its nondiscretionary duty under § 7410(c).

In complaining of EPA's inaction, the plaintiffs have incorrectly assessed the effect of the control strategies for particulates, sulfur oxides, and photochemical oxidants imposed by the 1977 Amendments. These specific procedural and substantive requirements, discussed above, effectively supersede the 1976 Notices of Required Revisions.

The legislative history of the Amendments indicates that EPA's attempts to enforce SIP revisions following the original 1975 compliance deadline were considered to be inadequate and required additional statutory guidance.* * *

Choosing to preserve the primary role of the states in attaining national standards, the Conference Committee adopted the Senate's approach for mandatory SIP revisions as a precondition for permitting major new stationary sources to locate in a nonattainment area. §§ 7501–08, 7410(a)(2)(I). With no indication to the contrary, it is reasonable to conclude that the 1977 Amendments' design for nonattainment plan revisions and deadline extensions operates in the same way as the Senate Committee's proposal, on which it is based, to nullify the effect of the outstanding Notices of Required Revision.

The facts in the present case illustrate the logic of so construing the Amendments. Of the nonattainment areas for oxidants and particulates for which revisions were required under the 1976 Notices, all but three were designated nonattainment for the same pollutants by EPA on March 3, 1978, under the amended § 7407(d) procedure. This * * * means that the revisions called for in 1976 relate to the same nonattainment problems that New York and New Jersey would have to confront in submitting 1979 SIP revisions under Part D of the amended Act, §§ 7501–7508. Both New York and New Jersey have submitted proposed SIP revisions pursuant to Part D. These revisions will be assessed by EPA as to whether they will attain national standards in the nonattainment areas designated on March 3, 1978, and as to whether they will prevent stationary sources in nonattainment areas from causing or contributing to violations of the national standards in Connecticut.

[6]For purposes of this opinion, various air quality designations or deadlines under the Clean Air Act for "New York" or "New Jersey" pertain, except where otherwise described, to the New York portion or the New Jersey portion, respectively, of the New York–New Jersey–Connecticut Interstate Air Quality Control Region. Appendix A to the Complaint enumerates the counties included in both portions.

It would make no sense as a practical matter for EPA to promulgate SIP revisions premised on the now-superseded 1976 notices, only to have them eclipsed by the 1979 revisions. Moreover, EPA action at this time would frustrate the obvious statutory purpose in delaying the deadline for submission of Part D revisions until January 1, 1979: to allow integrated state and local consideration of the most appropriate mix of stationary source and transportation controls to meet national air quality standards. See § 7401(a)(3) (pollution control is the "primary responsibility of States and local governments").

The submission of New York's and New Jersey's 1979 revisions has initiated the administrative review process established by the statute. EPA will have to approve or disapprove the states' submissions, and, if the proposed revisions are found inadequate to prohibit stationary sources in these states from affecting Connecticut's attainment of air quality standards, the states will have 60 days or a period prescribed by the Administrator to revise further the SIPs. After that time, if the states fail to act, EPA must publish regulations setting forth the necessary SIP revisions. § 7410(c). If plaintiffs were to consider the promulgated revisions still inadequate, they will have an opportunity to petition for review in the court of appeals for the appropriate circuit. § 7607(b).

Until EPA's review of the newly submitted SIPs is completed, neither EPA nor the plaintiffs can determine a need for additional control measures to prevent interstate pollution. The Administrator will grant approval only when the SIP, as revised, meets all the requirements of §§ 7410(a)(2) and 7502(b), and "[d]etermining whether such is the case requires the fusion of technical knowledge and skills with judgment which is the hallmark of duties which are discretionary." *Kennecott Copper Corp. v. Costle*, 572 F.2d 1349, 1354 (9th Cir. 1978). Once EPA has performed its review duties, and if the states then have failed to make any required further revisions of their SIPs, the Administrator may well have a mandatory duty to act in the manner prescribed by § 7410(c)(1)(C), *Natural Resources Defense Council v. Train*, 545 F.2d 320 (2d Cir. 1976), but the Agency has no statutory obligation at this time to conform the SIPs to the requirements of the 1976 notices.

* * *

3. *EPA Review of the Approved Variance for LILCO's Electricity Generating Plants*

On August 26, 1977, EPA allegedly approved, by its authority under § 7410(a)(3)(A), a revision to the New York SIP that allowed a "special limitation" for the use of high sulfur fuel by LILCO at its electricity generating plants in Northport and Port Jefferson on the north shore of Long Island. The special limitation permits these facilities to use fuel oil having a maximum 2.8% sulfur content until May 31, 1980. The New York State regulation for sulfur content in fuel oil had provided a general limitation of 1% for plants in Suffolk County.

Plaintiffs allege that the use of 2.8% sulfur fuel by LILCO plants increases the levels of sulfur dioxide, particulate matter, and sulfates in Connecticut, and thereby interferes with Connecticut's measures to prevent significant deterioration of its air quality and to attain national air quality standards for these pollutants in violation of § 7410(a)(2)(E). Plaintiffs claim that the Administrator has failed to perform his non-discretionary duty to revise the New York SIP so as to meet the requirements of § 7410(a)(2)(E). Therefore, this Court allegedly has jurisdiction to order EPA to revoke its conditional approval of LILCO's variance.

The 1977 Amendments significantly altered SIP requirements with respect to the abatement of interstate air pollution. Section 7410(a)(2)(E) was added to require that each SIP prohibit any stationary source within the state from emitting pollutants that would interfere with measures taken by another state to attain or maintain national air quality standards or to prevent significant deterioration of its existing air quality. This basic prohibition is implemented by Title I, Part C of the Act, §§ 7470–

7491, entitled "Prevention of Significant Deterioration of Air Quality" ("PSD"). According to § 7471, each SIP must contain emission limitations and other measures necessary, as determined by applicable agency regulations, to prevent significant deterioration of air quality in any region that has been designated "unclassifiable" for sulfur oxides or particulate matter, § 7407(d)(1)(D), or "in attainment" or "unclassifiable" for any other pollutant, § 7407(d)(1)(E). Section 7473 sets numerical increments defining the maximum amounts of sulfur oxides or particulates that any "unclassifiable" region may allow to be added to the existing levels over a certain time period. Stricter standards of protection are established for control regions containing national parks and wilderness areas, defined as Federal class I areas under § 7472(a), than for control regions without such areas. See §§ 7473(b)(1), 7491.

Since the 1977 Amendments and applicable legislative history do not establish a separate and unique date for submission of SIP revisions under these sections, the deadline for action by the states is set by § 406(d)(2) of P.L. 95–95, 91 Stat. 796. Section 406(d)(2) provides that each state that is required to revise its SIP by reason of any of the 1977 Amendments must adopt and submit the proposed changes before the later of one year from the date of enactment (*i. e.*, August 7, 1978) or nine months after promulgation of EPA regulations necessary for the approval of such revisions.

In the March 3, 1978 publication of air quality statuses, the Administrator designated the boroughs of New York as either unclassifiable or in attainment for sulfur dioxide and particulates. 43 Fed.Reg. 9018 (1978). On June 19, 1978, the Administrator promulgated final PSD regulations. 43 Fed.Reg. 26380 (1978). Therefore, New York was required to submit its applicable SIP revisions no later than nine months after promulgation of the PSD regulations, *i. e.*, by March 19, 1979.

Although failing to act in a timely fashion, New York apparently has submitted proposed revisions on or about June 12, 1979, to administer and enforce the PSD regulations. * * * The Administration has a non-discretionary duty to approve or disapprove these proposals within four months of the date required for submission. § 7410(a)(2). In assessing the sufficiency of the New York revisions, the Administrator must determine whether the PSD regulations and the general prohibition on significant interstate pollution are met. §§ 7410(a)(2)(E) and (J). In doing so, the Administrator will have to reckon with the interstate impact of LILCO's use of high sulfur oil. The statutory time period for examination of the New York proposals has not yet passed, however, and this Court cannot now order the EPA to assess the revisions or take other action.

Consequently, this aspect of plaintiffs' claim is also premature.[12]

4. *Promulgation of Photochemical Oxidant Control Measures*

In Count V of the complaint, plaintiffs charge EPA with violation of a non-discretionary duty to promulgate federal regulations to control the transport to Connecticut of photochemical oxidants generated in New York. Plaintiffs assert that this duty arises under the "purposes and directives" of the Clean Air Act, the National Environmental Policy Act (42 U.S.C. §§ 4331 and 4332), the Fifth Amendment, and the federal common law of nuisance.

EPA has no mandatory duty under the Act to issue the regulations that plaintiffs seek. The legislative history of the 1977 Amendments is replete with indications that

[12]EPA argues additionally that this count of the complaint should be dismissed for the plaintiffs' failure to exhaust the administrative remedy available in § 7426(b). That section permits a state or political subdivision to petition EPA for a finding that a major stationary source emits pollutants that interfere with air quality control in the petitioning state. It is clear that the petition procedure is not a prerequisite to institution of this civil suit. By its express terms, § 7426 applies only to "any state or political subdivision," and would not bar a claim by the non-municipal plaintiffs.

Congress acknowledged the severity of oxidant nonattainment problems and of the oxidant transport phenomenon. But, the Act on its face, and the committee reports describing the statutory scheme, clearly vest primary authority in the states to deal with these problems, under guidance from EPA.

Section 7502(a)(2) allows an extension to states with serious photochemical oxidant and carbon monoxide attainment difficulties, from the normal attainment deadline of December 31, 1982, until December 31, 1987, at the latest. Initial SIP revisions, due on January 1, 1979, must assure that the emission levels for these pollutants will be reduced by reasonably available technology in the interim. § 7502(b). While final enforcement measures need not be promulgated by the states before July 1, 1982, the states are required to undertake regional planning to "determine which elements of a revised implementation plan will be planned for and implemented or enforced by the State and which . . . by local governments or regional agencies, or any combination of local governments, regional agencies, or the State." §§ 7502(c), 7504.

These provisions preserve and reemphasize the policy of state control of pollutant sources, a policy orginating in the 1970 Act. They embody the traditional "carrot and stick" philosophy by creating incentives for effective state and local planning to protect public health while still permitting industrial and commercial growth. The Senate Report expressed the belief that "States and communities, given additional time and flexibility, would be more willing to take the difficult steps necessary both to reduce the emission output from direct sources of pollution and to adopt the kinds of transportation and land use control necessary to reduce the causes of pollution." S.Rep.No. 95–127, 95th Cong., 1st Sess. 3 (May 10, 1977).

Therefore, a state whose 1979 plan revisions demonstrate that oxidant or carbon monoxide standards will not be met by 1982 may adopt a compliance schedule that is "more closely related to the performance of the auto industry with respect to the statutory standards." *Id.* This would allow a state to "choose whatever mix of continuous emission reduction measures and strategies it wants to meet the requirements of this section."

In return, the 1979 revisions must require alternative site analyses for major emitting facilities that propose to locate in a nonattainment area, establish a schedule for implementing a vehicle inspection and maintenance program, and require that funds reasonably available to state or local governments be used to improve public transportation.* * *

EPA could not promulgate regulations at this time to control oxidant emission and transport within the tri-state area without undermining this statutory scheme. As previously discussed, EPA will not be in a position to issue oxidant regulations for New York and New Jersey until it has evaluated their 1979 SIP revisions and determined whether the states qualify for the oxidant attainment deadline extension, and only then if the proposed SIPs are found inadequate and the states fail to submit satisfactory corrections.

Plaintiffs also fail to state a colorable claim under the Fifth Amendment, NEPA, and the federal common law of nuisance. Plaintiffs allege no specific theory by which EPA has denied them due process of law or equal protection of the laws, and none is apparent. Congress' general declaration of a national environmental policy in 42 U.S.C. §§ 4331 and 4332 does not create an enforceable duty for the EPA to act in a manner inconsistent with the express terms of its enabling statute. Finally, any non-discretionary duty of the EPA to act in its regulatory capacity arises from the Clean Air Act, and not from federal common law; therefore, no right of action derives from federal common law to enforce such a duty. *Cf. Wheeldin v. Wheeler*, 373 U.S. 647, 651, 83 S.Ct. 1441, 10 L.Ed.2d 605 (1963) (federal statute governing issuance of subpoenas allegedly violated; no common law cause of action for abuse of subpoena power implied from existence of the statute).

5. *Identity of Major Stationary Pollutant Sources in New Jersey*

Both plaintiffs and defendant seek summary judgment on Count VI, paragraph 80(e) of the Complaint, which charges EPA with a non-discretionary duty to revise the New Jersey SIP in compliance with § 7426(a)(2). This section provides that each applicable implementation plan must identify all major existing stationary sources that either would be subject to PSD measures in Part C of Title I, or may significantly contribute to interstate pollution, and that notice of such sources must be given to all nearby states no later than November 7, 1977.

Plaintiffs had originally alleged that New Jersey did not revise its plan pursuant to that provision, and therefore EPA had a mandatory duty under § 7410(c)(1)(A) to conform the New Jersey SIP. EPA responded that New Jersey had made its § 7426 (a)(2) submission in a timely fashion, and attached a copy of the document as Appendix 7 to its Memorandum in Support of the Motion for Summary Judgment (filed October 30, 1978). Plaintiffs now argue that the submission is plainly inadequate to satisfy the requirements of § 7426.

The Administrator's duty to prepare and publish revisions to a SIP becomes obligatory under § 7410(c)(1)(A) when "the State fails to submit an implementation plan which meets the requirements of this section." In order for a plan or plan revision to fulfill the requirements of § 7410(a)(2)(E), it must "contain adequate provisions . . . (ii) insuring compliance with the requirements of section 7426 of this title, relating to interstate pollution abatement."

Any non-discretionary duty on EPA's part to promulgate a SIP for New Jersey, and thereby to notify Connecticut of the identity of major stationary pollutant sources in New Jersey that may have significant interstate impact, can arise only if New Jersey does not discharge its responsibilities under § 7426.

It is not for this Court to decide whether the New Jersey revision is sufficient under § 7426. Such a determination rests with the Administrator in approving or disapproving the revision under § 7410(a)(3)(A), see *Northern Ohio Lung Association v. EPA*, 572 F.2d 1143 (6th Cir. 1978), and a review of that decision is available only in the court of appeals. In replying to defendant's motion, plaintiffs assert that the EPA has not acted on the New Jersey proposal, in violation of its non-discretionary duty, and has therefore precluded them from initiating a § 7607 proceeding. Although plaintiffs may have a substantial claim, their complaint does not allege failure of EPA to act on the New Jersey submission, and EPA has had no opportunity to respond. The claim, as presented in subparagraph 80(e) of the Complaint is dismissed, with leave to amend within 20 days, and the cross-motions for summary judgment with respect to this subparagraph are dismissed as moot.

6. *Limitations on Awarding Federal Grants*

In their prayer for relief, plaintiffs seek to restrain EPA from awarding any federal grants to New York or New Jersey until the states have promulgated and enforced required SIP revisions. EPA's obligation to withhold federal assistance from states that are out of compliance with the requirements of the Act is circumscribed by § 7506. The conditions for denial of an award have not yet occurred, and any sanction by the EPA under that section is clearly not warranted. Therefore, prayer 10 of the Complaint is stricken.

Section 7506 provides:

> (a) The Administrator shall not approve any projects or award any grants authorized by this chapter . . . in any air quality control region—
>
> (1) in which any national primary ambient air quality standard has not been attained
>
> (2) where transportation control measures are necessary for the attainment of such standard, and

(3) where the Administrator finds after July 1, 1979, that the Governor has not submitted an implementation plan which considers each of the elements required by section 7502 of this title (nonattainment plan provisions) or that reasonable efforts toward submitting such an implementation plan are not being made.

Since both New York and New Jersey have submitted nonattainment plan revisions, the sanction under subsection (a) will not be available until July 1, 1979, at the earliest. If the states are permitted an extension for the attainment of photochemical oxidant or carbon monoxide air quality standards, enforcement of subsection (a) with respect to those pollutants in not appropriate until July 1, 1982. Obviously, plaintiffs' attempt to compel EPA's denial of federal grants under subsection (a) is premature.

The Suit Against LILCO

LILCO, the sole private defendant in this action, is charged only in Count III of the Complaint. Court III alleges that LILCO maintains a federal common law nuisance by burning oil containing 2.8% sulfur at its Long Island electricity generating plants. The New York SIP allegedly provides a general 1% sulfur content limitation for that area, whereas Connecticut maintains a state-wide limitation of 0.5%

* * * LILCO moves to dismiss on numerous grounds, including lack of subject matter jurisdiction, lack of *in personam* jurisdiction, improper venue, insufficiency of service, and failure to state a claim. Without considering all of the alleged bases for subject matter jurisdiction, it is sufficient to observe that this Court's jurisdiction is properly predicated on 28 U.S.C. § 1331(a) to consider the federal common law claim. Although the defenses of lack of *in personam* jurisdiction, improper venue, and insufficiency of process relate to the propriety of maintaining this action in the District Court of Connecticut, this Court's disposition makes an examination of these contentions unnecessary. Assuming that plaintiffs have standing to assert a claim of federal common law nuisance, they have failed to state a claim upon which relief can be granted.

The federal common law of nuisance developed to guarantee to the states a right of protection against impairment of their environmental resources by outside polluters. The Courts created federal common law where they perceived a definite federal interest that was inadequately protected by existing federal legislation. See *Illinois v. City of Milwaukee*, 406 U.S. 91, 103, 92 S.Ct. 1385, 31 L.Ed.2d 712 (1972); Only a federal common law basis could provide an adequate means of dealing with interstate environmental disputes, at least "[u]ntil the field has been made the subject of comprehensive legislation or authorized administrative standards." *Texas v. Pankey, supra*, 441 F.2d at 241.

The defendant contends that the Clean Air Act and EPA's substantive rulings have entirely preempted the federal common law of nuisance. Although several courts have found that the application of federal common law in the context of interstate water pollution is not inconsistent with the purposes and operation of federal legislation, no case has yet determined whether the federal common law regarding air quality has been preempted in whole or in part by the Act and promulgated regulations. This Court need not reach the issue of preemption, however. Even if some common law of nuisance survives, plaintiffs are not entitled to equitable relief under these circumstances.

The parties do not dispute that LILCO's conduct was authorized by a variance to the New York SIP that was approved by the EPA on August 26, 1977. Complaint ¶ 77. In approving the special limitation, the EPA was required to determine that LILCO's use of 2.8% sulfur oil would not unduly interfere with Connecticut's pollution control measures. §§ 7410(a)(3)(A) and (a)(2)(E). This Court will not devise an equitable remedy to proscribe the very conduct that the EPA, acting in its regulatory capacity pursuant to statutory mandate, has specifically legitimated.[21]

In summary, all claims of the complaint are dismissed for failure to state a claim on which relief can now be granted. This dismissal is without prejudice to the filing of an amended complaint within 20 days, failing which the action will be dismissed. To some extent this ruling has considered uncontested matters beyond the scope of the pleadings and therefore could be considered a ruling for summary judgment, Fed. R.Civ.P. 12(c), but since the plaintiffs are being given leave to amend, the Court's ruling is being made with respect to the sufficiency of the complaint.

---

c. *Approval of State Implementation Plans* (*SIPs*)

One of the basic premises of the Clean Air Act is that each state has the primary responsibility for ensuring air quality within its geographic boundaries. However, the Act provides that the states are to meet the national air quality standards within a specified period of time, which period has been extended by Congress in periodic amendments. Each state is required to submit to EPA a plan designed to achieve and maintain the air quality standards. The plan must include emission limitations, schedules and timetables for compliance and other measures necessary to attain and maintain those standards. EPA prescribes the rules for the preparation of the state implementation plan (SIP). EPA may reject a SIP and may regulate the subject directly until a satisfactory SIP is accepted. In addition, if the proposed SIP is unsatisfactory, EPA may withhold support and permits required for major new growth that increases air pollution, i.e., highway and sewer grants.

The details of the components of a SIP are discussed in a later section describing the role of the states. *Train v. Natural Resources Defense Council, Inc.* and *Union Electric Co. v. EPA*, below illustrate the role of EPA in reviewing **state implementation plans**.

---

[21]The relief sought by plaintiffs' action would have a substantial impact upon the implementation of a specific agency determination. Plaintiffs' claim against LILCO's conduct as a federal common law nuisance is, in effect, an attack upon the validity of the EPA-approved variance. It is mere sophistry to argue that a challenge to LILCO's operation in compliance with the special limitation is not a challenge to the legality of the limitation itself. The expansion of the common law of nuisance to accommodate plaintiffs' action would, however, undercut the explicit statutory scheme of judicial review. Congress intended that the courts of appeals consider all claims against the validity of performance standards approved by final decision of the Administrator. *See Oljato Chapter of Navajo Tribe v. Train*, 169 U.S.App. D.C. 195, 199–202, 515 F.2d 654, 658–61 (D.C. Cir. 1975) (litigation seeking revision of stationary source pollutant standard must be brought as a direct appeal under § 7607). "Congress, of course, is the primary source of federal law, and the federal courts must adhere to the intent of Congress whenever this intent is discernible." *United States v. Carson*, 372 F.2d 429, 432 (6th Cir. 1967).

TRAIN
v.
NATURAL RESOURCES DEFENSE COUNCIL, INC.

421 U.S. 60 (1975)

Mr. Justice REHNQUIST delivered the opinion of the Court.

We granted certiorari in this case, 419 U.S. 823, 95 S.Ct. 39, 42 L.Ed.2d 46 (1974), to review a judgment of the Court of Appeals for the Fifth Circuit which required petitioner Administrator of the Environmental Protection Agency to disapprove a portion of the implementation plan submitted to him by the State of Georgia pursuant to the Clean Air Amendments of 1970.[1] The case presents an issue of statutory construction which is illuminated by the anatomy of the statute itself, by its legislative history, and by the history of congressional efforts to control air pollution.

I

Congress initially responded to the problem of air pollution by offering encouragement and assistance to the States. In 1955 the Surgeon General was authorized to study the problem of air pollution, to support research, training, and demonstration projects, and to provide technical assistance to state and local governments attempting to abate pollution. 69 Stat. 322. In 1960 Congress directed the Surgeon General to focus his attention on the health hazards resulting from motor vehicle emissions.

* * *

The Clean Air Act of 1963, 77 Stat. 392, authorized federal authorities to expand their research efforts, to make grants to state air pollution control agencies, and also to intervene directly to abate *interstate* pollution in limited circumstances. Amendments in 1965, § 101, 79 Stat. 992, and in 1966, 80 Stat. 954, broadened federal authority to control motor vehicle emissions and to make grants to state pollution control agencies.

The focus shifted somewhat in the Air Quality Act of 1967, 81 Stat. 485. It reiterated the premise of the earlier Clean Air Act "that the prevention and control of air pollution at its source is the primary responsibility of States and local governments." *Ibid.* Its provisions, however, increased the federal role in the prevention of air pollution, by according federal authorities certain powers of supervision and enforcement. But the States generally retained wide latitude to determine both the air quality standards which they would meet and the period of time in which they would do so.

The response of the States to these manifestations of increasing congressional concern with air pollution was disappointing. Even by 1970, state planning and implementation under the Air Quality Act of 1967 has made little progress. Congress reacted by taking a stick to the States in the form of the Clean Air Amendments of 1970, Pub.L. 91–604, 84 Stat. 1676, enacted on December 31 of that year. These Amendments sharply increased federal authority and responsibility in the continuing

[1]Natural Resources Defense Council, Inc. v. EPA, 489 F.2d 390 (1974).

effort to combat air pollution. Nonetheless, the Amendments explicitly preserved the principle: "Each State shall have the primary responsibility for assuring air quality within the entire geographic area comprising such State. . . ." § 107(a) of the Clean Air Act, as added, 84 Stat. 1678, 42 U.S.C. § 1857c–2(a). The difference under the Amendments was that the States were no longer given any choice as to whether they would meet this responsibility. For the first time they were required to attain air quality of specified standards, and to do so within a specified period of time.

The Amendments directed that within 30 days of their enactment the Environmental Protection Agency should publish proposed regulations describing national quality standards for the "ambient air," which is the statute's term for the outdoor air used by the general public. After allowing 90 days for comments on the proposed standards, the Agency was then obliged to promulgate such standards. § 109(a)(1) of the Clean Air Act, as added, 84 Stat. 1679, 42 U.S.C. § 1857c–4(a)(1). The standards were to be of two general types: "primary" standards, which in the judgment of the Agency were "requisite to protect the public health," § 109(b)(1), and "secondary" standards, those that in the judgment of the Agency were "requisite to protect the public welfare from any known or anticipated adverse effects associated with the presence of such air pollutant in the ambient air." § 109(b)(2).

Within nine months after the Agency's promulgation of primary and secondary air quality standards, each of the 50 States was required to submit to the Agency a plan designed to implement and maintain such standards within its boundaries. § 110(a)(1) of the Clean Air Act, as added, 84 Stat. 16080, 42 U.S.C. § 1857c–5(a)(1). The Agency was in turn required to approve each State's plan within four months of the deadline for submission, if it had been adopted after public hearings and if it satisfied eight general conditions set forth in § 110(a)(2). Probably the principal of these conditions, and the heart of the 1970 Amendments, is that the plan provide for the attainment of the national primary ambient air quality standards in the particular State "as expeditiously as practicable but . . . in no case later than three years from the date of approval of such plan." § 110(a)(2)(A). In providing for such attainment, a State's plan must include "emission limitations, schedules, and timetables for compliance with such limitations"; it must also contain such other measures as may be necessary to insure both timely attainment and subsequent maintenance of national ambient air standards. § 110(a)(2)(B).

Although the Agency itself was newly organized, the States looked to it for guidance in formulating the plans they were required to submit. On April 7, 1971—scarcely three months after the enactment of the Clean Air Amendments—the Agency published proposed guidelines for the preparation, adoption, and submission of such plans. 36 Fed.Reg. 6680. After receiving numerous comments, including those from respondent Natural Resources Defense Council, Inc. (NRDC), it issued final guidelines on August 14, 1971, 36 Fed.Reg. 1586. See 40 CFR Part 51 (1974). The national standards themselves were timely promulgated on April 30, 1971, 36 Fed.Reg. 8186. See 40 CFR Part 50 (1974).

No one can doubt that Congress imposed upon the Agency and States a comprehensive planning task of the first magnitude which was to be accomplished in a relatively short time. In the case of the States, it was soon realized that in order to develop the requisite plans within the statutory nine-month deadline, efforts would have to be focused on determining the stringent emission limitations necessary to comply with national standards. This was true even though compliance with the standards would not be necessary until the attainment date, which normally would be three years after Agency approval of a plan. The issue then arose as to how these stringent limitations, which often could not be satisfied without substantial research and investment, should be applied during the period prior to that date.

One approach was that adopted by Florida, under which the plan's emission limitations would not take effect until the attainment date. Under this approach, no source is subject to enforcement actions during the preattainment period, but all are put on notice of the limitations with which they must eventually comply.[3] Since the Florida approach basically does not require preattainment date pollution reductions on the part of those sources which might be able to effect them, the Agency encouraged an alternative approach. Under it a State's emission limitations would be immediately effective. The State, however, would have the authority to grant variances to particular sources which could not immediately comply with the stringent emission limitations necessary to meet the standards.

Georgia chose the Agency's preferred approach. Its plan provided for immediately effective categorical emission limitations, but also incorporated a variance procedure whereby particular sources could obtain individually tailored relief from general requirements. This variance provision, Ga.Code Ann. § 88–912 (1971), was one of the bases upon which the Agency's approval of the Georgia plan was successfully challenged by respondents in the Court of Appeals. It is the only aspect of that court's decision as to which the Agency petitioned for certiorari.

II

The Agency's approval of Georgia's variance provision was based on its interpretation of § 110(a)(3), which provides that the Agency shall approve any revision of an implementation plan which meets the § 110(a)(2) requirements applicable to an original plan. The Agency concluded that § 110(a)(3) permits a State to grant individual variances from generally applicable emission standards, both before and after the attainment date, so long as the variance does not cause the plan to fail to comply with the requirements of § 110(a)(2). Since that section requires, *inter alia*, that primary ambient air standards be attained by a particular date, it is of some consequence under this approach whether the period for which the variance is sought extends beyond that date. If it does not, the practical effect of treating such preattainment date variances as revisions is that they can be granted rather freely.

This interpretation of § 110(a)(3) was incorporated in the Agency's original guidelines for implementation plans, 40 CFR §§ 51.6(c), 51.32(f) (1973).

* * *

III

Both of the sections in controversy are contained in § 110 of the amended Clean Air Act, which is entitled "Implementation Plans." Section 110(a)(3) provides in pertinent part:

"(A) The Administrator shall approve any revision of an implementation plan applicable to an air quality control region if he determines that it meets the requirement of paragraph (2) and has been adopted by the State after reasonable notice and public hearings."

Section 110(f) provides:

"(1) Prior to the date on which any stationary source or class of moving sources is required to comply with any requirement of an applicable implementation plan the Governor of the State to which such plan applies may apply to the Administrator to postpone the applicability of such requirement to such source (or class) for not more than one year. If the Administrator determines that—

"(A) good faith efforts have been made to comply with such requirement before such date,

[3]While sources would not be subject to enforcement actions based on their levels of emissions prior to the attainment date, they could be required to adhere to schedules for the planning, contracting, and construction necessary to assure that their emissions would be within permissible levels as of the attainment date. See 40 CFR §§ 51.15(c), 52.524(b) (1974).

"(B) such source (or class) is unable to comply with such requirement because the necessary technology or other alternative methods of control are not available for a sufficient period of time,

"(C) any available alternative operating procedures and interim control measures have reduced or will reduce the impact of such source on public health, and

"(D) the continued operation of such source is essential to national security or to the public health or welfare,

"then the Administrator shall grant a postponement of such requirement."

As previously noted, respondents contended that "variances" applicable to individual sources—for example, a particular factory—may be approved only if they meet the stringent procedural and substantive standards set forth in § 110(f). As is apparent from the text of § 110(f), its postponements may be for no more than one year, may be granted only if application is made prior to the date of required compliance, and must be supported by the Agency's determination that the source's continued operation "is essential to national security or to the public health or welfare." Petitioners, on the other hand, rely on the revision authority of § 110(a)(3) for the contention that a state plan may provide for an individual variance from generally applicable emission limitations so long as the variance does not cause the plan to fail to comply with the requirements of § 110(a)(2). Since a variance would normally implicate only the § 110(a)(2)(A) requirement that plans provide for attainment and maintenance of national ambient air standards, treatment as revisions would result in variances being readily approved in two situations: first, where the variance does not defer compliance beyond the attainment date; and second, where the national standards have been attained and the variance is not so great that a plan incorporating it could not insure their continued maintenance. Moreover, a § 110(a)(3) revision may be granted on the basis of hearings conducted by the State, whereas a § 110(f) postponement is available only after the Agency itself conducts hearings.

There is thus considerable practical importance attached to the issue of whether variances are to be treated as revisions or as postponements, or for that matter, as the First Circuit would have it, as neither until the mandatory attainment date but as postponements thereafter. This practical importance reaches not merely the operator of a particular source who believes that circumstances justify his receiving a variance from categorical limitations. It also reaches the broader issue of whether Congress intended the States to retain any significant degree of control of the manner in which they attain and maintain national standards, at least once their initial plans have been approved or, under the First Circuit's approach, once the mandatory attainment date has arrived. To explain our conclusion as to Congress' intent, it is necessary that we consider the revision and postponement sections in the context of other provisions of the amended Clean Air Act, particularly those which distinguish between national ambient air standards and emission limitations.

As we have already noted, primary ambient air standards deal with the quality of outdoor air, and are fixed on a nationwide basis at levels which the Agency determines will protect the public health. It is attainment and maintenance of these national standards which § 110(a)(2)(A) requires that state plans provide. In complying with this requirement a State's plan must include "emission limitations," which are regulations of the composition of substances emitted into the ambient air from such sources as power plants, service stations, and the like. They are the specific rules to which operators of pollution sources are subject, and which if enforced should result in ambient air which meets the national standards.* * *

We believe that the foregoing analysis of the structure and legislative history of the Clean Air Amendments shows that Congress intended to impose national ambient air standards to be attained within a specific period of time. It also shows that in §§ 110(e) and (f) Congress carefully limited the circumstances in which timely attainment and subsequent maintenance of these standards could be compromised. We also believe that Congress, consistent with its declaration that "[e]ach State shall have the primary responsibility for assuring air quality" within its boundaries, § 107(a), left to the States considerable latitude in determining specifically how the standards would be met. This discretion includes the continuing authority to revise choices about the mix of emission limitations. We therefore conclude that the Agency's interpretation of §§ 110(a)(3) and 110(f) was "correct," to the extent that it can be said with complete assurance that any particular interpretation of a complex statute such as this is the "correct" one. Given this conclusion, as well as the facts that the Agency is charged with administration of the Act, and that there has undoubtedly been reliance upon its interpretation by the States and other parties affected by the Act, we have no doubt whatever that its construction was sufficiently reasonable to preclude the Court of Appeals from substituting its judgment for that of the Agency.

* * *

VI

For the foregoing reasons, the Court of Appeals for the Fifth Circuit was in error when it concluded that the postponement provision of § 110(f) is the sole method by which may be obtained specific ameliorative modifications of state implementation plans. The Agency had properly concluded that the revision mechanism of § 110(a)(3) is available for the approval of those variances which do not compromise the basic statutory mandate that, with carefully circumscribed exceptions, the national primary ambient air standards be attained in not more than three years, and maintained thereafter. To the extent that the judgment of the Court of Appeals for the Fifth Circuit was to the contrary, it is reversed and the cause is remanded for further proceedings consistent with this opinion.

It is so ordered.

Mr. Justice DOUGLAS dissents.

Mr. Justice POWELL took no part in the consideration or decision of this case.

UNION ELECTRIC COMPANY
v.
E.P.A.

427 U.S. 246 (1976)

MR. JUSTICE MARSHALL delivered the opinion of the Court.

After the Administrator of the Environmental Protection Agency (EPA) approves a state implementation plan under the Clean Air Act, the plan may be challenged in a court of appeals within 30 days, or after 30 days have run if newly discovered or available information justifies subsequent review. We must decide whether the operator of a regulated emission source, in a petition for review of an EPA-approved state plan filed after the original 30-day appeal period, can raise the claim that it is economically or technologically infeasible to comply with the plan.

I

We have addressed the history and provisions of the Clean Air Amendments of 1970, Pub. L. 91–604, 84 Stat. 1676, in detail in *Train* v. *Natural Resources Defense Council* (*NRDC*), 421 U.S. 60 (1975), and will not repeat that discussion here. Suffice it to say that the Amendments reflect congressional dissatisfaction with the progress of existing air pollution programs and a determination to "tak[e] a stick to the States," *id.*, at 64, in order to guarantee the prompt attainment and maintenance of specified air quality standards. The heart of the Amendments is the requirement that each State formulate, subject to EPA approval, an implementation plan designed to achieve national primary ambient air quality standards—those necessary to protect the public health—"as expeditiously as practicable but . . . in no case later than three years from the date of approval of such plan." § 110(a)(2)(A) of the Clean Air Act, as added, 84 Stat. 1680, 42 U.S.C. § 1857c–5(a)(2)(A). The plan must also provide for the attainment of national secondary ambient air quality standards—those necessary to protect the public welfare—within a "reasonable time." *Ibid.* Each State is given wide discretion in formulating its plan, and the Act provides that the Administrator "shall approve" the proposed plan if it has been adopted after public notice and hearing and if it meets eight specified criteria. § 110(a)(2).[1]

[1]Section 110(a)(2), 42 U.S.C. § 1857c–5(a)(2), provides in full:

"The Adminstrator shall, within four months after the date required for submission of a plan under paragraph (1), approve or disapprove such plan or each portion thereof. The Administrator shall approve such plan, or any portion thereof, if he determines that it was adopted after reasonable notice and hearing and that—

"(A)(i) in the case of a plan implementing a national primary ambient air quality standard, it provides for the attainment of such primary standard as expeditiously as practicable but (subject to subsection (e)) in no case later than three years from the date of approval of such plan (or any revision thereof to take account of a revised primary standard); and (ii) in the case of a plan implementing a national secondary ambient air quality standard, it specifies a reasonable time at which such secondary standard will be attained;

"(B) it includes emission limitations, schedules, and timetables for compliance with such limitations, and such other measures as may be necessary to insure attainment and maintenance of such primary or secondary standard, including, but not limited to, land-use and transportation controls;

"(C) it includes provision for establishment and operation of appropriate devices, methods, systems, and procedures necessary to (i) monitor, compile, and analyze data on ambient air quality and, (ii) upon request, make such data available to the Administrator;

"(D) it includes a procedure, meeting the requirements of paragraph (4), for review (prior to construction or modification) of the location of new sources to which a standard of performance will apply;

"(E) it contains adequate provisions for intergovernmental cooperation, including measures necessary to insure that emissions of air pollutants from sources located in any air quality control region will not interfere with the attainment or maintenance of such primary or secondary standard in any portion of such region outside of such State or in any other air quality control region;

"(F) it provides (i) necessary assurance that the State will have adequate personnel, funding, and authority to carry out such implementation plan, (ii) requirements for installation of equipment by owners or operators of stationary sources to monitor emissions from such sources, (iii) for periodic reports on the nature and amounts of such emissions; (iv) that such reports shall be correlated by the State agency with any emission limitations or standards

On April 30, 1971, the Administrator promulgated national primary and secondary standards for six air pollutants he found to have an adverse effect on the public health and welfare. 40 CFR pt. 50 (1975). See § 108(a) of the Act, as added, 84 Stat. 1678, 42 U.S.C. § 1857c–3(a). Included among them was sulfur dioxide, at issue here. 40 CFR §§ 50.4–50.5 (1975). After the promulgation of the national standards, the State of Missouri formulated its implementation plan and submitted it for approval. Since sulfur dioxide levels exceeded national primary standards in only one of the State's five air quality regions—the Metropolitan St. Louis Interstate region, 40 CFR § 52.1321 (1975)—the Missouri plan concentrated on a control strategy and regulations to lower emissions in that area. The plan's emission limitations were effective at once, but the State retained authority to grant variances to particular sources that could not immediately comply. Mo. Rev. Stat. § 203.110 (1972). The Administrator approved the plan on May 31, 1972. See 40 CFR § 52.1320 *et seq*. (1975).

Petitioner is an electric utility company servicing the St. Louis metropolitan area, large portions of Missouri, and parts of Illinois and Iowa. Its three coal-fired generating plants in the metropolitan St. Louis area are subject to the sulfur dioxide restrictions in the Missouri implementation plan. Petitioner did not seek review of the Administrator's approval of the plan within 30 days, as it was entitled to do under § 307(b)(1) of the Act, as added, 84 Stat. 1708, 42 U.S.C. § 1857h–5(b)(1), but rather applied to the appropriate state and county agencies for variances from the emission limitations affecting its three plants. Petitioner received one-year variances, which could be extended upon reapplication. The variances on two of petitioner's three plants had expired and petitioner was applying for extensions when, on May 31, 1974, the Administrator notified petitioner that sulfur dioxide emissions from its plants violated the emission limitations contained in the Missouri plan. See 40 Fed. Reg. 3566 (1975). Shortly thereafter petitioner filed a petition in the Court of Appeals for the Eighth Circuit for review of the Administrator's 1972 approval of the Missouri implementation plan.

Section 307 (b)(1) allows petitions for review to be filed in an appropriate court of appeals more than 30 days after the Administrator's approval of an implementation plan only if the petition is "based solely on grounds arising after such 30th day." Petitioner claimed to meet this requirement by asserting, *inter alia*, that various economic and technological difficulties had arisen more than 30 days after the Administrator's approval and that these difficulties made compliance with the emission limitations impossible. The Court of Appeals ordered briefing on the question of its subject-matter jurisdiction to hear the case and, after argument, granted the motions of the EPA and intervenor-respondents, the Attorney General of Missouri and the Missouri Air Conservation Commission, to dismiss the petition for review for lack of jurisdiction.

The court held that "only matters which, if known to the Administrator at the time of his action [in approving a state implementation plan], would justify setting aside

---

established pursuant to this Act, which reports shall be available at reasonable times for public inspection; and (v) for authority comparable to that in section 303, and adequate contingency plans to implement such authority;

"(G) it provides, to the extent necessary and practicable, for periodic inspection and testing of motor vehicles to enforce compliance with applicable emission standards; and

"(H) it provides for revision, after public hearings, of such plan (i) from time to time as may be necessary to take account of revisions of such national primary or secondary ambient air quality standard or the availability of improved or more expeditious methods of achieving such primary or secondary standard; or (ii) whenever the Administrator finds on the basis of information available to him that the plan is substantially inadequate to achieve the national ambient air quality primary or secondary standard which it implements."

that action are properly reviewable after the initial 30 day review period." 515 F. 2d 206, 216 (1975). Since, in the court's view, claims of economic and technological infeasibility could not properly provide a basis for the Administrator's rejecting a plan, such claims could not serve—at any time—as the basis for a court's overturning an approved plan. Accordingly, insofar as petitioner's claim of newly discovered or available information was grounded on an assertion of economic and technological infeasibility, the court held itself to be without jurisdiction to consider the petition for review, and so dismissed the petition. In so holding the Court of Appeals considered and rejected the contrary or partially contrary holdings of three other Circuits.* * *

We granted certiorari to resolve the conflict among the Circuits, 423 U. S. 821 (1975), and we now affirm.

II

A

We reject at the outset petitioner's suggestion that a claim of economic or technological infeasibility may be considered upon a petition for review based on new information and filed more than 30 days after approval of an implementation plan even if such a claim could not be considered by the Administrator in approving a plan or by a court in reviewing a plan challenged within the original 30-day appeal period. In pertinent part § 307 (b)(1) provides:

> "A petition for review of the Administrator's action in approving or promulgating any implementation plan under section 110 . . . may be filed only in the United States Court of Appeals for the appropriate circuit. Any such petition shall be filed within 30 days from the date if such petition is based solely on grounds arising after such 30th day."

Regardless of when a petition for review is filed under § 307 (b)(1), the court is limited to reviewing "the Administrator's action in approving . . . [the] implementation plan . . . ." Accordingly, if new "grounds" are alleged, they must be such that, had they been known at the time the plan was presented to the Administrator for approval, it would have been an abuse of discretion for the Administrator to approve the plan. To hold otherwise would be to transfer a substantial responsibility in administering the Clean Air Act from the Administrator and the state agencies to the federal courts.

B

Since a reviewing court—regardless of when the petition for review is filed—may consider claims of economic and technological infeasibility only if the Administrator may consider such claims in approving or rejecting a state implementation plan, we must address ourselves to the scope of the Administrator's responsibility. The Administrator's position is that he has no power whatsoever to reject a state implementation plan on the ground that it is economically or technologically infeasible, and we have previously accorded great deference to the Administrator's construction of the Clean Air Act. See *Train* v. *NRDC*, 421 U. S., at 75. After surveying the relevant provisions of the Clean Air Amendments of 1970 and their legislative history, we agree that Congress intended claims of economic and technological infeasibility to be wholly foreign to the Administrator's consideration of a state implementation plan.

As we have previously recognized, the 1970 Amendments to the Clean Air Act were a drastic remedy to what was perceived as a serious and otherwise uncheckable problem of air pollution. The Amendments place the primary responsibility for formulating pollution control strategies on the States, but nonetheless subject the

States to strict minimum compliance requirements. These requirements are of a "technology-forcing character," *Train* v. *NRDC, supra*, at 91, and are expressly designed to force regulated sources to develop pollution control devices that might at the time appear to be economically or technologically infeasible.

This approach is apparent on the face of § 110 (a)(2). The provision sets out eight criteria that an implementation plan must satisfy, and provides that if these criteria are met and if the plan was adopted after reasonable notice and hearing, the Administrator "shall approve" the proposed state plan. The mandatory "shall" makes it quite clear that the Administrator is not to be concerned with factors other than those specified, *Train* v. *NRDC, supra*, at 71 n. 11, 79, and none of the eight factors appears to permit consideration of technological or economic infeasibility.[5] Nonetheless, if a basis is to be found for allowing the Administrator to consider such claims, it must be among the eight criteria, and so it is here that the argument is focused.

It is suggested that consideration of claims of technological and economic infeasibility is required by the first criterion—that the primary air quality standards be met "as expeditiously as practicable but . . . in no case later than three years . . ." and that the secondary air quality standards be met within a "reasonable time." § 110 (a)(2)(A). The argument is that what is "practicable" or "reasonable" cannot be determined without assessing whether what is proposed is possible. This argument does not survive analysis.

Section 110 (a)(2)(A)'s three-year deadline for achieving primary air quality standards is central to the Amendments' regulatory scheme and, as both the language and the legislative history of the requirement make clear, it leaves no room for claims of technological or economic infeasibility. The 1970 congressional debate on the Amendments centered on whether technology forcing was necessary and desirable in framing and attaining air quality standards sufficient to protect the public health, standards later termed primary standards. The House version of the Amendments was quite moderate in approach, requiring only that health-related standards be met "within a reasonable time." H. R. 17255, 91st Cong., 2d Sess., § 108 (c)(1)(C)(i) (1970). The Senate bill, on the other hand, flatly required that, possible or not, health-related standards be met "within three years." S. 4358, 91st Cong., 2d Sess., § 111 (a)(2)(A) (1970).

The Senate's stiff requirement was intended to foreclose the claims of emission sources that it would be economically or technologically infeasible for them to achieve emission limitations sufficient to protect the public health within the specified time. As Senator Muskie, manager of the Senate bill, explained to his chamber:

> " 'The first responsibility of Congress is not the making of technological or economic judgments—or even to be limited by what is or appears to be technologically or economically feasible. Our responsibility is to establish what the public interest requires to protect the health of persons. This may mean that people and industries will be asked to do what seems to be impossible at the present time.' " 116 Cong. Rec. 32901–32902 (1970).

[5]See n. 1, *supra*. Comparison of the eight criteria of § 110 (a)(2) with other provisions of the Amendments bolsters this conclusion. Where Congress intended the Administrator to be concerned about economic and technological infeasibility, it expressly so provided. Thus, §§ 110 (e), 110 (f), 111 (a)(1), 202 (a), 211 (c)(2)(A), and 231 (b) of the Amendments all expressly permit consideration, *e. g.*, "of the requisite technology, giving appropriate consideration to the cost of compliance." § 231 (b), as added, 84 Stat. 1704, 42 U. S. C. § 1857f–9 (b). See also 42 U. S. C. §§ 1857c–5 (e), 1857c–5 (f), 1857c–6 (a)(1), 1857f–1 (a), 1857f–6c (c)(2)(A). Section 110 (a)(2) contains no such language.

See also *id.*, at 32919 (remarks of Sen. Cooper); 33115 (remarks of Sen. Prouty). This position reflected that of the Senate committee:

"In the Committee discussions, considerable concern was expressed regarding the use of the concept of technical feasibility as the basis of ambient air standards. The Committee determined that 1) the health of people is more important than the question of whether the early achievement of ambient air quality standards protective of health is technically feasible; and 2) the growth of pollution load in many areas, even with application of available technology, would still be deleterious to public health.

"Therefore, the Committee determined that existing sources of pollutants either should meet the standard of the law or be closed down . . . ." S.Rep. No. 91–1196, pp. 2–3 (1970).

The Conference Committee and, ultimately, the entire Congress accepted the Senate's three-year mandate for the achievement of primary air quality standards, and the clear import of that decision is that the Administrator must approve a plan that provides for attainment of the primary standards in three years even if attainment does not appear feasible. In rejecting the House's version of reasonableness, however, the conferees strengthened the Senate version. The Conference Committee made clear that the States could not procrastinate until the deadline approached. Rather, the primary standards had to be met in less than three years if possible; they had to be met "as expeditiously as practicable." § 110 (a)(2)(A). Whatever room there is for considering claims of infeasibility in the attainment of primary standards must lie in this phrase, which is, of course, relevant only in evaluating those implementation plans that attempt to achieve the primary standard in less than three years.

* * *

In sum, we have concluded that claims of economic or technological infeasibility may not be considered by the Administrator in evaluating a state requirement that primary ambient air quality standards be met in the mandatory three years. And, since we further conclude that the States may submit implementation plans more stringent than federal law requires and that the Administrator must approve such plans if they meet the minimum requirements of § 110 (a)(2), it follows that the language of § 110 (a)(2)(B) provides no basis for the Administrator ever to reject a state implementation plan on the ground that it is economically or technologically infeasible. Accordingly, a court of appeals reviewing an approved plan under § 307 (b)(1) cannot set it aside on those grounds, no matter when they are raised.

III

Our conclusion is bolstered by recognition that the Amendments do allow claims of technological and economic infeasibility to be raised in situations where consideration of such claims will not substantially interfere with the primary congressional purpose of prompt attainment of the national air quality standards. Thus, we do not hold that claims of infeasibility are never of relevance in the formulation of an implementation plan or that sources unable to comply with emission limitations must inevitably be shut down.

Perhaps the most important forum for consideration of claims of economic and technological infeasibility is before the state agency formulating the implementation plan. So long as the national standards are met, the State may select whatever mix of control devices it desires, *Train* v. *NRDC, supra*, at 79, and industries with particular economic or technological problems may seek special treatment in the plan itself. Cf. 40 CFR §§ 51.2 (b), (d) (1975); S. Rep. No. 91–1196, p. 36 (1970). Moreover, if the industry is not exempted from, or accommodated by, the original plan, it may obtain a variance, as petitioner did in this case; and the variance, if granted after notice and a hearing, may be submitted to the EPA as a revision of the plan. § 110 (a)(3)(A), as amended, 88 Stat. 256, 42 U. S. C. § 1857c–5 (a)(3)(A) (1970 ed., Supp. IV). Lastly, an industry denied an exemption from the implementation plan, or denied a subsequent variance, may be able to take its claims of economic or technological infeasibility to the state courts. See, *e. g.*, Mo. Rev. Stat. § 203.130 (1972); Cal. Health & Safety Code § 39506 (West 1973); Pa. Stat. Ann., Tit. 71, § 1710.41 (1962).

While the State has virtually absolute power in allocating emission limitations so long as the national standards are met, if the state plan cannot meet the national standards, the EPA is implicated in any postponement procedure. There are two ways that a State can secure relief from the EPA for individual emission sources, or classes of sources, that cannot meet the national standards. First, if the Governor of the State so requests at the time the original implementation plan is submitted, and if the State provides reasonable interim controls, the Administrator may allow a two-year extension of the three-year deadline for attainment of primary air quality standards if he finds, *inter alia*, that it is technologically infeasible for the source to comply. § 110 (e). Second, again upon application of the Governor of the State, the Administrator may allow a one-year postponement of any compliance date in an implementation plan if he finds, *inter alia*, that compliance is technologically infeasible and that "the continued operaton of [the emission source] is essential to national security or to the public health or welfare . . . ." § 110 (f). See *Train* v. *NRDC*, 421 U. S., at 81.

Even if the State does not intervene on behalf of an emission source, technological and economic factors may be considered in at least one other circumstance. When a source is found to be in violation of the state implementation plan, the Administrator may, after a conference with the operator, issue a compliance order rather than seek civil or criminal enforcement. Such an order must specify a "reasonable" time for compliance with the relevant standard, taking into account the seriousness of the violation and "any good faith efforts to comply with applicable requirements." § 113 (a)(4) of the Clean Air Act, as added, 84 Stat. 1686, 42 U. S. C. § 1857c–8 (a)(4). Claims of technological or economic infeasibility, the Administrator agrees, are relevant to fashioning an appropriate compliance order under § 113 (a)(4). Brief for Respondent EPA 36 n. 34.[18]

In short, the Amendments offer ample opportunity for consideration of claims of technological and economic infeasibility. Always, however, care is taken that consideration of such claims will not interfere substantially with the primary goal of prompt attainment of the national standards. Allowing such claims to be raised by appealing the Adminstrator's approval of an implementation plan, as petitioner suggests, would frustrate congressional intent. It would permit a proposed plan to be struck down as infeasible before it is given a chance to work, even though Congress clearly contemplated that some plans would be infeasible when proposed. And it would permit the Administrator or a federal court to reject a State's legislative choices in regulating air pollution, even though Congress plainly left with the States, so long as the national standards were met, the power to determine which sources would be burdened by regulation and to what extent. Technology forcing is a concept some-

[18]If he chooses not to seek a compliance order, or if an order is issued and violated, the Administrator may institute a civil enforcement proceeding. § 113 (b). Additionally, violators of an implementation plan are subject to criminal penalties under § 113 (c) and citizen enforcement suits under § 304, as added, 84 Stat. 1706, 42 U. S. C. § 1857h–2. Some courts have suggested that in criminal or civil enforcement proceedings the violator may in certain circumstances raise a defense of economic or technological infeasibility. See *Buckeye Power, Inc.* v. *EPA*, 481 F. 2d 162, 173 (CA6 1973); *Indiana & Michigan Electric Co.* v. *EPA*, 509 F. 2d 839, 847 (CA7 1975). We do not address this question here.

what new to our national experience and it necessarily entails certain risks. But Congress considered those risks in passing the 1970 Amendments and decided that the dangers posed by uncontrolled air pollution made them worth taking. Petitioner's theory would render that considered legislative judgment a nullity, and that is a result we refuse to reach.

Affirmed.

---

d. *Emission Standards for Specified New Sources (NSPS)*

The system of regulation of the Clean Air Act places the responsibility for regulation of air pollution of *existing* stationary sources of air pollution on the state in which the pollution is created. However, Congress gave EPA the power to set standards for *new* facilities, known as **New Source Performance Standards (NSPS)**. Section 111 of the Clean Air Act requires EPA to prescribe standards of performance for new sources of air pollution that reflect the best system of emission reduction after considering the cost of achieving the emission reduction as well as the health, energy and environmental impact of those standards.

The emission standard for new sources of air pollution will depend upon whether the site for the proposed new sources is in a **Nonattainment Area (NAA)** or a **Prevention of Significant Deterioration Area (PSD)**. If the proposed new source is in a Nonattainment Area the source must meet the **Lowest Achievable Emission Rate (LAER)** and achieve the net effect of *reduced* emissions. If the proposed new source is in a PSD area a permit can be issued only if the new source meets the **Best Available Control Technology (BACT,** or **BAT)** for that source at that location and must meet the other requirements of Section 165 of the Clean Air Act that regulates PSD areas.

EPA has been slow in implementing the New Source Performance Standards. Only fossil-fuel steam generators, incinerators, cement and acid plants have been regulated. Congress, in the 1977 Amendments, ordered EPA to promulgate the standards for the remaining industries within four years from adoption of the 1977 Amendments.

National Lime Association v. EPA, below, illustrates the difficulty that EPA has in establishing new source performance standards that are "achievable" by the industry. *ASARCO, Inc. v. EPA* illustrates the statutory problem of incorporating the **"bubble concept"** into the new source performance standards.

NATIONAL LIME ASSOCIATION
v.
E. P. A.

627 F.2d 416 (D.C.Cir. 1980)

WALD, Circuit Judge:

The National Lime Association (NLA), representing ninety percent of this country's commercial producers of lime and lime hydrate (the industry), challenges the new source performance standards (NSPS) for lime manufacturing plants issued by the Environmental Protection Agency (EPA, Administrator or Agency) under § 111 of the Clean Air Act (the Act), 42 U.S.C. § 7411 (Supp. I 1977). The standards limit the mass of particulate that may be emitted in the exhaust gas from all lime-hydrating and from certain lime-manufacturing facilities and limit the permitted visibility of exhaust gas emissions from some facilities manufacturing lime. We find inadequate support in the administrative record for the standards promulgated and therefore remand to the Administrator.

I.
RELEVANT PARTICULARS OF THE LIMESTONE INDUSTRY

A. *The Industry*

In sheer size and weight of production, the limestone industry ranks among the largest in this country. Limestone production in the United States ranks second only to sand and gravel in commodity tonnage and exceeds petroleum, coal and iron ore in volume produced. Limestone deposits can be found beneath an estimated fifteen to twenty percent of the surface of the United States and occur in every state. Total national production approximates twenty-two million tons annually and derives from plants in over forty states.

The recent development of two important industrial uses for lime has ensured the continuing growth of production despite a decline in agricultural use. The industry is capital-intensive with declining employment, but because so many other industrial processes depend on the use of lime, any decline in production would have "a large multiplier effect on U.S. employment."

B. *The Production of Lime from Limestone*

The process by which commercially valuable lime is produced is relatively simple. Limestone is quarried, crushed, sized and fed into a kiln where it is subjected to high temperatures (1100°C/2000°F). By a process known as "calcination," the heating ("burning") of limestone produces quicklime, a soft, porous, highly reactive material commonly used in industry. As might be expected, the process generates a substantial quantity of dust, or in the language of the Agency, particulate matter, sufficiently lightweight to be carried off in the hot exhaust gas and emitted from the kiln. The particulate matter thus released is composed of partially burned limestone, raw limestone feed, deadburned lime and quicklime. Typically, the process also releases sulfur dioxide (SO_2).[7]

Almost ninety percent of total United States lime production is processed in rotary kilns. Uncontrolled emissions from rotary kilns have been reported to run from 150 to 200 pounds per ton of lime produced, roughly five percent of the feed poundage and nine percent of the produce. A typical lime plant producing 500 tons per day from a rotary kiln, conforming to typical state pollution-control standards, emits about 150 megagrams (165 tons) of particulate matter per year. Rotary kilns produce a greater volume of particulate emissions than the formerly widely used vertical kilns but they are also the only kilns which can retain product quality while burning coal, a fuel on which the industry has become increasingly dependent.[11]

C. *The Production of Hydrated Lime*

A comparatively small amount (ten percent) of all lime produced is further processed into hydrated or slaked lime. This is done by adding water to lime and introducing the mixture into an agitated hydrator. An exothermic reaction occurs and a fluffy, dry, white powder, known as hydrated lime, is the result. Particulate matter is carried off in the steamy exhaust emitted from the hydration process.

D. *Emissions Control in the Production of Lime*

Rotary kilns here and abroad have employed several different methods of emissions controls, including the fabric filter baghouse, the electrostatic precipitator (ESP), the high energy scrubber, and the gravel bed filter. One survey showed that of eighty-five domestic rotary kilns, twenty-four percent used a baghouse, thirty-one percent used a high energy scrubber and eight percent used an ESP. However, use of the baghouse method is increasing because this method requires less energy and does not itself create additional problems of pollution control.

EPA has identified baghouses, ESPs and scrubbers as "best systems" of emissions control for rotary lime kilns.

Baghouses

The operation of baghouses and electrostatic precipitators was briefly explained in our initial review of EPA's performance standards for portland cement plants,

[7]Sulfur is found in most limestone and in all fuels used in calcination, except natural gas. SSEIS 3–9. However,

> [t]he sulfur in the limestone feed does not normally contribute to a substantial portion of the total SO_2 emissions from a rotary kiln. . . . The major concern with respect to SO_2 emissions from rotary kilns is the sulfur content of the fuel.

Id.

[11]SSEIS 3–5. Low sulfur coal supplies are dwindling; EPA estimates that by 1986, 50% of new plant capacity will be using high sulfur coal. SSEIS 3–5.

The increased use of coal, particularly high sulfur coal, can be expected to affect emissions. Use of high sulfur coal can result in "significant" SO_2 emissions; EPA projects 84 pounds per hour of SO_2 when 3.5% sulfur coal is burned in a "model" kiln producing 500 tons of lime per day. SSEIS 3–9—3–11. This compares with approximately 22 pounds per hour of SO_2 when low sulfur coal (one percent or less) is burned. The chemical composition of the limestone feed, the kiln temperature, the amount of excess oxygen in the kiln, and the amount of dust and particle size will all affect SO_2 emissions, but the major factor will be the sulfur content of the fuel. SSEIS 3–9.

The standards at issue here, however, expressly limit only particulate emissions. No standard has been set for emissions of sulfur dioxide in the lime industry.

Portland Cement Association v. Ruckelshaus, 486 F.2d 375, 390–91, (D.C.Cir. 1973), *cert. denied*, 417 U.S. 921, 94 S.Ct. 2628, 41 L.Ed.2d 226 (1974) [hereinafter cited as *Portland Cement I*]. The baghouse method employs fabric filters ("bags"), situated within an enclosed area (a "house"), to remove particulate from the kiln exhaust gas which is channeled through the house.

As the exhaust gas passes through, a dust cake forms on the filters. The cake itself improves filtration efficiency, but from time to time the filters must be cleaned. This is done by forcing a reverse gas flow through the fabric, thus releasing the cake for disposal.

EPA acknowledges that fabric filter effectiveness is primarily a function of kiln exhaust particle size distribution, fabric type, fabric age and maintenance history.

Electrostatic Precipitators

Under this method, "dust particles are charged [by discharge electrodes] and pass through an electrical field [collector plates] of the opposite charge, thus causing the dust to be precipitated out of the exhaust gas . . . ." *Portland Cement I*, 486 F.2d at 390. Two basic criteria must be met before an ESP can be utilized: (1) the suspended particle must be able to accept an electric charge; and (2) the particle must then pass through an electric field of sufficient strength to ensure removal of the particulate from the gas stream at the desired efficiency.

Precipitability is a function of the chemical composition of the dust particles, and will vary with the different kinds of material that make up the kiln exhaust dust (limestone, quicklime, fly ash, calcium sulfate, etc.). Assuming precipitability, the two main factors influencing the efficiency of a precipitator are the gas velocity and treatment time. The ESP method experiences a relatively low collection efficiency on submicron particles.

Although most particles collected by an ESP fall by gravity into waiting hoppers, programmed rapping of the electrodes is also required to keep the collector plates and discharge electrodes clean. As with the baghouse method, the dust collected is dry and may be disposed of in a variety of ways. A high level of maintenance skill is needed to keep an ESP in operation at design conditions.

Scrubbers

Scrubbers operate on the principle that wet particles are easier to control than dry. High pressure (or high energy) scrubbers of the type EPA considers capable of meeting the promulgated standards are those which because of their design increase the likelihood of contact between particle and water.

The most common high pressure drop scrubber used for controlling emissions from rotary lime kilns is the venturi scrubber. This scrubber operates by accelerating the velocity of the exhaust gas through a narrow venturi-shaped throat, where it is then brought into contact at great force with a spray of water. The particles thus dampened coalesce to form a slurry that can then be collected by a comparatively simple water-gas separation device. The separated gas is then released into the atmosphere.

The efficiency of particulate removal is a direct function of energy input, measured by pressure drop across the venturi throat. Gas-water contact in the venturi scrubber is so thorough that even submicron particles are removed. Although low pressure drop scrubbers use less energy than high pressure drop scrubbers, even a low efficiency scrubber requires more energy than either the baghouse or the ESP. The slurry which is the by-product of scrubber use is deposited in ponds, where the collected particulate settles out from the scrubbing water. The "clean" scrubbing water is then reused. Under present law settling ponds must be located so that they do not receive excessive rainwater run-off, causing overflow into local navigable waters.

E. *Emissions Control in the Production of Hydrated Lime*

Hydration emissions have been shown to be most effectively controlled by wet scrubbers and they are the *only* system of emissions reduction considered by EPA for lime hydrators.

The most common type of scrubber used on lime hydrators is the wetted fan type with centrifugal separation. In this scrubber water is sprayed into the center of a draft fan where it is forced to mix with the exhaust gas. More water is sprayed just after the fan into the duct carrying this gas-water mixture. The dust laden slurry water is then removed from the cleaned gas stream by centrifugal separation and the "scrubbed" gas is then vented to the atmosphere.

Slurry water is returned immediately to the hydrator for reuse; the hydration process requires the addition of water and the captured dust seems to contribute to, rather than interfere with, the production of hydrate. Recycling the slurry water eliminates the settling ponds and waste sludge disposal problems usually associated with particulate scrubbers.

II.
PROCEDURAL HISTORY

Section 111 of the Clean Air Act,* * * 42 U.S.C. § 7411 (Supp. I 1977), authorizes the Administrator to limit the air pollutants that can lawfully be emitted from newly constructed[22] or modified[23] plants. This the Administrator can do by promulgating new source performance standards requiring new or modified plants to meet standards which can be met through application of the best system of emission reduction (considering costs) which has been "adequately demonstrated." The purpose is to assure that new or modified plants will not create significant new air pollution problems.

On May 3, 1977, EPA added lime manufacturing plants to the list of sources that "may contribute significantly to air pollution which causes or contributes to the endangerment of public health or welfare" pursuant to section 111(b) of the Clean Air Act.* * *

At the same time, EPA proposed NSPS for lime plants.* * *

Although lime plants were determined to be sources of nitrogen oxides, carbon monoxide and sulfur dioxide as well as particulates, standards of performance were proposed and ultimately promulgated only with respect to particulate matter. Furthermore, of the various types of kilns that may be used in the calcination of limestone, only rotary kilns are regulated by the standards.[28]

[22]A "new source" is defined by the Act to mean:

> any stationary source, the construction or modification of which is commenced after the publication of regulations (or, if earlier, proposed regulations) prescribing a standard of performance under this section which will be applicable to such source.

[23]"Modification" of a source is defined to mean:

> any physical change in, or change in the method of operation of, a stationary source which increases the amount of any air pollutant emitted by such source or which results in the emission of any air pollutant not previously emitted. . .

Conversion of a kiln from natural gas or fuel oil to coal firing may constitute a "modification," triggering application of the NSPS here promulgated.

[28]The SSEIS identifies three other types of kilns in current use by the industry: the vertical kiln; the rotary hearth kiln; and the fluidized bed kiln. SSEIS 3–11—3–13. The focus on rotary kilns was attributed to the widespread use of such kilns in recent years and to the Agency's

The kiln standards limit emissions[29] to 0.15 kilogram of particulate matter per megagram of limestone feed (0.3 pound per ton) and ten percent "opacity."[30] The owner or operator of an affected facility is required by the regulations to monitor continuously the opacity of emissions. Where the scrubber method is used for control, both the opacity standard and the opacity monitoring requirement are waived, and the pressure drop and liquid supply pressure of the scrubber must be monitored instead.[33]

The standard proposed and promulgated for lime hydrators limits emissions to 0.075 kilogram of particulate matter per megagram of lime feed (0.15 pound per ton). No opacity standard was set. The hydrator standard requires that the electric current and the liquid supply pressure of the scrubbers used to control emissions be monitored continuously.

The standards promulgated for particulate emissions are considerably stricter than the average applicable state regulations already in effect. Plants conforming to the NSPS here would—in the case of rotary kilns—be required to emit less than one-third the particulate permitted under average state regulations and—in the case of hydrators—less than one-sixth the particulate permitted by these regulations. . . .

III.
PREVIOUS REVIEW UNDER SECTION 111

As amended in 1977, section 111 of the Clean Air Act requires the Administrator to prescribe standards of performance for new statutory sources that reflect

> the degree of emission limitation and the percentage reduction achievable through the application of the best technological system of continuous emission reduction which (taking into consideration the cost of achieving such emission reduction, any nonair quality health and environmental impact and energy requirements), the Administrator determines has been adequately demonstrated. . . .

42 U.S.C. § 7411(a) (Supp. I 1977). As the court of exclusive review for NSPS, we have examined section 111 standards on several prior occasions [Citations omitted]* * *

These decisions, viewed independently, have established a rigorous standard of review under section 111. We have not deviated from the approach applied to the first NSPS to reach this court. In that case, *Portland Cement I*, we acknowledged that

> [w]hile we remain diffident in approaching problems of this technical complexity, . . . the necessity to review agency decisions, if it is to be more than a meaningless exercise, requires enough steeping in technical matters to determine whether the agency "has exercised a reasoned discretion." . . . We cannot substitute our judgment for that of the agency, but it is our duty to consider whether "the decision was based on a consideration of the relevant factors and whether there

---

expectation that the suitability of these kilns to the burning of coal (*see* text at note 12, *supra*) would secure their preeminent place among the kilns used in the industry.

> It is expected that as supplies of natural gas and oil become more expensive or unavailable, all new kilns would be rotary lime kilns designed to burn coal.

[29]The standards regulate only kiln exhaust effluent. Particulate emissions from "fugitive" sources (*e.g.*, transfer points, screens or loading operations) are not regulated. "Fugitive" sources can account for up to 10% of all particulate emissions. SSEIS 3–16.

[30] " 'Opacity' means the degree to which emissions reduce the transmission of light and obscure the view of an object in the background."

[33]Water supply pressure and pressure drop across the venturi throat were both found by EPA relevant to the efficiency of the scrubber method of emissions control.

has been a clear error of judgment." . . . Ultimately, we believe that the cause of a clean environment is best served by reasoned decision-making.

486 F.2d at 402 (citations omitted)* * * The search for reasoned decisionmaking in a world of technical expertise must continue if judicial review is to have any meaning in the statutory scheme.

Section 111 requires that the emissions control system considered able to meet the standard be "adequately demonstrated" and the standard itself "achievable." 42 U.S.C. § 7411(a) (Supp. I 1977). We have in the past remanded section 111 standards for the "seeming refusal of the agency to respond to what seem to be legitimate problems with the methodology of the [ ]tests," *Portland Cement I*, 486 F.2d at 392; and the limited relevance and reliability of the tests relied upon in support of the standard. *Id.* at 396, 401 . . .

However, we think it serves little purpose to elaborate on the standard of review as applied before we explain how, under the general approach required by statute and our earlier decisions, we have evaluated petitioner's and respondents' contentions.

The issue presented here is primarily one of the adequacy of EPA's test data on which the industry standards are based. NLA disagrees with EPA's conclusion that the standards are achievable under the "best technological system of continuous emission reduction which . . . the Administrator determines has been adequately demonstrated." Specifically, NLA claims that the test data underlying the development of the standards do not support the Administrator's conclusion that the promulgated emission levels are in fact "achievable" on a continuous basis. Promulgation of standards based upon inadequate proof of achievability would defy the Administrative Procedure Act's mandate against action that is "arbitrary, capricious, an abuse of discretion, or otherwise not in accordance with law." 5 U.S.C. § 706 (1976).[45]

IV.

ASSESSMENT OF THE OBJECTIONS RAISED BY THE INDUSTRY

Our review has led us to conclude that the record does not support the "achievability" of the promulgated standards for the industry as a whole.[46]

* * *

[45]The "arbitrary and capricious" standard was expressly adopted as the standard of judicial review of, *inter alia*, NSPS under the 1977 Amendments to the Clean Air Act. 42 U.S.C. § 7607 (Supp. I 1977). For reasons noted we do not apply § 7607 as amended in 1977 to the proceedings here.

[46]An achievable standard need not be one already routinely achieved in the industry. *Essex Chemical*, 486 F.2d at 433–34, *citing Portland Cement I*. But, to be achievable, we think a uniform standard must be capable of being met under most adverse conditions which can reasonably be expected to recur and which are not or cannot be taken into account in determining the "costs" of compliance.

The statutory standard is one of achievability, given costs. Some aspects of "achievability" cannot be divorced from consideration of "costs." Typically one associates "costs" with the capital requirements of new technology. *See e.g., AFL-CIO v. Marshall*, 617 F.2d 636, 659 (D.C.Cir.1979). However, certain "costs" (*e.g.*, frequent systemic shutdown to service emissions control systems or use of feedstock of a certain size of composition in order to meet the new emissions standards) are more intimately intertwined with "achievability" than are the capital costs of new technology. In this case the lime industry attacks the standards as "unachievable." When questioned at oral argument, counsel for petitioner disclaimed any attack upon the expense of implementation, stating that he attacked the achievability of the standard "on any reliably repetitive basis," "because of the very variables in the production of lime."

This conclusion is a cumulative one, resulting from our assessment of the many points raised by the industry at the administrative level and in this court; no one point made is so cogent that remand would necessarily have followed on that basis alone.[48] In the analysis that follows, common threads will be discerned in our discussions of individual points. Chief among these common threads is a concern that the Agency consider the representativeness for the industry as a whole of the tested plants on which it relies, at least where its central argument is that the standard *is* achievable because it *has* been achieved (at the tested plants). The Agency's failure to consider the representativeness—along various relevant parameters—of the data relied upon is the primary reason for our remand. The locus of administrative burdens of going forward or of persuasion may shift in the course of a rulemaking proceeding, but we think an initial burden of promulgating and explaining a non-arbitrary, non-capricious rule rests with the Agency and we think that by failing to explain how the standard proposed is achievable under the range of relevant conditions which may affect the emissions to be regulated, the Agency has not satisfied this initial burden.* * *

The critical question presented here is whether the regulated industry, through its trade association, should have borne the entire burden of demonstrating the unreliability for the industry as a whole of the conclusions drawn by the EPA. In this connection we are candidly troubled by the industry's failure to respond, at a crucial

---

This necessarily asserts that a standard which does not account for certain routine variations in conditions is "unachievable." We agree, where, as here, there is no evidence in the record that the "costs" of adjusting for such routine variatons (assuming such adjustments be possible) were considered by the Agency in promulgating its standard.* * *

[48]In addition to the points made in connection with the achievability of the standard, NLA disputes EPA's determination that lime manufacturing plants "may contribute significantly to air pollution which causes or contributes to the endangerment of public health or welfare." 42 U.S.C. § 1857c–6(b)(1)(A) (1976) (repealed 1977). (*See* text at note 25, *supra*.)

EPA considers the significant production of particulate emissions itself to cause or contribute to air pollution (which may reasonably be anticipated to endanger public health or welfare). The Agency has made this determination for purposes of establishing national primary and secondary ambient air quality standards under § 109 of the Clean Air Act, now codified at 42 U.S.C. § 7408 (Supp. I 1977), and without regard to the harmful or beneficial effect of the material of which the particulate is composed. 36 Fed.Reg. 1502, 8137, 8138 (1971). When ambient air quality standards for particulate were first proposed, the Agency described some of the health effects of particulate matter:

> Particulate matter of technological origin is pervasive in its distribution and is associated with a variety of adverse effects on public health and welfare. Particulate matter in the respiratory tract may produce injury by itself, or it may act in conjunction with gases, altering their sites or their mode of action. Particles cleared from the respiratory tract by transfer to the lymph, blood, or gastro-intestinal tract may produce effects elsewhere in the body.* * *

We think the danger of particulate emissions' effect on health has been sufficiently supported in the Agency's (and its predecessor's) previous determinations to provide a rational basis for the Administrator's finding in this case. *See* Air Quality Criteria for Particulate Matter, *supra*. Moreover, whatever its impact on public health, we cannot say that a dust "nuisance" has no impact on public welfare. Congress has provided that with respect to the Clean Air Act:

> All language referring to effects on welfare includes, but is not limited to, effects on soils, water, crops, vegetation, manmade materials, animals, wildlife, weather, visibility, and climate, damage to and deterioration of property, and hazards to transportation, as well as effects on economic values and on personal comfort and well-being.* * *

juncture in the standards development process, to the Agency's invitation to submit data supporting a fundamental industry objection to the achievability of the standard. We would have expected the industry to have been eager to supply supporting data for its position, assuming the "cost" of obtaining such data were less than the "cost" of compliance with a standard that was argued to be unachievable on any reliably repetitive basis for the industry as a whole. We cannot help but wonder if the industry's failure to supply such data means that the data available or obtained would not be favorable to the industry's position. Nevertheless we remand because we think, on balance, EPA must affirmatively show that its standard reflects consideration of the range of relevant variables that may affect emissions in different plants.

The showing we require does not mean that EPA must perform repeated tests on every plant operating within its regulatory jurisdiction. It does, however, mean that due consideration must be given to the possible impact on emissions of recognized variations in operations and some rationale offered for the achievability of the promulgated standard given the tests conducted and the relevant variables identified.

A. *The Particulate Emission Standards*

1. *Rotary Kilns*

EPA tested emissions at six plants before it proposed its mass emission standard for rotary lime kilns. These six plants were selected for testing on the basis of visits to thirty-nine plants, during which the visibility of emissions was observed and information obtained on the emissions control systems employed. The thirty-nine plants were themselves selected because they had been identified as effectively controlled after a review of the literature and contact with industry representatives. SSEIS A-1. The results of the tests of one plant (Plant A) which could not meet the proposed standard were excluded from consideration because the plant was thought not to represent best technology. From what we can gather from the record, three plants were able to meet the standard consistently.

Our doubts about the representativeness of the data relied upon are grouped under three subheadings below: *Variations in Quantity of Particulate Generated in the Kiln*; *Variations in Controllability of Particulate Generated*; and *Explanation of Discarded Data from Plants A and F.* * * *

a. *Variations in Quantity of Particulate Generated in the Kiln*

That the quantity of dust produced in the kilns would affect the controllability of emissions and the achievability of the standards does not seem an unreasonable expectation. The Agency, however, appears to have taken conflicting positions on the reasonableness of this expectation and perhaps as a consequence has devoted inadequate attention to several variables which EPA's own documents and the industry suggest may affect the volume of dust produced in different kilns.

(1) *Feedstock Variations*

For example, the record suggests that the size and chemical composition of the limestone feedstock used will affect the amount of dust produced.* * *

The EPA did note in its SSEIS that "[r]otary kilns can handle a range of stone feed sizes between ¼ inch and 2½ inches," SSEIS 3–6, and that larger feed size generally results in lower dusting in the kiln. *See* SSEIS 3–14. The Agency also acknowledged that the grade and composition of limestone varies widely across the country. SSEIS 3–1. However, no data on stone size are included by the EPA in the summary data on plants tested (SSEIS App. C) and little information concerning the chemical composition of the feed used at the tested plants is provided.* * * We are, more importantly, left in the dark about which kinds of limestone can be expected to produce the greatest volume of emission dust and what, if any, processing adjustments can be expected of producers using particular kinds of feed in order to achieve the standard proposed. For all we know, the six plants tested could be using kinds and sizes of feed which are representative of only a small segment of the industry spectrum. If that were true the plants may not be "representative" and the regulation might not be "achievable" by the industry as a whole.

(2) *Gas Velocity and Operation Levels*

According to the MRI Report, quoted * * * dust generation is in part a function of *gas velocity* in the kiln. Gas velocity appears in turn to depend on several factors, including the percentage of capacity at which the kiln is operating. The MRI Report stated that kiln gas velocity has "the most [apparent] effect [on dust generation] when the kiln is operated close to 100 percent of design capacity," and noted that in one plant studied an increase in production—from 100% to 135% of design capacity—resulted in double the rate of emissions where a reduction from 100% to 75% resulted in only an eight percent reduction. This seems to mean that at levels close to or exceeding capacity, gas velocity and consequently dust generation increases at a faster rate than at lower levels of production. Thus the level of capacity at which the plant was operating at the time of sampling and the gas velocity would appear relevant to the representativeness of the test data.

Both in this court and at the administrative level the industry has addressed the possible atypicality of the production level of some of the test plants, which it alleges were not tested at full capacity and in doing so, it has echoed a concern expressed by this court in an earlier case.* * *

Having stated that much, however, the Agency did not explain how the range of test results fully takes account of any significant differences in operating conditions in the industry. The support document is totally devoid of analysis of the relevance or irrelevance of operating level or gas velocity to the achievability of the standard, notwithstanding assertions in the EPA's own contracted-for report that gas velocity bears upon dust generation rates.

(3) *Dust Levels at the Tested Plants*

The SSEIS asserts, without explaining how the conclusion was reached, that Kilns A, B and E each generated dust at a rate of twenty-two to twenty-five percent (pounds of dust collected per pound of lime produced), higher rates than the average rate of dust generation at the eleven plants for which data were submitted by the NLA. The NLA data, however, indicate a much greater range in dust generation levels than that suggested by the EPA's test plant figures.* * *

As laypersons it seems entirely logical to us to suppose that dust generation levels would directly affect emissions controllability, *viz.*, the higher the dust generation, the more difficult the achievability of the standard by the technological control device.

Our examination of the record thus yields a conflict: while in one breath EPA appears to acknowledge the relevance of dust generation levels to the proposed standard, in another breath the relevance is denied. In our view, the conflict is not adequately explained, nor is the industry-wide achievability of the standard adequately justified, in light of the acknowledged possibility that heavy dusting creates a more difficult control problem.* * * But the exact relationship between volume of dust generated and the efficiency of the emissions control systems is never clearly stated or explained by the Agency. Instead, the Agency sends us several mixed signals.

On the one hand, the Agency suggests both directly and indirectly that more dust means a more difficult control problem.* * * On the other hand, the Agency asserts that the amount of dust generated is irrelevant to the efficiency of at least one control method and therefore to the achievability of the standard.* * *

b. *Variations in Controllability of Particulate Generated*

The record points to other variables which were also given short shrift in the stated rationale: the use of coal to fuel the kiln (as it relates to controllability of emissions); and variations in size of emitted particles. The record strongly supports the relevance of coal usage to the effiiciency of at least the ESP control method and it also suggests a relationship between particle size and the efficiency of both the ESP and the baghouse control method. Nothing indicates how—if at all—variations in these factors were considered in proposing an "achievable" standard.

(1) *Coal Usage*

It is clear that the trend in the industry is not only toward coal, but toward high sulfur coal, as other energy sources become scarcer.* * * Moreover, conversion to coal is expected to be a major "modification" that will bring old plants into the regulatory orbit under section 111. Finally, Congress was especially concerned in passing the 1977 Clean Air Act Admendments that the increased use of coal enter into the Agency's regulatory approach.

However, the impact of high sulfur coal usage on the controllability of particulate emissions under any of the three "best" emissions control systems was not clearly or closely examined by EPA in the development of this standard.* * *

The support document acknowledged:

> The tests that were performed on the ESP-controlled kilns are not indicative of normal operation since the current trend in the lime manufacturing industry is toward the use of coal as fuel and the kilns that were tested were fired by oil and natural gas. It is expected that this use of coal would produce a more difficult control problem. However, with proper design of the ESP, it is EPA's judgment that the system could easily meet the level of the proposed standard.

EPA does not, however, explain the basis for its optimistic judgment that an ESP could meet the standard on a coal burning kiln. Although other factors may affect the chemical composition and hence the precipitability of emissions, EPA's failure adequately to consider the impact of coal usage is a particularly obvious omission.* * *

In addition, the record reflects little consideration of the impact of variations in the *sulfur* content of coal used. For example, the sulfur content at the coal burning plants tested was considerably smaller than the average projected sulfur content (3 percent) for all new lime plants in the near future.* * *

Given the high emphasis in the 1977 Clean Air Act Amendments on coal—especially high sulfur coal—as the fuel of choice, we think the effect on emissions of this fuel's use should have been specifically examined and a rationale offered to demonstrate the standard's "achievability"—under *any* of the best methods of emissions control—when high sulfur coal is burned.

(2) *Particle Size*

Although there is (a) considerable evidence in the record that the efficiency of available control technology varies with emitted particle size and (b) that lime dust particle size varies regionally (probably due to feedstock variation), the EPA (c) undertook no analysis of the impact of particle size distribution on the achievability of its standard.* * *

Thus, it seems likely that both dry-collection methods, the ESP and the baghouse, operate more efficiently when the proportion of large to small particles in the emissions is relatively high. It is therefore possible that a kiln which produces a high proportion of fine particulate may not be able to meet the standard, at least using energy-conserving dry collection methods.* * * When particle size was identified as a potentially important variable, both the Agency and the industry failed to pick up the ball.

c. *EPA's lack of analysis*

As far as we can tell the Agency gathered no data on particle size distribution at the tested plants or in the industry generally, either before or after the industry meeting which focused on this factor. Whether the EPA took particle size into account in developing and promulgating its proposed standard cannot be determined from this record.

Understandably, the Agency's main defense in court centers on the industry's total failure to respond positively to EPA's suggestion that the industry either suggest additional test sites or submit data on the basis of which EPA might reconsider or subcategorize the standard to conform to local variations. EPA's point is a sympathetic one, but not, we think, dispositive. EPA has a statutory duty to promulgate achievable standards. This requires that they approach that task in a systematic manner that identifies relevant variables and ensures that they are taken account of in analyzing test data. EPA's own support document recognizes particle size as a variable but enigmatically does not discuss it at any length or explain its importance in emissions control. That the industry did not assist the Agency in any meaningful way by data or even by suggestions for additional testing is certainly discouraging. But we do not think that inaction—lamentable though it may be—lifted the burden from the Agency of pursuing what appears to be a relevant variable or at the least discussing in its document why it was not considered important.

In this respect, we believe that the industry's comments, concerning particle size distribution, when viewed in light of the material contained in EPA's own support statement and in light of the background documents on which it relied, met a "threshold requirement of materiality," mandating an Agency response which was not forthcoming here.

d. *Explanation of Discarded Data from Plants A and F*

Finally (with respect to the rotary kiln particulate emission standard), a few words should be devoted to the mysterious Plant A and the plant controlled by a low-pressure venturi scrubber (Plant F). Test results obtained at Plant A were excluded from consideration and those obtained at Plant F were discounted (if not excluded entirely from consideration) in the rationale for the proposed standard. This was because after testing it was concluded these plants did not represent best technology. SSEIS 8–17, 8–18. At both plants the measured particulate emissions had significantly exceeded the proposed standard. The only reason—apart from the poor test result—given for the conclusion that Plant A did not represent best technology was as follows:

> The Plant A baghouse is not typical of those in use in the lime industry. Large quantities of dilution air infiltrate through the corrugated asbestos siding and doors into the clean air side of the baghouse. It is unknown how this affects the performance of the baghouse, but this baghouse did not perform as well as the two other baghouses (Plants B and E) that were source tested in conjunction with this study.

It would appear that EPA's observation of "large quantities of dilution air" at this plant is related to its measurement of high oxygen levels in the effluent. Yet when the oxygen determination at the plant was questioned as "thermodynamically impossible" (R. 139, 7, App. 189), EPA conceded error but offered no other reason to support its conclusion that Plant A did not represent best technology. We think it incumbent upon the Agency, at least where it chooses to propose a standard on a data base as apparently limited as this one, to offer some supportable reason for its conclusion that a tested plant, chosen as likely to be well-controlled, does not represent best technology. The mere fact that its test results were unsatisfctory is not enough.

If, for unexplained reasons, one-third of the test plants initially chosen by EPA for their well-controlled systems fail to meet the standard, the conclusion is just as plausible that the standard is not achievable as that the plants chosen did not have well-controlled systems. It is up to EPA to dispel such doubts, and they have not done so here.* * *

B. *The Opacity Standard and Continuous Monitoring Requirement*

1. *The Opacity Standard*

"Opacity" is defined by regulation to mean "the degree to which emissions reduce the transmission of light and obscure the view of an object in the background." 40 C.F.R. § 60.2(j) (1979). EPA explains that "[t]he opacity level of visible emissions is an indication of the mass concentration of a particular pollutant" and that "[v]arious studies have shown that opacity varies directly with mass concentrations of particulate matter." SSEIS 8–19. EPA considers opacity standards to be "a necessary supplement to particulate mass emission standards" basically because "[o]pacity test methods are quicker, easier to apply, and less costly that concentration/mass tests for particulate matter."

The performance standards prescribed by EPA for rotary lime kilns consist of both a mass emission standard (grams of particulate emission per gram of feed) and an opacity standard (ten percent). 43 Fed.Reg. 9453 (1978). Only those kilns using dry methods of emissions control are subject to the ten percent opacity standard.* * *

We have considered the various arguments made by the NLA and conclude that EPA's apparent failure to consider in this case some variables which were (1) given more careful consideration in the promulgation of earlier opacity standards and (2) given inadequate consideration in the companion mass emission standard requires us to remand the opacity standard to the Administrator for additional explanation or for revision.* * *

b. *Variables Inadequately Considered in Mass Emission Standard*

Opacity standards are intended to operate in tandem with mass emission standards, notwithstanding their independent enforceability. Ideally, a violation of an opacity standard should indicate a violation of a mass emission standard. For this reason the Agency relies on data from the same test plants to support both the opacity and the mass emission standard; but for this reason when the representativeness of data relied upon for one standard is inadequately shown, the representativeness of data relied upon for the other standard is drawn in question.

As discussed above, the Agency failed to consider the representativeness of the particle size produced at its test plants. This failure is particularly striking in connection with the opacity standard because variations in particle size have been given careful consideration in the development of earlier opacity standards.

We have already noted that the emissions control systems favored by the standards and by prevailing economic and technological trends may operate more efficiently when the predominant size of particulate emissions is large. As it happens, large particulate is also likely to appear less opague. Thus, it is possible that a plant would meet both standards only because the particles emitted are uniformly large and we cannot ascertain how the plants tested here "measure up."

c. *EPA's Arguments*

Both in this court and at the administrative level EPA emphasizes the overwhelming extent to which the plants tested were able to meet the ten percent opacity standard. But without knowing the representativeness of the plants tested or of test conditions, we cannot say that the standard is neither arbitrary nor capricious. Certainly the fact that virtually all plants tested were able to meet the standard is an important consideration, but our doubts are sufficient, when coupled with our doubts concerning the mass emissions standard (discussed above), to remand to the Agency for amplification of the record.

EPA has committed itself to take the possibility of inaccurate opacity measurement into account in the enforcement of the standard. It has also provided a type of "variance" mechanism under which new sources which meet the mass emission standard but which cannot meet the opacity standard may petition the Administrator to establish a separate opacity standard for that facility. 40 C.F.R. § 60.11(e) (1979), 39 Fed.Reg. 39872 (1974). The variance mechanism, however, seems clearly to have been intended to be narrowly construed.

The Agency relies upon the flexibility built into the regulatory scheme to support the rationality of its standards. The wisdom of such flexibility has been applauded on earlier occasions by this court, but the statutory scheme prescribes "achievable" standards and there is a limit to the flexibility with which the Agency is or should be endowed.* * *

2. *Continuous Monitoring*

On the opacity monitoring requirement, the petitioner's argument is simple: there is no adequately demonstrated technology for monitoring opacity. One company operating affected facilities (Dow Chemical) commented, "We have tried several continuous monitoring systems in the past and have been unable to find an instrument that will suitably do the job and can be maintained in operation."

The company cited high opacity readings attributable to instrument malfunctioning "as frequently as twice a day" and also remarked that "[t]he opacity readings [of the monitor] do not relate to the actual stack conditions as measured by visual observers."

EPA answers that the continuous monitoring data would not be used to determine compliance with the opacity standard but "to keep a check on the operation and maintenance of the control equipment," and to trigger performance checks by trained observers.* * *

The Agency argues that if the equipment gives any "indication" of changed opacity it is enough to justify a continuous monitoring requirement.* * *

It dismisses the industry's contention that reliable monitoring equipment is not available to perform this limited a function and shifts the burden to the industry to show "by supporting data," SSEIS II, 13, that it is not.

EPA maintains that it has had considerable experience with the use of continuous monitoring devices and that in its experience a monitor will show if an emissions control device is being properly operated and maintained and the opacity standards met. SSEIS II, 14; SSEIS 8–24. Thus monitoring will act as a needed warning alarm when the control system is out of kilter. The industry itself admits there is some value to a continuous monitoring requirement. Dow Chemical took a critical stance (adopted by NLA, Brief for Petitioner at 52) but also acknowledged that monitoring equipment "gives an indication of whether the opacity is increasing or decreasing." R. 148, 2, App. 328. Given this concession, we cannot find the continuous monitoring requirement arbitrary as an adjunct to a non-arbitrary, non-capricious opacity standard. We have today remanded the opacity standard for lime plants. If on remand an opacity standard is retained, EPA may continue to require continuous monitoring.

V.
THE STANDARD OF REVIEW AS APPLIED

Our requirement that the EPA consider the representativeness of the test data relied upon in the development and justification of its standard does not presage any new or more stringent standard of judicial review. The rigorousness of the review in which this court has engaged in previous NSPS decisions—known to some as the "hard look" standard—has already been described.

In enacting the Clean Air Act Amendments of 1977, Congress expressly approved the rigorous standard of review which the courts had theretofore applied to Agency decisions under the Clean Air Act. Although the judicial review provisions of the 1977 Amendments do not apply to this rule-making proceeding, Congress' express affirmance of the standards already developed fortifies our adherence to the learning of our earlier Clean Air Act decisions in reviewing the new source performance standards currently before us.

We think these decisions amply support our conclusion that a remand is appropriate in this case. Both decisions reviewing the NSPS and those reviewing other administrative determinations under the Clean Air Act evince a concern that variables be accounted for, that the representativeness of test conditions be ascertained, that the validity of tests be assured and the statistical significance of results determined. Collectively, these concerns have sometimes been expressed as a need for "reasoned decision-making" and sometimes as a need for adequate "methodology." However expressed, these more substantive concerns have been coupled with a requirement that assumptions be stated, that process be revealed, that the rejection of alternate theories or abandonment of alternate courses of action be explained and that the rational for the ultimate decision be set forth in a manner which permits the public to exercise its statutory prerogative of comment and the courts to exercise their statutory responsibility upon review. The standard we apply here is neither more rigorous nor more deferential than the standard applied in these earlier cases.

Our opinion should not suggest the necessity of "ninety-five percent certainty" in all the "facts" which enter into the Agency's decision. We would require only that the Agency provide sufficient data to demonstrate a systematic approach to problems, not that it adduce vast quantities of factual data. However, where the facts pertinent to the standard's feasibility are available and easily discoverable by conventional technical means, there is somewhat less reason for so limited a data base. Nothing in the record suggests the relevant facts are not readily accessible to the Agency; the number of plants is large, use of the control methods found by the Agency to represent the "best systems" is widespread, and stack emission measurement techniques have been known and applied for many years.

With respect to the standard's achievability we are thus not presented with the question how much deference is owed a judgment predicated on limited evidence when additional evidence cannot be adduced or adduced in the near future. We do not depart from some of the most carefully considered and closely reasoned decisions of this court which permit an agency latitude to exercise its discretion in accordance with the remedial purposes of the controlling statute where relevant facts cannot be ascertained or are on the frontiers of scientific inquiry.

A systematic approach may not necessarily require a conclusion grounded in actual test results. We do not intend to bridle the Agency's discretion to make well-founded assumptions even where the assumption could be replaced by valid test results, but we think first, the assumption should be stated and second, where test data *could* have verified the assumption, a reason for not testing or relying on such data should be given.

We recognize, for example, that the finding of facts, especially through elaborate testing, is costly and the costs of additional testing may be added by the Agency to the costs of delay in issuing the proposed rule and the sum of these costs weighed against the benefit of proposing a rule without additional data.

[Remanded.]

ASARCO, INC.
v.
E.P.A.

578 F.2d 319 (D.C.Cir. 1978)

J. SKELLY WRIGHT, Circuit Judge:

These cases involve challenges by ASARCO Incorporated, Newmont Mining Corporation, and Magma Copper Company (hereinafter referred to collectively as ASARCO) and the Sierra Club (Sierra) to regulations issued by the Environmental Protection Agency (EPA). The challenged provisions modify previous regulations implementing Section 111 of the Clean Air Act, 42 U.S.C. § 1857c–6 (1970 & Supp. V 1975), *as amended*, Pub.L.No. 95–95 § 109, 91 Stat. 685, 697–703 (1977), which mandates national emission standards for new stationary sources of air pollution, by introducing a limited form of what the parties call the "bubble concept."

I

A. *Section 111 and the "Bubble Concept"*

The 1970 amendments to the Clean Air Act were passed in reaction to the failure of the states to cooperate with the federal government in effectuating the stated purposes of the Act, especially the commitment "to protect and enhance the quality of the Nation's air resources so as to promote the public health and welfare and the productive capacity of its population." Clean Air Act § 101(b)(1), 4 U.S.C. § 1857(b)(1) (1970). *See generally* W. Rogers, Environmental Law § 3.1 (1977). The 1970 changes were designed "to improve the quality of the nation's air," 84 Stat. 1676 (1970), by increasing the federal government's role in the battle against air pollution. *Train v. Natural Resources Defense Council, Inc.*, 421 U.S. 60, 64, 95 S.Ct. 1470, 43 L.Ed.2d 731 (1975). The amendments require the states to develop pollution control programs (State Implementation Plans or SIPs) that will keep the levels of given pollutants in the atmosphere below the National Ambient Air Quality Standards (NAAQSs) set by EPA. Clean Air Act §§ 109, 110, 42 U.S.C. §§ 1857c–4, 1857c–5 (1970 & Supp V.

In addition, the 1970 amendments added Section 111, which is the focus of this litigation. This section directs EPA to set specific and rigorous limits on the amounts of pollutants that may be emitted from any "new source" of air pollution. The New Source Performance Standards (NSPSs) established under Section 111 are designed to force new sources to employ the best demonstrated systems of emission reduction.[6] Since the NSPSs are likely to be stricter than emission standards under

[6]The 1970 amendments provide that the NSPSs were to "reflect[] the degree of emission limitation achievable through the application of the best system of emission reduction which (taking into account the cost of achieving such reduction) the Administrator determines has been adequately demonstrated." Section 111(a)(1), 42 U.S.C. § 1857c–6(a)(1) (1970).

This language was amended in 1977, but the new provisions still reflect a commitment to requiring the best technology. The NSPSs must now "reflect the degree of emission limitation

State Implementation Plans, plant operations have an incentive to avoid application of the NSPSs.

The basic controversy in the cases before us concerns the determination of the units to which the NSPSs apply. Under the Act the NSPSs apply to "new sources." A "new source" is defined as "*any stationary source*, the *construction or modification* of which" begins after the NSPS covering that type of source is published. Section 111(a)(2), 42 U.S.C. § 1857c–6(a)(2) (1970) (emphasis added). Further statutory definitions explain the terms used in this one. A "'stationary source' means any building, structure, facility, or installation which emits or may emit any air pollutant." Section 111(a)(3), 42 U.S.C. § 1857c–6(a)(3) (1970). A "'modification' means any physical change in, or change in the method of operation of, a stationary source which increases the amount of any air pollutant emitted by such source or which results in the emission of any air pollutant not previously emitted." Section 111(a)(4), 42 U.S.C. § 1857c–6(a)(4) (1970). The statute thus directs that the NSPSs are to apply to any building, structure, facility, or installation which emits or may emit any air pollutant and which is either (1) newly constructed or (2) physically or operationally changed in such a way that *its* emission of any air pollutant increases.

The "bubble concept" is based on defining a *stationary source* as a *combination* of facilities, such as an *entire plant*, and applying the NSPSs only when a new *plant* is constructed or when an existing *plant* is physically or operationally changed in such a way that *net* emissions of any pollutant from the *entire plant* increase. If applied consistently, the bubble concept would allow the operator of an existing plant to avoid application of the strict NSPSs by offsetting any increase in pollution caused by a change in the plant (*e.g.*, modification or replacement of an existing facility, or even addition of a new facility) against a decrease in pollution from other units within the plant as a whole.

* * *

EPA acknowledges in its brief that it originally "defined the term *new source* as 'an affected *facility*' which in turn was defined as any apparatus to which a standard of performance is specifically applicable." Brief for EPA at 10 (emphasis added). Affected facilities, and thus new sources, were clearly not synonymous with entire plants.

* * *

In September 1974, the agency * * * proposed new regulations incorporating a limited version of the bubble concept.* * *

The new regulations would classify an entire plant as a single stationary source by embellishing the statutory definition of a stationary source as follows:

> "Stationary source" means any building, structure, facility, or installation which emits or may emit any air pollutant *and which contains any one or combination of the following:*
>
> *(1) Affected facilities.*
>
> *(2) Existing facilities.*
>
> *(3) Facilities of the type for which no standards have been promulgated in this part.*

40 C.F.R. § 60.2(d) (1976) (emphasis added). The italicized language is not included in the statutory definition of "stationary source" ("any building, structure, facility,

---

and the percentage reduction achievable through the application of the best technological system of continuous emission reduction which (taking into consideration the cost of achieving such emission reduction, any nonair quality health and environmental impact and energy requirements) the Administrator determines has been adequately demonstrated." Pub.L.No. 95–95 § 109(c)(1)(A), 91 Stat. 699–700.

or installation which emits or may emit any air pollutant"), nor was it included in the prior regulations. *See* 40 C.F.R. § 60.2(d) (1975). Thus the present regulations, instead of limiting the definition of "stationary source" to one "facility" as the statute does, make it cover "any one or combination of" facilities. The preamble to the new regulations makes it clear that the purpose of this change is to define a stationary source as an entire plant.[18]

Relying on this new definition of a stationary source, EPA applies the bubble concept to allow a plant operator who alters an existing facility in a way that increases its emissions to avoid application of the NSPSs by decreasing emissions from other facilities within the plant. The regulations provide that "[a] modification shall not be deemed to occur" unless the change in an existing facility results in a net increase in the emission of a pollutant from the whole "source."

The Sierra Club's basic contention is that the new regulations are inconsistent with the plain language of Section 111. The statute defines a *stationary source* as "*any* building, structure, *facility*, or installation which emits or may emit any air pollutant." Section 111(a)(3), 4 U.S.C. § 1857c–6(a)(3) (1970) (emphasis added). In contrast, the new regulations define stationary source to include "any * * * *combination* of * * * facilities * * *." 40 C.F.R. § 60.2(d) (1976) (emphasis added).

This change in the definition of a stationary source is essential to EPA's adoption of the bubble concept. By treating a combination of facilities as a single source, the regulations allow a facility whose emissions are increased by alterations to avoid complying with the applicable NSPS as long as emission decreases from other facilities within the same "source" cancel out the increase from the altered facility. Sierra argues forcefully that this result is incompatible with the statute's mandate that NSPSs should be applied to "*any* structure, building, facility, or installation" that undergoes "any physical change * * * or * * * change in the method of operation * * * which increases the amount of any air pollutant emitted by such [structure, building, facility, or installation]." 42 U.S.C. §§ 1857c–6(a)(3), 1857c–6(a)(4) (1970) (emphasis added). *See* brief for petitioner Sierra Club at 25–33.

EPA responds that the "broad" statutory definition of *stationary source* gives it "discretion" to define a *stationary source* as either a single facility or a combination of facilities. Brief for EPA at 13–16. We find this response unpersuasive. The regulations plainly indicate that EPA has attempted to change the basic unit to which the NSPSs apply from a *single* building, structure, facility, or installation—the unit prescribed in the statute—to a *combination* of such units. The agency has no authority to rewrite the statute in this fashion. *See, e.g., Ass'n of American Railroads v. Costle, supra; Lubrizol Corp. v. EPA, supra.*

Our conclusion that the regulations incorporating the bubble concept must be rejected as inconsistent with the language of the Act is reinforced when we consider the purpose of the Clean Air Act and Section 111, the confusion generated by the present regulations, and the weakness of EPA's arguments in favor of the bubble concept.

"[T]he goal of the Clean Air Act," as EPA admits in its brief, "is to *enhance* air quality and not merely to *maintain* it."

EPA's main argument in support of its regulations is that its version of the bubble concept is necessary to provide flexibility in applying the NSPSs to modified facilities because the cost of bringing *existing* facilities into compliance with NSPSs is allegedly much greater than the cost of bringing *new* facilities into compliance. This argument does not survive analysis. The record does not show that any version of the bubble concept is needed to provide flexibility to the operators of existing facilities.

[18]Generally speaking, "sources" are entire plants, while "facilities" are identifiable pieces of process equipment or individual components which when taken together would comprise a source.* * *

* * *We remand to the EPA for further proceedings not inconsistent with this opinion.

LEVENTHAL, Circuit Judge, concurring:

As the majority opinion points out, the manner in which the statute defines the terms "new source" and "stationary source" does not provide leeway for the agency to assign different meaning to "stationary source" depending on whether construction or modification is in question.

However, the statute does not totally prohibit the agency from making appropriate distinctions based on the realistic difference between new construction and modification. While costs may not be considered in determining whether a facility will be subject to an NSPS, as the bubble concept would have done, they may be considered in determining the level at which a standard should be set, and how it should be formulated.

---

e. *Hazardous Air Pollutants*

(1) *Emission Standards.* Under Section 112, EPA is required to publish a list of hazardous air pollutants and then establish emission standards with "an ample margin of safety to protect the public health" for each such pollutant. A "hazardous air pollutant" is defined in that section as "an air pollutant to which no ambient air quality standard is applicable and which . . . may cause, or contribute to, an increase in mortality or an increase in serious irreversible, or incapacitating reversible, illness. . . ." Until 1977 the only substances contained on EPA's list of hazardous substances were mercury, beryllium, asbestos, vinyl chloride and benzene. In the 1977 Amendments, Congress directed EPA to conduct studies to determine whether radioactive pollutants, cadmium, arsenic and polycyclic organic matter emissions endanger public health and, if appropriate, to add such substances to the list of hazardous substances.

ADAMO WRECKING CO.
v.
UNITED STATES

434 U.S. 275 (1978)

Mr. Justice REHNQUIST delivered the opinion of the Court.

The Clean Air Act authorizes the Administrator of the Environmental Protection Agency to promulgate "emission standards" for hazardous air pollutants "at the level which in his judgment provides an ample margin of safety to protect the public health." § 112(b)(1)(B), 84 Stat 1685, 42 USC § 1857c–7(b)(1)(B) [42 USCS § 1857c–7(b)(1)(B)]. The emission of an air pollutant in violation of an applicable emission standard is prohibited by § 112(c)(1)(B) of the Act, 42 USC § 1857c–7(c)(1)(B) [42 USCS § 1857c–7(c)(1)(B).] The knowing violation of the latter section, in turn, subjects the violator to fine and imprisonment under the provisions of § 113(c)(1)(C) of the Act, 42 USC § 1857c–8(c)(1)(C) (1970 ed Supp V) [42 USCS § 1857c–8(c)(1)(C)]. The final piece in this statutory puzzle is §307(b) of the Act, 84 Stat 1708, 42 USC § 1857h–5(b) (1970 ed Supp V) [42 USCS § 1857h–5(b)], which provides in pertinent part:

> "(1) A petition for review of action of the Administrator in promulgating . . . any emission standard under section 112 . . . may be filed only in the United States Court of Appeals for the District of Columbia. . . . Any such petition shall be filed within 30 days from the date of such promulgation or approval, or after such date if such petition is based solely on grounds arising after such 30th day.
>
> "(2) Action of the Administrator with respect to which review could have been obtained under paragraph (1) shall not be subject to judical review in civil or criminal proceedings for enforcement."

It is within this legislative matrix that the present criminal prosecution arose.

Petitioner was indicted in the United States District Court for the Eastern District of Michigan for violation of § 112(c)(1)(B). The indictment alleged that petitioner, while engaged in the demolition of a building in Detroit, failed to comply with 40 CFR § 61.22(d)(2)(i) (1975). That regulation, described in its caption as a "National Emission Standard for Asbestos," specifies procedures to be followed in connection with building demolitions, but does not by its terms limit emissions of asbestos which occur during the course of a demolition. The District Court granted petitioner's motion to dismiss the indictment on the ground that no violation of § 112(c)(1)(B), necessary to establish criminal liability under § 113(c)(1)(C), had been alleged, because the cited regulation was not an "emission standard" within the meaning of § 112(c). The United States Court of Appeals for the Sixth Circuit reversed, 545 F2d 1 (1976), holding that Congress had in § 307(b) precluded petitioner from questioning in a criminal proceeding whether a regulation ostensibily promulgated under § 112(b)(1)(B) was in fact an emission standard. We granted certiorari, 430 US 953, 51 L Ed 2d 802, 97 S Ct 1596 (1977), and we now reverse.

I

We do not intend to make light of a difficult question of statutory interpretation when we say that the basic question in this case may be phrased: "When is an emission standard not an emission standard?"

Because § 307(b) expressly applies only to "emission standards," we must still inquire as to the validity of the Government's underlying assumption that the Administrator's mere designation of a regulation as an "emission standard" is sufficient to foreclose any further inquiry in a criminal prosecution under § 113(c)(1)(C) of the Act. For the reasons hereafter stated, we hold that one such as respondent who is charged with a criminal violation under the Act may defend on the ground that the "emission standard" which he is charged with having violated was not an "emission standard" within the contemplation of Congress when it employed that term, even though the "emission standard" in question has not been previously reviewed under the provisions of § 307(b) of the Act.

II

The statutory basis for imposition of criminal liability under subchapter I of the Act, under which this indictment was brought, is § 113(c)(1), 84 Stat 1687, as amended, 42 USC § 1857c–8(c)(1) (1970 ed and supp V) 42 USCS § 1857c–8(c)(1)]:

"(c)(1) Any person who knowingly—

"(A) violates any requirement of an applicable implementation plan (i) during any period of Federally assumed enforcement, or (ii) more than 30 days after having been notified by the Administrator under subsection (a)(1) that such person is violating such requirement, or

"(B) violates or fails or refuses to comply with any order issued by the Administrator under subsection (a), or

"(C) violates section 111(e), section 112(c), or section 119(g)

"shall be punished by a fine of not more than $25,000 per day of violation, or by imprisonment for not more than one year, or by both. If the conviction is for a violation committed after the first conviction of such person under this paragraph, punishment shall be by a fine of not more than $50,000 per day of violation, or by imprisonment for not more than two years, or by both."

Each of the three separate subsections in the quoted language creates criminal offenses. The first of them, subsection (A), deals with violations of applicable implementation plans after receipt of notice of such violation. Under § 307(b)(1), judicial review of the Administrator's action in approving or promulgating an implementation plan is not restricted to the Court of Appeals for the District of Columbia Circuit, but may be had "in the United States Court of Appeals for the appropriate circuit." But § 307(b)(2) does provide that the validity of such plans may not be reviewed in the criminal proceeding itself.

Subsection (C), which we discuss before turning to subsection (B), provides criminal penalties for violations of three separate sections of the Act: § 111(e), 42 USC § 1857c–6(e) [42 USCS § 1857c–6(e)], which prohibits operation of new stationary sources in violation of "standards of performance" promulgated by the Administrator; § 112(c), which is the offense charged in this case; and § 119(g), 88 Stat 254, 42 USC § 1857c–10(g) (1970 ed Supp V) [42 USCS § 1857c–10(g)], which requires compliance with an assortment of administrative requirements.* * *

III

The conclusion we draw from [an] excursion into the complexities of the criminal sanctions provided by the Act are several. First, Congress has not chosen to prescribe *either* civil or criminal sanctions for violations of *every* rule, regulation, or order issued by the Administrator. Second, Congress, as might be expected, has imposed *civil* liability for a wider range of violations of the orders of the Administrator than those for which it has imposed *criminal* liability. Third, even where Congress has imposed criminal liability for the violation of an order of the Administrator, it has not uniformly precluded judicial challenge to the order as a defense in the criminal proceeding. Fourth, although Congress has applied the preclusion provisions of § 307(b)(2) to implementation plans approved by the Administrator, and it has in § 113(c)(1)(A) provided criminal penalties for violations of those plans, it has nonetheless required, under normal circumstances, that a violation continue for a period of 30 days after receipt of notice of the violation from the Administrator before the criminal sanction may be imposed.

These conclusions in no way detract from the fact that Congress *has* precluded judicial review of an "emission standard" in the court in which the criminal proceeding for the violation of the standard is brought. Indeed, the conclusions heighten the importance of determining what it was that Congress meant by an "emission standard," since a violation of *that* standard is subject to the most stringent criminal liability imposed by § 113(c)(1) of the Act: Not only is the Administrator's promulgation of the standard not subject to judicial review in the criminal proceeding, but no prior notice of violation from the Administrator is required as a condition for criminal liability. Since Congress chose to attach these stringent sanctions to the violation of an emission standard, in contrast to the violation of various other kinds of orders that might be issued by the Administrator, it is crucial to determine whether the Administrator's mere designation of a regulation as an "emission standard" is conclusive as to its character.

The stringency of the penalty imposed by Congress lends substance to petitioner's contention that Congress envisioned a particular type of regulation when it spoke of an "emission standard." The fact that Congress dealt more leniently, either in terms of liability, of notice, or of available defenses, with other infractions of the Administrator's orders suggests that it attached a peculiar importance to compliance with "emission standards." All of this leads us to conclude that Congress intended, within broad limits, that "emission standards" be regulations of a certain type, and that it did not empower the Administrator, after the manner of Humpty Dumpty in Through the Looking-Glass, to make a regulation an "emission standard" by his mere designation.

The statutory scheme supports the conclusion that § 307(b)(2), in precluding judicial review of the validity of emission standards, does not relieve the Government of the duty of proving, in a prosecution under § 113(c)(1)(C), that the regulation allegedly violated is an emission standard. Here, the District Court properly undertook to resolve that issue.

The District Court did not presume to judge the wisdom of the regulation or to consider the adequacy of the procedures which led to its promulgation, but merely concluded that it was not an emission standard.

In sum, a survey of the totality of the statutory scheme does not compel agreement with the Government's contention that Congress intended that the Administrator's designation of a regulation as an emission standard should be conclusive in a criminal prosecution. At the very least, it may be said that the issue is subject to some doubt. Under these circumstances, we adhere to the familiar rule that, "where there is ambiguity in a criminal statute, doubts are resolved in favor of the defendant."* * *

We conclude, therefore, that a federal court in which a criminal prosecution under § 113(c)(1)(C) of the Clean Air Act is brought may determine whether or not the regulation which the defendant is alleged to have violated is an "emission standard" within the meaning of the Act.

* * *

IV

It remains to be seen whether the District Court reached the correct conclusion with regard to the regulation here in question. In the Act, Congress has given a substantial indication of the intended meaning of the term "emission standard." Section 112 on its face distinguishes between emission standard and the techniques to be utilized in achieving those standards. Under § 112(c)(1)(B)(ii), the Administrator is empowered temporarily to exempt certain facilities from the burden of compliance with an emission standard, "if he finds that such period is necessary for the installation of controls." In specified circumstances, the President, under § 112(c)(2), has the same power, "if he finds that the technology to implement such standards is not available." Section 112(b)(2) authorizes the Administrator to issue information on "pollution control techniques."

[7a] Most clearly supportive of petitioner's position that a standard was intended to be a quantitative limit on emissions is this provision of § 112(b)(1)(B): "The Administrator shall establish any such standard *at the level* which in his judgment provides an ample margin of safety to protect the public health from such hazardous air pollutant." (Emphasis added.) All these provisions lend force to the conclusion that a standard is a quantitative "level" to be attained by use of "techniques," "controls," and "technology." This conclusion is fortified by recent amendments to the Act, by which Congress authorized the Administrator to promulgate a "design, equipment, work practice, or operational standard" when "it is not feasible to prescribe or enforce an emission standard." Clean Air Act Amendments of 1977, Pub L 95–95, § 110.91 Stat 703.

This distinction, now endorsed by Congress, between "work practice standards" and "emission standards" first appears in the Administrator's own account of the development of this regulation. Although the Administrator has contended that a "work practice standard" is just another type of emission standard, the history of this regulation demonstrates that he chose to regulate work practices only when it became clear he could not regulate emissions. The regulation as originally proposed would have prohibited all visible emissions of asbestos during the course of demolitions. 36 Fed Reg 23242 (1971). In adopting the final form of the regulation, the Administrator concluded "that the no visible emission requirement would prohibit repair or demolition in many situations, since it would be impracticable, if not impossible, to do such work without creating visible emissions." 38 Fed Reg 8821 (1973). Therefore the Administrator chose to "specif[y] certain work practices" instead. Ibid.

[8a, 9a] The Government concedes that, prior to the 1977 Amendments, the statute was ambiguous with regard to whether a work-practice standard was properly classified as an emission standard, but argues that this Court should defer to the Administrator's construction of the Act. Brief for United States 32, and circumstances, in this case the 1977 Amendments to the Clean Air Act tend to undercut the administrative construction. The Senate Report reiterated its "strong preference for numerical emission limitations," but endorsed the addition of § 112(e) to the Act to allow the use of work-practice standards "in a very few limited cases." S Rep No. 95–127, p 44 (1977). Although the Committee agreed that the Amendments would authorize the regulation involved here, it refrained from endorsing the Administrator's view that the regulation had previously been authorized as an emission standard under § 112(c). The clear distinction drawn in § 112(e) between work-practice standards and emission standards practically forecloses any such inference, Cf. Red Lion Broadcasting Co. v. FCC, 395 US 367, 380–381, 23 L Ed 2d 371 89 S Ct 1794 (1969).

For all of the foregoing reasons, we conclude that the work-practice standard involved here was not an emission standard. The District Court's order dismissing the indictment was therefore proper, and the judgment of the Court of Appeals is reversed.

The provision of the 1977 Amendments referred to by the Supreme Court in the *Adamo* case follows:

EMISSION STANDARDS FOR HAZARDOUS AIR POLLUTANTS

Section 112 of the Clean Air Act is amended by adding the following new subsection at the end thereof:

"(e)(1) For purposes of this section, if in the judgment of the Administrator, it is not feasible to prescribe or enforce an emission standard for control of a hazardous air pollutant or pollutants, he may instead promulgate a design, equipment, work practice, or operational standard, or combination thereof, which in his judgment is adequate to protect the public health from such pollutant or pollutants with an ample margin of safety. In the event the Administrator promulgates a design, or equipment standard under this subsection, he shall include as part of such standard such requirements as will assure the proper operation and maintenance of any such element of design or equipment.

"(2) For the purpose of this subsection, the phrase 'not feasible to prescribe or enforce an emission standard' means any situation in which the Administrator determines that (A) a hazardous pollutant or pollutants cannot be emitted through a conveyance designed and constructed to emit or capture such pollutant, or that any requirement for, or use of, such a conveyance would be inconsistent with any Federal, State, or local law, or (B) the application of measurement methodology to a particular class of sources is not practicable due to technological or economic limitations.

* * *

The Administrator shall establish any such standard at the level which in his judgment provides an ample margin of safety to protect the public health from such hazardous air pollutant.

---

(2) *Imminent Hazard Emergency Powers.* Section 303 of the Clean Air Act gives EPA the power to seek an injunction from a federal district court to stop emissions that "constitute an imminent and substantial endangerment" to health. The issue that will arise when such an injunction is sought is whether the circumstances of the case constitute an **imminent and substantial endangerment**. No decisions have interpreted the meaning of those words under the Clean Air Act. However, a similar issue has arisen under the Federal Insecticide, Fungicide and Rodenticide Act, where the Secretary of Agriculture is given power to suspend the registration of an insecticide "to prevent an imminent hazard to the public." In *Environmental Defense Fund v. Ruckelshaus*, 429 F.2d 615 (D.C. Cir. 1970) the court said that a hazard may be "imminent" even if its impact will not be apparent for many years and that the most important element of an "imminent hazard" is a serious threat to the public health.

2. REGULATION OF MOBILE SOURCES

Motor vehicles cause over 40 percent, by weight, of all the air pollution in the country. Approximately one-half of all of the hyrdrocarbons in the air *come from motor vehicle emissions*; two thirds of all carbon monoxide and nitrogen oxide emissions, as well as over ninety percent of lead bearing particles, *come from motor vehicles*. Most of these emissions come from the exhaust and can be reduced by engine modifications that cause more efficient combustion and afterburning devices, such as catalytic converters, that can reduce the emission of carbon monoxide and hydrocarbons even further.

The system of regulation of motor vehicles included in the Clean Air Act is composed of two parts: (*1*) new car emission standards and (*2*) fuel additive limitations.

a. *New Car Emission Standards*

The primary method by which Congress sought to reduce air pollution created by mobile sources was to require automobile manufacturers to redesign their products to reduce emissions of each of the pollutants by a specified percentage by a specified period of time. In the 1970 Clean Air Act, Congress prescribed a 90% reduction in hydrocarbons by 1975, a 90% reduction in carbon monoxide by 1976 and a 90% reduction in nitrogen oxides by 1976. After the energy crisis became apparent in 1974, Congress adopted the Energy Supply and Environmental Coordination Act, in which the emission objectives were lowered to a 75% reduction in hydrocarbons and carbon monoxide by 1977 and a 75% reduction in nitrogen oxides by 1978. When it became apparent that American automakers were not going to be able to meet these emission standards by the specified dates Congress postponed the deadlines again in the 1977 Amendments to a 90% reduction in hydrocarbons by 1981 and an 80% reduction in carbon monoxide by 1980. If EPA determines that it is not technologically feasible for the auto industry to meet the 80% reduction by 1980 it may postpone the deadline for an additional two years. The 1977 Amendments also provide a waiver of four years of the nitrogen oxide standard for diesel engines and other innovative technologies.

In 1975 most American automakers began to use the **catalytic converter** to reduce exhaust emissions of hydrocarbons and carbon monoxide. There are several disadvantages of this technique: it increases the emission of sulfuric acid and nitrogen oxides and loses it effectiveness after about 50,000 miles of use. In addition it can be rendered ineffective by the use of gasoline containing lead.

b. *Unleaded Gas Requirement*

In the early 1920's it was discovered that when lead "antiknock" compounds are added to gasoline the fuel's octane rating increases substantially and results in greater automobile engine efficiency. By the 1970s about 90 percent of gasoline made in the United States contained lead additives. When catalytic converters came into widespread use in the mid-1970s, EPA required a separate grade of lead-free gasoline to protect the catalytic converter made ineffective by lead in gasoline. In *Amoco Oil Co. v. EPA*, 501 F.2d 722 (D.C. Cir. 1974) this regulation was upheld.

Section 211(c)(1)(A) of the Clean Air Act authorizes the EPA to regulate **gasoline additives** whose emission products "will endanger the public health or welfare." Pursuant to this authorization EPA determined that the automobile emissions caused by leaded gasoline present a significant risk of harm to the public and promulgated regulations that phased out the use of lead in gas over a period of time. EPA cannot act under Section 211 until after "considering all relevant medical and scientific evidence available to [them] including consideration of other technologically or economically feasible means of achieving emission standards." The EPA regulations of the lead content of gas were upheld in *Ethyl Corp. v. EPA*, 541 F.2d 1 (D.C.Cir. 1976).

In a lengthy and carefully written opinion by Circuit Judge J. Skelly Wright, the court reviewed the statute and the evidence and concluded that there was sufficient evidence for the EPA Administrator to determine that automobile emissions caused by leaded gasoline present a significant risk of harm to justify the EPA regulations.

D. State Regulation: State Implementation Plans

The Clean Air Act contemplates a system of joint control of air pollution by the federal and state governments. Under the Act each state is required to prepare implementation plans to achieve the ambient air quality standards adopted by the federal government. The original 1970 Clean Air Act provided, in Section 110(a)(2), for the attainment of primary standards within 3 years and the attainment of secondary standards within a reasonable time. EPA was authorized to review **state implementation plans** and to prescribe rules for the preparation of those plans. Those rules are contained in 40 C.F.R. 51 et seq.

Included in these rules is a description of each of the elements of a State Implementation Plan (SIP). Every plan must contain the following elements:[1]

1. Legal Authority

The plan must show that the state has the necessary legal authority to prepare and implement the plan. More specifically the plan must provide evidence that there is legal authority to:

a. Adopt emission standards and other measures necessary to attain and maintain the national air quality standards.
b. Enforce all applicable laws, including the ability to seek injunctions.

[1]Material in this section is derived from, EPA, *A Citizen's Guide to Clean Air.*

c. Take emergency action to abate pollution which substantially endangers human health.
d. Obtain any information needed to determine whether sources are in compliance with applicable laws, including inspection and record-keeping requirements.
e. Prevent construction, modification or operation of any stationary source at any location where its emission will prevent the attainment of maintenance of air quality standards.
f. Require stationary sources to install, maintain and use emission monitoring devices and to periodically report the amounts of emissions.

2. CONTROL STRATEGY

The SIP must adopt a **"control strategy"** that includes, among other things, the following components:

a. Emission limitations.
b. Economic incentives or disincentives such as emission charges or taxes.
c. Closing or relocation of residential, commercial or industrial facilities.
d. Changes in schedules or methods of operation of stationary sources.
e. Periodic inspection of motor vehicles.
f. Installation of emission control devices.
g. Measures to reduce motor traffic such as commuter toll charges, gas rationing, parking restrictions, staggered hours.
h. Expansion of mass transportation.
i. Land use or transportation control measures. However, in the 1977 Amendments, Congress provided that a SIP cannot be rejected because of its failure to contain controls on indirect sources of pollution Sec. 110(a)(5)(A)(i).

3. COMPLIANCE SCHEDULES

Every SIP should provide for **compliance schedules** prepared by each source of pollution within a control region and containing a detailed, step-by-step schedule of measures it will take to bring it within compliance of the objectives of the plan. This schedule must be negotiated with each major source of pollution and once negotiated and agreed upon is to be legally enforceable. The rules also contain prescribed procedures for variances and exemptions from the compliance schedules.

4. EMERGENCY EPISODE PROCEDURES

Every SIP should also contain, in appropriate control regions, a contingency plan covering the emergency measures to be taken when there is a liklihood that pollution will reach levels that constitute "imminent and substantial endangerment to the health of persons." A potential emergency is divided into three stages:

First stage—"Alert"—When adverse meterological conditions and pollutant concentrations approach levels at which preventive action becomes necessary.

Second stage—"Warning"—If the situation continues to deteriorate.

Third Stage—"Emergency"—When air quality continues to "degrade toward a level of significant harm to the health of persons."

The contingency plan must also specify the control measures to be taken at each stage, including such measures as prohibition or restriction on motor vehicle traffic; curtailment of retail, commercial or industrial activities; prohibition or limit on incinerators; and combustion of specified fuels.

5. Surveillance Systems

Every SIP must contain two different surveillance systems:

Ambient air surveillance systems. These systems monitor pollution levels in the ambient air. There must be at least one sampling site in each control region located in the area of estimated maximum concentration of each pollutant.

Individual source surveillance systems. Every owner or operator of a stationary source must maintain records and periodically report on the nature and amounts of emissions.

6. Review of New Sources

The SIP must contain legally enforceable procedures that will enable the state to prevent the construction or modification of any stationary source that would, directly or indirectly, interfere with attainment or maintenance of the air quality standards.

7. Resources

The plan must describe the manpower and funds necessary to carry out the plan for five years and for additional 1-, 3- and 5-year intervals. Manpower needs must include administrative, engineering, technical and enforcement services.

8. Interstate Cooperation

The plan must provide for exchange of all necessary information among agencies in each control region whose boundaries lie in more than one state. This information includes data on emissions, air quality, proposed new industrial sites, etc.

9. Public Participation

Public Hearings. Public hearings must be held in each state before the state adopts an implementation plan and sends it to EPA for approval.

Public Reporting. States are required to gather emission data from individual sources, correlate this information with the standards established under the Act and make this information available to the public.

Under the Clean Air Act, the EPA administrator is required to reject a SIP if he finds that the plan will fail to meet all of the requirements of the Act, including the requirement to meet ambient air quality standards. *Bunker Hill Co. v. EPA*, below, illustrates the complexity of this decision in a situation where the EPA administrator determined that there was an alternative technological method that should have been prescribed in the SIP to abate a source of pollution.

BUNKER HILL CO.
v.
E.P.A.

572 F.2d 1286 (1977)

SNEED, Circuit Judge:

Petitioner challenges the actions of the Environmental Protection Agency (EPA) in rejecting portions of the State of Idaho's implementation plan under the Clean Air Act, 42 U.S.C.A. §§ 1857, et seq. (Supp. 1977), and substituting therefor its own regulations. The rejected portions of the Idaho implementation plan deal with the control of sulfur dioxide (SO_2) from the Idaho plant of petitioner. The petitioner's challenge relies on several grounds. While we find in favor of the Administrator on various legal and procedural issues, we remand this proceeding to the EPA for further consideration of the technological feasibility of certain modifications of petitioner's smelter operations which would be required by the substituted regulations.

I.
History of the Case.

Bunker Hill's Kellogg, Idaho operations include lead and zinc smelters that emit substantial amounts of SO_2 gas. Some of the So_2 gas presently is vented directly to the atmosphere; the remainder is treated in three acid plants—two servicing the zinc operations, and the third handling the lead smelter. There is no dispute that, as presently operated, Bunker Hill's Idaho plant is not meeting the federal ambient air quality standards for SO_2.[1] The primary issue before us is what modifications Bunker

[1]The Clean Air Act provides for pollution control through a joint effort of the state and federal governments. Under the Act, it is the responsibility of each state to formulate implementation plans (such as the one under review here) that guarantee the attainment within the state of ambient air quality standards set by the EPA. 42 U.S.C.A. § 1857c–5(a)(2)(A) (Supp. 1977). The Administrator is directed by the Act to set two types of ambient air quality

Hill must make in its operations in order to satisfy the requirements of the Clean Air Act. To understand this issue the administrative proceedings culminating in this challenge will be outlined and thereafter the focus will be upon the technological feasibility of the control technology made necessary by EPA's substituted regulations. Our disposition of this challenge will conclude with a discussion of certain other issues raised by petitioner and with our instructions pertaining to the procedure on remand to the EPA.

On January 3, 1975, the Idaho Department of Health and Welfare (IDHW) adopted a regulation requiring Bunker Hill to "capture" 72 percent of its SO_2 emissions;[2] the IDHW had decided, after lengthy hearings, that this percentage emission control was the maximum percentage feasible under currently available technology.[3] This level of emission control would be achieved through a series of specific emission limitations: (1) a 4000 parts per million (ppm) SO_2 limitation on the emissions from each of Bunker Hill's acid plants and from its zinc plant main stack, based on eight-hour averages; (ii) a 100 tons per day limitation on emissions from the lead plant main stack; and (iii) a 1200 tons per week limitation on emissions from the entire smelting complex.

Since even this level of emission control would not meet the ambient air quality standards, the Idaho plan also would require Bunker Hill to supplement its control program with whatever dispersion enhancement techniques[4] prove necessary to

---

standards. "Primary" ambient air quality standards are to be set "the attainment and maintenance of which in the judgment of the Administrator, . . . and allowing an adequate margin of safety, are requisite to protect the public health." 42 U.S.C.A. § 1857c–4(b)(1) (Supp. 1977). Generally, the Administrator will state the primary standards both in terms of a yearly maximum average and in terms of a maximum concentration of pollutant during a limited number of hours that cannot be exceeded more than once per year. The Administrator is also to set "secondary" standards "the attainment and maintenance of which in the judgment of the Administrator . . . [are] requisite to protect the public welfare from any known or anticipated adverse effects associated with the presence of such air pollutants in the ambient air." 42 U.S.C.A. § 1857c–4(b)(2) (Supp. 1977). In most cases, although not all, the secondary standards will be higher and more difficult to attain than the primary standards. This is reflected in the provisions of the Act requiring the primary standards to be met as expeditiously as practicable and in no case later than three years after approval of the state implementation plan, but requiring secondary standards to be met only at some "reasonable time" thereafter. 42 U.S.C.A. § 1857c–5(a)(2)(A) (Supp. 1977).

[2]There are two basic forms of pollution abatement techniques. The first, "emission controls," *limit the amount* of SO_2 emitted from the pollution source; thus, an "emission limitation" constricts the amount of pollutant that a source can actually emit to the atmosphere. It is this form of abatement technique that is referred to when one speaks of "capturing" a certain percentage of SO_2 emissions. The second set of abatement techniques, "dispersion enhancement techniques," do not reduce the concentration of pollutants emitted, but instead *increase the dispersion* of the pollutants through the atmosphere away from high-concentration areas and toward lower-concentration areas.

[3]As discussed *infra*, polluting sources must use the maximum level of emission control that is economically and technologically feasible in meeting the federal ambient air quality standards. Dispersion enhancement techniques are to assume a secondary role in attaining the standards, to be used only where the maximum emission control still will not guarantee that the standards will be met. *See* 41 Fed.Reg. 7450; cases cited *infra* at pp. 1292–1293. Thus, a key issue in this case is what level of emission control is the maximum feasible under current technology.

[4]There are two basic types of dispersion enhancement techniques. "Supplementary control systems" involve staggering the hours of operation of the polluting facilities, with the facilities operating more extensively when meteorological conditions are favorable to dispersion, and sometimes even temporarily closing when meteorological conditions are unfavorable. The

meet these standards. Bunker Hill would be held responsible for violations in the Kellogg Valley of any federal ambient air quality standard, although, in the case of the primary annual standard, a 30-day investigation period would be provided for purposes of determining whether other undetected and uncontrolled sources might have been the actual cause of the violation, in which case Bunker Hill would not be held liable. Finally, Bunker Hill would be required to conduct reasearch and development aimed at improving emission control techniques; as these techniques became feasible, Bunker Hill's emission limitations would be tightened.

The EPA refused to approve Idaho's proposed emission limitations and instead substituted standards that would guarantee 82 percent control. On the basis of a study commissioned by EPA of Bunker Hill's operation, together with other evidence, the EPA held that 82 percent, rather than 72 percent, was the maximum level of control technologically and economically feasible for Bunker Hill. The EPA study (prepared for EPA by Mr. Tim Browder, an expert in SO_2 control technology—hereinafter referred to as the Browder Study) contended that various efficiency problems presently plaguing Bunker Hill's control process could be solved by modifying Bunker Hill's acid plants. In particular, the Browder Study argued that adding sulfur burners to the acid plants would guarantee sustained autothermality.[6]* * * Since even 82 percent control would not guarantee attainment of the air quality standards, dispersion enhancement techniques would again be required. As under the Idaho provisions, Bunker Hill would be held accountable for any violations of the federal ambient air quality standards; however, the EPA made no provision for a 30-day investigation period. Again, Bunker Hill would be required to carry on a research and development program with the objective of raising over the years the level of constant emission control.

Bunker Hill focuses its attack on the EPA's determination that Bunker Hill can feasibly achieve 82 percent emission control. First, it argues that the EPA was bound by the contrary conclusion of the IDHW that only a 72 percent control level is feasible. Second, even assuming that the EPA was free to reconsider the question of the maximum feasible control level, Bunker Hill argues that the EPA's determination was "arbitrary and capricious" and was marred by various procedural irregularities. Bunker Hill also attacks the EPA's decision to eliminate the 30-day review period provided for in the original Idaho regulations.

Our study of the administrative record cast considerable doubt on whether the sulfur burner system proposed in the Browder Study, a necessary element in EPA's proposed 82 percent emission control standard, is indeed technologically feasible. In particular, Bunker Hill's principal expert witness contended that sulfur burners could not track, or be coordinated with, the wide fluctuations in SO_2 concentration that plague Bunker Hill's smelter gases. Mr. Browder failed to respond fully and satisfactorily.* * *

Despite this clarification in dealing with a technical subject with respect to which we are not experts and ever mindful of our limited authority in reviewing the Administrator's actions, we nonetheless reluctantly are compelled, on the basis of the record as augmented, to conclude that the Administrator has not "exercised a reasoned discretion" in concluding that the Browder sulfur burner proposals, and hence an 82 percent emission control standard, are technologically feasible.* * *

---

other major dispersion technique is tall stacks, which by emitting pollutants at higher altitudes disperse the pollutants over a wider area.

[6]As defined *infra* at p. 1295, an acid plant operates "autothermally" when the heat necessary to efficiently convert the SO_2 into So_3 (and ultimately into sufuric acid) is provided by the transformation process itself.

II.
Maximum Feasible Control Technology.

The importance of the technological feasibility of the Browder sulfur burner proposal has its source in the fact that cases in this and other circuits have established that the national ambient air quality standards must be met, to the maximum extent possible, by constant emission controls (such as acid plants augmented or not by sulfur burners); dispersion enhancement techniques (such as tall stacks) are to be used only in a supplemental role where necessary to meet the air quality standards. [Citations Omitted]

The Clean Air Act, as interpreted by these cases, requires pollution sources to achieve the highest emission control level that is technologically and economically feasible. *Id.* Conversely, the EPA cannot require a level of control technology that is technologically and economically infeasible. Thus, if the Browder sulfur burner proposals are technologically feasible, their use is required because only then will constant emission controls be in use to the maximum extent possible. If not, their use cannot be required.* * *

A. *EPA's Ability to Reexamine State Determinations of Feasibility.*

Bunker Hill, however, argues that the technological feasibility of constant emission controls is fixed by the Idaho state plan. Thus, it insists that EPA cannot require the implementation of the Browder sulfur burner proposals because Idaho, by not requiring their implementation, has conclusively established their technological infeasibility. We disagree.

The Clean Air Act requires that the Administrator disapprove any state implementation plan that he "determines" fails to meet any of the requirements of 42 U.S.C.A. § 1857c–5(a)(2) (Supp.1977). One of these requirements is the maximum feasible use of constant control systems. No argument has been suggested for why, on the one hand, the Administrator can examine some state findings in reviewing a state implementation plan (e. g., a finding that the plan assures that attainment of the various ambient air quality standards) but, on the other hand, be bound by state findings of feasibility or infeasibility. The Clean Air Act requires that the Administrator "determine" that a state plan meets *all* of the requirements of section 1857c–5(a)(2) before approving the plan, and one of these requirements is the maximum feasible use of constant control systems. Bunker Hill's reading would reduce EPA's approval of the Idaho implementation plan to a rubber stamp, a result which, we are certain, Congress did not intend.[12] To the extent that the recent district court opinion in *Kennecott Copper Corp. v. Train*, 424 F.Supp. 1217, 1231 (D.Nev.1976) (holding that the Administrator was bound by a state finding of economic infeasibility) suggests to the contrary, we believe it to be in error.

B. *Review of the EPA's Feasibility Findings.*

Although EPA is not bound by Idaho's determination of technological feasibility, its rejection of the state plan must not be "arbitrary, capricious, an abuse of

[12]*Cf. Union Electric Co. v. EPA*, 427 U.S. 246, 96 S.Ct. 2518, 49 L.Ed.2d 474 (1976). While the Court notes that "[p]erhaps the most important forum for consideration of claims of economic and technological infeasibility is before the state agency formulating the implementation plan," *id.* at 266, 96 S.Ct. at 2529, it goes on to hold: "Economic and technological factors may be relevant in determining whether the minimum conditions are met. Thus, the Administrator may consider whether it is economically or technologically possible for the state plan to proceed more rapidly than it does. If he determines that it is, he may reject the plan as not moving 'as expeditiously as practicable' in achieving primary standards or as failing to attain secondary standards within a 'reasonable time.'"

discretion, or otherwise not in accordance with law."* * * It is clear that, before requiring 82 percent control, the Administrator was required to find that this level of emission control *is* economically and technologically feasible *for Bunker Hill* to achieve. In reaching this determination, the Administrator must have exercised "reasoned discretion."

The Administrator's finding must have been "based on a consideration of the relevant factors" and not "a clear error of judgment."

The technological feasibility of the EPA standards for Bunker Hill is dependent on a finding that sulfur burners are technologically capable of curing the problems of fluctuating SO_2 concentrations facing Bunker Hill. The feasibility of Browder's sulfur burner proposal could have been established in two ways. First, EPA could have located contemporary examples of sulfur burners being used to cure a similar problem in a similar context. Second, even if the proposed sulfur burner system was not in current use, EPA could have relied on expert testimony demonstrating that sulfur burners under present technology can cure Bunker Hill's SO_2 concentration problem. This second method of establishing technological feasibility, however, carries a "significant burden of proof. The demonstration of feasibility must not be based on a "subjective understanding of the problem or 'crystal ball inquiry.'" * * *The expert testimony must clearly demonstrate that the technology is available and must answer cogent criticisms of opposing experts. The proposed technology must not be "at a level that is purely theoretical or experimental." * * * On the basis of the record before us, we cannot say that the Browder sulfur burner proposal is other than "purely theoretical or experimental."

1. *Bunker Hill's Problem.*

To validate this view it is necessary that the manner in which Bunker Hill operates be described in some detail. Its problem fundamentally is whether, given its operational necessities, the 2600 ppm acid plant limitation can be met. A significant percentage of current SO_2 emissions from Bunker Hill's lead and zinc smelters is controlled through the use of their three acid plants. These acid plants convert SO_2 into SO_3 and ultimately into sulfuric acid,which can either be sold or neutralized. A necessary element to this catalytic process is heat, which can be provided, at least in part, by circulating back the heat given off by the transformation process itself. The more concentrated the gas being converted the more heat will be given off by the transformation process. If the gas stream being emitted into the acid plant has a sufficient SO_2 concentration, then the heat given off by the transformation process will be sufficient in itself to run the transformation process almost indefinitely. This condition of operation is known as autothermality.

At Bunker Hill, there are frequent periods during which the three acid plants cannot operate autothermally. During these periods, either SO_2 must be vented from the smelters directly to the atmosphere, or the acid plants must be operated at abnormally low efficiencies (resulting in emissions significantly greater than 2600 ppm). None of Bunker Hill's three acid plants can achieve autothermality immediately upon start-up of operations because the gas initially emitted from the operations is very low in SO_2 concentration. These difficulties particularly trouble the acid plant servicing the lead sintering process (hereinafter referred to as the "lead-smelter acid plant"). The sintering machine conveyor belt is stopped and started several times a day. During the stopped period, which is typically one or two hours, lead concentrate remaining on the belt continues to smolder, producing a low level of SO_2 emission. When the sintering machine in restarted, a strong but widely fluctuating SO_2 gas stream is produced that can continue for extended periods of time.* * *

EPA does not dispute the significance of these efficiency problems, at least with respect to the lead-smelter acid plant.* * *

However, on the basis of the Browder Study, EPA contends that these problems can be solved and a more efficient operation obtained by various modifications in the acid plants, in particular the addition of sulfur burners.

2. *Feasibility of Sulfur Burners.*

The Original Record:

The Browder Study concluded that the problem of fluctuating SO_2 content could be successfully overcome by the use of sulfur burners.* * * Bunker Hill's expert, Mr. J. R. Donavan, strongly disagreed in a series of rebuttal comments. In particular, according to Donovan, sulfur burners

> "can only be used where by-product SO_2 gas streams contain a relatively low concentration of SO_2 which may vary to some small degree, but typically not to the extent experienced at Bunker Hill's facilities. The major purpose of using auxiliary sulfur burning facilities in such plants is to increase SO_2 concentration to levels which can be handled readily in sulfuric acid plants and/or to increase sulfuric acid production to meet market needs."

In summary, according to Donovan, sulfur burners have been used successfully to upgrade weak SO_2 concentrations (with minor fluctuations in strength) but have never been used, and, given current technology, probably cannot be used, to even out wide fluctuations in SO_2 streams, the problem presented by the Bunker Hill operations.

The original record nowhere contains a reasoned refutation of Donovan's objections. Nor does it contain anything approaching an adequate demonstration of the feasibility of sulfur burners. * * *

As Donovan admitted in his own testimony, sulfur burners *are* used on acid plants; the issue presented by Donovan is whether sulfur burners have been used on a plant similar to Bunker Hill's plants. Browder's list is meaningless without any discussion of the analogousness of the acid plants listed to the problem confronted.* * * And, of course, all must admit that the fact that sulfur burners are being *installed* at a lead smelter does not prove that the sulfur burners are feasible means of meeting the problems of Bunker Hill's lead smelter emissions.* * *

In summary, there was no evidence in the original record demonstrating that sulfur burners are presently utilized by acid plants with similar input problems to those confronted by Bunker Hill. None of the acid plants cited by EPA as using sulfur burners were claimed to be, let alone shown to be, analogous to Bunker Hill's acid plants. Furthermore, considerable doubt was cast on the validity of many of the purported examples of sulfur burner use. EPA made no attempt through detailed expert testimony to demonstrate that the SO_2 concentration problems outlined by Donovan could be overcome. Thus, on the basis of the original record, we would be forced to conclude that to require Bunker Hill's acid plants to meet a 2600 ppm emission limitation would be arbitrary and capricious.* * *

The Augmented Record:

* * *EPA's brief virtually concedes that the East Helena smelter is not a relevant analogy in evaluating the feasibility of Browder's sulfur burner proposal.* * * And no evidence was presented documenting any case where sulfur burners have been or are being used to cure fluctuation problems similar to those encountered at Bunker Hill.* * * Browder's "proposed control method of measuring fluctuations in SO_2 content and gas volume and adjusting sulfur burning rates to produce a more uniform gas stream are impractical and unworkable."* * *

Given these significant and unresolved criticisms of the Browder proposal, a remand to the EPA for further consideration of the feasibility of its standards becomes necessary. Even read in the deferential light required of a reviewing court, the record before use merely establishes that Browder's sulfur burner proposal might work. As we noted above, this is not enough. The record must establish that the required technology is feasible, not merely *possibly* feasible. Approval of EPA's standards on the basis of this record would seriously risk closing down a major smelting operation on the strength of a showing that does no more than demonstrate that the technology on which EPA relies is only "theoretical or experimental."

3. *Extent to Which the 2600 ppm Standard Would Be Met Assuming the Feasibility of the Sulfur Burners.*

Our remand provides an opportunity for the EPA to clarify an additional area of uncertainty which would exist even had EPA succeeded in establishing adequately the feasibility of Browder's sulfur burner proposal. It concerns the percentage of time the proposal would enable Bunker Hill to meet the 2600 ppm standard. According to the original Browder Study, the modifications proposed by the Study, if feasible, would "produce equivalent average stack losses of [1500–2000] ppm for most of the time." J.A. 729. In later portions of the original record, Mr. Browder translates "most of the time" to mean 85 percent-plus of the time. J.A. 769, 775. It is unclear from these statements, however, whether the Browder Study modifications would guarantee that Bunker Hill could meet the 2600 ppm standard *all of the time* as required by the EPA regulations.

Clarifying materials submitted by EPA in augmentation of the record have not resolved this uncertainty.* * *

We agree with EPA that it need not show that its standards can be met 100 percent of the time. Given the possibility of mechanical failure, etc., a showing that the standards can be met 99 percent-plus of the time is sufficient. Furthermore, assuming that Browder's guarantees are valid, we would agree with EPA that the measure of performance has been met. However, doubts are raised by Bunker Hill as to whether Mr. Browder's interpretation of his earlier statements is consistent with the proposals that he is making.* * * Given the possible inconsistency in Mr. Browder's interpretation of his 85 percent-plus guarantee, the EPA should clarify upon remand the percentage of the time that Browder's proposals will ensure Bunker Hill's meeting the 2600 ppm standard.* * *

III.

The 30-Day Investigation Period.

Bunker Hill also objects to EPA's disapproval of Idaho's provision for a 30-day investigation period following a violation in the Kellogg Valley of the primary annual ambient air quality standard. Under the Idaho regulations, the period would be used to determine whether other undetected and uncontrolled sources might have been the actual cause of the violation.

EPA's proposal, on the other hand, would make Bunker Hill liable for any violation of the standard and no formal opportunity to prove that it was not the cause of the violation would be available. We believe EPA's decision to eliminate the investigation period as reasonably necessary for the EPA's proper enforcement of the ambient air quality standards represents an exercise of reasoned discretion.

Section 1857c–5(a)(2) of the Clean Air Act requires that the EPA Administrator, before approving any portion of a state implementation plan, determine that the plan will meet the ambient air quality standards; this determination must include the adequacy of enforcement procedures. As noted by the EPA in its disapproval of the 30-day investigation period, it is extremely difficult to determine who is responsible for a violation of the ambient air quality standard where dispersion enhancement techniques are being used to meet the standards. Because of this difficulty, "it is reasonable to condition the use of [dispersion enhancement techniques] on the assumption of responsibility for violations of the ambient standards by a source which is overwhelmingly responsible for the emissions in a particular area. Bunker Hill contributes approximately 99.8 percent of the SO_2 emissions in the Kellogg Valley [sic]. . . . EPA believes that the 30-day review provisions might allow Bunker Hill to avoid the legal responsibility which it must assume if an unpredictable system such as [dispersion enhancement techniques] is to be a method of air pollution control."

This strikes us as sensible; therefore, EPA's decision to eliminate the review period is not arbitrary or capricious.* * *

IV.
Procedure on Remand.

* * *We also recognize, however, that the present dispute has already lasted more than four years and has seriously delayed implementation of the goals of the Clean Air Act in the Kellogg Valley. All parties are anxious for a quick but fair resolution of the questions involved. An expedited remand and review process, therefore, is required. We instruct the EPA to enter its final order in this matter within six months, after giving Bunker Hill an opportunity to cross-examine its technical experts and at least 30 days to comment on the evidence on which EPA intends to rely. If Bunker Hill is dissatisfied with the Administrator's final action, it shall have ten days to file its objections with this court. An accelerated briefing schedule would then be set.

REMANDED.

On Petition for Rehearing

The Administrator's petition for rehearing has been carefully considered by this court. We have been mindful during our deliberations of the enactment of the Clean Air Act Amendments of 1977, Pub.Law 95–95, 91 Stat. 685 (1977), subsequent to the filing of our opinion in this case.

We find nothing in the 1977 Amendments or otherwise to alter our position that national ambient air quality standards must be met, to the extent possible by constant emission controls. Whatever doubt there may have been about the correctness of that position was eliminated by the 1977 Amendments. *See* Section 301, Clean Air Act Amendments of 1977. To the extent a state plan does not require such controls it may be modified by the Administrator to bring it into line with this basic necessity. 42 U.S.C. § 1857c–5(c)(1).

In our opinion we indicated that the Administrator could mandate a particular constant emission control when it was technologically and economically feasible. Because we were unable on the basis of the record before us to concude that the Administrator's required constant emission control was technologically feasible, rather than "purely theoretical or experimental," we remanded the case for further consideration of the issue of technological feasibility and did not address Bunker Hill's objections as to economic feasibility. The Administrator, in his petition for rehearing, urges us to delete economic feasibility as a consideration in determining whether a particular constant emission control is possible. He insists that this deletion is required by the 1977 Amendments. We recognize that this contention is not without force. However, we believe it better at the present time to defer any consideration of this issue. For present purposes it is sufficient to recognize that the issue is an open one and that our opinion must be read as modified to the extent such recognition so requires it to be. Our remand, therefore, remains, as before, limited to the technological feasibility of the proposed EPA standards.

The Administrator in his petition for rehearing also contends that our opinion imposes on him the burden of designing and engineering the control technology modification needed by a source to comply with an emission limitation. Moreover, he insists that our opinion suggests that the burden of persuasion is upon him to show that a specific control technology is technologically and economically feasible. In our opinion we do not focus on burden of proof issues. We reviewed the actions of the EPA in rejecting the State of Idaho's plan in accordance with the usual standards of review employed by courts in reviewing actions by administrative agencies. Such actions must reflect an exercise by the administrator of "reasoned discretion" and not a "crystal ball inquiry." We held, and on this rehearing do not depart from that holding, that the Browder sulfur burner proposal on the basis of the present record is purely theoretical and experimental. It follows from that holding that the Administrator's action in rejecting the state plan on the basis of the Browder proposal did not reflect an exercise of "reasoned discretion" and thus was arbitrary and capricious. We said no more than this is our opinion.

The Administrator's petition for rehearing raises many interesting additional issues regarding the effect of the 1977 Amendments which we decline to pursue. To do so in the present setting of this case would involve our rendering an advisory opinion. This we cannot do.

The Administrator's petition for rehearing, except as indicated herein, is denied. The six-month period within which the EPA is required to enter its final order in this matter shall commence with the date this order is filed.

E. Local Regulation

Local governments have the power to regulate only those subjects authorized by the state legislature or state constitution. Environmental problems are usually considered to be **matters of state concern** and are usually regulated by the state rather than by municipal governments. Nevertheless there are several areas where direct local regulations of air pollution as well as indirect regulation of more traditional local matters can involve significant issues of air quality control.

1. Direct Local Regulation

Local government may be authorized to prohibit air pollution as part of its grant of police power over iocal affairs. The validity of such local regulation may depend on several factors. For example, an ordinance of the city of Des Moines prohibiting the emission of dense smoke as a nuisance and requiring the remodeling of practically all furnaces within the city to meet the standards was upheld by the United States Supreme Court as not in violation of the due process or equal protection clauses of the United States Constitution. See *Northwestern Laundry v. Des Moines*, 239 U.S. 486 (1916). On the other hand, local regulations are vulnerable to the argument that the subject was pre-empted by federal or state regulation of the subject. See *City of Burbank v. Lockheed Air Terminal Inc., supra.*

Local regulation may be held invalid where the ordinance is too vague and indefinite, such as an ordinance that makes it a criminal offense to create "foul or obnoxious odors" or that "allows noxious fumes to escape." *Verona v. Shalit*, 92 N.J. Super. 65, 222 A.2d 145 (1966). On the other hand, where the ordinance is carefully drawn it will be upheld against arguments that it is unreasonable, discriminatory or vague. *Sittner v. Seattle*, below, provides such an example.

SITTNER v. CITY OF SEATTLE

384 P.2d 859 (Wash. 1963)

HUNTER, Judge.

This is an appeal from the dismissal of an action seeking a declaratory judgment in which plaintiffs (appellants) prayed that Ordinance No. 90000, section 60, of the defendant (respondent), city of Seattle, be declared void and, in addition, that the defendant be permanently enjoined from enforcing such section of the ordinance.

The plaintiffs consist of 25 individuals and corporations, 20 of which are engaged in the auto wrecking business and five of which are engaged in the iron and metal business. As an incident of their business operations, which are all located within the city of Seattle, they burn salvaged metals in order to prepare them for reuse by foundries. Such scrap metal is desired by the foundries only if it is thoroughly cleaned. As the metal is cleaned by the burning process, smoke is emitted into the air.

Ordinance No. 90000 is entitled:

"AN ORDINANCE relating to air pollution, creating an air Pollution Control Advisory Board, regulating emissions of air contaminants, defining offenses and prescribing penalties."

Section 60 of Ordinance No. 90000 controls the emission of "smoke" by making it "unlawful to cause, suffer or allow emissions of smoke from any source other than heat processing equipment, the opacity of which is equal to or more than forty per cent," with certain exceptions relating to emissions for temporary periods of time. To measure the allowable opacity, the ordinance utilizes what is known as the Ringelmann Smoke Chart."

Smoke is defined as:

"An air contaminant consisting of a visible air-borne concentration of combustion produced solid particles and other matter."

Section 80 of Ordinance No. 90000 controls the emission of "dust" from heat processing equipment or from the milling, grinding, crushing or handling or any material. Section 80 sets forth a table which provides for the maximum dust emissions allowable per hour in relation to the process weight per hour. It defines dust as:

"An air contaminant consisting of solid particles, capable of being air-borne."

The plaintiffs contend section 60 of Ordinance No. 90000 is unconstitutional because the "opacity" standard used and the mandatory application of the Ringelmann Smoke Chart thereto does not have a reasonable relationship to the prevention of air pollution. It is their position that, first, the "opacity" standard does not measure the contents of the smoke, e. g., the toxic content thereof, and, second, the Ringelmann Smoke Chart does not measure opacity but colorations of smoke.

An ordinance to be void for unreasonableness must be plainly and clearly unreasonable. Seattle v. Hurst, 50 Wash. 424, 97 P. 454, 18 L.R.A.,N.S., 169 (1908). Although the "opacity" standard may not detect all of the air contaminants which pollute the air, we cannot say that it is not a reasonable means by which to detect some of the contaminating particles which smoke contains. It is no defense that the "opacity" standard does not regulate all air contamination but permits some emissions to go unpunished since a law designed to prevent one evil is not void because it does not prevent another. Ballentine v. Nester, 350 Mo. 58, 164 S.W.2d 378 (1942). Similarly, while it is true that the Ringelmann Smoke Chart measures coloration and not opacity, it does not necessarily follow that the chart may not be reasonably used as a basis for determining opacity. The Ringelmann Smoke Chart has been widely accepted throughout the United States as a measurement of air pollution by both legislatures and courts, and we find ourselves in agreement with the wisdom of this acceptance.

The trial court did not err in finding that the Ringelmann Smoke Chart is a reasonable standard of measurement and that, in respect to the "opacity" standard, section 60 of Ordinance No. 90000 is not unreasonable.

The plaintiffs contend section 60 of Ordinance No. 90000 is unconstitutional for the reason that the exemption of "heat processing equipment" from the restriction of section 60, under which the plaintiffs are regulated, is arbitrary and capricious.

This contention requires the determination of whether the city of Seattle has made a reasonable classification by exempting heat processing equipment from section 60. With respect to testing the constitutionality of legislative classifications, we stated in Clark v. Dwyer, 56 Wash.2d 425, 353 P.2d 941 (1960):

"Article 1, § 12 of the state constitution and the fourteenth amendment to the Federal Constitution, prohibiting special privileges and immunities and guaranteeing equal protection of the laws, require that class legislation must apply alike to all persons within a class, and reasonable ground must exist for making a distinction between those within, and those without, a designated class. Within the limits of these restrictive rules, the legislature has a wide measure of discretion, and its determination, when expressed in statutory enactment, cannot be successfully attacked unless it is manifestly arbitrary, unreasonable, inequitable, and unjust.* * *"

The plaintiffs contend that, under section 60 of Ordinance No. 90000, they are forbidden to emit air contaminants in the form of smoke whch exceeds 40 per cent opacity whereas heat processing equipment is permitted to contaminate the air with smoke in any amount it wishes. The defendant's reply to this contention is that the exemption of heat processing equipment from section 60 is not unreasonable inasmuch as it is, instead, directly controlled by section 80 which regulates the emission of dust from such equipment.

The plaintiffs' contention is premised on the assumption that dust and smoke are different air contaminants, and that the following finding of fact of the trial court is the law of the case since no exception was taken thereto: "That a logical and reasonable distinction in fact does exist between dust and smoke as defined in the ordinance."

We determine the foregoing purported finding of fact to involve no factual issue; that it is a construction of the ordinance and thus constitutes a conclusion of law which is not binding on this court.* * * An examination of the ordinance on its face appears to support the plaintiffs' contention that smoke and dust are different air contaminants since smoke and dust are defined and controlled separately. However, the ordinance must be considered in its entirety. It cannot be limited to labels or definitions, but must be considered from the standpoint of the contents of such definitions in relation to the purpose of the ordinance.

We believe the primary purpose of Ordinance No. 90000 is the regulation of air contaminants in the form of solid particles, inasmuch as the measurements which are used to test air contaminants, *viz.*, the process weight table and the Ringelmann Smoke Chart, are primarily designed to measure the amount of solid particle contaminants emitted into the air. The ordinance defines "dust" as "An air contaminant consisting of *solid particles*, capable of being air-borne." (Italics ours.) "Smoke" is defined as "An air contaminant consisting of a visible air-borne concentration of *combustion produced solid particles* and other matter." (Italics ours.) We therefore conclude that, within the purview of the ordinance, "smoke" consists substantially of air-borne solid particles which fall within the definition of "dust" and that the regulation of "dust" inherently constitutes the regulation of "smoke."

The municipality of Seattle, in the exercise of its police power for the protection of the public health and welfare, may reasonably regulate the emission of air contaminants in the form of solid particles according to any reasonable classification. The question then remains whether the regulation of solid particles emitted from heat processing equipment on the basis of the process weight table and the regulation of solid particles emitted from burning conducted by the plaintiffs on the basis of the Ringelmann Smoke Chart constitute reasonable regulations based upon reasonable classifications.

It is conceivable that emissions from heat processing equipment raise problems of detecting solid particles that are not combustion produced. The Ringelmann Smoke Chart is designed primarily for the detection of combustion produced black soot particles. See Faith, Air Pollution Control, pp. 84–86 (1959). It therefore follows that the emission of solid particles from heat processing sources, conceivably, can be more effectively regulated by measuring the content of the emission by the process weight table rather than by the Ringelmann Chart.

We conclude that the use of process weight tables for the control of solid particles emitted from heat processing equipment and the use of the Ringelmann Chart for the control of solid particles emitted from other sources of burning are reasonable regulations based upon reasonable classifications. The plaintiffs have therefore failed to establish that the control exercised by the ordinance over their burning activities is discriminatory and in contravention of Art. 1, § 12 of the state constitution and the fourteenth amendment to the Federal constitution.

The plaintiffs contend that compliance with the ordinance makes it economically infeasible for continuation of their business and that the ordinance is therefore oppressive and a taking of their property without due compensation. Economic hardships often invitably result from laws and ordinances enacted or adopted for the protection of the public health and welfare; this, however, cannot affect their constitutional validity unless they are shown to be clearly unreasonable and discriminatory.* * * The plaintiffs have not shown that Ordinance No. 90000 is unreasonable or discriminatory, and their contention, therefore, cannot be sustained.

The other contentions raised by the plaintiffs challenging the constitutionality of the ordinance are unsupported by authority, and we find them to be without merit.

The judgment of the trial court is affirmed.

---

2. LAND USE CONTROLS

State enabling legislation authorizes local governments to regulate land use. The power to adopt zoning laws authorizes local governments to determine the location and intensity of land use within the municipality. Areas zoned for high-intensity industrial use, for example, will create problems of air pollution not likely to be produced in areas zoned for low-density residential use. One obvious method of avoiding air pollution is to zone out pollution-creating activities. This solution to the problem of air pollution may be too simplistic to a local governing body that seeks to encourage the creation of jobs for its residents and tax revenue to pay for required services.

3. TRANSPORTATION CONTROLS

Transportation controls are controls designed to limit the use of automobiles. The objective is to reduce auto-caused air pollution by placing restrictions on the extent to which the automobile is used. Under Section 110(a)(2)(B) of the Clean Air Act, 42 U.S.C. 1857c-5(a)(2)(B)(1970), SIPS must include "emission limitations, schedules and timetables for compliance with such limitations, and such other measures as may be necessary to insure attainment and maintenance of such primary or secondary air quality standards, including, but not limited to *land use* and transportation controls" (emphasis added).

The following are some of the transportation control techniques that may be used to control air pollution:

- Encourage mass transit
- Create special bus lanes
- Offer car pool bonuses
- Impose or increase bridge tolls
- Stagger working hours
- Reduce parking spaces in the central city
- Ban cars in selected areas
- Change traffic patterns
- Require after hours delivery
- Promote rail shipment
- Promote waterfront facilities

Friends of the Earth v. EPA, below, resulted in three decisions involving litigation dealing with the approval of New York City's Transportation Control Plan that was a part of New York State's SIP.

FRIENDS OF THE EARTH
v.
E.P.A.

499 F.2d 1118 (1974)

(FRIENDS I)

LUMBARD, Circuit Judge:

Pursuant to § 307(b)(1) of the Clean Air Act, 42 U.S.C. § 1857h–5(b)(1), petitioners, a group of environmental and public interest organizations concerned with the quality of New York's air, ask this court to review the approval of New York's transportation control plan for the New York City metropolitan area by the Administrator of the Environmental Protection Agency (EPA). We grant review in part and deny review in part.

I.

By enacting the Clean Air Amendments of 1970, Pub.L. No. 91–604, 84 Stat. 1676, Congress amended the Clean Air Act, 42 U.S.C. §§ 1857–1858a, to require that states meet national standards for air quality within a few years. Briefly stated, under § 109 of the Act, 42 U.S.C. § 1857c–4, the Administrator is to promulgate national primary ambient air quality standards and national secondary ambient air quality standards. Primary standards are for protection of the public health, while secondary standards are for protection of the public welfare. On April 30, 1971, the Administrator promulgated primary standards for six air pollutants—particulate matter, sulfur oxides, nitrogen dioxide, carbon monoxide, hydrocarbons, and photochemical oxidants. Under § 110 of the Act, 42 U.S.C. § 1857c–5, the states after notice and public hearings were to adopt and submit to the Administrator, within nine months after promulgation of an air quality standard, a plan to implement the standard. Primary standards were to be implemented as expeditiously as possible but in any case within three years of the Administrator's approval of the plan; secondary standards were to be implemented within a reasonable time. The Administrator can extend the period for meeting a primary standard by two years, upon application of the governor of the state, if certain sources of emissions are unable to comply with the requirement because necessary technology or alternatives are not available and if the state had considered and applied other reasonably available alternative means of achieving the standard and has justifiably concluded that the standard cannot be implemented in three years. If the state fails to submit a plan meeting the requirements of the Act, the Administrator is empowered to prepare and promulgate his own implementation plan for the state.

At issue here is New York's plan to control transportation within the New York city metropolitan area as part of its effort to meet the primary standards for carbon monoxide, hydrocarbons, and photochemical oxidants. According to the implementation plan, motor vehicles are responsible for roughly 95 percent of the carbon monoxide emissions, 65 percent of the hydrocarbons emissions, and 50 percent of the photochemical oxidants. The controls on new automobile emissions mandated by § 202 of the Act, 42 U.S.C. § 1857f–1, will only achieve about 40 percent of the reduction in pollutants necessary to fulfill the EPA's primary standards. Therefore,

New York's implementation plan had to consider other methods of limiting or dispersing automobile emissions if the standards were to be met.

Earlier this year, we considered a challenge to the principal New York implementation plan, Natural Resources Defense Council, Inc. v. EPA, 494 F.2d 519 (2d Cir. 1974). That plan did not include transportation control measures because the EPA had advised New York and several other states that transportation control plans did not have to be filed until February 15, 1973, and did not have to meet the primary standards until May 31, 1977, allowing for the full two-year extension permissible under § 110. The reason for this advise was that the EPA and the states lacked practical experience in developing transportation control measures that would meet air quality standards. However, this blanket extension was challenged and in Natural Resources Defense Council, Inc. v. EPA, 154 U.S.App.D.C. 384, 475 F.2d 968 (1973), the District of Columbia Circuit held that, although the Administrator had acted in good faith, he had not met the requirements of § 110 in granting the two-year extension. He was ordered to rescind the extension and to require those states which had not yet submitted plans fully complying with § 110 to do so by April 15, 1973. These plans had to meet all requirements of § 110 and be capable of meeting the primary air quality standards by May 31, 1975. If extensions of up to two years were requested, the Administrator had to determine in each case that all requirements of § 110(e) for granting an extension had been met.

The EPA did rescind its extension and the State of New York prepared an implementation plan concerning transportation controls in the New York City area. The plan as adopted has four levels of strategies for reducing pollutants—primary stage strategies which have to be followed if the 1975 deadline is to be met, maintenance stage strategies which are of little effect in meeting the 1975 deadline but necessary to maintaining air quality after 1975, a contingency stage strategy which is required if primary stage strategies fail, and secondary stage strategies which may be beneficial but need further study. The primary strategies as listed by the plan together with the designation letter and number given to each are: vehicle turnover as new automobiles with emission controls replace old vehicles (A–1); retrofitting heavy-duty vehicles with catalytic converters (A–2); thrice yearly emission inspections of all livery vehicles (A–3); semi-annual emission inspections of heavy-duty vehicles (A–4); emission inspections of passenger cars (A–5); training of mechanics (A–6); maintenance and inspection of diesel buses (A–7); retrofitting of light-duty vehicles with catalytic converters (A–8); elimination of leaded gasoline (A–9); reciprocal retrofit and fuel regulations in New Jersey and Connecticut (A–10); enforcement of traffic and parking regulations (B–1A); traffic management (B–1B); selective ban on taxicab cruising (B–1C); reduction in the number of parking places in Manhattan business districts (B–3); expanded use of exclusive bus lanes and increased express bus service (B–5); staggering of work hours and days (C–8); and citizen participation in the planning process and public information (E–4). A contingency stage strategy would be to ban all private automobiles from Manhattan's business districts (B–2). A table in the margin shows the reduction in air pollutants that New York expected each primary strategy to achieve, although it acknowledged that the success of any one strategy depended on the success of several others.[3]

New York submitted the plan to the EPA on April 17, 1973, and in an accompanying letter Governor Rockefeller requested a two-year extension for meeting the photochemical oxidants standard and an eighteenth-month extension for meeting the carbon monoxide standard. The letter explained that achieving the required standards required installing catalytic converters on all existing passenger cars and that it was not technologically feasible to do so since sufficient numbers of converters could not be produced and installed in time and their reliability was unproven. Also it was doubted that the petroleum industry could supply in time sufficient quantities of lead-free gasoline necessary for catalytic converters. Rockefeller added as new primary strategies a requirement that all 1975 model taxis be equipped with a "California package" for emission controls (A–11), a requirement that deliveries to stores, factories, and office buildings be made after business hours (D–3), and a requirement that tolls be imposed on all East River and Harlem River Bridges (B–7).

On June 22, 1973, the Administrator approved New York's plan and granted a nineteen-month extension for meeting both the photochemical oxidants and carbon monoxide standards. 38 Fed.Reg. 16560–61. He also promulgated amendments of 40 C.F.R. § 52.1670, a table that listed the dates by which New York had to meet air quality standards. Another regulation, 40 C.F.R. § 52.1683, was revised to require that New York submit by July 30, 1973 the legislative authority needed to carry out the strategies and by December 30, 1973 the necessary adopted regulations and administrative policies needed to implement such strategies. 38 Fed.Reg. 16567.

[3]TABLE

Impact of Primary Stage Transportation Control Strategies
(1975 Emissions Relative to 1970 Emissions)

	PERCENT REDUCTION			
	Carbon Monoxide		Hydrocarbons-Oxidants	Nitrogen Dioxide
Strategy	Downtown	Midtown	Analysis Zone	Analysis Zone
Stationary source Controls	4	4	18*	11
A-1	29	48	30	1
A-2	21	8	6**	–
A-3	Included in Strategy A-1 and A-8			
A-4	Included in Strategy A-2			
A-5	Included in Strategy A-1 and A-8			
A-6	–	–	–	–
A-7	–	–	–	–
A-8	7	10	14**	3
A-9	–	–	–	–
A-10	Included in Strategy A-1 and A-8			
B-1A	7	5	2	1
B-1B	Included in Strategy B-1A			
B-1C	2	1	–	–
B-3	8	2	–	–
B-5	–	–	–	–
C-8	–	–	–	–
E-4	–	–	–	–
TOTAL	78	78	70	16***
Needed	78		69	32

*Hydrocarbon emission reduction amounts to 8%; however, solvent reformulation will reduce oxidant concentrations by another 10%.

**Older vehicle operators will choose not to retrofit; therefore, reductions in vehicle miles traveled from these classes will occur. Emission reductions are estimated at 10% of the respective class total.

***Nitrogen dioxide emissions reduction through transportation control measures will not achieve the up to 32% reduction. New York is awaiting guidance from the Environmental Protection Agency on sampling before imposing additional controls on oxides of nitrogen emissions.

II.

What is the scope of judicial review in this case? For the most part we are concerned with whether the Administrator was correct in his factual determinations.* * * Although this inquiry into the facts is to be searching and careful, the ultimate standard of review is a narrow one. The court is not empowered to substitute its judgment for that of the agency.* * *

III.

The first challenge, however, is to the legal sufficiency of New York's implementation plan. It is argued that the plan is too vague because the strategies, in particular the reduction in parking strategy, do not indicate precisely what actions will be taken. In addition, it is claimed that the plan does not comply with the requirement of § 110(a)(2)(B) that it contain "emission limitations, schedules, and timetables for compliance with such limitations."

On the first point we agree that the plan is not as specific as it could be. In discussing the parking strategy, the plan says,

> Since parking policy is to be the primary strategy for reducing passenger car VMT [vehicle miles traveled] (by approximately 50 per cent in the Manhattan business districts), it is estimated that available parking spaces also should be reduced by 30 to 40 per cent. A practical approach to the goal is a strongly enforced, complete ban on on-street parking south of 60th Street in Manhattan during the business day, gradual reduction in the number of off-street parking spaces and a change in pricing policies to discourage passenger car . . . commuting rather than to encourage it. One third to one half of the remaining off-street parking spaces should be relocated to fringe lots along the Hudson riverfront. Jitney service for shoppers will be established between these lots and the business area.

The argument is that this statement and others like it are deficient in that there is no mention of what particular off-street facilities will be eliminated or how they will be selected.

The Administrator, however, has chosen to interpret the Act to allow states to postpone promulgating detailed regulations for several months after submission and acceptance of a plan, here December 30, 1973. The Administrator has said allowing postponement of regulations "does not defer the necessity for the States to choose their strategies and make firm commitments to put them into effect. It merely means that the detailed procedures involved can be approved later. If the plan did not provide adequate assurance that this later stage would be essentially procedural, so that substantial difficulties would not arise then, the plan was not approved." 38 Fed.Reg. 16554.

We think that this interpretation of the requirements of the Act is a reasonable one and that we should defer to the Administrator's judgment. After all, the Administrator has the difficult and complex job of supervising the implementation of plans to achieve air quality standards in all fifty states plus the District of Columbia, Puerto Rico, the Virgin Islands, Guam, and American Samoa. See 42 U.S.C. § 1857h(d). The Administrator has not been rubber-stamping his approval of state transportation control plans. On June 22, 1973, out of transportation control plans for 43 regions, it was anticipated that all but nine would require some modification by EPA, and 24 would require substantial EPA modification or promulgation. See 38 Fed.Reg. 16554. The Administrator's interpretation requires that there be sufficient commitment and detail so that achievement of the air quality standards is ensured. While New York's plan does not commit itself to banning parking on any particular street, the EPA or a private citizen could in an appropriate enforcement action require New York to implement a plan reducing business district parking by thirty to forty per cent. So long as the plan is detailed enough that the proposed strategies will achieve national air quality standards and there is no reason to believe that the delay in promulgating detailed regulations would interfere with the requirement that such standards be achieved "as expeditiously as practicable," § 110(a)(2)(A)(i), we see no good reason not to allow a state some additional time to submit more specific details of their implementation plan.

As far as the alleged lack of schedules for implementation is concerned, suffice it to say that the plan does contain such schedules. While here too there may not be the detail petitioners would like, we think that it is sufficient for the purposes of the Act. Therefore, we do not agree with the petitioners on this point.

IV.

Petitioners' next challenge accuses the Administrator of making three unjustified assumptions in approving the parking ban strategy which plays a major role in achieving the goal of a fifty per cent drop in passenger car VMT. It is claimed that the Administrator mistakenly assumed that without implementing the strategies the percentage of commuters using the various modes of transportation will remain constant. In particular it is argued that in the past fare increases have always resulted in decreased ridership on mass transit facilities and since the plan makes no provision for maintaining current fares, it is possible that fare increases could cause so many commuters to use their cars despite reductions in parking space that the parking ban strategy will not work. But the plan does not aim at attracting riders to mass transit; it admits that there is no sure way to do that. Rather it aims at compelling them to use other modes of travel besides private automobile by denying them parking space. Increased use of express buses with special highway lanes is intended to provide an acceptable alternative to those displaced. We, therefore, do not think the Administrator acted unreasonably in approving a plan that did not provide for maintaining current mass transit fares.

Another argument is that even if there is a reduction in parking spaces, there may not be a great enough decline in passenger car VMT because many commuters will park illegally anyway. The plan does admit that most cars parked on the street in the central business districts are parked illegally, but the plan also provides for stepped-up enforcement of traffic regulations by a paraprofessional staff. We think that the Administrator acted reasonably in concluding that increased enforcement would solve the problem.

Petitioners' most troublesome challenge is that the Administrator assumed that the total supply of parking spaces in the central business districts is currently equal to the total demand. That this may have been assumed appears in an evaluation prepared by the EPA staff for the Administrator where it is said that it is assumed that a fifty percent reduction in parking places will result in a fifty percent reduction in miles traveled by passenger vehicles. Petitioners challenge this by pointing to a New York City intradepartmental memorandum, dated July 13, 1973, which found an average vacancy rate in midtown Manhattan parking garages of about forty-three percent. This means that a reduction in parking spaces may not achieve the fifty percent reduction in passenger car VMT that the plan hoped for. An even greater reduction in parking spaces may be necessary to achieve the desired reduction in VMT.

We do not conclude that the Administrator was necessarily in error. The relationship between parking spaces and VMT would appear to depend upon complex and varied factors, including, at least in part, public perception concerning how many parking spaces are available reasonably close to commuter destinations. But we believe that a further explanation by the Administrator is necessary. The petition for review of this point is therefore granted, and this matter is remanded for further explanation by the Administrator on why he concluded that the parking ban strategy would achieve its goals.

V.

The next challenge is that New York did not give adequate assurances that there would be sufficient funds to implement the plan. Although § 105 of the Clean Air Act, 42 U.S.C. § 1857c, allows the Administrator to make grants to defray part of the costs of achieving national air quality standards, the Act places primary responsibility for providing funds upon the states. Section 110(a)(2)(F)(i) requires that the state plan contain "necessary assurances that the State will have adequate personnel, funding, and authority to carry out such implementation plan."

Here the Administrator has not explained how he determined that New York has provided the requisite necessary assurances concerning personnel and funding. The plan does provide a detailed list of what funds and staff will be required in implementing the plan but does not say from where these resources will be derived. In his letter accompanying the plan, Governor Rockefeller stated that new funding was required and bluntly said, "Congress has mandated; Congress should provide the necessary funds." We, therefore, cannot tell how the Administrator determined that there were adequate assurances.

In Natural Resources Defense Council, Inc. v. EPA, *supra*, 494 F.2d at 527, we faced a similar situation. Adopting the test announced by the First Circuit in Natural Resources Defense Council, Inc. v. EPA, 478 F.2d 875, 890–891 (1st Cir. 1973), we said that this situation calls for the Administrator's reasoned judgment on the adequacy of state resources and directed the Administrator to provide a detailed statement of his rationale in determining that New York had provided the needed necessary assurances on funding and personnel. Since we do not know the basis of the Administrator's determination on this matter, we again direct the Administrator to provide a detailed statement of his rationale on this matter.

VI.

As noted above, the Administrator granted New York a nineteen-month extension in meeting the photochemical oxidants and carbon monoxide primary air quality standards in the New York City metropolitan area. Before such an extension can be granted the Administrator must determine that one or more emission sources or class of sources are unable to comply with the plan which implements a primary standard because necessary technology or other alternatives are not available or will not be available soon enough and that the state has considered reasonably available alternative means of achieving the standard. In addition the Administrator must determine that the remaining parts of the plan will be implemented by May 31, 1975, and that there are reasonable interim standards for those parts that cannot be implemented.

Petitioners do not challenge New York's contention that there will not be sufficient catalytic converters available in 1975 to retrofit all passenger vehicles and heavy-duty vehicles. Instead they argue that New York has not exhausted all reasonably available means of achieving the standards by May 31, 1975. They offer five alternatives: a greater reduction in taxi cruising, increased car pool incentives, control of gasoline sales, elimination of commuter discounts for tolls on Hudson River bridges and tunnels, and expedited imposition of tolls on toll-free Harlem and East River bridges.

We faced a similar challenge in Natural Resources Defense Council, Inc. v. EPA, *supra*, 494 F.2d at 524–525, and said there that rather than have the Administrator disprove "a thousand negatives" to conclude that all reasonable alternatives have been explored, that petitioners must carry the burden of going forward with "a reasonable claim of something important overlooked." We think it is clear that three of petitioners' alternatives, increased car pool incentives, elmination of commuter discounts, and imposition of tolls on all bridges, do not meet this burden. There is no showing that these strategies would accomplish anything more than a successful parking ban strategy. Additionally, ending commuter discounts at Hudson River crossings apparently would have to be done by the Port of New York Authority, an independent organization formed by compact between New York and New Jersey.

A control on gasoline sales, if successful, would undoubtedly result in a decrease in VMT. The Administrator in his determination that an extension was called for did not specifically reject gasoline rationing. The evaluation of New York's plan mentions gasoline rationing along with other alternatives, but states, apparently without support in the record, that once VMT is reduced fifty percent, the remaining VMT contributes little to the carbon monoxide problem.

We would therefore have difficulty in upholding the Administrator's determination on this issue if he had not elsewhere provided an explanation. The EPA considered requiring limitation on gasoline supplies in the plans it proposed for several states whose plans were inadequate. The Administrator concluded that such limitations are not a reasonably available alternative sufficient to prevent an extension since "[t]he possibilities of evasion, the likelihood of noncompliance, and the difficulties of enforcement are too great to make this measure practicable." 38 Fed.Reg. 30632 (Nov. 6, 1973). This explanation is a reasonable one and we see no reason to go through the formality of remanding this case to the Administrator to receive a similarly worded explanation.

Finally, it is suggested that New York could ban all cruising by taxicabs looking for passengers. New York's plan provides for a twenty percent cut in taxi cruising. The plan states that taxicabs contribute almost sixty percent of the vehicle miles traveled in midtown Manhattan and almost half this mileage is cruising without passengers. The plan estimated that a total ban on cruising in midtown could result in as much as a twenty percent reduction in carbon monoxide levels. The plan instead would institute only a partial ban on certain streets and relies on other strategies to achieve the primary standards. The reason a total ban was not instituted was taxi industry pressure. Originally a total ban was proposed, but in a compromise a partial ban was agreed to. The plan states, "The industry acknowledged that they would do almost anything to insure their freedom to cruise."

While such a compromise would be acceptable if national primary air quality standards are achieved, the Clean Air Act does not contemplate allowing extension in achieving the standards merely because reasonably available means are unacceptable to any special group. [CITATIONS OMITTED]

The twenty percent reduction in carbon monoxide mentioned in the plan would go a long way in making up for the unavailability of the retrofitting strategies.

This twenty percent figure, however, may be inflated since the plan says a one or two percent reduction will be caused by a twenty percent reduction in cruising. Furthermore, the requirement that all 1975 model taxis have the "California package" of emission controls conceivably could lessen the environmental impact that a ban on taxi cruising would have. The Administrator gave no explanation concerning this matter in approving the plan, and the EPA staff evaluation report only notes that the Department of Transportation has urged a more drastic ban and states that New York State should consider such a ban "in the event that additional reductions are deemed necessary as the attainment date approaches." Which date, May 31, 1975, or nineteen months later is not made clear, and the EPA has not required that New York consider this matter before the May 31 deadline. We, therefore, must remand this matter for a further explanation by the Administrator on why he determined that a total ban, or a substantially larger ban than twenty per cent, on cruising of taxis was not a reasonably available means of achieving primary air quality standards by May 31, 1975.

VII.

Finally, we are asked to order either the EPA or the State of New York to promulgate the detailed regulations for implementing the plans.* * *

At argument, the EPA joined in petitioners' request that we order New York to comply with the EPA regulation and begin implementing its plan. Although counsel for the respondent Governor did not argue against such an order, we have concluded that we lack jurisdiction to issue such an order. Our jurisdiction here under § 307(b)(1) of the Act, 42 U.S.C. § 1857h–5(b)(1), is limited to reviewing the correctness of the Administrator's approval of the state plan. For this purpose, actual compliance with an adequate plan is irrelevant. Congress has provided in the Clean Air Act specific measures for enforcing the plan. Under § 110 the Administrator can promulgate a revised plan if the original plan proves to be inadequate and the state refuses to act. Under § 113, 42 U.S.C. § 1857c–8, the Administrator can bring suit in the appropriate district court to enforce his orders or an implementation plan. Finally under § 304, 42 U.S.C. § 1857h–2, private citizens, subject to whatever constraints the Eleventh Amendment may provide, can bring suit in the district courts to enforce implementation plans. By providing these methods, Congress must have intended that judicial enforcement of implementation plans be instituted in the district courts where a factual record can be developed. Accordingly, we decline to order New York to comply with the implementation plan.

VIII.

The petition to review is granted to the extent that the Administrator is required to explain further his determinations regarding the parking ban strategy, the necessary assurances concerning funding and personnel, and the twenty percent ban on taxicab cruising. In all other respects, the petition is denied.

So ordered.

FRIENDS OF THE EARTH
v.
CAREY

535 F.2d 165 (1976)

(FRIENDS II)

* * *

CONCLUSION

We are aware that enforcement of the air quality plan might well cause inconvenience and expense to both governmental and private parties, particularly when a congested metropolitan community provides the focal point of the controversy. But Congress decreed that whatever time and money otherwise might be saved should not be gained at the expense of the lungs and health of the community's citizens:

> "The protection of public health—as required by the national ambient air quality standards and as mandated by provisions for the elimination of emissions of extremely hazardous pollution agents—will require major action throughout the Nation. Many facilities will require major investments in new technology and new processes. Some facilities will need altered operating procedures or a change of fuels. Some facilities may be closed.

"The requirements for State action will be broadened. And the obligation of polluters will be greatly increased. What has been a program focused on uniquely critical areas, underfunded and inadequately manned, will become truly national in scope and will require an immediate increase in personnel and funding." [CITATIONS OMITTED]

The record before us is one that cries out for prompt and effective relief if the congressional clean air mandate is to have any meaning and effect in New York City. We cannot disregard the frank statement made by New York State's Assistant Attorney General some two years ago, that this "is a legally enforceable plan, . . . a legally adequate plan," and that "[i]f there is a valid legal ground for . . . a refusal [to enforce the plan], we have not been able to find it. . . ." Yet it is beyond serious dispute that the defendants are now almost a year in default in carrying out the principal strategies of the mandated Plan, which are central to achieving the primary ambient air quality standards prescribed by Congress, with the result that the public of New York City is exposed to carbon monoxide pollution that has in the meantime climbed to over five times the federal health standards. The court cannot consistently with its duty be a party to the delaying process that has led to this situation. The Senate Committee on Public Works, discussing the purpose of the citizen suit provision in its Report on the Clean Air Act Amendments of 1970, made this clear:

"If the Secretary and State and local agencies should fail in their responsibility, the public would be guaranteed the right to seek vigorous enforcement action under the citizen suit provisions of section 304.

* * * * * *

"The Committee believes that if the timetables established throughout the Act with respect to ambient air quality standards necessary to protect public health are to be met, the threat of sanction must be real, and enforcement provisions must be swift and direct. Abatement orders, penalty provisions, and rapid access to the Federal District Court should accomplish the objective of compliance." Accordingly . . . we reverse the district court's decision and remand the case to that court with the following instructions: . . . Partial summary judgment should be entered in favor of plaintiffs, directing enforcement . . . the court to take such further steps as are necessary to insure enforcement of these strategies;

Further hearings should be held promptly to determine whether the defendants are in default in carrying out any of the remaining strategies and, if so, the court should enter such orders and take such other steps as are necessary to enforce those strategies being violated by the State.

Since time is of the essence in providing such relief as may be appropriate in this case, we direct that the case be given priority on remand and that, if Judge Duffy's schedule precludes his handling it promptly, the case be reassigned to another judge who is in a position to do so.

The mandate shall issue forthwith.

In *Friends III*, 552 F.2d 25 (1977), the court held that New York State and New York City could be compelled, via a § 304 citizen suit, to enforce the air quality provisions of their SIPS. The court ordered compliance without further delay. Application for stay by New York City was denied, 434 U.S. 1310.

4. INDIRECT SOURCE CONTROLS

Indirect sources of air pollution are facilities that attract vehicles that cause emissions. Typical examples include parking facilities, shopping centers, office complexes, airports, highways, and recreation, amusement, sports and entertainment facilities. Local governments can control indirect sources through their land use regulatory powers. The state and federal governments have an interest in indirect sources of air pollution because the Clean Air Act lists indirect source controls as one of the components of a SIP. Indirect source controls include requirements that **preconstruction reviews** be undertaken for all major indirect sources of air pollution. In *City of Highland Park v. Train*, below, plaintiff's action to prevent construction of a large shopping center failed because of jurisdictional and procedural defects. However, the case illustrates the possibilities for the use of this provision of the Clean Air Act to oppose a shopping center or other indirect source of air pollution. In 1977 Congress amended this section by providing that a SIP may not be rejected for the reason that it does not contain indirect source controls. This provision makes indirect source controls a voluntary component of a SIP.

CITY OF HIGHLAND PARK
v.
TRAIN

519 F.2d 681 (1975)

TONE, Circuit Judge.

In the principal case before us in these consolidated proceedings, No. 74–1271, plaintiffs sue to block the construction of a shopping center and the extension and widening of the road along which the shopping center is to be built, relying upon the Clean Air amendments of 1970, the National Environmental Protection Act, and the Equal Protection Clause of the Fourteenth Amendment. They seek to compel the Administrator of the Environmental Protection Agency to promulgate "indirect source" and "significant deterioration" regulations which they hope would preclude the construction of the shopping center and the road expansion (Counts I and II) and to enjoin the road expansion until the Department of Transportation has filed an environmental impact statement pursuant to the National Environmental Protection Act (Count III). Plaintiffs also allege that the Village of Northbrook has denied them equal protection by the adoption of a zoning ordinance which permits the construction of the shopping center (Count IV).

The District Court dismissed the claims under the Clean Air Amendments for failure to comply with the 60-day notice requirement of section 304, 42 U.S.C. § 1857h–2, for failure to state a claim on which relief can be granted, and on the ground that some of the relief requested was already the subject of orders issued by other federal courts. Finding it undisputed that there was no federal involvement in the road expansion project, the court granted summary judgment on the claim that an environmental impact statement should have been filed. The equal protection claim was also held to be without merit. The court entered an order dismissing the action, *City of Highland Park v. Train*, 374 F.Supp. 758 (N.D.Ill.1974), from which plaintiffs appeal and which we affirm.

Plaintiffs are two municipalities adjacent to the site of the proposed shopping center, a non-profit corporation dedicated to protecting the environment in the area, and various individuals who reside near the site. The defendants are the Administrator of the Environmental Protection Agency, the agency itself, the Secretary of the Department of Transportation, the department itself, the Department of Highways of Cook County, Illinois, the developers of the shopping center, proposed tenants of the shopping center, the Village of Northbrook, in which the shopping center will be located, and the trustees of the village.

The right of way of Lake-Cook Road extends from Lake Michigan along the entire boundary between Lake and Cook Counties to the western end of the boundary and continues on west to the Fox River. Between Milwaukee Avenue and Rand Road, the road is not completed. Where it is completed, it is, for the most part, two lanes wide. In 1967 the Cook County Highway Department initiated plans to expand the completed portions of the road to four lanes and to construct a four-lane extension on the right-of-way where no actual roadway presently exists.

In January, 1973, certain of the defendants announced a plan for the construction of a shopping center on the south side of Lake-Cook Road between Skokie Highway and Waukegan Road. The shopping center, according to the complaint, will occupy one million square feet, having a parking lot accommodating 5,000 cars, and generate 28,400 vehicle trips per day. Ninety percent or more of this traffic will be carried by Lake-Cook Road, the only through-street which provides access to the shopping center. Plaintiffs allege that this traffic "will overwhelm even the proposed four lane expanded roadway," and cause "intolerable" congestion at the intersections of Lake-Cook Road and Skokie Highway and Waukegan Road. As a result, residents of the area will be subjected to substantial "noise and discomfort in the use of their homes and in the use of the streets in their community" and will be exposed to increases in the concentration of carbon monoxide in the ambient air by more than 66 percent over existing levels.

The Clean Air Amendments and Their Implementation

To explain plaintiffs' claims under the Clean Air Amendments of 1970, it is necessary to begin by summarizing pertinent parts of that legislation and its implementation by actions of the Administrator and the states and by certain court decisions. The background and a more complete history of the amendments and their implementation to date appear in Mr. Justice Rehnquist's opinion for the Supreme Court in *Train v. Natural Resources Defense Council, Inc.*, 421 U.S. 60, 95 S.Ct. 1470, 43 L.Ed.2d 731 (1975).

When the states did not act to fulfill their "primary responsibility" for prevention of air pollution under earlier federal clean air legislation, "Congress reacted by taking a stick to the States in the form of the Clean Air Amendments of 1970.* * * The 1970 Amendments established a program to control air pollution to be carried out by the federal government and the states. The parts of the Amendments pertinent here may be summarized as follows:

The Administrator was required, before specified dates, to publish a list of air pollutants and issue "air quality criteria" containing information about each listed pollutant and its effects on the air. (Section 108, 42 U.S.C. § 1857c–3.) He was also required to establish national "ambient air quality standards" for each air pollutant for which air quality criteria were issued. (Section 109, 42 U.S.C. § 1857c–4.) The states have primary authority to establish "implementation plans" to achieve these standards, but these plans are subject to review by the Administrator. (Section 110, 42 U.S.C. § 1857c–5.)

Two sets of standards were to be prescribed by the Administrator, "primary standards," the "attainment and maintenance of which, in the judgment of the Administrator, based on [air quality] criteria and allowing an adequate margin of safety, are requisite to protect the public health;" and "secondary standards," which "shall specify a level of air quality the attainment and maintenance of which in the judgment of the Administrator, based on such criteria, is requisite to protect the public welfare from any known or anticipated adverse effects associated with the presence of such air pollutant in the ambient air." (Section 109(b), 42 U.S.C. §1857–4(b).) The Administrator prescribed these standards within the time allowed him by the Act.

Within nine months after the Administrator's promulgation of the national standards, each state was to submit to him a plan providing for the "implementation, maintenance, and enforcement" of the standards. (Section 110(a)(1), 42 U.S.C. § 1857c–5(a)(1).) Each state plan was required to provide for the attainment of the national primary standards "as expeditiously as practicable" and not later than three years after the date the Administrator approved the plan. (Section 110(a)(2)(A)(i), 42 U.S.C. § 1857c–5(a)(2)(A)(i).) The national secondary standards were to be met within a "reasonable time" to be specified in the plan. (Section 110(a)(2)(A)(ii), 42 U.S.C. § 1857c–5(a)(2)(A)(ii).) Each state plan was to include "emission limitations, schedules, and timetables for compliance with such limitation, and such other measures as may be necessary to insure attainment and maintenance of such primary or secondary standard, including, but not limited to, land-use and transportation controls." (Section 110(a)(2)(B), 42 U.S.C. § 1857c–5(a)(2)(B).) Other prerequisites to approval by the Administrator are set forth in the Act. (Section 110(a)(2)(C) through (H), 42 U.S.C. § 1857c–5(a)(2)(C) through (H).)

Within four months after the date a state plan was required to be submitted, the Administrator was required to review the plan to determine whether it satisfied the statutory requirements and to approve or disapprove the plan or each portion thereof. (Section 110(a), 42 U.S.C. § 1857c–5(a).) If the Administrator determined that a state's plan or any portion thereof did not satisfy the statutory requirements, he was to disapprove the plan, or the offending portion thereof, and, within six months after the date the plan was required to be submitted, promulgate his own implementation plan or portion thereof for that state. (Section 110(c)(1), 42 U.S.C. § 1857c–5(c)(1).)

Significant Deterioration Regulations

During the period he was reviewing state plans, the Administrator questioned his authority to require those plans to protect against "significant deterioration" of air quality in areas in which the air was cleaner than required by the national standards, when that significant deterioration would not result in pollution violative of the national standards. He took the position that he would not demand such provisions in state plans. [Citations Omitted]

In the *Sierra Club* case the court held, on motion for preliminary injunction, that the Administrator had a non-discretionary duty to protect the air quality from significant deterioration and issued a preliminary injunction prohibiting him from approving state plans "which allow pollution levels of clean air to rise to the secondary level of pollution." 344 F.Supp. at 256. The court ordered the Administrator to promulgate proposed significant deterioration regulations within six months as to any state plan which permitted or failed to take measures sufficient to prevent significant deterioration. 2 E.L.R. 20262, 20263.

As a result of that decision, the Administrator again reviewed all state implementation plans and disapproved them to the extent that they failed to prevent significant deterioration of air quality. One of the plans affected was that of Illinois.* * *

In response to his duty under the court's order in the *Sierra Club* case the Administrator proposed (38 Fed.Reg. 18,986 (July 16, 1973)) and reproposed (39 Fed.Reg. 31,000 (Aug. 27, 1974)) rules on the prevention of significant air quality deterioration. Eventually he promulgated regulations for two of the six air pollutants for which he had earlier promulgated national ambient air quality standards under his statutory duty.[2] (39 Fed.Reg. 42,510 (Dec. 5, 1974).) These regulations are intended to prevent significant deterioration in the quality of air for two pollutants, particulate matter and sulfur dioxide, by limiting increases in the concentrations of those pollutants in areas where the present level of pollution is less than required by the national ambient air quality standards. This is to be accomplished by dividing those areas in which the level of pollution does not presently exceed the national ambient air quality standards into three classes in whch increases in concentration of the two pollutants are limited by different amounts. The Administrator originally classified all areas, but the states, after a public hearing and subject to other requirements, may submit to the Administrator proposals for reclassification of areas. No final regulations have been promulgated for the other four pollutants as of yet. The Administrator, therefore, has not yet complied with the *Sierra Club* order.

Indirect Source Regulations

When the Administrator gave partial approval to the Illinois implementation plan on May 26, 1972, he also granted to Illinois, as he did to a number of other states, extensions until February 15, 1973, to submit the transportation portion of its implementation plan. Several other states were given until mid-1977 to attain the national primary standards.* * * The court established a new time schedule under which the Administrator was to review the maintenance provisions of the state plans and disapprove those which he determined did not contain sufficient measures for maintenance of the primary standard. (*Id.* at 972.) In this re-examination, the Administrator found that none of the state plans, including that of Illinois, contained adequate provisions for insuring the maintenance of national standards, but granted the states another opportunity to develop adequate programs.

The Administrator, pursuant to the order of the Court of Appeals for the District of Columbia in *Natural Resources Defense Council, Inc. v. EPA*, then promulgated regulations to insure the maintenance of national standards by requiring state implementation plans to contain procedures for review of any new stationary source

[2]The six pollutants originally identified were sulfur dioxide, particulate matter, carbon monoxide, photochemical oxidants, hydrocarbons, and nitrogen dioxide. (40 C.F.R. §§ 50.4–50.11 (1974).) The original proposed rules referred to in the text broadened "nitrogen dioxide" to "nitrogen oxide" and omitted photochemical oxidants, apparently because they are formed from hydrocarbons and nitrogen dioxides and do not exist otherwise, and therefore do not require separate treatment. This part of the proposed rules required only that the best possible technology be used.

or modification that might "interfere with attainment or maintenance of a standard either directly because of emissions from it, or indirectly, because of emissions resulting from mobile source activities associated with it."* * *

An indirect source is defined by the regulation as "a facility, building, structure, or installation which attracts or may attract mobile source activities that results in emissions or a pollutant for which there is a national standard," for example a "[p]arking facility." (40 C.F.R. § 52.22(b)(i) (1974).) The regulation applies to any indirect source on which construction or modification is to commence after December 31, 1974. The Administrator later amended the indirect source regulations in respects not material here.

Counts I and II: The Regulations

In Count I of their complaint plaintiffs allege that the Administrator has been in violation of the provisions of the Act requiring him to issue two kinds of regulations: (a) significant deterioration regulations, preventing the significant deterioration of air quality in areas with air cleaner than national standards (as stated above, such regulations as to two of the six pollutants in question have now been promulgated); and (b) indirect source regulations, preventing violations of the national air quality standards by indirect sources (as stated above, these regulations have now been promulgated). They seek an order requiring him to promulgate those regulations and to halt further construction of the shopping center until its plans have been reviewed by the Administrator under both sets of regulations he is required to promulgate. In Count II the plaintiffs reallege that the Administrator has been in violation of his statutory duty to promulgate significant deterioration and indirect source regulations. In this count, however, they seek to halt construction of the Lake-Cook Road expansion and improvement project until its plans have been reviewed by the Administrator under both sets of regulations. To facilitate understanding of our analysis, we will divide our discussion of plaintiffs' claims by considering separately plaintiffs' rights to obtain promulgation of the two sets of regulations rather than by considering separately Counts I and II of their complaint.

Review of the Indirect Source Regulations

The Administrator having promulgated indirect source regulations after the complaint was filed, plaintiffs' grievance now is that those regulations exempt indirect sources on which construction was commenced before January 1, 1975, as it was on the shopping center involved in this case.

Section 307(b)(1) of the Amendments, 42 U.S.C. § 1857h–5(b)(1), provides in pertinent part:

> "A petition for review of the Administrator's action in . . . promulgating any implementation plan under section 1857c–5 of this title [section 110 of the Amendments] . . . may be filed only in the United States Court of Appeals for the appropriate circuit."

The indirect source regulations are subject to this section. Entitled "Review of Indirect Sources" (39 Fed.Reg. 7270 7285 (Feb. 25, 1974)), they purport to be promulgated pursuant to section 110, 42 U.S.C. § 1857c–5. It is so stated in the Administrator's comments in the first part of the regulations. Furthermore, the regulations contain the subtitle, "Approval and Promulgation of Implementation Plans," which is the statutory language used in section 307. The regulations set out the national standards for regulation of indirect sources, disapprove various parts of state implementation plans, and incorporate the federal standards into those plans. For example, Subpart O deals with Illinois and provides:

"Subpart O–Illinois

"25. Subpart O is amended by adding § 52.736 as follows:
"§ 52.736 Review of new sources and modifications.

"(a) The requirements of § 51.18 of this chapter are not met because the State failed to submit a plan for review of new or modified indirect sources.

"(b) *Regulation for review of new or modified indirect sources*. The provisions of § 52.22(b) of this chapter are hereby incorporated by reference and made a part of the applicable implementation plan for the State of Illinois." 39 Fed.Reg. at 7281.

Since the regulations incorporate the federal standards into the state plans, the Administrator is in effect promulgating implementation plans where state plans are deficient, in accordance with section 110(c) (42 U.S.C. § 1857c–5), which is to be reviewed only under section 307(b)(1) (42 U.S.C. § 1957h–5(b)(1)).

* * *

Plaintiffs attempt to characterize the regulations' exemption of any facility on which construction was started before January 1, 1975 as a failure to promulgate regulations with respect to such facilities. We think, however, that a provision defining the scope of regulations and their effective date is as much a part of the regulations as the substantive parts.* * *

The Failure to Promulgate Significant Deterioration Regulations for Automobile-Related Pollutants

Regulations for two air pollutants, particulate matter and sulfur dioxide, having been promulgated after the complaint was filed (see note 2, *supra*), plaintiffs now seek to require the Administrator to promulgate regulations for carbon monoxide and the other automobile-related pollutants for which he had established national ambient air standards.

As the District Court pointed out, the Administrator has already been ordered in *Sierra Club v. Ruckelshaus, supra*, to promulgate significant deterioration regulations. Counsel for the government, in their brief in this court, represented that the Administrator had complied with this order, and "[t]herefore, since the significant deterioration regulations have already been published, the issue of any prior failure to promulgate them is rendered moot." Because, as is apparent from the regulations and the Administrator's introductory statement accompanying them and as counsel for the government acknowledged during oral argument, the regulations that have been promulgated relate to only two of the six identified pollutants, the case is not moot as to this point. Whether there is a need for a second order against the Administrator to do that which he has already been ordered to do in the *Sierra Club* case is a question we need not reach, because we find that this claim is not maintainable by plaintiffs at this time.

Section 304(a) of the Amendments, 42 U.S.C. § 1857h–2(a), provides in pertinent part as follows:

"Except as provided in subsection (b) of this section, any person may commence a civil action on his own behalf—

* * *

"(2) against the Administrator where there is alleged a failure of the Administrator to perform any act or duty under this Act which is not discretionary with the Administrator."

Subsection (b), 42 U.S.C. § 1857h–2(b), imposes the following limitation upon this right to sue:

"No action may be commenced—

* * *

"(2) under subsection (a)(2) of this section prior to 60 days after the plaintiff has given notice of such action to the Administrator . . . ."

Plaintiffs failed to give the Administrator sixty days notice prior to commencing suit, which the District Court held was fatal to its jurisdiction under section 304. The court reasoned that the purpose of the sixty-day notice requirement was to give the Administrator time to assess and respond to difficult, multicount lawsuits, to deploy attorneys from Washington, if necessary, and to arrange for the on-going process of regulatory development and other substantive EPA concerns despite the interruption caused by a pending lawsuit.* * *

The legislative history of section 304 shows Congress's determination that citizen participation in the enforcement of standards and regulations under the Clean Air Act of 1970 be established. It also shows, however, that Congress intended to provide for citizens' suits in a manner that would be least likely to clog already burdened federal courts and most likely to trigger governmental action which would alleviate any need for judicial relief. It was in response to these concerns that the statutory notice provisions were included in section 304.* * *

Disposition as to Counts I and II

Since neither judicial review of the indirect source regulations nor mandatory relief to compel the promulgation of significant deterioration regulations for pollutants related to automobiles is available in the proceedings before us, there is no basis in the allegations of Counts I and II for plaintiffs' demand for an injunction against further construction on the highway expansion and the shopping center until their claims concerning these regulations are finally resolved. We cannot find at this stage a sufficient likelihood that regulations entitling plaintiffs to such injunctive relief will ultimately be promulgated to justify an award of injunctive relief. We therefore affirm the dismissal of Counts I and II.

The Petition for Review

On January 6, 1975, plaintiffs filed in this court a petition for review, No. 75–1006, seeking review of the significant deterioration regulations promulgated by the Administrator on December 5, 1974. That petition which states as petitioners' sole grievance the Administrator's failure to promulgate significant deterioration regulations with respect to carbon monoxide and other automobile related pollutants was consolidated with No. 74–1271 on the representation by petitioners that the same substantive issues were involved in the two cases, the court viewing the petition for review as an attempt by petitioners to "safeguard their jurisdictional grounds." * * * The appropriate procedure for compelling the Administrator to act is that provided in section 304(a), *supra*, which expressly provides for an action in the district court "against the Administrator when there is alleged a failure of the Administrator to perform any act or duty under this Act which is not discretionary with the Administrator." Plaintiffs recognized this when they brought their action under section 304(a), but they failed to give statutory notice that would have made their action viable. The petition for review is dismissed.* * *

Part Three

Water Pollution

Part Three

Water Pollution

A. Introduction: Basic Concepts and Definitions

1. Types of Water Pollutants

Our nation has been fortunate in having water resources in substantial quantity and in relatively good quality. Many recent incidents resulting in water pollution have directed attention to current problems of water contamination. However, pollution of water is an old problem. A century ago the primary cause of water pollution was its contamination by typhoid bacteria in human fecal matter. This problem was relatively easily resolved by the construction of sewage treatment plants and by other techniques of sanitary engineering. In recent years the problem of water pollution has been complicated by the introduction of many new chemical contaminants whose effect is more indirect, latent and more difficult to diagnose and eliminate.

In *A Primer on Waste Water Treatment*, Environmental Protection Agency (CWA-12, 1971), EPA describes eight types of pollutants that affect our water supply:

Oxygen-demanding wastes. These are the traditional organic wastes and ammonia contributed by domestic sewage and by industrial wastes of plant and animal origin. In addition to human sewage, such wastes result from food processing, paper production, tanning, and other manufacturing processes. These wastes are usually destroyed by bacteria if there is sufficient oxygen in the water. Since fish and other aquatic life depend on oxygen for life, the oxygen-demanding wastes must be controlled, or the fish die.

Disease-causing agents. This category includes infectious organisms which are carried into surface and ground water by sewage from cities and institutions and by certain kinds of industrial wastes, such as those from tanning and meat packing plants. Man or animals come in contact with these microbes either by drinking the water or while, for example, swimming or fishing. Although modern disinfection techniques have greatly reduced the danger of this type of pollutant, potential problem areas must be monitored continually.

Plant nutrients. These are the substances in the food chain of aquatic life such as algae and water weeds which support and stimulate their growth. Carbon, nitrogen and phosphorus are the three chief nutrients present in natural water. Large amounts of these nutrients are produced by sewage, certain industrial wastes, and drainage from fertilized lands. Biological waste treatment processes do not remove the phosphorus and nitrogen to any substantial extent—in fact, they convert the organic forms of these substances to mineral form, making them more usable by plant life. The problem starts when an excess of these nutrients overstimulates the growth of water plants, causing unsightly conditions, interfering with treatment processes, and causing unpleasant and disagreeable tastes and odors in the water.

Synthetic organic chemicals. Included in this category are detergents and other household aids, all the new synthetic organic pesticides, synthetic industrial chemicals, and the wastes from their manufacture. Many of these substances are toxic to fish and aquatic life and are possibly harmful to humans. They cause taste and odor problems and resist conventional waste treatment. Some are known to be highly poisonous at very low concentrations. What the long-term effects of small doses of toxic substances may be is not yet known.

Inorganic chemicals and mineral substances. A vast array of metal salts, acids, solid matter, and many other chemical compounds is included in this group. They reach our waters from mining and manufacturing processes, oil field operations, agricultural practices, and natural sources. Water used in irrigation picks up large amounts of minerals as it filters down through the soil on its way to the nearest stream. Acids of a wide variety are discharged as wastes by industry, but the largest single source of acid in our water comes from mining operations and mines that have been abandoned. Many of these types of chemicals are being created each year. They interfere with natural stream purification; destroy fish and other aquatic life; cause excessive hardness of water supplies; corrode expensive water treatment equipment; increase commercial and recreational boat maintenance costs; and increase the cost of waste treatment.

Sediments. These are the particles of soils, sands, and minerals washed from the land and paved areas of communities into the water. Construction projects are often large sediment producers. While not as insidious as some other types of pollution, sediments are a major problem because of the sheer magnitude of the amount reaching our waterways. Sediments fill stream channels and harbors, requiring expensive dredging, and they fill reservoirs, reducing their capacities and useful life. They erode power turbines and pumping equipment, and reduce fish and shellfish populations by blanketing fish nests and food supplies. More important, sediments reduce the amount of sunlight penetrating the water. The sunlight is required by green aquatic plants in producing the oxygen necessary to normal stream balance. Sediments greatly increase the treatment costs for municipal and industrial water supply and for sewage treatment where combined sewers are in use.

Radioactive substances. Radioactive pollution results from the mining and processing of radioactive ores; from the use of refined radioactive materials in power reactors and for industrial, medical and research purposes; and from fallout following nuclear weapons testing. Increased use of these substances poses a potential public health problem. Since radiation accumulates in humans, control of this type of pollution must take into consideration total exposure in the human environment—water, air, food, occupation and medical treatment.

Heat. Heat reduces the capacity of water to absorb oxygen. Tremendous volumes of water are used by power plants and industry for cooling. Most of the water, with the added heat, is returned to streams, raising their temperatures. With less oxygen, the water is not as efficient in assimilating oxygen-consuming wastes and in supporting fish and aquatic life. Unchecked waste-heat discharges can seriously alter the ecology of a lake, a stream, or even part of the sea.

Water in lakes or stored in impoundments can be greatly affected by heat. Summer temperatures heat up the surfaces, causing the water to form into layers, with the cooler water forming the deeper layers. Decomposing vegetable matter from natural and man-made pollutants deplete the oxygen from these cooler lower layers, with harmful effects on the aquatic life. When the oxygen-deficient water is discharged from the lower gates of a dam, it may have serious effects on downstream fish life and reduce the ability of the stream to assimilate downstream pollution.

Municipal wastes usually contain oxygen-consuming pollutants, synthetic organic chemicals such as detergents, sediments, and other types of pollutants. The same is true of many industrial wastes, which may contain, in addition, substantial amounts of heat from cooling processes. Water that drains off the land usually contains great amounts of organic matter in addition to sediment. Also, land drainage may contain radioactive substances and pollutants washed from the sky, vegetation, buildings, and streets during rainfall.

To complicate matters, most of our wastes are a mixture of the eight types of pollution, making the problems of treatment and control that much more difficult.

2. Water-Quality Standards and Criteria

One of the first steps in a rational process of regulation of the causes of water pollution is to determine the **standards** by which water quality will be evaluated and to establish the **criteria** by which each of the contaminants will be measured.

There is general agreement that the quality of water may be measured by the following **general standards**:

- Amount of oxygen dissolved in water (DO)
- Biochemical oxygen demand (BOD) of the wastes discharged
- Acidity and alkalinity (*ph*) of the water
- Solids in the water
- Turbidity (cloudiness)
- Color
- Temperature
- Taste and odor
- Organisms living in the water
- Other properties, such as radioactivity and salinity

In addition to the above water-quality standards, attention has been directed to the question of water-quality criteria because of Section 304(a) of the Federal Water Pollution Control Act Amendments of 1972. That section directs the Administrator of EPA to develop and publish "criteria for water quality" that reflect the latest scientific knowledge about the kind and extent of all identifiable effects of pollutants in water on health and the biological community. In response to this directive EPA has published *Quality Criteria For Water* (1976), in which it has specified the criteria for over 50 water pollutants. The report defines "water-quality criteria" as "a designated concentration of a constituent that, when not exceeded, will protect an organism, an organism community, or a prescribed water use or quality with an adequate degree of safety." The following are some examples of quality criteria set forth in this report:

Fecal Coliform Bacteria:

Bathing Waters. Based on a minimum of five samples taken over a 30-day period, the fecal coliform bacterial level should not exceed a log mean of 200 per 100 ml, nor should more than 10 percent of the total samples taken during any 30-day period exceed 400 per 100 ml.

Shellfish Harvesting Waters. The median fecal coliform bacterial concentration should not exceed 14 MPN (most probable number) per 100 ml with not more than 10 percent of samples exceeding 43 MPN per 100 ml for the taking of shellfish.

Lead

0.3 mg/l for domestic water supplies (welfare).
1.0mg/l for freshwater aquatic life.

3. METHODS OF SEWAGE TREATMENT

Most of the effort and expenditures for water pollution control has been directed to the construction of sewer systems and waste treatment plants. The following excerpts from A Primer on Waste Water Treatment, EPA (No.

CWA-12, 1971) provide basic information about the processes of sewage treatment.

A PRIMER ON WASTE WATER TREATMENT

Environmental Protection Agency (1971)

Collecting and Treating Wastes

The most common form of pollution control in the United States consists of a system of sewers and waste treatment plants. The sewers collect the waste water from homes, businesses, and many industries and deliver it to the plants for treatment to make it fit for discharge into streams or for reuse.

There are two kinds of sewer systems—combined and separate. Combined sewers carry away both water polluted by human use and water polluted as it drains off homes, streets, or land during a storm.

In a separated system, one system of sewers, usually called sanitary, carries only sewage. Another system of storm sewers takes care of the large volumes of water from rain or melting snow.

Each home has a sewer or pipe which connects to the common or lateral sewer beneath a nearby street. Lateral sewers connect with larger sewers called trunk or main sewers. In a combined sewer system, these trunk or main sewers discharge into a larger sewer called an interceptor. The interceptor is designed to carry several times the dry-weather flow of the system feeding into it.

During dry weather when the sewers are handling only the normal amount of waste water, all of it is carried to the waste treatment plant. During a storm when the amount of water in the sewer system is much greater, part of the water, including varying amounts of raw sewage, is allowed to bypass directly into the receiving streams. The rest of the wastes are sent to the treatment plant. If part of the increased load of water were not diverted, the waste treatment plant would be overloaded and the purifying processes would not function properly. (A research, development and demonstration program is being conducted to solve this urban runoff pollution problem. The aim is to develop technology that will control and/or treat combined sewer overflows, storm water discharges and general washoff of rainwater polluted by dirt or other contaminants on the land.)

Interceptor sewers are also used in sanitary sewer systems as collectors of flow from main sewers and trunks, but do not normally include provisions for bypassing. A waste treatment plant's basic function is to speed up the natural processes by which water purifies itself. In many cases, nature's treatment process in streams and lakes was adequate before our population and industry grew to their present size.

When the sewage of previous years was dumped into waterways, the natural process of purification began. First, the sheer volume of clean water in the stream diluted the small amount of wastes. Bacteria and other small organisms in the water consumed the sewage or other organic matter, turning it into new bacterial cells, carbon dioxide, and other products.

But the bacteria normally present in water must have oxygen to do their part in breaking down the sewage. Water acquires this all-important oxygen by absorbing it from the air and from plants that grow in the water itself. These plants use sunlight to turn the carbon dioxide present in water into oxygen.

The life and death of any body of water depend mainly upon its ability to maintain a certain amount of dissolved oxygen. This dissolved oxygen—or DO—is what fish breathe. Without it they suffocate. If only a small amount of sewage is dumped into a stream, fish are not affected and the bacteria can do their work and the stream can quickly restore its oxygen loss from the atmosphere and from plants. Trouble begins when the sewage load is excessive. The sewage will decay and the water will begin to give off odors. If carried to the extreme, the water could lose all of its oxygen, resulting in the death of fish and beneficial plant life.

Since dissolved oxygen is the key element in the life of water, the demands on it are used as a measure in telling how well a sewage treatment plant is working. This measuring device is called biochemical oxygen demand, or BOD. If the effluent or the end-product from a treatment plant has a high content of organic pollutants, the effluent will have a high BOD. In other words, it will demand more oxygen from the water to break down the sewage and consequently will leave the water with less oxygen (and also dirtier).

With the growth of the nation, the problems of pollution have become more complex. The increased amounts of wastes and the larger demands for water have reduced the capacity of running water to purify itself. Consequently, cities and industry have had to begin thinking about removing as much as possible of the oxygen-demanding pollutants from their sewage.

Adequate treatment of wastes along with providing a sufficient supply of clean water has become a major concern.

Primary Treatment

At present, there are two basic ways of treating wastes. They are called primary and secondary. In primary treatment, solids are allowed to settle and are removed from the water. Secondary treatment, a further step in purifying waste water, uses biological processes.

As sewage enters a plant for primary treatment, it flows through a screen. The screen removes large floating objects such as rags and sticks that may clog pumps and small pipes. The screens vary from coarse to fine—from those with parallel steel or iron bars with openings of about half an inch or more to screens with much smaller openings.

Screens are generally placed in a chamber or channel in an inclined position to the flow of the sewage to make cleaning easier. The debris caught on the upstream surface of the screen can be raked off manually or mechanically.

Some plants use a device known as a comminutor which combines the functions of a screen and a grinder. These devices catch and then cut or shred the heavy solid material. In the process, the pulverized matter remains in the sewage flow to be removed later in a settling tank.

After the sewage has been screened, it passes into what is called a grit chamber where sand, grit, cinders, and small stones are allowed to settle to the bottom. A grit chamber is highly important for cities with combined sewer systems because it will remove the grit or gravel that washes off streets or land during a storm and ends up at treatment plants.

The unwanted grit or gravel from this process is usually disposed of by filling land near a treatment plant.

In some plants, another screen is placed after the grit chamber to remove any further material that might damage equipment or interfere with later processes.

With the screening completed and the grit removed, the sewage still contains dissolved organic and inorganic matter along with suspended solids. The latter consist of minute particles of matter that can be removed from the sewage by treatment in a sedimentation tank. When the speed of the flow of sewage through one of these tanks is reduced, the suspended solids will gradually sink to the bottom. This mass of solids is called raw sludge.

Various methods have been devised for removing sludge from the tanks.

In older plants, sludge removal was done by hand. After a tank has been in service for several days or weeks, the sewage flow was diverted to another tank. The sludge in the bottom of the out-of-service tank was pushed or flushed with water to a pit near the tank, and then removed, usually by pumping, for further treatment or disposal.

Almost all plants built within the past 30 years have had a mechanical means for removing the sludge from sedimentation tanks. Some plants remove it continuously while others remove it at intervals.

To complete the primary treatment, the effluent from the sedimentation tank is chlorinated before being discharged into a stream or river. Chlorine gas is fed into the water to kill and reduce the number of disease-causing bacteria. Chlorination also helps to reduce objectionable odors.

Although 30 percent of the municipalities in the United States give only primary treatment to their sewage, this process by itself is considered entirely inadequate for most needs.

Today's cities and industry, faced with increased amounts of wastes and wastes that are more difficult to remove from water, have turned to secondary and even advanced waste treatment.

Secondary Treatment

Secondary treatment removes up to 90 percent of the organic matter in sewage by making use of the bacteria in it. The two principal types of secondary treatment are trickling filters and the activated-sludge process.

The trickling filter process or the activated sludge process is used mostly today. After the effluent leaves the sedimentation tank in the primary stage of treatment, it flows or is pumped to a facility using one or the other of these processes. A trickling filter is simply a bed of stones from three to ten feet deep through which the sewage passes. Bacteria gather and multiply on these stones until they can consume most of the organic matter in the sewage. The cleaner water trickles out through pipes in the bottom of the filter for further treatment.

The sewage is applied to the bed of stones in two principal ways. One method consists of distributing the effluent intermittently through a network of pipes laid on or beneath the surface of the stones.

Attached to these pipes are smaller, vertical pipes which spray the sewage over the stones.

Another much-used method consists of a vertical pipe in the center of the filter connected to rotating horizontal pipes which spray the sewage continuously upon the stones.

The trend today is toward the use of the activated sludge process instead of trickling filters. This process speeds up the work of the bacteria by bringing air and sludge heavily laden with bacteria into close contact with the sewage.

After the sewage leaves the settling tank in primary treatment, it is pumped to an aeration tank where it is mixed with air and sludge loaded with bacteria and allowed to remain for several hours. During this time, the bacteria break down the organic matter.

From the aeration tank, the sewage, now called mixed liquor, flows to another sedimentation tank to remove the solids. Chlorination of the effluent completes the basic secondary treatment.

The sludge, now activated with additional millions of bacteria and other tiny organisms, can be used again by returning it to an aeration tank for mixing with new sewage and ample amounts of air.

The activated sludge process, like most other techniques, has advantages and limitations. The size of the units necessary for this treatment is small, thereby requiring less land space and the process is free of flies and odors. But it is more costly to operate than the trickling filter, and the activated sludge process sometimes loses its effectiveness when faced with difficult industrial wastes.

An adequate supply of oxygen is necessary for the activated sludge process to be effective. Air is mixed with sewage and biologically active sludge in the aeration tanks by three different methods.

The first, mechanical aeration, is accomplished by drawing the sewage from the bottom of the tank and spraying it over the surface, thus causing the sewage to absorb large amounts of oxygen from the atmosphere.

In the second method, large amounts of air under pressure are piped down into the sewage and forced out through openings in the pipe. The third method is a combination of mechanical aeration and the forced air method.

The final phase of the secondary treatment consists of the addition of chlorine, as the most common method of disinfection, to the effluent coming from the trickling filter or the activated sludge process. Chlorine is usually purchased in liquid form, converted to a gas, and injected into the effluent 15 to 30 minutes before the treated water is discharged into a watercourse. If done properly, chlorination will kill more than 99 percent of the harmful bacteria in an effluent.

Lagoons and Septic Tanks

There are many well-populated areas in the United States that are not served by any sewer systems or waste treatment plants. Lagoons and septic tanks may act as less than satisfactory alternatives at such locations.

A septic tank is simply a tank buried in the ground to treat the sewage from an individual home. Waste water from the home flows into the tank where bacteria in the sewage may break down the organic matter and the cleaner water flows out of the tank into the ground through sub-surface drains. Periodically the sludge or solid matter in the bottom of the tank must be removed and disposed of.

In a rural setting, with the right kind of soil and the proper location, the septic tank may be a reasonable and temporary means of disposing of strictly domestic wastes. Septic tanks should always be located so that none of the effluent can seep into sources used for drinking.

Lagoons, or as they are sometimes called, stabilization or oxidation ponds also have several advantages when used correctly.

They can give sewage primary and secondary treatment or they can be used to supplement other processes.

A lagoon is a scientifically constructed pond, usually three to five feet deep, in which sunlight, algae, and oxygen interact to restore water to a quality that is often equal to or better than effluent from secondary treatment. Changes in the weather may change the effectiveness of lagoons.

When used with other waste treatment processes, lagoons can be very effective. A good example of this is the Santee, California, water reclamation project. After conventional primary and secondary treatment by activated sludge, the town's waste water is kept in a lagoon for 30 days. Then the effluent, after chlorination, is pumped to land immediately above a series of lakes and allowed to trickle down through sandy soil into the lakes. The resulting water is of such good quality, the residents of the area can swim, boat, and fish in the lake water.

Advanced Methods of Treating Wastes

These new problems of a modern society have placed additional burdens upon our waste treatment systems. Today's pollutants are more difficult to remove from the water. And increased demands upon our water supply aggravate the problem. During the dry season, the flow of rivers decreases to such an extent that they have difficulty in assimilating the effluent from waste treatment plants.

In the future, these problems will be met through better and more complete methods of removing pollutants from water and better means for preventing some wastes from even reaching our streams in the first place.

The best immediate answer to these problems is the widespread application of existing waste treatment methods. Many cities that have only primary treatment need secondary treatment. Many other cities need enlarged or modernized primary and secondary systems.

But this is only a temporary solution. The discharge of oxygen-consuming wastes will increase despite the universal application of the most efficient waste treatment processes now available. And these are the simplest wastes to dispose of. Conventional treatment processes are already losing the battle against the modern-day, tougher wastes.

The increasing need to reuse water now calls for better and better waste treatment. Every use of water—whether in the home, in the factory, or on the farm—results in some change in its quality.

To return water of more usable quality to receiving lakes and streams, new methods for removing pollutants are being developed. The advanced waste treatment techniques under investigation range from extensions of biological treatment capable of removing nitrogen and phosphorus nutrients to physical-chemical separation techniques such as adsorption, distillation, and reverse osmosis.

These new processes can achieve any degree of pollution control desired and, as waste effluents are purified to higher and higher degrees by such treatment, the point is reached where effluents become "too good to throw away."

Such water can be deliberately and directly reused for agricultural, industrial, recreational, or even drinking water supplies. This complete water renovation will mean complete pollution control and at the same time more water for the Nation.

Coagulation–Sedimentation

The application of advanced techniques for waste treatment, at least in the next several years, will most likely take up where primary and secondary treatment leave off. Ultimately, entirely new systems will no doubt replace the modern facilities of today.

The process known as coagulation–sedimentation may be used to increase the removal of solids from effluent after primary and secondary treatment. Besides removing essentially all of the settleable solids, this method can, with proper control and sufficient addition of chemicals, reduce the concentration of phosphate by over 95 percent.

In this process, alum, lime, or iron salts are added to effluent as it comes from the secondary treatment. The flow then passes through flocculation tanks where the chemicals cause the smaller particles to floc or bunch together into large masses.

The larger masses of particles or lumps will settle faster when the effluent reaches the next step—the sedimentation tank.

Although used for years in the treatment of industrial wastes and in water treatment, coagulation–sedimentation is classified as an advanced process because it is not usually applied to the treatment of municipal wastes. In many cases, the process is a necessary pre-treatment for some of the other advanced techniques.

Adsorption

Technology has also been developed to effect the removal of refractory organic materials. These materials are the stubborn organic matter which persists in water and resists normal biological treatment.

The effects of the organics are not completely understood, but taste and odor problems in water and fish kills have been attributed to such materials.

Adsorption consists of passing the effluent through a bed of activated carbon granules which will remove more than 98 percent of the organics. To cut down the cost of the procedure, the carbon granules can be cleaned by heat and used again.

An alternative system utilizing powdered carbon is under study. Rather than pass the effluent through a bed of granules, the powdered carbon is put directly into the stream. The organics stick to the carbon and then the carbon is removed from the effluent by using coagulating chemicals and allowing the coagulated carbon particles to settle in a tank.

The use of this finely ground carbon will improve the rate at which the refractory organics are removed. The potential widespread use of powdered carbon adsorption depends largely on the effectiveness of regenerating the carbon for use again.

Except for the salts added during the use of water, municipal waste water that has gone through the previous advanced processes will be restored to a chemical quality almost the same as before it was used.

When talking of salts in water, salt is not limited to the common kind that is used in the home for seasoning food. In waste treatment language, salts mean the many minerals dissolved by water as it passes through the air as rainfall, as it trickles through the soil and over rocks, and as it is used in the home and factory.

Electrodialysis

Electrodialysis is a rather complicated process by which electricity and membranes are used to remove salts from an effluent. A membrane is usually made of chemically treated plastic. The salts are forced out of the water by the action of an electric field. When a mineral salt is placed in water it has a tendency to break down into ions. An ion is an atom or a small group of atoms having an electrical charge.

As an example, the two parts of common table salt are sodium and chlorine. When these two elements separate as salt dissolves in water, the sodium and chlorine particles are called ions. Sodium ions have a positive charge while chlorine ions have a negative charge.

When the effluent passes through the electrodialysis cell, the positive sodium ions are attracted through a membrane to a pole or electrode that is negatively charged. The negatively charged chlorine ions are pulled out of the water through another membrane toward an electrode with a positive charge.

With the salts removed by the action of the two electrodes, the clean water flows out of the electrodialysis cell for reuse or discharge into a river or stream.

As a city uses its water, the amount of salts in the water increases by 300–400 milligrams per liter. Fortunately, electrodialysis can remove this buildup of salts.

In other words, this process returns the salt content of the water back to where it was or even better than when the city first received the water.

Common Sewage Treatment Terminology

Activated Sludge process removes organic matter from sewage by saturating it with air and adding biologically active sludge.

Adsorption is an advanced way of treating wastes in which activated carbon removes organic matter from waste water.

Aeration Tank serves as a chamber for injecting air into water.
Algae are plants which grow in sunlit waters. They are a food for fish and small aquatic animals and, like all plants, put oxygen in the water.
Bacteria are small living organisms which often consume the organic constituents of sewage.
BOD, or biochemical oxygen demand, is the dissolved oxygen required by organisms for the aerobic decomposition of organic matter present in water. It is used as a measure in determining the efficiency of a sewage treatment plant.
Chlorinator is a device for adding chlorine gas to sewage to kill infectious germs.
Coagulation is the clumping together of solids to make them settle out of the sewage faster. Coagulation of solids is brought about with the use of certain chemicals such as lime, alum and iron salts.
Combined Sewer carries both sewage and storm water run-off.
Comminutor is a device for the catching and shredding of heavy solid matter in the primary stage of waste treatment.
Diffused Air is a technique by which air under pressure is forced into sewage in an aeration tank. The air is pumped down into the sewage through a pipe and escapes out through holes in the side of the pipe.
Digestion of sludge takes place in tanks when the materials decompose, resulting in partial gasification, liquefaction, and mineralization of pollutants.
Distillation in waste treatment consists of heating the effluent and then removing the vapor or steam. When the steam is returned to a liquid it is almost pure water. The pollutants remain in the concentrated residue.
Effluent is the liquid that comes out of a treatment plant after completion of the treatment process.
Electrodialysis is a process which utilizes direct current and an arrangement of permeable-active membranes to achieve separation of the soluble minerals from the water.
Floc is a clump of solids formed in sewage by biological or chemical action.
Flocculation is the process by which clumps of solids in sewage are made to increase in size by chemical, physical, or biological action.
Fungi are small, non-chlorophyll-bearing plants which may play a useful role in trickling filter treatment operations.
Incineration consists of burning the sludge to remove the water and reduce the remaining residues to a safe, non-burnable ash. The ash can then be disposed of safely on land, in some waters, or into caves or other underground locations.
Interceptor sewers in a combined system control the flow of the sewage to the treatment plant. In a storm, they allow some of the sewage to flow directly into a receiving stream. This protects the treatment plant from being overloaded in case of a sudden surge of water into the sewers. Interceptors are also used in separate sanitation systems to collect the flows from main and trunk sewers and carry them to the points of treatment.
Ion is an electrically charged atom or group of atoms which can be drawn from waste water during the electrodialysis process.
Lateral sewers are the pipes that run under the streets of a city and into which empty the sewers from homes or businesses.
Lagoons are ponds, usually man-made to rigid specifications, in which sunlight, algae, and oxygen interact to restore water to a reasonable state of purity.
Mechanical Aeration uses mechanical energy to inject air into water, causing the waste stream to absorb oxygen from the atmosphere.
Microbes are minute plant or animal life. Some microbes which may cause disease exist in sewage.
Mixed Liquor is a mixture of activated sludge and waters containing organic matter undergoing activated sludge treatment in the aeration tank.

Organic Matter is the carbonaceous waste contained in plant or animal matter and originating from domestic or industrial sources.

Oxidation is the addition of oxygen which breaks down organic wastes or chemicals in sewage by bacterial and chemical means.

Oxidation Pond is a man-made lake or body of water in which wastes are consumed by bacteria. It is used most frequently with other waste treatment processes. An oxidation pond is basically the same as a sewage lagoon.

Primary Treatment removes the material that floats or will settle in sewage. It is accomplished by using screens to catch the floating objects and tanks for the heavy matter to settle in.

Pollution results when animal, vegetable, mineral or heat wastes or discharges reach water, making it less desirable for domestic, recreation, industry, or wildlife uses.

Polyelectrolytes are synthetic chemicals used to speed the removal of solids from sewage. The chemicals cause the solids to flocculate or clump together more rapidly than chemicals like alum or lime.

Receiving Waters are rivers, lakes, oceans, or other water courses that receive treated or untreated waste waters.

Salts are the minerals that water picks up as it passes through the air, over and under the ground, and through household and industrial uses.

Sand Filters remove some suspended solids from sewage. Air and bacteria decompose additional wastes filtering through the sand. Cleaner water drains from the bed. The sludge accumulating at the surface must be removed from the bed periodically.

Sanitary Sewers, in a separate system, are pipes in a city that carry only domestic waste water. The storm water runoff is taken care of by a separate system of pipes.

Secondary Treatment is the second step in most waste treatment systems in which bacteria consume the organic parts of the wastes. It is accomplished by bringing the sewage and bacteria together in trickling filters or in the activated sludge process.

Sedimentation Tanks help remove solids from sewage. The waste water is pumped to the tanks where the solids settle to the bottom or float on the top as scum. The scum is skimmed off the top, and solids on the bottom are pumped to incineration, digestion, filtration or other means of final disposal.

Septic Tanks are used for domestic wastes when a sewer line is not available to carry them to a treatment plant. The wastes are piped to underground tanks directly from the home or homes. The bacteria in the wastes decompose the organic waste and the sludge settles on the bottom of the tank. The effluent flows out of the tank into the ground through drains. The sludge is pumped out of the tanks, usually by commercial firms, at regular intervals.

Sewers are a system of pipes that collect and deliver waste water to treatment plants or receiving streams.

Sludge is the solid matter that settles to the bottom, floats, or becomes suspended in the sedimentation tanks and must be disposed of by filtration and incineration or by transport to appropriate disposal sites.

Storm Sewers are a separate system of pipes that carry only runoffs from buildings and land during a storm.

Sterilization is the destruction of all living organisms. In contrast, disinfection is the destruction of most of the living organisms.

Suspended Solids are the small particles of solid pollutants which are present in sewage and which resist separation from the water by conventional means.

Trickling Filter is a support medium for bacterial growth, usually a bed of rocks or stones. The sewage is trickled over the bed so the bacteria can break down the organic wastes. The bacteria collect on the stones through repeated use of the filter.

Waste Treatment Plant is a series of tanks, screens, filters, and other processes by which pollutants are removed from water.
Virus is the smallest form of micro-organism capable of causing disease.

B. Private Rights and Remedies

Before the adoption of the system of regulation provided by the federal government in the Federal Water Pollution Control Act, also known as the Clean Water Act, the rights of private persons to clean water were determined by common-law principles such as riparian rights, the nuisance doctrine and the constitutional protection against having government take private property without the payment of just compensation. These common law and constitutional principles continue to provide the basis of private rights and remedies in addition to rights arising from federal and state water pollution control legislation.

1. Riparian Rights

Riparian rights are the various rights that belong to the owners of land adjoining a body of water. Technically, "riparian" is used to describe land adjoining a river or stream and "littoral" is used for land on a lake or ocean. However, in most discussions of the issue, the word "riparian" is used to describe both situations. The important distinction is that these rights do not belong to the public at large but are incidental to the ownership of land adjoining water.

There are two different theories of riparian rights in use in different sections of the country. In the northeastern sections of the country most states have adopted the **reasonable-use** or **natural-flow** principle to determine the respective rights of upstream and downstream owners of land. Under the "reasonable use" theory, each riparian owner may make full use of the adjoining water-course as long as it does not unreasonably interfere with the beneficial use of other riparian owners. Under the "natural flow" theory, each riparian owner has the right to have the flow of water across his land maintained in its natural state, without significant diminution of quality or quantity. As a practical matter, many courts in the northeastern section of the country have combined the two theories to protect a riparian owner's right to natural flow subject to reasonable use by other riparian owners.

In the western sections of the country many states have adopted a theory known as the **prior-appropriation** or "first come, first served" principle. This general principle has been modified to some extent by state legislation.

In *Westville v. Whitney Home Builders*, the court discusses the various theories of riparian rights. This decision is followed by *Restatement, Torts*, Section 853, that proposes specific factors to be considered in determining the relative utility of use of the water by competing riparian owners. Following that are sections of an Oklahoma statute and the Colorado Constitution that illustrate the attitude of the western states on riparian rights.

WESTVILLE
v.
WHITNEY HOME BUILDERS, INC.

40 N.J.Super. 62, 122 A.2d 233 (1956)

CONFORD, J.A.D.

The plaintiff, Borough of Westville, is a municipality in Gloucester County. It is situated on the outskirts of Camden, near the Delaware River. The Township of Deptford adjoins it on the south. The defendant, Whitney Home Builders, Inc., has been engaged in the construction of a one-family residential development in Deptford, near the Westville line.* * *

Under plans approved by the State Board of Health in the summer of 1954, the defendant sewerage company has constructed in Deptford, near the Westville boundary, a sewage treatment plant geared to handle and treat the sewage from 300 homes. The plant went into operation the latter part of December 1954. At the time of the trial of this cause in April and May 1955, some 30 homes were being serviced. The gravamen of this action concerns the disposition of the liquid effluent of the treated sewage. It is discharged into a small natural stream or ditch which traverses the property of the defendants and flows thence in a northeasterly direction through Westville somewhat less than a mile and then empties into a pond, which, with part of the ditch, is situated in the borough's principal park. The park land was acquired by the borough by tax foreclosure in 1939. The pond drains over a spillway on its easterly bank into an outlet to the waters of Big Timber Creek, some 1,000 feet away, a tributary of the nearby Delaware.

Both the ditch and the pond originate in natural watercourses fed by surface waters. In 1940 the pond was improved in the course of a federal W. P. A. project for conversion of the foreclosed land into a park. The pond averages two to three feet in depth and is now about 500 feet in length. It has been used for many years by the public for skating in winter and by boys for fishing and, occasionally, wading in summer. Wading in recent years has apparently been infrequent. Since the construction of the park it has been a recreational center of the borough. There are benches around the pond and basketball and baseball play areas. It is the locale for all public patriotic exercises and the situs of memorials for veterans of both world wars. A newly erected schoolhouse is situated west of the park, near the pond.* * *

The plaintiffs named in the complaint, which was filed August 2, 1954, were the borough and the local board of health. They alleged the impending construction of the sewerage system, the proposed discharge of the sewage effluent into the ditch and its consequent flow from the ditch into and through the park pond. The threatened use of the ditch was described as "deleterious" and plaintiffs charged:

> "(a) that they have a right that the surface waters which heretofore have flowed through said ditch shall not be contaminated or polluted by the discharge of the effluent from said proposed sewerage disposal plant; and
>
> "(b) that the discharge of said effluent, if permitted, would create a public nuisance and be productive of a hazard to the public health."

and demanded judgment of injunction and damages.* * *

A pretrial conference produced a pretrial order, filed February 18, 1955, wherein the remaining count of the complaint is paraphrased as a cause of action by the borough, "as lower riparian proprietor, to restrain defendants, as upper riparian proprietors, from unreasonably contaminating or polluting, or further unreasonably contaminating or polluting, the waters" of the ditch * * * "by the discharge of sewage effluent into said ditch."

* * *

The trial court concluded that there had been no showing of contamination as it defined the term—"increase of bacteria and organisms," or of any "appreciable pollution." The showing as to prospective "putrescence" and decay from increased vegetation in the pond was found "too speculative" to found a claim for relief. The plaintiff's grievance was assessed as one solely "psychological or esthetic" in nature, and not, as such, the appropriate subject of injunctive relief. Judgment was entered on the merits for defendants.* * *

Plaintiff purports at the opening of its argument to rely solely for its right to injunctive relief upon the asserted inherent offensiveness and loathesomeness of the sewage effluent, no matter how efficient defendants' treatment plant and relatively free from impurities the effluent, analytically speaking. It urges that the flow into the ditch and pond *ipso facto* introduces a self-evident "noisome substance" into the common watercourse, Worthen & Aldrich v. White Spring Paper Co., 74 N.J.Eq. 647, 654, 70 A. 468 (Ch.1908), affirmed 75 N.J.Eq. 624, 78 A. 1135 (E. & A.1909), this amounting to an invasion of its property rights in its status as a riparian owner, which entitles it to relief without regard to the existence of damages in any other sense.* * *

Water pollution is generally measured in important degree in terms of bacteria count and index of coliform micro-organisms (B coli), the latter reflecting the degree of animal (including human) excrement. Analysis of the waters of the ditch and pond by an expert for defendants prior to the construction of the plant, on July 27, 1954, showed "gross pollution" at points above and below the proposed site of the sewage plant and in the pond, in terms both of bacteria and B coli. The measure of dissolved oxygen at the mouth of the pond was 1.9 parts per million in July, 1954, an indication of the beginning of putrefaction. All the witnesses testified that the polluted condition of the ditch and pond stemmed from the normal floatage of impurities on surface waters in such a semi-urban area.* * *

The only other tangible, rather than psychological, objection advanced by plaintiff was to the possibilities of odor or stench. There was some evidence that when the plant operates at full capacity and there is simultaneously a period of low natural flow in the ditch, the volume of effluent may be expected to exceed that of the natural stream flow. Corson stated that at such times there would be stench in the pond, attributable to depletion of dissolved oxygen in the sewage. But this is seen to be without warrant.* * *

The conclusion of the trial court that the evidence of potential odors from vegetation or putrescence is speculative seems to us a fair characterization, on the present record.* * *

Defendants contend that, in effect, this is an action to enjoin a public nuisance, a remedy assertedly granted but rarely, and then only at the suit of the Attorney-General. But see Mayor, etc., of Alpine v. Brewster, 7 N.J. 42, 52, 80 A.2d 297 (1951), as to cases where an individual has also sustained special damage over and above the public injury. We need not pursue that legal inquiry, as it is not now claimed by the plaintiff borough or apparent to us that it is here sought to enjoin a public nuisance. We take it that plaintiff seeks only to vindicate its proprietary right as a riparian owner to have abated what it conceives to be a misuse to its detriment by another riparian proprietor of the common watercourse. The maintenance of such an action is clearly its right notwithstanding its status as a municipal corporation. 11 McQuillin, Municipal Corporations (3rd ed. 1950) § 31.19, p. 215; cf. Paterson v. East Jersey Water Co., 74 N.J.Eq. 49, 70 A. 472 (Ch.1908), affirmed 77 N.J.Eq. 588, 78 A. 1134 (E. & A.1910). Its ownership of the land in the park and its use of the pond for recreational purposes supports its authority to apply to the courts for relief against such actions as it conceives to be wrongful and injurious to the public in its enjoyment of the facilities maintained by the municipality.* * *

We thus come to a consideration of the law governing the mutual rights and obligations of riparian owners, *inter sese*, in respect to the use of the water flow. It will be seen that this subject, in New Jersey as elsewhere in this country, is in a state of some doctrinal confusion. The early history of this field is summarized by the American Law Institute in the Restatement, Torts, chapter 41, scope note, pp. 341, 342:

> "In the early English Common Law there was little litigation over the private use of water. The uses for water were limited mainly to use for domestic purposes and for running small grist mills, and the law in respect to such uses was relatively simple: 'First come, first served.' Each landowner was regarded as having the privilege of using the water on his land for his own ordinary purposes irrespective of the effect on others, but this was not as harsh a rule as it might seem, for the simple reason that such use seldom had any material effect on others. There was water enough for all because there were no such things as public waterworks, sewage disposal systems, large factories, and power plants.
>
> "With the beginning of the industrial revolution, however, the situation changed. There arose many new uses for water which either consumed large quantities of it or polluted it to such an extent that it was of little use to others. The resulting conflict of interests in the use of water demanded a more equitable rule than 'first come, first served.' Story and Kent, with their knowledge of Roman Law, seized upon the law of Riparian Rights and applied it to these new and 'extraordinary' uses. In brief, that theory of law embodied the principle that all riparian proprietors on a watercourse or lake have equal rights in respect to the use of the water, and that none can use to the extent of depriving others of an equal opportunity to use.

* * *

While the "first come, first served" concept referred to above became firmly imbedded in a doctrine of "prior appropriation" in many western states, by decision and statute, because of the geography of aridity and the incidents of frontier history, Comment, 19 Mo.L.Rev. 138, 139 (1954), it has been customary to say that most of the American states transmuted the philosophy of "equal rights" into one or the other of two particular rationales, the "natural flow" theory and the "reasonable use" doctrine.

The natural flow theory, long held in England, contemplates that it is the right of every riparian proprietor to have the flow of water across his land maintained in its natural state, not sensibly diminished in quantity or impaired in quality. Each may use the water for "natural purposes," or for extraordinary needs when there is no material effect upon the water and the use is on or in connection with the use of the riparian land.* * *

The reasonable use doctrine does not concern itself with the impairment of the natural flow or quality of the water but allows full use of the watercourse in any way that is beneficial to the riparian owner provided only it does not unreasonably interfere with the beneficial uses of others, the court or jury being the arbiter as to what is unreasonable.* * *

The American Law Institute has said:

> "Most courts, either not realizing that there are two distinct theories [natural flow and reasonable use] or not fully grasping their fundamental differences, attempt to apply both theories, with results that are not only illogical but weirdly inconsistent at times," Restatement, Torts, chapter 41, scope note, p. 346.

The Acquackanonk Water Co. case, supra, is a good example of such a mixture of concepts. After referring conventionally to the equal right of flow "without diminution or alteration" (29 N.J.Eq. at page 369), the opinion goes on (at page 370):

> "The owner must so use and apply the water as to work no *material* injury or annoyance to his neighbor below him, who has an equal right to the subsequent use of the same water. * * * All that the law requires of the party by or over whose land a stream passes is, that he should use the water in a *reasonable* manner, and so as not to destroy or render useless, or *materially diminish or affect* the application of the water by the proprietors above or below on the stream." (Emphasis added.)

This excerpt is substantially the reasonable use rule, and it clearly reflects the court's philosophy in the particular case. There may be "alteration" of the natural state of the water if the use is reasonable and there is no material effect upon the reasonable use of another.* * *

See also the discussion in 93 C.J.S., Waters, where, in successive asseverations, a riparian owner is said to have a "natural easement" "to have the water flow pure and undefiled", and that right is nevertheless stated to be "subject to the right of each riparian proprietor to use the stream to a reasonable extent, and whether or not a pollution of the waters of a stream is an actionable injury to a lower riparian proprietor depends on whether it is the result of such a reasonable use of the stream as the upper owner is entitled to make or of an unreasonable use in excess of his rights." § 43, p. 688, citing many cases exemplifying the reasonable use doctrine.

An illuminating variant of the reasonable use doctrine is its expression in terms of "fair participation" between riparian owners. In Sandusky Portland Cement Co. v. Dixon Pure Ice Co., 221 F. 200, L.R.A. 1915E, 1210 (7th Cir.1915), certiorari denied 238 U.S. 630, 35 S.Ct. 793, 59 L.Ed. 1497 (1915), a lower owner who manufactured ice from river water was held entitled to an injunction against the heating of the water by an upper proprietor to an extent which materially retarded the formation of ice. The court said (221 F. at page 204):

> "Complainant may not insist on such a use of the water by the defendant as will deprive the latter of any use thereof which may be necessary for its business purposes, provided complainant can by reasonable diligence and effort make the flowing water reasonably answer its own purposes. There must be a fair participation between them. * * * But where, as in the present case, it is shown by the evidence that defendant's use of the river water, while essential for its own purposes, entirely destroys the right of complainant thereto, there can be no claim by defendant that its use thereof is reasonable. In other words, the emergency of defendant's needs is not the measure of its rights in the water."* * *

On principle, we conclude that the interests of a changing, complex and technologically mushrooming society call for the application of the "reasonable use" doctrine in this field; a rule which enables judicial arbitration, in the absence of controlling legislation, of the fair participation in common waters of those who have a right of property therein on the basis of what all of the attendant circumstances shows to be reasonable.* * *

It remains to apply the foregoing principles to the special problem presented here. We have already taken notice of the plea of plaintiff that the effluent flowing into the ditch and pond is "noisome" and necessarily a pollutant because its origin in association with human *excreta* and *secreta* engenders such revulsion in the average person as assertedly must substantially impair the use of the pond as an important part of the public recreational and park area. The synthesis of the evidence set out in II, supra, cannot help but lead to the fair conclusion that the effluent is not reasonably to be regarded as a threat to health, nor offensive, now or in fair prospect, to the senses of sight or smell. No user of the park not knowing of the discharge of the effluent is ever apt to suffer lessened enjoyment ascribable to its flow. Indeed the contrary may be true in times of drought. As recognized by trial court and counsel the question is substantially one of psychological impairment of the recreational function of the park.

We by no means make light of plaintiff's grievance. The problem presented has impressed us as of considerable import. As conceded by the trial court the people of Westville cannot be expected to be happy over the continuous presence of sewage effluent in their park pond, no matter how relatively pure. However, as will be more particularly developed presently, it cannot be said that the discharge of treated sewage effluent into a running stream is *per se* an unreasonable riparian use in today's civilization. Under the reasonable use approach we are called upon to counterweigh social uses and harms. And this we must do in a realistic rather than a theoretical way, and on the basis of the evidence of record, rather than on emotion or runaway imagination.

At the time of the trial the plant had been in operation almost five months. Only two citizens of Westville testified as witnesses, one the borough clerk and the other the borough attorney. Neither gave any evidence of actually lessened use or enjoyment of the park by the citizenry in a recreational sense. We recognize, of course, that the five-month period did not include the summer months, when the height of recreational use is reached. We entertain no doubt that an actual impairment of the use of the pond for psychological reasons associated with defendants' operations would call for serious consideration by the court. But we cannot deal with a different record than that before us. The " 'state of a man's mind is as much a fact as the state of his digestion.' " Rubenstein v. Rubenstein, 20 N.J. 359, 368, 120 A.2d 11, 15 (1956). We cannot assume, without evidence to the contrary, that, whatever the extent of public knowledge in Westville of the existence of the effluent, a pond and ditch not sensibly different in any apparent respect from what it has always been will not constitute substantially the same setting for park and recreational purposes that it has in the past. Initial public revulsion, if present, may or may not give way to acceptance of a situation which eventualities prove to involve no unpleasantness or actual harm. On the contrary, unpleasantness or harm may arise.* * *

On the other scale of the balance, we find the defendant sewerage company, certificated as a public utility pursuant to legislation, serving a function plainly essential to the public health, and by an instrumentality expressly approved, both as to plant and outlet, by the State Board of Health, pursuant to R.S. 58:12–3, N.J.S.A.

* * *

On the basis of the entire case we cannot conclude that the denial of injunctive relief by the trial court was erroneous. We do not rest our conclusion on the premise, which plaintiff has properly been at pains to dissipate, that there is required a showing of any particular kind of damages or injury other than psychological where there has, indeed, been the invasion of a property right. See Holsman v. Boiling Spring Bleaching Co., supra (14 N.J.Eq., at pages 342, 343). Our conception is, rather, that a determination as to the existence of an actionable invasion of the unquestionable property right of a riparian owner in the flow of a watercourse depends upon a weighing of the reasonableness, under all the circumstances, of the use being made by the defendant and of the materiality of the harm, if any found to be visited by such use upon the reasonable uses of the water by the complaining owner. For all of the reasons we have set out, we do not consider that the balance of uses and harms reflected by this record points to an injunction. We trust that what we have said will not be read in anywise to impugn the appropriateness of plaintiff's use of the ditch and pond for recreational and park purposes as a riparian owner. If defendants' future operation of the treatment plant is ever shown to be such, in fact, as unreasonably to affect the use and enjoyment by the people of Westville of their park and pond, nothing herein determined upon the basis of the present record will, of course, preclude appropriate relief.

Judgment affirmed.

---

4 RESTATEMENT TORTS

Sec. 853 (1939)

§ 853. UTILITY OF USE—FACTORS CONSIDERED.

In determining the utility of a use of water causing intentional harm to another riparian proprietor through a non-trespassory invasion of his interest in the use of water in a watercourse or lake, the following factors are to be considered:

(a) the social value which the law attaches to the primary purpose for which the use is made;
(b) the suitability of the use to the watercourse or lake, and to the customs and usages existing with respect to it;
(c) the impracticability of preventing or avoiding the harm; and
(d) the classification of the use as riparian or non-riparian (§ 855).

* * *

Comment on Clause (a):

c. Primary purpose of the use. By primary purpose of the use of water is meant the actor's main or predominant objective in making it when he knows that it is interfering or will interfere with another's use.* * *

Comment on Clause (b):

f. Suitability of use to watercourse or lake. The water in a watercourse or lake is a common asset of all the riparian proprietors thereon, and each is entitled to a fair share in its use.* * *

Comment on Clause (c):

g. Impracticability of preventing or avoiding the harm. When a riparian proprietor knows to a substantial certainty that his use of water will interfere with another's use of water, his use lacks utility unless he has taken all practicable steps to avoid or minimize the harm.* * *

h. Other factors. The factors stated in this Section are not intended to be exhaustive. They are the most important, but in some cases where the harmful use has considerable utility but the gravity of the harm is also great, other factors may be considered. For example, the fact that the stream or lake is the only source of water available to the particular proprietor may make the utility of his use greater than it would be if he could obtain water without too much difficulty from a spring, well or other source.

* * *

OKLAHOMA STATUTES

Sec. 82:26 (1952)

§ 26. Engineer to issue license

On or before the date set for the application of the water to a beneficial use, the State Engineer shall cause the works to be inspected, after due notice to the owner of the permit. Upon the completion of such inspection, the State Engineer shall issue a license to appropriate water to the extent and under the conditions of the actual application thereof to a beneficial use, but in no manner extending the rights described in the permit: Provided, that the inspection to determine the amount of water applied to a beneficial use shall be made at the same time as that of the constructed work, if requested by the owner, and if such action is deemed proper by the State Engineer.
R.L.1910, § 3653.

COLO. CONST.

Art. XVI, sec. 6.

Section 6. Diverting unappropriated water—priority preferred uses.—The right to divert the unappropriated waters of any natural stream to beneficial uses shall never be denied. Priority of appropriation shall give the better right as between those using the water for the same purpose; but when the waters of any natural stream are not sufficient for the service of all those desiring the use of the same, those using the water for domestic purposes shall have the preference over those claiming for any other purpose, and those using the water for agricultural purposes shall have preference over those using the same for manufacturing purposes.

---

2. THE NUISANCE DOCTRINE

Where the pollution of water results in a substantial and unreasonable interference with the use and enjoyment of one's property, the **nuisance doctrine** may be invoked to protect the rights of and provide a remedy to the injured party. *Whalen v. Union Bag & Paper Co.*, 208 N.Y. 1, 101 N.E. 805 (1913) is the landmark decision that upheld an injunction to prevent a paper company from discharging its effluent into a stream where the defendant's paper mill had a value of over $1,000,000 and employed between 400 and 500 persons and where the plaintiff's damages were only $100.00. The decision in *Freitas v. City of Atwater*, presented below, illustrates the issues that arise where the nuisance created by the pollution of a stream is caused by more than one defendant.

FREITAS
v.
CITY OF ATWATER

196 Cal.App.2d 289, 16 Cal.Rptr. 393 (1961)

SCHOTTKY, J.—The city of Atwater, the Foremost Food and Chemical Company, Inc., a corporation, and the Davis Canning Company, a corporation, have appealed from an order granting plaintiffs an injunction which restrained the appellants as follows:

1. The city of Atwater was permanently enjoined from (a) delivering to the Atwater Main any more water than the capacity of its three pipelines into it, or delivering any cannery waste or any sewage effluent from the city's new sewer treatment plant; and (b) enlarging in any way the size of its three pipelines or increasing the burden on the Atwater Main.
2. The Davis Canning Company was permanently enjoined from conveying any water, cannery waste or other substance from its cannery or ponds into the Atwater Main situated on the plaintiffs' property.

3. The Foremost Food and Chemical Company, Inc. (The Blue Dairy Products Company) was permanently enjoined from conveying water or other substance into any portion of the Atwater Main situated on the plaintiffs' property.

* * *

The plaintiffs, who are primarily dairymen, live in the vicinity of the Atwater Main, which is south of the city of Atwater. The object of the plaintiff was to prevent the three appealing defendants and one other from continuing to use the Atwater Main for the disposal of their waste water and to prevent the city from discharging the chlorinated effluent from its new sewage treatment plant (which was under construction at the time this action was being tried) into the Atwater Main.* * *

The evidence introduced at the trial disclosed that the Atwater Main was built in 1916 through the lands the plaintiffs now own by a drainage improvement district, which subsequently conveyed the easement for the ditch to the Merced Irrigation District, a public corporation. The Merced Irrigation District is not a party to the action.

Commencing with its incorporation in 1922, the city has used the Atwater Main for the discharge of waters from its storm drainage system and from its municipal swimming pool. This discharge, which is directly into the Atwater Main, has increased as the population of the city has increased. At no time has the city ever obtained permission from anyone to use the Atwater Main.

The cannery and its predecessor have used the Atwater Main since 1940 for disposal of its waste water. In that year the Merced Irrigation District entered into an agreement with the Ripon Canning Company, Inc., whereby the latter was granted a license to dispose of 1,000 gallons of clear water per minute into the Atwater Main. In 1945 a contract was entered into by the Merced Irrigation District and the Scientific Nutrition Corporation whereby the latter was granted a license to discharge 2,000 gallons per minute of clear uncontaminated water into the Atwater Main. In 1950 a similar agreement was made with the predecessor of the Davis Canning Company, Atwater Packing Corporation. The record also discloses that in 1957 the Merced Irrigation District terminated the license after complaints were received.* * *

According to the testimony introduced by the plaintiffs, the pollution of the water in the Atwater Main first became objectionable in 1956. Obnoxious odors emanated from the water of the Atwater Main. In addition, there was evidence that the gases emanating from the Atwater Main burned the eyes. The trial judge, upon stipulation by all parties, made a personal examination of the Atwater Main and found dead fish.

The court found substantially as follows:

That the city of Atwater had established a limited prescriptive right to drain storm water and surface water from a portion of the city through three pipelines into the Atwater Main because of the fact that the pipelines were constructed openly at a considerable expense without objection and the city had used the pipelines for many years.

That the city had not acquired a right to dispose of any additional amount of water either from its new sewer plant or any other source, nor had it acquired the right to dispose of cannery waste or sewer effluent into the Atwater Main.

That Davis Canning Company had not established a prescriptive right to put any cannery waste or water into the Atwater Main; that the only right it ever had was a permissive right obtained from the Merced Irrigation District.

That the Davis Canning Company had been conveying a part of its waste through pipelines into totally inadequate settling ponds, which resulted in odors offensive to the senses.

That the remaining waste from the canning company, which consisted of fruit and vegetable juices and portions of fruits and vegetables, passed directly into the Atwater Main; that part of the waste material from the cannery attaches to the banks of the Atwater Main and there decays, causing a slimy substance which produces a strong offensive odor.

That the method used by the canning company in disposing of the waste matter from the cannery constituted a public and private nuisance.

That the Foremost Food and Chemical Company, Inc., had not created a nuisance during the time it had used the Atwater Main; that its right to use the Atwater Main was only a permissive right which had been terminated; and that the creamery had not established a prescriptive right to use the Atwater Main.* * *

In arguing for a reversal of the judgment appellant canning company contends that it had established a prescriptive right to dispose of its cooler water into the Atwater Main.

* * *

Since the question of adverse use is one of fact, the question before this court is whether there is substantial evidence in the record to support the decision of the trial court that the cannery did not acquire a prescriptive right to use the Atwater Main as against the plaintiffs. There is evidence in the record that the cannery's predecessors in interest obtained permission from the Merced Irrigation District to discharge water into the Atwater Main. A fee was paid for the license, both by Davis and its predecessors. Under such circumstances the court could well find that Davis Canning Company did not have the proper state of mind to create an adverse use. Here there was evidence of submission to the right of the Merced Irrigation District. This was sufficient to support the finding of the trial court that the use was not adverse to anyone.

The canning company also contends that it obtained a claim of right to put its wash water into the Atwater Main (water used to wash the fruit and carry off any unprocessable substance from the fruit). The evidence most favorable to the respondents discloses that the manner in which the settling pond was used constituted a public and private nuisance. The evidence also shows that permission to use the Atwater Main had been obtained from the Merced Irrigation District. If the use were permissive and not adverse, which would be a question of fact, no prescriptive right was obtained and any discussion of nuisance is moot. In any event, the cannery could not obtain a prescriptive right to maintain a public nuisance. (*Wright* v. *Best*, 19 Cal.2d 368 [121 P.2d 702].)

"[A] public nuisance may also be a private one, when it interferes with the enjoyment of land, . . ." (Prosser on Torts (2d ed.), p. 391.) There was evidence that the effluent from the settling pond killed fish in the Atwater Main. This would be a public nuisance. (Prosser on Torts (2d ed.), p. 402.) There was also evidence that the pollution of the Atwater Main caused injury to plaintiffs' cattle and that the gases exuded were injurious to health. One disinterested witness testified the odors reminded him "of stepping into a chemical lab, like sulphuric acid. It burned your nose. It actually burned, and it made your eyes water. It was terrific." Another witness who lived approximately 500 feet from the Atwater Main described the odors as "like something decaying." He also testified that the gases caused a person's eyes, nose, throat and ears to burn. There was additional testimony to the same effect. This also would be a nuisance, but probably only a private one. (See Prosser on Torts (2d ed.), p. 402, where he states that the pollution of a stream which merely inconveniences a number of riparian owners is a private nuisance.) The respondents contended that the pollution of the Atwater Main first became bad in 1956 or 1957, so the right to pollute the stream had not ripened into a prescriptive right at the time this suit was instituted. Respondents, of course, could seek equitable relief to enjoin the private nuisance.

Appellant city of Atwater contends that its prescriptive right to use the drain for the disposal of its waste water includes the right to dispose of the purified effluent from its new municipal sewage treatment plant. First it should be pointed out that effluent from the old sewage plant never was a part of the prescriptive right the city obtained in the Atwater Main. The city's prescriptive right was to use the Atwater Main for the disposal of storm drainage waters and water from the municipal swimming pool. This would not be true even under section 479 of the Restatement of Property, which reads: "In ascertaining whether a particular use is permissible under an easement appurtenant created by prescription there must be considered, in addition to the factors enumerated in section 478, the needs which result from a normal evolution in the use of the dominent tenement and the extent to which the satisfaction of those needs increases the burden on the servient tenement."

In comment (c) of section 479 of the Restatement of Property it is stated that "prescriptive interests do not include the privilege to make uses necessitated by a development of the dominant tenament not foreseeable during the prescriptive period as a normal development of that tenement."

Here the foreseeable use was storm drainage waters. Effluent from a sewage treatment plant was not foreseeable, particularly since the effluent from the old sewage plant did not flow into the Atwater Main.* * *

Both the city and the cannery contend that the trial court erred in issuing a permanent injunction. We do not agree with this contention. A permanent injunction will issue to prevent a wrongful act if its continuance may ripen into an easement in favor of a defendant which will deprive plaintiff of the use and enjoyment of his property or take from him the substance of his estate. (27 Cal.Jur.2d 157.)

The injunction was proper to prevent both the cannery and the city from acquiring a prescriptive right to use the Atwater Main. The injunction only enjoined the city from discharging its sewage effluent into the Atwater Main. It was proper to prevent the threatened injury under the facts of the instant case. If the city by the exercise of the right of eminent domain obtains the land, the city will be free to use the Atwater Main for the discharge of the effluent from its new plant and the injunction issued in the instant case would be moot.* * *

The judgment is affirmed.

---

3. Inverse Condemnation

Where pollution of a body of water is caused by the discharge of pollutants by a governmental agency, such as a municipal sewage treatment plant, the issue will arise whether such action by the government constitutes a taking for which just compensation is required by the constitution. In *City of Walla Walla v. Conkey*, set forth in Part One, the court held that the defendant city's sewage disposal activities provided the basis for an action in **inverse condemnation.**

C. The Federal Clean Water Act

1. Goals, Objectives, Planning, Grants and Regulation

In 1972 Congress adopted the Federal Water Pollution Control Act, in which the federal government undertook a major program to eliminate water pollution. The goals and objectives of that Act may be summarized as follows:

(*1*) Eliminate the discharge of pollutants into navigable waters by 1985
(*2*) Achieve an interim goal of water quality high enough to protect fish

and recreation in and on water by 1983 (the so-called **"fishable and swimmable"** standard)

(*3*) Prohibit the discharge of toxic pollutants

(*4*) Construct publicly owned waste treatment works

(*5*) Planning: Develop area-wide waste treatment management planning processes

(*6*) Develop the technology to eliminate the discharge of pollutants

To achieve these objectives Congress authorized grants for planning, construction of waste treatment plants, research and also adopted a system of regulation of water pollution.

a. *Grants for Planning*

The purpose of the federal grants for planning is to establish a procedure for the development of comprehensive and coordinated plans to find workable solutions to the problems of water pollution and then to establish management structures to ensure that the proposed solutions will be implemented.

Funding for the most comprehensive system of planning was provided under Section 208 of the Act, which created a program for **area-wide waste treatment and management planning.** The scope of the planning included in this program can be seen by the following list of subjects that must be contained in a **Section 208 areawide plan:**

(*1*) A description of all the waste water systems within the area, including the location and capacities of all facilities, the treatment levels and type of treatment in each and the method of disposing of the waste products from each

(*2*) Identification of all anticipated municipal and industrial waste treatment works needed to maintain acceptable water quality for a 20-year period

(*3*) Identification of all stormwater run-off control systems

(*4*) Establishment of construction priorities for 5-year and 20-year periods

(*5*) Establishment of a regulatory program to provide for waste treatment management on an area-wide basis; provide for identification, evaluation and control of all pollution sources; regulate the location, modification and construction of all new waste discharging facilities; and ensure that industrial or commercial wastes discharged into publicly owned treatment works meet applicable **pretreatment requirements**

(*6*) Identification of **nonpoint sources of pollution**, including those related to agriculture, forestry, mining, construction and certain forms of salt water intrusion and the identification of procedures and methods, including land use regulations, to control those sources of pollution

(*7*) Identification of processes to control the disposition of residual waste and land disposal of pollutants to protect ground water and surface water quality

(*8*) Identification of agencies necessary to construct, operate and maintain facilities required by the plan and otherwise carry out the plan

(*9*) Selection of a management agency and **institutional arrangements** to implement the plan and identification of the major management alternatives including enforcement, financing, land use and other regulatory measures and associated management authorities and practices

(*10*) Schedule for implementing all elements of the plan, including identification of the monetary costs and economic, social and environmental impact of implementation

(*11*) Required certifications relating to consistency with other plans and to public participation in the planning process and plan adoption

(*12*) A statement of the recommendations of appropriate local governmental bodies

The 208 planning process is intended to involve local, regional, state and federal officials. The local officials advise the governor about the designation of the planning areas and agencies. They or their representatives may serve on the planning agency. If the governor does not designate the planning area, local officials may designate their own. Local officials also help determine the management structure capable of implementing the plan. The governor designates the planning areas within his state and the planning agencies. He must certify the plan before it is forwarded to EPA for approval. State agencies may oversee the planning process and its management and implementation. EPA must approve the planning area, the planning agencies and the plan and its management structure. The federal government provides technical assistance and grants to pay for the planning process.

The federal government also provides grants for other forms of waste water management planning. **Section 201** of the Federal Water Pollution Control Act authorizes funding for **facilities planning**, i.e., construction or modification of a sewage treatment plant and facilities, including sewer lines. **Section 303** provides funds for **river basin planning**, i.e., planning for the area drained by a river and its tributaries. The river basin plan assesses the extent to which a basin's waters are polluted and defines the nature and volume of pollutants that can be discharged without violating minimum standards of water quality. It also establishes priorities for the construction or modification of treatment plants in the basin. **Section 209** provides funds for planning for **water resources basins.** These plans are broader in scope than water treatment facilities. In addition Section 209 provides plans for water supply, recreation, transportation and other resources derived from the basin.

b. *Grants For Waste Treatment Plants*

At the time of the adoption of the Federal Water Pollution Act in 1972, untreated and improperly treated sewage comprised over 20 percent of the total amount of pollutants discharged into the nation's waters each year. To overcome this problem, Congress authorized federal grants to pay for up to 75 percent of the cost of planning and construction of sewage treatment facilities.

To be eligible for these federal grants, municipalities must agree to comply with a long list of conditions prescribed by the EPA and intended to ensure that the goals of the Act will be achieved. Included among the conditions of eligibility for a sewage treatment facility construction grant are the following:

(*1*) The facility must use the **best practicable waste treatment technology.** This has been interpreted to mean that secondary (but not tertiary) treatment is required for sewage.
(*2*) The facility must be revenue-producing, i.e., a charge is to be made to municipalities using the plant and attempts are to be made to produce revenue from the sale of sludge for fertilizer.
(*3*) Where the sludge cannot be processed and sold for fertilizer it should be disposed of in a manner that will not cause environmental hazards.
(*4*) Connecting sewer systems must be designed and constructed to avoid excessive infiltration.
(*5*) All facilities must be incorporated into regional or area-wide plans.
(*6*) Industries that discharge into the facility must meet **pretreatment standards**, i.e., must pretreat their wastes to remove any substances that might harm the plant's processes or pass through the plant untreated.
(*7*) Although combined storm water and sewage systems are permitted, their design and maintenance must meet EPA standards.

c. *Grants for Research and Training*

Congress recognized that technological improvements and trained personnel would be necessary to meet its objective of reducing water pollution to zero. To encourage the development of that technology and skilled personnel, grants were authorized for research and training. For example, up to 75 percent of the cost of research and demonstration programs are authorized for programs that investigate such problems as sludge removal, waste oil reuse, ship discharge, etc.

d. *Systems of Regulation*

In addition to the billions of dollars provided for the construction of municipal waste treatment plants and for research, Congress also provided a system of regulation to achieve its stated goal to eliminate the discharge of pollutants into navigable waters by 1985. That regulatory system calls for (*1*) **effluent limitations** for publicly owned treatment works and industries, (*2*) a **national permit program,** the **National Pollutant Discharge Elimination System (NPDES),** to control the discharge of pollutants, (*3*) a **system of regulation of new sources** of water pollution, **New Source Performance Standards (NSPS),** (*4*) a system of **regulation of toxic substances** and (*5*) **prohibition of the discharge of hazardous substances** and funding for the clean-up thereof.

2. Regulation By Technology-Based Effluent Standards

The stated goals of the Federal Water Pollution Control Act of 1972, and reaffirmed in the Clean Water Act of 1977 (which also changed the name of the Act to "The Clean Water Act") are to make the nation's waters clean enough for fishing and swimming by 1983 and *no discharges by 1985.* The basic concept in the Act is set forth in Section 301(a), which declares that "the discharge of any pollutant by any person shall be unlawful." The Act then establishes an interim, three-step procedure for the achievement of that goal. A lower standard is set for 1977; a stricter standard is set for 1983; and the goal of no discharge of pollutants is established for 1985.

a. *The 1977 Standard for Industries*

EPA has established **technology-based effluent limitations** and standards for categories of industries. There are over 30 industries for which such "Effluent Limitation Guideline Regulations" have been promulgated. In determining the effluent limitation for a given industry, EPA will consider such factors as age of the plants, raw materials used, manufacturing processes, the products produced, available treatment technology, energy requirements and cost.

The 1977 standard for industries is: **best practicable control technology currently available (BPT)**. An effluent standard based on BPT is one that is based on the *average of the best existing performance by plants of various sizes, ages, and unit processes within each industrial category.*

b. *The 1977 Standard for Municipal Treatment Plants*

EPA has established secondary treatment as the standard for effluent limitation of publicly owned waste-water treatment plants. Using this standard, EPA limits the discharge of biochemical oxygen demand (BOD), suspended solids, and fecal coliform bacteria and the range of acceptable *pH.*

c. *The 1983 Standard for Industries*

The Clean Water Act of 1977 creates three separate categories of pollutants and establishes technology-based effluent standards for each. The 1977 Act also extends the deadline dates:

(*1*) *Conventional Pollutants.* Industries that discharge "conventional pollutants" must meet effluent limitations based on the "best conventional pollutant control technology" (BCT). **Conventional pollutants** are defined as sewage type pollutants such as biological oxygen-demanding, suspended solids, fecal coliform and those influencing *pH*. **Best conventional pollutant control technology" (BCT)** has not been defined precisely but is considered to be a standard whose strictness falls somewhere in between **"best practical control technology currently available" (BPT)** and the most strict, **"best available technology economically achievable" (BAT)**. The deadline for the application of the BCT standard to conventional pollutants is July 1, 1984.

(*2*) *Toxic Pollutants.* Industries that discharge **"toxic pollutants"** must meet effluent limitations based on "best available technology economically achievable" (BAT). The 1977 Clean Water Act extends the deadline for achieving this standard for one year to July 1, 1984. The Act lists 65 toxic substances and authorizes EPA to add to or delete other substances from that list. When a substance is added to the toxic pollutant list the discharger must comply with the effluent limitations within three years from the publication of those limitations. EPA may not issue waivers from effluent limitations for toxic pollutants.

(*3*) *Nonconventional Pollutants.* Industries that discharge **"nonconventional pollutants"** must meet effluent limitations based on "best available technology economically achievable" (BAT) within three years from the time that such standards are established, but in no event later than July 1, 1987. A "nonconventional pollutant" is a pollutant that is neither a conventional pollutant (i.e., sewage type) nor a toxic pollutant. Unlike the other two classifications, waivers may be issued for nonconventional pollutants if the discharger sustains the burden of proving that such extension will not result in an unacceptable health or environmental risk.

The following summarizes the effluent limitation standards and the deadline dates for each of the three pollutants described in the 1977 Amendments of the Clean Water Act:

Pollutant	Standard	Deadline Date
Conventional	BCT	July 1, 1984—no waivers
Toxic	BAT	July 1, 1984—no waivers
Nonconventional	BAT	July 1, 1987—waivers allowed

Each of the standards for effluent limitations is defined as follows:

Best practical control technology currently available (BPT). Effluent limitations based on BPT will be based on *the average of the best existing performance* by plants of various sizes, ages and unit processes within each industrial category. In determining BPT the EPA considers "the total cost of application of technology in relation to the effluent reduction benefits to be achieved from such applications"; i.e., EPA uses a cost–benefit analysis when using the BPT standard to establish an effluent limitation for an industry.

Best available technology economically achievable (BAT). Effluent limitations based on BAT will be based on the existing performance of *the best performer* in any industrial category. EPA does not use a cost–benefit analysis to compare the relative benefits and costs to be achieved from the proposed effluent limitations. However, EPA is bound by a test of reasonableness to establish a standard that is "economically achievable."

Best conventional pollutant control technology (BCT). Effluent limitations based on BCT will be based on a standard that is somewhere between BPT, the least strict standard, and BAT, the most strict standard. A cost–benefit analysis is required for BCT as well as BPT. However, when making the cost–benefit comparison for BCT, if it would be less expensive but equally efficient to deal with conventional pollutants by using a municipal waste treatment plant such alternative seems to be authorized under the BCT standard, but not under the BPT standard.

The following cases illustrate some of the problems involved in controlling water pollution through the regulation of industries on the basis of technology-based effluent standards. In *American Frozen Food Institute v. Train*, the court took the opportunity to review the legislative history of the statute before dealing with several issues, one of which was the authority of EPA to use Section 301 rather than the Section 402 permit program as the basic enforcement mechanism. In *California & Hawaiian Sugar Co. v. EPA* the court reviewed the factors to be considered by the EPA Administrator in establishing effluent limitations to determine whether the effluent limitations were reasonable. *E. I. du Pont de Nemours & Co. v. Train* raises several questions including the applicability of effluent limitations to the entire industry instead of establishing effluent limitations for each discharger. In *EPA v. National Crushed Stone Assoc.* the United States Supreme Court resolved the question of whether EPA's regulations providing for a variance modifying effluent limitations based on best practical control technology currently available (BPT) have to allow for consideration of the economic capability of an individual discharger to afford the costs involved in complying with these limitations.

AMERICAN FROZEN FOOD INSTITUTE
v.
TRAIN

539 F.2d 107 (D.C.Cir. 1976)

EDWARDS, Circuit Judge.

This case requires this court to review and interpret the Federal Water Pollution Control Act Amendments of 1972.

* * *

In its Declaration of Goals and Policy, the Act imposes on American industry (and the American public through passed-on product costs) the economic burden of ending all discharges of pollutants by the year 1985. Section 101(a), 33 U.S.C. § 1251(a) (Supp. III, 1973). In some instances the statute clearly contemplates the closing of marginal plants which cannot function economically with the costs added by water pollution controls.* * *

Petitioners, who are representatives of the potato processing industry, attack on a broad front the Environmental Protection Administrator's actions under and his interpretation of the Federal Water Pollution Control Act Amendments of 1972 in applying the Act to the industry concerned. Certain other industry representatives have filed briefs amici curiae claiming that this court has no jurisdiction in this case.

The principal questions presented by this case are:

Does the United States Court of Appeals have jurisdiction to review the actions here complained of?

Did the Administrator violate the Act by combining in one document issued on one day his response to the requirements of Sections 301, 304 and 306 of the Act, thereby necessitating that his orders be set aside?

* * *

I.
THE STRUCTURE OF THE ACT

In Title I of the Act, we find the following sweeping Declaration of Goals and Policy:

DECLARATION OF GOALS AND POLICY

Sec. 101. (a) The objective of this Act is to restore and maintain the chemical, physical, and biological integrity of the Nation's waters. In order to achieve this objective it is hereby declared that, consistent with the provisions of this Act—

(1) *it is the national goal that the discharge of pollutants into the navigable waters be eliminated by 1985;*

(2) it is the national goal that wherever attainable, an interim goal of water quality which provides for the protection and propagation of fish, shellfish, and wildlife and provides for recreation in and on the water be achieved by July 1, 1983;

(3) it is the national policy that the discharge of toxic pollutants in toxic amounts be prohibited;

(4) it is the national policy that Federal financial assistance be provided to construct publicly owned waste treatment works;
(5) it is the national policy that area-wide waste treatment management planning processes be developed and implemented to assure adequate control of sources of pollutants in each State; and
(6) it is the national policy that a major research and demonstration effort be made to develop technology necessary to eliminate the discharge of pollutants into the navigable waters, waters of the contiguous zone, and the oceans.
33 U.S.C. § 1251(a) (Supp. III, 1973) (Emphasis added.)

Concern about pollution of the nation's lakes, rivers, harbors and contiguous oceans is by no means new:

The Federal Water Pollution Control Act . . . was originally enacted by act June 30, 1948.* * *

However, the Federal Water Pollution Control Act Amendments of 1972 are not mere amendments to previous control attempts. Preceding pollution control measures were fundamentally designed to determine what lakes and streams had become polluted beyond toleration and then to locate the particular polluters and suppress the discharges that were causing the condition. Determination of which polluter caused what pollution proved over the years to be an impractical task. Congress was confronted by failure of efforts which its leaders estimated to have cost $20 billion of public funds. It also was confronted by continuing and increasing massive pollution which was turning many American rivers into open sewers, was threatening the extinction of marine life in several of the Great Lakes, as well as our ocean harbors, and was endangering the purity of our waters for drinking, for water recreation, for crop irrigation, and for industrial usage.

By 1972 Congress determined upon a wholly new approach. The basic concept of the Act we construe in this case is an ultimate flat prohibition upon all discharges of pollutants:

Sec. 301. (a) Except as in compliance with this section and sections 302, 306, 307, 318, 402, and 404 of this Act, the discharge of any pollutant by any person shall be unlawful.
Sec. 301(a), 33 U.S.C. § 1311(a)(Supp. III, 1973).

The fantastic disruption of economic life which would be occasioned by immediate implementation of this enactment is alleviated by a complex set of statutory exceptions provided for under federal and state permit programs—all designed to require decreasing levels of pollutant discharges and aimed at achieving by 1985 the ultimate national goal of eliminating the discharge of all pollutants in any American lakes, rivers, or contiguous seas.

In the interim period the act provides for national standards called "effluent limitations" applicable to statutorily name categories and classes of industrial and commercial dischargers. The first purpose of the effluent limitations is to achieve by July 1, 1977 "*the best practicable control technology currently available.*" (§ 1311(b)(1)(A), 33 U.S.C. § 1311(b)(1)(A)). The effluent limitations are to be based on "effluent limitations guidelines" published after carefully devised study procedures (§ 304, 33 U.S.C. § 1314).

The Act further requires by July 1, 1983, "effluent limitations for categories and classes of point sources . . . that shall require application of "*the best available technology economically achievable for each category or class.*" (§ 301(b)(2)(A), 33 U.S.C. § 1311(b)(2)(A)).

Where application of "the best available technology" does not result in the complete elimination of discharges of pollutants, the Act calls for continuing periodic review, presumably until all discharges are terminated. (§ 301(d), 33 U.S.C. § 1311(d)).

This same standard, *i. e.* "best available technology," is mandated forthwith for all new plant construction (new point sources) by § 306, 33 U.S.C. § 1316. This section also allows a 10-year period of amortization of costs before any higher standard may be imposed.

The Act sets forth machinery for state enforcement of these nationally set standards through state permit programs when the Administrator determines that the state concerned "has the capability of administering a permit program which will carry out the objective of this Act. . . . (§ 402(a)(5), 33 U.S.C. § 1342(a)(5)). As to nonparticipating states, direct enforcement through a federal permit program is retained in the hands of the federal Administrator. (§ 402(a)(1), (2), (3), 33 U.S.C. § 1342(a)(1), (2), (3)). In addition, as to participating states the Act clearly gives the federal Administrator ultimate enforcement power and responsibility if a state fails in its permit issuing or enforcement responsibilities under the Act. (§ 402(c), 33 U.S.C. § 1342(c)).

Enforcement of the permit program described above is provided for by both civil and criminal proceedings in the United States District Court as set forth in § 309, 33 U.S.C. § 1319, of the Act. In addition, under § 505, 33 U.S.C. § 1365, private suits by adversely affected citizens to enforce the provisions of the Act can be brought in the United States District Courts.

The Administrator is given statutory authority to "prescribe such regulations as are necessary to carry out his functions" under the Act. (§ 501(a), 33 U.S.C. § 1361).

Judicial review of the actions of the federal Administrator is provided for by original action in the various United States Courts of Appeals. (§ 509, 33 U.S.C. § 1369).

What has been set forth above represents only the skeletal structure of the Act as it applies to industrial and commercial pollutant discharges.

II.
LEGISLATIVE HISTORY

The legislative history of this Act is readily available. It is fully compiled in two volumes entitled "A Legislative History of the Water Pollution Control Act Amendments of 1972." From this work we select principally those statements which deal specifically with effluent limitations, as set forth in § 301 and § 306, their relationship to the information and guideline program of § 304, the permit program outlined in § 402, the enforcement program outlined in § 309, and judicial review as called for in § 509.

The Joint Conference Report deals directly with one of the major issues in this appeal by squarely rejecting plant-by-plant determination of effluent limitations:

> The conferees intend that the Administrator or the State, as the case may be, will make the determination of the economic impact of an effluent limitation on the basis of classes and categories of point sources, as distinguished from a plant by plant determination. However, after July 1, 1977, the owner or operator of a plant may seek relief from the requirement to achieve effluent limitations based on best available technology economically achievable. The burden will be on him to show that modified requirements will represent the maximum use of technology within his economic capability and will result in reasonable further progress toward the elmination of the discharge of pollutants. If he makes this showing, the Administrator may modify the requirements applicable to him. *Leg. Hist.* at 304.

The central importance of § 301 to the total Congressional plan is enunciated in the Committee Report which follows. In addition, this Senate Report on the Bill indicates clearly that the best practicable level of enforcement by 1977 is to be set at least as high as *an average of the best performers* in the category or class of industry concerned while the best available level of performance required by 1983 is to be set, "at a minimum," in relation to *the best performer* in any such industrial category:

> *It is the Committee's intention that pursuant to subsection 301(b)(1)(A), and Section 304(b) the Administrator will interpret the term "best practicable" when applied to various categories of industries as a basis for specifying clear and precise effluent limitations to be implemented by January 1, 1976.* In defining best practicable for any given industrial category, the Committee expects the Administrator to take a number of factors into account. These factors should include the age of the plants, their size and the unit processes involved and the cost of applying such controls. *In effect, for any industrial category, the Committee expects the Administrator to define a range of discharge levels, above a certain base level applicable to all plants within that category. In applying effluent limitations to any individual plant, the factors cited above should be applied to that specific plant. In no case, however, should any plant be allowed to discharge more pollutants per unit of production than is defined by that base level.*
>
> The Administrator should *establish the range of best practicable levels based upon the average of the best existing performance by plants of various sizes, ages, and unit processes within each industrial category.* It is acknowledged that in those industrial categories where present practices are uniformly inadequate, *the Administrator may determine best practicable to require higher levels of control than any currently in place if he determines the technology to achieve those higher levels can be practicably applied.*
>
> Best practicable can be assumed to substitute for the present terminology "equivalent of secondary treatment for industry["] but this interpretation should not be construed as limiting the authority of the Administrator.
>
> Under the Phase II the Committee intends that effluent limitations be based upon application of best available technology as defined by the Administrator. *In making the determination of "best available" the Committee expects the Administrator to apply the same principles involved in making the determination of best practicable as outlined above except that rather than the range of levels established in reference to the average of the best performers in an industrial category the range should at a minimum be referenced to the best performer in any industrial category.*
>
> The distinction between best practicable and best available is intended to reflect the Committee's intent press toward increasingly higher levels of control, applied over five year periods. Through research and development of new processes, modifications, replacement of obsolete plants and processes, and other improvements in technology, the Committee anticipates that it should be possible, taking into account the cost of controls, to achieve, by 1981, levels of control approaching 95–99 percent reduction of pollutants discharged in most cases and complete recycling in the remainder.
>
> *Leg.Hist.* at 1468–69. (Emphasis added.)

The critical importance of "nationally uniform effluent limitations" is emphasized by these comments from Senator Muskie:

> Senators will recall from the November debate on the Senate bill that there were three essential elements to it: Uniformity, finality, and enforceability. Without these elements a new law would not constitute any improvement on the old; we would not bring a conference agreement to the floor without them.
>
> *As far as uniformity and finality are concerned, the conference agreement provides that each polluter within a category or class of industrial sources will be required to achieve nationally uniform effluent limitations based on "best practicable" technology no later than July 1, 1977.* This does not mean that the Administrator cannot require compliance by an earlier date; *it means that these limitations must be achieved no later than July 1, 1977, that they must be uniform, and that they will be final upon the issuance of a permit under section 402 of the bill.*
>
> * * *

> The third critical element that concerned the Senate in its consideration of this legislation was enforceability. Enforceability is assured through the provisions of the permit program and through section 309, the enforcement section of the act. *The Administrator has the responsibility to determine the effluent limitations to be applied to each category or class of polluter, to set forth those limitations in a permit issued pursuant to section 402 of the act*, and to enforce those limitations through the provisions of section 309.

Leg.Hist. at 162–63. (Emphasis added.)

The same Senator also introduced the following exhibit concerning the relationship between §§ 301 and 304 and how "the best practicable technology" to be required by 1977 will be determined:

> The Conference agreement establishes a two phase program for the application and enforcement of effluent limitations. The first phase requires point sources to achieve that level of effluent reduction identified as "best practicable control technology" no later than July 1, 1977. The Conferees attempted to clarify what was intended by the term "best practicable control technology."
>
> *It is the intention that pursuant to subsection 301(b)(1)(A) and Section 304(b), the Administrator will interpret the term "best practicable" when applied to various categories of industries as a basis for specifying clear and precise effluent limitations to be implemented by July 1, 1977.* In defining "best practicable" for any given industrial category, the Committee expects the Administrator to take a number of factors into account. These factors should include the age of the plants, their size, the unit processes involved, and the cost of applying such controls.
>
> *The Administrator should establish the range of "best practicable" levels based upon the average of the best existing performance by plants of various sizes, ages, and unit processes within each industrial category. In those industrial categories where present practices are uniformly inadequate, the Administrator should interpret "best practicable" to require higher levels of control than any currently in place if he determines that the technology to achieve those higher levels can be practicably applied.*
>
> "Best practicable" can be interpreted as the equivalent of secondary treatment for industry, but this interpretation should not be construed to limit the authority of the Administrator.
>
> The modification of subsection 304(b)(1) is intended to clarify what is meant by the term "practicable". The balancing test between total cost and effluent reduction benefits is intended to limit the application of technology only where the additional degree of effluent reduction is wholly out of proportion to the costs of achieving such marginal level of reduction for any class or category of sources.
>
> *The Conferees agreed upon this limited cost-benefit analysis in order to maintain uniformity within a class and category of point sources subject to effluent limitations, and to avoid imposing on the Administrator any requirement to consider the location of sources within a category or to ascertain water quality impact of effluent controls, or to determine the economic impact of controls on any individual plant in a single community.*
>
> *It is assumed, in any event, that "best practicable technology" will be the minimal level of control imposed on all sources within a category or class during the period subsequent to enactment and prior to July 1, 1977.*
>
> The Conference agreement requires that implementation plans and compliance schedules in existing water quality standards be adhered to, to the extent that those plans and schedules require compliance no later than July 1, 1977, and to the extent that they call for a degree of pollution control no less stringent than that defined by "best practicable control technology."

Leg.Hist. at 169–70. (Emphasis added.)

This same document states the Congressional pupose of employment of "the best available technology" by 1983—"without regard to cost":

> The Conference agreement applies a different test to the Administrator's determination of "best available demonstrated technology". In determining the degree of effluent reduction to be achieved for a category or class of sources by 1983, the Administrator may consider a broader range of technological alternatives and should, at a minimum, review capabilities which exist in operation or which can be applied as a result of public and private research efforts.
>
> In making the determination of "best available" for a category or class, the Administrator is expected to apply the same principles involved in making the determination of "best practicable" (outlined above), except as to cost-benefit analysis. Also, rather than establishing the range of levels in reference to the average of the best performers in an industrial category, the range should, at a minimum, be established with reference to the best performer in any industrial category.
>
> The distinction between "best practicable" and "best available" is intended to reflect the need to press toward increasingly higher levels of control in six-year stages. Through the research and development of new processes, modifications, replacement of obsolete plans and processes, and other improvements in technology, it is anticipated that it should be possible, taking into account the cost of controls, to achieve by 1983 levels of control which approach and achieve the elimination of the discharge of pollutants.
>
> As to the cost of "best available" technology, the Conferees agreed upon the language of the Senate bill in Section 304(b)(2). While cost should be a factor in the Administrator's judgment, no balancing test will be required. *The Administrator will be bound by a test of reasonableness. In this case, the reasonableness of what is "economically achievable" should reflect an evaluation of what needs to be done to move toward the elimination of the discharge of pollutants and what is achievable through the application of available technology—without regard to cost.*
>
> *Leg.Hist.* at 170. (Emphasis added.)

The harshness of the proceding paragraph is subject to relief under § 301(c) which gives the Administrator the power to modify the effluent limitation as to any particular point source which is 1) employing the best available technology within its economic capability, and 2) making reasonable further progress toward elimination of discharge of pollutants. This is made clear in the following paragraph from Senator Muskie's exhibit:

> The Conferees have provided, however, a mechanism for individual point-source-by-source consideration in section 301(c). That section provides that the Administrator may modify any effluent limitation based on "best available technology" to be achieved by July 1, 1983, with respect to any point source, upon a showing by the owner or operator of such point source that an effluent limitation so modified will represent the maximum use of technology within the economic capability of the operator and will result in reasonable further progress toward the goal of the elimination of the discharge of pollutants.
>
> *Leg.Hist.* at 172.

Senator Muskie also detailed the relationship contemplated between the guideline section, § 304, and the effluent limitation section, § 301:

> Section 304(b), as agreed to by the Conferees, *requires that the Administrator publish regulations which shall provide guidelines for the establishment of the effluent limitations to be achieved by categories and classes of point sources* (other than publicly owned treatment works) *pursuant to section 301(b)* of the Act.

> Section 304(b) identifies certain factors to be taken into account by the Administrator in determining the "best practicable" treatment and the "best available" treatment applicable to categories or classes of point sources. Among these factors are considerations of costs. *In determining the "best practicable technology" for a particular class or category of point sources, the Administrator is directed to consider the relationship between the total cost of the application of such technology and the effluent reduction benefits to be achieved from such application within that category or class.*
>
> In determining the "best available technology" for a particular category or class of point sources, the Administrator is directed to consider the cost of achieving effluent reduction. *The Conferees intend that the factors described in section 304(b) be considered only within classes or categories of point sources and that such factors not be considered at the time of the application of an effluent limitation to an individual point source within such a category or class.*
>
> *Except as provided for in section 301(c) of the Act, the intent is that effluent limitations applicable to individual point sources within a given category or class be as uniform as possible. The Administrator is expected to be precise in his guidelines so as to assure that similar point sources with similar characteristics, regardless of their location or the nature of the water into which the discharge is made, will meet similar effluent limitations.*
>
> *Leg.Hist.* at 171–72. (Emphasis added.)

The Senate Report makes clear that § 304(b) requires guidelines for setting effluent limitations under § 301 "which will be imposed as conditions of permits issued under § 402":

> Subsection (b) of this section requires the Administrator, within one year after enactment, to publish guidelines for setting effluent limitations reflecting the mandate of section 301, which will be imposed as conditions of permits issued under section 402. These guidelines would identify what constituted the "best practicable control technology currently available" and the "best available control measures and practices," and the degree of effluent reduction attainable through the application of each. Thus, these guidelines would define the effluent limitations required by the first and second phases of the program established under section 301. In addition, the Administrator would identify control measures and practices available to eliminate the discharge of pollutants from any category of point sources, to allow the full implementation of the objectives of the Act.
>
> *Leg.Hist.* at 1469.

In the House, phased compliance with nationally uniform standards and the critical dates of 1977 and 1983 were emphasized. Rep. Jones of Alabama said:

> Title III of the conference report contains many of the basic provisions for standards and enforcement. Included are section 301(b)(1)(A), which requires point sources to achieve by July 1, 1977, effluent limitations which require the application of "best practicable control technology currently available" and section 301(b)(2)(A) which requires point sources to achieve by July 1, 1983, effluent limitations which require the application of "best available technology economically achievable."
>
> *It is the intention of the managers that the July 1, 1977, requirements be met by phased compliance and that all point sources will be in full compliance no later than July 1, 1977.* Discharge permits issued by the Administrator or by the States should include any applicable implementation plans established under existing water quality standards.
>
> If the owner or operator of a given point source determines that he would rather go out of business than meet the 1977 requirements, the managers clearly expect

that any discharge issued in the interim would reflect the fact that all discharges not in compliance with such "best practicable control technology currently available" would cease by June 30, 1977. In any event, the discharge would have to be consistent with any applicable water quality standards including implementation plans.

By the term "best practicable" the managers mean that all factors set forth in section 304(b)(1)(B) are to be taken into consideration. With the exception of modifications of section 301 requirements for the discharges of heat which may be made pursuant to section 316(a), the determination of the "best practicable control technology currently available" is not to be based upon the existing quality of the receiving waters. *The managers expect that the total cost of application of technology in relation to the effluent limitation benefits to be achieved will always be a factor used by the Administrator in his determination of "best practicable control technology currently available" for a given category or class of point source.*

The term "total cost of application of technology" as used in section 304(b)(1)(B) is meant to include those internal, or plant, costs sustained by the owner or operator and those external costs such as potential unemployment, dislocation, and rural area economic development sustained by the community, area, or region.

By the term "control technology" the managers mean the treatment facilities at the end of a manufacturing, agricultural, or other process, rather than control technology within the manufacturing process itself.

By the term "currently available" the managers mean the control technology, which, by demonstration projects, pilot plans, or general use, has demonstrated a reasonable level of engineering and economic confidence in the viability of the process at the time of commencement of actual construction of the control facilities.

The House managers were determined and successful in their efforts to make sure that the factors in sections 304(b)(1)(B) and 304(b)(2)(B) relating to the assessment of "best practicable control technology currently available" and "best available technology economically achievable," respectively, included consideration of nonwater quality environmental impact, including energy requirements. The managers believe that it would be foolhardy to credit one environmental account and debit another by the same action. Their intent is that the assessment of "best practicable control technology currently available" shall be such that the net effect on water and other environmental needs will be positive and beneficial, and that other impacts of water quality environmental efforts would not negate the overall benefit of the achievement of higher water quality.

Leg.Hist. at 231–32 (Emphasis added.)

Representative Dingell specifically noted that effluent limitations should not be set on a plant-by-plant basis:

Eighth, the bill, *in section 301, establishes a two-phase program for application and enforcement of effluent limitations.* The first phase requires achievement by July 1, 1977, of that level of effluent reduction identified as "best practicable control technology." It should be emphasized that the term "best practicable" does not mean a reliance on secondary treatment. The second phase provides a higher degree of effluent reduction to be achieved by 1983. *The distinction between "best practicable" and "best available" is intended to reflect the need to press toward increasingly higher levels of control.*

The conference report emphasizes on page 121 a very important point. The report states: The conferees intend that the Administrator or the State, as the case may be, will make the determination of the economic impact of an effluent limitation on the basis of classes and categories of point sources, as distinguished from a plant-by-plant determination.

Thus, a plant-by-plant determination of the economic impact of an effluent limitation is neither expected, nor desired, and, in fact, it should be avoided.

The report also states on page 171:* * * after July 1, 1977, the owner or operator of a plant may seek relief from the requirement to achieve effluent limitations based on best available technology economically achievable. The burden will be on him to show that modified requirements will represent the maximum use of technology within his economic capability and will result in reasonable further progress toward the elimination of the discharge of pollutants. If he makes this showing, the Administrator may modify the requirements applicable to him.

This provision could be troublesome, if EPA does not administer it properly. This is, of course, an area where the public participation requirement of section 101(e) of the bill will be most important. In order to avoid any possibility of a weakening of the after-1977 requirement, EPA must establish procedures for the public to participate in modified effluent limitations such as may result from such "relief" requests. The applicant's showing must be available to the public for comment, as well as EPA's proposed determination.

In making this determination, EPA should assure itself that, even if such "relief" is granted, it will still result in "further progress toward elimination of the discharge of pollutants" from point sources than has resulted from the pre-1977 requirements.

Leg.Hist. at 254–55. (Emphasis added.)

Representative Wright stated that the effluent limitations called for in § 301 were to be promulgated as "regulations":

Subsection *104(t)* provides that the Administrator shall conduct continuing comprehensive *studies of the effects and methods of control of thermal discharges.* The results of these studies shall be reported by the Administrator no later than 270 days after enactment, and shall be considered by the Administrator in proposing regulations with respect to thermal discharges under section 316 and by the States in proposing thermal water quality standards. These studies will provide needed data and should be very helpful to the Administrator in proposing regulations. *The Administrator should consider the results of these studies promulgating regulations not only under section 316 but also under other sections of the act where thermal discharges may be regulated, including section 301 on effluent limitations*, section 303 on water quality standards, and section 306 on new source performance standards.

Leg.Hist. at 264 (Emphasis added.)

The discussion of the section on judicial review of the actions of the Administrator by the United States Courts of Appeals (§ 509) emphasizes 1) that review is to be expedited and 2) that it should not impede enforcement. *See Leg.Hist.* at 330–31, 822–23, 1502–03.

In pursuance of these goals the statute itself provides for expedited review by the Courts of Appeals and prohibits any later review of actions of the Administrator, subject to § 509 review, in enforcement proceedings. *See* § 509(b)(2), 33 U.S.C. § 1369(b)(2) (Supp. III, 1973).

Finally, the Committee Report from the House makes clear that "guidelines" under § 304 are not in themselves enforcible until "promulgated" under other sections of the Bill—particularly §§ 301 and 306. It also makes clear that if a point source has a valid permit under § 402, compliance with that permit and its terms is compliance with §§ 301 and 306 for purposes of enforcement program provided for in §§ 309 and 505:

> *The Committee points out, as it did in the discussion of section 401, that the term "applicable" used in section 402 has two meanings. It means that the requirement which the term "applicable" refers to must be pertinent and apply to the activity and the requirement must be in existence by having been promulgated or implemented.*
>
> *The Committee further recognizes that the requirements under sections 301, 302, 306, 307, 308, 316 and 403 will not all be promulgated immediately upon enactment of this bill. Nevertheless, it would be unreasonable to delay issuing of permits until all the implementing steps are necessary.* Therefore, subsection (a)(2) provides that prior to the taking of the necessary implementing actions relating to all such requirements, the Administrator may issue permits during this interim period with such conditions as he determines are necessary to carry out the provisions of this Act. Thus, the new permit program may be initiated without undue delay upon enactment of this Act.
>
> Subsection (a)(2) requires the Administrator to prescribe conditions for these permits to assure compliance with the requirements of subsection (a)(1), including conditions on data and information collection, reporting and such other requirements as he deems appropriate.
>
> Subsection (a)(3) provides that the Administrator's permit program and the permits he issues will be subject to the same terms, conditions, requirements as apply to a state permit program and permit issued under subsection (b).
>
> *Leg.Hist.* at 812–13. (Emphasis added.)
>
> *Subsection (1) provides that compliance with a permit issued pursuant to section 402 shall be considered to be compliance for purposes of sections 309 and 505, with section 301, 302, 306, 307, 316 and 403, except any standard imposed upon section 307 for a toxic pollutant injurious to public health. The purpose of this provision is to assure that the mere promulgation of any effluent limitation or other limitation, a standard, or a thermal discharge regulation, by itself will not subject a person holding a valid permit to prosecution. However, once such a requirement is actually made a condition of the permit, then the permittee will be held to comply with the terms thereof.*
>
> *Leg.Hist.* at 815. (Emphasis added.)

This review of the language and structure of the Act and its legislative history leads us to four final conclusions and two tentative conclusions.

Final Conclusions

The Act, although entitled "Amendments," is an entirely new approach to water pollution control.

The prinicipal purpose of the Act is to achieve the complete elimination of all discharges of pollutants into the nation's waters by 1985 or as soon thereafter as may be.

The authors of the Act clearly foresaw that its impact would be very costly to both the public and private sectors and determined to proceed *in spite of the cost*.

The authors of the Act were much concerned about timely implementation, and specified implementation dates of 1977, 1983 and 1985 for different phases of achievement of the principal purpose of elimination of all pollutants.

Tentative Conclusions

Section 301 of the Act is the fundamental control section and contemplates national standards of effluent limitations (rather than individual plant standards).

Review of all standards (including § 301 effluent limitations) promulgated by the

Administrator is provided for in the various United States Courts of Appeals by § 509 of the Act.

Further analysis of the tentative conclusions will follow in answers to the issues presented in this case.

III. THE STATUTORY ISSUES

1. *Jurisdiction* (and EPA's § 301 authority). The Act gives the Courts of Appeals of the United States wide and exclusive jurisdiction to review the actions of the Administrator:

> (b)(1) Review of the Administrator's action (A) in promulgating any standard of performance under section 306, (B) in making any determination pursuant to section 306(b)(1)(C), (C) in promulgating any effluent standard, prohibition, or treatment standard under section 307, (D) in making any determination as to a State permit program submitted under section 402(b), *(E) in approving or promulgating any effluent limitation or other limitation under section 301, 302, or 306*, and (F) in issuing or denying any permit under section 402, *may be had by any interested person in the Circuit Court of Appeals of the United States for the Federal judicial district in which such person resides or transacts* such business upon application by such person. Any such application shall be made within ninety days from the date of such determination, approval, promulgation, issuance or denial, or after such date only if such application is based solely on grounds which arose after such ninetieth day.
>
> (2) Action of the Administrator with respect to which review could have been obtained under paragraph (1) of this subsection shall not be subject to judicial review in any civil or criminal proceeding for enforcement.
>
> § 509(b), 33 U.S.C. § 1369(b) (Supp. III, 1973). (Emphasis added.)

On the other hand the role of the United States District Courts under the applicable portions of this Act is directed to enforcement proceedings against alleged polluters:

* * *

The specific language of § 509(b) grants this court authority to review the "effluent limitations" issued by the Administrator under § 301, § 302 and § 306. The petitioners and the respondent in this case agree that this court has such jurisdiction. Amici from the chemical and oil industries, however, present a different point of view. They contend that the statute gives the Administrator no authority to issue nationwide effluent limitations under § 301. They argue that the guidelines called for in § 304 are the controlling regulations. Therefore, since § 509 contains no specific authority for the Courts of Appeals to renew the "guidelines" issued by the Administrator under § 304, this court is without authority to review the issues in this case. They also contend that § 304 "guidelines" applicable to the industries concerned can only be reviewed in the United States District Courts.

In this regard they cite and rely upon *CPC International Inc. v. Train*, 515 F.2d 1032 (8th Cir. 1975). We disagree with amici in this case.* * *

From the express language of the Act and its legislative history, we have no doubt that the Act provides for issuance of "guidelines" under § 304(b) for categories of pollution point sources and that these "guidelines" were intended by Congress as a source of guidance to the Administrator in issuance of "effluent limitations" under § 301 for categories and classes of pollution point sources. Further, the "guidelines" and "effluent limitations" were intended to serve as controlling standards for state permit programs under § 402.

It is important to remember—in direct contrast to the arguments of amici in this case and the interpretation of the Act set forth in the Eighth Circuit's opinion in *CPC*

International—that § 301 is the basic enforcement mechanism relied upon by Congress:* * *

The very first sentence in § 301(a) provides the fundamental prohibition: "Except as in compliance with this section and sections 302, 306, 307, 318, 402, and 404 of this Act, the discharge of any pollutant by any person shall be unlawful." Significantly, this fundamental sentence makes no reference at all to § 304(b). Further, as noted above, there is no provision in the Act for enforcement of the § 304(b) guidelines against polluters. But § 301(e) specifically provides:

> (e) Effluent limitations established pursuant to this section or section 302 of this Act shall be applied to all point sources of discharge of pollutants in accordance with the provisions of this Act. 33 U.S.C. § 1311(e) (Supp. III, 1973).

We note, of course, the argument of amici curiae and the Eighth Circuit that § 301 does not expressly direct the Administrator to promulgate the "effluent limitations" which § 301 says "should be achieved." This argument, based on the employment of the passive tense in relation to effluent limitations, ignores the fact that § 301 begins with the fundamental statutory prohibition that (with named exceptions) "the discharge of any pollutant by any person shall be unlawful." This prohibition which is central to the entire Act is statutory and requires no promulgation. The Administrator's function is to set the interim levels of pollutant discharge allowable until absolute cessation is required. Effluent limitations are both required by § 301 and made enforceable against violators by criminal and civil penalties under § 309. Section 309(a) specifically provides for enforcement of any "limitation which implements section 301. . . ." 33 U.S.C. § 1319(a) (Supp. III, 1973). The drafters' intent that the Administrator promulgate such standards is made clear by § 509 (quoted in full above) which specifically provides for review of the Administrator's action "in approving *or promulgating* any effluent limitation or other limitation under section 301. . . ." § 509(b)(1)(E), 33 U.S.C. § 1369(b)(1)(E) (Supp. III, 1973).

Further, if anything more be needed, the Administrator is given wide authority to issue regulations. Section 501(a) specifically provides: "The Administrator is authorized to prescribe such regulations as are necessary to carry out his functions under this Act." Under this statute, as we read it, the Administrator has no more important function than carrying out the fundamental purposes of the Act spelled out in § 301.

This is demonstrated by the fact that both the federal and state permit programs called for by § 402 are required to be in compliance with "the requirements . . . of § 301." There is no such command applicable to § 304. Thus, without the national standards required by § 301, the fifty states would be free to set widely varying pollution limitations. These might arguably be different for every permit issued.

In sum, giving effect to the argument advanced by amici and the Eighth Circuit's *CPC International* opinion would effectively emasculate the act. The plainly expressed purpose of Congress to require nationally uniform interim limitations upon like sources of pollution would be defeated. States would be motivated to compete for industry by establishing minimal standards in their individual permit programs. Enforcement would proceed on an individual point source basis with the courts inundated with litigation. The elimination of all discharge of pollutants by 1985 would become the impossible dream.

* * *

2. *Simultaneous Issuance*. Petitioners' primary attack (as opposed to that of amici curiae) upon EPA's interpretation of the act concerns the Agency's telescoping of the requirements of § 301 and § 304(b) so that the "guidelines" called for by § 304(b) were issued at the same time as the "effluent limitations" called for by § 301. The petitioners argue that the Administrator violated the Act by failing to publish the guidelines first and the limitations thereafter as a subsequent "phase" and that by seeking to satisfy the statutory requirements in one document, he has succeeded in

publishing regulations which were valid neither as guidelines under § 304(b) nor as limitations under § 301.

We agree with petitioners that one very logical interpretation of the statute is that it contemplates issuance of the guidelines first and the limitations afterwards. This is particularly true since the limitations are required to be based upon the guidelines. The two sections of the statute with which we are currently concerned, however, contain only one time requirement as to issuance of the guidelines and the limitation. In § 304(b) the Statute requires the Administrator to publish "guidelines for effluent limitations" within "one year of enactment of this title."

The Act became effective October 18, 1972, and the effluent limitations contained in Appendix B were promulgated nearly six months late on March 12, 1974, to be effective May 20, 1974. 40 C.F.R. §§ 407.10–407.56 (1975). While the statute sets no date for publication of the effluent limitations, they are required by § 301 to be made effective as legally enforceable on industries which were point sources for pollutants at least by July 1, 1977. The Administrator had obviously not been able to achieve the time limitation mandated by the Act as to the guidelines. If he had continued to delay issuance of effluent limitations, he would have been subject to the charge of giving inadequate time to industry for ordering and manufacturing equipment and constructing facilities which would be required to meet the effluent limitations by the July 1977 deadline.

It seems clear to us that the Administrator, having already failed to meet the statutory deadline for issuance of the guidelines, elected to take a shortcut. Our questions are: Did that shortcut represent an impermissible interpretation of the Act, and, as claimed by plaintiffs, does that shortcut require our invalidation of both the § 304 guidelines and the § 301 limitations which are under attack in this case?

We answer both of these questions in the negative.

As to both § 304 guidelines and § 301 effluent limitations, the essentials of informal rule-making had been carried out by the Administrator. The industry affected had had full opportunity (in all except one respect affecting the fecal coli standard) to offer comment—and, indeed, as this record demonstrates, had done so both before and after the publication of the proposed rule. We can find no deprivation of petitioners' statutory rights in the procedure followed. Invalidation would have as its principal effect simply further delay of the implementation of the national policy of purification of America's waters.

Additionally, however, we observe that the Administrator's intepretation of this complex Act is not without logic. The statute contains no language which forbids the issuance of § 304(b) guidelines and § 301 limitations in the same document on the same day. Obviously, the guidelines and the effluent limitations are closely related. To propose each separately through separate rulemaking procedures would have occasioned considerable additional delay. Congressional insistence upon prompt action by the Administrator in implementing the statutory purposes may be found throughout both the legislative history and the terms of the Act itself. Such insistence doubtless came to weigh heavily on the Administrator; and, indeed, it does upon us.

* * *

We conclude that the Administrator's decision to issue "guidelines" under § 304 and "effluent limitations" under § 301 through the same procedures, on the same day, and in the same document was a permissible interpretation of the statute which we are required to accept.

CALIFORNIA & HAWAIIAN SUGAR CO.
v.
E.P.A.

553 F.2d 280 (2d Cir. 1977)

FEINBERG, Circuit Judge:

In March 1974, the Environmental Protection Agency (EPA) promulgated final regulations requiring curtailment of water pollution by crystalline cane sugar refineries in the United States.

* * *

C&H challenges the EPA's action as arbitrary and capricious in various respects, and urges us to vacate the regulations and remand for further consideration by the agency. For the reasons set forth below, we conclude that the agency acted reasonably. We therefore uphold the regulations.

* * *

Statutory Regulations

Disposal of the waste water is governed by the Federal Water Pollution Control Act, as amended, 33 U.S.C. § 1251 et seq. (Supp. IV 1974). Since its amendment in 1972, Pub.L. No. 92–500, the Act has focused attention on the discharges from each "point source" of pollutants rather than on the pollutant levels in the public waterways themselves. All discharges are prohibited, under § 301 of the Act, 33 U.S.C. § 1311, unless authorized by a permit issued pursuant to another section of the Act. The permit section relevant here, § 402, 33 U.S.C. § 1342, directs the EPA to transfer authority for issuance of permits to the states as soon as they develop programs that meet the Act's requirements. Section 301(b)(1)(A) requires that by July 1, 1977, each point source must comply with effluent limitations fixed by the EPA on the basis of the "best practicable control technology currently available" (BPT). By 1983, the sources must meet a different, presumably stiffer, standard based on the "best available technology economically achievable" (BAT). In setting the standards, the EPA is directed to consider six factors, all but one of which are phrased in identical terms for both BPT and BAT: age of equipment and facilities involved, the process employed, the engineering aspects of the application of various types of control techniques, process changes, and nonwater quality environmental impact (including energy demands). The remaining factor involves costs, and the phrasing for the two standards differs. For BPT, the 1977 standard, the Act refers the EPA to "total cost of application of technology in relation to the effluent reduction benefits to be achieved by such application . . ." Section 304(b)(1)(B) of the Act, 33 U.S.C. § 1314(b)(1)(B). For BAT, the 1983 standard, the Act mandates consideration of "the cost of achieving such effluent reduction." Section 304(b)(2)(B).

* * *

C&H challenges the regulations in four respects: It argues (1) the agency created an impermissibly inflexible regulatory scheme by imposing specific number limitations, rather than defining a range of limitations, and by failing to specify factors to be considered for individual permit applications; (2) the EPA acted arbitrarily and capriciously in concluding that certain treatment technology could be borrowed from other industries to enable the cane sugar refiners to comply with both the 1977 and the 1983 standards; (3) the agency failed adequately to consider the adverse environmental effects of the recommended effluent treatment; and (4) the high costs of the required measures are not justified by the environmental benefits achieved.

Flexibility of the Regulations

C&H contends that the agency should not have fixed precise numerical limitations for the discharge of pollutants from every point source. According to C&H, the Act's authors intended the agency to define a range of permissible discharge levels, so that the limit for each individual plant could be set after consideration of the various factors enumerated in § 304. Application of this flexible approach would eventually be entrusted to the states, thus facilitating further accommodation of the different situations of the refineries. C&H tells us that the uncertainty associated with transplanting technology from other industries makes this flexibility especially important.

This argument cannot stand in the face of our decision in *Hooker Chemicals & Plastic Corp. v. Train*, supra. In that case, chemical companies challenged effluent limitation guidelines for the phosphate-manufacturing industry on various bases, including failure to establish ranges and to specify factors to be considered for point sources in each category and subcategory. We concluded:

> [W]henever Congress spoke of "ranges" in the debates over the Act, it meant only the spectrum comprised of varying discharge levels on a subcategorical, rather than individual, basis. [*E. I. duPont de Nemours & Co. v. Train*, 4 Cir., 541 F.2d 1018] *De Nemours II,, supra* at 1209. Although variances are conceivable at the permit-granting stage (see our accompanying opinion *Natural Resources Defense Council v. Environmental Protection Agency*, 2 Cir., 537 F.2d 642), Congress intended that the regulations establish a single discharge level for a given subcategory. This is implicit in the Congressional choice of the superlative form in the statutory language requiring achievement of the degree of effluent reduction attainable by application of "*best*" technology.

537 F.2d at 630. The Supreme Court, in *E. I. duPont de Nemours & Co. v. Train*, supra, recently considered this question, and in response to an argument based on the same language that C&H cites in the legislative history of the Act, said:

> If construed to be consistent with the legislative history we have already discussed, and with what we have found to be the clear statutory language, this language can be fairly read to allow the use of subcategories based on factors such as size, age, and unit processes, with effluent limitations for each subcategory normally based on the performance of the best plants in that subcategory.
> 430 U.S. at 112, n.21, 97 S.Ct. at 976.

Thus, the EPA's use of specific number limitations for the whole subcategory is permissible if accomplished on the basis of the appropriate factors. And the regulations as published recite the fact that

> [i]n establishing the limitations set forth in this section, EPA took into account all information it was able to collect, develop and solicit with respect to factors (such as age and size of plant, raw materials, manufacturing processes, products produced, treatment technology available, energy requirements and costs) which can affect the industry subcategorization and effluent levels established.

39 Fed.Reg. 10525 (1974). The Development Document bears out this assertion. Furthermore, the agency expressly adverted to the possibility of adjusting the limitations for individual plants with "fundamentally different" attributes. Id. We

therefore conclude that the agency properly fixed precise limitations on the discharge of pollutants, took sufficient account to the factors prescribed in the Act and allowed adequate tailoring of the limitations to peculilarities of specific point sources.

Transferability of Technology

The EPA established BOD and TSS limitations for both 1977 (BPT) and 1983 (BAT) on the basis of its determination that treatment techniques employed by other industries could work effectively on sugar refining waste. Neither the Act nor the agency requires the use of any particular treatment method at any point source; the regulations speak only of the quantity and quality of pollutants discharged. But the stringent limitations require substantial reduction of the discharges produced by the present refining process. To accomplish this, the EPA recommended that for the 1977 standard the refiners treat the process water stream by exposing it to active biota while it undergoes aeration. The EPA felt that this "activated sludge" process was "currently available" even though no cane sugar refiner employs it.

* * *

Congress clearly intended the concept of BPT to encompass transferred technology. See Congressional Research Service, A Legislative History of the Water Pollution Control Act Amendments of 1972, at 169–70 (1973). Restricting the EPA to treatment technology already in use in a particular industry would only insulate industrial categories in which present practices might be uniformly inadequate. C&H argues, however, that the efficacy of activated sludge treatment for cane sugar refining waste is so uncertain that it cannot be considered for the 1977 standard.

* * *

In the light of this alleged insufficient support for the EPA's conclusion that the transferred technology will enable cane sugar refiners to comply with the BPT and BAT limitations, C&H urges us to vacate the regulations

* * *

We find adequate support for the agency's determination. The record indicates that the EPA collected data on the use of biological treatment in various industries with high carbonaceous wastes similar to cane sugar refining wastes, in municipal treatment systems that receive cane sugar process water, in combined cane sugar factory-refineries, and in bench and pilot scale tests. While it may be that none of these completely duplicated the actual conditions in a cane sugar refinery, they were all relevant sources for the EPA to consult for information.

The factory-refineries and the municipal facilites indicate that cane sugar wastes could respond well to biological treatment.

* * *

To appraise the efficacy of activated sludge treatment in the industrial context, the EPA looked to the various industries whose discharges resembled cane sugar refining discharges in important respects.

* * *

These numerous sources of data provided sufficient support for the agency's decision on the transferability of activate sludge technology.

* * *

Other Environmental Effects

C&H complains that the EPA failed to account for a number of non-water quality environmental problems that will flow from the new regulations. The activated sludge treatment plants will require additional land, possibly a problem for refineries in urban areas. Moreover, disposal of the resulting bacterial sludge as landfill may not endear the refiners to local public health authorities. The EPA, however, did consider that the many activated sludge treatment plants already in industrial and municipal use are able to dispose of their sludge without undue difficulty, and an agency pilot scale test indicated that drying the sludge was possible.

* * *

Finally, C&H informs us that the cooling towers may cause serious fogging and noise and that the fog may imperil traffic on roads near the refineries. The EPA correctly points out that the comments it received on this point were based more on speculation than facts. Nonetheless, the agency acknowledged that these problems might develop. Development Document at 142. The record contains no evidence that any of the five refineries presently using cooling towers has encountered them, however. Moreover, the agency took into consideration the likelihood that design modification and careful placement could abate the noise and fogging problems.

* * *

Under these circumstances, the EPA's determination was not arbitrary.

Costs

As indicated above, § 304 directs the EPA to consider the cost of treatment technologies recommended for use as BPT and BAT. C&H complains that in doing so the EPA used 1971 cost data, understated the cost of capital and land, and overstated industry income, investment and cash flow, with the result that the EPA's cost estimate was one-third of the real figure for BPT, and one-half the real price of BAT. C&H also emphasizes that the EPA should not just compute the price of the new treatment systems, but also must ascertain the specific resulting environmental benefits. Instead, C&H says, the agency merely parroted the boilerplate statement that "[i]t is not feasible to quantify in economic terms . . . the costs resulting from the discharge of these pollutants to our Nation's Waterways." 39 Fed.Reg. 1054 (1974). According to C&H, the expensive cooling towers will treat water containing only "minute" concentration of BOD, which the EPA has not shown to threaten aquatic life or suitability for human use.

The EPA, however, need not document specifically the benefits to society from the curtailment of pollutants from a particular point source. Congress has established as a national goal the complete elimination of pollutant discharges by 1985. 33 U.S.C. § 1251(a)(1) (Supp. IV 1974). The EPA must lead industry toward that goal through the 1977 and 1983 standards, and the agency's discretion is necessarily broad. See *FMC Corp. v. Train*, supra, 539 F.2d at 978–79. In its consideration in this proceeding, the EPA apparently did use the most recent cost information available, and focused its economic analysis narrowly on cane sugar refining, instead of the entire food processing industry, which C&H apparently used in reaching its higher cost estimates. As to C&H's numerous other charges of specific inaccuracies in the EPA cost figures, the agency has presented data to support its estimates. We believe that the EPA estimates fall within the realm of reason on the basis of information in the record. See id. at 979. In short, this is not a case like *Hooker*, upon which C&H relies, where there was an "absence of any practical consideration of costs." 537 F.2d at 635.

We have considered all of C&H's arguments, and we uphold the effluent limitations guidelines as promulgated by the EPA. The petition for review is denied.

E.I. DU PONT DE NEMOURS & CO.
v.
TRAIN

430 U. S. 112 (1977)

Mr. Justice STEVENS delivered the opinion of the Court.

* * *

These cases present three important questions of statutory construction: (1) whether EPA has the authority under § 301 of the Act to issue industrywide regulations limiting discharges by existing plants; (2) whether the Court of Appeals, which admittedly is authorized to review the standards for new sources, also has jurisdiction under § 509 to review the regulations concerning existing plants; and (3) whether the new-source standards issued under § 306 must allow variances for individual plants.* * *

The Statute

The statute, enacted on October 18, 1972, authorized a series of steps to be taken to achieve the goal of eliminating all discharges of pollutants into the Nation's waters by 1985, § 101(a)(1).

The first steps required by the Act are described in § 304, which directs the Administrator to develop and publish various kinds of technical data to provide guidance in carrying out responsibilities imposed by other sections of the Act. Thus, within 60 days, 120 days, and 180 days after the date of enactment, the Administrator was to promulgate a series of guidelines to assist the States in developing and carrying out permit programs pursuant to § 402. §§ 304(h), (f), (g). Within 270 days, he was to develop the information to be used in formulating standards for new plants pursuant to § 306. § 304(c). And within one year he was to publish regulations providing guidance for effluent limitations on existing point sources. Section 304(b) goes into great detail concerning the contents of these regulations. They must identify the degree of effluent reduction attainable through use of the best practicable or best available technology for a class of plants. The guidelines must also "specify factors to be taken into account" in determining the control measures applicable to point sources within these classes. A list of factors to be considered then follows. The Administrator was also directed to develop and publish, within one year, elaborate criteria for water quality accurately reflecting the most current scientific knowledge, and also technical information on factors necessary to restore and maintain water quality. § 304(a). The title of § 304 describes it as the "information and guidelines" portion of the statute.

Section 301 is captioned "effluent limitations." Section 301(a) makes the discharge of any pollutant unlawful unless the discharge is in compliance with certain enumerated sections of the Act. The enumerated sections which are relevant to this case are § 301 itself, § 306, and § 402. A brief word about each of these sections is necessary.

Section 402 authorizes the Administrator to issue permits for individual point sources, and also authorizes him to review and approve the plan of any State desiring to administer its own permit program. These permits serve "to transform generally applicable effluent limitations . . . into the obligations (including a timetable for compliance) of the individual discharger[s]. . . ." *EPA v. California ex rel. State Water Resources Control Board*, 26 U.S. 200, 205, 96 S.Ct. 2022 , 2025, 48 L.Ed.2d 578. Petitioner chemical companies' position in this litigation is that § 402 provides the only statutory authority for the issuance of enforceable limitations on the discharge of pollutants by existing plants. It is noteworthy, however, that although this section authorizes the imposition of limitations in individual permits, the section itself does not mandate either the Administrator or the State to use permits as the method of prescribing effluent limitations.

Section 306 directs the Administrator to publish within 90 days a list of categories of sources discharging pollutants and, within one year thereafter, to publish regulations establishing national standards of performance for new sources within each category. Section 306 contains no provision for exceptions from the standards for individual plants; on the contrary, subsection (e) expressly makes it unlawful to operate a new source in violation of the applicable standard of performance after its effective date. The statute provides that the new-source standards shall reflect the greatest degree of effluent reduction achievable through application of the best available demonstrated control technology.

Section 301(b) defines the effluent limitations that shall be achieved by existing point sources in two stages. By July 1, 1977, the effluent limitations shall require the application of the best *practicable* control technology currently available; by July 1, 1983, the limitations shall require application of the best *available* technology economically achievable. The statute expressly provides that the limitations which are to become effective in 1983 are applicable to "categories and classes of point sources"; this phrase is omitted from the description of the 1977 limitations. While § 301 states that these limitations "shall be achieved," it fails to state who will establish the limitations.

Section 301(c) authorizes the Administrator to grant variances from the 1983 limitations. Section 301(e) states that effluent limitations established pursuant to § 301 shall be applied to all point sources.

To summarize, § 301(b) requires the achievement of effluent limitations requiring use of the "best practicable" or "best available" technology. It refers to § 304 for a definition of these terms. Section 304 requires the publication of "regulations, providing guidelines for effluent limitations." Finally, permits issued under § 402 must require compliance with § 301 effluent limitations. Nowhere are we told who sets the § 301 effluent limitations, or precisely how they relate to § 304 guidelines and § 402 permits.

* * *

The Issues

The broad outline of the parties' respective theories may be stated briefly. EPA contends that § 301(b) authorizes it to issue regulations establishing effluent limitations for classes of plants. The permits granted under § 402, in EPA's view, simply incorporate these across-the-board limitations, except for the limited variances allowed by the regulations themselves and by § 301(c). The § 304(b) guidelines, according to EPA, were intended to guide it in later establishing § 301 effluent-limitation regulations. Because the process proved more time consuming than Congress assumed when it established this two-stage process, EPA condensed the two stages into a single regulation.

In contrast, petitioners contend that § 301 is not an independent source of authority for setting effluent limitations by regulation. Instead, § 301 is seen as merely a description of the effluent limitations which are set for each plant on an individual basis during the permit-issuance process. Under the industry view, the § 304 guidelines serve the function of guiding the permit issuer in setting the effluent limitations.

The jurisdictional issue is subsidiary to the critical question whether EPA has the power to issue effluent limitations by regulation. Section 509(b)(1), 86 Stat. 892, 33 U.S.C. § 1369(b)(1), provides that "[r]eview of the Administrator's action . . . (E) in approving or promulgating any effluent limitation . . . under section 301" may be had in the courts of appeals. On the other hand, the Act does not provide for judicial review of § 304 guidelines. If EPA is correct that its regulations are "effluent limitation[s] under section 301," the regulations are directly reviewable in the Court of Appeals. If industry is correct that the regulations can only be considered § 304 guidelines, suit to review the regulations could probably be brought only in the District Court, if anywhere. Thus, the issue of jurisdiction to review the regulations is intertwined with the issue of EPA's power to issue the regulations.

We think § 301 itself is the key to the problem. The statutory language concerning the 1983 limitation, in particular, leaves no doubt that these limitations are to be set by regulation. Subsection (b)(2)(A) of § 301 states that by 1983 "effluent limitations *for categories and classes* of point sources" are to be achieved which will require "application of the best available technology economically achievable *for such category or class*." (Emphasis added.) These effluent limitations are to require elimination of all discharges if "such elimination is technologically and economically achievable for a *category or class* of point sources." (Emphasis added.) This is "language difficult to reconcile with the view that individual effluent limitations are to be set when each permit is issued." *American Meat Institute v. EPA*, 526 F.2d 442, 450 (C.A.7 1975). The statute thus focuses expressly on the characteristics of the "category or class" rather than the characteristics of individual point sources. Normally, such classwide determinations would be made by regulation, not in the course of issuing a permit to one member of the class.

Thus, we find that § 301 unambiguously provides for the use of regulations to establish the 1983 effluent limitations. Different language is used in § 301 with respect to the 1977 limitations. Here, the statute speaks of "effluent limitations for point sources," rather than "effluent limitations for categories and classes of point sources." Nothing elsewhere in the Act, however, suggests any radical difference in the mechanism used to impose limitations for the 1977 and 1983 deadlines. See *American Iron & Steel Institute v. EPA*, 526 F.2d 1027, 1042 n.32 (C.A.3 1975). For instance, there is no indication in either § 301 or § 304 that the § 304 guidelines play a different role in setting 1977 limitations. Moreover, it would be highly anomalous if the 1983 regulations and the new-source standards were directly reviewable in the Court of Appeals, while the 1977 regulations based on the same administrative record were reviewable only in the District Court. The magnitude and highly technical character of the administrative record involved with these regulations makes it almost inconceivable that Congress would have required duplicate review in the first instance by different courts. We conclude that the statute authorizes the 1977 limitations as well as the 1983 limitations to be set by regulation, so long as some allowance is made for variations in individual plants, as EPA has done by including a variance clause in its 1977 limitations.

The question of the form of § 301 limitations is tied to the question whether the Act requires the Administrator or the permit issuer to establish the limitations. Section 301 does not itself answer this question, for it speaks only in the passive voice of the achievement and establishment of the limitations. But other parts of the statute leave little doubt on this score. Section 304(b) states that "[f]or the purpose of adopting or revising effluent limitations . . . the Administrator shall" issue guideline regulations; while the judicial-review section, § 509(b)(1), speaks of "the Administrator's action . . . in approving or promulgating any effluent limitation or other limitation under section 301. . . ." See *infra*, at 979. And § 101(d) requires us to resolve any ambiguity on this score in favor of the Administrator. It provides that "[e]xcept as otherwise *expressly* provided in this Act, the Administrator of the

Environmental Protection Agency . . . shall administer this Act." (Emphasis added.) In sum, the language of the statute supports the view that § 301 limitations are to be adopted by the Administrator, that they are to be based primarily on classes and categories, and that they are to take the form of regulations.

The legislative history supports this reading of § 301. The Senate Report states that "pursuant to subsection 301(b)(1)(A), and Section 304(b)" the Administrator is to set a base level for all plants in a given category, and "[i]n no case . . . should any plant be allowed to discharge more pollutants per unit of production than is defined by that base level." S.Rep. No. 92–414, p. 50 (1971), Leg.Hist. 1468, U.S.Code Cong. & Admin.News 1972, pp. 3668, 3716. The Conference Report on § 301 states that "the determination of the economic impact of an effluent limitation [will be made] on the basis of classes and categories of point sources, as distinguished from a plant by plant determination." Sen.Conf.Rep. No. 92–1236, p. 121 (1972), Leg.Hist. 304; U.S.Code Cong. & Admin. News 1972, p. 3799. In presenting the Conference Report to the Senate, Senator Muskie, perhaps the Act's primary author, emphasized the importance of uniformity in setting § 301 limitations. He explained that this goal of uniformity required that EPA focus on classes or categories of sources in formulating effluent limitations. Regarding the requirement contained in § 301 that plants use the "best practicable control technology" by 1977, he stated:

> "The modification of subsection 304(b)(1) is intended to clarify what is meant by the term 'practicable.' The balancing test between total cost and effluent reduction benefits is intended to limit the application of technology only where the additional degree of effluent reduction is wholly out of proportion to the costs of achieving such marginal level of reduction for *any class or category* of sources.
>
> "The Conferees agreed upon this limited cost-benefit analysis in order to maintain *uniformity within a class and category* of point sources subject to effluent limitations, and to avoid imposing on the Administrator any requirement to consider the location of sources within a category or to ascertain water quality impact of effluent controls, or to determine the economic impact of controls on any individual plant in a single community." 118 Cong.Rec. 33696 (1972), Leg. Hist. 170 (emphasis added).

He added that:

> "The Conferees intend that the factors described in section 304(b) be considered only within classes or categories of point sources and that such factors not be considered at the time of the application of an effluent limitation to an individual point source within such a category or class." 118 Cong.Rec. 33697 (1972), Leg.Hist. 172

This legislative history supports our reading of § 301 and makes it clear that the § 304 guidelines are not merely aimed at guiding the discretion of permit issuers in setting limitations for individual plants.

What, then, is the function of the § 304(b) guidelines? As we noted earlier, § 304(b) requires EPA to identify the amount of effluent reduction attainable through use of the best practicable or available technology and to "specify factors to be taken into account" in determining the pollution control methods "to be applicable to point sources . . . within such categories or classes." These guidelines are to be issued "[f]or the purpose of adopting or revising effluent limitations under this Act." As we read it, § 304 requires that the guidelines survey the practicable or available pollution-control technology for an industry and assess its effectiveness. The guidelines are then to describe the methodology EPA intends to use in the § 301 regulations to determine the effluent limitations for particular plants. If the technical complexity of the task had not prevented EPA from issuing the guidelines within the statutory deadline, they could have provided valuable guidance to permit issuers, industry, and the public, prior to the issuance of the § 301 regulations.

Our construction of the Act is supported by § 501(a), which gives EPA the power to make "such regulations as are necessary to carry out" its functions, and by § 101(d), which charges the agency with the duty of administering the Act. In construing this grant of authority, as Mr. Justice Harlan wrote in connection with a somewhat similar problem:

> "'[C]onsiderations of feasibility and practicality are certainly germane' to the issues before us. *Bowles v. Willingham*, [321 U.S. 503, at 517, 64 S.Ct. 641, at 648, 88 L.Ed. 892]. We cannot, in these circumstances, conclude that Congress has given authority inadequate to achieve with reasonable effectiveness the purposes for which it has acted." *Permian Basin Area Rate Cases*, 390 U.S. 747, 777, 88 S.Ct. 1344, 1365, 20 L.Ed.2d 312.

The petitioners' view of the Act would place an impossible burden on EPA. It would require EPA to give individual consideration to the circumstances of each of the more than 42,000 dischargers who have applied for permits, Brief for Respondents in No. 75–978, p. 30 n.22, and to issue or approve all these permits well in advance of the 1977 deadline in order to give industry time to install the necessary pollution-control equipment. We do not believe that Congress would have failed so conspicuously to provide EPA with the authority needed to achieve the statutory goals.

Both EPA and petitioners refer to numerous other provisions of the Act and fragments of legislative history in support of their positions. We do not find these conclusive, and little point would be served by discussing them in detail. We are satisfied that our reading of * * *301 is consistent with the rest of the legislative scheme.

* * *

Consequently, we hold that EPA has the authority to issue regulations setting forth uniform effluent limitations for categories of plants.

II

Our holding that § 301 does authorize the Administrator to promulgate effluent limitations for classes and categories of existing point sources necessarily resolves the jurisdictional issue as well. For, as we have already pointed out, § 509(b)(1) provides that "[r]eview of the Administrator's action . . . in approving or promulgating any effluent limitation or other limitation under section 301, 302, or 306, . . . may be had by any interested person in the Circuit Court of Appeals of the United States for the Federal judicial district in which such person resides or transacts such business. . . ."

* * *

III

The remaining issue in this case concerns new plants. Under § 306, EPA is to promulgate "regulations establishing Federal standards of performance for new sources. . . ." § 306(b)(1)(B). A "standard of performance" is a "standard for the control of the discharge of pollutants which reflects the greatest degree of effluent reduction which the Administrator determines to be achievable through application of the best available demonstrated control technology, . . . including, where practicable, a standard permitting no discharge of pollutants." § 306(a)(1). In setting the standard, "[t]he Administrator may distinguish among classes, types, and sizes within categories of new sources . . and shall consider the type of process employed (including whether batch or continuous)." § 306(b)(2). As the House Report states, the standard must reflect the best technology for "that category of sources, and for class, types, and sizes within categories." H.R.Rep. No. 92–911, p. 111 (1972), Leg.Hist. 798.

The Court of Appeals held:

> "Neither the Act nor the regulations contain any variance provision for new sources. The rule of presumptive applicability applies to new sources as well as existing sources. On remand EPA should come forward with some limited escape mechanism for new sources." *Du Pont II*, 541 F.2d, at 1028.

The court's rationale was that "[p]rovisions for variances, modifications, and exceptions are appropriate to the regulatory process." *Ibid.*

The question, however, is not what a court thinks is generally appropriate to the regulatory process; it is what Congress intended for these regulations. It is clear that Congress intended these regulations to be absolute prohibitions. The use of the word "standards" implies as much. So does the description of the preferred standard as one "permitting *no* discharge of pollutants." (Emphasis added.) It is "unlawful for *any* owner or operator of *any* new source to operate such source in violation of any standard of performance applicable to such source." § 306(e) (emphasis added). In striking contrast to § 301(c), there is no statutory provision for variances, and a variance provision would be inappropriate in a standard that was intended to insure national uniformity and "maximum feasible control of new sources." S.Rep. No. 92–414, p. 58 (1971), Leg.Hist. 1476.

That portion of the judgment of the Court of Appeals in 541 F.2d 1018 requiring EPA to provide a variance procedure for new sources is reversed. In all other aspects, the judgments of the Court of Appeals are affirmed.

ENVIRONMENTAL PROTECTION AGENCY v. NATIONAL CRUSHED STONE ASSOCIATION

449 U.S. 64 (1980)

JUSTICE WHITE delivered the opinion of the Court.

In April and July 1977 the Environmental Protection Agency (EPA), acting under the Federal Water Pollution Control Act Amendments of 1972 (ACT) . . . promulgated pollution discharge limitations for the coal industry and for that portion of the mineral mining and processing industry comprising the crushed stone, construction sand, and gravel categories. Although the Act does not expressly authorize or require variances from the 1977 limitation, each set of regulations contained a variance provision. Respondents sought review of the regulations in various courts of appeals, challenging both the substantive standards and the variance clause. All of the petitions for review were transferred to the Court of Appeals for the Fourth Circuit, In *National Crushed Stone Association* v. *EPA*, 601 F. 2d 111 (CA4 1979), and in *Consolidation Coal Company v. Costle*, 604 F. 2d 239 (CA4 1979), the Court of Appeals set aside the variance provision as "unduly restrictive" and remanded the provision to EPA for reconsideration.

To obtain a variance from the 1977 uniform discharge limitations a discharger must demonstrate that the "factors relating to the equipment or facilities involved, the process applied, or other such factors relating to such discharger are fundamentally different from the factors considered in the establishment of the guidelines." Although a greater than normal cost of implementation will be considered in acting on a request for a variance, economic ability to meet the costs will not be considered. A variance, therefore, will not be granted on the basis of the applicant's economic inability to meet the costs of implementing the uniform standard.

The Court of Appeals for the Fourth Circuit rejected this position. It required EPA to "take into consideration, among other things, the statutory factors set out in § 301 (c)," which authorizes variances from the more restrictive pollution limitations to become effective in 1987 and which specifies economic capability as a major factor to be taken into account. The court held that

> "'if [a plant] is doing all that the maximum use of technology within its economic capability will permit and if such use will result in reasonable further progress toward the elimination of the discharge of pollutants . . . no reason appears why [it] should not be able to secure such a variance should it comply with any other requirements of the variance.'" 601 F. 2d, at 124, quoting from *Appalachian Power Co.* v. *Train*, 545 F. 2d 1351, 1378 (CA4 1976).

We granted certiorari to resolve the conflict between the decision below and *Weyerhauser Co.* v. *Costle*,—U.S. App. D. C.—, 590 F.2d 1001 (1978), in which the variance provision was upheld.

I

We shall first briefly outline the basic structure of the Act, which translates Congress' broad goal of eliminating "the discharge of pollutants into the navigable waters," 35 U. S. C. 1251 (a)(1), into specific requirements that must be met by individual point sources.

Section 301 (b) of the Act, 33 U. S. C. § 1311 (b), authorizes the Administrator to set effluent limitations for categories of point sources. With respect to existing point sources, the section provides for implementation of increasingly stringent effluent limitations in two steps. The first step, to be accomplished by July 1, 1977, requires all point sources to meet standards based on "the application of the best practicable control technology currently available [BPT] as defined by the Administrator. . . ." § 301 (b)(1)(A). The second step, to be accomplished by July 1, 1987, requires all point sources to meet standards based on application of the "best available technology economically achievable [BAT] for such category or class. . . ." § 301 (b)(2)(A). Both sets of limitations—BPT's followed within 10 years by BAT's—are to be based upon regulatory guidelines established under § 304 (b).

Section 304 (b) of the Act, 33 U. S. C. § 1314 (b), is again divided into two sections corresponding to the two levels of technology, BPT and BAT. Under § 304 (b)(1) the Administrator is to quantify "the degree of effluent reduction attainable through the application of the best practicable control technology currently available [BPT] for classes and categories of point sources. . . ." In assessing the BPT the Administrator is to consider:

> "the total cost of application of technology in relation to the effluent reduction benefits to be achieved from such application, . . . the age of equipment and facilities involved, the process employed, the engineering aspects of the application of various types of control techniques, process changes, non-water quality environmental impact (including energy requirements), and such other factors as the Administrator deems appropriate."

Similar directions are given the Administrator for determining effluent reductions attainable from the BAT except that in assessing BAT total cost is no longer to be considered in comparison to effluent reduction benefits.

Section 402 authorizes the establishment of the National Pollutant Discharge Elimination System (NPDES), under which every discharger of pollutants is required to obtain a permit. The permit requires the discharger to meet all the applicable requirements specified in the regulations issued under § 301. Permits are issued by either the Administrator or state agencies that have been approved by the Administrator. The permit "transform[s] generally applicable effluent limitations . . . into the obligations (including a timetable for compliance) of the individual discharger. . . ." *EPA* v. *California ex rel. State Water Resources Control Board*, 426 U. S. 200, 205 (1976).

Section 301 (c) of the Act explicitly provides for modifying the 1987 (BAT) effluent limitations with respect to individual point sources. A variance under § 301 (c) may be obtained upon a showing "that such modified requirements (1) will represent the maximum use of technology within the economic capability of the owner or operator; and (2) will result in reasonable further progress toward elimination of the discharge of pollutants." Thus, the economic ability of the individual operator to meet the costs of effluent reductions may in some circumstances justify granting a variance from the 1987 limitations.

No such explicit variance provision exists with respect to BPT standards, but in *E. I. du Pont de Nemours* v. *Train*, 430 U. S. 112 (1977), we indicated that a variance provision was a necessary aspect of BPT limitations applicable by regulations to classes and categories of point sources. 430 U. S., at 128. The issue in this case is whether the BPT variance provision must allow consideration of the economic capability of an individual discharger to afford the costs of the BPT limitation. For the reasons that follow, our answer is in the negative.

II

The plain language of the statute does not support the position taken by the Court of Appeals. Section 301 (c) is limited on its face to modifications of the 1987 BAT limitations. It says nothing about relief from the 1977 BPT requirements. Nor does the language of the Act support the position that although § 301 (c) is not itself applicable to BPT standards, it requires that the affordability of the prescribed 1977 technology be considered in BPT variance decisions. This would be a logical reading of the statute only if the factors listed in § 301 (c) bore a substantial relationship to the considerations underlying the 1977 limitations as they do to those controlling the 1987 regulations. This is not the case.

The two factors listed in § 301 (c)—"maximum use of technology within the economic capability of the owner or operator" and "reasonable further progress toward the elimination of the discharge of pollutants"—parallel the general definition of BAT standards as limitations that "require application of the best available technology economically achievable for such category or class, which will result in reasonable further progress toward . . . eliminating the discharge of all pollutants. . . ." § 301 (b)(2). A § 301 (c) variance, thus, creates for a particular point source a BAT standard that represents for it the same sort of economic and technological commitment as the general BAT standard creates for the class. As with the general BAT standard, the variance assumes that the 1977 BPT has been met by the point source and that the modification represents a commitment of the maximum resources economically possible to the ultimate goal of eliminating all polluting discharges. No one who can afford the best available technology can secure a variance.

There is no similar connection between § 301 (c) and the considerations underlying the establishment of the 1977 BPT limitations. First, § 301 (c)'s requirement of "reasonable further progress" must have reference to some prior standard. BPT serves as the prior standard with respect to BAT. There is, however, no comparable, prior standard with respect to BPT limitations. Second, BPT limitations do not require an industrial category to commit the maximum economic resources possible to pollution control, even if affordable. Those point sources already using a satisfactory pollution control technology need take no additional steps at all. The § 301 (c) variance factor, the "maximum use of technology within the economic capability of the owner or operator," would therefore be inapposite in the BPT context. It would not have the same effect there that it has with respect to BAT's, *i. e.*, it would not apply the general requirements to an individual point source.

More importantly, to allow a variance based on the maximum technology affordable by the point source, even if that technology fails to meet BPT effluent limitations, would undercut the purpose and function of BPT limitations. Rather than the 1987 requirement of the best measures economically and technologically feasible, the statutory provisions for 1977 contemplate regulations prohibiting discharges from any point source in excess of the effluent produced by the best practicable technology currently available in the industry. The Administrator was referred to the industry and to existing practices to determine BPT. He was to categorize point sources, examine control practices in exemplary plants in each category, and after weighing benefits and costs and considering other factors specified by § 304, determine and define the best practicable technology at a level that would effect the obvious statutory goal for 1977 of substantially reducing the total pollution produced by each category of the industry. Necessarily, if pollution is to be diminished, limitations based on BPT must forbid the level of effluent produced by the most pollution-prone segment of the industry, that segment not measuring up to "the average of the best existing performance." So understood, the statute contemplated regulations that would require a substantial number of point sources with the poorest performances either to conform to BPT standards or to cease production. To allow a variance based on economic capability and not to require adherence to the prescribed minimum technology would permit the employment of the very practices that the Administrator had rejected in establishing the best practicable technology currently in use in the industry.

To put the matter another way, under § 304, the Administrator is directed to consider the benefits of effluent reductions as compared to the costs of pollution control in determining BPT limitations. Thus, every BPT limitation represents a conclusion by the Administrator that the costs imposed on the industry are worth the benefits in pollution reduction that will be gained by meeting those limits. To grant a variance because a particular owner or operator cannot meet the normal costs of the technological requirements imposed on him, and not because there has been a recalculation of the benefits compared to the costs, would be inconsistent with this legislative scheme and would allow a level of pollution inconsistent with the judgment of the Administrator.

In terms of the scheme implemented by BPT limitations, the factors that the Administrator considers in granting variances do not suggest that economic capability must also be a determinant. The regulations permit a variance where "factors relating to the equipment or facilities involved, the process applied, or such other factors relating to such discharger are fundamentally different from the factors considered in the establishment of the guidelines." If a point source can show that its situation, including its costs of compliance, is not within the range of circumstances considered by the Administrator, then it may receive a variance, whether or not the source could afford to comply with the minimum standard. In such situations, the variance is an acknowledgement that the uniform BPT limitation was set without reference to the full range of current practices, to which the Administrator was to refer. Insofar as a BPT limitation was determined without consideration of a current practice fundamentally different from those that were considered by the Administrator, that limitation is incomplete. A variance based on economic capability, however, would not have this character: it would allow a variance simply because the point source could not afford a compliance cost that is not fundamentally different from those the Administrator has already considered in determining BPT. It would force a displacement of calculations already performed, not because those calculations were incomplete or had unexpected effects, but only because the costs happened to fall on one particular operator, rather than on another who might be economically better off.

Because the 1977 limitations were intended to reduce the total pollution produced by an industry, requiring compliance with BPT standards necessarily imposed additional costs on the segment of the industry with the least effective technology. If the statutory goal is to be achieved, these costs must be borne or the point source eliminated. In our view, requiring variances from otherwise valid regulations where dischargers cannot afford normal costs of compliance would undermine the purpose and the intended operative effect of the 1977 regulations.

III

The Administrator's present interpretation of the language of the statute is amply supported by the legislative history, which persuades us that Congress understood that the economic capability provision of § 301 (c) was limited to BAT variances; that Congress foresaw and accepted the economic hardship, including the closing of some plants, that effluent limitations would cause; and that Congress took certain steps to alleviate this hardship, steps which did not include allowing a BPT variance based on economic capability.

There is no indication that Congress intended § 301 (c) to reach further than the limitations of its plain language. The statement of the House managers of the Act described § 301 (c) as "not intended to justify modifications which would not represent an upgrading over the July 1, 1977, requirements of 'best practicable control technology.'" 1 Leg. Hist. 232. The Conference Report noted that a § 301 (c) variance could only be granted after the effective date of BPT limitations and could only be applied to BAT limitations. Similarly, the Senate Report on the Conference action emphasized that one of the purposes of the BPT limitation was to avoid imposing on the "Administrator any requirement . . . to determine the economic impact of controls on any individual plant in a single community." 1 Leg. Hist. 170.

Nor did Congress restrict the reach of § 301 (c) without understanding the economic hardships that uniform standards would impose. Prior to passage of the Act, Congress had before it a report jointly prepared by EPA, the Commerce Dept., and the Council on Environmental Quality on the impact of the pollution control measures on industry. That report estimated that there would be 200 to 300 plant closings caused by the first set of pollution limitations. Comments in the Senate debate were explicit: "There is no doubt that we will suffer some disruptions in our economy because of our efforts; many marginal plants may be forced to close." 2 Leg. Hist. 1282 (Sen. Bentsen). The House managers explained the Conference position as follows:

> "If the owner or operator of a given point source determines that he would rather go out of business than meet the 1977 requirements, the managers clearly expect that any discharge issued in the interim would reflect the fact that all discharges not in compliance with such 'best practicable technology currently available' would cease by June 30, 1977." 1 Leg. Hist. 231.

Congress did not respond to this foreseen economic impact by making room for variances based on economic impact. In fact, this possibility was specifically considered and rejected:

> "This alternative [to a loan program] would be waiving strict environmental

> standards where economic hardship could be shown. But the approach of giving variances to pollution controls based on economic grounds has long ago shown itself to be a risky course: All too often, the variances become a tool used by powerful political interests to obtain so many exemptions for pollution control standards and timetables on the filmsiest [*sic*] of pretenses that they become meaningless. In short, with variances, exceptions to pollution cleanup can become the rule, meaning further tragic delay in stopping the destruction of our environment." 2 Leg. Hist. 1355 (Sen. Nelson).

Instead of economic variances, Congress specifically added two other provisions to address the problem of economic hardship.

First, provision was made for low-cost loans to small businesses to help them meet the cost of technological improvements. § 8, amending 15 U. S. C. § 636. The Conference Report described the provision as authorizing the Small Business Administration "to make loans to assist small business concerns . . . if the Administrator determines that the concern is likely to suffer substantial economic injury without such assistance." 1 Leg. Hist. 153. Senator Nelson, who offered the amendment providing for these loans, saw the loans as an alternative to the dangers of an economic variance provision that he felt might otherwise be necessary. Several Congressmen understood the loan program as an alternative to forced closings: "It is the smaller business that is hit hardest by these laws and their enforcement. And it is the same class of business that has the least resources to meet the demands of this enforcement. . . . Without assistance, many of these businesses may face extinction." 2 Leg. Hist. 1359 (Sen. McIntyre).

Second, an employee protection provision was added, giving EPA authority to investigate any plant's claim that it must cut back production or close down because of pollution control regulations. § 507 (e), 33 U. S. C. § 1367 (e). This provision had two purposes: to allow EPA constantly to monitor the economic effect on industry of pollution control rules and to undercut economic threats by industry that would create pressure to relax effluent limitation rules. Congressman Fraser explained this second purpose as follows:

> "[T]he purpose of the amendment is to provide for a public hearing in the case of an industry claim that enforcement of these water-control standards will force it to relocate or otherwise shut down operations. . . . I think too many companies use the excuse of compliance, or the need for compliance, to change operations that are going to change anyway. It is this kind of action that gives the whole antipollution effort a bad name and causes a great deal of stress and strain in the community." 1 Leg. Hist. 659.

The only protection offered by the provision, however, is the assurance that there will be a public inquiry into the facts behind such an economic threat. The section specifically concludes that "nothing in this subsection shall be construed to require or authorize the Administrator to modify or withdraw any effluent limitation or order issued under this Act." § 507 (e).

As we see it, Congress anticipated that the 1977 regulations would cause economic hardship and plant closings: "[T]he question . . . is not what a court thinks is generally appropriate to the regulatory process; it is what Congress intended for *these* regulations." *Du Pont, supra*, at 138.

IV

It is by now a commonplace that "when faced with a problem of statutory construction, this Court shows great deference to the interpretation given the statute by the officers or agency charged with its administration." *Udall* v. *Tallman*, 380 U. S. 1, 16 (1965). The statute itself does not provide for BPT variances in connection with permits for individual point sources, and we had no occasion in *du Pont* to address the adequacy of the Administrator's 1977 variance provision. In the face of § 301 (c)'s explicit limitation and in the absence of any other specific direction to provide for variances in connection with permits for individual point sources, we believe that the Administrator has adopted a reasonable construction of the statutory mandate.

In rejecting EPA's interpretation of the BPT variance provision, the Court of Appeals relied on a mistaken conception of the relation between BPT and BAT standards. The court erroneously believed that since BAT limitations are to be more stringent than BPT limitations, the variance provision for the latter must be at least as flexible as that for the former with respect to affordability. The variance permitted by § 301 (c) from the 1987 limitations, however, can reasonably be understood to represent a cost in decreased effluent reductions that can only be afforded once the minimal standard expressed in the BPT limitation has been reached.

We conclude, therefore, that the Court of Appeals erred in not accepting EPA's interpretation of the Act. EPA is not required by the Act to consider economic capability in granting variances from its uniform BPT regulations.

The judgment of the Court of Appeals is *Reversed.*

---

3. REGULATION UNDER THE NATIONAL PERMIT SYSTEM (NPDES)[1]

Section 402 of the Federal Water Pollution Control Act (FWPCA), subsequently renamed the Clean Water Act (CWA), creates the **National Pollutant Discharge Elimination System (NPDES)** as the primary regulatory mechanism for source-by-source control of the discharge of pollutants into the nation's waters. The NPDES permit is the mechanism for insuring that effluent limitations are met, the necessary technology is applied, and all requirements for controlling discharges and complying with water quality standards are met on schedule.

The Clean Water Act makes it illegal to discharge any pollutant without an NPDES permit. The law applies to all "point" sources, defined to include municipal waste treatment plants, manufacturing plants, agriculture, forestry, mining and fishing operations and other service, wholesale, retail and commercial establishments. The discharge of pollutants without a permit, or in violation of the permit conditions, is punishable by a fine up to $10,000 per day. Willful or negligent violations are punishable by a fine of up to $25,000 a day and one year in prison for the first offense, and up to $50,000 a day and two years in prison for subsequent violations. EPA is authorized to require compliance with permit conditions by issuing administrative orders that are enforceable in a federal court. The permit system also requires dischargers to monitor their discharges and to report the amount and nature of all waste components.

A permit is not intended to be a license to pollute. It sets specific limits on the amount of each pollutant to be discharged. If the discharger cannot

[1]The information in this section is derived from *Toward Cleaner Water: The New Permit Program To Control Water Pollution*, EPA, 1974.

comply immediately with the limits, the permit will require the discharger to agree to reduce or eliminate the discharges in accordance with a schedule that specifies the amount of reductions at specified dates. Each step of this compliance schedule is enforceable in court.

a. *Role of the States*

Initially the NPDES program is administered by the federal government through the EPA. However, the law requires EPA to turn over the permit-issuing to any state that requests this authority and agrees to operate its own program to meet the following requirements:

Equal in Scope. The state program must be at least equal in scope and effectiveness to the EPA program.

Funding. The program must be adequately funded and staffed with qualified personnel. The state must submit proposed costs and describe available funds.

Illegal to Discharge. The state law must make it illegal to discharge pollutants except as allowed under the permit.

Enforceable. The program must be legally enforceable in state courts. The state must have the power to compel compliance with national and state effluent standards and limitations and water quality standards. Civil and criminal penalties must be at least equal to those in the federal law.

Inspection and Monitoring. The state must have the power to enter, inspect and monitor sources of pollution, and the authority to require polluters to install monitoring equipment, keep records, and file reports.

Imminent Dangers. The state must have the power to immediately stop discharges that pose an imminent or substantial danger to public health or welfare. If the state does not have this power, it must have a procedure for immediately notifying EPA by telephone of actual or threatened emergencies.

Conflicts of Interest. Anyone who receives, or has received in the two prior years, a significant portion of his income, directly or indirectly, from permit-holders or applicants for a permit may not serve on the state board or agency that approves permit applications.

Planning. The state must have an EPA-approved continuing planning process designed to produce water quality management plans for all navigable waters within the state. The plans should include: (*1*) analysis of effluent reductions needed to meet water quality standards, (*2*) compliance schedules, (*3*) priorities for building new waste treatment facilities, and (*4*) schedules for issuing permits.

Public Access. The state's permit program must provide for public access to all information, except trade secrets, generated in the permit process.

Public Hearing. The state's procedure must provide an opportunity for a public hearing before a permit is issued or denied.

Even if the state operates its own permit program, EPA still has the authority to veto a proposed state permit if EPA believes that the permit does not comply with the law or EPA regulations, or if the waters of another state will be adversely affected by the proposed discharge. Furthermore, if a discharge fails to comply with the terms of a state permit, EPA can step in and take enforcement action if the state fails to do so. EPA may also revoke a state's permit authority if the program is not administered in compliance with federal requirements. Such revocation may take place only after the state has failed to take remedial action after notice from EPA and a public hearing is held on the proposed revocation.

b. *Contents of a Permit*

A permit issued by either EPA or a state permit program must contain the following elements:

Pollutants Specified. The permit must specify each pollutant to be discharged and must set the average and maximum daily limits on each pollutant. The permitted discharge must meet water quality standards and other federal and state requirements.

Compliance Schedule. If the discharge is not in compliance with all applicable standards and effluent limits the permit must require the discharger to take specific steps to achieve compliance. If compliance cannot be achieved within nine months, progress reports must be submitted within two weeks after each interim deadline and the final compliance date.

Monitoring and Reporting. The discharger must monitor all major discharges and all discharges of toxic pollutants, whether major or not, and must report the monitoring data at least once a year.

Expiration Date. The permit must be limited to a fixed period of time, not to exceed five years. The discharger may apply for a reissuance of the permit at least 80 days before the expiration date.

Conditions. All permits issued must be subject to the following conditions:

- The discharger must report any new or increased discharges in a new application.
- Any discharge of a new pollutant, or more frequent or excess discharge of a pollutant authorized by the permit, will constitute a violation of the permit.
- If any of the terms or conditions of the permit is violated the permit may be revoked, suspended or modified. The permit may be revoked, suspended or modified if it was obtained by misrepresentation or failure to disclose all relevant facts.
- The discharger will allow EPA or state water pollution control officials to enter and inspect the plant, inspect and copy records required to be kept under terms of the permit, inspect monitoring equipment required by the permit and sample pollution discharges.
- The discharger will keep his pollution control system in good working order and operating as efficiently as possible to comply with the permit.

• The discharges will comply with toxic effluent limitations.

There are several additional conditions that must be met when the discharger is a *publicly owned waste treatment plant*:

• If the treatment plant handles discharges from industries, the permit holder must report any new pollutants coming from those sources or any substantial change in the volume or nature of the industrial discharges.

• Publicly owned treatment plants must require industries to pretreat their wastes to get rid of pollutants that cannot be treated by, or would interfere with, the operation of the treatment plant. It should be noted here that industries discharging directly into a publicly owned waste treatment system do not need a permit for such discharges, but must meet the pretreatment standards set by the public system.

In the following cases, *Ford Motor Co. v. EPA* involves an appeal of an EPA veto of a proposed modification of an existing NPDES permit; *Save the Bay, Inc. v. EPA* involves the validity of the procedure adopted by EPA to review state permits; and *Cleveland Electric Illuminating Co. v. EPA* illustrates the limits of EPA authority to reject a permit approved under a state permit program.

FORD MOTOR COMPANY
v.
E.P.A.

567 F.2d 661 (6th Cir. 1977)

Before WEICK and ENGEL, Circuit Judges, and WEINMAN, Senior District Judge.

WEICK, Circuit Judge.

The principal question before us is whether the Environmental Protection Agency [EPA] properly vetoed modifications in Ford Motor Company's [Ford] existing National Pollutant Discharge Elimination System [NPDES] permit which were proposed by the Michigan Water Resource Commission [MWRC] pursuant to the Federal Water Pollution Control Act of 1972 [FWPCA] §§ 101, *et seq.*, 33 U.S.C. §§ 1251, *et seq*. Ford has petitioned for review of EPA's veto of the permit modifications. We hold that the veto of EPA was invalid because it was not based upon any published regulation or guideline or on any express statutory provision.

* * *

I

In order fully to understand the issues, a review of the pertinent provisions of the

FWPCA is necessary. Congress declared that the objective of the Act was "to restore and maintain the chemical, physical and biological integrity of the Nation's waters" § 101(a), 33 U.S.C. § 1251(a). One of the national goals of the Act was to eliminate by 1985 "the discharge of pollutants into navigable waters." § 101(a)(1). Furthermore, Congress proclaimed by the Act its policy to have the States participate in the prevention, reduction and elimination of pollution. § 101(b). Congress also stressed the need for public participation "in the development, revision and enforcement of any regulation, standard, effluent limitation, plan or program established by the Administrator or any State" and required the publication of "regulations specifying minimum guidelines for public participation in such processes." § 101(e).

The Supreme Court in *EPA v. State Water Resources Control Bd.*, 426 U.S. 200, 204–05, 96 S.Ct. 2022, 2024–25, 48 L.Ed.2d 578 (1976), noted one of the purposes of the Act:

> First, the Amendments are aimed at achieving maximum "effluent limitations" on "point sources," as well as achieving acceptable water quality standards. A point source is "any discernible, confined and discrete conveyance . . . from which pollutants are or may be discharged."[9] An "effluent limitation" in turn is "any restriction established by a State or the Administrator on quantities, rates, and concentrations of chemical, physical, biological, and other constituents which are discharged from point sources . . . including schedules of compliance."[10] Such direct restrictions on discharges facilitate enforcement by making it unnecessary to work backward from an overpolluted body of water to determine which point sources are responsible and which must be abated. In addition, a discharger's performance is now measured against strict technology-based[11] effluent limitations—specified levels of treatment—to which it must conform, rather than against limitations derived from water quality standards to which it and other polluters must collectively conform.[12]

The EPA Administrator was required after consultation with the appropriate federal and state agencies and other interested persons, to adopt regulations providing guidelines for effluent limitations no later than October 18, 1973 and annually thereafter. § 304(b)(2), 33 U.S.C. § 1314(b)(2). Once these guidelines were provided they were to be followed when NPDES permits were issued and were "to serve as the basis of the administrator's veto of objectionable permits." *CPC Int'l, Inc. v. Train*, 515 F.2d 1032, 1039 (8th Cir. 1975). *Compare E. I. duPont deNemours & Co. v. Train*, 430 U.S. 112, 133, n. 24, 97 S.Ct. 965, 51 L.Ed.2d 204 (1977).

The EPA Administrator also was authorized to promulgate effluent limitations for classes and categories of existing point sources which necessarily serve as a basis for denial of a permit. *See* § 301, 33 U.S.C. § 1311; *E. I. duPont deNemours & Co. v.*

[9]§ 502(14), 33 U.S.C. § 1362(14) (1970) ed., Supp. IV). The terms "pollutant" and "discharge of pollutant" are defined in §§ 502(6), (12), 33 U.S.C. §§ 1362(6), (12) (1970 ed., Supp. IV).

[10]§ 502(11), 33 U.S.C. § 1362(11) (1970 ed., Supp. IV). Section 502(17) defines a "schedule of compliance" to be "a schedule of remedial measures including an enforceable sequence of actions or operations leading to compliance with an effluent limitation, other limitation, prohibition, or standard." 33 U.S.C. § 1362(17) (1970 ed., Supp. IV).

[11]Point sources other than publicly owned treatment works must achieve effluent limitations requiring application of the "best practicable control technology currently available" by July 1, 1977, and application of the "best available technology economically achievable" by July 1, 1983. §§ 301(b)(1)(A), (2)(A), 33 U.S.C. §§ 1311(b)(1)(A), (2)(A) (1970 ed., Supp. IV).

[12]Water quality standards are retained as a supplementary basis for effluent limitations, however, so that numerous point sources, despite individual compliance with effluent limitations, may be further regulated to prevent water quality from falling below acceptable levels. See §§ 301(e), 302, 303, 33 U.S.C. §§ 1311(e), 1312, 1313 (1970 ed., Supp. IV).

Train, supra; and *American Iron and Steel Inst. v. EPA*, 526 F.2d 1027, 1041 (3d Cir. 1975).

The Court in the *duPont* case explained at 130 of 430 U.S., at 976 of 97 S.Ct. the function of the § 304(b) guidelines and at the same time their relation to § 301 regulations:

> As we noted earlier, § 304(b) requires EPA to identify the amount of effluent reduction attainable through use of the best practicable or available technology and to "specify factors to be taken into account" in determining the pollution control methods "to be applicable to point sources . . . within such categories or classes." These guidelines are to be issued "[f]or the purpose of adopting or revising effluent limitations under this Act." As we read it, § 304 requires that the guidelines survey the practicable or available pollution control technology for an industry and assess its effectiveness. The guidelines are then to describe the methodology EPA intends to use in the § 301 regulations to determine the effluent limitations for particular plants. [footnote omitted]

Congress also provided a plan for implementing water quality standards, which addressed the problem of concentration of pollutants in particular bodies of water, to meet the purposes and goals of the FWPCA.

Section 303(a), 33 U.S.C. § 1313(a) provides for state-adopted water quality standards including those state standards adopted prior to the FWPCA, which standards meet the requirements of the FWPCA unless otherwise determined by the EPA Administrator. For instance, on September 21, 1973 the State of Michigan, pursuant to the FWPCA, approved new water quality standards which went into effect on December 12, 1973. Michigan Water Quality Standards, Michigan Administrative Code Part 4; Rule 323.1041, *et seq*. Because EPA took no action on the Michigan standards, they became the federal water quality standards in that state. *See* § 303(c)(3), 33 U.S.C. § 1313(c)(3).

Moreover, the EPA Administrator, after issuing notice and holding a public hearing, has authority to establish more restrictive effluent limitations to "discharges of pollutants from a point source or group of point sources" which (even though the effluent limitations under § 301(b)(2) (best available control technology) are applied to the point sources) would still be interfering "with the attainment or maintenance of the water quality in a specific portion of the navigable waters . . .". § 302(a) and (b), 33 U.S.C. § 1312(a) and (b).

The Supreme Court in the *State Water Resources* case also explained a second purpose of FWPCA, 426 U.S. at 205, 96 S.Ct at 2025:

> Second, the Amendments establish the National Pollutant Discharge Elimination System (NPDES)[13] as a means of achieving and enforcing the effluent limitations. Under NPDES, it is unlawful for any person to discharge a pollutant without obtaining a permit and complying with its terms.[14] An NPDES permit serves to transform generally applicable effluent limitations and other standards—including those based on water quality—into the obligations (including a timetable for compliance) of the individual discharger, and the Amendments provide for direct administrative and judicial enforcement of permits. §§ 309 and 505, 33 U.S.C. §§ 1319, 1365 (1970 ed., Supp. IV). With

[13]§ 402, 33 U.S.C. § 1342 (1970 ed., Supp. IV).

[14]Section 301(a), 33 U.S.C. § 1311(a) (1970 ed., Supp. IV), makes unlawful "the discharge of any pollutant by any person" except in compliance with numerous provisions of the Amendments, including § 402 which establishes NPDES.

In effect, the NPDES terminates operation of the Refuse Act permit program. §§ 402(a)(4), (5), 402(k), 33 U.S.C. §§ 1342(a)(4), (5), 1342(k) (1970 ed., Supp. IV).

> few exceptions, for enforcement purposes a discharger in compliance with the terms and conditions of an NPDES permit is deemed to be in compliance with those sections of the Amendments on which the permit conditions are based. § 402(k), 33 U.S.C § 1342(k) (1970 ed., Supp. IV). In short, the permit defines, and facilitates compliance with an enforcement of, a preponderance of a discharger's obligations under the Amendments.

EPA is empowered by Congress to issue these permits. § 402, 33 U.S.C. § 1342. However, the Act also provide that these permits may be issued by the States. If a State desires to administer the program pursuant to the Congressional policy of State control over water pollution, EPA must first approve the State's permit program. *See* § 402(b). Once the Administrator's approval is given, the State may issue NPDES permits as long as the permits meet the requirements of the FWPCA. Among its duties under the permit program, the State must "provide an opportunity for public hearing before a ruling on each such application [for a permit]" and provide the Administrator with "notice of each application [including a copy thereof] for a permit." § 402(b)(3) and (4). On October 17, 1973 the EPA Administrator approved the permit program of the State of Michigan. 39 F.R. 26061 (July 16, 1974).

In addition to EPA's possible withdrawal of its approval of a State's permit program under § 402(c), EPA also retains a veto power over a State's issuance of an individual permit. Section 402(d)(2)(B) provides:

> No permit shall issue . . . if the Administrator within ninety days of the date of transmittal of the proposed permit by the State objects in writing to the issuance of such permit as being *outside the guidelines and requirements of [the Act]*. [Emphasis added]

The aggrieved party has ninety days from the date of denial of the permit under § 402 in which to seek review of the Administrator's action, by petition therefor filed in the appropriate United States Court of Appeals. § 509(B)(1)(F), 33 U.S.C. § 1369(b)(1)(F).

Ford operates a stamping plant in Monroe, Michigan. Each day the plant produces 40,000 steel automobile wheels, 16,000 bumpers and numerous coil springs. The plant discharges into the Raisin River less than one mile above the river's point of entry into Lake Erie, various metals, such as chromium, copper, nickel and zinc.

* * *

On December 20, 1974 the State of Michigan, pursuant to the approval of MWRC, issued Ford the NPDES permit on its Monroe Plant. The permit included the mixing zone as suggested to EPA by MWRC, *supra*. EPA did not veto the permit and it became effective.

On July 11, 1975 MWRC, at Ford's suggestion, sent to EPA a proposed modification of Ford's Monroe Plant permit. Among other things, MWRC proposed use of flow augmentation for Ford to meet water quality standards. Ford, in its brief to this Court, stated:

> The term "flow augmentation" as described in the proposal permit refers to the mixing of the treated effluent from the plant with other waters (from a mixing canal on the plant property [which water was obtained from Lake Erie]) in order to reduce the concentration of pollutants to levels specified in the permit and to assure compliance with the concentration limits in the water quality standard for the river into which the effluent is ultimately discharged.

The proposed modification was succinctly stated by Jeffrey G. Miller, EPA Deputy Assistant Administrator for Water Enforcement:

> The relevant facts are that the best practicable technology will achieve necessary reduction in pounds of pollutants discharged but that the resulting concentra-

tion in the volume of process effluent is still greater than concentration limits specified in the Michigan Water Quality Standards. The State proposes to allow flow augmentation (dilution) to meet the water quality standard concentration limitations. Monitoring for compliance with the BPT limitations is to be done prior to dilution. Monitoring for compliance with the water quality standards concentration limitations is to be done at the downstream edge of the mixing zone. The mixing zone for purposes of evaluating compliance with the State's water quality standards is defined as the total flow in the Raisin River from the point of discharge to the Detroit Edison Power Plant intake, a distance of approximately 900 feet. The State concedes that a mixing zone generally should not include an entire river but claims that Michigan biologists are confident that fish passage will be assured if the concentration limits are not exceeded.

* * *

On January 22, 1976 Mr. Bryson of EPA informed . . . MWRC by letter that MWRC's proposed permit modifications on the Ford Monroe Plant were denied. Bryson stated that "[t]reatment to BPT supplemented by dilution to meet water quality standards is not compatible with the requirements of [the FWPCA]." Attached to the letter was Miller's memorandum of January 14, 1976, *supra*, as justification for EPA's action. EPA stated to MWRC that Miller's memorandum made "two important points about the inconsistency of the proposed permit with national policy." These two points were stated as follows:

1. Flow augmentation is not consistent with the requirements of the instream concentration limits contained in water quality standards.
2. BPT or any more stringent limitation of pounds derived from load allocation of assimilative capacity or other water quality standards must be met before the question of flow augmentation to achieve diffusion oriented limitations can be considered.

On April 20, 1976 pursuant to § 509(b)(1)(F) of the Act, 33 U.S.C. § 1369(b)(1)(F), Ford petitioned this Court to review the January 22, 1976 decision of EPA denying the permit modifications for the Monroe Plant.

* * *

Although the issue as to whether the proposed permit modifications are or are not outside the guidelines and requirements of the FWPCA is the main question to be decided in this case, there is little doubt that EPA has limited review powers over the issuance of a proposed permit submitted by a State pursuant to the State's own NPDES permit program under § 402. The FWPCA does vest final review authority with the Administrator for permits issued by the states (see the *duPont* case, *supra*, at 137 n. 27, 97 S.Ct. 965) but since it was "believed that the states would shoulder the primary burden of issuing permits to individual dischargers," the "EPA duties were to be restricted to assuring that the state followed the procedural guidelines and to reviewing individual permits of major significance." *Natural Resources Defense Council Inc. v. Train*, 166 U.S.App.D.C. 312, 329, 510 F.2d 692, 709 (1975). *See* 1972 U.S.Code Cong. & Ad.News, p. 3737. *Cf. Mianus River Preservation Comm. v. Administrator, EPA, supra.*

The permit involved raises an issue of "major significance," namely, the use of low-flow augmentation to meet water quality standards. This issue may have a major impact on many dischargers in the United States.

* * *

Ford argues that EPA objected to the use of low-flow augmentation to meet water quality standards under the FWPCA solely upon EPA's own ad hoc policy determination as to effluent limitations at the Monroe Plant. Ford further contends that there are no published regulations, guidelines or specific statutory requirements under the FWPCA prohibiting the use of low-flow augmentation to meet water quality standards. Ford concludes therefore, that EPA exceeded its veto authority when it denied Ford the permit modification because § 402(d)(2)(B) allows EPA to object only to the issuance of NPDES permits which are *outside the guidelines and requirements of* the FWPCA, and not upon the EPA's private policy determination. In fact, Ford maintains that EPA's action in the present case denied Ford, as a permittee, its statutory right to a hearing on the issues related to the permit. Ford argues that although § 402(b)(3) provides the permittee a right to a hearing under a state's permit program, EPA in effect renders this statutory right to a hearing a nullity when it declines to issue a NPDES permit for any policy reason, rather than upon "previously promulgated generic guidelines." We believe that the main thrust of Ford's argument is well taken.

It is clear from the record in this appeal that EPA had no prior well-established agency policy which prohibited the use of low-flow augmentation to meet water quality standards. In fact, in August 1975 two EPA officials appear to have indicated initially that flow augmentation was proper. When Bryson, the Region V EPA Deputy Director, in October 1975 requested from Miller of EPA a memorandum of flow augmentation, Bryson did not even know the national policy of the agency on flow augmentation. Miller's response in a memorandum, the basis for EPA's veto of the proposed permit modifications, did not cite any statutory provision, regulation or guideline. As already noted, Miller stated:

> [I]t would not appear that any policy guideline can be laid down either flatly prohibiting or approving flow augmentation to achieve a given water quality standard, nor that the decision for or against such dilution in a given case can be cited as a precedent for a general position.

EPA's November 1976 memorandum from the office of its General Counsel, on the subject of low-flow augmentation, contains this statement:

> The [FWPCA] is silent on the question of whether this alternative is proper and legal as a method of meeting water quality standards based on concentrations.

Nonetheless, this memorandum stated that the EPA policy clearly discouraged the use of flow augmentation or dilution "as an alternative to treatment for meeting water quality standards," developing its reasoning from analogies on the statutory requirements under § 102(b)(1) of the Act, 33 U.S.C. § 1252(b)(1), and § 110(a)(2)(B) of the Clean Air Act, 42 U.S.C. § 1857c–5(a)(2)(B). Such a position would undoubtedly be a good reason for publishing regulations or guidelines in the future on this subject, but it can hardly be a justification for vetoing the proposed permit modifications in the present case when the reasoning was adopted ten months after the veto.

* * *

An examination of the various statutory provisions of the FWPCA indicates that Congress among other things, directed EPA to publish guidelines and regulations setting forth the effluent limitations applicable to point sources.

* * *

EPA has not met with difficulty in publishing necessary regulations and guidelines within the time framework contemplated by Congress for most industries.

The absence of such regulations and guidelines however, as well as the lack of specific statutory requirements under the Act relating to the use of flow augmenttion to meet water quality standards precludes EPA's denial of a modification on a NPDES permit as the flow augmentation under § 402(d)(2)(B) because such modification is not "outside the guidelines and requirements" of the Act. *Cf. Republic Steel Corp. v. Train*, 557 F.2d 91 (6th Cir. 1977). Without such guidelines and requirements, EPA could arbitrarily deny permit modifications and render state

NPDES permit programs a farce. An industry would have difficulty in preparing its application for a permit without such guidelines. As Ford argued, a permittee would effectively be denied a hearing on issues related to the permit. In other words, EPA would be making decisions unfettered by administrative constraints, despite the congressional policy specifically providing therefore. § 101(e).

In the present case we are unable to find *any* "guidelines and requirements" in the FWPCA, or guidelines promulgated pursuant thereto upon which EPA on January 22, 1976 relied, to deny the NPDES permit modifications on the Ford Monroe Plant. Therefore, EPA's veto action under § 402(d)(2)(B) was a clear error in judgment and was arbitrary, capricious and an abuse of discretion. Ad hoc national policy determinations developed through internal agency memoranda standing alone without promulgating regulations or guidelines through public notice and/or an opportunity for a public hearing, are not proper procedures for EPA to enforce the FWPCA.

* * *

If the State of Michigan conducts further hearings on the proposed permit modifications at the Ford Monroe Plant, Ford and EPA may appear at these hearings to present their respective contentions with respect thereto.

Accordingly, EPA's veto of the proposed permit modifications at the Ford Monroe Plant is set aside. This case is remanded for further proceedings not inconsistent with this opinion.

ENGEL, Circuit Judge, dissenting.

I respectfully dissent. The practical effect of the majority opinion is to hold that if a pollution discharge is not expressly forbidden by the FWPCA, EPA regulations or state-adopted water quality standards, it is permitted.* * *

SAVE THE BAY, INC.
v.
ADMINISTRATOR OF E.P.A.

556 F.2d 1282 (5th Cir. 1977)

GOLDBERG, Circuit Judge:

The 1972 amendments to the Federal Water Pollution Control Act joined the Environmental Protection Agency and the fifty states in a delicate partnership charged with controlling and eventually eliminating water pollution throughout the United States. The petition before us raises several questions concerning the role of the federal appellate and district courts in scrutinizing EPA's performance within this partnership.

The Mississippi Air and Water Pollution Control Commission is a member of this pollution battling alliance. In 1975 the Commission granted to E. I. DuPont de Nemours & Co. a permit to operate a titantium dioxide plant at Bay St. Louis, Mississippi. EPA acquiesced in this action by its partner; petitioner here challenges that acquiescence. Petitioner specifically claims, first, that the Commission so mishandled DuPont's permit application that the EPA should have revoked the Commission's authority to grant such permits. Second, petitioner would have this court review EPA's failure to block the DuPont permit.

EPA strenuously urges that this court is without jurisdiction to consider either of petitioner's contentions. We conclude that this court has both the authority and obligation to review EPA decisions to withdraw or not to withdraw a state's delegated permit authority. Certain preconditions to that review are here missing, however, and preclude our determination of the merits of petitioner's first claim. Second, we conclude that this court lacks jurisdiction to review EPA's failure to veto the permit. To the extent EPA's action in this regard is reviewable, original jurisdiction must lie in the district courts. Accordingly, we dismiss the original petition filed in this court.

I.
Legislative and Factual Background

The Federal Water Pollution Control Act Amendments of 1972, 33 U.S.C. §§ 1251–1376 (hereinafter "Amendments") substantially overhauled the nation's system of water quality control, declaring "the national goal that the discharge of pollutants into the navigable waters be eliminated by 1985." § 101(a)(1), 33 U.S.C. § 1251(a)(1). Toward that end the Amendments introduced a system of "effluent limitations" on "point sources" of pollutants.[1] Formerly federal water pollution control efforts centered on standards of water quality specifying acceptable levels of pollution in interstate navigable waters. Through the shift in the 1972 Amendments to strict limitations applicable to each individual point of discharge, Congress intended to "facilitate enforcement by making it unnecessary to work backward from an overpolluted body of water to determine which point sources are responsible and which must be abated." *EPA v. California ex rel. State Water Resources Control Board*, 426 U.S. 200, 204, 96 S.Ct. 2022, 2024–25, 48 L.Ed.2d 528 (1976).

To enforce the effluent limitations, the Amendments created the National Pollution Discharge Elimination System (NPDES), a scheme for issuing permits to individual dischargers of pollutants. *See* § 402, 33 U.S.C. § 1342. Without an NPDES permit, one may not lawfully discharge a pollutant. *See* § 301(a), 33 U.S.C. § 1311(a). Discharge in compliance with the terms of an NPDES permit, on the other hand, is with few exceptions deemed compliance with the Amendments for enforcement purposes. *See* § 402(k), 33 U.S.C. § 1342(k). Thus the terms of individual NPDES permits provide the chief means of implementing the strict national standards mandated by the Amendments.

Congress vested this all-important permit issuing authority in EPA as an original matter. *See* § 402(a)(1), 33 U.S.C. § 1342(a)(1). In keeping with congressional desire "to recognize, preserve, and protect the primary responsibilities and rights of States to prevent, reduce, and eliminate pollution," Amendments § 101(b), 33

[1]A point source is "any discernible, confined and discrete conveyance . . . from which pollutants are or may be discharged." § 502(14), 33 U.S.C. § 1362(14). An effluent limitation is "any restriction established by a state or the Administrator on quantities, rates, and concentrations of chemical, physical, biological, and other constituents which are discharged from point sources . . ." § 502(11), 33 U.S.C. § 1362(11). The Amendments base the effluent limitations on particular technologies. With the exception of publicly owned treatment works, point sources had to achieve effluent limitations requiring application of the "best practicable control technology currently available" by June 1, 1977, and must achieve limitations requiring application of the "best available technology economically achievable" by June 1, 1983. §§ 301(b)(1)(A), 301(b)(2)(A), 33 U.S.C §§ 1311(b)(1)(A), 1311(b)(2)(A).

U.S.C. 1251(b), the 1972 legislation also offered states the opportunity to obtain permit issuing authority. Under § 402(b), 33 U.S.C. § 1342(b), a state may submit to EPA a proposed permit program governing discharges into navigable waters within its borders. The state must demonstrate that it will apply the effluent limitations and the Amendments' other requirements in the permits it grants and that it will monitor and enforce the terms of those permits. Unless the Administrator of EPA determines that the proposed state program does not meet these requirements, he must approve the proposal.

Upon approval of a state program, EPA must suspend its own issuance of permits covering those navigable waters subject to the program. § 402(c)(1), 33 U.S.C. § 1342(c)(1). Although its role as issuer of NPDES permits thereupon ceases, the federal agency retains review authority and responsibility over an approved state program. The two aspects of this supervisory role form the subjects of the case at bar.

First, EPA may withdraw its approval of a state program upon determining, after notice and an opportunity to respond, that the program is not being administered in compliance with the requirements of § 402, 33 U.S.C. § 1342. *See* § 402(c)(3), 33 U.S.C. § 1342(c)(3). Second, EPA may veto individual permits issued under approved state programs. Section 402(d)(1), 33 U.S.C. § 1342(d)(1), requires a state to send EPA a copy of each permit application it receives and to notify EPA of every action related to the application, including any proposed permit. Section 402(d)(2)(B), 33 U.S.C. § 1342(d)(2)(B), provides that no permit shall issue

> if the Administrator within ninety days of the date of transmittal of the proposed permit by the State objects in writing to the issuance of such permit as being outside the guidelines and requirements of this chapter.

The Administrator may waive his right to object to any individual permit application. § 402(d)(3), 33 U.S.C. § 1342(d)(3). Additionally, at the time he approves a state program the administrator may waive as to any category of point sources the requirement that the state transmit proposed permit applications and related action as well as his veto power over permits within the category. § 402(e), 33 U.S.C. § 1342(e). The Administrator may also promulgate regulations, applicable to every approved state program, designating categories of point sources within which the transmittal requirements and veto power will not apply. § 402(f), 33 U.S.C. § 1342(f).

In both the committee reports and floor debates Congress devoted significant attention to the EPA veto power over individual permits granted under state NPDES programs. In that version of the Amendments first passed by the Senate, § 402(d) provided that no permit under a state program could issue "until the Administrator is satisfied that the conditions to be imposed by the State meet the requirements of this Act." S. 2770, 92nd Cong., 2d Sess. § 402(d) (1972). Like the legislation now in effect, the Senate bill authorized EPA waiver of this review requirement on an individual permit or categorical basis. The Public Works Committee explained its understanding of the veto provision:

> Although the Administrator is given the authority to review any permit before it is issued by a State, the Committee expects that, after delegation, the Administrator will withhold his review of proposed permits which are not of major significance.

S. Rep. No. 92–414, 92d Cong., 1st Sess. (1971), *reprinted in* [1972] U.S.Code Cong. & Ad.News, pp. 3668, 3737.

The House rejected the individual permit veto in the version of the Amendments it passed. It authorized EPA to interpose an objection to a state permit only upon notification by another state claiming adverse impact from the proposed permit. H.R. 11896, 92d Cong., 2d Sess. §§ 402(b)(5), 402(d)(2) (1972). The House Public Works Committee explained its failure to include a permit-by-permit veto power in the following terms:

> The Committee considered extensively the proposition that all the permits issued by the States ought to be subject to review and possible veto by the Administrator. During the Committee's hearings, the Governors and other representatives of the States, almost unanimously, stressed the need to put the maximum responsibility for the permit program in the States. They deplored the duplication and second guessing that could go on if the Administrator could veto the State decisions. The Committee believes that the States ought to have the opportunity to assume the responsibilities that they have requested. If, however, a State fails to carry out its obligations and misuses the permit program, the Administrator is fully authorized under subsection (c)(3) of this section to withdraw his approval of a State program.

H.Rep. No. 92–911, 92d Cong., 2d Sess. 127 (1972). During the floor debates in the House, the sponsors of the legislation echoed these arguments for disapproval of the veto power. Proponents of the veto power contended that it was necessary to deter states from relaxing enforcement to attract industry and that EPA's power to revoke a state's NPDES authority was too unwieldy and drastic a tool to be a useful alternative. The House nevertheless rejected an amendment vesting in EPA a permit-by-permit veto authority similar to that passed by the Senate. *See* 118 Cong.Rec. 10664 (1972).

The Senate view with slight modification prevailed at conference. The conference committee draft, adopted by both houses, reinstated EPA's power to stop issuance of an individual permit by objecting to it as "outside the guidelines and requirements of [the Federal Water Pollution Control Act]." Amendments § 402(d)(2), 33 U.S.C. § 1342(d)(2). The conference committee also brought forward the features of the Senate bill allowing EPA to waive its permit veto power on an individual or categorical basis.

Senator Muskie, the principal author of the Amendments, their sponsor and floor manager in the Senate, and the Senate leader at conference negotiations, prepared for the Senate a statement of his understanding of the conference agreement. Regarding the revival of the permit veto power, he commented as follows:

> The Conference agreement provides that the Administrator may review any permit issued pursuant to this Act as to its consistency with the guidelines and requirements of the Act. Should the Administrator find that a permit is proposed which does not conform to the guidelines issued under section 304 [33 U.S.C. § 1314] and other requirements of the Act, he shall notify the State of his determination, and the permit cannot issue until the Administrator determines that the necessary changes have been made to assure compliance with such requirements.

118 Cong.Rec. 33698 (1972).

In returning to the House with a bill including the EPA veto that body had previously rejected, the conferees stressed their understanding of the supervisory role EPA would occupy once it approved a state NPDES program. Representative Jones of Alabama explained as follows:

> If the State fails to carry out its responsibility or misuses the permit program, the Administrator is fully authorized to withdraw his approval of the State plan or in the case of an individual permit which does not meet regulations and guidelines in the Act, preclude the issuance of such permit. It is intended, however, that the Administrator shall not take such action except upon a clear showing of failure on the part of the State to follow the guidelines or otherwise to comply with the law.
>
> * * *

Both houses passed the legislation as revised by conference committee. Both subsequently voted to override a presidential veto.

This legislative history forms the backdrop to the dispute before this court. Mississippi submitted a proposed NPDES program for EPA approval in August 1973. The federal agency gave its approval on May 1, 1974, transferring authority to issue NPDES permits for dischargers in Mississippi to the Mississippi Air and Water Pollution Control Commission (hereinafter "Commission").

On August 28, 1974, the Commission sent EPA a copy of DuPont's application for a permit to discharge from a proposed titanium dioxide manufacturing plant to be located on St. Louis Bay. The company proposed one discharge point into the Bay and two into a deep well injection system.

EPA did not waive its authority to review the DuPont proposal. Rather the agency undertook consideration of the matter in consultation with the Commission's staff. EPA suggested certain changes in the Commission's proposed permit, including increased monitoring requirements of the deep well discharges and a requirement that DuPont conduct a study to determine the present levels of various elements in the Bay.

On January 17, 1975, the Commission sent EPA a final draft permit, incorporating the requested changes. EPA informed the Commission it would not veto the permit as drafted, but requested further changes. On February 3, 1975, the Commission issued the DuPont permit, which again incorporated all EPA's requests.

Save the Bay, Inc., an incorporated association concerned with environmental protection, filed its petition in this court on March 11, 1975. Petitioner presses two claims. First, it asserts that the Commission so violated federal guidelines in handling the DuPont permit that EPA should have revoked the state's NPDES authority pursuant to § 402(c)(3), 33 U.S.C. § 1342(c)(3). Second, petitioner claims EPA should have vetoed the permit as "outside the guidelines and other requirements" of the Amendments. EPA vigorously responds that this court lacks jurisdiction over either of petitioner's claims. Our jurisdiction, if any, must be found in § 509(b)(1) of the Amendments, 33 U.S.C. § 1369(b)(1), a limited grant of original jurisdiction to the Court of Appeals:

> (b)(1) Review of the Administrator's action (A) in promulgating any standard of performance under section 1316 of this title, (B) in making any determination pursuant to section 1316(b)(1)(C) of this title, (C) in promulgating any effluent standard, prohibition, or pretreatment standard under section 1317 of this title, (D) in making any determination as to a State permit program submitted under section 1342(b) of this title, (E) in approving or promulgating any effluent limitation or other limitation under section 1311, 1312, or 1316 of this title, and (F) in issuing or denying any permit under section 1342 of this title, may be had by any interested person in the Circuit Court of Appeals of the United States for the Federal judicial district in which such person resides or transacts such business upon application by such person.

II.
Failure to Withdraw Mississippi's NPDES Authority

Save the Bay alleges that the Commission's treatment of the DuPont permit demonstrated that the state authority is operating contrary to EPA guidelines in several areas, including providing for public participation and policing conflicts of interest. Petitioner contends that EPA's failure to respond by withdrawing the Commission's authority is directly reviewable here as "Administrator's action . . . (D) in making any determination as to a State permit program submitted under section 1342(b) of this title . . ." § 509(b)(1)(D), 33 U.S.C. § 1369(b)(1)(D). EPA responds that the agency has made no "determination" regarding revocation of the Commission's authority for this court to review.

* * *

EPA's contention is rather that the administrative process regarding revocation has not moved sufficiently forward to generate a "determination" for this court to review. The agency at oral argument expressed the position that full administrative development should precede litigation over claims that a state program's permit authority should be withdrawn. Following the approach taken to a very similar problem in *Oljato Chapter of Navajo Tribe v. Train*, 169 U.S.App.D.C. 195, 515 F.2d 654 (1975), we agree.

In *Oljato*, petitioners claimed that new information required EPA revision of Clean Air Act standards applicable to certain coal-fired electric generating stations. The D.C. Circuit found that the Clean Air Act, § 307(b)(1), 42 U.S.C. § 1857h–5(b)(1), vested it with original jurisdiction to review a decision whether to revise standards on the basis of new information. The court rejected, however, the suggestion that it consider directly the information proffered by petitioners and that it determine whether the data sufficed to require revision of the challenged standard. Instead the court required submission of the information to the agency with an opportunity for its response as a condition precedent to judicial review:

* * *

As in *Oljato*, the parties' positions on revocation of the Commission's authority, even regarding matters of fact, have developed in the context of litigation and outside the very limited administrative record before us on review. This petition came only 18 days after EPA received Save the Bay's letter characterizing the failure to withdraw the Commission's NPDES authority as an accomplished violation for which the organization would file suit; here was no proffer of information and request for investigation and a hearing. EPA quickly found itself in the position of justifying past behavior, not considering the most desirable present course of action.

Accordingly, we cannot proceed to the merits of this claim. Under the procedure fashioned in *Oljato*, a request that EPA revoke a state's NPDES authority and an EPA response are prerequisites to our review.

* * *

We must emphasize the limited nature of our ultimate review over a decision not to revoke a state's NPDES authority, which would encompass the familiar inquiry whether the decision was "arbitrary, capricious, an abuse of discretion, or otherwise not in accordance with law". 5 U.S.C. § 706(2)(A); *see Citizens to Preserve Overton Park*, 401 U.S. 402, 91 S.Ct. 814, 28 L.Ed.2d 136 (1971). Finally, we must express some skepticism whether a state authority's unsatisfactory handling of a single permit would ever warrant EPA revocation of NPDES authority, much less judicial reversal of a decision not to revoke. Certainly only the most egregious flouting of federal requirements in the context of an individual permit could justify that sanction. A complaint relating to the treatment of a single permit application therefore seems more appropriately addressed to EPA's veto power over individual permits, to which we now turn. Petitioner's claim that EPA should have revoked the Commission's NPDES authority is dismissed without prejudice to refiling after compliance with the procedural requirements set forth above.

III.
Failure to Veto a Permit:
Court of Appeals Review

Save the Bay's primary concern before this Court is the DuPont permit. The organization contends that alleged defects in the permit required EPA to block its issuance. Petitioner asks this court to review the agency's failure to do so.

Our immediate concern is not whether there exists any federal judicial review of the Administrator's decisions whether to veto permits issued under state NPDES programs. Rather it is whether those decisions fall within the limited categories of administrative action over which § 509, 33 U.S.C. § 1369, grants this court original jurisdiction. We conclude that § 509 does not encompass EPA's omission to veto a proposed permit under a state program. The language of § 509 suggests this conclusion. The state of the administrative record compiled in consideration of a permit which does not end in a veto supports it.

Section 509(b)(1)(F), 33 U.S.C. § 1369(b)(1)(F), provides this court with jurisdiction to review the Administrator's action "in issuing or denying any permit under section 1342". In states that have not obtained approval for their own NPDES programs, this provision unquestionably vests in us review over EPA decisions to issue or deny permits to applicants. In states with approved NPDES programs, however, the role of this provision is less clear, for although EPA's failure to veto a proposed permit leads indirectly to issuance by the state, such EPA action does not necessarily constitute "issuing" for purposes of § 509, 33 U.S.C. § 1369.

The quandary presented by the case at bar is thus the following: when an approved state NPDES authority proposes to grant a permit, does EPA's omission to veto constitute "action in issuing" a permit?

The language of the 1972 Amendments is consistently to the contrary. Permits granted under state NPDES programs are state-issued permits, not EPA-issued. Upon the approval of a state NPDES program, § 402(c)(1), 33 U.S.C. § 1342(c)(1), requires the Administrator to "suspend the issuance of permits under subsection (a)", the subsection authorizing EPA itself to issue permits. Before approving a state program, the Administrator must determine that under the program adequate authority exists "to issue" permits in accordance with the requirements of the Amendments. § 402(b), 33 U.S.C. § 1342(b). Among the materials a state program must transmit to EPA in connection with individual permit applications is "each permit proposed to be *issued by such State.*" § 402(d)(1), 33 U.S.C. § 1342(d)(1) (emphasis added).

The legislative history also suggests that the Administrator's exercise of supervisory review over proposed permits forwarded by state programs is distinct from "issuance" of the permits, which is left to the states.

* * *

Accordingly, we conclude that the Administrator's consideration of a permit proposed to be issued by a State NPDES authority and his decision not to object to the permit do not constitute "action in issuing" a permit within the jurisdictional grant of § 509(b)(1)(F), 33 U.S.C. § 1369(b)(1)(F).

* * *

V.
Conclusion

We have been called upon to examine a statutory scheme that has the potential for the optimum of federalism. The legislation contains problems of accommodation that will require additional interstitial interpretation and environmental exploration as the partners pirouette. The success of their federalist venture will depend not only upon the grace, but also the substance of movement by both partners in the ballet. We have endeavored to ink a most self-effacing role for the federal judiciary, one which should foster a harmonious background to the dance and necessitate intervention only when a point of unmelodious discord seriously threatens the contrapuntal balance.

The petition of Save the Bay, Inc., insofar as it claims the Administrator has unlawfully failed to revoke the NPDES authority of the Mississippi Commission, is DISMISSED WITHOUT PREJUDICE. Insofar as it seeks review of the failure to veto the DuPont permit, it is

DISMISSED.

CLEVELAND ELECTRIC ILLUMINATING CO.
v.
E. P. A.

603 F.2d 1 (6th Cir. 1979)

LIVELY, Circuit Judge.

In this case we consider a petition for review of action of the United States Environmental Protection Agency (U.S. EPA) under the Federal Water Pollution Control Act Amendments of 1972, Pub.L. 92–500, 86 Stat. 816, codified at 33 U.S.C. § 1251 *et seq.* (1972 Amendments). The particular question for review is whether U.S. EPA acted lawfully in rejecting a proposed permit for The Cleveland Electric Illuminating Company (CEI) to discharge effluents into navigable waters in Ohio. The permit was proposed by the Ohio Environmental Protection Agency (Ohio EPA), but was withdrawn when U.S. EPA objected in writing. We grant the petition for review, vacate the action of U.S. EPA and remand for further proceedings.

I.

The goals and policy of Congress in enacting the 1972 Amendments are clearly stated in § 101(a) which begins: "The objective of this chapter is to restore and maintain the chemical, physical, and biological integrity of the Nation's waters." As the means of achieving this objective Congress adopted as a national goal the elimination of all discharges of pollutants into the navigable waters of the nation by 1985. To this end all such discharges are declared illegal unless made in compliance with provisions of the statute.

Recognizing the magnitude of its undertaking, Congress provided for reduction of discharges by reference to the development of technology for controlling and eliminating the discharge of pollutants. Thus, section 301 of the 1972 Amendments establishes a two-stage plan for meeting an interim goal of water quality to be achieved by July 1, 1983. Under this timetable, no later than July 1, 1977, effluent limitations are required to be achieved for all "point sources [facilities or installations which emit pollutants] which shall require the application of the best practicable control technology currently available" as defined by U.S. EPA. § 301(b)(1)(A). This requirement is referred to as BPT. The second stage is to be achieved no later than July 1, 1983. By that time effluent limitations are required to be achieved for all "categories and classes of point sources . . . which [ ] shall require application of the best available technology economically achievable for such category or class, which will result in reasonable further progress toward the national goal of eliminating the discharge of all pollutants," as determined in accordance with regulations of U.S. EPA. § 301(b)(2)(A). This requirement is referred to as BAT.

One of the methods devised by Congress for achieving the ultimate goal of the 1972 Amendments involves the issuance of permits to dischargers who meet the BPT and BAT requirements. This permit program is referred to as the National Pollutant Discharge Elimination System (NPDES). § 402. The permits under NPDES are issued by U.S. EPA unless a particular state has established a permit program which meets the requirements of the statute. If a state establishes an approved permit system, U.S. EPA no longer issues permits with respect to the navigable waters subject to the state program. § 402(c). However, each state is required to send U.S. EPA a copy of each permit application and to notify it of each permit which the state proposes to issue. If U.S. EPA objects in writing within 90 days on grounds that a proposed permit is outside the guidelines and requirements of the 1972 Amendments the permit may not be issued. § 402(d).

The effluent limitations applicable to steam electric generating plants are contained in 40 C.F.R. Part 423. Effluent limitations effective July 1, 1977 to be attained by application of BPT are set forth as guidelines in 40 C.F.R. § 423.12. Those to be attained no later than July 1, 1983 by application of BAT are established by the guidelines contained in 40 C.F.R. § 423.13. Both sections contain "variance provisions." As originally promulgated by U.S. EPA the variance provision of § 423.12(a), with which this opinion is concerned, read as follows:

> (a) In establishing the limitations set forth in this section, EPA took into account all information it was able to collect, develop and solicit with respect to factors (such as age and size of plant, utilization of facilities, raw materials, manufacturing processes, non-water quality environmental impacts, control and treatment technology available, energy requirements and costs) which can affect the industry subcategorization and effluent levels established. It is, however, possible that data which would affect these limitations have not been available and, as a result, these limitations should be adjusted for certain plants in this industry. An individual discharger or other interested person may submit evidence to the Regional Administrator (or to the State, if the State has the authority to issue NPDES permits) that factors relating to the equipment or facilities involved, the process applied, or such other factors related to such discharger are fundamentally different from the factors considered in the establishment of the guidelines. On the basis of such evidence or other available information, the Regional Administrator (or the State) will make a written finding that such factors are or are not fundamentally different for that facility compared to those specified in the Development Document. If such fundamentally different factors are found to exist, the Regional Administrator or the State shall establish for the discharger effluent limitations in the NPDES permit either more or less stringent than the limitations established herein, to the extent dictated by such fundamentally different factors. Such limitations must be approved by the Administrator of the Environmental Protection Agency. The Administrator may approve or disapprove such limitations, specify other limitations, or initiate proceedings to revise these regulations.

* * *

When U.S. EPA approved Ohio's program for issuing NPDES permits the applications of CEI were transmitted to Ohio EPA. Proposed permits were prepared by Ohio EPA and forwarded to U.S. EPA. However, CEI requested an adjudication hearing on these permits and the proceedings returned to Ohio EPA.

The major pollutant which CEI discharges is burned coal residue consisting of bottom ash and fly ash. Ash laden water is pumped into ponds and lagoons where the ash solids eventually settle to the bottom. The ponds are cleaned out periodically and the sediment is disposed of at an off-site landfill. However, there is overflow from these settling ponds and the guidelines and standards require that the solids stay in the ponds long enough to settle completely before water flows out. The four generating plants of CEI are located in an urban area on relatively small sites. CEI successfully contended before Ohio EPA that these sites do not contain enough unoccupied space to permit enlargement of the settling ponds to a sufficient degree to meet the July 1, 1977 standards of adequate settling time. Following lengthy informal proceedings CEI and Ohio EPA entered into "consent agreements" with respect to each of CEI's four generating plans in October 1976.

The consent agreements contained findings, *inter alia*, that even though CEI had installed equipment not required by applicable regulations which had significantly reduced total suspended solids in discharges from the ash ponds and clarifiers, "the existing ponds and clarifiers are incapable of providing adequate retention time and pond stability to comply with certain 1977 standards." The Ohio EPA issued final orders with each consent agreement. These orders were to be issued as NPDES permits if approved by the U.S. EPA.

* * *

The Ohio EPA orders were rejected as NPDES permits by U.S. EPA "because the dates for compliance with final limitations required to achieve best practicable control technology (BPT) or water standards extend beyond July 1, 1977 in violation of Section 301 of the Act . . . ." Noting that proposed construction schedules extended into 1980, U.S. EPA stated, "This is particularly disturbing since the company may be putting itself in the position where at the completion of construction to meet BPT requirements it would have to start immediately to redesign and construct new or additional facilities to meet the 1983 Best Available Treatment (BAT) requirements."

III.

In seeking review of U.S. EPA's refusal to approve the proposed permits, CEI contends that it produced evidence during the informal proceedings which supports the findings of Ohio EPA that certain effluent limitations contained in the final guidelines are "inappropriate" for its generating facilities. It asserts that certain "unique, insoluble" problems made it impossible to comply with some of the limitations by July 1, 1977. These conditions all relate to the size of the sites of the four generating plants, approximately 100 acres each.

* * *

U.S. EPA supports its action on the basis of its determination that the proposed permits were clearly outside the guidelines. It argues that the effluent limitations are final and binding on all power plant operators in the absence of a variance and that no variance was obtained by CEI. It further contends that the "Development Document for Effluent Limitations Guidelines" shows that the question of the amount of land needed for disposal of burned coal residues was carefully considered in promulgating the regulations. After such consideration U.S. EPA concluded that "special consideration of land needs was unwarranted because treatment technology includes small-sized configurated equipment as well as lagoon type facilities." Thus, asserts U.S. EPA, the size of a plant site is not a "fundamentally different factor [ ]" which would render a particular generating plant atypical from those considered in the Development Document. The existence of fundamentally different factors is the only basis for a variance under 40 C.F.R. § 423.12(a), *supra*. Further, CEI never attempted to obtain a variance or to prove the existence of fundamentally different factors, according to U.S. EPA. In effect, U.S. EPA contends that the only variance procedure available to a discharger is that described in § 423.12(a). It argues that this procedure provides sufficient flexibility to protect a discharger with unique problems from an otherwise unfair application of the general effluent limitations.

On the other hand, CEI asserts that the variance provisions of § 423.12(a) were invalidated by the Fourth Circuit in *Appalachian Power Co. v. Train*, 545 F.2d 1351 (1976). This occurred while it was engaged in informal negotiations with Ohio EPA. Thus CEI contends that there were no prescribed criteria for granting variances when Ohio EPA determined that some of the BPT limitations were inappropriate for its four installations. Under these circumstances, argues CEI, it was within the authority of Ohio EPA to issue permits on the basis of the record before it.

* * *

Ohio EPA proposed to issue permits which allowed partial exemption from the

BPT requirements for two reasons: (1) the limited size of the sites on which the four CEI units were located made full achievement of the July 1, 1977 limitations by application of BPT impracticable, and (2) by foregoing attainment of some of the 1977 limitations and proceeding immediately to construction and installation of facilities required to reach BAT limitations, the more stringent BAT requirements would be met in 1980, approximately 3 years before the date required by the 1972 Amendments.

When U.S. EPA acted on the Ohio EPA proposal there was no variance procedure for electric generating units because 40 C.F.R. § 423.12(a) as adopted in 1974 had been set aside in *Appalachian Power Co., supra*, and no replacement had been adopted. The effect of the Ohio EPA proposed permit was to grant a variance based on plant-specific factors. In its brief before this court U.S. EPA argued that since Ohio EPA did not make an explicit finding that fundamentally different factors existed at CEI's plants, U.S. EPA was not required to consider its factual findings and orders. We believe that U.S. EPA failed to consider all of the relevant factors and committed a clear error of judgment. *Citizens to Preserve Overton Park, supra.* Under a statutory scheme which gives initial authority to a state agency, subject to approval of its recommendations by a federal agency, considerations of comity require the reviewing agency to consider the findings of the initiating agency. This arbitrary determination by U.S. EPA is completely unsupportable, particularly in view of the finding of the court of appeals in *Appalachian Power Co.* that the "fundamentally different factors" requirement is "unduly restrictive." 545 F.2d at 1359.

More significant than U.S. EPA's failure to consider Ohio EPA's findings because they did not refer to "fundamentally different" factors is its failure to consider the finding that CEI would achieve BAT requirements three years in advance of the statutory deadline if permitted to adopt alternate BPT limitations and accelerate installations required to achieve BAT limitations. As noted earlier in this opinion, U.S. EPA in vetoing the proposed permits, commented on the possibility of CEI's being required to begin immediately to redesign and construct new facilities at completion of construction to meet BPT requirements. This comment indicates that U.S. EPA failed either to consider or to comprehend fully an important finding of Ohio EPA which it viewed as a critical element of its recommendation that CEI be permitted to comply with alternative effluent limitations between 1977 and 1980.

We conclude that CEI is entitled to have the proposed NPDES permits considered under the amended regulation. In considering these proposed permits U.S. EPA must give due regard to the findings of Ohio EPA. In view of the fact that the BPT standard is the first of two interim requirements—the second being the more stringent BAT standard—U.S. EPA must consider the finding that CEI will be able to attain the BAT limitations some three years prior to the statutory deadline if exempted from compliance with a portion of the 1977 limitations.

The ultimate justification for every regulation and guideline pertaining to discharges is its effectiveness in promoting the achievement of the goals of Congress in enacting the 1972 Amendments. The primary goal is restoration of the navigable waters of the nation to a condition of "chemical, physical, and biological integrity." § 101(a). Upon remand U.S. EPA is to consider whether this goal is better served by permitting CEI to accelerate its achievement of BAT limitations rather than requiring it to follow a sequential pattern by first complying with all BPT limitations.

The petition for review is granted. The action of U.S. EPA declining to approve the NPDES permits proposed by Ohio EPA is vacated and the cause is remanded to U.S. EPA for further proceedings consistent with this opinion.

---

4. REGULATION OF NEW SOURCES (NATIONAL STANDARDS OF PERFORMANCE FOR NEW SOURCES)

Section 306 directs the EPA Administrator to establish federal standards of performance for **new sources** of water pollution produced by specified industries that are notorious polluters of water. Included in the 20 categories of sources listed in the statute are pulp and paper mills, meat product rendering, grain mills, canned and preserved fruits and vegetable processing, textile mills, electroplating, plastic and synthetic materials manufacturing, soap and detergents, fertilizer manufacturing and petroleum refining.

The **standard of performance** for new sources of water pollution is defined as a standard for the control of the discharge of pollutants that reflects the greatest degree of effluent reduction that is achievable through application of the **best available demonstrated control technology.** When establishing such standards the EPA Administrator is directed to take into consideration the *cost* of achieving such effluent reduction as well as other nonwater environmental impact and energy requirements.

A state may develop its own procedure for applying and enforcing standards of performance for new sources within the state. If the EPA approves, the state standards of performance will be applied to new sources of pollution in that state.

Section 306 contains a provision that ensures a discharger that any new source constructed to meet all applicable standards shall not be subject to any more stringent standard of performance for a period of 10 years after completion of such construction.

CPC International Inc. v. Train illustrates the recurring issue that arises where a discharger claims that the new source standard prescribed by EPA is not "achievable" or "demonstrated" within the meaning of Section 306.

CPC INTERNATIONAL, INC.
v.
TRAIN

515 F.2d 1032 (8th Cir. 1975)

HEANEY, Circuit Judge.

The petitioners are engaged in the processing of corn into starch, syrup, dextrose, animal feed and corn oil. They file petitions for direct review of three distinct groups of regulations promulgated by the Administrator of the Environmental Protection Agency under the Federal Water Pollution Control Act Amendments of 1972. 33 U.S.C. §§ 1251 et seq. The regulations relate to the "Corn Wet Milling Subcategory" of the "Grain Mills Point Source Category," and consist of:

(1) Standards of performance for *new* plants, promulgated under § 306(b);

(2) Pretreatment standards for *new* plants which discharge wastes into municipal treatment plants, promulgated under § 307(c);* * *

A. THE SCHEME OF THE 1972 ACT.

The Federal Water Pollution Control Act Amendments of 1972 restructure the federal program for water pollution control. The 1972 Act was enacted against a background of frustration and ineffectiveness in controlling the quality of the nation's waters. The keystone of the pre-1972 program had been the setting of "water quality standards" for interstate navigable waters. Under that program, if wastes discharged into receiving waters reduced the quality below permissible standards, legal action could be commenced against the discharger. To establish that a given polluter had violated the federal legislation, a plaintiff had to cross a virtually unbridgeable causal gap by demonstrating that the cause of the unacceptable water quality was the effluent being discharged by the defendant. The enforcement mechanism of the prior legislation was so unwieldy that only one case had reached the courts in more than two decades. *See* S.Rep.No.92–414, 92d Cong., 1st Sess. (1971), *reported in* A Legislative History of the Water Pollution Control Act Amendments of 1972 at 1423 (1973), U.S. Code Cong. & Admin.News, 1972, p. 3668.

The 1972 Act brought about a major change in the enforcement mechanism by shifting the focus from water quality standards to effluent limitations. *See id.* at 1425. It provides in §301(a) that the discharge of any pollutant is unlawful unless it is in compliance with conditions (effluent limitations) contained in a permit issued under § 402. Permits are to be issued by the EPA, or by those states whose permit programs have been approved by the EPA pursuant to § 402(a)(5).

The Act declares that "it is the national goal that the discharge of all pollutants into the navigable waters be eliminated by 1985." § 101(a)(1). To move the country toward this goal, the Act establishes a system of standards and guidelines under which permit conditions are to become more and more restrictive, culminating hopefully in a "zero-discharge" condition.

For new sources, the Administrator is directed to categorize sources and to "publish regulations establishing Federal standards of performance." § 306(b)(1)(B). The new source standards are to reflect

> * * * the greatest degree of effluent reduction which the Administrator determines to be achievable through application of the best available demonstrated control technology, processes, operating methods, or other alternatives, including, where practicable, a standard permitting no discharge of pollutants.

§ 306(a)(1).

* * *

II. THE NATIONAL STANDARDS OF PERFORMANCE FOR NEW SOURCES.

Our review of the Administrator's action in promulgating the national standards of performance for new sources is limited to a determination of whether the Administrator's decision was "arbitrary, capricious, an abuse of discretion, or otherwise not in accordance with law." 5 U.S.C. § 706(2)(A); Citizens to Preserve Overton Park v.

Volpe, 401 U.S. 402, 416, 91 S.Ct. 814, 28 L.Ed.2d 136 (1971). *Cf.* Union Electric Co. v. Environmental Protection Agency, 515 F.2d 206, at 214 (8th Cir. 1975). As the Supreme Court noted in Citizens to Preserve Overton Park v. Volpe, *supra*, 401 U.S. at 416, 91 S.Ct. at 823, the scope of this review is a limited one:

> * * * [T]he court must consider whether the decision was based on a consideration of the relevant factors and whether there has been a clear error of judgment. * * * Although this inquiry into the facts is to be searching and careful, the ultimate standard of review is a narrow one. The court is not empowered to substitute its judgment for that of the agency.

The new source standards for the corn wet milling subcategory set maximum allowable discharge levels or "loads" for three pollutant measurements: five-day biochemical oxygen demand (BOD_5), total suspended solids (TSS), and pH. The BOD_5 and TSS load levels are expressed in terms of pounds per thousand standard bushels (MSBu) of corn processed. For BOD_5, the new source standards permit a maximum average of daily values for thirty consecutive calendar days of 20 pounds per MSBu. For TSS, the standards permit a thirty-day average of 10 pounds per MSBu. The maximum allowable discharge level on any single day is three times the thirty-day average, or 60 pounds of BOD_5 and 30 pounds of TSS per MSBu. *See* 40 C.F.R. § 406.15.

The petitioners assert that the new source standards are arbitrary and capricious and are not in accordance with law, because there is no adequate basis in the record for the EPA's conclusion that the standards can be met by utilization of

> * * * the best available demonstrated control technology, processes, operating methods, or other alternatives * * *

§ 306(a)(1).

Specifically, the petitioners contend that the new source standards are predicated on the existence and efficacy of technology which is neither "available" nor "demonstrated" within the meaning of the Act.

Initially, we must examine the EPA's justification for the new source standards. Those standards are identical to the 1983 guidelines for existing plants. 40 C.F.R. § 406.13. The 1983 guidelines assume the technology available to meet the 1977 guidelines will be supplemented by additional technology in 1983.

The 1977 guidelines are predicated on a technology consisting essentially of recirculated cooling water, aerated equalization, activated sludge, and good housekeeping practices. The EPA concluded that this technology would be sufficient to permit compliance with the 1977 guidelines, which consist of 50 pounds each of BOD_5 and TSS per MSBu on a thirty-day average, with three times that amount permitted on any single day. *See* 40 C.F.R. § 406.12.

The 1983 guidelines/new source standards are predicated on the availability of the 1977 technology plus the addition of deep bed filtration. The EPA concluded that deep bed filtration will result in the removal of approximately 30 more pounds of BOD_5 and 40 more pounds of TSS per MSBu.

The correctness of the EPA's conclusion that the new source standards can be met thus hinges on the validity of four intermediate conclusions: (1) that the 1977 technology is "demonstrated" and "available" for new plants; (2) that the 1977 technology will be sufficient to remove all but 50 pounds each of BOD_5 and TSS per MSBu; (3) that the incremental deep bed filter technology is "demonstrated" and "available" for new plants; and (4) that the incremental technology will be sufficient to remove an additional 30 pounds of BOD_5 and 40 pounds of TSS per MSBu.

The petitioners concede that the 1977 technology is available for implementation in new plants. They contend, however, that it will not perform up to EPA expectations and that its use will not bring compliance with the 1977 guidelines. They rest their case on the premise that the CPC Plant at Pekin, Illinois, has not been able to meet the 1977 guidelines, despite its implementation of "most" of the 1977 technology. Their reliance is misplaced, for the record indicates that the Pekin Plant discharges 6,000 pounds of BOD_5 daily in once-through barometric cooling water without treatment—a practice which does not square with the 1977 technology's requirement that cooling water be recirculated and treated. If the Pekin Plant recirculated this cooling water, treated it in accordance with approved technology, and maintained effective inplant controls, it would, on the basis of the record, be able to meet 1977 discharge guidelines.

* * *

The EPA, on the other hand, based its conclusions as to the performance capabilities of the 1977 technology on the following reasoning:

(1) Data from existing plant operations indicates that the best existing plants have made substantial progress in reducing BOD_5 and TSS by using an activated sludge process plus some in-plant controls;

(2) The best existing plants fail to treat large quantities of BOD_5 and TSS because they use barometric condensers and discharge the waste from these condensers directly into receiving waters;

(3) By using surface condensers—a demonstrated technology—the raw effluent could be concentrated and subjected to activated sludge treatment thereby achieving significantly greater BOD_5 and TSS reductions;

(4) None of the best known in-plant controls are being used in combination in any one plant;

(5) By combining the best known in-plant controls in one plant, greater reductions of BOD_5 and TSS would be achievable;

(6) There are no practical reasons which would preclude the implementation of the complete 1977 technology in a new plant.

We conclude that the data was sufficient, the projected results were reasonable, and the petitioners have not demonstrated that the EPA made a clear error of judgment in determining that the 1977 technology, when employed in a new plant, would enable it to comply with the 1977 guidelines.

The remaining question, therefore, is whether the record supports the Administrator's conclusion that the technology necessary to achieve the incremental removal of 30 pounds of BOD_5 and 40 pounds of TSS per MSBu is available for use in new plants. We conclude that it does not.

The EPA's supporting documents concede that the deep bed filtration technology has not been "demonstrated" within the corn wet milling industry. *See Development Document* at 87, 121. This does not end the inquiry, for new source standards may properly be based on a technology which has been demonstrated outside the industry, if that technology is transferable to it. The EPA contends that deep bed filtration has been proven effective elsewhere and that it is readily transferable to corn wet milling.

To base its standards on transfer technology, the EPA must: (1) determine that the transfer technology—in this case, deep bed filtration—is available outside the industry; (2) determine that the technology is transferable to the industry; and (3) make a *reasonable* prediction that the technology, if used in the industry, will be capable of removing the increment required by the new source standards. *Cf.* Portland Cement Association v. Ruckelshaus, 158 U.S.App.D.C. 308, 468 F.2d 375, 391–392 (1973); International Harvester Co. v. Ruckelshaus, 155 U.S.App.D.C. 411, 478 F.2d 615, 628–629 (1973).

The petitioners concede that deep bed filtration has been successfully used in other industries and in municipal treatment works. They deny, however, that deep bed filtration is adaptable to the corn wet milling industry and deny that the use of such filters in the industry will result in the removal of the incremental 30 pounds of

BOD_5 and 40 pounds of TSS per MSBu. The basis for their contention is the fact that corn wet milling industry effluent is subject to "shockloads," and contains such high concentrations of suspended solids that clogging of the filtration system is to be expected.

Given the unique nature of the corn wet milling effluent, and the apparent relevance of its uniqueness to the efficacy of deep bed filtration, the EPA cannot rely on a presumption of transferability of that technology. Its conclusion that the technology is transferable, and its prediction that the use of the technology within the industry will result in removal of the 30 and 40 pound increments must be supported by evidence in the record. The District of Columbia Circuit, in examining new source standards under the Clean Air Act, has stated the matter well:

> * * * The Administrator may make a projection based on existing technology, though that projection is subject to the restraints of reasonableness and cannot be based on "crystal ball" inquiry. * * * [T]he question of availability is partially dependent on "lead time", the time in which the technology will have to be available. Since the standards here put into effect will control new plants immediately, as opposed to one or two years in the future, the latitude of projection is correspondingly narrowed. If actual tests are not relied on, but instead a prediction is made, "its validity as applied to this case rests on the reliability of [the] prediction and the nature of [the] assumptions." *International Harvester*, at 45 [155 U.S.App.D.C. at 438, 478 F.2d at 642].

Portland Cement Ass'n v. Ruckelshaus, *supra*, at 391–392.

We conclude that the prediction as to the efficacy of deep bed filtration in the corn wet milling industry is not a reasonable one, because there is no support in the record for the prediction. The sum total of the evidence in the record as to the efficacy of deep bed filtration in or outside of the corn wet milling industry consists of the following:

(1) A statement that deep bed filtration has been used outside the industry for several years, and produces a "high quality effluent." *Development Document* at 121.

This statement is not supported in the record and the degree of BOD_5 and TSS reduction obtained by other industries and municipalities is nowhere quantified.

(2) Statements that:

"It is *anticipated* that the technology of removing biological solids by filtration will improve rapidly * * *." *Id.* at 120 (Emphasis supplied.).

"Deep bed filtration will remove most of the remaining suspended solids * * *." *Id.* at 121.

"[I]t is * * * *felt* that" the new performance standards can be met with the technology. *Id.* at 126 (Emphasis supplied.).

The technology "*should* significantly reduce the raw waste loads" and the new source standards "*should* be achievable." *Id.* at 127 (Emphasis supplied.).

The Clinton Plant "*should* demonstrate" the transferability of the technology to the industry. *Id.* at 121 (Emphasis supplied.).

These statements are likewise not supported in the record. We can find no concrete data, test results, literature, or expert opinion tending to support the EPA's feelings, anticipations and prophecies.

To the contrary, the EPA originally proposed a 1977 guideline of 35 pounds per MSBu of TSS, only to raise it to 50 pounds in the final regulations, with the following comment:

> * * * EPA believes that while the 30 lb limit might be attainable, the technology is not yet available to achieve this effluent level on a routine basis.* * *

39 Fed.Reg. 10512 (1974).

Further doubt is cast on the achievability of the new source standards in a letter sent by the Department of Agriculture to the EPA on July 25, 1973:

> If the Level II (July 1, 1983) standards are to be applied immediately to any new construction, this would appear to delay any new construction by several years because of recognized lack of proven control and treatment technologies for economically achieving the proposed levels. Is such delay acceptable?

It follows that, on the basis of *this record*, we have no alternative but to reject the new source standards. There remains the question of remedy. The Act directs that the standards should have been promulgated more than one year ago. *See* § 306(b)(1). We believe that this mandate to proceed expeditiously would not be furthered if we simply held that the new source standards are unacceptable. Accordingly, we remand to the EPA with directions set forth below, and retain jurisdiction pending the remand. *See* South Terminal Corp. v. Environmental Protection Agency, 504 F.2d 646, 665–667 (1st Cir. 1974); International Harvester Co. v. Ruckelshaus, *supra*, at 649; Kennecott Copper Corp. v. Environmental Protection Agency, 149 U.S.App.D.C. 231, 462 F.2d 846, 850–851 (1972). *Cf.* 28 U.S.C. § 2106.

The proceedings in the EPA on remand shall be conducted in accordance with the procedural requirements of the Act, except that the time periods shall be shortened so as to permit the EPA to enter its final order in the matter within 120 days. Within that time, the EPA shall either furnish support for the new source standards previously published, or establish new ones which can be achieved with the best available demonstrated control technology. If the petitioners are dissatisfied with the Administrator's final action, they shall have ten days to file with this Court any objections to his final order. In that event, an accelerated briefing schedule shall be arranged with the clerk of this Court to review the Administrator's action.

On remand, we instruct the EPA to deal with one other matter which is not adequately covered in the record. Section 306(b)(1)(B) directs the Administrator to consider the issue of costs in adopting new source standards. This consideration is particularly important here, since the record indicates that capital and operating costs may be of more significance in this industry than in some others, due to low profit margins, the highly volatile nature of raw material prices, and competitive substitutes which make it difficult to pass on increased costs to consumers. *Compare* Portland Cement Ass'n v. Ruckelshaus, *supra* at 387–388, 390.

The current record concerning costs for new sources is unsatisfactory in two major respects. First, the EPA has not projected separate operating and capital cost figures for new plants, but has relied on those prepared with respect to modifying existing plants to comply with the 1983 guidelines. It must correct this defect on remand. It may well be that these costs will be less for new plants than for modified ones, but we cannot assume this to be the case. Second, the EPA based its cost figures on 1971 prices, even though the *Development Document* and the regulations were published in March of 1974. More current figures than this are available, and should be used by the EPA in setting forth projected capital and operating costs for new plants.* * *

After this case was remanded to EPA, the agency established a record to support the new source performance standards which were upheld in *CPC International, Inc. v. Train*, 540 F.2d 1329 (8th Cir. 1976), *cert. denied* 430 U.S. 966 (1977).

---

5. TOXIC AND PRETREATMENT EFFLUENT STANDARDS

Section 307 authorizes EPA to regulate **toxic pollutants** and to provide for **pretreatment standards** for the introduction of pollutants into publicly owned treatment plants. The provisions of the 1972 Act required EPA to publish a list of toxic pollutants for which effluent limitations were to be established. For the first five years of administration of the statute, EPA directed most of its efforts to the regulation of industry by technology-based effluent standards and neglected the provisions available for regulation of toxic substances under Section 307. Only six toxic chemicals had been regulated in the first five years of enforcement, namely, aldrin/dieldrin, endrin, DDT, toxaphene, benzidene and PCBs. Several suits were brought against EPA seeking an order requiring it to expand the list of toxic substances and an order requiring EPA to promulgate effluent standards for those toxics. These suits were combined and settled in a consent decree in *NRDC v. Train*, 545 F.Supp. 320 (D.D.C. 1976) in which EPA agreed to set effluent standards for 65 pollutants listed therein.

The 1977 Amendments to the Clean Water Act incorporated this list by reference and further authorized EPA to add or subtract from this list at its discretion without a public hearing. Section 307 also lists six factors to be considered by EPA when adding to or removing substances from the list and when setting the effluent standards for each, namely: (*1*) toxicity of the pollutant, (*2*) persistence, (*3*) degradability, (*4*) the usual or potential presence in the affected organisms in any waters, (*5*) the importance of the affected organisms and (*6*) the nature and extent of the effect of the toxic pollutant on such organisms. EPA is directed to consider these same factors, plus an additional factor, when setting effluent limitations for each toxic pollutant. The additional factor to be considered is (*7*) the extent to which effective control is being or may be achieved under other regulatory authority. In addition to the seven factors listed above, the statute specifically directs the Administrator to set the effluent standard at a level that provides an **ample margin of safety**.

The second half of Section 307 requires the EPA to promulgate regulations establishing pretreatment standards for pollutants to be discharged by industry into publicly owned treatment plants. The purpose of these regulations is to protect the treatment plants from pollutants that would interfere with the operation of the plants or would not be susceptible to treatment therein.

In the cases that follow, *Hercules, Inc. v. EPA* raises the question whether EPA should consider the issues of **cost and technological feasibility** when setting effluent standards for toxic pollutants; *Inland Steel Co. v. EPA* involves the relationship between effluent standards under Section 307 and permits issued under the Section 402 NPDES program. In the excerpt from *CPC International, Inc. v. Train*, supra, the court discusses the pretreatment standards for new sources.

HERCULES, INC.
v.
E.P.A.

598 F.2d 91 (D.C.Cir. 1978)

TAMM, Circuit Judge:

We are called upon in these consolidated cases to review challenges to the Environmental Protection Agency's (EPA) first regulations limiting discharges into the nation's waterways of two toxic substances, toxaphene and endrin, under the Federal Water Pollution Control Act Amendments. For the reasons that follow, we uphold EPA's regulations.

I.
FACTS AND PRIOR PROCEEDINGS

A. *Factual Background.*

Endrin is a chlorinated hydrocarbon first introduced about 1950. It has been used as a pesticide for several decades, and is currently used for pest control on crops including cotton and sugar cane. At present, there is only one domestic manufacturer of endrin, Velsicol Chemical Corp. (Velsicol), which produces three to six million pounds a year. 42 Fed.Reg. 2595, 2600 (1977). Its endrin manufacturing plant is located at Memphis, Tennessee, and its discharges eventually reach the Mississippi River and are carried through the lower Mississippi to the Gulf of Mexico.

* * *

Toxaphene is also a chlorinated hdyrocarbon pesticide. It has been used for several decades, and is currently used for pest control on cotton and livestock. In the recent past, toxaphene was produced by four manufacturers. *See* 41 Fed.Reg. 23590 (1976). Hercules, Inc. (Hercules) contends that it is now the only manufacturer that discharges any toxaphene into waterways, and thus, the only manufacturer affected by these regulations.

* * *

On June 10, 1976, EPA proposed standards for endrin and toxaphene. 41 Fed.Reg. 23576 (1976). The standards were of two kinds: *concentration* limitations on the concentration of pollutant allowed in the discharges, and *mass* limitations on the amount of pollutant allowed in the discharges.

* * *

On January 3, 1977, the Administrator filed his final decision concerning endrin and toxaphene with the EPA hearing clerk, and on January 12, the decision was published. 42 Fed.Reg. 2588. The final decision adopted the proposed concentration limitations for endrin and toxaphene, but adopted relaxed mass limitations of 0.0006 kg/kkg of endrin produced and 0.00003 kg/kkg of toxaphene produced.

II.
APPLICABLE LAW.

EPA adopted the regulations now under review pursuant to authority conferred by the Federal Water Pollution Control Act Amendments of 1972 (1972 Act or the

Act), 33 U.S.C. §§ 1251–1376 (1976). Almost one year after EPA published its final regulations, while this case awaited oral argument in this court, Congress amended the toxics provision of the 1972 Act in section 53 of the Clean Water Act of 1977 (1977 Amendments or the Amendments), 33 U.S.C.A. § 1317 (1977). Velsicol argues that the subsequent congressional action requires us to remand the toxic effluent standards for endrin for new proceedings under the 1977 Amendments. We do not agree. Courts apply the statutory law as it exists at the time of decision unless the intent of Congress is otherwise. *Bradley v. School Board*, 416 U.S. 696, 715–16 & n.21, 94 S.Ct. 2006, 40 L.Ed.2d 476 (1974). We conclude that this is a case in which it was intended that the new legislation not affect regulations that were awaiting judicial review prior to enactment of the legislation.

* * *

Congress passed the 1972 Act in an effort to deal with the regulatory problems that had hindered efforts to control water pollution. *EPA v. State Water Resources Control Board*, 426 U.S. 200, 202–03, 96 S.Ct. 2022, 48 L.Ed.2d 578 (1976). The 1972 Act solved some regulatory problems, but not others. By 1977, Congress concluded that the toxics provision of the 1972 Act, which provided for regulation based on health criteria, had been a failure. As a reaction to inadequacy of the 1972 toxics provision, EPA commenced a new program to issue regulations under other provisions of the 1972 Act: it would regulate toxic discharges on an industry-by-industry basis and set standards based on the feasibility of control technology. EPA would also continue to issue health-based standards. EPA's new program was sanctioned by the judicial decree in *NRDC v. Train*, 8 ERC (BNA) 2120, 2122 (D.D.C.1976) ("Flannery decree"), *rev'd in part on other grounds sub nom. NRDC v. Costle*, 183 U.S.App.D.C. 11, 561 F.2d 904 (1977). In the 1977 Amendments, Congress remodeled the toxics provision based on the judicial decree in *NRDC v. Train*.

In section 53(a) of the 1977 Amendments, 33 U.S.C.A. § 1317(a)(2) (1977), Congress directed EPA to take into account, in issuing health-based regulations, "the extent to which effective control is being or may be achieved under other regulatory authority," particularly EPA's authority to promulgate feasibility-based regulations. *See* 33 U.S.C.A. § 1311(b)(2)(C) (1977). Velsicol contends that this provision shows that Congress intended EPA to withdraw the health-based toxics regulations promulgated under the 1972 Act, particularly the endrin regulations, and to regulate endrin discharges using feasibility-based criteria. EPA responds that the 1977 Amendments were intended to supplement its authority, and were not intended in any way to impede promulgation of health-based regulations.

On a question of statutory interpretation such as this one, involving legislation enacted with EPA's advice and cooperation, EPA's view of the legislative intent concerning its ongoing efforts deserves some deference.

* * *

Congress knew that EPA's health-based regulations were in effect and were awaiting judicial review.

* * *

Moreover, its attititude was not that EPA had done too much and should start all over, but rather that EPA had done too little. "Frankly, [Section 307(a)] has failed. . . . [O]nly six toxic chemicals—aldrin/dieldrin, endrin, DDT, toxaphene, benzidene and PCB's—*have been regulated*. Six chemicals in 5 years." *Id.* at H12927 (remarks of Rep. Roberts) (emphasis added). Congress's strong support for continuing health-based regulation is shown not only by its impatience with EPA's pace, but also by the great emphasis placed in the 1977 Amendments on making it *easier* for EPA to promulgate health-based regulations as a supplement to feasibility-based regulation.

* * *

The provision relied on by Velsicol merely directs EPA to "take into account" its "other regulatory authority"; it created no new threshold barrier in health-based regulation. Senator Muskie stated that the test for regulating a pollutant under health-based criteria instead of feasibility-based criteria is simply whether "there is sufficient information on toxicity to establish a separate nationwide effluent standard for that pollutant." 123 Cong.Rec. S19649 (daily ed. Dec. 15, 1977). EPA's lengthy and detailed final decision on endrin, 42 Fed.Reg. 2590–601, both demonstrates and supports its view that there is sufficient information on endrin to establish such a standard.

Velsicol emphasizes that Congress listed endrin among the sixty-five families of toxic substances in the 1977 Amendments. It maintains this must have been intended to require EPA to reconstruct its regulations under the feasibility-based provisions of the 1977 Amendments. However, the list of substances in the 1977 Amendments was modeled, in large measure, on the judicial decree in *NRDC v. Train*. *See* note 14 *supra*. That decree expressly directed EPA to proceed with health-based regulation of endrin at the same time as it proceeded with feasibility-based regulation of other substances. 8 ERC (BNA) at 2128–29. The 1977 Amendments required, "at a minimum," section 307(a)(2), that EPA publish effluent limitations based upon best-available technology for all pollutants on the list; the list was in no way intended to preclude health-based standards if they were warranted. 123 Cong.Rec. S19663 (daily ed. Dec. 15, 1977) (remarks of Sen. Randolph).

Thus, we conclude that the 1977 Amendments were intended to aid, not to impede, EPA's health-based regulation. In accordance with EPA's view that this intent would be frustrated if the regulations were nullified, we conclude that the applicable law in this proceeding is the 1972 Act and that no remand is necessary.

* * *

The court has discussed the standards of section 307(a), 33 U.S.C. § 1317(a) (1976), in *EDF v. EPA [PCBs]*, 194 U.S.App.D.C. at ____, 598 F.2d at 79–81. As explained there, section 307(a)(2) of the 1972 Act lists six factors for EPA to "take into account" in proposing a toxic effluent standard: "the toxicity of the pollutant, its persistence, degradability, the usual or potential presence of the affected organisms in any waters, the importance of the affected organisms and the nature and extent of the effect of the toxic pollutant on such organisms." EPA is to set discharge standards that provide an "ample margin of safety." Section 307(a)(4). Under the "ample margin of safety" directive, EPA's standards must protect against incompletely understood dangers to public health and the environment, in addition to well-known risks.

Hercules' challenge to the regulations concentrates on the last three factors in section 307(a): "the usual or potential presence of the affected organisms in any waters, the importance of the affected organisms and the nature and extent of the effect of the toxic pollutant on such organisms." Hercules argues that these factors preclude EPA from basing its calculations upon experiments performed on the pinfish, and require it to focus exclusively on organisms actually found in the particular receiving waters into which Hercules discharges. EPA's testing scheme, Hercules contends, is "contrary to the statutory requirement that EPA design its standards to fit the characteristics of *specific water bodies* in terms of 'the toxicity of the pollutant' *in those waters* and 'the importance of the affected organisms' *in those waters*." Brief of Petitioner Hercules at 59 (emphasis added).

* * *

We agree with EPA's interpretation of the statute. *See, e.g., E. I. du Pont de Nemours & Co. v. Train*, 430 U.S. at 134–35, 97 S.Ct. 965. As reported, the House version of the 1972 Act, H.R. 11896, 92d Cong., 2d Sess. § 307(a)(1) & (2) (1972) (emphasis added), contained a factor for toxic standards related to local conditions, as Hercules would prefer: "the usual or potential presence of the affected organisms *in* [*the receiving*] waters." The Senate version did not include any factors relating to "affected organisms." S. 2770, 92nd Cong., 1st Sess. § 307 (1971). In conference, the House factors were accepted, but the phrase "in the receiving waters" was replaced by "in any waters." The Conference Report notes:

> Sections 307(a)(1) and (2) are the same as the comparable provisions of the House amendment, except that the Administrator is required to take into account the usual or potential presence of the affected organisms *in any water rather than in the receiving waters* as is provided in the House amendment.

1 Senate Comm. on Public Works, 93d Cong., 1st Sess., A Legislative History of the Water Pollution Control Act Amendments of 1972 (hereafter, Legislative History) at 312 (Comm.Print 1973) (emphasis added). Senator Muskie, a conference manager, explained that the substitution was a compromise to preserve the "categorical determination" established by the Senate in lieu of the focus on particular "receiving waters" in the House version:

> With regard to toxic pollutant control, the Senate bill and the House amendment differed in provisions for determining whether a pollutant would, in fact, be toxic. The House amendment proposed that there be an examination of the effect of a pollutant on receiving waters to determine toxicity. The Senate bill established a general test in order to assure a categorical determination as to which pollutants were toxic and which were not. The Conference agreement provides specific tests for toxicity as proposed by the House *but retains the categorical determination* established by the Senate.

1 Legislative History at 173 (emphasis added).

The Conference Committee's focus on a "categorical determination" rather than on specific "receiving waters" reflected a drafters' leitmotif in the 1972 Act. Pre-1972 attempts at water pollution control had been based upon characteristics of local bodies of receiving water. For this reason, in part, they failed:

> The earliest version of the Federal Water Pollution Control Act was passed in 1948 and amended five times before 1972. Throughout that 24 year period, Congress attempted to use receiving water quality as a basis for setting pollution standards. W. Rodgers, Environmental Law 355–57(1977). At the end of that period, Congress realized not only that its water pollution efforts until then had failed, but also that reliance on receiving water capacity as a crucial test for permissible pollution levels and contributed greatly to that failure. *EPA v. State Water Resources Control Board*, 426 U.S. 200, 202, 96 S.Ct. 2022, 48 L.Ed.2d 578 (1976).

Weyerhaeuser Co. v. Costle, 191 U.S.App. D.C. 309 at 340, 590 F.2d 1011 at 1042 (1978). The 1972 Act remedied that short-coming by shifting its focus from difficult-to-measure conditions and benefits in local receiving waters to readily determinable categorical consideration.

> Congress concluded that water pollution seriously harmed the environment, and that although the cost of control would be heavy, the nation would benefit from controlling that pollution. Yet scientific uncertainties made it difficult to assess the benefits to particular bodies of receiving water. . . . Under the new statutory scheme, Congress clearly intended us to avoid such problems of proof so that a set of regulations with enforceable impact is possible.

Id. at 337–340, 590 F.2d at 1039–1042. *See also E. I. du Pont de Nemours & Co. v. Train*, 430 U.S. at 127, 97 S.Ct. 965.

Applying a categorical approach, EPA did not limit its study to the aquatic life found in receiving waters from toxaphene discharges. Instead, EPA tested six important marine species, and from the results of these tests, it inferred the likely sensitivity of other species. Specifically, it chose the most sensitive species actually tested (pinfish), and used the test results from that species to set the ambient water criterion.

The choice of the most sensitive species actually tested may be understood on at least two levels. Legally, section 307(a)(4)'s fundamental instruction is that EPA's standards should provide an "ample margin of safety." Basing the scheme upon the most sensitive species actually tested provides a margin of safety for less sensitive species.

* * *

Further, we uphold EPA's decision to set a mass limitation restating its effluent discharge standard. *See* text at ___ of 194 U.S.App.D.C., at 193–104 of 598 F.2d *supra*. EPA set a mass limitation in order that its effluent discharge standard would not be subverted; its standard would thus be met, not by dilution of effluent with uncontaminated water, but by treatment of the effluent. The 1972 Act favors toxic substance abatement rather than dilution. Section 101(a)(3), 33 U.S.C. § 1251(a)(3) (1976) (emphasis added) expresses a "national policy that the discharge of toxic pollutants in toxic *amounts* be prohibited." Obviously, this national policy will be frustrated if discharge of a toxic substance continues in the same amount, but merely in diluted form. During public hearings on the 1972 Act, then-Administrator Ruckelshaus testified that "we don't believe that the solution to pollution is dilution." 2 Legislative History at 1228. Congress accepted his position and "[t]he Conference substitute [for the Senate and House bills] specifically bans pollution dilution as an alternative to waste treatment." 1 Legislative History at 284.

* * *

We find EPA's determination of the effluent discharge and mass limitation standards supported by substantial evidence and within the zone of reasonableness.

* * *

Velsicol's principal argument for invalidating the endrin standard is that EPA was required to give consideration to the feasibility of achieving the standard with existing pollution control technology, but failed to do so adequately. It contends that consideration of feasibility is required by "reasoned decision making" and principles of "rational" consideration. Velsicol maintains that the standard under review is, in fact, not achievable.

* * *

EPA defends its standard on alternative grounds. It contends that section 307(a) simply does not require it to give any consideration to economic and technological feasibility. Reviewing the factors listed in that section, it points out that "[a]bsent from the list is any requirement that the Administrator consider technological feasibility or economic impact." Brief for Respondent in No. 77 1349 at 41. *See also id*. at 53 & n. 30. EPA also contends that the endrin standard is, in fact, feasible. *Id* at 53.

We agree with EPA's contention that section 307(a) does not require it to consider economic and technological factors.

* * *

Section 307(a)(2) requires EPA to "take into account" six factors in proposing toxics standards that comprehensively cover the fate of toxic substances in the environment, their effects on living organisms in general, and their effects on some organisms present and important in particular. *EDF v. EPA [PCBs]*, 194 U.S.App.D.C. at ___, 598 F.2d at 79–80. None of the six factors speaks explicitly to the technical means used to control the discharge of substances, nor is there present any term commonly used to denote a feasibility consideration, *e.g.*, feasibility, achievability, practicability, economic impact, or cost.

* * *

Section 307(a) itself provides for consideration of no other factors.

* * *

An examination of other provisions of the 1972 Act reinforces this interpretation of section 307(a). Section 307(a)(4) directs EPA to set standards providing "an ample margin of safety," without any mention of feasibility criteria. Further, we do not believe that section 307(a)(5) introduces feasibility criteria into the statutory scheme. Section 307(a)(5) states that "[w]hen proposing or promulgating any effluent standard (or prohibition) under this section, the Administrator shall designate the category or categories of sources to which the effluent standard (or prohibition) shall apply." The legislative history makes clear that categories would be differentiated not by the feasibility *vel non* of pollution control, but by the extent to which a toxic substance is present in the industrial process.

The legislative background explains why Congress focused on public and environmental protection, rather than discharge control technology, in the setting of toxic standards. The regulatory scheme is similar to that of the Clean Air Act Amendments of 1970, Pub.L.No. 91–604, 84 Stat. 1676, which distinguished between pollutants subject to technology-based regulation under section 111, and hazardous substances, subject to health-based regulation under section 112. Recognizing that "certain pollutants" required special treatment because of risk to health, Congress enacted section 112, dealing with hazardous pollutants, without provision for considerations of feasibility.

* * *

The 1972 Act continued this distinction, adopting technology-based standards for pollutants in general and health-based standards for toxic pollutants. *Compare* sections 301 & 304(b), 33 U.S.C. §§ 1311 & 1314(b) (1976) *with* section 307(a). "The Committee considers that the discharge of toxic pollutants are much too dangerous to be permitted on merely economic grounds." 1 Legislative History at 800 (House Report). In light of this clear statutory wording and legislative history, it is not surprising that numerous commentators agree that considerations of technological and economic feasibility do not play a part in standard-setting for toxic substances.

Velsicol argues that, if feasibility is not considered, the regulations will be promulgated at an irrationally strict level. However, the congressional selection of factors is a legislative determination that the need of the public and the environment for protection from toxic chemicals is more important than the problems of stringent regulation. This congressional determination is a rational response to the dangers presented by toxic substances. The meaning of the statute being clear, it is not this court's prerogative to impose considerations of feasibility.

* * *

We have concluded that section 307(a) does not include feasibility as a factor for consideration. However, the fact that EPA considered evidence about feasibility does not require that the regulations be vacated. It is apparent that EPA calculated its endrin standards using health-based, not feasibility-related, evidence. It conducted bioassays of aquatic species, determined the maximum long-term dose of endrin that the most sensitive tested species could tolerate, set an ambient water criterion, and calculated effluent standards and mass limitations. Only then, upon calculating its standards, did it consider evidence about feasibility to provide an additional test. 42 Fed.Reg. 2597 600. It found that the standards were, in fact, feasible. Although consideration of feasibility is not contemplated by section 307(a), EPA's consideration of it did not affect its conclusions based on the factors specified by section 307(a), but constituted an attempt to confer additional legitimacy on its conclusions.

* * *

Under the 1972 Act's regulatory scheme, EPA sets discharge standards under the various statutory sections, and the standards are then incorporated into permits issued to dischargers which permit the maximum amount of pollutants that may be discharged. However, a special exception to this scheme is made in the area of toxic pollutant regulation. "Compliance with a permit issued pursuant to this section shall be deemed compliance [with the statutory standards] . . . except any standard imposed under [section 307] for a toxic pollutant *injurious to human health*." Section 402(k) of the Act, 33 U.S.C. § 1342(k) (1976) (emphasis added). Thus, dischargers must meet newly established toxics standards even before their permits have been (or may be) revised to include them. EPA contends this provision applies to its toxaphene and endrin standards. Hercules responds that toxaphene is not "injurious to human health" within the meaning of the statute, because the current level of toxaphene discharges is not creating a human health hazard. Velsicol also argues that the one-year compliance period should be extended because section 53(b) of the Clean Water Act of 1977, 33 U.S.C.A. § 1317(a)(6) (1977) allows EPA to set a longer time for compliance than the maximum specified in the 1972 Act (if it determines that compliance within that time is technologically infeasible for a category of sources).

We reject petitioners' arguments and uphold EPA's requirement of swift compliance with the newly set toxics standards. The 1972 Act is replete with declarations that swift compliance with toxics standards is the normal, not the exceptional, circumstance that petitioners would make it. Section 307(a)(6) provides that "[a]ny effluent standard (or prohibition) established pursuant to this section shall take effect on such date or dates as specified in the order promulgating such standard, but in no case, more than one year from the date of such promulgation." As the legislative history of the 1972 Act explains:

> Because of the hazards posed by toxic substances, the committee considers the need for compliance with promulgated standards for toxic substances to be especially urgent. Language in section [307(a)(6)] is thus intended to convey that one year be an *absolute maximum time* allowed for compliance with standards promulgated under this section, and that compliance be required *as early as possible* within this limit.

2 Legislative History at 1479 (Senate Report) (emphasis added). This command is reinforced by the declaration of purpose in section 101(a)(3) of the Act, 33 U.S.C. § 1251(a)(3) (1976), that "it is the national policy that the discharge of toxic pollutants in toxic amounts be prohibited." This policy, in contrast to others declared in section 101(a), was intended to be implemented rapidly. *See* note 67 *supra.* Because of EPA's failure to carry out Congress's mandate for rapid action concerning toxics, *see EDF v. EPA [PCBs]*, 189 U.S.App.D.C. at —, 598 F.2d at 68–69, it is easy to lose sight of Congress's original intention that toxics be dealt with quickly. However, we will not interpret the 1972 Act as though delay in toxics control were an acceptable result.

Hercules points out that the term "injurious to human health" must have been intended to distinguish some toxic substances that are "injurious" from others that are not. It contends that since all toxic substances are likely to be "injurious" in some amount, for the term to make a meaningful distinction, it must require proof that the toxic substance creates a human health hazard in the amount now being discharged. EPA concluded that a less restrictive view of the term would make it meaningful. As EPA interpreted the statute, the test should be whether the toxic substance would injure humans in "relatively small quantities." 42 Fed.Reg. 2601.

We adopt EPA's interpretation. Nowhere in the Act's approach to toxics is there any requirement that EPA determine what quantities of a toxic substance are now being discharged. Hercules' view would require EPA to investigate and determine local discharge conditions, while EPA's view allows a categorical approach to toxicity measurements similar to that used in section 307(a). *See* text accompanying notes 23–27 *supra*. Velsicol's argument based on the Clean Water Act of 1977 is similarly unpersuasive. The fact that the Clean Water Act of 1977 gave EPA discretionary authority to allow a longer compliance time does not necessarily imply or suggest that the pre-existing maximum one-year period was always to be considered excessively stringent.

VII. CONCLUSION.

For the foregoing reasons, we uphold EPA's regulations setting standards for discharges of endrin and toxaphene.

So ordered.

INLAND STEEL CO. v. E.P.A.

574 F.2d 367 (7th Cir. 1978)

Before SWYGERT and TONE, Circuit Judges, and SHARP, District Judge.

TONE, Circuit Judge.

This is a petition for review of an order of the Environmental Protection Agency granting a permit under § 402 of the Federal Water Pollution Control Act Amendments of 1972, 33 U.S.C. § 1342, allowing Inland Steel Company to discharge certain pollutants in waste water from its Indiana Harbor Works in East Chicago, Indiana. The question raised is whether EPA may properly include in the permit a condition that the permit will be modified to reflect subsequently adopted toxic pollutant standards under § 307(a) of the Act that are more stringent than the standards contained in the permit as issued. Inland contends that such a condition is beyond EPA's power to impose and, in fact, is specifically prohibited by § 402(k) of the Act. We disagree and therefore uphold this condition of the permit.

The Indiana Harbor Works is an integrated steel manufacturing facility that uses Lake Michigan water in its production processes and, after treatment, discharges the water into the Indiana Harbor Canal. Inland applied for a National Pollutant Discharge Elimination System (NPDES) permit for the plan under § 402 of the Act. The initial permit was issued in 1974, and an amended permit was issued on July 23, 1976 for a period of three years. The following provision appears in Inland's permit:

> [I]f a toxic effluent standard or prohibition (including any schedule of compliance specified in such effluent standard or prohibition) is established under Section 307(a) of the Act for a toxic pollutant which is present in the discharge and such standard or prohibition is more stringent than any limitation for such pollutant in this permit, this permit shall be revised or modified in accordance with the toxic effluent standard or prohibition and the permittee so notified.

This requirement was included in the permit in accordance with the following NPDES regulation promulgated by EPA pursuant to the authority granted it under the Act:

> (a) Regional Administrators shall insure that the terms and conditions of all issued permits provide for and insure the following:
>
> * * *
>
> > (6) That if a toxic effluent standard or prohibition (including any schedule of compliance specified in such effluent standard or prohibition) is established under section 307(a) of the Act for a toxic pollutant which is present in the permittee's discharge and such standard or prohibition is more stringent than any limitation upon such pollutant in the permit, the Regional Administrators shall revise or modify the permit in accordance with the toxic effluent standard or prohibition and so notify the permittee.

40 C.F.R. § 125.22(a)(6).

After receiving its permit, Inland requested and was granted an adjudicatory hearing under the authority of 40 C.F.R. § 125.36(b). In the ensuing administrative proceeding, Inland challenged the modification provision set forth above, although there were, and are as yet, no toxic pollutant standards applicable to the Indiana Harbor Works. The Administrator upheld the toxic pollutant provision in Inland's NPDES permit, and this petition for review followed.

Although Inland frames its attack as one upon the toxic pollutant provision of the permit, it necessarily challenges the validity of the regulation upon which the provision is based, which, as we have noted, requires that an EPA Regional Administrator issuing a permit include in that permit a condition to the effect that any subsequently promulgated more stringent toxic pollutant effluent standard will be incorporated into the permit. We therefore must decide, with the question of the Administrator's authority to impose the modification condition in the permit, the underlying question of his authority to promulgate the regulation.

* * *

The issuance of NPDES permits, such as the one issued to Inland, is governed by § 402 of the Act. Paragraph (a)(1) of that section provides that the Administrator of EPA may

> issue a permit for the discharge of any pollutant, or combination of pollutants, notwithstanding § 301(a) [making the discharge of any pollutant by any person unlawful except in compliance with specified sections of the Act], upon condition that such discharge will meet either all applicable requirements under §§ 301, 302, 306, 307, 308, and 403 of this Act, or prior to the taking of necessary implementing actions relating to all such requirements, such conditions as the Administrator determines are necessary to carry out the provisions of this Act.

Paragraph (a)(2) directs the Administrator to "prescribe conditions for such permits to assure compliance with the requirements of paragraph (1) of this subsection . . ." Permits "are for fixed terms not exceeding five years." Section 402(b)(1)(B).

Section 402(k), upon which Inland Steel bases its principal argument, states as follows:

> Compliance with a permit issued pursuant to this section shall be deemed compliance, for purposes of sections 309 and 505, with sections 301, 302, 306, 307, and 403, except any standard imposed under section 307 for a toxic pollutant injurious to human health. Until December 31, 1974, in any case where a permit for discharge has been applied for pursuant to this section, but final administrative disposition of such application has not been made, such discharge shall not be a violation of (1) section 301, 306, or 402 of this Act, or (2) section 13 of the Act of

> March 3, 1899, unless the Administrator or other plaintiff proves that final administrative disposition of such application has not been made because of the failure of the applicant to furnish information reasonably required or requested in order to process the application. For the 180-day period beginning on the date of enactment of the Federal Water Pollution Control Act Amendments of 1972, in the case of any point source discharging any pollutant or combination of pollutants immediately prior to such date of enactment which source is not subject to section 13 of the Act of March 3, 1899, the discharge by such source shall not be a violation of this Act if such a source applies for a permit for discharge pursuant to this section within such 180-day period.

Sections 309 and 505, referred to in the first sentence, are enforcement provisions. The former authorizes the Administrator to issue compliance orders, bring suits, and seek penalties to enforce the Act, including permit conditions and requirements. Section 505 authorizes citizens to bring actions against the Administrator for not performing nondiscretionary duties and also against dischargers for violations of the Act.

Inland argues that the first sentence of § 402(k) makes the terms of the permit irrevocable during the life of the permit, except with respect to a standard imposed for a toxic pollutant injurious to human health. Our reading of that sentence in the context of the rest of the Act and of the legislative history leads us to reject that argument.

To begin with, § 402(k) does not purport to address the question of permit modification. Its concern is what constitutes compliance with the Act for the purpose of an enforcement proceeding brought under § 309 or § 505. It allows the permit holder an absolute defense if he can demonstrate compliance with his permit, unless the standard sought to be enforced is a toxic pollutant standard relating to human health. The obvious reason for the exception is that protection of human health should not be delayed while proceedings are undertaken to modify the permits of those dischargers who are discharging that pollutant.

The legislative history confirms this reading. Referring to the paragraph that ultimately became § 402(k), the House Report on the bill states as follows:

> The purpose of the provision is to assure that the mere promulgation of any effluent limitation or other limitation, a standard, or a thermal discharge regulation, by itself will not subject a person holding a valid permit to prosecution. However, once such a requirement is actually made a condition of the permit, then the permittee will be held to comply with the terms thereof.

* * *

Other sections of the Act confirm the interpretation we place upon § 402(k). We begin with § 307 itself. Paragraph (a) of that section requires the Administrator to promulgate effluent standards for toxic pollutants, which are not to be limited to those injurious to human health. Subparagraph (6) of that paragraph requires that the effective date of a standard be no later than one year after the promulgation date. Under paragraph (d),

> [a]fter the effective date of any effluent standard or prohibition . . . under this section, it shall be unlawful for any owner or operator of any source to operate any source in violation of any such effluent standard or prohibition.

There is nothing in § 307 or elsewhere in the Act to indicate that Congress intended to excuse permit holders from full compliance with that section.

It is apparent from § 402 that Congress contemplated that permits would be issued as soon as possible. Relatively short periods of exemption from enforcement were provided for applicants under paragraph (k) as we have seen. Paragraph (a)(1) authorizes the Administrator to issue permits without waiting for "the taking of necessary implementing actions" such as the formulation and adoption of toxic pollutant standards. Congress must have realized that many permits would be issued before some or all of the toxic standards could be made effective. An intention to excuse all permit holders who obtained their permits before a toxic standard became effective from compliance with that standard during the life of the permit seems highly unlikely, especially in view of the importance Congress attached to prompt compliance with toxic pollutant standards.

When Congress wished to limit the Administrator's authority to modify permits, it did so in explicit language. Under § 306, "standards of performance" (defined in § 306(a)(1) to mean only standards adopted under that section) for new point sources are to be revised from time to time § 306(b)(1)(B), but a more stringent standard of performance may not be imposed on an individual source for ten years after completion of construction or until the facility is fully depreciated or amortized, whichever is earlier, § 306(d). It is inferable from Congress' special treatment of new sources that it determined to afford protection of a limited kind to new sources but not to extend the same protection to existing sources or to restrict the effectiveness of § 307 standards even upon new sources.

* * *

The notion that Congress intended to withhold from the Administrator the authority to include in a permit a provision authorizing modification of the permit to incorporate a subsequently adopted more stringent toxic pollutant standard is hard to square with the alternative that concededly is open to the Administrator. He could choose to issue permits of extremely short duration instead of the five-year maximum permitted by § 402(b)(1)(B), or the three years fixed for Inland's final permit, and thus assure that any new or amended toxic pollutant standard would be complied with promptly. Having given the Administrator this power, Congress would have had no reason of which we can conceive for withholding the authority he claims in this case.

Finally, the Administrator is given a broad discretion to choose the means by which he will carry out his responsibilities. He is authorized by § 501(a) "to prescribe such regulations as are necessary to carry out his functions under this Act." He also has the responsibility under § 402(a)(1) for imposing as a condition to the issuance of a permit that the discharge meets "all applicable requirements under," *inter alia*, § 307. In addition, when a permit is issued before the promulgation of standards applicable to the subject plant's discharges, as was the permit here with respect to toxic pollutant standards, that permit is to be subject, under § 402(a)(1), to "such conditions as the Administrator determines are necessary to carry out the provisions of this Act."

* * *

Inland also argues that its right to equal protection rooted in the due process clause of the Fifth Amendment has been violated because the Administrator did not include similar modification provisions in the permits issued to two of its competitors. EPA points out that it has issued numerous permits to steel manufacturers and other dischargers in the area and Inland has only pointed to two, and further that Inland is incorrect as to one of these. Without some showing to the contrary, we are entitled to assume that the Administrator has complied in good faith with his regulations in issuing the thosuands of NPDES discharge permits other than the two referred to by Inland. Moreover, in the absence of some showing of intentionally invidious and discriminatory enforcement of the regulations against Inland, *cf. Oyler v. Boles*, 368 U.S. 448, 456, 82 S.Ct. 501, 7 L.Ed.2d 446 (1962); *Bordenkircher v. Hayes*, ——— U.S.———, ———, 98 S.Ct. 663, 54 L.Ed.2d 604 (1978), its selective enforcement argument is without merit.

REVIEW DENIED.

CPC INTERNATIONAL, INC.
v.
TRAIN

515 F.2d 1032 (8th Cir. 1975)

* * *

III.
THE PRETREATMENT STANDARDS FOR NEW SOURCES

Section 307(c) of the Act provides that the Administrator shall promulgate pretreatment standards for new plants which introduce their pollutants into publicly owned treatment works. The pretreatment standards promulgated for new plants in the corn wet milling industry, 40 C.F.R. § 406.16, incorporate by reference a general set of pretreatment standards earlier promulgated in Part 128 of title 40 of the Code of Federal Regulations. *See* 38 Fed.Reg. 30982–84 (1973). Those standards split pollutants into two categories: "compatible" and "incompatible." Compatible pollutants include BOD, TSS and pH. *See* 40 C.F.R. § 128.121. Under the general pretreatment standards incorporated by the new source pretreatment standards, a plant is not required to pretreat its effluent for removal of compatible pollutants, except as required by 40 C.F.R. § 128.131 or by a state or municipality. *See id.* § 128.132. Since the corn wet milling effluent is a compatible one within the meaning of the regulations, new plants in the industry need worry only about the applicability of § 128.131. That section provides:

> No waste introduced into a publicly owned treatment works shall interfere with the operation or performance of the works. Specifically, the following wastes shall not be introduced into the publicly owned treatment works:
>
> (a) Wastes which create a fire or explosion hazard in the publicly owned treatment works.
>
> (b) Wastes which will cause corrosive structural damage to treatment works, but in no case wastes with a pH lower than 5.0, unless the works is designed to accommodate such wastes.
>
> (c) Solid or viscous wastes in amounts which would cause obstruction to the flow in sewers, or other interference with the proper operation of the publicly owned treatment works.
>
> (d) Wastes at a flow rate and/or pollutant discharge rate which is excessive over relatively short time periods so that there is a treatment process upset and subsequent loss of treatment efficacy.

The petitioners complain that this standard is not really a standard, because it is too vague and uncertain. While their attack on § 128.131 is in the form of a general broadside, their only real complaint concerns subparagraph (d). We conclude that the petitioners' objection to that subparagraph is well taken. The record clearly indicates that corn wet milling effluent is subject to shockloads. A new plant operator whose shockload is determined to be "excessive over [a] relatively short time period * * * [causing] loss of treatment efficacy," would be subject under subparagraph (d) to substantial civil or criminal penalties. *See* § 309. This standard is too vague to warn the industry of the scope of prohibited conduct. On remand, therefore, the EPA shall review subparagraph (d) of § 128.131, as it applies to the corn wet milling industry, and shall amend the regulation so as to define in a reasonably specific manner what it considers to be an excessive discharge to a municipal plant over relatively short periods of time. We do not require, as the petitioners would have us do, that the regulations must be amended to provide that a new corn wet milling plant may discharge all compatible wastes into municipal treatment works without limitation.

We recognize that the Administrator's task in defining those shockloads which will upset municipal treatment works is a difficult one. Obviously such a definition is dependent on the size and capabilities of the particular works which is receiving the waste. Nevertheless, this is a difficulty with which the Administrator must grapple.

The pretreatment standards for new plants are remanded for reconsideration and amendment of the incorporated § 128.131(d), as it relates to new sources in the corn wet milling industry. The Administrator shall complete his action in that regard within the time limits and procedural requirements set forth in Part II of this opinion. This Court retains jurisdiction in the matter, and will hear objections to the Administrator's action on remand in accordance with the provisions of Part II of this opinion.

IV.
SUMMARY.

The petitions challenging the validity of the guidelines for existing sources are dismissed. The new source standards and the pretreatment standards for new sources are remanded to the Administrator of the EPA for proceedings consistent with this opinion. Each party to this proceeding shall bear its own costs.

---

6. Prohibition of Discharge of Hazardous Substances

Section 311 of the Clean Water Act prohibits the discharge of **"hazardous substances"** in "harmful quantities." Pursuant to authority provided in this Section, EPA has identified over 270 substances as "hazardous." Once a substance is included on this list a discharger must report any "spilling, leaking, pumping, pouring, emitting, emptying or dumping" of such substance and is liable for the cleanup costs. Under the 1977 Amendments, EPA may take action to clean up the spill and add the costs to a penalty to be assessed against the discharger. In addition, owners or operators are now liable for expenses incurred by the federal government or state government in restoring natural resources damaged or destroyed as a result of the oil spill for which the discharger is liable.

An owner or operator is not liable if he can prove that the discharge was caused by: (*1*) an "act of God" defined as "an act occasioned by an unanticipated grave natural disaster," (*2*) an act of war, (*3*) negligence on the part of the United States government, (*4*) an act of omission of a third party whether or not negligent or (*5*) any combination of these. On the other hand, if it can be proved that the discharge was "the result of willful negligence or willful misconduct within the privity and knowledge of the owner, such owner or operator will be liable to the United States for the full amount of such costs." However, the statute provides for limits of liability for both onshore and offshore facilities.

In the case that follows, *Manufacturing Chemists Association v. Costle*, the court reviews the EPA regulations under this section, including the definition of "hazardous quantities."

MANUFACTURING CHEMISTS ASSOCIATION
v.
COSTLE

455 F. Supp. 968 (W.D. La. 1978)

VERON, District Judge.

This action challenges certain regulations promulgated by the Environmental Protection Agency ("EPA") pursuant to Section 311 of the Federal Water Pollution Control Act, ("the Act").* * * These regulations identify some 271 chemicals as "hazardous substances" and thereby trigger a comprehensive reporting, liability and cleanup scheme for discharges of hazardous substances from offshore facilities, vessels and onshore facilities.

* * *

Plaintiff/Manufacturing Chemists Association ("MCA") is a nonprofit trade association of 196 member companies representing more than 90% of the production capacity of basic industrial chemicals in the United States.

* * *

Plaintiffs' motion for summary judgment, put very simply, rests on the assertion that the regulations promulgated by EPA under Section 311 are arbitrary and capricious and contrary to the underlying statutory mandate. It is therefore urged that this court find the regulations legally invalid, and grant a permanent injunction to prevent their implementation and enforcement. Defendants, on the other hand, argue that the regulations are a valid and enforceable result of the rulemaking powers and practices of an administrative agency. It is contended that this court's authority to review administrative actions is extremely limited in scope and that the regulations, though perhaps not as rational as they could be, certainly meet the threshold tests for validity.

* * *

I.

Plaintiffs first attack EPA's selection of the one pound unit (and multiples thereof) for purposes of determining "hazardous quantities."

* * *

". . . Section 311(b)(3) of the Act prohibits discharges of hazardous substances 'in harmful quantities' into navigable waters. Violations of this provision give rise to penalties, an obligation to notify the appropriate federal agency, and liability for the cost of removal under Sections 311(b)(5), (6) and (f). Determination of a 'harmful quantity' is critical to the implementation of the remedial provisions. Section 311(b)(4) defines 'harmful quantities' and directs the EPA to determine:

> 'those quantities of . . . any hazardous substance the discharge of which, *at such times, locations, circumstances and conditions*, will be harmful to the public health or welfare.'

The EPA's attempt to implement this directive is found in Part 118 of the final regulations. The list of 271 hazardous substances is divided into 5 categories based upon their relative toxicity. EPA then chooses one pound (the smallest common commercial container size) as the 'harmful quantity' for all substances in the most toxic category. Larger multiples of the one pound unit are then applied to the remaining categories in ascending order as their toxicity decreases. Thus, a discharge of one pound of a substance in category 'X' is deemed to be 'harmful' for purposes of triggering the provisions regarding penalties and notification, while those who discharge 10 pounds of a substance in category 'A' (that category of substances slightly less toxic than those in category 'X') or 100 pounds of a substance in category 'B' (a group of substances which are still less toxic) will find their actions subject to the same provisions. All such quantities must have been discharged within a 24 hour period.

The final regulations, on their face, do not appear to comport with the statutory mandate. Nowhere in Part 118 do we find reference to the considerations specifically required by Section 311(b)(4). Such factors as 'times, locations, circumstances and conditions' are not mentioned, nor can their influence be found in the 'one pound' rule. As counsel for the plaintiffs aptly noted, the choice of a 'one pound bottle' as the basic unit of trade by the chemical industry was the result of many different considerations, none of which concerns the impact of the chemical within the container on the environment. Packaging, marketing, pricing and easy use of products (the factors normally taken into account by manufacturers) have no relationship to the purposes or intentions of the Act and regulations. It would appear, then, that the EPA has not complied with the statutory requisites in promulgating the challenged regulations.* * * The harm that will result from the discharge of a given amount of a hazardous substance may be determined as much by characteristics of the receiving water body as by the toxicity of the substance itself. Conditions of the receiving body which will have an impact on the concentration of the pollutant include type, flow rate and size of the water body, and salinity, hardness, alkalinity, biological population and buffering capacity of the water.

"Counsel for the EPA argued that the harmful quantity test finally adopted by the regulations was chosen because it was 'clear and easily comprehensible' and was therefore more easily understood by all interested parties. Counsel also urged that the 'one pound' test would be an effective incentive for compliance with the notification requirements of Section 311. While it is conceivable that the test finally selected may accomplish the ends urged by the EPA, such goals should not be attained through totally arbitrary means. The Acting Chief of the U. S. Coast Guard Office of Marine Environment and Systems accurately described the 'one pound' rule chosen by the EPA:

> 'The method for determining harmful quantity of hazardous substances, while having some merit in its simplicity, ignores the relationship between quantity discharged and the receiving water and *has no sound technical basis.*'* * *

For the foregoing reasons we now hold that the "one pound" method of determining "hazardous quantities" is, in fact, arbitrary and capricious and contrary to the statutory mandate.

* * *

II.

Plaintiffs further urge that the method in which EPA treated the question of "removability" of the "hazardous substances" (for purposes of applying two different sets of penalty provisions) was arbitrary and contrary to the statute. As we understand the basic intent of Congress and the statute, two systems of penalties were established and were to act as deterrents against the discharge of any "hazardous substances." Sections 311(c) and (f)(2) provided that any discharge of hazardous substances, in an amount deemed to be harmful to the environment, would be met with an effort to clean up or mitigate the harmful effects of such a discharge. The cost of such efforts would be borne by the spiller or discharger, up to the limit of $50 million.

At the same time, however, it was clear that certain of these substances immediately dissolved in water and any attempts to remove them or mitigate the resulting damage after discharges would be completely unsuccessful. For spillers and dischargers of that type of substance Section 311(b)(2)(B)(iii) set up a structure of special penalties which would act as a deterrent in cases where the "clean-up liability" would obviously not do so. It therefore became necessary for the EPA to determine which of the 271 "hazardous substances" were "removable" and which ones were not in order to determine which of the parallel systems of penalties was applicable in a given spill or discharge situation.

The EPA, relying on the words "actually being removed" found in Section 311(b)(2)(B)(i), decided that Congress intended for it to determine which substances could be physically removed from the water into which it had been discharged, and that those substances which could not be so removed were to be subject both to the clean-up cost penalty (to cover any expense resulting from efforts to mitigate the effects of the "non-removable" substance upon the water and the environment) and to the special penalties which serve as deterrents to discharges of non-removable substances. The EPA therefore concluded that it would treat the ten substances which had characteristics similar to oil (which is actually removable from water under certain circumstances) to be found on the list of 271 "hazardous substances" as being "removable" for purposes of Section 311(b)(2)(B) and would treat the remaining 261 substances as "non-removable" when applying the relevant penalty provisions.

* * *

We do not believe that the EPA properly defined or applied the term "removable" in making its determinations and we find the resulting regulations to be arbitrary and therefore invalid on that basis. Section 311(a)(8) defines the terms "remove" and "removal" to include:

> ". . . removal of the oil or hazardous substances from the water and shorelines or the taking of such other acts as may be necessary to minimize or mitigate [the] damage to the public health or welfare . . ."

A rational and reasonable reading of this definition, coupled with what we believe to be the clear intent of Congress to set up two parallel and independent systems of penalties, leads inexorably to the conclusion that a standard of "removability" must not be limited to actual physical removal from a receiving water body. Rather, mitigation of harm, through neutralization of a harmful substance, fits squarely within the statutory definition of removability.

* * *

We therefore find that the EPA's decision to ignore mitigability in determining "removability" of "hazardous substances" was arbitrary and capricious and contrary to the statutory mandate of Section 311.

* * *

III.

The final issue raised by the parties for decision in the case at bar is the interrelationship (or lack thereof) between the control of discharges of "hazardous substances" under Section 311 and the already existing NPDES permit system for continuous industrial discharges established under Section 402 of the Act, 33 U.S.C. § 1342. EPA has taken the position that those continuous dischargers currently operating under valid NPDES permits (most of those permits being silent with regard to the amount of any of the 271 "hazardous substances" that may permissibly be discharged) must file applications for amended permits. These applications would, in themselves, delay the immediate enforcement of Section 311 against industrial dischargers until the NPDES permit agency has had an opportunity to evaluate the application and issue an amended permit which would include specific limitations concerning discharge of the 271 substances. It is still unclear what would be the source of these specific limitations since "guideline regulations" normally relied upon by the permit agencies in issuing permits as yet have not been developed for the newly designated "hazardous substances." Finally, EPA contends that any discharger which receives the required amended permit would be subject to the penalty provisions under both Sections 311 and 402 should it suffer the misfortune of not complying with its new permit. (Indeed, it is urged that the penalties under Section 311 would be based on the total amount of the offending discharge rather than simply on the amount of the discharge which exceeds the limitations set by permit.)

Plaintiffs' opinion is diametrically opposed to the one espoused by EPA. First, it is argued that EPA has no authority under Section 311 to require holders of permits to apply for amended ones. This position, it is urged, is supported by the apparent provision in the Section 402 permit structure which indicates that once a permit is issued the permittee is entitled to assume that so long as it complies with the requirements of its permit it may assume that no new limitations will be placed on its discharges during the lifetime of its permit. Second, plaintiffs assert that the penalties in Section 311 are in no way related to the permit system and should not be applied to violations of NPDES permits.

Having considered the relevant statutory provisions this court concludes that EPA does, in fact, have the limited authority to require applications for amended permits. Section 402 provides for changes in permits and the enforcement of more stringent controls over discharges, even during the life of an existing permit, in cases where circumstances have changed since the issuance of the original permit. We find that the designation of 271 substances as "hazardous" is just such a change in circumstances as would give rise to allowable changes in permit requirements. However, those new limitations must be issued and implemented in a manner which is reasonable and fair, and which attempts to cause as little economic inconvenience to the dischargers whose permits are being revised as is possible under the circumstances. For example, the EPA would certainly be ill advised if it were to simply apply its "harmful quantities" from Section 311 to the amended NPDES permits without closely studying the "best practicable control technology." Further, we would expect EPA to delay issuing amended permits until new "guideline regulations" have been developed for at least the most hazardous substances in order to guarantee uniformity of discharge requirements for those substances. Finally, a reasonable amount of time would have to be granted for purposes of monitoring discharges and preparing applications for amendments.

Deciding that a better designed and developed set of regulations could validly require holders of NPDES permits to apply for amended permits does not mean, however, that violation of those amended permits (or of the already existing permits which happen to mention any of the 271 new "hazardous substances") properly would be met with penalties arising both under Section 311 and Section 402. The latter statute contains a detailed system of penalties to be applied to those who fail to comply with their permits. The reporting provisions and financial penalties found in Section 402 act as sufficient deterrent to the undesirable activities and would make application of the penalties under Section 311 redundant and wholly unnecessary.

Further, the rational underpinnings for the limitations to be found in NPDES permits are completely different from those which form the bases of the new regulations. The penalty systems should therefore be maintained as separate and distinct entities. NPDES limitations are founded upon the ascertainment of the "best practicable control technology" which can be applied to relevant discharges coming from relevant industries. Considerations of "harm to the environment" are indirect and subliminal at best. Conversely, environmental harm is of paramount importance within the Section 311 scheme. It would therefore seem unreasonable to penalize a permit violator under both statutory frameworks. (Even if Section 311 were to be applied such penalties should certainly be applied only to the amount of discharge which exceeded the total amount allowed by permit.) This court concludes that the only rational course would be to require applications for amended permits to be filed (through a more reasonable and ordered process) and then to penalize permit violations solely under the provisions of Section 402.* * *

---

7. Enforcement

The regulatory provisions of the Clean Water Act may be enforced by several methods. The primary basis of enforcement is through the **NPDES permit program.** Upon receipt of evidence that any of the conditions of a permit is violated, the EPA Administrator may notify the discharger and the state agency of such finding. If the state does not take appropriate action to require compliance with the permit condition the Administrator may issue a federal order of compliance. If the Administrator determines that there are widespread violations of permit conditions, indicating a state failure to enforce the permit program, he may notify the appropriate state official of that determination and begin proceedings after 30 days to reassume federal jurisdiction over the permit process.

a. *Civil Proceedings*

If the Administrator determines that a discharger is violating effluent limitations or has failed to comply with any of the conditions of the discharge permit he may seek compliance by injunction or civil penalty in a federal court. Any person who violates a permit limitation or condition or compliance order is liable for a civil penalty not to exceed $10,000 per day for each violation.

The Clean Water Act also authorizes the Coast Guard to assess a civil penalty for discharges of oil into navigable waters. In *United States v. Marathon Pipe Line Co.*, below, the court deals with the issue of whether a discharger is liable for such penalty even though he was without fault and where the spill was caused by a third party.

UNITED STATES
v.
MARATHON PIPE LINE CO.

589 F.2d 1305 (7th Cir. 1978)

CASTLE, Senior Court Judge.

Marathon Pipe Line Company appeals from the district court's enforcement by way of summary judgment of a $2,000 civil penalty assessed by the United States Coast Guard against Marathon under section 1321(b)(6) of the Federal Water Pollution Control Act (FWPCA) for a discharge of oil into navigable waters in violation of section 1321(b)(3) of the Act. The issue presented is whether section 1321(b)(6) permits the Coast Guard to assess more than a nominal civil penalty against the owner of a discharging facility where the owner is without fault and the spill was caused by a third party. Affirming the district court, we hold that section 1321(b)(6) is an absolute liability provision which contemplates a substantial penalty even in the absence of fault and, accordingly, that the Coast Guard did not abuse its discretion in assessing a $2,000 civil penalty for a discharge of 19,992 gallons of crude oil.

On November 20, 1975 Marathon was notified by local police that a pipeline owned by it had ruptured and was discharging crude oil into the Kaskaskia River in southern Illinois. The company immediately took steps to contain the spill and reported the occurrence to the United States Environmental Protection Agency. In all, 19,992 gallons of crude oil were discharged from the pipeline and 10,920 gallons were recovered or burned, so that approximately 9,072 gallons escaped downriver. Subsequent investigation by the company revealed that a bulldozer had struck the four-inch buried pipe back in June or July of 1975 while hired to dig an irrigation ditch for the owners of the land. The bulldozer operator had reported the damage to the landowners, but as the latter thought that the pipeline was no longer in use, neither ever reported the damage to Marathon. The location of the pipeline was a matter of public record, the easement having been duly recorded with the local recorder's office, and the pipeline was marked in accordance with all federal regulations. It is undisputed that the eventual split in the line resulted from the bulldozer damage and that Marathon was in no way at fault in not learning of either the digging or the damage at any time prior to the spill.

The Statutory Scheme

The FWPCA was enacted "to restore and maintain the chemical, physical and biological integrity of the Nation's waters." 33 U.S.C. § 125(a). Toward that end Congress set the goal of eliminating the discharge of all pollutants into navigable waters by 1985. § 1251(a)(1). Section 1321, dealing with oil and hazardous substance liability, sets a "no discharge" policy of immediate effect and prohibits any discharge in harmful quantities.§§ 1321(b)(1) & (3). The section holds owners or operators of discharging facilities liable for clean-up costs, subject to the defenses of act of God, act of war, negligence of the United States Government, or act or omission of a third party. § 1321(f). If the discharged substance is nonremovable, the owner or operator is liable to a variable civil penalty dependent on the amount and toxicity of the substance spilled. This "liquidated damages liability" is again subject to the four enumerated defenses. § 1321(b)(2)(B)(iii). Finally, section 1321(b)(6), the immediate focus of our concern here, makes owners and operators liable to a civil penalty of up to $5,000, with no provision for any defenses but with the amount of the penalty to be determined by the Coast Guard, which is instructed to take into account ability to pay and "gravity of the violation."

Marathon's Statutory and Abuse of Discretion Claims

The civil penalty provision is clearly one of strict liability since fault is not even a requisite for clean-up or liquidated damages liability, and every court which has considered the question has so held.

* * *

However, Marathon claims that, although civil penalty liability attaches without regard to fault, a nominal amount only may be assessed in the absence of any fault on its part.

* * *

In effect, Marathon would have us read into the statute a strict standard of liability for a nominal penalty and a negligence standard of liability for a substantial penalty. We do not believe the plain language of the statute supports different standards for a substantial as opposed to a nominal penalty. We must construe a statute according to its ordinary meaning unless Congress clearly did not intend it to have such meaning, as determined from other parts of the statute or legislative history, or unless Congress could not have intended it to have such a meaning because it would render the statute unconstitutional.

* * *

We believe the intent of Congress, as manifested in section 1321 taken as a whole, is to impose a substantial civil penalty on owners or operators even in the absence of fault and that such an intent is well within the constitutional powers of Congress.

Marathon does not directly address the issue of congressional intent, arguing instead that the Coast Guard misapplied its own administrative guidelines in fixing the amount of the penalty. The statute directs the Coast Guard to consider, in setting a penalty, the owner's ability to pay and the "gravity of the violation." The Coast Guard has interpreted the latter to include size of the spill, the owner's prior record, and the "degree of culpability." Thus degree of fault is but one of several factors the Coast Guard will consider in setting a penalty. There is no allegation here that the Coast Guard did not consider absence of fault as a mitigating factor, and the evidence indicates that it did, as it is the Coast Guard's stated policy to assess a penalty at or near the maximum of $5,000, and Marathon has offered no evidence to show that a spill of crude oil of this magnitude would not ordinarily result in the maximum penalty. Accordingly, we find that the statute allows a substantial penalty in the circumstances of this case and that the Coast Guard did not abuse its discretion in assessing one.

* * *

Aside from the deference we would in any event have to accord Congress in the field of economic regulation, Marathon's claim suffers from the more basic defect that deterrence is not the sole purpose of the civil penalty, or for that matter of strict liability in general. Strict liability, though performing a residual deterrent function, is based on the economic premise that certain enterprises ought to bear the social costs of their activities. In the FWPCA in general, Congress has made a legislative determination that polluters rather than the public should bear the costs of water pollution. In section 1321, the clean-up, liquidated damages, and civil penalty liabilities all serve to shift the cost of oil and hazardous substance pollution onto the private sector. The economic, rather than deterrent, rationale underlying section 1321 is evidenced by the fact that none of the three liabilities created by the section is conditioned on a finding of fault. The fact that Congress carved out very narrow defenses (not including absence of fault) to the first two liabilities does not invalidate a third liability not accorded any defenses at all. Congress had the power to impose a full enterprise liability on the private sector but instead opted for the compromise position of narrow defenses for the first two liabilities and no defense to the third and most limited liability, which in any event could not exceed $5,000.

The purpose of the FWPCA and of section 1321 is to achieve the result of clean water as well as to deter conduct causing spills. The civil penalty serves the Act's goal of pollution-free water by providing a means of funding the administration and enforcement of the Act. Under section 1321(k) the proceeds of civil penalty collections are to be deposited in a revolving fund which is to be used to finance a National Contingency Plan for the containment, dispersal, and removal of spills; the clean-up of maritime disaster discharges; the reimbursement of clean-up costs incurred by owners or operators who are able to establish one of the four defenses; and the administration of the act. §§ 1321(c), (d), (i), and (*l*). The principle of financing regulation through a penalty or forfeiture imposed on regulatees is not novel, *One Lot Emerald Cut Stones v. United States*, 409 U.S. 232, 93 S.Ct. 489, 34 L.Ed.2d 438 (1972), nor is basing such penalty or forfeiture on ownership of the offending thing, regardless of fault, violative of due process, *Calero-Toledo v. Pearson Yacht Leasing Co.*, 416 U.S. 663, 94 S.Ct. 2080, 40 L.Ed.2d 452 (1974) (ownership of yacht on which marijuana was found), *Edelberg v. Illinois Racing Bd.*, 540 F.2d 279 (7th Cir. 1976) (ownership of drugged horse).

Conclusion

The plain language of the statute as well as its interpretation by the Coast Guard permit the assessment of a substantial penalty in the absence of fault. Such a penalty is rationally related to the FWPCA's economic purpose of placing the financial burden of achieving and maintaining clean water on owners or operators of polluting facilities.

The district court's enforcement of the $2,000 civil penalty is Affirmed.

---

b. *Criminal Proceedings*

Any person who willfully or negligently violates the effluent standards or permit conditions or limitations under the Clean Water Act may be punished by fine of not less than $2500 nor more than $25,000 per day of violation, or by imprisonment of not more than one year, or by both. There are also criminal penalties for knowingly making false statements or tampering with monitoring devices required under the Act.

In *U.S. v. Frezzo Brothers, Inc.*, below, the defendant argued that EPA must either give notice of alleged violations of the Act or start a civil action before instituting criminal proceedings.

UNITED STATES
v.
FREZZO BROTHERS, INC.

602 F.2d 1123 (3d Cir. 1979)

ROSENN, Circuit Judge.

Since the enactment in 1948 of the Federal Water Pollution Control Act, 62 Stat. 1155 ("the Act"), the Government has, until recent years, generally enforced its provisions to control water pollution through the application of civil restraints. In this case, however, the Government in the first instance has sought enforcement of the Act as amended in 1972, 33 U.S.C.A. §§ 1251–1376 (Supp. 1973), against an alleged corporate offender and its officers by criminal sanctions. Whether the Government may pursue the criminal remedies under the Act before instituting a civil action or before giving written notice of the alleged violation is the principal issue presented in this appeal.

The appellants were convicted by a jury on six counts of willfully or negligently discharging pollutants into a navigable water of the United States without a permit, in violation of 33 U.S.C. §§ 1311(a), 1319(c). The corporate defendant, Frezzo Brothers, Inc., was fined $50,000, and the individual defendants, Guido and James Frezzo received jail sentences of thirty days each and fines aggregating $50,000. The Frezzos appeal from the trial court's final judgment of sentence. We affirm.

* * *

The Frezzos first argue that the Administrator of the Environmental Protection Agency must either give them some notice of alleged violations of the Federal Water Pollution Control Act, or institute a civil action before pursuing criminal remedies under the Act. . . .

* * *

The enforcement provisions of the Act are contained in 33 U.S.C. § 1319. The criminal provision of the Act, § 1319(c) provides in relevant part:

> (1) Any person who willfully or negligently violates section 1311 . . . of this title . . . shall be punished by a fine of not less than $2,500 nor more than $25,000 per day of violation, or by imprisonment for not more than one year, or by both. . . .

This provision is preceded by § 1319(a) dealing with state enforcement and compliance orders, and § 1319(b) governing civil actions. There is conflicting legislative history with respect to whether a compliance order or a civil suit by the Administrator should be a prerequisite to the Government's institution of criminal proceedings under § 1319(c).

* * *

There is nothing in the text of § 1319(c) that compels the conclusion that prior written notice, other administrative or civil remedies are prerequisite to criminal proceedings under the Act. The Senate acceded to the House in not making civil enforcement mandatory upon the Administrator under section 1319. *Legislative*

History, supra at 174. Hence, we can only conclude that whatever support existed for the position urged by the Frezzos did not prevail in the enactment of the final Bill.

Further, we see no reason why the Government should be hampered by prerequisites to seeking criminal sanctions under the Act. The Frezzos urge that it can only be through prior notification, followed by continued polluting in the face of such notice, that willful violations of the Act can be established. We find this argument unconvincing. Although continued discharges after notification could be one way for the Government to prove scienter, it is certainly not the only way to establish willful violations. The Government could logically argue, as it did in this case, that the circumstances surrounding the alleged discharges manifested willful violations of the Act and that it had the power to pursue criminal rather than civil sanctions. Furthermore, in view of the broad responsibilities imposed upon the Administrator of the EPA, he should be entitled to exercise his sound discretion as to whether the facts of a particular case warrant civil or criminal sanctions. We therefore hold that the Administrator of the EPA is not required to pursue administrative or civil remedies, or give notice, before invoking criminal sanctions under the Act.

The Frezzos next contend that the indictment should have been dismissed because the EPA had not promulgated any effluent standards applicable to the compost manufacturing business. The Frezzos argue that before a violation of § 1311(a) can occur, the defendants must be shown to have not complied with existing effluent limitations under the Act. The district court disagreed, finding no such requirement. 461 F.Supp. at 268–69. We agree with the district court.

The core provision of the Act is found in § 1311(a) which reads:

> Except as in compliance with this section and sections 1312, 1316, 1317, 1328, 1342, and 1344 of this title, the discharge of any pollutants by any person shall be unlawful.

Section 1311(b) then sets out a timetable for the promulgation of effluent limitations for point sources and section 1312 provides for the establishment of water quality related effluent limitations. The Frezzos contend that they cannot have violated the Act because the EPA has not yet promulgated effluent limitations which they can be held to have violated. Appellants rely primarily on *United States v. GAF Corporation*, 389 F.Supp. 1379 (S.D. Texas 1975) as support for their position. That case did hold that before an abatement order may be issued pursuant to § 1319(a)(3) of the Act, the defendants must be shown to have violated an applicable effluent limitation. 389 F.Supp. at 1385–86. The Government argues, however, that the decision is incorrect and cites *American Frozen Food Institute v. Train*, 176 U.S.App.D.C. 105, 113, 539 F.2d 107, 115 (1976) for the proposition that:

> By 1972 Congress determined upon wholly a new approach. The basic concept of the Act [section 1311(a)] we construe in this case is an ultimate flat prohibition upon all discharges of pollutants. . . .

Indeed, the court specifically noted that "[t]his prohibition which is central to the entire Act is statutory and requires no promulgation." *Id.*, 176 U.S.App.D.C. at 126, 539 F.2d at 128.

* * *

The *GAF* court appropriately recognized that the legislative history of the Act was "curiously incomplete" on the issue in question. *Id.* We therefore must interpret the statute in a fashion that best effectuates the policies of the Act. The basic policy of the Act is to halt uncontrolled discharges of pollutants into the waters of the United States. 33 U.S.C. § 1251. In fact, the Act sets forth "the national goal that the discharge of [all] pollutants into the navigable waters be eliminated by 1985." *Id.* § 1251(a)(1); *United States v. Hamel, supra* at 109. We see nothing impermissible with allowing the Government to enforce the Act by invoking § 1311(a), even if no effluent limitations have been promulgated for the particular business charged with polluting. Without this flexibility, numerous industries not yet considered as serious threats to the environment may escape administrative, civil, or criminal sanctions merely because the EPA has not established effluent limitations. Thus, dangerous pollutants could be continually injected into the water solely because the administrative process has not yet had the opportunity to fix specific effluent limitations. Such a result would be inconsistent with the policy of the Act.

We do not believe, as did the court in *GAF*, that the permit procedure urged by the Government is unduly burdensome on business. If no effluent limitations have yet been applied to an industry, a potential transgressor should apply for a permit to discharge pollutants under section 1342(a).

The Administrator may then set up operating conditions until permanent effluent limitations are promulgated by EPA. The pendency of a permit application, in appropriate cases, should shield the applicant from liability for discharge in the absence of a permit. 33 U.S.C. § 1342(k). *See Stream Pollution Con. Bd. of Ind. v. U.S. Steel Corp.*, 512 F.2d 1036, 1041 n. 12 (7th Cir. 1975). EPA cannot be expected to have anticipated every form of water pollution through the establishment of effluent limitations. The permit procedure, coupled with broad enforcement under § 1311(a) may, in fact, allow EPA to discover new sources of pollution for which permanent effluent standards are appropriate.

In the present case, it is undisputed that there was no pending permit to discharge pollutants; nor had Frezzo Brothers, Inc., ever applied for one. This case, therefore, appears to be particularly compelling for broad enforcement under sections 1311(a), 1319(c)(1). The Frezzos, under their interpretation of the statute, could conceivably have continued polluting until EPA promulgated effluent limitations for the compost operation. The Government's intervention by way of criminal indictments brought to a halt potentially serious damage to the stream in question, and has no doubt alerted EPA to pollution problems posed by compost production. We therefore hold that the promulgation of effluent limitation standards is not a prerequisite to the maintenance of a criminal proceeding based on violation of section1311(a) of the Act.

(c) *Private (Citizen) Suits*

Section 505 authorizes any "citizen" to bring a civil suit against any person who is alleged to be in violation of effluent standards or limitations under the Act. A "citizen" may also bring suit against the EPA Administrator for alleged failure to perform any nondiscretionary duty under the Act. However, the citizen may not start a suit if the Administrator has already begun a civil or criminal action and is prosecuting it diligently.

The word "citizen" is defined in the Act as "a person . . . having an interest which is or may be adversely affected." This definition is intended to limit the private suit provision to persons having "standing to sue" under the ruling in *Sierra Club v. Morton*, 405 U.S. 727 (1972), set forth in the first chapter.

Section 505 provides that a citizen must give 60 days notice to the Administrator and to the state in which the violation is alleged to have occurred. See *Middlesex County Sewer Authority v. Sea Clammers*, in Part One, for a discussion of the consequences of failure to comply strictly with this notice provision.

D. Federal Safe Drinking Water Act

1. Public Water Supply Systems

The purpose of the **Safe Drinking Water Act** is to ensure that the **public water supply systems** meet national standards for the protection of public health. The term "public water supply systems" is defined as a piped water supply that has 15 or more service connections or regularly serves 25 or more persons. The regulations contained in 40 C.F.R. 141 (Dec. 24, 1974) divide public water systems into two types:

Community system. Serves at least 15 service connections or 25 residents on a year round basis.

Noncommunity system. Serves an average of 25 persons daily at least 60 days of the year. This category includes such sources of public water supply as gas stations, factories, campgrounds, mobile home parks, parks, schools, restaurants, motels and other facilities that have their own water systems.

2. Primary Drinking Water Regulations

The Act authorizes EPA to establish **primary national drinking water regulations** for all public water systems in a two-stage procedure. The first stage is the promulgation of **interim regulations**, whose purpose is to protect health to the extent feasible, using technology, treatment techniques, and other means that are generally available, taking costs into consideration. These regulations became effective on June 24, 1977. They require (*1*) minimum sampling and testing frequencies; (*2*) maximum contaminant level for bacteria, turbidity, ten inorganic chemicals, six organic pesticides or herbicides and radionuclides; (*3*) samples to be tested in approved laboratories; (*4*) reporting of deviations from standards; and (*5*) maintenance of records. In 1978 EPA issued interim regulations for synthetic organics resulting from chlorination. The proposed regulations sought to require drinking water systems serving 75,000 or more people to install granual activated carbon (GAC) filtration systems.

The second stage calls for the development of **revised national primary drinking water regulations**. The National Academy of Sciences (NAS) is designated as the entity to conduct a study to determine the maximum contaminant levels of drinking water to protect the public health. NAS is also to determine whether there are contaminants whose levels in drinking water cannot be determined but which may have an adverse affect on the health of persons. Based on the information furnished by the NAS, the Administrator is to publish the recommended maximum contaminant levels for each of the listed contaminants together with revised national primary drinking water regulations.

EPA is authorized, but not required, to promulgate *secondary* regulations that will deal with taste, odor and appearance of drinking water.

3. Enforcement of the Regulations

Sections 300g-2 and 300g-3 of the Safe Drinking Water Act establish the system of enforcing the primary regulations. Initially, the federal government is authorized to enforce the primary regulations. A procedure is established by which a state may assume primary enforcement responsibility. To do so the states must meet federal standards. If they do they are eligible for federal grants to help pay the cost of enforcement. To be eligible for the grant program a state must agree to: (*1*) adopt adequate statutory authority to enforce compliance with the primary regulations; (*2*) apply the regulations to all public water supplies; (*3*) bring suit in state courts to enforce the regulations; (*4*) provide for a right of entry into places of public water supply; (*5*) require suppliers to keep records and give public notice of violations; (*6*) impose civil and criminal penalties for violations; (*7*) adopt state primary drinking water regulations that are no less stringent than federal regulations; (*8*) establish a program for certification of laboratories that analyze drinking water supplies and (*9*) adopt emergency procedures.

If a state does not elect to assume primary enforcement responsibility, or is denied such responsibility because it fails to meet the requirements, EPA must assume the responsibility. If the state assumes this responsibility EPA may reassume enforcement responsibility only where (*1*) the Administration determines that the specific criteria for state primary enforcement responsibility is not be satisfied; (*2*) a public water system is not complying with the primary regulations, or the terms of a variance or exemption thereunder; (*3*) the governor of the state requests EPA enforcment; or (*4*) in emergency situations.

EPA's enforcement responsibilities are limited in two respects. Under the provisions of Section 300g-3, the Administrator has **discretion** to decide whether or not enforcement proceedings will be brought. This is to be contrasted to the Clean Water Act where the Administrator has a **mandatory** duty to enforce violations of regulations under the Act. The second limitation of EPA under the Safe Drinking Water Act is that enforcement action is limited to the bringing of a civil suit, i.e., EPA does not have the power to issue administrative compliance orders under the Safe Drinking Water Act as it may under the Clean Water Act.

4. Variances and Exemptions

Sections 300g-4 and 300g-5 provide for **variances** and **exemptions** from primary drinking water regulations. EPA or the state may permit a variance from the regulations under two circumstances: (*1*) where the characteristics of the water supply make compliance impossible, despite the application of best technology treatment techniques generally available (taking costs into consideration). However a schedule must be established to bring the system into compliance within a prescribed period of time; (*2*) where the applicant can demonstrate that the quality of the water before treatment makes the utilization of the prescribed treatment technique unnecessary to protect the public health. There is a third situation where EPA, but not a state agency, can issue a variance: (*3*) where the applicant public water system can show that an alternative treatment technique not included in the primary regulations is at least as efficient in lowering the level of the contaminant as the prescribed regulations.

It is also possible for EPA or the state to determine that a public water system is **exempt** from primary drinking water regulations on a finding that compelling factors, including economic factors, make it impossible to comply with a contaminant level or treatment technique prescribed in the regulations. To issue an exemption, EPA or the state agency must find that the public water system was operating prior to the effective date of the regulations and that the exemption will not create an unreasonable risk to health. In addition, a compliance schedule must be adopted to bring the system into compliance by a prescribed date.

5. Underground Injections and Areas with Only One Aquifer

Section 300h creates a program to protect underground sources of water supply from **underground injections**, defined as "the subsurface emplacement of fluids by well injection." A permit is required for a new underground injection well and for penalties provided for violation of the conditions of such a permit or the injection of fluids without a permit.

Section 300h-3(e) provides for special protection of **areas with only one aquifer**. This section provides that where the Administrator determines that an area has an aquifer which is the **sole or principal drinking water source for the area**, which if contaminated would create a significant hazard to public health, he will publish notice of that determination. Once this determination is made the federal government will not be able to provide funds for any project which may contaminate such aquifer so as to create a significant hazard to public health. A subsequent proviso permits such federal funding for federal programs only if the plan or design of the project ensures that the aquifer will not be contaminated.

6. Emergency Powers

Section 300i provides for emergency powers. The Administrator is authorized to take such action as he deems necessary to protect the public health where he receives information that a contaminant is present in or is likely to enter a public water system and presents an imminent and substantial endangerment to the health of persons where the state or local officials have not acted. The Administrator is required, where practicable, to first consult with state and local officials. The Administrator may issue administrative orders to protect the health of persons using the water system and may bring civil action for appropriate relief, including an injunction. Failure to comply with the Administrator's orders is punishable by a fine, not to exceed $5,000, for each day of noncompliance.

7. CITIZEN SUITS

Section 300j-8 provides for citizens' civil suits. It authorizes "any person" to bring suit against (*1*) any person alleged to be in violation of any requirement prescribed under the Act, and (*2*) the Administrator where it is alleged that he failed to perform any nondiscretionary act or duty prescribed under the Act. Notice of such violation must be given to the alleged violator and EPA or state agency and notice of intention to bring suit must be given to the Administrator at least 60 days before suit is brought.

For additional information about the Safe Drinking Water Act see Douglas, *Safe Drinking Water Act of 1974—History and Critique*, 5 ENVIRONMENTAL AFFAIRS 501 (1976).

Shortly after adoption of interim primary drinking water regulations by EPA, the Environmental Defense Fund challenged their adequacy. In *Environmental Defense Fund, Inc. v. Costle*, below, the court reviewed the legislative history of the Safe Drinking Water Act and reviewed the validity of specific regulations for both organic and inorganic contaminants in drinking water.

ENVIRONMENTAL DEFENSE FUND, INC.
v.
COSTLE

578 F.2d 337 (D.C.Cir. 1978)

LEVENTHAL, Circuit Judge:

This case calls on us to consider the duties of the Environmental Protection Agency (EPA) under the Safe Drinking Water Act passed on December 18, 1974.

I.
INTRODUCTION

In this statute, Congress responded to accumulating evidence that our drinking water contains unsafe levels of a large variety of contaminants. The Act requires the Environmental Protection Agency to promulgate regulations restricting the concentration of such substances in drinking water.

The present action is brought by the Environmental Defense Fund (EDF), a nonprofit organization concerned with environmental issues. EDF challenges the adequacy of interim regulations promulgated under the Act, urging that they fail to restrict levels of certain substances that may be harmful, and fail to require adequate monitoring of other substances.

The EPA responds by stressing the poverty of clearcut information concerning the harmfulness of the substances in question, and the lack of a satisfactory method for determining their levels in drinking water. These considerations, argues the Agency, make it unfeasible to formulate more extensive regulations at the present time. The Agency's position is reinforced by the fact that the challenged regulations are interim; the statutory scheme provides for the development of more definitive regulations at a later time.

The dispute poses for this court the difficult task of determining whether the agency has exceeded the bounds of its permissible discretion, in any area characterized by scientific and technological uncertainty. Where administrative judgment plays a key role, as is unquestionably the case here, this court must proceed with particular caution, avoiding all temptation to direct the agency in a choice between rational alternatives. At the same time, we must be cognizant of our duty to scrutinize with care the actions under challenge, to determine whether a rational basis for them may be discerned. Our responsibility is particularly weighty where, as here, serious issues of public health are involved on a potentially vast scale.

II.
THE STATUTORY SCHEME

The Safe Drinking Water Act provides that the Administrator of the Environmental Protection Agency shall promulgate national drinking water standards in three phases. The first phase leads to the promulgation of "interim primary drinking water regulations" (interim regulations). These regulations set maximum contaminant levels (MCL) for substances that the Administrator finds may have an adverse effect on health, or, where that is not feasible, specify treatment techniques to reduce the level of the contaminant. They are intended to "protect health to the extent feasible, using technology, treatment techniques, and other means, which the Administrator determines are generally available (taking costs into consideration) on the date of enactment of this title." Proposed interim primary drinking water regulations were to be published within 90 days after the passage of the Act. Final interim regulations were to be promulgated 180 days after passage of the Act. The interim regulations were to take effect eighteen months after the date of their promulgation.

The second phase results in the promulgation of "revised national primary drinking water regulations" (revised regulations). These regulations also set MCL's or specify treatment techniques. They must be formulated to reduce contaminant levels as nearly as is feasible to levels at which no adverse effects on health occur. Feasibility is to be determined with reference to the best technology generally available, taking cost into consideration.

To lay the groundwork for phase two, the Act directs the Administrator to enter into an appropriate arrangement with the National Academy of Sciences or another independent scientific organization to conduct a study to determine the existence of drinking water contaminants that may pose a health problem and, where possible, to establish safe maximum contaminant levels for these substances. A report of the results of this study is to be made to Congress within two years after passage of the Act and a summary of the report is to be published in the Federal Register. Within 90 days after publication of the report, the Administrator is required to formulate proposed revised national primary drinking water regulations, based on the findings contained in the report. Within 180 days after the date of the proposed revised regulations, the Administrator must promulgate revised regulations. These regulations are to take effect 18 months after promulgation.

The third and final phase of regulation generates "national secondary drinking water regulations" (secondary regulations). The Administrator is required to publish proposed "national secondary drinking water regulations" within 270 days after the date of the Act's passage. Within 90 days after publication of such proposed regulations, he must promulgate secondary regulations. The Act does not specify when these regulations are to take effect.

Regulations promulgated in all three phases may be amended.

III.
CHALLENGES TO THE INTERIM REGULATIONS

Pursuant to statute, on March 14, 1975, the Administrator published proposed interim regulations for public comment. In the course of the proceedings, EDF challenged the adequacy of the proposed regulations. Subsequently, on December 10, 1975, the Administrator promulgated the interim regulations. In this appeal, EDF challenges four specific aspects of these regulations: 1) the failure to fully control organic contaminants in drinking water; 2) the adequacy of the MCL for fluoride; 3) the failure to regulate sodium and sulfates; 4) the adequacy of the monitoring required for cadmium and lead. It will be helpful to detail the nature of the dispute on each point.

A. *Regulation of Organics*

The interim regulations provide MCL's for only six organic contaminants out of the large number of such substances known to be present in drinking water. They do not specify treatment techniques for reducing organics. EDF argues that the legislative intent was that comprehensive regulation of organics should commence with the interim regulations. It points to accumulating evidence not only of the presence of large numbers of organic substances in drinking water, but of correlations between such contaminants and human health consequences, including cancer. It urges the need to set a limit on *total* organic content of drinking water, by adoption of some chemical measure which would serve as a surrogate for total organic content.

The EPA responds that the interim regulations were meant to be less comprehensive than the revised regulations and, more specifically, that Congress did not anticipate a comprehensive regulation of organics under the interim regulations. The EPA further stresses that the effects of long-term ingestion of organic contaminants in drinking water are not yet clear, making it difficult to set MCL's for these substances. In addition, argues the EPA, information on the efficacy and expense of available treatment techniques is incomplete. Thus, its decision to limit regulation of organics to six substances is presented as a legitimate exercise of agency discretion.

B. *Regulation of Inorganic Substances*

1. *Fluoride*

The MCL for fluoride specified by the interim regulations is based on the principle that drinking water may usefully contain sufficient fluoride to provide optimal protection against dental caries, but that the amount by which such levels are exceeded should be limited, so as to avoid undue side-effects—primarily mottling of the teeth (fluorosis), a condition with only esthetic significance. The MCL established by the Administrator permits fluoride levels up to two times the optimal protective level. EDF argues that the permitted level is too high: the severity of fluorosis is proportional to fluoride concentrations; thus, permitting levels to greatly exceed the optimal therapeutic level violates the duty of the Administrator to formulate interim regulations that will protect health "to the extent feasible."

In response, the EPA cites authority to the effect that the levels in question do not pose a health hazard. The EPA views the matter as essentially one of line-drawing, in which it properly exercised reasonable discretion.

2. *Sodium and Sulfates*

Neither of these substances is controlled under the interim regulations. The EDF argues that the health effects of these substances are well established and that regulation was mandated by the Act.

The EPA believes that the setting of MCL's for these substances would have been inappropriate, since individual response to their presence in drinking water varies over a broad continuum. While monitoring of these levels and notification of those concerned might be desirable, EPA concluded that it lacked authority under the Act to require such programs.

3. *Cadmium and Lead*

The interim regulations set MCL's for both of these substances. The parties do not dispute the fact that their presence in drinking water represents a potential danger to health. Rather, EDF focuses on the manner in which the level of these contaminants in drinking water are to be monitored under the interim regulations. While levels are monitored at the tap (thus insuring that contributions from the distribution and plumbing systems will be reflected), samples are required to be tested only annually, and the size and distribution of sampling is not specified. EDF objects that more frequent sampling, of a specified size and distribution, is needed in order adequately to control the contributions of cadmium and lead from distribution sources, which vary widely in the extent to which they are responsible for these substances in drinking water.

The EPA defends its monitoring requirements on the ground that, in its judgment, more extensive monitoring cannot be justified in light of the added expense. The agency points out that injurious effects from these substances result from long-term exposure, thus permitting correction of deviation from safe levels before harm to the public has resulted. The agency thus views its monitoring requirements as an appropriate exercise of its discretion.

IV.
THE INTENT OF THE LEGISLATURE

This case involves conflicting contentions as to the nature of our present state of knowledge in the pertinent areas. We begin, however, by noting that the parties differ in their apprehension of the legislative intent, and by making our own effort to discern the will of Congress.

A. *The Statutory Language*

The phased structure of the statutory scheme suggests that formulation of the regulations is intended to be progressive in nature, adapting to increasing knowledge and experience in the area. Yet the statutory language does not dispose of the general issue presented by petitioners: How comprehensive did Congress intend the interim regulations to be?

The opening section of the Act defines the term "primary drinking water regulation" (which includes both interim and revised regulations) as a regulation "which specifies contaminants which . . . . may have any adverse effect on the health of persons. . . ." Petitioner EDF, stressing the word "may," urges that this language reflects a legislative intent that interim, as well as revised, regulations should cover *all* substances in drinking water that may adversely affect health. While there is room for argument, it is our view that the language is more naturally read as a definition—which it purports to be—than a legisltive command.

In another provision, § 1412(a)(2) of the Act states that interim primary regulations "shall protect health to the extent feasible, using technology, treatment techniques, and other means whch the Administrator determines are generally available (taking costs into consideration) on the date of enactment of this Act [December 16,

1974]." Read by itself, this language can be taken as extremely comprehensive. We think, however, that the Congressional intent to avoid a requirement of broadcast comprehensiveness is discernible when the above language is read alongside the statutory language concerning the (greater) comprehensiveness of *revised* regulations. Section 1412(b) of the Act requires the revised primary reglations to

> specify a maximum contaminant level or require the use of treatment techniques for each contaminant for which a recommended maximum contaminant level is established or which is listed in a rule under paragraph (1)(B). The maximum contaminant level specified in a revised national primary drinking water regulation for a contaminant shall be as close to the recommended maximum contaminant level established under paragraph (1)(B) for such contaminant as is feasible. A required treatment technique for a contaminant for which a recommended maximum contaminant level has been established under paragraph (1)(B) shall reduce such contaminant to a level which is as close to the recommended contaminant level as is feasible. A required treatment technique for a contaminant which is listed under paragraph (1)(B) shall require treatment necessary in the Administrator's judgment to prevent known or anticipated adverse effects on the health of persons to the extent feasible. For purposes of this paragraph, the term "feasible" means feasible with the use of the best technology, treatment techniques, and other means, which the Administrator finds are generally available (taking cost into consideration).

This provision in paragraph (3) of § 1421(b) must be read in conjunction with paragraph (1)(B) of that section, which requires the Administrator to establish recommended maximum contaminant levels for, or at least list, *each* contaminant which, in his judgement, may have any adverse effect on health. Hence the passage from paragraph (3) quoted above requires in turn that he specify a MCL, or a mandatory treatment technique, for *each* contaminant which *may* pose a threat to health. The statutory langauge is thus unambiguous (though perhaps labyrinthine) in its requirement that the revised regulations be fully comprehensive in scope. The language of section 1412(a) which seems universal when taken by itself is perceived on study to be silent as to scope of the interim regulations, and in contrast with the wording for revised regulations, There is more room for administrative discretion than first appears.

There is also a tightening between sections 1412(a) and section 1412(b) as to substantive content. Both sections use the term "feasible," and there is flexibility to consider costs. But section 1412(a) provides that the interim regulations shall protect health to the extent feasible using technology generally available on December 16, 1974, while section 1412(b) provides that the revised regulations shall use the *best* technology generally available.

The text of the statute indicates that the regulations are to become progressively more comprehensive and demanding. The words used give some signals of intent. However, it is the history of the legislation that is more enlightening and reenforcing of what we glean initially from the words alone.

B. *The Legislative History*

Prior to the passage of the Safe Drinking Water Act, the only enforceable federal standards for drinking water were directed at communicable waterborne diseases. These were promulgated under the Public Health Service Act. Under that law, the Public Health Service published, in 1962, *recommended—i.e.*, nonenforceable—guidelines for drinking water contaminants unrelated to communicable disease.

Congress passed the Safe Drinking Water Act in response to increasing indications of a serious threat to health from contaminants in our drinking water not related to communicable disease. The legislative history contains abundant evidence that Congress intended the rapid implementation of broad mandatory controls over impurities. The Report of the House Committee on Interstate and Foreign Commerce sets a general tone of urgency in stating that

> the lack of comprehensive cost, health effects, technological assessment, and monitoring data cannot justify any further delay in Congressional and administrative action. While it would be desirable to have complete health effects research, effective treatment technology, and acurate, inexpensive monitoring systems in operation prior to commencing a system of regulation, this is simply not possible. It is the . . . intent [of the Committee] that EPA, the States, and the public water systems begin now to maximize protection of the public health insofar as possible, and to continue and expand these efforts as new more accurate data, technology, and monitoring equipment become available.

Specifically, the House Report indicates that controls were not to be delayed pending the development of more refined data on health effects and more efficient detection and treatment technology.

> Primary regulations [i.e., both interim and revised] must specify contaminants which in the judgment of the Administrator may have an adverse effect on the health of persons when found in drinking water. The words used by the Committee were carefully chosen. Because of the essential preventive purpose of the legislation, the vast number of contaminants which may need to be regulated, and the limited amount of knowledge presently available on the health effects of various contaminants in drinking water, the Committee did not intend to require conclusive proof that any contaminant *will* cause adverse health effects as a condition for regulation of a suspect contaminant. Rather, all that is required is that the Administrator make a reasoned and plausible judgment that a contaminant *may* have such an effect.

A further suggestion of the legislature's intent with regard to organic contaminants is seen in its expectation that the interim regulations "would be based largely on a review and updating of the United States Public Health Service drinking water standards" as conducted by the EPA Advisory Committee on the Revision and Application of the Drinking Water Standards in 1973. House Report at 17; U.S.Code Cong. & Admin.News 1974, p. 6470. Both the 1962 Public Health Service Drinking Water Standards and the 1973 recommendations of the EPA Advisory Committee on the Revision and Application of the Drinking Water Standards include a surrogate for total organics.

V.
EVALUATION OF THE CHALLENGED REGULATIONS IN LIGHT OF THE LEGISLATIVE INTENT

We are persuaded that the legislature intended the EPA to undertake rapid and comprehensive measures in coping with the problem of unsafe drinking water. It seems particularly clear from the legislative history that Congress contemplated prompt regulation, whenever feasible, of every contaminant identified as possibly injurious to health.

While the urgency of the legislature's plan is undeniable, a second aspect of its plan, of perhaps equal importance, is apparent. Regulation in this area, to proceed most efficiently, must remain attuned to our rapidly expanding knowledge and technology. The phase structure of the statutory scheme wisely reflects such an awareness. Heavy investment in measures of uncertain value may prove costly not only in financial terms but also, and more importantly, on a human scale. It would be simplistic to read the legislative will as mandating an undifferentiated and full-scale commitment of resources to programs based entirely on the present state of our knowledge. We do not understand petitioners to adopt such a position.

The notion of attuning national efforts to the progressive development of our capabilities in the area has reverberations, we think, for the proper role of the judiciary in a dispute such as the one before us. In our response to the challenge directed against administrative action, we must be wary lest our interim adjudications hinder pursuit of the legislative goals. In circumstances such as confront us here, judicial efforts may be more profitably expended in assuring that future agency action will effectively promote the goals of the legislature than in fashioning remedies to "correct" earlier agency missteps.

With these thoughts in mind, we proceed to examine the challenged regulations.

A. *Regulation of Organics*

As we have indicated above, we believe the legislature contemplated that the interim regulations would, where feasible, control every contaminant that may prove injurious to health. The failure of the challenged regulations to do so thus becomes suspect. In light of the clear language of the legislative history, the incomplete state of our knowledge regarding the health effects of certain contaminants and the imperfect nature of the available measurement and treatment techniques cannot serve as justification for delay in controlling contaminants that may be harmful.

There is ample evidence establishing the fact that our drinking water is contaminated with a large variety of organic substances, of demonstrated carcinogenicity in animals. Most of these substances are not controlled under the interim regulations. Methods of monitoring the total organic content of water are available and, while not perfect, they make possible the exercise of significant control over the drinking water content of a wide range of organic substances. The argument of the EPA that the use of such imperfect measures may lead to a false sense of security cannot be accepted in light of the clear language in the House Report requiring prompt action despite defects in our monitoring capabilities. Finally, there is material in the record before us to indicate that feasible methods for lowering the level of organic contaminants in drinking water may be available at a reasonable cost. This would of course be a matter of EPA determination in the first instance, but the EPA has not stated that its course has been based on a contrary assumption.

While there is therefore serious question whether the EPA's failure to control total organics in the interim regulations has been responsive to the statute's provisions, we defer final resolution of this question. Considerations already identified suggest the wisdom of this course of action. During the pendency of this litigation, information bearing upon the problem of organic contaminants in drinking water has continued to accumulate. The National Academy of Sciences has submitted to Congress a report of its study of contaminants in driking water, undertaken pursuant to section 1412(e) of the Act. The EPA has solicited views and data concerning the control of organic contaminants in drinking water, preparatory to considering amendment of the interim regulations. These are but two examples of potential new sources of data that may aid the agency in reformulating its present approach to contaminants so as to keep pace with scientific and technological developments.

Congress has authorized the appellate courts to adopt such procedure, including orders of remand and requirement of further proceedings, "as may be just under the circumstances." In cases like this, the court of appellate juridiction has been given authority to review actions of agencies in order to assure adherence to legislative mandate and furtherance of the legislative will. In our view, it would not be consistent with sound procedure, and hence would not be just to all concerned in the circumstances, to insist on agency application of resources and effort to reconsideration or revision of the interim regulations, as if that were the only process before the agency. The statute itself delineates an ongoing process, and we are informed of the potential of agency revision of its interim regulations. The court cannot wear blinders in a litigation involving an ongoing administrative process, and its rulings and relief must take account of the world as it exists as of the time of the decree.

In furtherance of our function and responsibility, we remand the record with a request to EPA to report to this court within 60 days regarding significant changes that have occurred, since the promulgation of the interim regulations, in its assessment of the problem of controlling organic contaminants in drinking water, and to advise the court of its determinations—as of the time of the report—as to whether it plans to propose amended interim regulations in light of newly acquired data.

B. *Regulation of Inorganic Substances*

We find the dispute concerning the EPA's handling of inorganic contaminants susceptible of more definitive resolution at this time. This issue is not characterized by the extremely rapid scientific and technological development that give a special dimension to the problem of organics. Current knowledge of injurious effects is more well-developed and stable. The costs and efficacy of monitoring and treatment procedures are similarly more well established.

The task of the agency here is largely one of line drawing. Agency expertise and judgment must be applied in determining the optimal balance between promotion of the public welfare and avoidance of unnecessary expense. We will not interfere so long as the agency strikes a balance that reasonable promotes the legislative purpose.

Applying this standard we find that the challenged actions concerning the regulation of inorganic substances fall within the limits of discretion delegated to the agency under the Act, and reasonably promote the legislative intent. Our views may be summarized briefly.

1. Fluoride: The interim regulations permit fluoride levels to reach twice the optimal level for protection against dental caries. The EDF accepts that these levels may exceed the optimal therapeutic level, but argues that the MCL should be set at 1.5 times the optimal therapeutic level. The cosmetically undesirable mottling of the tooth enamel that results from excessive fluoride occurs in a severity proportional to the concentration of fluoride in the drinking water. Nevertheless, because of the expense of removing fluoride from drinking water in areas where it occurs naturally in high concentration, some determination must be made of the level beyond which it is not feasible to require a further reduction of fluoride. The parties both recognize that there has been considerable controversy as to what this level should be. No evidence has been introduced that demonstrates that the level chosen by the EPA for the interim regulations fails to protect the public health to the extent feasible. We must conclude that the balance struck by the agency is well within its discretion under the Act.

2. Sodium and sulfates: The EPA did not promulgate interim regulations covering sodium and sulfates. The record before us does not require, as a matter of law, that the agency find that these substances, in the concentrations found in drinking water, have a significant impact on the health of most individuals. As has already been noted, the response of those who are affected varies considerably from one individual to the next. The decision not to impose MCL's for sodium and sulfates comports with these considerations, and is consonant with the views of the EPA Advisory Committee on the Revision and Application of the Drinking Water Standards, and of the National Drinking Water Advisory Council.

The EDF does not object to the EPA's failure to set MCL's for sodium and sulfates, but only to its failure to require monitoring of these substances and notice to customers when certain levels are exceeded. EDF finds authority for requiring such monitoring and notification in sections 1412(a)(2), 1445(a), and 1450(a)(1) of the Act, the provisions of which are noted in the margin.

Given the deference that the Supreme Court has proclaimed is due on the part of a court to the agency charged with putting a new statute in motion, we are in no position to say that the EPA has violated the statute by its failure to establish monitoring and notification requirments in the interim regulations. Section 1445(a) authorizes EPA to require water suppliers to monitor supplies for the purpose of aiding the Administrator in establishing regulations. It is for the EPA to consider, at least in the first instance, whether such monitoring may be established for the purpose of advice to the public, and whether in any event monitoring can be required in the absence of regulations specifying MCL's or treatment techniques, and whether any monitoring reports made to EPA must or should be available to the public, under the Freedom of Information Act or otherwise. An agency such as EPA is confronted with a host of complex and difficult questions all at one time; an attempt to tackle them holus-bolus may be unfeasible and counterproductive. Only where a statutory direction is clear is a court warranted in issuing a mandate directing it to take particular actions.

Section 1450(a)(1) constitutes a general authorization for the Administrator to promulgate regulations necessary to his functions under the Act. Such language invests the agency with a latitude that is considerable but not untrammeled. The matter of sodium and sulfates has not been swept aside. The study carried out by the National Academy of Sciences pursuant to section 1412(e) of the Act has addressed the matter, and the report of its findings may aid the agency in reevaluating its approach to these substances. The relief prayed by petitioners will not be granted.

3. Lead and Cadmium: The interim regulations set MCL's for both of these substances. EDF challenges the standards set by the regulations for monitoring the levels of these substances. Monitoring is required once a year for community water systems using surface water, and once every three years for systems using ground water. There is no requirement as to the number of, and locations at which, samples are to be taken. EDF appears to press for more frequent sampling, and for express requirements concerning the number of samples and times and locations at which samples are to be taken, so as to assure detection of harmful levels that may be present in only part of a particular system, or at only certain times.

As to frequency of sampling, the EPA stresses that the harmful effects of lead and cadmium in drinking water generally result from chronic exposure to the contaminants, a point with which the EDF appears to agree. EDF does not call our attention to any evidence that would indicate that the challenged sampling intervals are not sufficiently frequent to detect changes in contaminant levels before harm results. On this record, we cannot overturn the frequency established by the EPA as an abuse of discretion.

We turn to the issue of the samples to be taken within a given water supply system, their number, frequency and locations. Corrosion of supply pipes and plumbing fixtures concededly constitutes a significant source of lead and cadmium in drinking water. Consequently, levels of these substances may vary, even within the same water supply system, depending upon variations in the corrosiveness of the water at different times, in the periods of time during which water remains in the pipes, and in the age and composition of the pipes in different parts of the system. It is possible that an annual sampling of water at a single location in a water supply system may fail to detect such variations—even for long periods of time.

Section 1401(1)(D) of the Act states that primary drinking water regulations (*i.e.*, interim and revised regulations) must contain "criteria and procedures to assure [compliance] with . . . maximum contaminant levels; including quality controls and testing procedures to insure compliance with such levels and to insure proper operation and maintenance of the system . . ." It is plausible to put it that Congress contemplated monitoring that will detect variations within a system.

However, considerations of feasibility must be weighed in determining the extent to which intra-system variations are unacceptable under the Act. The House Report explains that "[m]onitoring should insure *to the extent feasible* the detection of a violation before such violation causes or contributes to any adverse health effect." While it can be argued that *all* water supply systems should be required to sample widely within the system, at specified locations and frequencies, such an approach might unnecessarily burden those systems for which intra-system variation is not a problem. The House Report suggests that monitoring requirements were intended to be more finely tuned:

> More frequent monitoring should be required by regulation for classes of systems facing local conditions which justify such increased monitoring. In prescribing regulations requiring more frequent monitoring or sampling than the minimum, the Administrator is expected to take into account, among other facts, the nature and type of the water source, historical data characterizing the water quality, anticipated variations in water quality, vulnerability of the source to accidental or deliberate contamination, the population at risk, the type of treatment provided, and the level of the contaminant which is generally found as it relates to the established limit.

While this passage from the House Report speaks only of frequency of sampling, its approach seems equally applicable to other aspects of monitoring.

The degree to which monitoring requirements can be tailored to detect local variations in contaminant levels depends upon the access of the EPA to information concerning such variations. The EPA maintains that it did not have detailed information of this sort available at the time of promulgation of the interim regulations. In an effort to obtain such data, it has encouraged the states to conduct sanitary surveys of water systems which would help to identify local drinking water problems.

An agency has discretion in selecting the techniques appropriate for grappling with a problem and carrying out its functions. We cannot at this point say that EPA's approach to the formulation of monitoring regulations is without a rational basis. As data accumulate on local variations in lead and cadmium levels, the agency will be in a position to formulate a more refined approach to monitoring—either by amending the interim regulations or by designing the revised and secondary regulations to reflect such local conditions. Should the agency fail to do so, we will have another case before us.

* * *

Subsequent to the preparation of the foregoing, the EPA has initiated further regulation of organics in drinking water. Regulations proposed by the Agency on January 25, 1978, would limit the presence of trihalomethanes, including chloroform, to under 100 parts per billion in the drinking water of communities with a population of more than 75,000; and would require, in these communities, the application of a special purification technique—filtration by granular activated carbon—to the treatment plants of systems whose water sources are polluted. The presence of chloroform in drinking water has been of particular concern because of its demonstarted carcinogenicity in laboratory animals and widespread presence in municipal water systems.

* * *

Insofar as the petition for review presents challenges as to inorganic contaminants, it is denied. As to the challenge to the regulation of organic contaminants, we remand the record for a report by the EPA, as set forth in this opinion.

Affirmed.

MacKINNON, Circuit Judge, concurring in part and dissenting in part: The majority opinion concludes with respect to *organics*:

> In furtherance of our function and responsibility, we remand the record with a request to EPA to report to this court within 60 days regarding significant changs

> that have occurred, since the promulgation of the interim regulations, in its assessment of the problem of controlling organic contaminants in drinking water, and to advise the court of its determinations—as of the time of the report—as to whether it plans to propose amended interim regulations in light of newly acquired data.

188 U.S.App.D.C. at ———, 578 F.2d at 346. I concur in this part of the opinion. However, I dissent from the affirmance of the Agency's action with respect to lead and cadmium. The Agency defends its regulation by statistics that are based on *source water*, not on statistics gathered at the point of final distribution. It also relies on testimony that in my view is not sufficiently extensive, particularly in view of the fact that lead and cadmium pollution is admittedly caused by spotty factors, *i. e.*, somewhat by the type of conduits used in various locations and the corrosiveness of the water. The contentions of the Fund, in this respect, seem to me to be logical; and since they are not answered by the Agency, I would remand those portions of the regulations for more extensive testing and reconsideration in the light thereof.

With respect to the Agency's regulations on inorganic substances, I would uphold them, in the main, for the reasons outlined in the majority opinion, but I would not confine the study of fluoride to its dental effects when it is also suspect of causing some changes in bone density.

Part Four

Control of Population Growth and Distribution

Part Four

Control of Population Growth and Distribution

A. Introduction: Why Is Population Growth an Environmental Issue?

The quality of the environment can easily be impaired by the two-pronged demographic phenomenon of too many people and too many people concentrated in specific places. The problem of accommodating too many people is relatively recent in world history. In the first million years of man's existence, it is estimated that world population was under three million persons. It reached five million about 8000 B.C. and about 500 million in 1650. World population in 1980 was about 4.5 billion and is expected to increase by 2 billion more by the year 2000.

In 1980 *The Global 2000 Report to the President* was prepared for and presented to President Carter by the Council on Environmental Quality and the U.S. State Department. The report sought to make projections of world population, resources and condition of the environment and make recommendations of United States policy to respond to the problems that will arise from population growth and concentration by the year 2000.

The following are some of the principal findings and conclusions of that study.

1. *Population*

Between 1980 and the year 2000, almost 2 billion more people will be added to the present world population of 4.5 billion. Ninety percent of the growth will occur in low-income countries. Population growth in richer countries, though much slower, is also of concern because consumption of resources per capita is very much higher.

2. Food and Agriculture

Population increases will place great stress on world food supply. Although food production may expand 90 percent (under optimistic assumptions) by the year 2000, the increase will be less than 15 percent on a per-capita basis. However, regional disparities in food supplies are expected to continue: food availability and nutrition levels may not improve very much in South Asia and the Middle East and may actually decline in the poorer parts of Africa. Of particular concern is the ability to improve world agricultural yields in the face of pressures leading to degradation of agricultural soil and water resources and the conversion of some of the best cropland to other uses.

The report called attention to American croplands being already under heavy pressure from erosion, loss of soil fertility, and conversion to nonagricultural uses.

3. Renewable Energy Resources and Conservation

Most countries, both rich and poor, have had to adjust to soaring oil prices. The developing countries, without their own oil resources, are hardest hit. They spend $50 billion per year to buy oil—almost twice the amount they receive collectively from all outside sources for development assistance. At the same time, the world's poorest half, most of whom rely mainly on traditional fuels such as firewood and agricultural waste, face another energy crisis: dwindling supplies of firewood. This combination is aggravating already severe economic and ecological problems, adding to the difficulties of achieving economic growth.

4. Tropical Forests

The conversion of forested land to agricultural use and the demand for firewood and forest products are depleting the world's forests at an alarming rate—as much as 18–20 million hectares annually, an area one-half the size of California. Most of the loss is in the tropical regions of developing nations, where some 40 percent of the remaining forests may disappear by the year 2000. Hundreds of millions of people are already directly affected by this extremely serious and growing global environmental problem.

5. Biological Diversity

The accelerating destruction and pollution of habitats of wild animals and plants threaten extinction of species in the next 20 years on an unprecedented scale. As much as 15–20 percent of all species on earth could be lost in the next 20 years, about one-half because of the loss and degradation of tropical forests and the rest principally in fresh water, coastal and reef ecosystems. (This estimate includes insects, other invertebrates and plants, as well as mammals, birds and vertebrate animals.)

6. Coastal and Marine Resources

Growing threats to coastal and marine ecosystems come from urban and industrial development and destruction of productive coastal wetlands and reefs; pollutants washed from the land, dumped or discharged into the ocean, or deposited from the atmosphere; and uncontrolled exploitation of world fisheries. The worldwide harvest of fish—a major component of the world's food supply—has leveled off and by the year 2000 may contribute less to the world's nutrition, on a per capita basis, than it does today. A special concern is the lack of data regarding the degree of pollution and disturbance and the longevity of impact in the open oceans.

7. Water Resources

Human needs for water will greatly increase over the next 20 years; in one-half of the countries of the world, population growth alone will cause demands to double. Data on water availability and quality is exceptionally poor, but it is clear that problems of water supply will be serious in many regions. Parts of the world, especially the Third World, are already suffering severe water shortages and drought, and water-borne disease is endemic in many areas. Without concerted efforts to the contrary, reliable water supplies will be disrupted increasingly because of damage to watersheds, and contamination is likely to increase.

8. Global Pollution

The earth's life-support systems are threatened by certain byproducts of economic development and industrial growth. Contamination from hazardous substances and nuclear waste, man-induced climate modification from the buildup of CO_2, damage to the stratospheric ozone layer, and acid precipitation could adversely affect virtually every aspect of the earth's ecosystems and resource base and, ultimately, mankind.

9. Sustainable Development

Many of the world's most severe environmental problems are in part a consequence of extreme poverty: deprived people are forced to undermine the productivity of the land on which they live in their necessary quest for food, fuel and shelter. People who have no other choice in getting their living plant crops on poor, erodible soils, graze their stock on marginal land that turns to desert from overuse, cut trees that are needed to stabilize soils and water supplies, and burn dung needed to fertilize and condition agricultural soils.

The problems of overpopulation were succinctly summarized by Johnson C. Montgomery in his article "The Population Explosion and United States Law," 22 *Hastings L. J.* 629 (1971), in which he suggests that among the results of overpopulation are: (*1*), Malnutrition, starvation and the possibility of worldwide famine; (*2*) Antisocial behavior and the disintegration of established social orders; (*3*) Environmental pollution of staggering proportions; and (*4*) Increasing economic costs to every segment of the society, including the individual taxpayer.

The *Global 2000 Report to the President* recommended a wide range of federal action at the international level, from international programs of family planning to direct programs of financial aid for food, agricultural improvement, research, education and technical assistance. At the national and local levels, the problem of overpopulation raises serious legal questions relating to the validity of techniques of regulating **population growth** and direct and indirect techniques of regulating **population distribution**.

B. Regulation of Population Growth

Every student of demography has been taught that the three **factors determining changes in population** in a given area are: (*1*) the number of births, (*2*) the number of deaths, and (*3*) the difference between in-migration and out-migration in the area. The ability of government to regulate each of these factors is severely limited. Generally accepted principles of morality limit the ability of government to affect the death rate (other than the ability to engage in warfare) to programs that tend to decrease, and not to increase, the death rate. Regulation of the migration of persons will be discussed later.

This section will deal with the validity of techniques by which the birth rate may be regulated. Governmental regulation of the birth rate has taken two conflicting forms: (*1*) *direct* restriction of the individual's right to procreate, and (*2*) *direct* restriction of the individual's right *not* to procreate. In addition, governmental action may take the form of (*3*) *indirect* measures that tend to discourage procreation.

1. Direct Restrictions on the Right to Procreate

Direct restrictions on the right to procreate may take the form of (*1*) criminal penalties for having more than a prescribed number of children, (*2*) compulsory abortion and (*3*) compulsory sterilization. Because of the extreme intrusion into personal privacy involved, there has been only limited use of such restrictions and only limited judicial statements to determine their validity. The general attitude of the judiciary may have been summarized best by the statement of Justice Goldberg in his concurring opinion in *Griswold v. Connecticut, infra*, in which he said:

> "Surely, the government, absent a showing of a *compelling state interest*, could not decree that all husbands and wives must be sterilized after two children have been born to them. . . . The personal liberty guaranteed by the Constitution does . . . include protection against such totalitarian limitation of family size, which is at complete variance with our constitutional concepts." (emphasis added)

This statement leaves open the possibility that some circumstances may provide the basis for a "compelling state interest" to justify such extreme measures as compulsory sterilization. The decisions in *Buck v. Bell* and *Skinner v. Oklahoma*, below, explore that possibility.

BUCK v. BELL

274 U.S. 200 (1927)

Mr. Justice Holmes delivered the opinion of the Court.

This is a writ of error to review a judgment of the Supreme Court of Appeals of the State of Virginia, affirming a judgment of the Circuit Court of Amherst County, by which the defendant in error, the superintendent of the State Colony for Epileptics and Feeble Minded, was ordered to perform the operation of salpingectomy upon Carrie Buck, the plaintiff in error, for the purpose of making her sterile. 143 Va. 310. The case comes here upon the contention that the statute authorizing the judgment is void under the Fourteenth Amendment as denying to the plaintiff in error due process of law and the equal protection of the laws.

Carrie Buck is a feeble minded white woman who was committed to the State Colony above mentioned in due form. She is the daughter of a feeble minded mother in the same institution, and the mother of an illegitimate feeble minded child. She was eighteen years old at the time of the trial of her case in the Circuit Court, in the latter part of 1924. An Act of Virginia, approved March 20, 1924, recites that the health of the patient and the welfare of society may be promoted in certain cases by the sterilization of mental defectives, under careful safeguard, &c.; that the sterilization may be effected in males by vasectomy and in females by salpingectomy, without serious pain or substantial danger to life; that the Commonwealth is supporting in various institutions many defective persons who if now discharged would become a menace but if incapable of procreating might be discharged with safety and become self-supporting with benefit to themselves and to society; and that experience has shown that heredity plays an important part in the transmission of insanity, imbecility, &c. The statute then enacts that whenever the superintendent of certain institutions including the above named State Colony shall be of opinion that it is for the best interests of the patients and of society that an inmate under his care should be sexually sterilized, he may have the operation performed upon any patient afflicted with hereditary forms of insanity, imbecility, &c., on complying with the very careful provisions by which the act protects the patients from possible abuse.* * *

The attack is not upon the procedure but upon the substantive law. It seems to be contended that in no circumstances could such an order be justified. It certainly is contended that the order cannot be justified upon the existing grounds. The judgment finds the facts that have been recited and that Carrie Buck "is the probable potential parent of socially inadequate offspring, likewise afflicted, that she may be sexually sterilized without detriment of her general health and that her welfare and that of society will be promoted by her sterilization," and thereupon makes the order. In view of the general declarations of the legislature and the specific findings of the Court, obviously we cannot say as matter of law that the grounds do not exist, and if they exist they justify the result. We have seen more than once that the public welfare may call upon the best citizens for their lives. It would be strange if it could not call upon these lesser sacrifices, often not felt to be such by those concerned, in order to prevent our being swamped with incompetence. It is better for all the world, if instead of waiting to execute degenerate offspring for crime, or to let them starve for their imbecility, society can prevent those who are manifestly unfit from continuing their kind. The principle that sustains compulsory vaccination is broad enough to cover cutting the Fallopian tubes. *Jacobson v. Massachusetts*, 197 U. S. 11. Three generations of imbeciles are enough.

But it is said, however it might be if this reasoning were applied generally, it fails when it is confined to the small number who are in the institutions named and is not applied to the multitudes outside. It is the usual last resort of constitutional arguments to point out shortcomings of this sort. But the answer is that the law does all that is needed when it does all that it can, indicates a policy, applies it to all within the lines, and seeks to bring within the lines all similarly situated so far and so fast as its means allow. Of course so far as the operations enable those who otherwise must be kept confined to be returned to the world, and thus open the asylum to others, the equality aimed at will be more nearly reached.

Judgment affirmed.

SKINNER v. OKLAHOMA

316 U.S. 535 (1942)

MR. JUSTICE DOUGLAS delivered the opinion of the Court.

This case touches a sensitive and important area of human rights. Oklahoma deprives certain individuals of a right which is basic to the perpetuation of a race—the right to have offspring. Oklahoma has decreed the enforcement of its law against petitioner, overruling his claim that it violated the Fourteenth Amendment. Because that decision raised grave and substantial constitutional questions, we granted the petition for certiorari.

The statute involved is Oklahoma's Habitual Criminal Sterilization Act. Okla. Stat. Ann. Tit. 57, §§ 171, *et seq.*; L. 1935, pp. 94 *et seq.* That Act defines an "habitual criminal" as a person who, having been convicted two or more times for crimes "amounting to felonies involving moral turpitude," either in an Oklahoma court or in a court of any other State, is thereafter convicted of such a felony in

Oklahoma and is sentenced to a term of imprisonment in an Oklahoma penal institution. § 173. Machinery is provided for the institution by the Attorney General of a proceeding against such a person in the Oklahoma courts for a judgment that such person shall be rendered sexually sterile. §§ 176, 177. Notice, an opportunity to be heard, and the right to a jury trial are provided. §§ 177–181. The issues triable in such a proceeding are narrow and confined. If the court or jury finds that the defendant is an "habitual criminal" and that he "may be rendered sexually sterile without deteriment to his or her general health," then the court "shall render judgment to the effect that said defendant be rendered sexually sterile" (§ 182) by the operation of vasectomy in case of a male, and of salpingectomy in case of a female. § 174. Only one other provision of the Act is material here, and that is § 195, which provides that "offenses arising out of the violation of the prohibitory laws, revenue acts, embezzlement, or political offenses, shall not come or be considered within the terms of this Act."

Petitioner was convicted in 1926 of the crime of stealing chickens, and was sentenced to the Oklahoma State Reformatory. In 1929 he was convicted of the crime of robbery with firearms, and was sentenced to the reformatory. In 1934 he was convicted again of robbery with firearms, and was sentenced to the penitentiary. He was confined there in 1935 when the Act was passed. In 1936 the Attorney General instituted proceedings against him. Petitioner in his answer challenged the Act as unconstitutional by reason of the Fourteenth Amendment. A jury trial was had. The court instructed the jury that the crimes of which petitioner had been convicted were felonies involving moral turpitude, and that the only question for the jury was whether the operation of vasectomy could be performed on petitioner without detriment to his general health. The jury found that it could be. A judgment directing that the operation of vasectomy be performed on petitioner was affirmed by the Supreme Court of Oklahoma by a five to four decision. 189 Okla. 235, 115 P.2d 123.

Several objections to the constitutionality of the Act have been pressed upon us. It is urged that the Act cannot be sustained as an exercise of the police power, in view of the state of scientific authorities respecting inheritability of criminal traits. It is argued that due process is lacking because, under this Act, unlike the Act upheld in *Buck* v. *Bell*, 274 U.S. 200, the defendant is given no opportunity to be heard on the issue as to whether he is the probable potential parent of socially undesirable offspring. See *Davis* v. *Berry*, 216 F. 413; *Williams* v. *Smith*, 190 Ind. 526, 131 N.E. 2. It is also suggested that the Act is penal in character and that the sterilization provided for is cruel and unusual punishment and violative of the Fourteenth Amendment. See *Davis* v. *Berry, supra.* Cf. *State* v. *Feilen*, 70 Wash. 65, 126 P. 75; *Mickle* v. *Henrichs*, 262 F. 687. We pass those points without intimating an opinion on them, for there is a feature of the Act which clearly condemns it. That is, its failure to meet the requirements of the equal protection clause of the Fourteenth Amendment.

We do not stop to point out all of the inequalities in this Act. A few examples will suffice. In Oklahoma, grand larceny is a felony. Okla. Stats. Ann. Tit. 21, §§ 1705, 5. Larceny is grand larceny when the property taken exceeds $20 in value. *Id.* § 1704. Embezzlement is punishable "in the manner prescribed for feloniously stealing property of the value of that embezzled." *Id.* § 1462. Hence, he who embezzles property worth more than $20 is guilty of a felony. A clerk who appropriates over $20 from his employer's till (*id.* § 1456) and a stranger who steals the same amount are thus both guilty of felonies. If the latter repeats his act and is convicted three times, he may be sterilized. But the clerk is not subject to the pains and penalties of the Act no matter how large his embezzlements nor how frequent his convictions.* * *

The instant legislation runs afoul of the equal protection clause, though we give Oklahoma that large deference which the rule of the foregoing cases requires. We are dealing here with legislation which involves one of the basic civil rights of man.

Marriage and procreation are fundamental to the very existence and survival of the race. The power to sterilize, if exercised, may have subtle, far-reaching and devastating effects. In evil or reckless hands it can cause races or types which are inimical to the dominant group to wither and disappear. There is no redemption for the individual whom the law touches. Any experiment which the State conducts is to his irreparable injury. He is forever deprived of a basic liberty. We mention these matters not to reexamine the scope of the police power of the States. We advert to them merely in emphasis of our view that strict scrutiny of the classification which a State makes in a sterilization law is essential, lest unwittingly, or otherwise, invidious discriminations are made against groups or types of individuals in violation of the constitutional guaranty of just and equal laws. The guaranty of "equal protection of the laws is a pledge of the protection of equal laws." *Yick Wo* v. *Hopkins*, 118 U.S. 356, 369. When the law lays an unequal hand on those who have committed intrinsically the same quality of offense and sterilizes one and not the other, it has made as invidious a discrimination as if it had selected a particular race or nationality for oppressive treatment. *Yick Wo* v. *Hopkins, supra; Gaines* v. *Canada*, 305 U.S. 337. Sterilization of those who have thrice committed grand larceny, with immunity for those who are embezzlers, is a clear, pointed, unmistakable discrimination.* * *

In *Buck* v. *Bell, supra*, the Virginia statute was upheld though it applied only to feeble-minded persons in institutions of the State. But it was pointed out that "so far as the operations enable those who otherwise must be kept confined to be returned to the world, and thus open the asylum to others, the equality aimed at will be more nearly reached." 274 U.S. p. 208. Here there is no such saving feature. Embezzlers are forever free. Those who steal or take in other ways are not.* * *

Reversed.

---

2. Direct Restrictions on the Right Not to Procreate

Governmental regulation of sexual activity and limitations on the freedom of reproductive decision making intrude into one of the most intimate aspects of personal privacy. Nevertheless, there are many illustrations of state regulation of sexual activity that are commonly accepted, such as criminal penalties for adultery and fornication, prohibitions of polygamy and incestuous marriages and minimum-age limitations on marriage. Direct governmental restrictions on the right of people to limit their family size raise serious questions of constitutional law. The constitutional issues are similar, but distinguishable, where the right not to procreate involves **avoidance of pregnancy** through contraception rather than **termination of pregnancy** through abortion.

a. *Contraceptive Devices and Information*

There is no specific provision of the United States Constitution that guarantees sexual or reproductive freedom. The extent to which such freedom is protected is implied by other constitutional provisions as interpreted by several decisions of the United States Supreme Court. The landmark decision *Griswold v. Connecticut*, set forth below, involves an old Connecticut statute that prohibited the use of birth-control devices. The purpose of the statute was to discourage illicit sexual relations. As a practical matter, it did not in fact curtail premarital and extramarital sexual relations but only prevented poor married couples from obtaining information and medical assistance relating to methods of birth control. In *Eisenstadt v. Baird*, following the *Griswold* decision, the court determined the scope of the constitutional protection of reproductive freedom when it reviewed the validity of a state statute that permitted married persons, but prohibited single persons, from obtaining contraceptive devices.

GRISWOLD v. CONNECTICUT

381 U.S. 479 (1965)

MR. JUSTICE DOUGLAS delivered the opinion of the Court.

Appellant Griswold is Executive Director of the Planned Parenthood League of Connecticut. Appellant Buxton is a licensed physician and a professor at the Yale Medical School who served as Medical Director for the League at its Center in New Haven—a center open and operating from November 1 to November 10, 1961, when appellants were arrested.

They gave information, instruction, and medical advice to *married persons* as to the means of preventing conception. They examined the wife and prescribed the best contraceptive device or material for her use. Fees were usually charged, although some couples were serviced free.

The statutes whose constitutionality is involved in this appeal are §§ 53–32 and 54–196 of the General Statutes of Connecticut (1958 rev.). The former provides:

> "Any person who uses any drug, medicinal article or instrument for the purpose of preventing conception shall be fined not less than fifty dollars or imprisoned not less than sixty days nor more than one year or be both fined and imprisoned."

Section 54–196 provides:

> "Any person who assists, abets, counsels, causes, hires or commands another to commit any offense may be prosecuted and punished as if he were the principal offender."

The appellants were found guilty as accessories and fined $100 each, against the claim that the accessory statute as so applied violated the Fourteenth Amendment. The Appellate Division of the Circuit Court affirmed. The Supreme Court of Errors affirmed that judgment. 151 Conn. 544, 200 A. 2d 479. We noted probable jurisdiction. 379 U. S. 926.* * *

Coming to the merits, we are met with a wide range of questions that implicate the Due Process Clause of the Fourteenth Amendment.* * *

The association of people is not mentioned in the Constitution nor in the Bill of Rights. The right to educate a child in a school of the parents' choice—whether public or private or parochial—is also not mentioned. Nor is the right to study any particular subject or any foreign language. Yet the First Amendment has been construed to include certain of those rights.* * *

In other words, the State may not, consistently with the spirit of the First Amendment, contract the spectrum of available knowledge. The right of freedom of speech and press includes not only the right to utter or to print, but the right to distribute, the right to receive, the right to read (*Martin* v. *Struthers*, 319 U. S. 141, 143) and freedom of inquiry, freedom of thought, and freedom to teach (see *Wieman* v. *Updegraff*, 344 U. S. 183, 195)—indeed the freedom of the entire university community. *Sweezy* v. *New Hampshire*, 354 U. S. 234, 249–250, 261–263; *Barenblatt* v. *United States*, 360 U. S. 109, 112; *Baggett* v. *Bullitt*, 377 U. S. 360, 369. Without those peripheral rights the specific rights would be less secure. And so we reaffirm the principle of the *Pierce* and the *Meyer* cases.

In *NAACP* v. *Alabama*, 357 U. S. 449, 462, we protected the "freedom to associate and privacy in one's associations," noting that freedom of association was a peripheral First Amendment right.* * *

In other words, the First Amendment has a penumbra where privacy is protected from governmental intrusion. In like context, we have protected forms of "association" that are not political in the customary sense but pertain to the social, legal, and economic benefit of the members.

* * *

The right of "association," like the right of belief (*Board of Education* v. *Barnette*, 319 U. S. 624), is more than the right to attend a meeting; it includes the right to express one's attitudes or philosophies by membership in a group or by affiliation with it or by other lawful means. Association in that context is a form of expression of opinion; and while it is not expressly included in the First Amendment its existence is necessary in making the express guarantees fully meaningful.

The foregoing cases suggest that specific guarantees in the Bill of Rights have penumbras, formed by emanations from those guarantees that help give them life and substance.* * *

The Fourth and Fifth Amendments were described in *Boyd* v. *United States*, 116 U. S. 616, 630, as protection against all governmental invasions "of the sanctity of a man's home and the privacies of life." We recently referred in *Mapp* v. *Ohio*, 367 U. S. 643, 656, to the Fourth Amendment as creating a "right to privacy, no less important than any other right carefully and particularly reserved to the people." See Beaney, The Constitutional Right to Privacy, 1962 Sup. Ct. Rev. 212; Griswold, The Right to be Let Alone, 55 Nw. U. L. Rev. 216 (1960).

We have had many controversies over these penumbral rights of "privacy and repose." See, *E. g.*, *Breard* v. *Alexandria*, 341 U. S. 622, 626, 644; *Public Utilities Comm'n* v. *Pollak*, 343 U. S. 451; *Monroe* v. *Pape*, 365 U. S. 167; *Lanza* v. *New York*, 370 U. S. 139; *Frank* v. *Maryland*, 359 U. S. 360; *Skinner* v. *Oklahoma*, 316 U. S. 535, 541. These cases bear witness that the right of privacy which presses for recognition here is a legitimate one.

The present case, then, concerns a relationship lying within the zone of privacy created by several fundamental constitutional guarantees. And it concerns a law which, in forbidding the *use* of contraceptives rather than regulating their manufacture or sale, seeks to achieve its goals by means having a maximum destructive impact upon that relationship. Such a law cannot stand in light of the familiar principle, so often applied by this Court, that a "governmental purpose to control or prevent activities constitutionally subject to state regulation may not be achieved by means which sweep unnecessarily broadly and thereby invade the area of protected freedoms." *NAACP* v. *Alabama*, 377 U. S. 288, 307. Would we allow the police to search the sacred precincts of marital bedrooms for telltale signs of the use of contraceptives? The very idea is repulsive to the notions of privacy surrounding the marriage relationship.

We deal with a right of privacy older than the Bill of Rights—older than our political parties, older than our school system. Marriage is a coming together for better or for worse, hopefully enduring, and intimate to the degree of being sacred. It is an association that promotes a way of life, not causes; a harmony in living, not political faiths; a bilateral loyalty, not commercial or social projects. Yet it is an association for as noble a purpose as any involved in our prior decisions.* * *

Reversed.

Mr. Justice Goldberg, whom The Chief Justice and Mr. Justice Brennan join, concurring.

* * * The language and history of the Ninth Amendment reveal that the Framers of the Constitution believed that there are additional fundamental rights, protected from governmental infringement, which exist alongside those fundamental rights specifically mentioned in the first eight constitutional amendments.

The Ninth Amendment reads, "The enumeration in the Constitution, of certain rights, shall not be construed to deny or disparage others retained by the people." The Amendment is almost entirely the work of James Madison. It was introduced in Congress by him and passed the House and Senate with little or no debate and virtually no change in language. It was proffered to quiet expressed fears that a bill of specifically enumerated rights could not be sufficiently broad to cover all essential rights and that the specific mention of certain rights would be interpreted as a denial that others were protected.[4]* * *

Mr. Justice Black, with whom Mr. Justice Stewart joins, dissenting.

I agree with my Brother Stewart's dissenting opinion. And like him I do not to any extent whatever base my view that this Connecticut law is constitutional on a belief that the law is wise or that its policy is a good one. In order that there may be no room at all to doubt why I vote as I do, I feel constrained to add that the law is every bit as offensive to me as it is to my Brethren of the majority and my Brothers Harlan, White and Goldberg who, reciting reasons why it is offensive to them, hold it unconstitutional. There is no single one of the graphic and eloquent strictures and criticisms fired at the policy of this Connecticut law either by the Court's opinion or by those of my concurring Brethren to which I cannot subscribe—except their conclusion that the evil qualities they see in the law make it unconstitutional.

* * *

The Court talks about a constitutional "right of privacy" as though there is some constitutional provision or provisions forbidding any law ever to be passed which might abridge the "privacy" of individuals. But there is not.* * *

EISENSTADT v. BAIRD

405 U.S. 438 (1972)

MR. JUSTICE BRENNAN delivered the opinion of the Court.

Appellee William Baird was convicted at a bench trial in the Massachusetts Superior Court under Massachusetts General Laws Ann., c. 272, § 21, first, for exhibiting contraceptive articles in the course of delivering a lecture on contraception to a group of students at Boston University and, second, for giving a young woman a package of Emko vaginal foam at the close of his address. The Massachusetts Supreme Judicial Court unanimously set aside the conviction for exhibiting contraceptives on the ground that it violated Baird's First Amendment rights, but by a four-to-three vote sustained the conviction for giving away the foam. *Commonwealth* v. *Baird*, 355 Mass. 746, 247 N. E. 2d 574 (1969). Baird subsequently filed a petition for a federal writ of habeas corpus, which the District Court dismissed. 310 F. Supp. 951 (1970). On appeal, however, the Court of Appeals for the First Circuit vacated the dismissal and remanded the action with directions to grant the writ discharging Baird. 429 F. 2d 1398 (1970). This appeal by the Sheriff of Suffolk County, Massachusetts, followed, and we noted probable jurisdiction. 401 U. S. 934 (1971). We affirm.

Massachusetts General Laws Ann., c. 272, § 21, under which Baird was convicted, provides a maximum five-year term of imprisonment for "whoever . . . gives away . . . any drug, medicine, instrument or article whatever for the prevention of conception," except as authorized in § 21A. Under § 21A, "[a] registered physician may administer to or prescribe for any married person drugs or articles intended for the prevention of pregnancy or conception. [And a] registered pharmacist actually engaged in the business of pharmacy may furnish such drugs or articles to any married person presenting a prescription from a registered physician." As interpreted by the State Supreme Judicial Court, these provisions make it a felony for anyone, other than a registered physician or pharmacist acting in accordance with the terms of § 21A, to dispense any article with the intention that it be used for the prevention of conception. The statutory scheme distinguishes among three distinct classes of distributees—*first*, married persons may obtain contraceptives to prevent pregnancy, but only from doctors or druggists on prescription; *second*, single persons may not obtain contraceptives from anyone to prevent pregnancy; and, *third*, married or single persons may obtain contraceptives from anyone to prevent, not pregnancy, but the spread of disease. This construction of state law is, of course, binding on us. *E. g., Groppi* v. *Wisconsin*, 400 U. S. 505, 507 (1971).

The legislative purposes that the statute is meant to serve are not altogether clear. In *Commonwealth* v. *Baird, supra*, the Supreme Judicial Court noted only the State's interest in protecting the health of its citizens: "[T]he prohibition in § 21," the court declared, "is directly related to" the State's goal of "preventing the distribution of articles designed to prevent conception which may have undesirable, if not dangerous, physical consequences." 355 Mass., at 753, 247 N. E. 2d, at 578. In a subsequent decision, *Sturgis* v. *Attorney General*, 358 Mass. 37, ———, 260 N. E. 2d 687, 690

(1970), the court, however, found "a second and more compelling ground for upholding the statute"—namely, to protect morals through "regulating the private sexual lives of single persons." The Court of Appeals, for reasons that will appear, did not consider the promotion of health or the protection of morals through the deterrence of fornication to be the legislative aim. Instead, the court concluded that the statutory goal was to limit contraception in and of itself—a purpose that the court held conflicted "with fundamental human rights" under *Griswold* v. *Connecticut*, 381 U. S. 479 (1965), where this Court struck down Connecticut's prohibition against the use of contraceptives as an unconstitutional infringement of the right of marital privacy. 429 F. 2d, at 1401–1402.

We agree that the goals of deterring premarital sex and regulating the distribution of potentially harmful articles cannot reasonably be regarded as legislative aims of §§ 21 and 21A. And we hold that the statute, viewed as a prohibition on contraception *per se*, violates the rights of single persons under the Equal Protection Clause of the Fourteenth Amendment.

* * *

II

The basic principles governing application of the Equal Protection Clause of the Fourteenth Amendment are familiar. As THE CHIEF JUSTICE only recently explained in *Reed* v. *Reed*, 404 U. S. 71, 75–76 (1971):

> "In applying that clause, this Court has consistently recognized that the Fourteenth Amendment does not deny to States the power to treat different classes of persons in different ways.* * *
>
> The Equal Protection Clause of that amendment does, however, deny to States the power to legislate that different treatment be accorded to persons placed by a statute into different classes on the basis of criteria wholly unrelated to the objective of that statute. A classification 'must be reasonable, not arbitrary, and must rest upon some ground of difference having a fair and substantial relation to the object of the legislation, so that all persons similarly circumstanced shall be treated alike.' *Royster Guano Co.* v. *Virginia*, 253 U. S. 412, 415 (1920)."

The question of our determination in this case is whether there is some ground of difference that rationally explains the different treatment accorded married and unmarried persons under Massachusetts General Laws Ann., c. 272, §§ 21 and 21A. For the reasons that follow, we conclude that no such ground exists.

First. Section 21 stems from Mass. Stat. 1879, c. 159, § 1, which prohibited, without exception, distribution of articles intended to be used as contraceptives. In *Commonwealth* v. *Allison*, 227 Mass. 57, 62, 116 N. E. 265, 266 (1917), the Massachusetts Supreme Judicial Court explained that the law's "plain purpose is to protect purity, to preserve chastity, to encourage continence and self restraint, to defend the sanctity of the home, and thus to engender in the State and nation a virile and virtuous race of men and women." Although the State clearly abandoned that purpose with the enactment of § 21A, at least insofar as the illicit sexual activities of married persons are concerned, see n. 3, *supra*, the court reiterated in *Sturgis* v. *Attorney General, supra*, that the object of the legislation is to discourage premarital sexual intercourse. Conceding that the State could, consistently with the Equal Protection Clause, regard the problems of extramarital and premarital sexual relations as "[e]vils . . . of different dimensions and proportions, requiring different remedies," *Williamson* v. *Lee Optical Co.*, 348 U. S. 483, 489 (1955), we cannot agree that the deterrence of premarital sex may reasonably be regarded as the purpose of the Massachusetts law.

It would be plainly unreasonable to assume that Massachusetts has prescribed pregnancy and the birth of an unwanted child as punishment for fornication, which is a misdemeanor under Massachusetts General Laws Ann., c. 272, § 18. Aside from the scheme of values that assumption would attribute to the State, it is abundantly clear that the effect of the ban on distribution of contraceptives to unmarried persons has at best a marginal relation to the proffered objective. What Mr. Justice Goldberg said in *Griswold* v. *Connecticut, supra*, at 498 (concurring opinion), concerning the effect of Connecticut's prohibition on the use of contraceptives in discouraging extramarital sexual relations, is equally applicable here. "The rationality of this justification is dubious, particularly in light of the admitted widespread availability to all persons in the State of Connecticut, unmarried as well as married, of birth-control devices for the prevention of disease, as distinguished from the prevention of conception." See also *id.*, at 505–507 (WHITE, J., concurring in judgment). Like Connecticut's laws, §§ 21 and 21A do not at all regulate the distribution of contraceptives when they are to be used to prevent, not pregnancy, but the spread of disease. *Commonwealth* v. *Corbett*, 307 Mass. 7, 29 N. E. 2d 151 (1940), cited with approval in *Commonwealth* v. *Baird*, 355 Mass., at 754, 247 N. E. 2d, at 579. Nor, in making contraceptives available to married persons without regard to their intended use, does Massachusetts attempt to deter married persons from engaging in illicit sexual relations with unmarried persons. Even on the assumption that the fear of pregnancy operates as a deterrent to fornication, the Massachusetts statute is thus so riddled with exceptions that deterrence of premarital sex cannot reasonably be regarded as its aim.

Moreover, §§ 21 and 21A on their face have a dubious relation to the State's criminal prohibition on fornication. As the Court of Appeals explained, "Fornication is a misdemeanor [in Massachusetts], entailing a thirty dollar fine, or three months in jail. Massachusetts General Laws Ann. c. 272 § 18. Violation of the present statute is a felony, punishable by five years in prison. We find it hard to believe that the legislature adopted a statute carrying a five-year penalty for its possible, obviously by no means fully effective, deterrence of the commission of a ninety-day misdemeanor." 429 F. 2d, at 1401. Even conceding the legislature a full measure of discretion in fashioning means to prevent fornication, and recognizing that the State may seek to deter prohibited conduct by punishing more severely those who facilitate than those who actually engage in its commission, we, like the Court of Appeals, cannot believe that in this instance Massachusetts has chosen to expose the aider and abetter who simply *gives away* a contraceptive to *20* times the *90-day* sentence of the offender himself. The very terms of the State's criminal statutes, coupled with the *de minimis* effect of §§ 21 and 21A in deterring fornication, thus compel the conclusion that such deterrence cannot reasonably be taken as the purpose of the ban on distribution of contraceptives to unmarried persons.

Second. Section 21A was added to the Massachusetts General Laws by Stat. 1966, c. 265, § 1. The Supreme Judicial Court in *Commonwealth* v. *Baird, supra*, held that the purpose of the amendment was to serve the health needs of the community by regulating the distribution of potentially harmful articles. It is plain that Massachusetts had no such purpose in mind before the enactment of § 21A. As the Court of Appeals remarked, "Consistent with the fact that the statute was contained in a chapter dealing with 'Crimes Against Chastity, Morality, Decency and Good Order,' it was cast only in terms of morals. A physician was forbidden to prescribe contraceptives even when needed for the protection of health. Commonwealth v. Gardner, 1938, 300 Mass. 372, 15 N. E. 2d 222." 429 F. 2d, at 1401. Nor did the Court of Appeals "believe that the legislature [in enacting § 21A] suddenly reversed its field and developed an interest in health. Rather, it merely made what it thought to be the precise accommodation necessary to escape the *Griswold* ruling." *Ibid.*

Again, we must agree with the Court of Appeals. If health were the rationale of § 21A, the statute would be both discriminatory and overbroad. Dissenting in *Commonwealth* v. *Baird*, 355 Mass., at 758, 247 N. E. 2d, at 581, Justices Whittemore and Cutter stated that they saw "in § 21 and § 21A, read together, no public health purpose. If there is need to have a physician prescribe (and a pharmacist dispense) contraceptives, that need is as great for unmarried persons as for married persons." The Court of Appeals added: "If the prohibition [on distribution to unmarried persons] . . . is to be taken to mean that the same physician who can prescribe for married patients does not have sufficient skill to protect the health of patients who lack a marriage certificate, or who may be currently divorced, it is illogical to the point of irrationality." 429 F. 2d, at 1401.[8] Furthermore, we must join the Court of Appeals in noting that not all contraceptives are potentially dangerous. As a result, if the Massachusetts statue were a health measure, it would not only invidiously discriminate against the unmarried, but also be overbroad with respect to the married, a fact that the Supreme Judicial Court itself seems to have conceded in *Sturgis* v. *Attorney General*, 358 Mass., at ___, 260 N. E. 2d, at 690, where it noted that "it may well be that certain contraceptive medication and devices constitute no hazard to health, in which event it could be argued that the statute swept too broadly in its prohibition." "In this posture," as the Court of Appeals concluded, "it is impossible to think of the statute as intended as a health measure for the unmarried, and it is almost as difficult to think of it as so intended even as to the married." 429 F. 2d, at 1401.

But if further proof that the Massachusetts statute is not a health measure is necessary, the argument of Justice Spiegel, who also dissented in *Commonwealth* v. *Baird*, 355 Mass., at 759, 247 N. E. 2d, at 582, is conclusive: "It is at best a strained conception to say that the Legislature intended to prevent the distribution of articles 'which may have undesirable, if not dangerous, physical consequences.' If that was the Legislature's goal, § 21 is not required" in view of the federal and state laws *already* regulating the distribution of harmful drugs. See Federal Food, Drug, and Cosmetic Act, § 503, 52 Stat. 1051, as amended, 21 U. S. C. § 353; Mass. Gen. Laws Ann., c. 94, § 187A, as amended. We conclude, accordingly, that, despite the statute's superficial earmarks as a health measure, health, on the face of the statute, may no more reasonably be regarded as its purpose than the deterrence of premarital sexual relations.

Third. If the Massachusetts statute cannot be upheld as a deterrent to fornication or as a health measure, may it, nevertheless, be sustained simply as a prohibition on contraception? The Court of Appeals analysis "led inevitably to the conclusion that, so far as morals are concerned, it is contraceptives per se that are considered immoral—to the extent that *Griswold* will permit such a declaration." 429 F. 2d, at 1401–1402. The Court of Appeals went on to hold, *id*., at 1402:

> "To say that contraceptives are immoral as such, and are to be forbidden to unmarried persons who will nevertheless persist in having intercourse, means that such persons must risk for themselves an unwanted pregnancy, for the child, illegitimacy, and for society, a possible obligation of support. Such a view of morality is not only the very mirror image of sensible legislation; we consider that it conflicts with fundamental human rights. In the absence of demonstrated harm, we hold it is beyond the competency of the state."

[8]Appellant insists that the unmarried have no right to engage in sexual intercourse and hence no health interest in contraception that needs to be served. The short answer to this contention is that the same devices the distribution of which the State purports to regulate when their asserted purpose is to forestall pregnancy are available without any controls whatsoever so long as their asserted purpose is to prevent the spread of disease. It is inconceivable that the need for health controls varies with the purpose for which the contraceptive is to be used when the physical act in all cases is one and the same.

We need not and do not, however, decide that important question in this case because, whatever the rights of the individual to access to contraceptives may be, the rights must be the same for the unmarried and the married alike.

If under *Griswold* the distribution of contraceptives to married persons cannot be prohibited, a ban on distribution to unmarried persons would be equally impermissable. It is true that in *Griswold* the right of privacy in question inhered in the marital relationship. Yet the marital couple is not an independent entity with a mind and heart of its own, but an association of two individuals each with a separate intellectual and emotional makeup. If the right of privacy means anything, it is the right of the *individual*, married or single, to be free from unwarranted governmental intrusion into matters so fundamentally affecting a person as the decision whether to bear or beget a child.* * *

On the other hand, if *Griswold* is no bar to a prohibition on the distribution of contraceptives, the State could not, consistently with the Equal Protection Clause, outlaw distribution to unmarried but not to married persons. In each case the evil, as perceived by the State, would be identical, and the underinclusion would be invidious. Mr. Justice Jackson, concurring in *Railway Express Agency* v. *New York*, 336 U. S. 106, 112–113 (1949), made the point:

> "The framers of the Constitution knew, and we should not forget today, that there is no more effective practical guaranty against arbitrary and unreasonable government than to require that the principles of law which officials would impose upon a minority must be imposed generally. Conversely, nothing opens the door to arbitrary action so effectively as to allow those officials to pick and choose only a few to whom they will apply legislation and thus to escape the political retribution that might be visited upon them if larger numbers were affected. Courts can take no better measure to assure that laws will be just than to require that laws be equal in operation."

Although Mr. Justice Jackson's comments had reference to administrative regulations, the principle he affirmed has equal application to the legislation here. We hold that by providing dissimilar treatment for married and unmarried persons who are similarly situated, Massachusetts General Laws Ann., c. 272, §§ 21 and 21A, violate the Equal Protection Clause. The judgment of the Court of Appeals is

Affirmed

---

b. *Antiabortion Statutes*

Until 1973 many states had statutes that made abortion a crime unless the mother's life was in danger. Such laws usually impose criminal penalties for anyone who performs or aids in an abortion. Other state statutes provided for a complicated procedure for approval of abortions that effectively prevented their performance. Antiabortion statutes have been adopted for many reasons. Based on religious, moral or "scientific" reasons, many people believe that "life" begins at conception and that abortion constitutes a destruction of that life. Others have argued that a fetus is a "person" entitled to the protections of the Fourteenth Amendment. Others have supported antiabortion laws as a regulation intended to protect pregnant women from the dangers of a dangerous operation by unskillful and unscrupulous medical practitioners. Still others support antiabortion laws as an expression of disapproval of a morality that encourages premarital and extramarital sexual relations.

In *Roe v. Wade*, set forth below, the United States Supreme Court faced up to what it characterized as "the sensitive and emotional nature of the abortion controversy . . . and the seemingly absolute convictions that the subject inspires" and set down the principles for determining the validity of state antiabortion statutes. In the years that followed, several state legislatures sought to adopt abortion regulation statutes that would comply with these principles. In New Jersey, the state legislature adopted a statute that required doctors to tell women of the psychological and physical dangers of abortion and to explain alternatives. It also required women to sign a written consent form which doctors would be required to keep for one year. It also required all abortions after 12 weeks of pregnancy to be performed in a hospital. The parents of minor girls would have to be notified before an abortion was performed and doctors who violated these provisions would be subject to criminal penalties of up to six months in jail. Governor Brendan Byrne vetoed the bill and the state legislature was unable to muster enough votes to override the governor's veto.

In other states abortion regulation statutes were adopted and their validity challenged. In *Doe v. Bolton*, the United States Supreme Court examined the validity of a statute that imposed restrictions on facilities used to perform abortions. In *Planned Parenthood v. Danforth* the statute in question gave husbands of pregnant women a veto over a decision to have an abortion. In *Colautti v. Franklin* the court examined the complex question of "fetal viability," i.e., when a fetus can survive outside the women's body. In *Bellotti v. Baird* the court defined the circumstances when a state statute may require a pregnant minor to obtain parental consent to an abortion.

During this period, Representative Henry J. Hyde, Republican from Illionois, succeeded in attaching the following rider to the 1976 federal budget: "None of the funds provided for in this paragraph shall be used to perform abortions except where the life of the mother would be endangered if the fetus were carried to term; or except for such medical procedures necessary for the victims of rape or incest, where such rape or incest has been reported promptly to a law enforcement agency or public health service." The validity of this provision, known as the Hyde Amendment, was challenged on the grounds that it (1) violated the constitutional prohibition against the establishment of religion, (2) violated the equal protection rights of poor women who need abortions and (3) violated the due process rights of indigent women. These arguments were evaluated by the United States Supreme Court in *Harris v. McRae*. At stake in this decision were Medicaid funds that had been used to finance the cost of from 250,000 to 300,000 abortions each year.

ROE v. WADE

410 U.S. 113 (1973)

Mr. Justice BLACKMUN delivered the opinion of the Court.

This Texas federal appeal and its Georgia companion, Doe v. Bolton, *post*, ___ U.S. ___, 93 S.Ct. 739, 34 L.Ed.2d ___, present constitutional challenges to state criminal abortion legislation. The Texas statutes under attack here are typical of those that have been in effect in many States for approximately a century.* * *

We forthwith acknowledge our awareness of the sensitive and emotional nature of the abortion controversy, of the vigorous opposing views, even among physicians, and of the deep and seemingly absolute convictions that the subject inspires. One's philosophy, one's experiences, one's exposure to the raw edges of human existence, one' religious training, one's attitudes toward life and family and their values, and the moral standards one establishes and seeks to observe, are all likely to influence and to color one's thinking and conclusions about abortion.

In addition, population growth, pollution, poverty, and racial overtones tend to complicate and not to simplify the problem.

Our task, of course, is to resolve the issue by constitutional measurement free of emotion and of predilection. We seek earnestly to do this, and, because we do, we have inquired into, and in this opinion place some emphasis upon, medical and medical-legal history and what that history reveals about man's attitudes toward the abortive procedure over the centuries. We bear in mind, too, Mr. Justice Holme's admonition in his now vindicated dissent in Lochner v. New York, 198 U.S. 45, 76, 25 S.Ct. 539, 547, 49 L.Ed. 937 (1905):

> "It [the Constitution] is made for people of fundamentally differing views, and the accident of our finding certain opinions natural and familiar, or novel, and even shocking, ought not to conclude our judgment upon the question whether statutes embodying them conflict with the Constitution of the United States."* * *

The Texas statutes that concern us here are Arts. 1191–1194 and 1196 of the State's Penal Code,[1] Vernon's Ann.P.C. These make it a crime to "procure an abortion," as therein defined, or to attempt one, except with respect to "an abortion procured or attempted by medical advice for the purpose of saving the life of the mother." Similar statutes are in existence in a majority of the States.

[1]"Article 1191. Abortion.

"If any person shall designedly administer to a pregnant woman or knowingly procure to be administered with her consent any drug or medicine, or shall use towards her any violence or means whatever externally or internally applied, and thereby procure an abortion, he shall be confined in the penitentiary not less than two nor more than five years; if it be done without her consent, the punishment shall be doubled. By 'abortion' is meant that the life of the fetus or embryo shall be destroyed in the woman's womb or that a premature birth thereof be caused.

"Art. 1192. Furnishing the means

Texas first enacted a criminal abortion statute in 1854. Texas Laws 1854, c. 49, § 1, set forth in 3 Gammel, Laws of Texas, 1502 (1898). This was soon modified into language that has remained substantially unchanged to the present time. See Texas Penal Code of 1857, Arts. 531–536; Paschal's Laws of Texas, Arts. 2192–2197 (1866); Texas Rev.Stat., Arts. 536–541 (1879); Texas Rev.Crim.Stat., Arts. 1071–1076 (1911). The final article in each of these compilations provided the same exception, as does the present Article 1196, for an abortion by "medical advice for the purpose of saving the life of the mother."

* * *

Jane Roe, a single woman who was residing in Dallas County, Texas, instituted this federal action in March 1970 against the District Attorney of the county. She sought a declaratory judgment that the Texas criminal abortion statutes were unconstitutional on their face, and an injunction restraining the defendant from enforcing the statutes.

Roe alleged that she was unmarried and pregnant; that she wished to terminate her pregnancy by an abortion "performed by a competent, licensed physician, under safe, clinical conditions"; that she was unable to get a "legal" abortion in Texas because her life did not appear to be threatened by the continuation of her pregnancy; and that she could not afford to travel to another jurisdiction in order to secure a legal abortion under safe conditions. She claimed that the Texas statutes were unconstitutionally vague and that they abridged her right of personal privacy, protected by the First, Fourth, Fifth, Ninth, and Fourteenth Amendments. By an amendment to her complaint Roe purported to sue "on behalf of herself and all other women" similarly situated.

James Hubert Hallford, a licensed physician, sought and was granted leave to intervene in Roe's action. In his complaint he alleged that he had been arrested previously for violations of the Texas abortion statutes and that two such prosecutions were pending against him. He described conditions of patients who came to him seeking abortions, and he claimed that for many cases he, as a physician, was unable to determine whether they fell within or outside the exception recognized by Article 1196. He alleged that, as a consequence, the statutes were vague and uncertain, in violation of the Fourteenth Amendment, and that they violated his own and his patients' rights to privacy in the doctor-patient relationship and his own right to practice medicine, rights he claimed were guaranteed by the First, Fourth, Fifth, Ninth, and Fourteenth Amendments.

"Whoever furnishes the means for procuring an abortion knowing the purpose intended is guilty as an accomplice.

"Art. 1193. Attempt at abortion

"If the means used shall fail to produce an abortion, the offender is nevertheless guilty of an attempt to produce abortion, provided it be shown that such means were calculated to produce that result, and shall be fined not less than one hundred nor more than one thousand dollars.

"Art. 1194. Murder in producing abortion

"If the death of the mother is occasioned by an abortion so produced or by an attempt to effect the same it is murder.

"Art. 1196. By medical advice

"Nothing in this chapter applies to an abortion procured or attempted by medical advice for the purpose of saving the life of the mother."

The foregoing Articles, together with Art. 1195, comprise Chapter 9 of Title 15 of the Penal Code. Article 1195, not attacked here, reads:

"Art. 1195. Destroying unborn child

"Whoever shall during parturition of the mother destroy the vitality of life in a child in a state of being born and before actual birth, which child would otherwise have been born alive, shall be confined in the penitentiary for life or for not less than five years."

John and Mary Doe, a married couple, filed a companion complaint to that of Roe. They also named the District Attorney as defendant, claimed like constitutional deprivations, and sought declaratory and injunctive relief.* * *

The two actions were consolidated and heard together by a duly convened three-judge district court. The suits thus presented the situations of the pregnant single woman, the childless couple, with the wife not pregnant, and the licensed practicing physician, all joining in the attack on the Texas criminal abortion statutes. Upon the filing of affidavits, motions were made to dismiss and for summary judgment. The court held that Roe and Dr. Hallford, and members of their respective classes, had standing to sue, and presented justiciable controversies, but that the Does had failed to allege facts sufficient to state a present controversy and did not have standing. It concluded that, with respect to the requests for a declaratory judgment, abstention was not warranted. On the merits, the District Court held that the "fundamental right of single women and married persons to choose whether to have children is protected by the Ninth Amendment, through the Fourteenth Amendment," and that the Texas criminal abortion statutes were void on their face because they were both unconstitutionally vague and constituted an overbroad infringement of the plaintiffs' Ninth Amendment rights. The court then held that abstention was warranted with respect to the requests for an injunction. It therefore dismissed the Doe complaint, declared the abortion statutes void, and dismissed the application for injunctive relief. 314 F.Supp.1217 (N.D.Tex.1970).

The plaintiffs Roe and Doe and the intervenor Hallford, pursuant to 28 U.S.C. § 1253, have appealed to this Court from that part of the District Court's judgment denying the injunction. The defendant District Attorney has purported to cross appeal, pursuant to the same statute, from the court's grant of declaratory relief to Roe and Hallford.

* * *

We are next confronted with issues of justiciability, standing, and abstention. Have Roe and the Does established that "personal stake in the outcome of the controversy," Baker v. Carr, 369 U.S. 186, 204, 82 S.Ct. 691, 703, 7 L.Ed.2d 663 (1962), that insures that "the dispute sought to be adjudicated will be presented in an adversary context and in a form historically viewed as capable of judicial resolution," Flast v. Cohen, 392 U.S. 83, 101, 88 S.Ct. 1942, 1953, 20 L.Ed.2d 947 (1968), and Sierra Club v. Morton, 405 U.S. 727, 732, 92 S.Ct. 1361, 1364, 31 L.Ed.2d 636 (1972)? And what effect did the pendency of criminal abortion charges against Dr. Hallford in state court have upon the propriety of the federal court's granting relief to him as a plaintiff-intervenor?

A. *Jane Roe*. Despite the use of the pseudonym, no suggestion is made that Roe is a fictitious person. For purposes of her case, we accept as true, and as established, her existence; her pregnant state, as of the inception of her suit in March 1970 and as late as May 21 of that year when she filed an alias affidavit with the District Court; and her inability to obtain a legal abortion in Texas.

Viewing Roe's case as of the time of its filing and thereafter until as late as May, there can be little dispute that it then presented a case or controversy and that, wholly apart from the class aspects, she, as a pregnant single woman thwarted by the Texas criminal abortion laws, had standing to challenge those statutes. * * *

The usual rule in federal cases is that an actual controversy must exist at stages of appellate or certiorari review, and not simply at the date the action is initiated. * * *

But when, as here, pregnancy is a significant fact in the litigation, the normal 266-day human gestation period is so short that the pregnancy will come to term before the usual appellate process is complete. If that termination makes a case moot, pregnancy litigation seldom will survive much beyond the trial stage, and appellate review will be effectively denied. Our law should not be that rigid. Pregnancy often comes more than once to the same woman, and in the general population, if man is to survive, it will always be with us. Pregnancy provides a classic justification for a conclusion of nonmootness. It truly could be "capable of repetition, yet evading review."* * *

We therefore agree with the District Court that Jane Roe had standing to undertake this litigation, that she presented a justiciable controversy, and that the termination of her 1970 pregnancy has not rendered her case moot.

B. *Dr. Hallford.* The doctor's position is different. He entered Roe's litigation as a plaintiff-intervenor.* * *

Dr. Hallford is therefore in the position of seeking, in a federal court, declaratory and injunctive relief with respect to the same statutes under which he stands charged in criminal prosecutions simultaneously pending in state court.* * *
We see no merit in that distinction.

* * *

Dr. Hallford's complaint in intervention, therefore, is to be dismissed. He is remitted to his defenses in the state criminal proceedings against him. We reverse the judgment of the District Court insofar as it granted Dr. Hallford relief and failed to dismiss his complaint in intervention.

C. *The Does.* In view of our ruling as to Roe's standing in her case, the issue of the Does' standing in their case has little significance. The claims they assert are essentially the same as those of Roe, and they attack the same statutes. Nevertheless, we briefly note the Does' posture.* * *

Their claim is that sometime, in the future, Mrs. Doe might become pregnant because of possible failure of contraceptive measures, and at that time in the future, she might want an abortion that might then be illegal under the Texas statutes.

This very phrasing of the Does' position reveals it speculative character. Their alleged injury rests on possible future contraceptive failure, possible future pregnancy, possible future unpreparedness for parenthood, and possible future impairment of health. Any one or more of these several possibilities may not take place and all may not combine. In the Does' estimation, these possibilities might have some real or imagined impact upon their marital happiness. But we are not prepared to say the the bare allegation of so indirect an injury is sufficient to present an actual case or controversy.* * *

The Does therefore are not appropriate plaintiffs in this litigation. Their complaint was properly dismissed by the District Court, and we affirm that dismissal.* * *

The principal thrust of appellant's attack on the Texas statutes is that they improperly invade a right, said to be possessed by the pregnant woman, to choose to terminate her pregnancy. Appellant would discover this right in the concept of personal "liberty" embodied in the Fourteenth Amendment's Due Process Clause; or in personal, marital, familial, and sexual privacy said to be protected by the Bill of Rights or its penumbras, see Griswold v. Connecticut, 381 U.S. 479, 85 S.Ct. 1678, 14 L.Ed.2d 510 (1965); Eisenstadt v. Baird, 405 U.S. 438 (1972); *id.*, at 460, 92 S.Ct. 1029, at 1042, 31 L.Ed.2d 349 (White, J., concurring); or among those rights reserved to the people by the Ninth Amendment, Griswold v. Connecticut, 381 U.S., at 486, 85 S.Ct., at 1682 (Goldberg, J., concurring). Before addressing this claim, we feel it desirable briefly to survey, in several aspects, the history of abortion, for such insight as that history may afford us, and then to examine the state purposes and interests behind the criminal abortion laws.

It perhaps is not generally appreciated that the restrictive criminal abortion laws in effect in a majority of States today are of relatively recent vintage. Those laws, generally proscribing abortion or its attempt at any time during pregnancy except when necessary to preserve the pregnant woman's life, are not of ancient or even of common law origin. Instead, they derive from statutory changes effected, for the most part, in the latter half of the 19th century.

1. *Ancient attitudes*. These are not capable of precise determination. We are told that at the time of the Persian Empire abortifacients were known and that criminal abortions were severely punished.We are also told, however, that abortion was practiced in Greek times as well as in the Roman Era, and that "it was resorted to without scruple." The Ephesian, Soranos, often described as the greatest of the ancient gynecologists, appears to have been generally opposed to Rome's prevailing free-abortion practices. He found it necessary to think first of the life of the mother, and he resorted to abortion when, upon this standard, he felt the procedure advisable. Greek and Roman law afforded little protection to the unborn. If abortion was prosecuted in some places, it seems to have been based on a concept of a violation of the father's right to his offspring. Ancient religion did not bar abortion.

2. *The Hippocratic Oath*.* * *

The Oath varies somewhat according to the particular translation, but in any translation the content is clear: "I will give no deadly medicine to anyone if asked, nor suggest any such counsel; and in like manner I will not give to a woman a pessary to produce abortion," or "I will neither give a deadly drug to anybody if asked for it, nor will I make a suggestion to this effect. Similarly, I will not give to a woman an abortive remedy.

Although the Oath is not mentioned in any of the principal briefs in this case or in Doe v. Bolton, *post*, ___ U.S. ___, 93 S.Ct. 739, 34 L.Ed.2d ___, it represents the apex of the development of strict ethical concepts in medicine, and its influence endures to this day.* * *

3. *The Common Law*. It is undisputed that at the common law, abortion performed *before* "quickening"—the first recognizable movement of the fetus *in utero*, appearing usually from the 16th to the 18th week of pregnancy was not an indictable offense. The absence of a common law crime for prequickening abortion appears to have developed from a confluence of earlier philosophical, theological, and civil and canon law concepts of when life begins. These disciplines variously approached the question in terms of the point at which the embryo or fetus became "formed" or recognizably human, or in terms of when a "person" came into being, that is, infused with a "soul" or "animated."* * *

Whether abortion of a *quick* fetus was a felony at common law, or even a lesser crime, is still disputed. Bracton, writing early in the 13th century, thought it homicide. But the later and predominant view, following the great common law scholars, has been that it was at most a lesser offense. In a frequently cited passage, Coke took the position that abortion of a woman "quick with childe" is "a great misprision no murder." Blackstone followed, saying that while abortion after quickening had once been considered manslaughter (though not murder), "modern law" took a less severe view. A recent review of the common law precedents argues, however, that those precedents contradict Coke and that even postquickening abortion was never established as a common law crime. This is of some importance because while most American courts ruled, in holding or dictum, that abortion of an unquickened fetus was not criminal under their received common law, others followed Coke in stating that abortion of a quick fetus was a "misprision," a term they translated to mean "misdemeanor." That their reliance on Coke on this aspect of the law was uncritical and, apparently in all the reported cases, dictum (due probably to the paucity of common law prosecutions for post-quickening abortion), makes it now appear doubtful that abortion was ever firmly established as a common law crime even with respect to the destruction of a quick fetus.

4. *The English statutory law*. England's first criminal abortion statute, Lord Ellenborough's Act, 43 Geo. 3, c. 58, came in 1803. It made abortion of a quick fetus, § 1, a capital crime, but in § 2 it provided lesser penalties for the felony of abortion before quickening, and thus preserved the quickening distinction.* * *

Recently Parliament enacted a new abortion law. This is the Abortion Act of 1967,

15 & 16 Eliz. 2, c. 87. The Act permits a licensed physician to perform an abortion where two other licensed physicians agree (a) "that the continuance of the pregnancy would involve risk to the life of the pregnant woman, or of injury to the physical or mental health of the pregnant woman or any existing children of her family, greater than if the pregnancy were terminated," or (b) "that there is a substantial risk that if the child were born it would suffer from such physical or mental abnormalities as to be seriously handicapped." The Act also provides that, in making this determination, "account may be taken of the pregnant woman's actual or reasonably foreseeable environment." It also permits a physician, without the concurrence of others, to terminate a pregnancy where he is of the good faith opinion that the abortion "is immediately necessary to save the life or to prevent grave permanent injury to the physical or mental health of the pregnant woman."

5. *The American law.* In this country the law in effect in all but a few States until mid-19th century was the pre-existing English common law. Connecticut, the first State to enact abortion legislation, adopted in 1821 that part of Lord Ellenborough's Act that related to a woman "quick with child." The death penalty was not imposed. Abortion before quickening was made a crime in the State only in 1860. In 1828 New York enacted legislation that, in two respects, was to serve as a model for early anti-abortion statutes. First, while barring destruction of an unquickened fetus as well as a quick fetus, it made the former only a misdemeanor, but the latter second-degree manslaughter. Second, it incorporated a concept of therapeutic abortion by providing that an abortion was excused if it "shall have been necessary to preserve the life of such mother, or shall have been advised by two physicians to be necessary for such purpose."* * *

It was not until after the War between the States that legislation began generally to replace the common law. Most of these initial statutes dealt severely with abortion after quickening but were lenient with it before quickening.* * *

Gradually, in the middle and late 19th century the quickening distinction disappeared from the statutory law of most States and the degree of the offense and the penalties were increased. By the end of the 1950's a large majority of the States banned abortion, however and whenever performed, unless done to save or preserve the life of the mother. The exceptions, Alabama and the District of Columbia, permitted abortion to preserve the mother's health. Three other States permitted abortions that were not "unlawfully" performed or that were not "without lawful justification," leaving interpretation of those standards to the courts. In the past several years, however, a trend toward liberalization of abortion statutes has resulted in adoption, by about one-third of the States, of less stringent laws, most of them patterned after the ALI Model Penal Code* * *

It is thus apparent that at common law, at the time of the adoption of our Constitution, and throughout the major portion of the 19th century, abortion was viewed with less disfavor than under most American statutes currently in effect. Phrasing it another way, a woman enjoyed a substantially broader right to terminate a pregnancy than she does in most States today. At least with respect to the early stage of pregnancy, and very possibly without such a limitation, the opportunity to make this choice was present in this country well into the 19th century. Even later, the law continued for some time to treat less punitively an abortion procured in early pregnancy.

6. *The position of the American Medical Association.* The anti-abortion mood prevalent in this country in the late 19th century was shared by the medical profession. Indeed, the attitude of the profession may have played a significant role in the enactment of stringent criminal abortion legislation during that period.* * *

In 1970, after the introduction of a variety of proposed resolutions, and of a report from its Boards of Trustees, a reference committee noted "polarization of the medical profession on this controversial issue"* * *

7. *The position of the American Public Health Association.* In October 1970, the Executive Board of the APHA adopted Standards for Abortion Services. These were five in number:

"a. Rapid and simple abortion referral must be readily available through state and local public health departments, medical societies, or other non-profit organizations.* * *

8. *The position of the American Bar Association.* At its meeting in February 1972 the ABA House of Delegates approved, with 17 opposing votes, the Uniform Abortion Act* * *

Three reasons have been advanced to explain historically the enactment of criminal abortion laws in the 19th century and to justify their continued existence.

It has been argued occasionally that these laws were the product of a Victorian social concern to discourage illicit sexual conduct. Texas, however, does not advance this justification in the present case, and it appears that no court or commentator has taken the argument seriously.* * *

A second reason is concerned with abortion as a medical procedure. When most criminal abortion laws were first enacted, the procedure was a hazardous one for the woman.* * *

Modern medical techniques have altered this situation.* * *

The third reason is the State's interest—some phrase it in terms of duty—in protecting prenatal life. Some of the argument for this justification rests on the theory that a new human life is present from the moment of conception. The State's interest and general obligation to protect life then extends, it is argued, to prenatal life. Only when the life of the pregnant mother herself is at stake, balance against the life she carries within her, should the interest of the embryo or fetus not prevail. Logically, of course, a legitimate state interest in this area need not stand or fall on acceptance of the belief that life begins at conception or at some other point prior to live birth. In assessing the State's interest, recognition may be given to the less rigid claim that as long as at least *potential* life is involved, the State may assert interests beyond the protection of the pregnant woman alone.

Parties challenging state abortion laws have sharply disputed in some courts the contention that a purpose of these laws, when enacted, was to protect prenatal life. Pointing to the absence of legislative history to support the contention, they claim that most state laws were designed solely to protect the woman. Because medical advances have lessened this concern, at least with respect to abortion in early pregnancy, they argue that with respect to such abortions the laws can no longer be justified by any state interest. There is some scholarly support for this view of original purpose. The few state courts called upon to interpret their laws in the late 19th and early 20th centuries did focus on the State's interest in protecting the woman's health rather than in preserving the embryo and fetus. Proponents of this view point out that in many States, including Texas, by statute or judicial interpretation, the pregnant woman herself could not be prosecuted for self-abortion or for cooperating in an abortion performed upon her by another. They claim that adoption of the "quickening" distinction through received common law and state statutes tacitly recognizes the greater health hazards inherent in late abortion and impliedly repudiates the theory that life begins at conception.

It is with these interests, and the weight to be attached to them, that this case is concerned.

The Constitution does not explicitly mention any right of privacy. In a line of decisions, however, going back perhaps as far as Union Pacific R. Co. v. Botsford, 141 U.S. 250, 251, 11 S.Ct. 1000, 1001, 35 L.Ed. 734 (1891), the Court has recognized that a right of personal privacy, or a guarantee of certain areas or zones of privacy, does exist under the Constitution. In varying contexts the Court or individual

Justices have indeed found at least the roots of that right in the First Amendment, Stanley v. Georgia, 394 U.S. 557, 564, 89 S.Ct. 1243, 1247, 22 L.Ed.2d 542 (1969); in the Fourth and Fifth Amendments; * * * in the Ninth Amendment, *id.*, at 486, 85 S.Ct. at 1862 (Goldberg, J., concurring); or in the concept of liberty guaranteed by the first section of the Fourteenth Amendment, see Meyer v. Nebraska, 262, U.S. 390, 399, 43 S.Ct. 625, 626, 67 L.Ed. 1042 (1923). These decisions make it clear that only personal rights that can be deemed "fundamental" or "implicit in the concept of ordered liberty," Palko v. Connecticut, 302 U.S. 319, 325, 58 S.Ct. 149, 152, 82 L.Ed. 288 (1937), are included in this guarantee of personal privacy. They also make it clear that the right has some extension to activities relating to marriage, Loving v. Virginia, 388 U.S. 1, 12, 87, S.Ct. 1817, 1823, 18 L.Ed.2d 1010 (1967), procreation, Skinner v. Oklahoma, 316 U.S. 535, 541–542, 62 S.Ct. 1110, 1113–114, 86 L.Ed. 1655 (1942), contraception, Eisenstadt v. Baird, 405 U.S. 438, 453–454, 92 S.Ct. 1029, 1038–1039, 31 L.Ed.2d 349 (1972); *id.*, at 460, 463–465, 92 S.Ct. at 1042, 1043–1044 (White, J., concurring), family relationships, Prince v. Massachusetts, 321 U.S. 158, 166, 64 S.Ct. 438, 442, 88 L.Ed. 645 (1944), and child rearing and education* * *

This right of privacy, whether it be founded in the Fourteenth Amendment's concept of personal liberty and restrictions upon state action, as we feel it is, or, as the District Court determined, in the Ninth Amendment's reservation of rights to the people, is broad enough to encompass a woman's decision whether or not to terminate her pregnancy. The detriment that the State would impose upon the pregnant woman by denying this choice altogether is apparent. Specific and direct harm medically diagnosable even in early pregnancy may be involved. Maternity, or additional offspring, may force upon the woman a distressful life and future. Psychological harm may be imminent. Mental and physical health may be taxed by child care. There is also the distress, for all concerned, associated with the unwanted child, and there is the problem of bringing a child into a family already unable, psychologically and otherwise, to care for it. In other cases, as in this one, the additional difficulties and continuing stigma of unwed motherhood may be involved. All these are factors the woman and her responsible physician necessarily will consider in consultation.

On the basis of elements such as these, appellants and some *amici* argue that the woman's right is absolute and that she is entitled to terminate her pregnancy at whatever time, in whatever way, and for whatever reason she alone chooses. With this we do not agree. Appellants' arguments that Texas either has no valid interest at all in regulating the abortion decision, or no interest strong enough to support any limitation upon the woman's sole determination, is unpersuasive. The Court's decisions recognizing a right of privacy also acknowledge that some state regulation in areas protected by that right is appropriate. As noted above, a state may properly assert important interests in safeguarding health, in maintaining medical standards, and in protecting potential life. At some point in pregnancy, these respective interests become sufficiently compelling to sustain regulation of the factors that govern the abortion decision. The privacy right involved, therefore, cannot be said to be absolute. In fact, it is not clear to us that the claim asserted by some *amici* that one has an unlimited right to do with one's body as one pleases bears a close relationship to the right of privacy previously articulated in the Court's decisions. The Court has refused to recognize an unlimited right of this kind in the past. Jacobsen v. Massachusetts, 197 U.S. 11, 25 S.Ct. 358, 49 L.Ed. 643 (1905) (vaccination); Buck v. Bell, 274 U.S. 200, 47 S.Ct. 584, 71 L.Ed. 1000 (1927) (sterilization).

We therefore conclude that the right of personal privacy includes the abortion decision, but that this right is not unqualified and must be considered against important state interests in regulation.

We note that those federal and state courts that have recently considered abortion law challenges have reached the same conclusion. * * * Most of these courts have agreed that the right of privacy, however based, is broad enough to cover the abortion decision; that the right, nonetheless, is not absolute and is subject to some limitations; and that at some point the state interests as to protection of health, medical standards, and prenatal life, become dominant. We agree with this approach.* * *

The appellee and certain *amici* argue that the fetus is a "person" within the language and meaning of the Fourteenth Amendment. In support of this they outline at length and in detail the well-known facts of fetal development. If this suggestion of personhood is established, the appellant's case, of course, collapses, for the fetus' right to life is then guaranteed specifically by the Amendment. The appellant conceded as much on reargument. On the other hand, the appellee conceded on reargument that no case could be cited that holds that a fetus is a person within the meaning of the Fourteenth Amendment.

The Constitution does not define "person" in so many words. Section 1 of the Fourteenth Amendment contains three references to "person." The first, in defining "citizens," speaks of "persons born or naturalized in the United States." The word also appears both in the Due Process Clause and in the Equal Protection Clause. "Person" is used in other places in the Constitution* * *

But in nearly all these instances, the use of the word is such that it has application only post-natally. None indicates, with any assurance, that it has any possible pre-natal application.

All this, together with our observation, *supra*, that throughout the major portion of the 19th century prevailing legal abortion practices were far freer than they are today, persuades us that the word "person," as used in the Fourteenth Amendment, does not include the unborn. This is in accord with the results reached in those few cases where the issue has been squarely presented. McGarvey v. Magee-Womens Hospital, 340 F.Supp. 751 (W.D.Pa.1972); Byrn v. New York City Health & Hospitals Corp., 31 N.Y.2d 194, 335 N.Y.S.2d 390, 286 N.E.2d 887 (1972), appeal pending; Abele v. Markle, ____ F.Supp. ____ (D.C.Conn.1972), appeal pending.* * *

This conclusion, however, does not of itself fully answer the contentions raised by Texas, and we pass on to other considerations.

The pregnant woman cannot be isolated in her privacy. She carries an embryo and, later, a fetus, if one accepts the medical definitions of the developing young in the human uterus. See Dorland's Illustrated Medical Dictionary, 478–479, 547 (24th ed. 1965). The situtation therefore is inherently different from marital intimacy, or bedroom possession of obscene material, or marriage or procreation, or education, with which *Eisenstadt, Griswold, Stanley, Loving, Skinner, Pierce,* and *Meyer* were respectively concerned. As we have intimated above, it is reasonable and appropriate for a State to decide that at some point in time another interest, that of health of the mother or that of potential human life, becomes significantly involved. The woman's privacy is no longer sole and any right of privacy she possesses must be measured accordingly.

Texas urges that, apart from the Fourteenth Amendment, life begins at conception and is present throughout pregnancy, and that, therefore, the State has a compelling interest in protecting that life from and after conception. We need not resolve the difficult question of when life begins. When those trained in the respective disciplines of medicine, philosophy, and theology are unable to arrive at any consensus, the judiciary, at this point in the development of man's knowledge, is not in a position to speculate as to the answer.* * *

Physicians and their scientific colleagues have regarded that event with less interest and have tended to focus either upon conception or upon live birth or upon the interim point at which the fetus becomes "viable," that is, potentially able to live outside the mother's womb, albeit with artificial aid. Viability is usually placed at about seven months (28 weeks) but may occur earlier, even at 24 weeks.* * *

We do not agree that, by adopting one theory of life, Texas may override the rights of the pregnant woman that are at stake. We repeat, however, that the State does have an important and legitimate interest in preserving and protecting the health of the pregnant woman, whether she be a resident of the State or a nonresident who seeks medical consultation and treatment there, and that it has still *another* important and legitimate interest in protecting the potentiality of human life. These interests are separate and distinct. Each grows in substantiality as the woman approaches term and, at a point during pregnancy, each becomes "compelling."

With respect to the State's important and legitimate interest in the health of the mother, the "compelling" point, in the light of present medical knowledge, is at approximately the end of the first trimester. This is so because of the now established medical fact, referred to above at p. 724, that until the end of the first trimester mortality in abortion is less than mortality in normal childbirth. It follows that, from and after this point, a State may regulate the abortion procedure to the extent that the regulation reasonably relates to the preservation and protection of maternal health. Examples of permissible state regulation in this area are requirements as to the qualifications of the person who is to perform the abortion; as to the licensure of that person; as to the facility in which the procedure is to be performed, that is, whether it must be a hospital or may be a clinic or some other place of less-than-hospital status; as to the licensing of the facility; and the like.

This means, on the other hand, that, for the period of pregnancy prior to this "compelling" point, the attending physician, in consultation with his patient, is free to determine, without regulation by the State, that in his medical judgment the patient's pregnancy should be terminated. If that decision is reached, the judgment may be effectuated by an abortion free of interference by the State.

With respect to the State's important and legitimate interest in potential life, the "compelling" point is at viability. This is so because the fetus then presumably has the capability of meaningful life outside the mother's womb. State regulation protective of fetal life after viability thus has both logical and biological justifications. If the State is interested in protecting fetal life after viability, it may go so far as to proscribe abortion during that period except when it is necessary to preserve the life or health of the mother.

Measured against these standards, Art. 1196 of the Texas Penal Code, in restricting legal abortions to those "procured or attempted by medical advice for the purpose of saving the life of the mother," sweeps too broadly. The statute makes no distinction between abortions performed early in pregnancy and those performed later, and it limits to a single reason, "saving" the mother's life, the legal justification for the procedure. The state, therefore, cannot survive the constitutional attack made upon it here.

This conclusion makes it unnecessary for us to consider the additional challenge to the Texas statute asserted on grounds of vagueness.* * *

To summarize and to repeat:

1. A state criminal abortion statute of the current Texas type, that excepts from criminality only a *life saving* procedure on behalf of the mother, without regard to pregnancy stage and without recognition of the other interests involved, is violative of the Due Process Clause of the Fourteenth Amendment.

(a) For the stage prior to approximately the end of the first trimester, the abortion decision and its effectuation must be left to the medical judgment of the pregnant woman's attending physician.

(b) For the stage subsequent to approximately the end of the first trimester, the

State, in promoting its interest in the health of the mother, may, if it chooses, regulate the abortion procedure in ways that are reasonably related to maternal health.

(c) For the stage subsequent to viability the State, in promoting its interest in the potentiality of human life, may, if it chooses, regulate, and even proscribe, abortion except where it is necessary, in appropriate medical judgment, for the preservation of the life or health of the mother.

2. The State may define the term "physician," as it has been employed in the preceding numbered paragraphs of this Part XI of this opinion, to mean only a physician currently licensed by the State, and may proscribe any abortion by a person who is not a physician as so defined.* * *

Our conclusion that Art. 1196 is unconstitutional means, of course, that the Texas abortion statutes, as a unit, must fall. The exception of Art. 1196 cannot be stricken separately, for then the State is left with a statute proscribing all abortion procedures no matter how medically urgent the case.

Although the District Court granted plaintiff Roe declaratory relief, it stopped short of issuing an injunction against enforcement of the Texas statutes. The Court has recognized that different considerations enter into a federal court's decision as to declaratory relief, on the one hand, and injunctive relief, on the other. Zwickler v. Koota, 389 U.S. 241, 252–255, 88 S.Ct. 391, 397–399, 19 L.Ed.2d 444 (1967); Dombrowski v. Pfister, 380 U.S. 479, 85 S. Ct. 1116, 14 L.Ed.2d 22 (1965). We are not dealing with a statute that, on its face, appears to abridge free expression, an area of particular concern under *Dombrowski* and refined in Younger v. Harris, 401 U.S., at 50, 91 S.Ct., at 753.

We find it unnecessary to decide whether the District Court erred in withholding injunctive relief, for we assume the Texas prosecutorial authorities will give full credence to this decision that the present criminal abortion statutes of that State are unconstitutional.

The judgment of the District Court as to intervenor Hallford is reversed, and Dr. Hallford's complaint in intervention is dismissed. In all other respects the judgment of the District Court is affirmed. Costs are allowed to the appellee.

It is so ordered.

Affirmed in part and reversed in part.

Mr. Justice REHNQUIST, dissenting.

PLANNED PARENTHOOD OF CENTRAL MISSOURI
v.
DANFORTH

428 U.S. 52 (1976)

Mr. Justice BLACKMUN delivered the opinion of the Court.

This case is a logical and anticipated corollary to Roe v. Wade, 410 U.S. 113 (1973), and Doe v. Bolton, 410 U.S. 179 (1973), for it raises issues secondary to those that were then before the Court. Indeed, some of the questions now presented were forecast and reserved in *Roe* and *Doe*. 410 U.S., at 165 n. 67.

I

After the decisions in *Roe* and *Doe*, this Court remanded for reconsideration a pending Missouri federal case in which the State's then existing abortion legislation, Mo.Rev.Stat. §§ 559.100, 542.380, and 563.300 (1969), was under constitutional challenge. Rodgers v. Danforth, 410 U.S. 949 (1973). A three-judge federal court for the Western District of Missouri, in an unreported decision, thereafter declared the challenged Missouri statutes unconstitutional and granted injunctive relief. On appeal here, that judgment was summarily affirmed. Danforth v. Rodgers, 414 U.S. 1035 (1973).

In June 1974, somewhat more than a year after *Roe* and *Doe* had been decided, Missouri's 77th General Assembly, in its Second Regular Session, enacted House Committee Substitute for House Bill no. 1211 (hereinafter referred to as the "Act"). The legislation was approved by the Governor on June 14, 1974, and became effective immediately by reason of an emergency clause contained in § A of the statute. The Act is set forth in full as the Appendix to this opinion. [Omitted.] It imposes a structure for the control and regulation of abortions in Missouri during all stages of pregnancy.

II

Three days after the Act became effective, the present litigation was instituted in the United States District Court for the Eastern District of Missouri. The plaintiffs are Planned Parenthood of Central Missouri, a not-for-profit Missouri corporation which maintains facilities in Columbia, Mo., for the performance of abortions; David Hall, M. D.; and Michael Freiman, M. D.* * *

The named defendants are the Attorney General of Missouri and the Circuit Attorney of the city of St. Louis "in his representative capacity" and "as the representative of the class of all similar Prosecuting Attorneys of the various counties of the State of Missouri." Complaint 10.

The plaintiffs brought the action on their own behalf and, purportedly, "on behalf of the entire class consisting of duly licensed physicians and surgeons presently performing or desiring to perform the termination of pregnancies and on behalf of the entire class consisting of their patients desiring the termination of pregnancy, all within the State of Missouri." Id., at 9. Plaintiffs sought declaratory relief and also sought to enjoin enforcement of the Act* * *

* * *

The case was presented to a three-judge District Court convened pursuant to the provisions of 28 U.S.C.A. §§ 2281 and 2284. 392 F.Supp. 1362 (1975).

* * *

On the issues as to the constitutionality of the several challenged sections of the Act, the District Court, largely by a divided vote, ruled that all except the first sentence of § 6(1) withstood the attack. That sentence was held to be constitutionally impermissible because it imposed upon the physician the duty to exercise at all stages of pregnancy "that degree of professional skill, care and diligence to preserve the life and health of the fetus" that "would be required * * * to preserve the life and health of any fetus intended to be born." Inasmuch as this failed to exclude the stage of pregnancy prior to viability, the provision was "unconstitutionally overbroad." Id., at 1371.

* * *

For convenience, we shall usually refer to the plaintiffs as "appellants" and to both named defendants as "appellees."

III

In Roe v. Wade the Court concluded that the "right of privacy, whether it be founded in the Fourteenth Amendment's concept of personal liberty and rstrictions upon state action, as we feel it is, or, as the District Court determined, in the Ninth Amendment's reservation of rights to the people, is broad enough to encompass a woman's decision whether or not to terminate her pregnancy." 410 U.S., at 153. It emphatically rejected, however, the proffered argument "that the woman's right is absolute and that she is entitled to terminate her pregnancy at whatever time, in whatever way, and for whatever reason she alone chooses." Ibid. Instead, this right "must be considered against important state interests in regulation." Id., at 154.

The Court went on to say that the "pregnant woman cannot be isolated in her privacy," for she "carries an embryo and, later, a fetus." Id., at 159. It was therefore "reasonable and appropriate for a State to decide that at some point in time another interest, that of health of the mother or that of potential human life, becomes significantly involved. The woman's privacy is no longer sole and any right of privacy she possess must be measured accordingly." Ibid. The Court stressed the measure of the State's interest in "the light of present medical knowledge." Id., at 163. It concluded that the permissibility of state regulation was to be viewed in three stages: "For the stage prior to approximately the end of the first trimester, the abortion decision and its effectuation must be left to the medical judgment of the pregnant woman's attending physician," without interference from the State. Id., at 164. The participation by the attending physician in the abortion decision, and his responsibility in that decision, thus, were emphasized. After the first stage, as so described, the State may, if it chooses, reasonably regulate the abortion procedure to preserve and protect maternal health. Ibid. Finally, for the stage subsequent to viability, a point purposefully left flexible for professional determination, and dependent upon developing medical skill and technical ability,[1] the State may regulate an abortion to protect the life of the fetus and even may proscribe abortion except where it is necessary, in appropriate medical judgment, for the preservation of the life or health of the mother. Id., at 163–165.

IV

* * *

Our primary task, then, is to consider each of the challenged provisions of the new Missouri abortion statute in the particular light of the opinions and decisions in *Roe*

[1] "Viability is usually placed at about seven months (28 weeks) but may occur earlier, even at 24 weeks." Roe v. Wade, 410 U.S. 113, 160 (1973).

and in *Doe*. To this we now turn, with the assistance of helpful briefs from both sides and from some of the *amici*.

A

The definition of viability. Section 2 (2) of the Act defines "viability" as "that stage of fetal development when the life of the unborn child may be continued indefinitely outside the womb by natural or artificial life-supportive systems." Appellants claim that this definition violates and conflicts with the discussion of viability in our opinion in *Roe*. 410 U.S., at 160, 163. In particular, appellants object to the failure of the definition to contain any reference to a gestational time period, to its failure of the definition to contain any reference to a gestational time period, to its failure to incorporate and reflect the three stages of pregnancy, to the presence of the word "indefinitely," and to the extra burden of regulation imposed. It is suggested that the definition expands the Court's definition of viability, as expressed in *Roe*, and amounts to a legislative determination of what is properly a matter for medical judgment. It is said that the "mere possibility of momentary survival is not the medical standard of viability." Brief for Appellants 67.

In *Roe*, we used the term "viable," properly we thought, to signify the point at which the fetus is "potentially able to live outside the mother's womb, albeit with artificial aid," and presumably capable of "meaningful life outside the mother's womb," 410 U.S., at 160, 163. We noted that this point "is usually placed" at about seven months or 28 weeks, but may occur earlier. Id., at 160.

We agree with the District Court and conclude that the definition of viability in the Act does not conflict with what was said and held in *Roe*. In fact, we believe that § 2(c), even when read in conjunction with § 5 (proscribing an abortion "not necessary to preserve the life or health of the mother * * * unless the attending physician first certifies with reasonable medical certainty that the fetus is not viable"), the constitutionality of which is not explicitly challenged here, reflects an attempt on the part of the Missouri General Assembly to comply with our observations and discussion in *Roe* relating to viability. Appellant Hall, in his deposition, had no particular difficulty with the statutory definition. As noted above, we recognized in *Roe* that viability was a matter of medical judgment, skill, and technical ability, and we preserved the flexibility of the term. Section 2(2) does the same. Indeed, one might argue, as the appellees do, that the presence of the statute's words "continued indefinitely" favor, rather than disfavor, the appellants, for, arguably, the point when life can be "continued indefinitely outside the womb" may well occur later in pregnancy than the point where the fetus is "potentially able to live outside the mother's womb." Roe v. Wade, 410 U.S., at 160.

In any event, we agree with the District Court that it is not the proper function of the legislature or the courts to place viability, which essentially is a medical concept, at a specific point in the gestation period. The time when viability is achieved may vary with each pregnancy, and the determination of whether a particular fetus is viable is, and must be, a matter for the judgment of the responsible attending physician. The definition of viability in § 2(2) merely reflects this fact. The appellees do not contend otherwise, for they insist that the determination of viability rests with the physician in the exercise of his professional judgment.[4]

[4]"The determination of when the fetus is viable rests, as it should, with the physician, in the exercise of his medical judgment, on a case-by-case basis." Brief for Appellees, 26. "Because viability may vary from patient to patient and with advancements in medical technology, it is essential that physicians make the determination in the exercise of their medical judgment." Id., at 28. "Defendant agrees that 'viability' will vary, that it is a difficult state to assess . . . and that it must be left to the physician's judgment." Id., at 29.

We thus do not accept appellants' contention that a specified number of weeks in pregnancy must be fixed by statute as the point of viability. See Wolfe v. Schroering, 388 F.Supp. 631, 637 (WD Ky.1974); Hodgson v. Anderson, 378 F.Supp. 1008, 1016 (Minn.1974) dism'd for want of jurisdiction sub nom. Spannaus v. Hodgson, 420 U.S. 903 (1975).[5]

We conclude that the definition in § 2 (2) of the Act does not circumvent the limitations on state regulation outlined in *Roe*. We therefore hold that the Act's definition of "viability" comports with *Roe* and withstands the constitutional attack made upon it in this litigation.

B

The woman's consent. Under § 3(2) of the Act, a woman, prior to submitting to an abortion during the first 12 weeks of pregnancy, must certify in writing her consent to the procedure and "that her consent is informed and freely given and is not the result of coercion." Appellants argue that this requirement is violative of Roe v. Wade, 410 U.S., at 164–165, by imposing an extra layer and burden of regulation on the abortion decision. See Doe v. Bolton, 410 U.S., at 195–200. Appellants also claim that the provision is overbroad and vague.

The District Court's majority relied on the propositions that the decision to terminate a pregnancy, of course, "is often a stressful one," and that the consent requirement of § 3(2) "insures that the pregnant woman retains control over the discretions of her consulting physician." 392 F.Supp., at 1368, 1369. The majority also felt that the consent requirement "does not single out the abortion procedure, but merely includes it within the category of medical operations for which consent is required."[6] Id., at 1369. The third judge joined the majority in upholding § 3(2), but added that the written consent requirement was "not burdensome or chilling" and manifested "a legitimate interest of the state that this important decision has in fact been made by the person constitutionally empowered to do so." 392 F.Supp., at 1374. He went on to observe that the requirement "in no way interposes the state or third parties in the decision-making process." Id., at 1375.

We do not disagree with the result reached by the District Court as to § 3 (2). It is true that *Doe* and *Roe* clearly establish that the State may not restrict the decision of the patient and her physician regarding abortion during the first stage of pregnancy. Despite the fact that apparently no other Missouri statute, with the exceptions referred to in n. 6, supra, requires a patient's prior written consent to a surgical procedure, the imposition by § 3(2) of such a requirement for termination of pregnancy even during the first stage, in our view, is not in itself an unconstitutional requirement. The decision to abort, indeed, is an important, and often a stressful one, and it is desirable and imperative that it be made with full knowledge of its nature and consequences. The woman is the one primarily concerned, and her awareness of the decision and its significance may be assured, constitutionally, by the State to the extent of requiring her prior written consent.

We could not say that a requirement imposed by the State that a prior written consent for any surgery would be unconstitutional. As a consequence, we see no constitutional defect in requiring it only for some types of surgery as, for example, an

[5]The Minnesota statute under attack in *Hodgson* provided that a fetus "shall be considered potentially 'viable' " during the second half of its gestation period. Noting that the defendants had presented no evidence of viability at 20 weeks, the three-judge district court held that that definition of viability was "unreasonable and cannot stand." 378 F.Supp., at 1016.

[6]Apparently, however, the only other Missouri statutes concerned with consent for general medical or surgical care relate to persons committed to the Missouri state chest hospital, Mo.Rev.Stat. § 199.240 (1969), or to mental or correctional institutions, id., § 105,700.

intracardiac procedure, or where the surgical risk is elevated above a specified mortality level, or, for that matter, for abortions.[8]

C

The spouse's consent. Section 3(3) requires the prior written consent ot the spouse of the women seeking an abortion during the first 12 weeks of pregnancy, unless "the abortion is certified by a licensed physician to be necessary in order to preserve the life of the mother."[9]

The appellees defend § 3(3) on the ground that it was enacted in the light of the General Assembly's "perception of marriage as an institution," Brief for Appellees 34, and that any major change in family status is a decision to be made jointly by the marriage partners. Reference is made to an abortion's possible effect on the woman's childbearing potential. It is said that marriage always has entailed some legislatively imposed limitations: reference is made to adultery and bigamy as criminal offenses; to Missouri's general requirement, Mo.Rev.Stat. § 453.030.3 (1969), that for an adoption of a child born in wedlock the consent of both parents is necessary; to similar joint consent requirements imposed by a number of States with respect to artificial insemination and the legitimacy of children so conceived; to the laws of two States requiring spousal consent for voluntary sterilization; and to the long-established requirement of spousal consent for the effective disposition of an interest in real property. It is argued that "[r]ecognizing that the consent of both parties is generally necessary * * * to begin a family, the legislature has determined that a change in the family structure set in motion by mutual consent should be terminated only by mutual consent," Brief for Appellees 38, and that what the legislature did was to exercise its inherent policymaking power "for what was believed to be in the best interests of all people of Missouri." Id., at 40.

The appellants, on the other hand, contend that § 3(3) obviously is designed to afford the husband the right unilaterally to prevent or veto an abortion, whether or not he is the father of the fetus, and that this not only violates *Roe* and *Doe* but is also in conflict with other decided cases. See, e. g., Poe v. Gerstein, 517 F. 2d 787, 794–796 (CA5 1975), Juris. Statement pending. No. 75–713; Wolfe v. Schroering, 388 F.Supp., at 636–637; Doe v. Rampton, 366 F.Supp. 189, 193 (Utah 1973). They also refer to the situation where the husband's consent cannot be obtained because he cannot be located. And they assert that § 3 (3) is vague and overbroad.

In *Roe* and *Doe* we specifically reserved decision on the question whether a requirement for consent by the father of the fetus, by the spouse, or by the parents, or a parent, of an unmarried minor, may be constitutionally imposed. 410 U.S., at 165 n. 67. We now hold that the State may not constitutionally require the consent of the spouse, as is specified under § 3(3) of the Missouri Act, as a condition for abortion during the first 12 weeks of pregnancy. We thus agree with the dissenting judge in the present case, and with the courts whose decisions are cited above, that the State cannot "delegate to a spouse a veto power which the state itself is absolutely

[8]The appellants' vagueness argument centers on the word "informed." One might well wonder, offhand, just what "informed consent" of a patient is. The three Missouri federal judges who comprised the three-judge District Court, however, were not concerned, and we are content to accept, as the meaning, the giving of information to the patient as to just what would be done and as to its consequences. To ascribe more meaning than this might well confine the attending physician in an undesired and uncomfortable straitjacket in the practice of his profession.

[9]It is of some interest to note that the condition does not relate, as most statutory conditions in this area do, to the preservation of the life or *health* of the mother.

and totally prohibited from exercising during the first trimester or pregnancy." 392 F.Supp. at 1375. Clearly, since the State cannot regulate or proscribe abortion during the first stage, when the physician and his patient make that decision, the State cannot delegate authority to any particular person, even the spouse, to prevent abortion during that same period.

We are not unaware of the deep and proper concern and interest that a devoted and protective husband has in his wife's pregnancy and in the growth and development of the fetus she is carrying. Neither has this Court failed to appreciate the importance of the marital relationship in our society. See e. g., Griswold v. Connecticut, 381 U.S. 479, 486 (1965); Maynard v. Hill, 125 U.S. 190, 211 (1888). Moreover, we recognize that the decision whether to undergo or to forego an abortion may have profound effects on the future of any marriage, effects that are both physical and mental, and possibly deleterious. Notwithstanding these factors, we cannot hold that the State has the constitutional authority to give the spouse unilaterally the ability to prohibit the wife from terminating her pregnancy, when the State itself lacks that right. See Eisenstadt v. Baird, 405 U.S. 438, 453 (1972).[11]

It seems manifest that, ideally, the decision to terminate a pregnancy should be one concurred in by both the wife and her husband. No marriage may be viewed as harmonious or successful if the marriage partners are fundamentally divided on so important and vital an issue. But it is difficult to believe that the goal of fostering mutuality and trust in a marriage, and of strengthening the marital relationship and the marriage institution, will be achieved by giving the husband a veto power exercisable for any reason whatsoever or for no reason at all. Even if the State had the ability to delegate to the husband a power it itself could not exercise, it is not at all likely that such action would further, as the District Court majority phrased it, the "interest of the state in protecting the mutuality of decisions vital to the marriage relationship." 392 F.Supp., at 1370.

We recognize, of course, that when a woman, with the approval of her physician but without the approval of her husband, decides to terminate her pregnancy, it could be said that she is acting unilaterally. The obvious fact is that when the wife and the husband disagree on this decision, the view of only one of the two marriage partners can prevail. Since it is the woman who physically bears the child and who is the more directly and immediately affected by the pregnancy, as between the two, the balance weighs in her favor. Cf. Roe v. Wade, 410 U. S., at 153.

[11]As the Court recognized in Eisenstadt Baird, "the marital couple is not an independent entity with a mind and heart of its own, but an association of two individuals each with a separate intellectual and emotional makeup. If the right of privacy means anything, it is the right of the *individual*, married or single, to be free from unwarranted governmental intrusion into matters so fundamentally affecting a person as the decision whether to bear or beget a child." 405 U. S., at 453 (emphasis in original).

The dissenting opinion of our Brother WHITE appears to overlook the implications of this statement upon the issue whether § 3(3) is constitutional. This section does much more than insure that the husband participate in the decision whether his wife should have an abortion. The State, instead, has determined that the husband's interest in continuing the pregnancy of his wife always outweighs any interest on her part in terminating it irrespective of the condition of their marriage. The State, accordingly, has granted him the right to prevent unilaterally, and for whatever reason, the effectuation of his wife's and her physician's decision to terminate her pregnancy. This state determination not only may discourage the consultation that might normally be expected to precede a major decision affecting the marital couple but also, and more importantly, the State has interposed an absolute obstacle to a woman's decision that *Roe* held to be constitutionally protected from such interference.

We conclude that §3(3) of the Missouri Act is inconsistent with the standards enunciated in Roe v. Wade, 410 U.S. at 164–165, and is unconstitutional. It is therefore unnecessary for us to consider the appellant's additional challenges to § 3(3) based on vagueness and overbreadth.

D

Parental Consent. Section 3(4) requires, with respect to the first 12 weeks of pregnancy, where the woman is unmarried and under the age of 18 years, the written consent of a parent or person *in loco parentis* unless, again, "the abortion is certified by a licensed physician as necessary in order to preserve the life of the mother." It is to be observed that only one parent need consent.

The appellees defend the statute in several ways. They point out that the law properly may subject minors to more stringent limitations than are permissible with respect to adults, and they cite, among other cases, Prince v. Massachusetts, 321 U.S. 158 (1944), and McKeiver v. Pennsylvania, 403 U.S. 528 (1971). Missouri law, it is said, "is replete with provisions reflecting the interest of the state in assuring the welfare of minors," citing statutes relating to a guardian *ad litem* for a court proceeding, to the care of delinquent and neglected children, to child labor, and to compulsory education. Brief for Appellees 42. Certain decisions are considered by the State to be outside the scope of a minor's ability to act in his own best interest or in the interest of the public, citing statutes proscribing the sale of firearms and deadly weapons to minors without parental consent, and other statutes relating to minors' exposure to certain types of literature, the purchase by pawnbrokers of property from minors, and the sale of cigarettes and alcoholic beverages to minors. It is pointed out that the record contains testimony to the effect that children of tender years (even ages 10 and 11) have sought abortions. Thus, a State's permitting a child to obtain an abortion without the counsel of an adult "who has responsibility or concern for the child would constitute an irresponsible abdication of the State's duty to protect the welfare of minors." Id., at 44. Parental discretion, too, has been protected from unwarranted or unreasonable interference from the State, citing Meyer v. Nebraska, 262 U.S. 390 (1923); Pierce v. Society of Sisters, 268 U.S. 510 (1925); Wisconsin v. Yoder, 406 U.S. 205 (1972). Finally, it is said that § 3(4) imposes no additional burden on the physician because even prior to the passage of the Act the physician would require parental consent before performing an abortion on a minor.

The appellants, in their turn, emphasize that no other Missouri statute specifically requires the additional consent of a minor's parent for medical or surgical treatment, and that in Missouri a minor legally may consent to medical services for pregnancy (excluding abortion), venereal disease, and drug abuse. Mo. Laws 1971, pp. 425–426, H.B. No. 73, §§ 1–3. The result of § 3(4), it is said, "is the ultimate supremacy of the parents' desires over those of the minor child, the pregnant patient." Brief for Appellants 93. It is noted that in Missouri a woman who marries with parental consent under the age of 18 does not require parental consent to abort, and yet her contemporary who has chosen not to marry must obtain parental approval.

The District Court majority recognized that, in contrast to § 3(3), the State's interest in protecting the mutuality of a marriage relationship is not present with respect to § 3(4). It found "a compelling basis," however, in the State's interest "in safeguarding the authority of the family relationship." 392 F.Supp., at 1370. The dissenting judge observed that one could not seriously argue that a minor must submit to an abortion if her parents insist, and he could not see "why she would not be entitled to the same right of self-determination now explicitly accorded to adult women, provided she is sufficiently mature to understand the procedure and to make an intelligent assessment of her circumstances with the advice of her physician." Id., at 1376.

Of course, much of what has been said above, with respect to § 3(3), applies with equal force to § 3(4). Other courts, that have considered the parental consent issue in the light of *Roe* and *Doe*, have concluded that a statute like § 3(4) does not withstand constitutional scrutiny. See, e. g., Poe v. Gerstein, 517 F.2d, at 792; Wolfe v. Schroering, 388 F.Supp., at 636–637; Doe v. Rampton, 366 F.Supp., at 192, 199; State v. Koome, 84 Wash.2d 901, 530 P.2d 260 (1975).

We agree with appellants and with the courts whose decisions have just been cited that the State may not impose a blanket provision, such as § 3(4), requiring the consent of a parent or person *in loco parentis* as a condition for abortion of an unmarried minor during the first 12 weeks of her pregnancy. Just as with the requirement of consent from the spouse, so here, the State does not have the constitutional authority to give a third party an absolute, and possibly arbitrary, veto over the decision of the physician and his patient to terminate the patient's pregnancy, regardless of the reason for withholding the consent.

Constitutional rights do not mature and come into being magically only when one attains the state-defined age of majority. Minors, as well as adults, are protected by the Constitution and possess constitutional rights. See, e. g., Breed v. Jones, 421 U.S. 519 (1975); Goss v. Lopez, 419 U.S. 565 (1975); Tinker v. Des Moines School District, 393 U.S. 503 (1969); In re Gault, 387 U.S. 1 (1967). The Court indeed, however, long has recognized that the State has somewhat broader authority to regulate the activities of children than of adults. Prince v. Massachusetts, 321 U.S., at 170; Ginsberg v. New York, 390 U.S. 629 (1968). It remains, then, to examine whether there is any significant state interest in conditioning an abortion on the consent of a parent or person *in loco parentis* that is not present in the case of an adult.

One suggested interest is the safe-guarding of the family unit and of parental authority. 392 F.Supp., at 1370. It is difficult, however, to conclude that providing a parent with absolute power to overrule a determination, made by the physician and his minor patient, to terminate the patient's pregnancy will serve to strengthen the family unit. Neither is it likely that such veto power will enhance parental authority or control where the minor and the nonconsenting parent are so fundamentally in conflict and the very existence of the pregnancy already has fractured the family structure. Any independent interest the parent may have in the termination of the minor daughter's pregnancy is no more weighty than the right of privacy of the competent minor mature enough to have become pregnant.

We emphasize that our holding that § 3(4) is invalid does not suggest that every minor, regardless of age or maturity, may give effective consent for termination of her pregnancy. See Bellotti v. Baird, post. The fault with § 3(4) is that it imposes a special consent provision, exercisable by a person other than the woman and her physician, as a prerequisite to a minor's termination of her pregnancy and does so without a sufficient justification for the restriction. It violates the strictures of *Roe* and *Doe*.

E

Saline amniocentesis. Section 9 of the statute prohibits the use of saline amniocentesis, as a method or technique of abortion, after the first 12 weeks of pregnancy. It describes the method as one whereby the amniotic fluid is withdrawn and "a saline or other fluid" is inserted into the amniotic sac. The statute imposes this proscription on the ground that the technique "is deleterious to maternal health," and places it in the form of a legislative finding. Appellants challenge this provision on the ground that it operates to preclude virtually all abortions after the first trimester. This is so, it is claimed, because a substantial percentage, in the neighborhood of 70% according to the testimony, of all abortions performed in the United States after the first trimester are effected through the procedure of saline amniocentesis. Appellants stress the fact that the alternative methods of hysterotomy and hysterectomy are significantly more dangerous and critical for the woman than the saline technique; they also point out that the mortality rate for normal childbirth exceeds that where saline amniocentesis is employed. Finally, appellants note that the perhaps safer alternative of prostaglandin installation, suggested and strongly relied upon by the appellees, at least at the time of the trial, is not yet widely used in this country.

We held in *Roe* that after the first stage, "the State in promoting its interest in the health of the mother, may, if it chooses, regulate the abortion procedure in ways that are reasonably related to maternal health." 410 U.S., at 164. The question with respect to § 9 therefore is whether the flat prohibition of saline amniocentesis is a restriction which "reasonably relates to the preservation and protection of maternal health." Id., at 163. The appellees urged that what the Missouri General Assembly has done here is consistent with that guideline and is buttressed by substantial supporting medical evidence in the record to which this Court should defer.

The District Court's majority determined, on the basis of the evidence before it, that the maternal mortality rate in childbirth does, indeed, exceed the mortality rate where saline amniocentesis is used. Therefore, the majority acknowledged, § 9 could be upheld only if there were safe alternative methods of inducing abortion after the first 12 weeks. 392 F.Supp. at 1373. Referring to such methods as hysterotomy, hysterectomy, "mechanical means of inducing abortion," and prostaglandin injection, the majority said that at least the latter two techniques were safer than saline. Consequently, the majority concluded, the restriction in § 9 could be upheld as reasonably related to maternal health.

We feel that the majority, in reaching its conclusion, failed to appreciate and to consider several significant facts. First, it did not recognize the prevalence, as the record conclusively demonstrates, of the use of saline amniocentesis as an accepted medical procedure in this country; the procedure, as noted above, is employed in a substantial majority (the testimony from both sides ranges from 68% to 80%) of all post-first trimester abortions. Second, it failed to recognize that at the time of trial, there were severe limitations on the availability of the prostaglandin technique, which, although promising, was used only on an experimental basis until less than two years before. See Wolfe v. Schroering, 388 F.Supp., at 637, where it was said that at that time (1974), "there are no physicians in Kentucky competent in the technique of prostaglandin amnio infusion." And the State offered no evidence that prostaglandin abortions were available in Missouri.[12] Third, the statute's reference to the

[12]In response to Mr. Justice WHITE'S criticism that the prostaglandin method of inducing abortion was available in Missouri, either at the time the Act was passed or at the time of trial, we make the following observations. First, there is no evidence in the record to which our Brother has pointed that demonstrates that the prostaglandin method was or is available in Missouri. Second, the evidence presented to the District Court does not support such a view. Until January 1974 prostaglandin was used only on an experimental basis in a few medical centers. And, at the time the Missouri General Assembly proscribed saline, the sole distributor of prostaglandin "restricted sales to around twenty medical centers from coast to coast." Brief for Appellee Danforth 68.

It is clear, therefore, that at the time the Missouri General Assembly passed the Act, prostaglandin was not available, in any meaningful sense of that term. Because of this undisputed fact, it was incumbent upon the State to show that at the time of trial in 1974 prostaglandin was available. It failed to do so. Indeed, the State's expert witness, on whose testimony the dissenting opinion relies, does not fill this void. He was able to state only that prostaglandin was used in a limited way until shortly before trial and that he "would think" that it was more readily available at the time of trial. R. 335. Such an experimental and limited use of prostaglandin throughout the country does not make it available or accessible to concerned persons in Missouri.

insertion of "a saline or other fluid" appears to include within its proscription the intra-amniotic injection of prostaglandin itself and other methods that may be developed in the future and that may prove highly effective and completely safe. Finally, the majority did not consider the anomaly inherent in § 9 when it proscribes the use of saline but does not prohibit techniques that are many times more likely to result in maternal death. See 392 F.Supp., at 1378 n. 8 (dissenting opinion).

These unappreciated or overlooked factors place the State's decision to bar use of the saline method in a completely different light. The State, through § 9, would prohibit the use of a method which the record shows is the one most commonly used nationally by physicians after the first trimester and which is safer, with respect to maternal mortality, than even continuation of the pregnancy until normal childbirth. Moreover, as a practical matter, it forces a woman and her physician to terminate her pregnancy by methods more dangerous to her health than the method outlawed.

As so viewed, particularly in the light of the present unavailability—as demonstrated by the record—of the prostaglandin technique, the outright legislative proscription of saline fails as a reasonable regulation for the protection of maternal health. It comes into focus, instead, as an unreasonable or arbitrary regulation designed to inhibit, and having the effect of inhibiting, the vast majority of abortions after the first 12 weeks. As such it does not withstand constitutional challenge. See Wolfe v. Schroering, 388 F.Supp., at 637.

Recordkeeping. Sections 10 and 11 of the Act impose recordkeeping requirements for health facilities and physicians concerned with abortions irrespective of the pregnancy stage. Under § 10, each such facility and physician is to be supplied with forms "the purpose and function of which shall be the preservation of maternal health and life by adding to the sum of medical knowledge through the compilation of relevant maternal health and life data and to monitor all abortions performed to assure that they are done only under and in accordance with the provisions of the law." The statute states that the information on the forms "shall be confidential and shall be used only for statistical purposes." The "records, however, may be inspected and health data acquired by local, state, or national public health officers." Under § 11 the records are to be kept for seven years in the permanent files of the health facility where the abortion was performed.

Appellants object to these reporting and recordkeeping provisions on the ground that they, too, impose an extra layer and burden of regulation, and that they apply throughout all stages of pregnancy. All the judges of the District Court panel, however, viewed these provisions as statistical requirements "essential to the advancement of medical knowledge," and as nothing that would "restrict either the abortion decision itself or the exercise of medical judgment in performing an abortion." 392 F.Supp., at 1374.

One may concede that there are important and perhaps conflicting interests affected by recordkeeping requirements. On the one hand, maintenance of records indeed may be helpful in developing information pertinent to the preservation of maternal health. On the other hand, as we stated in *Roe*, during the first stage of pregnancy the State may impose no restrictions or regulations governing the medical judgment of the pregnant woman's attending physician with respect to the termination of her pregnancy. 410 U.S., at 163, 164. Furthermore, it is readily apparent that one reason for the recordkeeping requirement, namely, to assure that all abortions in Missouri are performed in accordance with the Act, fades somewhat into insignificance in view of our holding above as to spousal and parental consent requirements.

Recordkeeping and reporting requirements that are reasonably directed to the preservation of maternal health and that properly respect a patient's confidentiality and privacy are permissible. This surely is so for the period after the first stage of pregnancy, for then the State may enact substantive as well as recordkeeping regulations that are reasonable means of protecting maternal health. As to the first stage, one may argue forcefully, as the appellants do, that the State should not be able to impose any recordkeeping requirements that significantly differ from those imposed with respect to other, and comparable, medical or surgical procedures. We conclude, however, that the provisions of §§ 10 and 11, while perhaps approaching permissible limits, are not constitutionally offensive in themselves. Recordkeeping of this kind, if not abused or overdone, can be useful to the State's interest in protecting the health of its female citizens, and may be a resource that is relevant to decisions involving medical experience and judgment. The added requirements for confidentiality, with the sole exception for public health officers, and for retention for seven years, a period not unreasonable in length, assist and persuade us in our determination of the constitutional limits. As so regarded, we see no legally significant impact or consequence on the abortion decision or on the physician-patient relationship. We naturally assume, furthermore, that these recordkeeping and record-maintaining provisions will be interpreted and enforced by Missouri's Division of Health in the light of our dicision with respect to the Act's other provisions, and that, of course, they will not be utilized in such a way as to accomplish, through the sheer burden of recordkeeping detail, what we have held to be an otherwise unconstitutional restriction. Obviously, the State may not require execution of spousal and parental consent forms that have been invalidated today.

G

Standard of care. Appellee Danforth in No. 74–1419 appeals from the unanimous decision of the District Court that § 6(1) of the Act is unconstitutional. That section provides:

> "No person who performs or induces an abortion shall fail to exercise that degree of professional skill, care and diligence to preserve the life and health of the fetus which such person would be required to exercise in order to preserve the life and health of any fetus intended to be born and not aborted. Any physician or person assisting in the abortion who shall fail to take such measures to encourage or to sustain the life of the child, and the death of the child results, shall be deemed guilty of manslaughter.* * * Further, such physician or other person shall be liable in an action for damages."

The District Court held that the first sentence was unconstitutionally overbroad because it failed to exclude from its reach the stage of pregnancy prior to viability. 392 F.Supp., at 1371.

The Attorney General argues that the District Court's interpretation is erroneous and unnecessary. He claims that the first sentence of § 6(1) establishes only the general standard of care that applies to the person who performs the abortion, and that the second sentence describes the circumstances when that standard of care applies, namely, when a live child results from the procedure. Thus, the first sentence, it is said, despite its reference to the fetus, has no application until a live birth results.

The appellants, of course, agree with the District Court. They take the position that § 6(1) imposes its standard of care upon the person performing the abortion even though the procedure takes place before viability. They argue that the statute on its face effectively precludes abortion and was meant to do just that.

We see nothing that requires federal court abstention on this issue. Wisconsin v. Constantineau, 400 U.S. 433, 437–439 (1971); Kusper v. Pontikes, 414 U.S. 51, 54–55 (1973). And, like the three judges of the District Court, we are unable to accept the appellee's sophisticated interpretation of the statute. Section 6 (1) requires the physician to exercise the prescribed skill, care, and diligence to preserve the life and health of the *fetus*. It does not specify that such care need be taken only after the stage of viability has been reached. As the provision now reads, it impermissibly requires the physician to preserve the life and health of the fetus, whatever the stage of pregnancy. The fact that the second sentence of § 6(1) refers to a criminal penalty where the physician fails "to take such measures to encourage or to sustain the life of the *child*, and the death of the *child* results" (emphasis supplied), simply does not modify the duty imposed by the previous sentence or limit that duty to pregnancies that have reached the stage of viability.

The appellees finally argue that if the first sentence of § 6(1) does not survive constitutional attack, the second sentence does, and, under the Act's severability provision, § B, is severable from the first. The District Court's ruling of unconstitutionality, 392 F.Supp., at 1371, made specific reference to the first sentence but its conclusion of law and its judgment invalidated all of § 6(1). Id., at 1374; Juris. Statement, No. 74–1419, A–34. Appellee Danforth's motion to alter or amend the judgment, so far as the second sentence of § 6(1) was concerned, was denied by the District Court. Id., at A–39.

We conclude, as did the District Court, that § 6(1) must stand or fall as a unit. Its provisions are inextricably bound together. And a physician's or other person's criminal failure to protect a liveborn infant surely will be subject to prosecution in Missouri under the State's criminal statutes.

The judgment of the District Court is affirmed in part and reversed in part and the case is remanded for further proceedings consistent with this opinion.

It is so ordered.

COLAUTTI
v.
FRANKLIN

439 U.S. 379 (1979)

Mr. Justice BLACKMUN delivered the opinion of the Court.

At issue here is the constitutionality of subsection (a) of § 5 of the Pennsylvania Abortion Control Act, 1974 Pa Laws, * * * This statute subjects a physician who performs an abortion to potential criminal liability if he fails to utilize a statutorily prescribed technique when the fetus "is viable" or when there is "sufficient reason to believe that the fetus may be viable." A three-judge Federal District Court declared § 5(a) unconstitutionally vague and overbroad and enjoined its enforcement. App 239a–244a. Pursuant to 28 USC § 1253 [28 USCS § 1253], we noted probable jurisdiction sub nom. Beal v. Franklin.

* * *

The Abortion Control Act was passed by the Pennsylvania Legislature, over the Governor's veto, in the year following this Court's decisions in Roe v Wade,* * *

Section 1 gave the Act its title. Section 2 defined, among other terms, "informed consent" and "viable." The latter was specified to mean "the capability of a fetus to live outside the mother's womb albeit with artificial aid." See Roe v Wade, 410 US, at 160, 35 L Ed 2d 147, 93 S Ct 705.

Section 3(a) proscribed the performance of an abortion "upon any person in the absence of informed consent thereto by such person." Section 3(b)(i) prohibited the performance of an abortion in the absence of the written consent of the woman's spouse, provided that the spouse could be located and notified, and the abortion was not certified by a licensed physician "to be necessary in order to preserve the life or health of the mother." Section 3(b)(ii), applicable if the woman was unmarried and under the age of 18, forbade the performance of an abortion in the absence of the written consent of "one parent or person in loco parentis" of the woman, unless the abortion was certified by a licensed physician "as necessary in order to preserve the life of the mother." Section 3(e) provided that whoever performed an abortion without such consent was guilty of a misdemeanor of the first degree.

Section 4 provided that whoever, intentionally and willfully, took the life of a premature infant aborted alive, was guilty of murder of the second degree. Section 5(a), set forth in n 1, supra, provided that if the fetus was determined to be viable, or if there was sufficient reason to believe that the fetus might be viable, the person performing the abortion was required to exercise the same care to preserve the life and health of the fetus as would be required in the case of a fetus intended to be born alive, and was required to adopt the abortion technique providing the best opportunity for the fetus to be aborted alive, so long as a different technique was not necessary in order to preserve the life or health of the mother. Section 5(d), also set forth in n 1, imposed a penal sanction for a violation of § 5(a).

Section 6 specified abortion controls. It prohibited abortion during the stage of pregnancy subsequent to viability, except where necessary, in the judgment of a licensed physician, to preserve the life or health of the mother. No abortion was to be performed except by a licensed physician and in an approved facility. It required that appropriate records be kept, and that quarterly reports be filed with the Commonwealth's Department of Health. And it prohibited solicitation or advertising with respect to abortions. A violation of § 6 was a misdemeanor of the first or third degrees, as specified.

Section 7 prohibited the use of public funds for an abortion in the absence of a certificate of a physician stating that the abortion was necessary in order to preserve the life or health of the mother. Finally, § 8 authorized the Department of Health to make rules and regulations with respect to performance of abortions and the facilities in which abortions were performed.* * *

Prior to the Act's effective date, October 10, 1974, the present suit was filed in the United States District Court for the Eastern District of Pennsylvania challenging, on federal constitutional grounds, nearly all of the Act's provisions. The three-judge court on October 10 issued a preliminary injunction restraining the enforcement of a number of those provisions. Each side sought a class-action determination; the plaintiffs', but not the defendants', motion to this effect was granted.

The case went to trial in January 1975. The court received extensive testimony from expert witnesses on all aspects of abortion procedures. The resulting judgment declared the Act to be severable, upheld certain of its provisions, and held other provisions unconstitutional. Planned Parenthood Assn. v Fitzpatrick, 401 F Supp 554 (1975). The court sustained the definition of "informed consent" in § 2; the facility-approval requirement and certain of the reporting requirements of § 6; § 8's authorization of rules and regulations; and, by a divided vote, the informed consent requirement of § 3(a). It overturned § 3(b)(i)'s spousal-consent requirement and, again by a divided vote, § 3(b)(ii)'s parental-consent requirement; § 6's reporting requirements relating to spousal and parental consent; § 6's prohibition of advertising; and § 7's restriction on abortion funding. The definition of "viable" in § 2 was declared void for vagueness and, because of the incorporation of this definition, § 6's proscription of abortions after viability, except to preserve the life or health of the woman, was struck down. Finally, in part because of the incorporation of the definition of "viable," and in part because of the perceived overbreadth of the phrase "may be viable," the court invalidated the viability-determination and standard-of-care provisions of § 5(a). 401 F Supp, at 594.

Both sides appealed to this Court. While the appeals were pending, the Court decided Virginia State Board of Pharmacy v Virginia Citizens Consumer Council.* * * Planned Parenthood of Central Missouri v Danforth, * * *, and Singleton v Wulff, * * * Virginia State Board shed light on the prohibition of advertising for abortion services. Planned Parenthood had direct bearing on the patient-spousal- and parental-consent issues and was instructive on the definition-of-viability issue. Singleton concerned the issue of standing to challenge abortion regulations. Accordingly, that portion of the three-judge court's judgment which was the subject of the plaintiffs' appeal was summarily affirmed. Franklin v Fitzpatrick. * * * And that portion of the judgment which was the subject of the defendants' appeal was vacated and remanded for further consideration in the light of Planned Parenthood, Singleton, and Virginia State Board. Beal v Franklin.* * *

On remand, the parties entered into a stipulation which disposed of all issues except the constitutionality of §§ 5(a) and 7. Relying on this Court's supervening decisions * * * the District Court found, contrary to its original view, * * * that § 7 did not violate either Tit XIX of the Social Security Act, as added, 79 Stat 343, and amended, 42 USC §§ 1396 et seq. [42 USCS §§ 1396 et seq.], or the Equal Protection Clause of the Fourteenth Amendment. App 241a. The court, however, declared: "After reconsideration of section 5(a) in light of the most recent Supreme Court decisions, we adhere to our original view and decision that section 5(a) is unconstitutional." Id., at 240a–241a. Since the plaintiffs-appellees have not appealed from the ruling with respect to § 7, the only issue remaining in this protracted litigation is the validity of § 5(a).

II

Three cases in the sensitive and earnestly contested abortion area provide essential background for the present controversy.

In Roe v Wade, * * *, this Court concluded that there is a right of privacy, implicit in the liberty secured by the Fourteenth Amendment, that "is broad enough to encompass a woman's decision whether or not to terminate her pregnancy."

This right, we said, although fundamental, is not absolute or unqualified, and must be considered against important state interests in the health of the pregnant woman and in the potential life of the fetus. "These interests are separate and distinct. Each grows in substantiality as the woman approaches term and, at a point during pregnancy, each becomes 'compelling.' "* * *

For both logical and biological reasons, we indicated that the State's interest in the potential life of the fetus reaches the compelling point at the stage of viability. Hence, prior to viability, the State may not seek to further this interest by directly restricting a woman's decision whether or not to terminate her pregnancy.[7] But after viability, the State, if it chooses, may regulate or even prohibit abortion except where necessary, in appropriate medical judgment, to preserve the life or health of the pregnant woman.* * *

We did not undertake in Roe to examine the various factors that may enter into the determination of viability. We simply observed that, in the medical and scientific communities, a fetus is considered viable if it is "potentially able to live outside the mother's womb, albeit with artificial aid."* * * We added that there must be a potentiality of "meaningful life,"* * *, not merely momentary survival. And we noted that viability "is usually placed at about seven months (28 weeks) but may occur earlier, even at 24 weeks."* * * We thus left the point flexible for anticipated advancements in medical skill.

Roe stressed repeatedly the central role of the physician, both in consulting with the woman about whether or not to have an abortion, and in determining how any abortion was to be carried out. We indicated that up to the points where important state interests provide compelling justifications for intervention, "the abortion decision in all its aspects is inherently, and primarily, a medical decision," * * * and we added that if this privilege were abused, "the usual remedies, judicial and intra-professional, are available."

* * *

Roe's companion case, Doe v Bolton, * * * underscored the importance of affording the physician adequate discretion in the exercise of his medical judgment. After the Court there reiterated that "a pregnant woman does not have an absolute constitutional right to an abortion on her demand." * * * the Court discussed, in a vagueness-attack context, the Georgia statute's requirement that a physician's decision to perform an abortion must rest upon "his best clinical judgment." The Court found it critical that that judgment "may be exercised in the light of all factors—physical, emotional, psychological, familial, and the woman's age—relevant to the well-being of the patient."

* * *

The third case, Planned Parenthood of Central Missouri v Danforth, * * *, stressed similar themes. There a Missouri statute that defined viability was challenged on the ground that it conflicted with the discussion of viability in Roe and that it was, in reality, an attempt to advance the point of viability to an earlier stage in gestation. The Court rejected that argument, repeated the Roe definition of viability, * * * and observed again that viability is "a matter of medical judgment, skill, and technical ability, and we preserved [in Roe] the flexibility of the term."* * * The Court also rejected a contention that "a specified number of weeks in pregnancy must be fixed by statute as the point of viability."

* * *

> "In any event, we agree with the District Court that it is not the proper function of the legislature or the courts to place viability, which essentially is a medical concept, at a specific point in the gestation period. The time when viability is achieved may vary with each pregnancy, and the determination of whether a particular fetus is viable is, and must be, a matter for the judgment of the responsible attending physician."

In these three cases, then, this Court has stressed viability, has declared its determination to be a matter for medical judgment, and has recognized that differing legal consequences ensue upon the near and far sides of that point in the human gestation period. We reaffirm these principles. Viability is reached when, in the judgment of the attending physician on the particular facts of the case before him, there is a reasonable likelihood of the fetus' sustained survival outside the womb, with or without artificial support. Because this point may differ with each pregnancy, neither the legislature nor the courts may proclaim one of the elements entering into the ascertainment of viability—be it weeks of gestation or fetal weight or any other single factor—as the determinant of when the State has a compelling interest in the life or health of the fetus. Viability is the critical point. And we have reognized no attempt to stretch the point of viability one way or the other.

With these principles in mind, we turn to the issues presented by the instant controversy.

III

The attack mounted by the plaintiffs-appellees upon § 5(a) centers on both the viability-determination requirement and the stated standard of care. The former provision, requiring the physician to observe the care standard when he determines that the fetus is viable, or when "there is sufficient reason to believe that the fetus may be viable," is asserted to be unconstitutionally vague because it fails to inform the physician when his duty to the fetus arises, and because it does not make the physician's good-faith determination of viability conclusive. This provision is also said to be unconstitutionally overbroad, because it carves out a new time period prior to the stage of viability, and could have a restrictive effect on a couple who wants to abort a fetus determined by genetic testing to be defective. The standard of care, and in particular the requirement that the physician employ the abortion technique "which would provide the best opportunity for the fetus to be aborted alive so long as a different technique would not be necessary in order to preserve the life or health of the mother," is said to be void for vagueness and to be unconstitutionally restrictive in failing to afford the physician sufficient professional discretion in determining which abortion technique is appropriate.

The defendants-appellants, in opposition, assert that the Pennsylvania statute is concerned only with post-viability abortions and with prescribing a standard of care for those abortions. They assert that the terminology "may be viable" correctly describes the statistical probability of fetal survival associated with viability; that the viability-determination requirement is otherwise sufficiently definite to be interpreted by the medical community; and that it is for the legislature, not the judiciary, to determine whether a viable but genetically defective fetus has a right to life. They contend that the standard-of-care provision preserves the flexibility required for sound medical practice, and that it simply requires that when a physician has a choice of procedures of equal risk to the woman, he must select the procedure least likely to be fatal to the fetus.

IV

We agree with plaintiffs-appellees that the viability-determination requirement of § 5(a) is ambiguous, and that its uncertainty is aggravated by the absence of a scienter requirement with respect to the finding of viability. Because we conclude that this portion of the statute is void for vagueness, we find it unnecessary to consider appellees' alternative arguments based on the alleged overbreadth of § 5(a).

A

It is settled that, as a matter of due process, a criminal statute that "fails to give a person of ordinary intelligence fair notice that his contemplated conduct is forbidden by the statute." United States v Harriss.* * *, or is so indefinite that "it encourages arbitrary and erratic arrests and convictions," Papachristou v Jacksonville, * * * is void for vagueness.* * * This appears to be especially true where the uncertainty induced by the statute threatens to inhibit the exercise of constitutionally protected rights.

Section 5(a) requires every person who performs or induces an abortion to make a determination, "based on his experience, judgment or professional competence," that the fetus is not viable. If such person determines that the fetus is viable, or if "there is sufficient reason to believe that the fetus may be viable," then he must adhere to the prescribed standard of care. See n 1, supra. This requirement contains a double ambiguity. First, it is unclear whether the statute imports a purely subjective standard, or whether it imposes a mixed subjective and objective standard. Second, it is uncertain whether the phrase "may be viable" simply refers to viability, as that term has been defined in Roe and in Planned Parenthood, or whether it refers to an undefined penumbral or "gray" area prior to the stage of viability.

The statute reuires the physician to conform to the prescribed standard of care if one of two conditions is satisfied: if he determines that the fetus "is viable," or "if there is sufficient reason to believe that the fetus may be viable." Apparently, the determination of whether the fetus "is viable" is to be based on the attending physician's "experience, judgment or professional competence," a subjective point of reference. But it is unclear whether the same phrase applies to the second triggering condition, that is, to "sufficient reason to believe that the fetus may be viable." In other words, it is ambiguous whether there must be "sufficient reason" from the perspective of the judgment, skill, and training of the attending physician, or "sufficient reason" from the perspective of a cross section of the medical community or a panel of experts. The latter, obviously, portends not an inconsequential hazard for the typical private practitioner who may not have the skills and technology that are readily available at a teaching hospital or large medical center.

[5a] The intended distinction between the phrases "is viable" and "may be viable" is even more elusive. Appellants argue that no difference is intended, and that the use of the "may be viable" words "simply incorporates the acknowledged medical fact that a fetus is 'viable' if it has that statistical 'chance' of survival recognized by the medical community." Brief for Appellants 28. The statute, however, does not support the contention that "may be viable" is synonymous with, or merely intended to explicate the meaning of, "viable."

Section 5(a) requires the physician to observe the prescribed standard of care if he determines "that the fetus is viable *or* if there is sufficient reason to believe that the fetus may be viable" (emphasis supplied). The syntax clearly implies that there are two distinct conditions under which the physician must conform to the standard of care. Appellants' argument that "may be viable" is synonymous with "viable" would make either the first or the second condition redundant or largely superfluous, in violation of the elementary canon of construction that a statute should be interpreted so as not to render one part inoperative.* * *

Furthermore, the suggestion that "may be viable" is an explication of the meaning of "viable" flies in the face of the fact that the statute, in § 2, already defines "viable." This, presumably, was intended to be the exclusive definition of "viable" throughout the Act. In this respect, it is significant that § 6(b) of the Act speaks only of the limited availability of abortion during the stage of a pregnancy "subsequent to viability." The concept of viability is just as important in § 6(b) as it is in § 5(a). Yet in § 6(b) the legislature found it unnecessary to explain that a "viable" fetus includes one that "may be viable."

Since we must reject appellants' theory that "may be viable" means "viable," a second serious ambiguity appears in the statute. On the one hand, as appellees urge and as the District Court found, * * * it may be that "may be viable" carves out a new time period during pregnancy when there is a remote possibility of fetal survival outside the womb, but the fetus has not yet attained the reasonable likelihood of survival that physicians associate with viability. On the other hand, although appellants do not argue this, it may be that "may be viable" refers to viability as physicians understand it, and "viable" refers to some undetermined stage later in pregnancy. We need not resolve this question. The crucial point is that "viable" and "may be viable" apparently refer to distinct conditions, and that one of these conditions differs in some indeterminate way from the definition of viability as set forth in Roe and in Planned Parenthood.

Because of the double ambiguity in the viability-determination requirement, this portion of the Pennsylvania statute is readily distinguishable from the requirement that an abortion must be "necessary for the preservation of the mother's life or health," upheld against a vagueness challenge in United States v Vuitch, * * * and the requirement that a physician determine, on the basis of his "best clinical judgment," that an abortion is "necessary," upheld against a vagueness attack in Doe v Bolton.* * * The contested provisions in those cases had been interpreted to allow the physician to make his determination in the light of all attendant circumstances—psychological and emotional as well as physical—that might be relevant to the well-being of the patient. The present statute does not afford broad discretion to the physician. Instead, it conditions potential criminal liability on confusing and ambiguous criteria. It therefore presents serious problems of notice, discriminatory application, and chilling effect on the exercise of constitutional rights.

B

The vagueness of the viability-determination requirement of § 5(a) is compounded by the fact that the Act subjects the physician to potential criminal liability without regard to fault. Under § 5(d), see n 1, supra, a physician who fails to abide by the standard of care when there is sufficient reason to believe that the fetus "may be viable" is subject "to such civil or criminal liability as would pertain to him had the fetus been a child who was intended to be born and not aborted." To be sure, the Pennsylvania law of criminal homicide, made applicable to the physician by § 5(d), conditions guilt upon a finding of scienter. See Pa Stat Ann, Tit 18, §§ 2501–2504 (Purdon 1973 and Supp 1978). The required mental state, however, is that of "intentionally, knowingly, recklessly or negligently caus[ing] the death of another human being." § 2501 (1973). Thus, the Pennsylvania law of criminal homicide requires scienter with respect to whether the physician's actions will result in the death of the fetus. But neither the Pennsylvania law of criminal homicide, nor the Abortion Control Act, requires that the physician be culpable in failing to find sufficient reason to believe that the fetus may be viable.

This Court has long recognized that the constitutionality of a vague statutory standard is closely related to whether that standard incorporates a requirement of mens rea.* * * Because of the absence of a scienter requirement in the provision directing the physician to determine whether the fetus is or may be viable, the statute is little more than "a trap for those who act in good faith."

The perils of strict criminal liability are particularly acute here because of the uncertainty of the viability determination itself. As the record in this case indicates, a physician determines whether or not a fetus is viable after considering a number of variables: the gestational age of the fetus, derived from the reported menstrual history of the woman; fetal weight, based on an inexact estimate of the size and condition of the uterus; the woman's general health and nutrition; the quality of the available medical facilities; and other factors. Because of the number and the imprecision of these variables, the probability of any particular fetus' obtaining meaningful life outside the womb can be determined only with difficulty. Moreover, the record indicates that even if agreement may be reached on the probability of survival, different physicians equate viability with different probabilities of survival, and some physicians refuse to equate viability with any numerical probability at all. In the face of these uncertainties, it is not unlikely that experts will disagree over whether a particular fetus in the second trimester has advanced to the stage of viability. The prospect of such disagreement, in conjunction with a statute imposing strict civil and criminal liability for an erroneous determination of viability, could have a profound chilling effect on the willingness of physicians to perform abortions near the point of viability in the manner indicated by their best medical judgment.

Because we hold that the viability-determination provision of § 5(a) is void on its face, we need not now decide whether, under a properly drafted statute, a finding of bad faith or some other type of scienter would be required before a physician could be held criminally responsible for an erroneous determination of viability. We reaffirm, however, that "the determination of whether a particular fetus is viable is, and must be, a matter for the judgment of the responsible attending physician." Planned Parenthood of Central Missouri v Danforth, * * * State regulation that impinges upon this determination, if it is to be constitutional, must allow the attending physician "the room he needs to make his best medical judgment." Doe v Bolton.

* * *

V

We also conclude that the standard-of-care provision of § 5(a) is impermissibly vague. The standard-of-care provision, when it applies, requires the physician to

> "exercise that degree of professional skill, care and diligence to preserve the life and health of the fetus which such person would be required to exercise in order to preserve the life and health of any fetus intended to be born and not aborted and the abortion technique employed shall be that which would provide the best opportunity for the fetus to be aborted alive so long as a different technique would not be necessary in order to preserve the life or health of the mother."

Plaintiffs-appellees focus their attack on the second part of the standard, requiring the physician to employ the abortion technique offering the greatest possibility of fetal survival, provided some other technique would not be necessary in order to preserve the life or health of the mother.

The District Court took extensive testimony from various physicians about their understanding of this requirement. That testimony is illuminating. When asked what method of abortion they would prefer to use in the second trimester in the absence of § 5(a), the plaintiffs' experts said that they thought saline amnio-infusion was the method of choice. This was described as a method involving removal of amniotic fluid and injection of a saline or other solution into the amniotic sac. See Planned Parenthood of Central Missouri v Danforth, * * * All physicians agreed, however, that saline amnio-infusion nearly always is fatal to the fetus, and it was commonly assumed that this method would be prohibited by the statute.

When the plaintiffs' and defendants' physician-experts respectively were asked what would be the method of choice under § 5(a), opinions differed widely. Preferences ranged from no abortion, to prostaglandin infusion, to hysterotomy, to oxytocin induction. Each method, it was generally conceded, involved disadvantages from the perspective of the woman. Hysterotomy, a type of Caesarean section procedure, generally was considered to have the highest incidence of fetal survival of any of the abortifacients. Hysterotomy, however, is associated with the risks attendant upon any operative procedure involving anesthesia and incision of tissue. And all physicians agreed that future children born to a woman having a hysterotomy would have to be delivered by Caesarean section because of the likelihood of rupture of the scar.

Few of the testifying physicians had had any direct experience with prostaglandins, described as drugs that stimulate uterin contractibility, inducing premature expulsion of the fetus. See Planned Parenthood of Central Missouri v Danforth, * * * It was generally agreed that the incidence of fetal survival with prostaglandins would be significantly greater than with saline amnio-infusion. Several physicians testified, however, that prostaglandins have undesirable side effects, such as nausea, vomiting, headache, and diarrhea, and indicated that they are unsafe with patients having a history of asthma, glaucoma, hypertension, cardiovascular disease, or epilepsy. * * * One physician recommended oxytocin induction. He doubted, however, whether the procedure would be fully effective in all cases, and he indicated that the procedure was prolonged and expensive.

The parties acknowledge that there is disagreement among medical authorities about the relative merits and the safety of different abortion procedures that may be used during the second trimester. See Brief for Appellants 24. The appellants submit, however, that the only legally relevant considerations are that alternatives exist among abortifacients, "and that the physician, mindful of the state's interest in protecting viable life, must make a competent and good faith medical judgment on the feasibility of protecting the fetus' chance of survival in a manner consistent with the life and health of the pregnant woman." Id., at 25. We read § 5(a), however, to be more problematical.

The statute does not clearly specify, as appellants imply, that the woman's life and health must always prevail over the fetus' life and health when they conflict. The woman's life and health are not mentioned in the first part of the stated standard of care, which sets forth the general duty to the viable fetus; they are mentioned only in the second part which deals with the choice of abortion procedures. Moreover, the second part of the standard directs the physician to employ the abortion technique best suited to fetal survival "so long as a different technique would not be *necessary* in order to preserve the life or health of the mother" (emphasis supplied). In this context, the word "necessary" suggests that a particular technique must be indispensable to the woman's life or health—not merely desirable—before it may be adopted. And "the life or health of the mother," as used in § 5(a), has not been construed by the courts of the Commonwealth, nor does it necessarily imply, that all factors relevant to the welfare of the woman may be taken into account by the physician in making his decision.* * *

Consequently, it is uncertain whether the statute permits the physician to consider his duty to the patient to be paramount to his duty to the fetus, or whether it requires the physician to make a "trade-off" between the woman's health and additional percentage points of fetal survival. Serious ethical and constitutional difficulties, that we do not address, lurk behind this ambiguity. We hold only that where conflicting duties of this magnitude are involved, the State, at the least, must proceed with greater precision before it may subject a physician to possible criminal sanctions.

Appellants' further suggestion that § 5(a) requires only that the physician make a good-faith selection of the proper abortion procedure finds no support in either the language or an authoritative interpretation of the statute. Certainly, there is nothing to suggest a mens rea requirement with respect to a decision whether a particular abortion method is necessary in order to preserve the life or health of the woman. The choice of an appropriate abortion technique, as the record in this case so amply demonstrates, is a complex medical judgment about which experts can—and do—disagree. The lack of any scienter requirement exacerbates the uncertainty of the statute. We conclude that the standard-of-care provision, like the viability-determination requirement, is void for vagueness.

The judgment of the District Court is affirmed.* * *

BELLOTTI
v.
BAIRD

428 U.S. 132 (1976)

Mr. Justice BLACKMUN delivered the opinion of the Court.

In this litigation, a three-judge District Court for the District of Massachusetts enjoined the operation of certain provisions of a 1974 Massachusetts statute that govern the type of consent required before an abortion may be performed on an unmarried woman under the age of 18. In so acting, the court denied by implication a motion by appellants that the court abstain from deciding the issue pending authoritative construction of the statute by the Supreme Judicial Court of Massachusetts. We hold that the court should have abstained, and we vacate the judgment and remand the cases for certification of relevant issues of state law to the Supreme Judicial Court, and for abstention pending the decision of that tribunal.

I

On August 2, 1974, General Court of Massachusetts (Legislature), over the Governor's veto, enacted legislation entitled "An Act to protect unborn children and maternal health within present constitutional limits." The Act, Mass Acts and Resolves 1974, c 706, § 1, amended Mass Gen Laws Ann, c 112 (Registration of Certain Professions and Occupations), by adding §§ 12H through 12R. Section 12P provides:

> "(1) If the mother is less than eighteen years of age and has not married, the consent of both the mother and her parents is required. If one or both of the mother's parents refuse such consent, consent may be obtained by order of a judge of the superior court for good cause shown, after such hearing as he deems necessary. Such a hearing will not require the appointment of a guardian for the mother.
>
> "If one of the parents has died or has deserted his or her family, consent by the remaining parent is sufficient. If both parents have died or have deserted their family, consent of the mother's guardian or other person having duties similar to a guardian, or any person who had assumed the care and custody of the mother is sufficient.
>
> "(2) The commissioner of public health shall prescribe a written form for such consent. Such form shall be signed by the proper person or persons and given to the physician performing the abortion who shall maintain it in his permanent files.
>
> "Nothing in this section shall be construed as abolishing or limiting any common law rights of any other person or persons relative to consent to the performance of an abortion for purposes of any civil action or any injunctive relief under section twelve R."

All nonemergency abortions are made subject to the provisions of § 12P by § 12N. Violations of § 12N are punishable under § 12Q by a fine of not less than $100 nor more than $2,000. Section 12R provides that the Attorney General or any person whose consent is required may petition the superior court for an order enjoining the performance of any abortion.

II

On October 30, 1974, one day prior to the effective date of the Act, plaintiffs, who are appellees here, filed this action in the United States District Court for the District of Massachusetts, asserting jurisdiction under 28 USC § 1343(3), 1331, and 2201 [28 USCS §§ 1343(3), 1331, and 2201], and 42 USC § 1983 [42 USCS § 1983] and claiming that § 12P violates the Due Process and Equal Protection Clauses of the Fourteenth Amendment. They sought injunctive and declaratory relief, and requested the empaneling of the three-judge court pursuant to 28 USC §§ 2281 and 2284 [28 USCS §§ 2281, 2284].

On October 31, the single District Judge issued an order temporarily restraining the enforcement of the parental-consent requirement of § 12P, and accepting the request for a three-judge court. Record Doc 2.

The plaintiffs, and the classes they purported to represent, are:

1. William Baird, a citizen of New York.

2. Parents Aid Society, Inc., a Massachusetts not-for-profit corporation. Baird is president of the corporation and is director and chief counselor of the center it operates in Boston for the purpose of providing, inter alia, abortion and counseling services. Baird and Parents Aid claim to represent all abortion centers and their administrators in Massachusetts who, on a regular and recurring basis, deal with pregnant minors. App 13, 43.

3. Mary Moes I, II, III, and IV, four minors under the age of 18, pregnant at the time of the filing of the suit, and residing in Massachusetts. Each alleged that she wished to terminate her preganancy and did not wish to inform either of her parents. Id., at 16–18, 19–22. The Moes claimed to represent all pregnant minors capable of, and willing to give, informed consent to an abortion, but who decline to seek the consent of both parents, as required by § 12P. Id., at 13, 43.

4. Gerald Zupnick, M.D., a physician licensed to practice in Massachusetts. He is the medical director of the center operated by Parents Aid. He claims to represent all physicians in Massachusetts who, without parental consent, see minor patients seeking abortions. Ibid.

The defendants in the action, who are the appellants in No. 75–73 (and who are hereinafter referred to as the appellants), are the Attorney General of Massachusettts, and the District Attorneys of all the counties in the Commonwealth.

Appellant in No. 75–109 (hereinafter referred to as the intervenor-appellant) is Jane Hunerwadel, a resident and citizen of Massachusetts, and parent of an unmarried minor female of childbearing age. Hunerwadel was permitted by the District Court to intervene as a defendant on behalf of herself and all others similarly situated App 24.

On November 13, appellants filed a "Motion to dismiss and/or for summary judgment," arguing, inter alia, that the district Court "should abstain from deciding any issue in this case." Id., at 23. In their momorandum to the court in support of that motion, appellants, in addition to other arguments, urged that § 12P, particularly in view of its judicial-review provision, "was susceptible of a construction by state courts that would avoid or modify any alleged federal constitutional question." Record Doc 5, p 12. They cited Railroad Comm'n v Pullman Co. * * *, and Lake Carriers' Assn. v MacMullan, * * * for the proposition that where an unconstrued state statute is susceptible of a constitutional construction, a federal court should abstain from deciding a constitutional challenge to the statute until a definitive state construction has been obtained.

The District Court held hearings on the motion for a preliminary injunction; these were later merged into the trial on the merits. It received testimony from various experts and from parties to the case, including Mary Moe I. On April 28, 1975, the three-judge District Court, by a divided vote, handed down a decision holding § 12P unconstitutional and void. 393 F Supp 847. An order was entered declaring § 12P "and such other portions of the chapter [112] insofar as they make specific reference thereto" void, and enjoining the defendants from enforcing them. App 45–46; Jurisdictional Statement in No. 75–73, pp A-33, A-34.

The majority held, inter alia, that appellees Mary Moe I, Doctor Zupnick, and Parents Aid had standing to challenge the operation of the statute, individually and as representatives of their proposed classes, 393 F Supp, at 850–852, and that the intervenor-appellant had standing to represent the interests of parents of unmarried minor women of childbearing age, id., at 849–850. It found that "a substantial number of females under the age of 18 are capable of forming a valid consent," and viewed the overall question as "whether the state can be permitted to restrain the free exercise of that consent, to the extent that it has endeavored to do so." Id., at 855.

In regard to the meaning of § 12P, the majority made the following comments:

> "1. The statute does not purport to require simply that parents be notified and given an opportunity to communicate with the minor, her chosen physician, or others. We mention this obvious fact because of the persistence of defendants and intervenor in arguing that the legislature could properly enact such a statute. Whether it could is not before us, and there is no reason for our considering it.
>
> "2. The statute does not exclude those capable of forming an intelligent consent, but applies to all minors. The statute's provision calling for the minor's own consent recognizes that at least some minors can consent, but the minor's consent must be supplemented in every case, either by the consent of both parents, or by a court order.
>
> "4. The statute does not purport simply to provide a check on the validity of the minor's consent and the wisdom of her decision from the standpoint of her interests alone. Rather, it recognizes and provides rights in both parents, independent of, and hence potentially at variance with, her own personal interests." 393 F Supp, at 855.
>
> "The dissent is seemingly of the opinion that a reviewing Superior Court Judge would consider only the interests of the minor. We find no room in the statute for so limited an interpretation." Id., at 855 n 10.
>
> "The parents not only must be consulted, they are given a veto." Id., at 856.

The majority observed that "'[n]either the Fourteenth Amendment nor the Bill of Rights is for adults alone,' In re Gault, * * * and, accordingly, held that the State cannot control a minor's abortion in the first trimester any more than it can control that of an adult. Re-emphasizing that "the statute is cast not in terms of protecting the minor . . . but in recognizing independent rights of parents," the majority concluded that "[t]he question comes, accordingly, do parents possess, apart from right to counsel and guide, competing rights of their own?" Ibid.

The majority found that in the instant situtión, unlike others, the parents' interests often are adverse to those of the minor and, specifically rejecting the contrary result in Planned Parenthood of Central Missouri v Danforth, * * *, concluded:

> "But even if it should be found that parents may have rights of a Constitutional dimension vis-a-vis their child that are separate from the child's, we would find that in the present area the individual rights of the minor outweigh the rights of the parents, and must be protected."* * *

The dissent argued that the parents of Mary Moe I, by not being informed of the action or joined as parties, "have been deprived of their legal rights without due process of law," ibid., that the majority erred in refusing to appoint a guardian ad litem for Moe I, and that it erred in finding that she had the capacity to give a valid and informed consent to an abortion. The dissent further argued that parents possess constitutionally cognizable rights in guiding the upbringing of their children, and that the statute is a proper exercise of state power in protection of those parental rights. Id., at 857–865.

Most important, however, the dissent's view of the statute differed markedly from the interpretation adopted by the majority. The dissent stated:

> "I find, therefore, no conceivable constitutional objection to legislation providing in the case of a pregnant minor an additional condition designed to make certain that she receive parental or judicial guidance and counselling before having the abortion. The requirement of consent of both parents ensures that both parents will provide counselling and guidance, each according to his or her best judgment. The statute expressly provides that the parents' refusal to consent is not final. The statute expressly gives the state courts the right to make a final determination. If the state courts find that the minor is mature enough to give an informed consent to the abortion and that she has been adequately informed about the nature of an abortion and its probable consequences to her, then we must assume that the courts will enter the necessary order permitting her to exercise her constitutional right to the abortion." Id., at 864.

The indicated footnote reads:

> "The majority speculate concerning possible interpretations of the 'for good cause shown' language. There is also some doubt whether the statute requires consent of one or both parents. The construction of the statute is a matter of state law. If the majority believe the only constitutional infirmities arise from their interpretation of the statute, the majority should certify questions of state law to the Supreme Judicial Court of Massachusetts pursuant to Rule 3:21 of that court in order to receive a definitive interpretation of the statute."* * *

Both appellants and intervenor-appellant appealed. We noted probable jurisdiction of each appeal and set the cases for oral argument with Planned Parenthood of Central Missouri v Danforth.* * *

III

Appellants and intervenor-appellant attack the District Court's majority decision on a number of grounds. They argue, inter alia, and each in their or her own way, that § 12P properly preserves the primacy of the family unit by reinforcing the role of parents in fundamental decisions affecting family members; that the District Court erred in failing to join Moe I's parents; that it abused its discretion by failing to appoint a guardian ad litem; and that it erred in finding the statute facially invalid when it was capable of a construction that would withstand constitutional analysis.

The interpretation placed on the statute by appellants in this Court is of some importance and merits attention, for they are the officials charged with enforcement of the statute.

Appellants assert, first, that under the statute parental consent may not be refused on the basis of concerns exclusively of the parent. Indeed, "the 'competing' parental right consists exclusively of the right to assess independently, for their minor child, what will serve that child's best interest. . . . [I]n operation, the parents' actual deliberation must range no further than would that of a pregnant adult making her own abortion decision." Brief for Appellants 23. And the superior court's review will ensure that parental objection based upon other considerations will not operate to bar the minor's abortion.* * *

Second, appellants argue that the last paragraph of § 12P preserves the "mature minor" rule in Massachusetts, under which a child determined by a court to be capable of giving informed consent will be allowed to do so. Appellants argue that under this rule a pregnant minor could file a complaint in superior court seeking authorization for an abortion, and, "[i]mportantly, such a complaint could be filed *regardless* of whether the parents had been consulted or had withheld their consent."* * * Appellants and the intervenor-appellant assert that the procedure employed would be structured so as to be speedy and nonburdensome, and would ensure anonymity.

* * *

Finally, appellants argue that under § 12P, a judge of the superior court may permit an abortion without parental consent for a minor incapable of rendering informed consent, provided that there is "good cause shown." Brief for Appellants 38. "Good cause" includes a showing that the abortion is in the minor's best interest. Id., at 39.

The picture thus painted by the respective appellants is of a statute that prefers parental consultation and consent, but that permits a mature minor capable of giving informed consent to obtain, without undue burden, an order permitting the abortion without parental consultation, and, further, permits even a minor incapable of giving informed consent to obtain an order without parental consultation where there is a showing that the abortion would be in her best interests. The statute, as thus read, would be fundamentally different from a statute that creates a "parental veto."

Appellees, however, on their part, take an entirely different view of the statute. They argue that the statute creates a right to a parental veto, that it creates an irrebuttable presumption that a minor is incapable of informed consent, and that the statute does not permit abortion without parental consent in the case of a mature minor or, in the case of a minor incapable of giving consent, where the parents are irrationally opposed to abortion.

Appellees specifically object to abstention. Their objection is based upon their opinion that "the statute gives to parents of minors an unbridled veto," Brief for Appelless 49, and that once that veto is exercised, the minor has the burden of proving to the superior court judge that "good cause" exists. Ibid. They view the "good cause" hearing as forcing the judge to choose "between the privacy rights of the young woman and the rights of the parents as established by the statute." Ibid. Assuming that "good cause" has a broader meaning, appellees argue that the hearing itself makes the statute unconstitutional, because of the burden it imposes and the delay it entails. Ibid.

IV

In deciding this case, we need go no further than the claim that the District Court should have abstained pending construction of the statute by the Massachusetts courts. As we have held on numerous occasions, abstention is appropriate where an unconstrued state statute is susceptible of a construction by the state judiciary "which might avoid in whole or in part the necessity for federal constitutional adjudication, or at least materially change the nature of the problem."* * *

We do not accept appellees' assertion that the Supreme Judicial Court of Massachusetts inevitably will interpret the statute so as to create a "parental veto," require the superior court to act other than in the best interests of the minor, or impose undue burdens upon a minor capable of giving an informed consent.

In Planned Parenthood of Central Missouri v Danforth, we today struck down a statute that created a parental veto.* * *

At the same time, however, we held that a requirement of written consent on the part of a pregnant adult is not unconstitutional unless it unduly burdens the right to seek an abortion. In this case, we are concerned with a statute directed toward minors, as to whom there are unquestionably greater risks of inability to give an informed consent. Without holding that a requirement of a court hearing would not unduly burden the rights of a mature adult, cf. Doe v Rampton, 366 F Supp 189 (Utah 1973), we think it clear that in the instant litigation adoption of appellant's interpretation would "at least materially change the nature of the problem" that appellants claim is presented.* * *

Whether the Supreme Judicial Court will so interpret the statute, or whether it will interpret the statute to require consideration of factors not mentioned above, impose burdens more serious than those suggested, or create some unanticipated interference with the doctor-patient relationship, we cannot now determine. Nor need we determine what factors are impermissible or at what point review of consent and good cause in the case of a minor becomes unduly burdensome. It is sufficient that the statute is susceptible of the interpretation offered by appellants, and we so find, and that such an interpretation would avoid or substantially modify the federal constitutional challenge to the statute, as it clearly would. Indeed, in the absence of an authoritative construction, it is impossible to define precisely the constitutional question presented.

Appellees also raise, however, a claim of impermissible distiction between the consent procedures applicable to minors in the area of abortion, and the consent required in regard to other medical procedures. This issue has come to the fore through the advent of a Massachusetts statute, enacted subsequent to the decision of the District Court, dealing with consent by minors to medical procedures other than abortion and sterilization. As we hold today in Planned Parenthood, however, not all distinction between abortion and other procedures is forbidden.

* * * The constitutionality of such distinction will depend upon its degree and the justification for it. The constitutional issue cannot now be defined, however, for the degree of distinction between the consent procedures for abortions and the consent procedures for other medical procedures cannot be established until the nature of the consent required for abortions is established. In these circumstances, the federal court should stay its hand to the same extent as in a challenge directly to the burdens created by the statute.

Finally, we note that the Supreme Judicial Court of Massachusetts has adopted a Rule of Court under which an issue of interpretation of Massachusetts law may be certified directly to that court for prompt resolution. * * * This court often has remarked that the equitable practice of abstention is limited by considerations of "'the delay and expense to which application of the abstention doctrine inevitably gives rise.'"

* * * As we have also noted, however, the availability of an adequate certification procedure "does, of course, in the long run save time, energy, and resources and helps build a cooperative judicial federalism."* * *

This Court has utilized certification procedures in the past, as have courts of appeals.* * *

The importance of speed in resolution of the instant litigation is manifest. Each day the statute is in effect, irretrievable events, with substantial personal consequences, occur. Although we do not mean to intimate that abstention would be improper in this case were certification not possible, the availability of certification greatly simplifies the analysis. Further, in light of our disapproval of a "parental veto" today in Planned Parenthood, we must assume that the lower Massachusetts courts, if called upon to enforce the statute pending interpretation by the Supreme Judicial Court, will not impose this most serious barrier. Insofar as the issue thus ceases to become one of total denial of access and becomes one rather of relative burden, the cost of abstention is reduced and the desirability of that equitable remedy accordingly increased.

V

We therefore hold that the District Court should have certified to the Supreme Judicial Court of Massachusetts appropriate questions concerning the meaning of § 12P and the procedure it imposes. In regard to the claim of impermissible discrimination due to the 1975 statute, a claim not raised in the District Court but subject to inquiry through an amended complaint, or perhaps by other means, we believe that it would not be inappropriate for the District Court, when any procedural requirement has been complied with, also to certify a question concerning the meaning of the new statute, and the extent to which its procedures differ from the procedures that must be followed under § 12P.

The judgment of the District Court is vacated, and the cases are remanded to that court for proceedings consistent with this opinion.

It is so ordered.

HARRIS v. MCRAE

448 U.S 297 (1980)

Mr. Justice STEWART delivered the opinion of the Court.

This case presents statutory and constitutional questions concerning the public funding of abortions under Title XIX of the Social Security Act, commonly known as the "Medicaid" Act, and recent annual appropriations acts containing the so-called "Hyde Amendment." The statutory question is whether Title XIX requires a State that participates in the Medicaid program to fund the cost of medically necessary abortions for which federal reimbursement is unavailable under the Hyde Amendment. The constitutional question, which arises only if Title XIX imposes no such requirement, is whether the Hyde Amendment, by denying public funding for certain medically necessary abortions, contravenes the liberty or equal protection guarantees of the Due Process Clause of the Fifth Amendment, or either of the Religion Clauses of the First Amendment.

I

The Medicaid program was created in 1965, when Congress added Title XIX to the Social Security Act, 79 Stat. 343, as amended, 42 U.S.C. § 1396 *et seq.* (1976 ed. and Supp. II), for the purpose of providing federal financial assistance to States that choose to reimburse certain costs of medical treatment for needy persons. Although participation in the Medicaid program is entirely optional, once a State elects to participate, it must comply with the requirements of Title XIX.

One such requirement is that a participating State agree to provide financial assistance to the "categorically needy" with respect to five general areas of medical treatment: (1) inpatient hospital services, (2) outpatient hospital services, (3) other laboratory and X-ray services, (4) skilled nursing facilities services, periodic screening and diagnosis of children, and family planning services, and (5) services of physicians. * * * Although a participating State need not "provide funding for all medical treatment falling within the five general categories, [Title XIX] does require that [a] state Medicaid plan[ ] establish 'reasonable standards . . . for determining . . . the extent of medical assistance under the plan which . . . are consistent with the objectives of [Title XIX].'* * *

Since September 1976, Congress has prohibited—either by an amendment to the annual appropriations bill for the Department of Health, Education, and Welfare or by a joint resolution—the use of any federal funds to reimburse the cost of abortions under the Medicaid program except under certain specified circumstances. This funding restriction is commonly known as the "Hyde Amendment," after its original congressional sponsor, Representative Hyde. The current version of the Hyde Amendment, applicable for fiscal year 1980, provides:

> "[N]one of the funds provided by this joint resolution shall be used to perform abortions except where the life of the mother would be endangered if the fetus were carried to term; or except for such medical procedures necessary for the victims of rape or incest when such rape or incest has been reported promptly to a law enforcement agency or public health service."

* * *

This version of the Hyde Amendment is broader than that applicable for fiscal year 1977, which did not include the "rape or incest" exception, Pub.L.No.94–439, § 209, 90 Stat. 1434, but narrower than that applicable for most of fiscal year 1978, and all of fiscal year 1979, which had an additional exception for "instances where severe and long-lasting physical health damage to the mother would result if the pregnancy were carried to term when so determined by two physicians."* * *

On September 30, 1976, the day on which Congress enacted the initial version of the Hyde Amendment, these consolidated cases were filed in the District Court for the Eastern District of New York. The plaintiffs—Cora McRae, a New York Medicaid recipient then in the first trimester of a pregnancy that she wished to terminate, the New York City Health and Hospitals Corp., a public benefit corporation that operates 16 hospitals, 12 of which provide abortion services, and others—sought to enjoin the enforcement of the funding restriction on abortions. They alleged that the Hyde Amendment violated the First, Fourth, Fifth, and Ninth Amendments of the Constitution insofar as it limited the funding of abortions to those necessary to save the life of the mother, while permitting the funding of costs associated with childbirth. Although the sole named defendant was the Secretary of Health, Education, and Welfare, the District Court permitted Senators James L. Buckley and Jesse A. Helms and Representative Henry J. Hyde to intervene as defendants.

After hearing, the District Court entered a preliminary injunction prohibiting the Secretary from enforcing the Hyde Amendment and requiring him to continue to provide federal reimbursement for abortions under the standards applicable before the funding restriction had been enacted. *McRae v. Mathews*, 421 F.Supp. 533. Although stating that it had not expressly held that the funding restriction was unconstitutional, since the preliminary injunction was not its final judgment, the District Court noted that such a holding was "implicit" in its decision granting the injunction. The District Court also certified the *McRae* case as a class action on behalf of all pregnant or potentially pregnant women in the State of New York eligible for Medicaid and who decide to have an abortion within the first 24 weeks of pregnancy, and of all authorized providers of abortion services to such women. *Id.*, at 543.

The Secretary then brought an appeal to this Court. After deciding *Beal v. Doe*, * * * we vacated the injunction of the District Court and remanded the case for reconsideration in light of those decisions.* * *

On remand, the District Court permitted the intervention of several additional plaintiffs, including (1) four individual Medicaid recipients who wished to have abortions that allegedly were medically necessary but did not qualify for federal funds under the versions of the Hyde Amendment applicable in fiscal year 1977 and 1978, (2) several physicians who perform abortions for Medicaid recipients, (3) the Women's Division of the Board of Global Ministries of the United Methodist Church (Women's Division), and (4) two individual officers of the Women's Division.

An amended complaint was then filed, challenging the various versions of the Hyde Amendment on several grounds. At the outset, the plaintiffs asserted that the District Court need not address the constitutionality of the Hyde Amendment because, in their view, a participating State remains obligated under Title XIX to fund all medically necessary abortions, even if federal reimbursement is unavailable. With regard to the constitutionality of the Hyde Amendment, the plaintiffs asserted, among other things, that the funding restriction violated the Religion Clauses of the First Amendment and the Due Process Clause of the Fifth Amendment.

After a lengthy trial, which inquired into the medical reasons for abortions and the diverse religious views on the subject, the District Court filed an opinion and entered a judgment invalidating all versions of the Hyde Amendment on Constitutional grounds. The District Court rejected the plaintiffs' statutory argument, concluding that even though Title XIX would otherwise have required a participating State to fund medically necessary abortions, the Hyde Amendment had substantively amended Title XIX to relieve a State of that funding obligation. Turning then to the constitutional issues, the District Court concluded that the Hyde Amendment, though valid under the Establishment Clause, violates the equal protection component of the Fifth Amendment's Due Process Clause and the Free Exercise Clause of the First Amendment. With regard to the Fifth Amendment, the District Court noted that when an abortion is "medically necessary to safeguard the pregnant woman's health, . . . the disentitlement to [M]edicaid assistance impinges directly on the woman's right to decide, in consultation with her physician and in reliance on his judgment, to terminate her pregnancy in order to preserve her health."[9] The court concluded that the Hyde Amendment violates the equal protection guarantee because, in its view, the decision of Congress to fund medically necessary services generally but only certain medically necessary abortions serves no legitimate governmental interest. As to the Free Exercise Clause of the First Amendment, the Court held that insofar as a woman's decision to seek a medically necessary abortion may be a product of her religious beliefs under certain Protestant and Jewish tenets, the funding restrictions of the Hyde Amendment violate that constitutional guarantee as well.

Accordingly, the District Court ordered the Secretary to "[c]ease to give effect" to the various versions of the Hyde Amendment insofar as they forbid payments for medically necessary abortions. It further directed the Secretary to "continue to aurthorize the expenditure of federal matching funds [for such abortions]." In addition, the Court recertified the *McRae* case as a nationwide class action on behalf

[9]The District Court also apparently concluded that the Hyde Amendment operates to the disadvantage of a "suspect class," namely, teenage women desiring medically necessary abortions. See n. 26, *infra*.

of all pregnant and potentially pregnant women eligible for Medicaid who wish to have medically necessary abortions, and of all authorized providers of abortions for such women.

* * *

II

It is well settled that if a case may be decided on either statutory or constitutional grounds, this Court, for sound jurisprudential reasons, will inquire first into the statutory question. This practice reflects the deeply rooted doctrine "that we ought not to pass on questions of constitutionality . . . unless such adjudication is unavoidable."* * *

According, we turn first to the question whether Title XIX requires a State that participates in the Medicaid program to continue to fund those medically necessary abortions for which federal reimbursement is unavailable under the Hyde Amendment. If a participating State is under such an obligation, the constitutionality of the Hyde Amendment need not be drawn into question in the present case, for the availability of medically necessary abortions under Medicaid would continue, with the participating State shouldering the total cost of funding such abortions.

The appellees assert that a participating State has an independent funding obligation under Title XIX because (1) the Hyde Amendment is, by its own terms, only a limitation on federal reimbursement for certain medically necessary abortions, and (2) Title XIX does not permit a participating State to exclude from its Medicaid plan any medically necessary service solely on the basis of diagnosis or condition, even if federal reimbursement is unavailable for that service. It is thus the appellees' view that the effect of the Hyde Amendment is to withhold federal reimbursement for certain medically necessary abortions, but not to relieve a participating State of its duty under Title XIX to provide for such abortions in its Medicaid plan.

The District Court rejected this argument. It concluded that although Title XIX would otherwise have required a participating State to include medically necessary abortions in its Medicaid program, the Hyde Amendment substantively amended Title XIX so as to relieve a State of that obligation. This construction of the Hyde Amendment was said to find support in the decisions of two Courts of Appeals, *Preterm, Inc. v. Dukakis*, 591 F.2d 121 (CA 1 1979), and *Zbaraz v. Quern*, 596 F.2d 196 (CA7 1979), and to be consistent with the understanding of the effect of the Hyde Amendment by the Department of Health, Education, and Welfare in the administration of the Medicaid program.

We agree with the District Court, but for somewhat different reasons. The Medicaid program created by Title XIX is a cooperative endeavor in which the Federal Government provides financial assistance to participating States to aid them in furnishing health care to needy persons. Under this system of "cooperative federalism," * * * if a State agrees to establish a Medicaid plan that satisfies the requirements of Title XIX, which include several mandatory categories of health services, the Federal Government agrees to pay a specified percentage of "the total amount expended . . . as medical assistance under the State plan . . ." 42 U.S.C. § 1396(a)(1). The cornerstone of Medicaid is financial contribution by both the Federal Government and the participating State. Nothing in Title XIX as originally enacted, or in its legislative history, suggests that Congress intended to require a participating State to assume the full costs of providing any health services in its Medicaid plan. Quite the contrary, the purpose of Congress in enacting Title XIX was to provide federal financial assistance for all legitimate state expenditures under an approved Medicaid plan.* * *

Since the Congress that enacted Title XIX did not intend a participating State to assume a unilateral funding obligation for any health service in an approved Medicaid plan, it follows that Title XIX does not require a participating State to include in its plan any services for which a subsequent Congress has withheld federal funding. Title XIX was designed as a cooperative program of shared financial responsibility, not as a device for the Federal Government to compel a State to provide services that Congress itself is unwilling to fund. Thus, if Congress chooses to withdraw federal funding for a particular service, a State is not obliged to continue to pay for that service as a condition of continued federal financial support of other services. This is not to say that Congress may not now depart from the original design of Title XIX under which the Federal Government shares the financial responsibility for expenses incurred under an approved Medicaid plan. It is only to say that, absent an indication of contrary legislative intent by a subsequent Congress, Title XIX does not obligate a participating State to pay for those medical services for which federal reimbursement is unavailable.[13]

Thus, by the normal operation of Title XIX, even if a State were otherwise required to include medically necessary abortions in its Medicaid plan, the withdrawal of federal funding under the Hyde Amendment would operate to relieve the State of that obligation for those abortions for which federal reimbursement is unavailable. The legislative history of the Hyde Amendment contains no indication whatsoever that Congress intended to shift the entire cost of such services to the participating States. See *Zbaraz v. Quern, supra*, 596 F.2d, at 200 ("no one, whether supporting or opposing the Hyde Amendment, ever suggested that state funding would be required"). Rather, the legislative history suggests that Congress has always assumed that a participating State would not be required to fund medically necessary abortions once federal funding was withdrawn pursuant to the Hyde Amendment. * * * Accordingly, we conclude that Title XIX does not require a participating State to pay for those medically necessary abortions for which federal reimbursement is unavailable under the Hyde Amendment.[16]

III

Having determined that Title XIX does not obligate a participating State to pay for those medically necessary abortions for which Congress has withheld federal funding, we must consider the constitutional validity of the Hyde Amendment. The appellees assert that the funding restrictions of the Hyde Amendment violate several rights secured by the Constitution—(1) the right of a woman, implicit in the Due Process Clause of the Fifth Amendment, to decide whether to terminate a pregnancy, (2) the prohibition under the Establishment Clause of the First Amendment against any "law respecting an establishment of religion," and (3) the right to freedom of religion protected by the Free Exercise Clause of the First Amendment. The appellees also contend that, quite apart from substantive constitutional rights, the Hyde Amendment violates the equal protection component of the Fifth Amendment.

It is well settled that, quite apart from the guarantee of equal protection, if a law "impinges upon a fundamental right explicitly or implicitly secured by the Constitution [it] is presumptively unconstitutional." * * * Accordingly, before turning to the equal protection issue in this case, we examine whether the Hyde Amendment violates any substantive rights secured by the Constitution.

[13]When subsequent Congresses have deviated from the original structure of Title XIX by obligating a participating State to assume the full costs of a service as a prerequisite for continued federal funding of other services, they have always expressed their intent to do so in unambiguous terms. See *Zbaraz v. Quern, supra*, 596 F.2d, at 200, n. 12.

[16]A participating State is free, if it so chooses, to include in its Medicaid plan those medically necessary abortions for which federal reimbursement is unavailable. We hold only that a state *need* not include such abortions in its Medicaid plan.

A

We address first the appellees' argument that the Hyde Amendment, by restricting the availability of certain medically necessary abortions under Medicaid, impinges on the "liberty" protected by the Due Process Clause as recognized in *Roe v. Wade*, 410 U.S. 113, 93 S.Ct. 705, 35 L.Ed.2d 147, and its progeny.

In the *Wade* case, this Court held unconstitutional a Texas statute making it a crime to procure or attempt an abortion except on medical advice for the purpose of saving the mother's life. The constitutional underpinning of *Wade* was a recognition that the "liberty" protected by the Due Process Clause of the Fourteenth Amendment includes not only the freedoms explicitly mentioned in the Bill of Rights, but also a freedom of personal choice in certain matters of marriage and family life. This implicit constitutional liberty, the Court in *Wade* held, includes the freedom of a woman to decide whether to terminate a pregnancy.

But the Court in *Wade* also recognized that a State has legitimate interests during a pregnancy in both ensuring the health of the mother and protecting potential human life. These state interests, which were found to be "separate and distinct" and to "grow[ ] in substantiality as the woman approaches term," *id.*, at 162–163, 93 S.Ct., at 731, pose a conflict with a woman's untrammeled freedom of choice. In resolving this conflict, the Court held that before the end of the first trimester of pregnancy, neither state interest is sufficiently substantial to justify any intrusion on the woman's freedom of choice. In the second trimester, the state interest in maternal health was found to be sufficiently substantial to justify regulation reasonably related to that concern. And, at viability, usually in the third trimester, the state interest in protecting the potential life of the fetus was found to justify a criminal prohibition against abortions, except where necessary for the preservation of the life or health of the mother. Thus, inasmuch as the Texas criminal statute allowed abortions only where necessary to save the life of the mother and without regard to the stage of the pregnancy, the Court held in *Wade* that the statute violated the Due Process Clause of the Fourteenth Amendment.

* * *

The Hyde Amendment, like the Connecticut welfare regulation at issue in *Maher*, places no governmental obstacle in the path of a woman who chooses to terminate her pregnancy, but rather, by means of unequal subsidization of abortion and other medical services, encourages alternative activity deemed in the public interest. The present case does differ factually from *Maher* insofar as that case involved a failure to fund nontherapeutic abortions, whereas the Hyde Amendment withholds funding of certain medically necessary abortions. Accordingly, the appellees argue that because the Hyde Amendment affects a significant interest not present or asserted in *Maher*—the interest of a woman in protecting her health during pregnancy—and because that interest lies at the core of the personal constitutional freedom recognized in *Wade*, the present case is constitutionally different from *Maher*. It is the appellees' view that to the extent that the Hyde Amendment withholds funding for certain medically necessary abortions, it clearly impinges on the constitutional principle recognized in *Wade*.

It is evident that a woman's interest in protecting her health was an important theme in *Wade*. In concluding that the freedom of a woman to decide whether to terminate her pregnancy falls within the personal liberty protected by the Due Process Clause, the Court in *Wade* emphasized the fact that the woman's decision carries with it significant personal health implications—both physical and psychological. 410 U.S., at 153, 93 S.Ct., at 726. In fact, although the Court in *Wade* recognized that the state interest in protecting potential life becomes sufficiently compelling in the period after fetal viability to justify an absolute criminal prohibition of nontherapeutic abortions, the Court held that even after fetal viability a State may not prohibit abortions "necessary to preserve the life or health of the mother." *Id.*, at

164, 93 S.Ct., at 732. Because even the compelling interest of the State in protecting potential life after fetal viability was held to be insufficient to outweigh a woman's decision to protect her life or health, it could be argued that the freedom of a woman to decide whether to terminate her pregnancy for health reasons does in fact lie at the core of the constitutional liberty identified in *Wade*.

But, regardless of whether the freedom of a woman to choose to terminate her pregnancy for health reasons lies at the core or the periphery of the due process liberty recognized in *Wade*, it simply does not follow that a woman's freedom of choice carries with it a constitutional entitlement to the financial resources to avail herself of the full range of protected choices. The reason why was explained in *Maher*: although government may not place obstacles in the path of a woman's exercise of her freedom of choice, it need not remove those not of its own creation. Indigency falls in the latter category. The financial constraints that restrict an indigent woman's ability to enjoy the full range of constitutionally protected freedom of choice are the product not of governmental restrictions on access to abortions, but rather of her indigency. Although Congress has opted to subsidize medically necessary services generally, but not certain medically necessary abortions, the fact remains that the Hyde Amendment leaves an indigent woman with at least the same range of choice in deciding whether to obtain a medically necessary abortion as she would have had if Congress had chosen to subsidize no health care costs at all. We are thus not persuaded that the Hyde Amendment impinges on the constitutionally protected freedom of choice recognized in *Wade*.[19]

Although the liberty protected by the Due Process Clause affords protection against unwarranted government interference with freedom of choice in the context of certain personal decisions, it does not confer an entitlement to such funds as may be necessary to realize all the advantages of that freedom. To hold otherwise would mark a drastic change in our understanding of the Constitution. It cannot be that because government may not prohibit the use of contraceptives, *Griswold v. Connecticut*, 381 U.S. 479, 85 S.Ct. 1678, 14 L.Ed.2d 510, or prevent parents from sending their children to a private school, *Pierce v. Society of Sisters*, 268 U.S. 510, 45 S.Ct. 571, 69 L.Ed. 1070, government, therefore, has an affirmative constitutional obligation to ensure that all persons have the financial resources to obtain contraceptives or send their children to private schools. To translate the limitation on governmental power implicit in the Due Process Clause into an affirmative funding obligation would require Congress to subsidize the medically necessary abortion of an indigent woman even if Congress had not enacted a Medicaid program to subsidize other medically necessary services. Nothing in the Due Process Clause supports such an extraordinary result.[20] Whether freedom of choice that is constitutionally protected warrants federal subsidization is a question for Congress to

[19]The appellees argue that the Hyde Amendment is unconstitutional because it "penalizes" the exercise of a woman's choice to terminate a pregnancy by abortion.* * *
This argument falls short of the mark.* * *
* * *regardless of how the claim was characterized, the *Maher* Court rejected the argument that Connecticut's refusal to subsidize protected conduct, without more, impinged on the constitutional freedom of choice. * * * Rather, the Hyde Amendment, like the Connecticut welfare provision at issue in *Maher*, represents simply a refusal to subsidize certain protected conduct. A refusal to fund protected activity, without more, cannot be equated with the imposition of a "penalty" on that activity.

[20]As this Court in *Maher* observed: "The Constitution imposes no obligation on the [Government] to pay the pregnancy-related medical expenses of indigent women, or indeed to pay any of the medical expenses of indigents." 432 U.S., at 469, 97 S.Ct., at 2380.

answer, not a matter of constitutional entitlement. Accordingly, we conclude that the Hyde Amendment does not impinge on the due process liberty recognized in *Wade*.

B

The appellees also argue that the Hyde Amendment contravenes rights secured by the Religion Clauses of the First Amendment. It is the appellees' view that the Hyde Amendment violates the Establishment Clause because it incorporates into law the doctrine of the Roman Catholic Church concerning the sinfulness of abortion and the time at which life commences. Moreover, insofar as a woman's decision to seek a medically necessary abortion may be a product of her religious beliefs under certain Protestant and Jewish tenets, the appellees assert that the funding limitations of the Hyde Amendment impinge on the freedom of religion guaranteed by the Free Exercise Clause.

1

It is well settled that "a legislative enactment does not contravene the Establishment Clause if it has a secular legislative purpose, if its principal or primary effect neither advances nor inhibits religion, and if it does not foster an excessive governmental entanglement with religion." *Committee for Pub. Ed. & Rel. Lib. v. Reagan*, 444 U.S. ____, ____, 100 S.Ct. 840, 846, 63 L.Ed.2d 94. Applying this standard, the District Court properly concluded that the Hyde Amendment does not run afoul of the Establishment Clause. Although neither a State nor the Federal Government can constitutionally "pass laws which aid one religion, aid all religions, or prefer one religion over another," *Everson v. Board of Education*, 330 U.S. 1, 15, 67 S.Ct. 504, 511, 91 L.Ed. 711, it does not follow that a statute violates the Establishment Clause because it "happens to coincide or harmonize with the tenets of some or all religions." *McGowan v. Maryland*, 366 U.S. 420, 442, 81 S.Ct. 1101, 1113, 6 L.Ed.2d 393. That the Judaeo-Christian religions oppose stealing does not mean that a State or the Federal Government may not, consistent with the Establishment Clause, enact laws prohibiting larceny. *Ibid.* The Hyde Amendment, as the District Court noted, is as much a reflection of "traditionalist" values towards abortion, as it is an embodiment of the views of any particular religion. See also *Roe v. Wade, supra*, 410 U.S., at 138–141, 93 S.Ct., at 719–721. In sum, we are convinced that the fact that the funding restrictions in the Hyde Amendment may coincide with the religious tenets of the Roman Catholic Church does not, without more, contravene the Establishment Clause.

* * *

C

It remains to be determined whether the Hyde Amendment violates the equal protection component of the Fifth Amendment. This challenge is premised on the fact that, although federal reimbursement is available under Medicaid for medically necessary services generally, the Hyde Amendment does not permit federal reimbursement of all medically necessary abortions. The District Court held, and the appellees argue here, that this selective subsidization violates the constitutional guarantee of equal protection.

The guarantee of equal protection under the Fifth Amendment is not a source of substantive rights or liberties, but rather a right to be free from invidious discrimination in statutory classifications and other governmental activity. It is well-settled that where a statutory classification does not itself impinge on a right or liberty protected by the Constitution, the validity of classification must be sustained unless "the classification rests on grounds wholly irrelevant to the achievement of [any legitimate governmental] objective." *McGowan v. Maryland, supra*, 366 U.S., at 425, 81 S.Ct., at 1105. This presumption of constitutional validity, however, disappears if a statutory classification is predicated on criteria that are, in a constitutional sense, "suspect," the principal example of which is a classification based on race, *e. g., Brown v. Board of Education*, 347 U.S. 483, 74 S.Ct. 686, 98 L.Ed. 873.

1

For the reasons stated above, we have already concluded that the Hyde Amendment violates no constitutionally protected substantive rights. We now conclude as well that it is not predicated on a constitutionally suspect classification. In reaching this conclusion, we again draw guidance from the Court's decision in *Maher v. Roe*. As to whether the Connecticut welfare regulation providing funds for childbirth but not for nontherapeutic abortions discriminated against a suspect class, the Court in *Maher* observed:

> "An indigent woman desiring an abortion does not come within the limited category of disadvantaged classes so recognized by our cases. Nor does the fact that the impact of the regulation falls upon those who cannot pay lead to a different conclusion. In a sense, every denial of welfare to an indigent creates a wealth classification as compared to nonindigents who are able to pay for the desired goods or services. But this Court has never held that financial need alone identifies a suspect class for purposes of equal protection analysis."* * *

Thus, the Court in *Maher* found no basis for concluding that the Connecticut regulation was predicated on a suspect classification.

It is our view that the present case in indistinguishable from *Maher* in this respect. Here, as in *Maher*, the principal impact of the Hyde Amendment falls on the indigent. But that fact does not itself render the funding restriction constitutionally invalid, for this Court has held repeatedly that poverty, standing alone is not a suspect classification. See, *e. .g., James v. Valtierra*, 402 U.S. 137, 91 S.Ct. 1331, 28 L.Ed.2d 678. That *Maher* involved the refusal to fund nontherapeutic abortions, whereas the present case involves the refusal to fund medically necessary abortions, has no bearing on the factors that render a classification "suspect" within the meaning of the constitutional guarantee of equal protection.

2

The remaining question then is whether the Hyde Amendment is rationally related to a legitimate governmental objective. It is the Government's position that the Hyde Amendment bears a rational relationship to its legitimate interest in protecting the potential life of the fetus. We agree.

In *Wade*, the Court recognized that the State has "[an] important and legitimate interest in protecting the potentiality of human life." 410 U.S., at 162, 93 S.Ct., at 731. That interest was found to exist throughout a pregnancy, "grow[ing] in substantially as the woman approaches term." * * * Moreover, in *Maher*, the Court held that Connecticut's decision to fund the costs associated with childbirth but not those associated with nontherapeutic abortions was a rational means of advancing the legitimate state interest in protecting potential life by encouraging childbirth.* * *

It follows that the Hyde Amendment, by encouraging childbirth except in the most urgent circumstances, is rationally related to the legitimate governmental objective of protecting potential life. By subsidizing the medical expenses of indigent women who carry their pregnancies to term while not subsidizing the comparable expenses of women who undergo abortions (except those whose lives are threatened), Congress has established incentives that make childbirth a more attractive alternative than abortion for persons eligible for Medicaid. These incentives bear a direct relationship to the legitimate congressional interest in protecting potential life. Nor is it irrational that Congress has authorized federal reimbursement for medically necessary services generally, but not for certain medically necessary abortions. Abortion is inherently different from other medical procedures, because no other procedure involves the purposeful termination of a potential life.

After conducting an extensive evidentiary hearing into issues surrounding the public funding of abortions, the District Court concluded that "[t]he interests of . . . the federal government . . . in the fetus and in preserving it are not sufficient, weighed in the balance with the woman's threatened health, to justify withdrawing medical assistance unless the woman consents . . . to carry the fetus to term." In making an independent appraisal of the competing interests involved here, the District Court went beyond the judicial function. Such decisions are entrusted under the Constitution to Congress, not the courts. It is the role of the courts only to ensure that congressional decisions comport with the Constitution.

Where, as here, the Congress has neither invaded a substantive constitutional right or freedom, nor enacted legislation that purposefully operates to the detriment of a suspect class, the only requirement of equal protection is that congressional action be rationally related to a legitimate governmental interest. The Hyde Amendment satisfies that standard. It is not the mission of this Court or any other to decide whether the balance of competing interests reflected in the Hyde Amendment is wise social policy. If that were our mission, not every Justice who has subscribed to the judgment of the Court today could have done so. But we cannot, in the name of the Constitution, overturn duly enacted statutes simply "because they may be unwise, inprovident, or out of harmony with a particular school of thought."* * *

Rather, "when an issue involves policy choices as sensitive as those implicated [here] . . . , the appropriate forum for their resolution in a democracy is the legislature."* * *

IV

For the reasons stated in this opinion, we hold that a State that participates in the Medicaid program is not obligated under Title XIX to continue to fund those medically necessary abortions for which federal reimbursement is unavailable under the Hyde Amendment. We further hold that the funding restrictions of the Hyde Amendment violate neither the Fifth Amendment nor the Establishment Clause of the First Amendment. It is also our view that the appellees lack standing to raise a challenge to the Hyde Amendment under the Free Exercise Clause of the First Amendment. Accordingly, the judgment of the District Court is reversed, and the case is remanded to that court for further proceedings consistent with this opinion.

It is so ordered.

---

3. Indirect Restrictions and Voluntary Methods of Population Control.

There are many policies and programs by which government may discourage the growth of population without blatant and direct limitation of the individual's ability to make his or her own decision about family size. Some of the measures suggested by Johnson C. Montgomery in "The Population Explosion and United States Law," *supra*, are:

- Repeal of all laws that limit sterilization, and adoption of state statutes that relieve doctors from liability for pregnancy that may occur after a sterilization procedure.

- Repeal of all laws that limit the right to abortion.
- Subsidization of contraception, sterilization and abortion by requiring all health insurance policies to cover the costs of such procedures and authorizing direct payment of such costs by welfare and medicare programs.
- Cash payments to individuals who are willing to undergo sterilization procedures.
- Payment of an annual subsidy to each woman of childbearing age who does not give birth during a given year.
- Revising the tax laws to (*1*) remove the exemption for children or for all children after the first two; (*2*) grant tax deductions, or a direct credit, for all monies spent for contraception, sterilization and abortion.
- Allocate funds for research on the technology of contraception, sterilization and abortion and methods of population control, including research into the process by which the sex of the offspring may be controlled.
- Provide women with fulfilling activity unrelated to childbearing; this includes programs to end sexual discrimination in education, employment, promotion and compensation.

Some of the measures listed above were incorporated into the Family Services and Population Research Act of 1970, Pub. L. No. 91-572, 84 Stat. 1504, that provided funding for family planning, including the voluntary use of contraceptives. The purposes of the Act, set forth in Section 2 thereof, are:

(*1*) To assist in making comprehensive voluntary family planning services readily available to all persons desiring such services; (*2*) To coordinate domestic population and family planning research with the present and future needs of family planning programs; (*3*) To improve administrative and operational supervision of domestic family-planning services and of population research programs related to such services; (*4*) To enable public and nonprivate entities to plan and develop comprehensive programs of family-planning services; (*5*) To develop and make readily available information (including education materials) on family planning and population growth to all persons desiring such information; (*6*) To evaluate and improve the effectiveness of family-planning service programs and population reasearch; (*7*) To assist in providing trained manpower needed to effectively carry out programs of population research and family planning services; and (*8*) To establish an Office of Population Affairs in the Department of Health, Education and Welfare [now Health and Human Services] as a primary focus within the federal government on matters pertaining to population research and family planning, through which the Secretary of Health, Education and Welfare . . . shall carry out the purposes of this Act.

There seems to be adequate constitutional authority for this federal legislation that is only an exercise of the spending power and does not impose family planning or restrict the right of anyone to determine family size. The issue becomes much more difficult when family-planning objectives are implemented by coercive measures. The attempt to limit the size of families receiving welfare assistance is an illustration of such governmental coercion. Supporters of this governmental policy frequently quote the statement in Swift's *Gulliver's Travels* (R. Greenberg, ed., 1961, at 43) that "[T]he Lilliputians thinking nothing can be more unjust, than that People, in Subservience to their own Appetities, should bring Children into the World, and leave the [burden] of supporting them on the Publick." On the basis of the value judgment conveyed by that statement some states have placed a limit on the total amount of public welfare assistance that may be paid under the Aid to Families with Dependent Children (AFDC) so that at some point an additional child will not increase the amount of assistance for which the family is eligible. Such restriction falls harshly on poor families and has been challenged on the ground that it discriminates against poor people and violates the Equal Protection Clause. The United States Supreme Court responded to this challenge in *Dandridge v. Williams*, below.

DANDRIDGE v. WILLIAMS

397 U.S. 471 (1970)

Mr. Justice STEWART delivered the opinion of the Court.

This case involves the validity of a method used by Maryland, in the administration of an aspect of its public welfare program, to reconcile the demands of its needy citizens with the finite resources available to meet those demands. Like every other State in the Union, Maryland participates in the Federal Aid to Families With Dependent Children (AFDC) program, 42 U. S. C. § 601 *et seq*. (1964 ed. and Supp. IV), which originated with the Social Security Act of 1935.* * *

The operation of the Maryland welfare system is not complex. By statute the State participates in the AFDC program. It computes the standard of need for each eligible family based on the number of children in the family and the circumstances under which the family lives. In general, the standard of need increases with each additional person in the household, but the increments become proportionately smaller. The regulation here in issue imposes upon the grant that any single family may receive an upper limit of $250 per month in certain counties and Baltimore City, and of $240 per month elsewhere in the State. The appellees all have large families, so that their standards of need as computed by the State substantially exceed the maximum grants that they actually receive under the regulation. The appellees urged in the District Court that the maximum grant limitation operates to discriminate against them merely because of the size of their families, in violation of the Equal Protection Clause of the Fourteenth Amendment. They claimed further that the regulation is incompatible with the purpose of the Social Security Act of 1935, as well as in conflict with its explicit provisions.

In its original opinion the District Court held that the Maryland regulation does conflict with the federal statute, and also concluded that it violates the Fourteenth Amendment's equal protection guarantee. After reconsideration on motion, the court issued a new opinion resting its determination of the regulation's invalidity entirely on the constitutional ground. Both the statutory and constitutional issues have been fully briefed and argued here, and the judgment of the District Court must, of course, be affirmed if the Maryland regulation is in conflict with either the federal statute or the Constitution. We consider the statutory question first, because if the appellees' position on this question is correct, there is no occasion to reach the constitutional issues. *Ashwander* v. *TVA*, 297 U. S. 288, 346–347 (Brandeis, J., concurring); *Rosenberg* v. *Fleuti*, 374 U. S. 449.

The appellees contend that the maximum grant system is contrary to § 402(a)(10) of the Social Security Act, as amended, which requires that a state plan shall

> provide . . . that all individuals wishing to make application for aid to families with dependent children shall have opportunity to do so, and that aid to families with dependent children shall be furnished with reasonable promptness to all eligible individuals.

The argument is that the state regulation denies benefits to the younger children in a large family. Thus, the appellees say, the regulation is in patent violation of the Act, since those younger children are just as "dependent" as their older siblings under the definition of "dependent child" fixed by federal law. See *King* v. *Smith*, 392 U.S. 309. Moreover, it is argued that the regulation, in limiting the amount of money any single household may receive, contravenes a basic purpose of the federal law by encouraging the parents of large families to "farm out" their children to relatives whose grants are not yet subject to the maximum limitation.

It cannot be gainsaid that the effect of the Maryland maximum grant provision is to reduce the per capita benefits to the children in the largest families. Although the appellees argue that the younger and more recently arrived children in such families are totally deprived of aid, a more realistic view is that the lot of the entire family is diminished because of the presence of additional children without any increase in payments.* * *

For the reasons that follow, we have concluded that the Maryland regulation is permissible under the federal law.

In *King* v. *Smith, supra*, we stressed the States' "undisputed power," under these provisions of the Social Security Act, "to set the level of benefits and the standard of need." *Id.*, at 334. We described the AFDC enterprise as "a scheme of cooperative federalism," *id.*, at 316, and noted carefully that "[t]here is no question that States have considerable latitude in allocating their AFDC resources, since each State is free to set its own standard of need and to determine the level of benefits by the amount of funds it devotes to the program."* * * Thus the starting point of the statutory analysis must be a recognition that the federal law gives each State great latitude in dispensing its available funds.

The very title of the program, the repeated references to families added in 1962, Pub. L. 87–543, § 104 (a)(3), 76 Stat. 185, and the words of the preamble quoted above, show that Congress wished to help children through the family structure. The operation of the statute itself has this effect. From its inception the Act has defined "dependent child" in part by reference to the relatives with whom the child lives. When a "dependent child" is living with relatives, then "aid" also includes payments and medical care to those relatives, including the spouse of the child's parent. 42 U.S.C. § 606(b) (1964 ed., Supp. IV). Thus, as the District Court noted, the amount of aid "is . . . computed by treating the relative, parent or spouse of parent, as the case may be, of the 'dependent child' as a part of the family unit."* * *

The States must respond to this federal statutory concern for preserving children in a family environment. Given Maryland's finite resources, its choice is either to support some families adequately and others less adequately, or not to give sufficient support to any family. We see nothing in the federal statute that forbids a State to balance the stresses that uniform insufficiency of payments would impose on all families against the greater abiilty of large families—because of the inherent economies of scale—to accommodate their needs to diminished per capita payments.* * *

For even if a parent should be inclined to increase his per capita family income by sending a child away, the federal law requires that the child, to be eligible for AFDC payments, must live with one of several enumerated relatives. The kinship tie may be attenuated but it cannot be destroyed.* * *

So long as some aid is provided to all eligible families and all eligible children, the statute itself is not violated.

This is the view that has been taken by the Secretary of Health, Education, and Welfare (HEW), who is charged with the administration of the Social Security Act and the approval of state welfare plans. The parties have stipulated that the Secretary has, on numerous occasions, approved the Maryland welfare scheme, including its provision of maximum payments to any one family, a provision that has been in force in various forms since 1947. Moreover, a majority of the States pay less than their determined standard of need, and 20 of these States impose maximums on family grants of the kind here in issue.* * *

Although a State may adopt a maximum grant system in allocating its funds available for AFDC payments without violating the Act, it may not, of course, impose a regime of invidious discrimination in violation of the Equal Protection Clause of the Fourteenth Amendment. Maryland says that its maximum grant regulation is wholly free of any invidiously discriminatory purpose or effect, and that the regulation is rationally supportable on at least four entirely valid grounds. The regulation can be clearly justified, Maryland argues, in terms of legitimate state interests in encouraging gainful employment, in maintaining an equitable balance in economic status as between welfare families and those supported by a wage-earner, in providing incentives for family planning, and in allocating available public funds in such a way as fully to meet the needs of the largest possible number of families. The District Court, while apparently recognizing the validity of at least some of these state concerns, nonetheless held that the regulation "is invalid on its face for overreaching," 297 F.Supp., at 468—that it violates the Equal Protection Clause "[b]ecause it cuts too broad a swath on an indiscriminate basis as applied to the entire group of AFDC eligibles to which it purports to apply. . . ." 297 F.Supp., at 469.

If this were a case involving government action claimed to violate the First Amendment guarantee of free speech, a finding of "overreaching" would be significant and might be crucial. For when otherwise valid governmental regulation sweeps so broadly as to impinge upon activity protected by the First Amendment, its very overbreadth may make it unconstitutional. See, *e. g., Shelton v. Tucker*, 364 U. S. 479. But the concept of "overreaching" has no place in this case. For there we deal with state regulation in the social and economic field not affecting freedoms guaranteed by the Bill of Rights, and claimed to violate the Fourteenth Amendment only because the regulation results in some disparity in grants of welfare payments to the largest AFDC families. For this Court to approve the invalidation of state economic or social regulation as "overreaching" would be far too reminiscent of an era when the Court thought the Fourteenth Amendment gave it power to strike down state laws "because they may be unwise, improvident, or out of harmony with a particular school of thought." *Williamson* v. *Lee Optical Co.*, 348 U. S. 483, 488. That era long ago passed into history. *Ferguson* v. *Skrupa*, 372 U. S. 726.

In the area of economics and social welfare, a State does not violate the Equal Protection Clause merely because the classifications made by its laws are imperfect. If the classification has some "reasonable basis," it does not offend the Constitution simply because the classification "is not made with mathematical nicety or because in practice it results in some inequality."* * *

Under this long-established meaning of the Equal Protection Clause, it is clear that the Maryland maximum grant regulation is constitutionally valid. We need not explore all the reasons that the State advances in justification of the regulation. It is enough that a solid foundation for the regulation can be found in the State's legitimate interest in encouraging employment and in avoiding discrimination between welfare families and the families of the working poor. By combining a limit on the recipient's grant with permission to retain money earned, without reduction in the amount of the grant, Maryland provides an incentive to seek gainful employment. And by keying the maximum family AFDC grants to the minimum wage a steadily employed head of the household receives, the State maintains some semblance of an equitable balance between families on welfare and those supported by an employed breadwinner.

It is true that in some AFDC families there may be no person who is employable. It is also true that with respect to AFDC families whose determined standard of need is below the regulatory maximum, and who therefore receive grants equal to the determined standard, the employment incentive is absent. But the Equal Protection Clause does not require that a State must choose between attacking every aspect of a problem or not attacking the problem at all. *Lindsley* v. *Natural Carbonic Gas Co.*, 220 U. S. 61. It is enough that the State's action be rationally based and free from invidious discrimination. The regulation before us meets that test.

We do not decide today that the Maryland regulation is wise, that it best fulfills the relevant social and economic objectives that Maryland might ideally espouse, or that a more just and human system could not be devised. Conflicting claims of morality and intelligence are raised by opponents and proponents of almost every measure, certainly including the one before us. But the intractable economic, social, and even philosophical problems presented by public welfare assistance programs are not the business of ths Court. The Constitution may impose certain procedural safeguards upon systems of welfare administration, *Goldberg* v. *Kelly, ante*, p. 254. But the Constitution does not empower this Court to second-guess state officials charged with the difficult responsibility of allocating limited public welfare funds among the myriad of potential recipients. Cf. *Steward Mach. Co.* v. *Davis*, 301 U. S. 548, 584–585; *Helvering* v. *Davis*, 301 U. S. 619, 644.

The judgment is reversed.

Mr. Justice Douglas, dissenting.

C. **Regulation of Population Distribution**

The 1980 census revealed significant changes in the distribution of population in the United States. In the decade between 1970 and 1980 the total population rose by 23.2 million people to 226,504,000. The major shift in population has been to the south and west. The three "sun-belt" states, Florida, Texas and California, increased by more than 10 million people between 1970 and 1980. The increase in population in these states is attributed to a migration of population from the "snow-belt" states as well as an increase in immigration of Hispanic people. The shift in national population is also attributed to a national preference for warm weather (and the lower energy costs related thereto), the availability of new jobs created in the sun-belt states and a new phenomenon of a growing national preference for places with lower population densities.

This new preference seems to be borne out by the changes in population of major cities and the differences in rate of growth of the states. Population of the 50 largest cities dropped 4% to 39 million; the next 50 largest cities increased by 5% to 10 million and the third 50 largest cities increased by 11 percent to over 6 million. This new preference for places with lower population densities is confirmed by the differences in the rate of growth among the states. Only two states, Rhode Island and New York, and the District of Columbia lost population. Among the states that grew at a slower rate than the national average are Pennsylvania, Massachusetts, Ohio, Connecticut, New Jersey and Illinois. Among the states that grew at a rate faster than the national average are Nevada, Arizona, Florida, Wyoming, Utah and Alaska.

As these shifts in population began to manifest themselves during the second half of the 1970s many government officials took notice and reconsidered their urban policies. In 1979, President Carter announced an "urban conservation" policy by which the federal government would weigh the advantages and disadvantages to cities of various federal programs and would redirect those federal loans and grants that would weaken established central business districts in distressed communities or promote unnecessary urban sprawl. The policy resulted from complaints of mayors and urban adivsors that the federal government, through its highway, sewer and water funds, had encouraged construction of outlying shopping centers that diverted business from the downtown areas.

In 1978, Governor Brown of California proposed "An Urban Strategy for California" in which he recommended, among other things, that new urban development in California be located according to the following priorities:

> "*First Priority*: Renew and maintain existing urban areas, both cities and suburbs.
>
> *Second Priority*: Develop vacant and underutilized land within existing urban and suburban areas and presently served by streets, water, sewer and other public services. Open space, historic buildings, recreational opportunities and the distinct identities of neighborhoods should be preserved.
>
> *Third Priority*: When urban development is necessary outside existing urban and suburban areas, use land that is immediately adjacent.

> Noncontiguous development would be appropriate when needed to accommodate planned open space, greenbelts, agricultural preservation or new town community development."

The California urban strategy included recommendations to increase the density of urban areas to help conserve existing urban development, protect existing neighborhoods, provide incentives for new private construction, save public dollars for capital facilities and energy, and to help protect agricultural land.

At the same time that the California urban strategy was being formulated, Brendan Byrne, then the governor of the highly urbanized frost-belt state of New Jersey, proposed a growth policy to direct population growth away from farmlands, pinelands and other valuable natural resources and to the cities and suburbs to stabilize their economies. The objective of the policy was to use the state's regulatory powers and public funds, such as water, sewer, energy and transportation, to direct the movement of population in the state instead of merely responding to the demands made by development. In Governor Byrne's sixth annual report to the state in 1980 he expressed the state administration's policy to shift population growth to already developed areas and away from fragile remaining natural resources.

During the decade of the 1970s many municipalities throughout the nation adopted programs and land-use laws to regulate the movement of population into their jurisdictions. The judicial decisions testing the validity of those programs and laws can be analyzed under the following categories: (*1*) programs of growth management to coordinate population growth with public services; (*2*) laws that discriminate against nonresidents; (*3*) land-use laws that exclude social and economic groups; (*4*) laws with racial discriminatory intent or effect.

1. Growth Management: Coordination of Population Growth

a. *Control of Growth Rate*

The essence of the planning process is the attempt to analyze the future needs and resources of a community for the purpose of providing for those needs in a rational, comprehenisve and coordinated manner. It is the nature of the planning process to attempt to determine the community's goals and objectives for future development and population growth and to provide for public services to meet the needs of future populations. Several communities have sought to implement such plans. The cases that follow provide some judicial responses to these plans.

Construction Industry Association v. City of Petaluma is now a landmark decision of the federal courts on the validity of a plan designed to regulate a community's rate of growth. The plan of the city of Petaluma, California set forth its growth control objectives unambiguously in its opening sentence: "In order to protect its small town character and surrounding open spaces, it shall be the policy of the City to control its future rate and distribution of growth." The plan consisted of several ordinances and statements of policy that sought to achieve the following:

(*1*) Limit new housing construction to 500 units per year.

(*2*) Draw an "urban extension line" to indicate the geographical outer limits of the city's growth for the next twenty years or more.

(*3*) Within the boundary of the urban extension line, prescribe zoning densities to limit the city's population to 55,000.

(*4*) Establish a policy by which the city would refuse to annex or to extend city facilities outside the urban extension line.

(*5*) Establish a complicated "Catch 22" application procedure for building permits that would tend to discourage builders from applying for permits.

(*6*) Although intended to last only to 1977, extend the plan at least to 1990 by official actions; e.g. the city entered into a contract with a water company until 1990, to provide water for a population of only 55,000.

The federal district court described each of the components of the Petaluma Plan in an extensive statement of its findings of fact. The court also found that if the Petaluma growth limits were adopted through the region it would result in: (*1*) regionwide increase in the cost of housing; (*2*) a decline in the quality of housing stock through the region; (*3*) a loss of mobility of residents of the region, which would tend to keep people in the cities; and (*4*) a regional increase in the percentage of substandard housing and a limitation of the choice of housing to persons with incomes under $14,000 per year.

Based on these findings of fact, the court then set forth its conclusion of law. At the outset, the court made it clear that its decision was based on decisions of the United States Supreme Court in a long line of cases that **freedom to travel** is a "fundamental right" protected by the Constitution, and this right includes the right to enter and live in any state or municipality in the nation. Having previously found that the express purpose and actual effect of the Petaluma Plan was to exclude substantial numbers of people who would otherwise have elected to migrate to the city, the court determined that this **limitation of population growth** could be defended only insofar as it furthered a "compelling state interest."

The city of Petaluma had argued that there were three such compelling interests that would support the exclusionary measure. First, the city asserted that its sewage treatment facilities were inadequate to serve an uncontrolled population growth. However, the court found that the city's facilities for expansion were sufficient to meet the needs of a growing population. The court then suggested that, even if the facilities were inadequate, they could be increased. The court proposed further, in dicta, that even though courts will not order citizens to vote for expenditure of funds, "neither Petaluma city officials, nor the local electorate may use their power to disapprove bonds at the polls as a 'weapon' to define or destroy fundamental constitutional rights."

The second argument made by the city was that its water supply was inadequate for enlarged population growth. However, the court rejected this argument on the finding that the city purposefully calculated its water needs based on the restricted population projections and contracted for its water supply to meet the limited population. Such an alleged inadequacy of water supply was self-created, easily overcome by contracting for an enlarged supply and therefore, not a compelling interest that would justify a population limitation.

The city's third argument was that the zoning power gave it the right to control its own rate of growth and to protect the character of the community. In response, the court held that a municipality capable of supporting a natural population expansion **may not limit growth simply because it does not prefer to grow** at the rate which would be dictated by prevailing market demand. It based this decision on the Supreme Court cases holding that the right to travel is a "fundamental right" and on the reasoning adopted by Pennsylvania courts which invalidated zoning ordinances that sought to exclude newcomers. The court cited with approval the following excerpts from those cases:

> The question posed is whether the township can stand in the way of the natural forces which send out growing population into hitherto undeveloped areas in search of a comfortable place to live. We have concluded not. A zoning ordinance whose primary purpose is to prevent the entrance of newcomers in order to avoid future burdens, economic or otherwise, upon the administration of public services and facilities cannot be held valid. . . . *National Land & Inv. Co. v. Kohn*, 215 A.2d 597 at 612 (1966).
>
> The implication of our decision in National Land is that communities must deal with the problems of population growth. They may not refuse to confront the future by adopting zoning regulations that effectively restrict population to near present levels. It is not for any given township to say who may or may not live within its confines, while disregarding the interests of the entire areas. If Concord Township is successful in unnaturally limiting its population growth through the use of exclusive zoning regulations, the people who would normally live there will inevitably have to live in another community, and the requirement that they do so is not a decision that Concord Township should alone be able to make. *Appeal of Kit-Mar Builders*, 268 A.2d 765 at 768–769 (1970).

Based on this analysis, the district court held that Petaluma's population growth limitations were not supported by any compelling governmental interest and were unconstitutional because they violated the right to travel. The court also declared that its decision is intended to encompass not only the limitation on the issuance of building permits but also "all other features of the plan which, directly or indirectly, seek to control population growth by any means other than market demands."

In 1975 the United States Court of Appeals (Ninth Circuit) reversed for the reasons expressed in the opinion set forth below. The United States Supreme Court refused to hear an appeal of this case.

City of Boca Raton v. Boca Villas Corp., set forth after the *Petaluma* decision, illustrates the need for careful documentation and preparation for a municipal ordinance that seeks to limit population growth. The Boca Raton ordinance sought to place a "cap" on population growth by providing that no building permits shall be issued when the total number of dwelling units within the city reaches 40,000. The testimony at the trial did not provide evidence of water, utility or public service need to justify this limitation on the growth of population. This case is sometimes cited as an illustration of how *not* to propose or adopt growth management legislation.

CONSTRUCTION INDUSTRY ASSOCIATION OF SONOMA COUNTY v. THE CITY OF PETALUMA

522 F.2d 897 (9th Cir. 1975)

CHOY, Circuit Judge:

The City of Petaluma (the City) appeals from a district court decision voiding as unconstitutional certain aspects of its five-year housing and zoning plan. We reverse.

Statement of Facts

The City is located in southern Sonoma County, about 40 miles north of San Francisco. In the 1950's and 1960's, Petaluma was a relatively self-sufficient town. It experienced a steady population growth from 10,315 in 1950 to 24,870 in 1970. Eventually, the City was drawn into the Bay Area metropolitan housing market as people working in San Francisco and San Rafael became willing to commute longer distances to secure relatively inexpensive housing available there. By November 1972, according to unofficial figures, Petaluma's population was at 30,500, a dramatic increase of almost 25 per cent in little over two years.* * *

To correct the imbalance between single-family and multi-family dwellings, curb the sprawl of the City on the east, and retard the accelerating growth of the City, the Council in 1972 adopted several resolutions, which collectively are called the "Petaluma Plan" (the Plan).

The Plan, on its face limited to a five-year period (1972–1977), fixes a housing development growth rate not to exceed 500 dwelling units per year. Each dwelling unit represents approximately three people. The 500-unit figure is somewhat misleading, however, because it applies only to housing units (hereinafter referred to as "development-units") that are part of projects involving five units or more. Thus, the 500-unit figure does not reflect any housing and population growth due to construction of single-family homes or even four-unit apartment buildings not part of any larger project.

The Plan also positions a 200 foot wide "greenbelt" around the City, to serve as a boundary for urban expansion for at least five years, and with respect to the east and north sides of the City, for perhaps ten to fifteen years. One of the most innovative features of the Plan is the Residential Development Control System which provides procedures and criteria for the award of the annual 500 development-unit permits. At the heart of the allocation procedure is an intricate point system, whereby a builder accumulates points for conformity by his projects with the City's general plan and environmental design plans, for good architectual design, and for providing low and moderate income dwelling units and various recreational facilities. The Plan further directs that allocations of building permits are to be divided as evenly as feasible between the west and east sections of the City and between single-family dwellings and multiple residential units (including rental units), that the sections of the City closest to the center are to be developed first in order to cause "infilling" of vacant area, and that 8 to 12 per cent of the housing units approved be for low and moderate income persons.* * *

Purpose of the Plan

The purpose of the Plan is much disputed in this case. According to general statements in the Plan itself, the Plan was devised to ensure that "development in the next five years, will take place in a reasonable, or orderly, attractive manner, rather than in a completely haphazard and unattractive manner." The controversial 500-unit limitation on residential development-units was adopted by the City "(i)n order to protect its small town character and surrounding open space." The other features of the Plan were designed to encourage an east-west balance in development, to provide for variety in densities and building types and wide ranges in prices and rents, to ensure infilling of close-in vacant areas, and to prevent the sprawl of the City to the east and north. The Construction Industry Association of Sonoma County (the Association) argues and the district court found, however, that the Plan was primarily enacted "to limit Petaluma's demographic and market growth rate in housing and in the immigration of new residents."

Market Demand and Effect of the Plan

In 1970 and 1971, housing permits were allotted at the rate of 1000 annually, and there was no indication that without some governmental control on growth consumer demand would subside or even remain at the 1000-unit per year level. Thus, if Petaluma had imposed a flat 500-unit limitation on *all* residential housing, the effect of the Plan would clearly be to retard to a substantial degree the natural growth rate of the City. Petaluma, however, did not apply the 500-unit limitation across the board, but instead exempted all projects of four units or less. Because appellees failed to introduce any evidence whatsoever as to the number of exempt units expected to be built during the five-year period, the effect of the 500 *development-unit* limitation on the natural growth in housing is uncertain. For purposes of this decision, however, we will assume that the 500 development-unit growth rate is in fact below the reasonably anticipated market demand for such units and that absent the Petaluma Plan, the City would grow at a faster rate.

According to undisputed expert testimony at trial, if the Plan (limiting housing starts to approximately 6 per cent of existing housing stock each year) were to be adopted by municipalities throughout the region, the impact on the housing market would be substantial. For the decade 1970 to 1980, the shortfall in needed housing in the region would be about 105,000 units (or 25 per cent of the units needed). Further, the aggregate effect of a proliferation of the Plan throughout the San Francisco region would be a decline in regional housing stock quality, a loss of the mobility of current and prospective residents and a deterioration in the quality and choice of housing available to income earners with real incomes of $14,000 per year or less. If, however, the Plan were considered by itself and with respect to Petaluma only, there is no evidence to suggest that there would be a deterioration in the quality and choice of housing available there to persons in the lower and middle income brackets. Actually, the Plan increases the availability of multi-family units (owner-occupied and rental units) and low-income units which were rarely constructed in the pre-Plan days.

Substantive Due Process

Appellees claim that the Plan is arbitrary and unreasonable and, thus, violative of the due process clause of the Fourteenth Amendment. According to appellees, the Plan is nothing more than an exclusionary zoning device, designed solely to insulate Petaluma from the urban complex in which it finds itself. The Association and the Landowners reject, as falling outside the scope of any legitimate governmental interest, the City's avowed purposes in implementing the Plan—the preservation of Petaluma's small town character and the avoidance of the social and environmental problems caused by an uncontrolled growth rate.

In attacking the validity of the Plan, appellees rely heavily on the district court's finding that the express purpose and the actual effect of the Plan is to exclude substantial numbers of people who would otherwise elect to move to the City. The existence of an exclusionary purpose and effect reflects, however, only *one* side of the zoning regulation. Practically all zoning restrictions have as a purpose and effect the *exclusion* of some activity or type of structure or a certain density of inhabitants. And in reviewing the reasonableness of a zoning ordinance, our inquiry does not terminate with a finding that it is for an exclusionary purpose. We must determine further whether the *exclusion* bears any rational relationship to a *legitimate state interest.* If it does not, then the zoning regulation is invalid. If, on the other hand, a legitimate state interest is furthered by the zoning regulation, we must defer to the legislative act. Being neither a super legislature nor a zoning board of appeal, a federal court is without authority to weigh and reappraise the factors considered or ignored by the legislative body in passing the challenged zoning regulation. The reasonableness, not the wisdom, of the Petaluma Plan is at issue in this suit.

It is well settled that zoning regulations "must find their justification in some aspect of the police power, asserted for the public welfare." The concept of the public welfare, however, is not limited to the regulation of noxious activities or dangerous structures. As the Court stated in *Berman v. Parker*, (1954):

The concept of the public welfare is broad and inclusive. The values it represents are spiritual as well as physical, aesthetic as well as monetary. It is within the power of the legislature to determine that the community should be beautiful as well as healthy, spacious as well as clean, well-balanced as well as carefully patrolled.

In determining whether the City's interest in preserving its small town character and in avoiding uncontrolled and rapid growth falls within the broad concept of "public welfare," we are considerably assisted by two recent cases, *Belle Terre*, and *Ybarra v. City of Town of Los Altos Hills*, each of which upheld as not unreasonable a zoning regulation much more restrictive than the Petaluma Plan, are dispositive of the due process issue in this case.* * *

Following the *Belle Terre* decision, the court in *Los Altos Hills* had an opportunity to review a zoning ordinance providing that a housing lot shall contain not less than one acre and that no lot shall be occupied by more than one primary dwelling unit. The ordinance as a practical matter prevented poor people from living in Los Altos Hills and restricted the density, and thus the population, of the town. This court, nonetheless, found that the ordinance was rationally related to a legitimate governmental interest—*the preservation of the town's rural evironment*—and, thus, did not violate the equal protection clause of the Fourteenth Amendment.

Both the Belle Terre ordinance and the Los Altos Hills regulation had the purpose and effect of permanently restricting growth; nonetheless, the court in each case upheld the particular law before it on the ground that the regulation served a legitimate governmental interest falling within the concept of the public welfare: the preservation of quiet family neighborhoods (Belle Terre) and the preservation of a rural environment (Los Altos Hills). Even less restrictive or exclusionary than the above zoning ordinances is the Petaluma Plan which, unlike those ordinances, does not freeze the population at present or near-present levels. Further, unlike the Los Altos Hills ordinance and the various zoning regulations struck down by state courts in recent years, the Petaluma Plan does not have the undesirable effect of welling out any particular income class nor any racial minority group.

Although we assume that some persons desirious of living in Petaluma will be excluded under the housing permit limitation and that, thus, the Plan may frustrate some legitimate regional housing needs, the Plan is not arbitrary or unreasonable. We agree with appellees that unlike the situation in the past most municipalties today are neither isolated nor wholly independent from neighboring municipalties and that, consequently, unilateral land use decisions by one local entity affect the needs and resources of an entire region.

It does not necessarily follow, however, that the *due process* rights of builders and landowners are violated merely because a local entity exercises in its own self-interest the police power lawfully delegated to it by the state. *See Belle Terre, supra; Los Altos Hills, supra.* If the present system of delegated zoning power does not effectively serve the state interest in furthering the general welfare of the region or entire state, it is the state legislature's and not the federal courts' role to intervene and adjust the system. As stated *supra*, the federal court is not a super zoning board and should not be called on to mark the point at which legitimate local interests in promoting the welfare of the community are outweighed by legitimate regional interests. *See* Note, *supra*, at 608–11.

We conclude therefore that under *Belle Terre* and *Los Altos Hills* the concept of the public welfare is sufficiently broad to uphold Petaluma's desire to preserve its small town character, its open spaces and low density of population, and to grow at an orderly and deliberate pace.

Reversed.

CITY OF BOCA RATON
v.
BOCA VILLAS CORP.

371 So.2d 154 (Fla. App. 1979)

PER CURIAM.

The City of Boca Raton amended its charter by the initiative and referendum method to establish a maximum number of dwelling units allowable within the city. This zoning device is commonly referred to as placing a "cap" on density, and the parties here refer to this amendment as the "cap." This charter amendment was implemented by ordinances reducing the density in single and multi-family residential zoning classifications.

The charter amendment passed by the city electorate provided:

> "The total number of dwelling units within the existing boundaries of the City is hereby limited to forty thousand (40,000). No building permit shall be issued for the construction of a dwelling unit within the City which would permit the total number of dwelling units within the City to exceed forty thousand (40,000)."

After passage of this charter amendment the City Council approved a City Planning & Zoning Board recommendation for an across-the-board density reduction of 50% for all multi-family zoning categories. Single family zoning categories were reduced to conform to the average of what had been constructed in the city prior to the charter amendment. Both the charter amendment and the implementing multi-family zoning ordinances were attacked in this suit by two property owners. After some twenty-seven days of trial the court entered an exhaustive final judgment holding that the charter amendment violated due process provisions of the State and Federal Constitutions because the cap did not bear a rational relationship to a permissible municipal objective and that the ordinances in question violated both due process and equal protection of the law. The judgment also held the current zoning of the property in question was confiscatory and directed the properties be rezoned no more restrictive than the judgment designated.

The trial judge held that the City had the power to establish a "cap" or maximum number of dwelling units allowable within the city boundaries. However, he opined that, as with any other zoning restriction, the "cap" must bear a rational relationship to a permissible municipal purpose, i. e., it must promote the public health, morals, safety or welfare. As one would imagine in a case of this nature, numerous experts were called by each side and in many respects they disagreed. It is apparent from the final judgment that the judge was not impressed by the testimony of some of the experts called to support the City's position that the "cap" and implementing ordinances were necessary to effectuate a valid municipal purpose. The judgment points to the testimony of the city Planning Director, city Engineering Director and engineering and planning consultants who contended that the City's present and future planning was quite adequate for a number of years without the cap. For example, Walter Young, the City Director of Planning, described Boca Raton's planning for the future "second to none," and that characterization is generally supported by the other expert planning witnesses. Yet in the formulation of the "cap" the city planning department was never consulted. The bottom line of Mr. Young's testimony was that, other than "community choice," he knew of no compelling reason for imposing a permanent fixed limitation on population or dwelling units. There are numerous other critical references to the quality of the city's proof to support its position, and the judgment contains specific findings of fact regarding "after-the-fact studies of the cap's relationship to public welfare" which support the conclusion reached in the judgment.

Based upon the testimony covering some 21 volumes, the trial judge made, among others, the following findings of fact bearing upon the contention that the cap lacks any rational relationship to a permissible municipal objective:

"1. Boca Raton's utility systems and services are presently adequate, were adequate prior to the Cap, and there are no present indications of undue strain as a result of further anticipated growth within densities allowed prior to the Cap.

"2. Boca Raton's school facilities are presently overcrowded but the adequacy or inadequacy of those facilities is beyond jurisdictional control of the City and therefore unrelated to purported limited growth benefits of a Cap. The court has already spoken to this issue in holding unconstitutional a Boca Raton ordinance requiring developers of unplatted subdivisions to obtain a letter of intent covering new school construction from the Palm Beach County, Florida School Board.

Further because of Boca Raton's population distribution, the Cap is most likely counterproductive to the entire Palm Beach County public school system. Fiscal studies of both parties confirm Boca Raton now generates a surplus of revenue for schools over and above the cost of school expenditures (including cost of new school construction).

"3. Cost-Revenue Studies by both parties establish greater fiscal surplus will result to general and capital funds of the City without the Cap.

"4. Boca Raton's water resources can abundantly withstand anticipated growth so long as proper management polices now in effect are maintained. One of the City's major factual justifications for the Cap was rooted in the 'water crop' theory, which purports to limit population by a budget of rainwater falling within City limits. The theory may be useful *regionally* as a factor in water management decision making. However, its argued use as support for the Cap requires the court completely disregard regional water resources until the city is assured other responsible governmental agencies (U.S. Corps of Engineers, Central and Southern Flood Control District and Lake Worth Drainage District) will continue to protect the municipal interest. Neither the court nor the city can be assured, but there is no creditable evidence these authorities will fail to carry out the responsibilities delegated to them. It is not rational to completely disregard past efforts, future plans and abundant alternative water resources available to Boca Raton through these regional water-management bodies. The record establishes Boca Raton's water resources can and will ultimately be managed regionally. Water resources will not depend upon a 'budget' which Boca Raton or other cities may impose, but rather will depend upon hard social choices involving agricultural priorities, environmental demands, quantity of water used in various sectors, and the cost which society is willing to pay. These are unresolved issues which directly relate to Southeastern Florida water demands and resources. A Cap predicated upon preservation of water resources is a preliminary and unnecessarily drastic solution to an area-water resource issue.

"5. Boca Raton's air quality and noise levels are normal for a community of its size and are well within state and federal standards and regulations. Anticipated growth will not cause those standards and regulations to be exceeded. The Gerrish Study of air pollution and the Peterson Study of background noise lend no credibility to the Cap or the Ashley-Veri report. Other than the water crop theory and these urban environmental studies, the Ashley-Veri report does not completely support the Cap. In fact, the report's final conclusion suggests as much when recommending (a) the Cap be raised and (b) that public funds be devoted to acquisition of vacant lands to reduce units.

"6. The City's current comprehensive plan and zoning maps were essentially prepared prior to and outside the Cap. There is no showing those plans would be jeopardized or materially affected if the Cap were removed.

"7. Much of the defendant's case hinged on expert opinion to the effect the Cap represents an important community goal. The case was largely presented in abstract and without specific factual showing of real necessity. Defendant argues unpersuasively that 'necessity is not the test for a city's right to amend its comprehensive plan.' The Cap may well be a firm planning goal embodied in legislation. However, legislation as far reaching as this Cap should not be adopted by trial and error. The court is unpersuaded the City's intended review by Ordinance No. 1966 adds present credence to the Cap. If the Cap is now irrational, a legislated promise to later amend, modify or repeal it adds nothing to present validity."

As we mentioned above the trial judge found the charter amendment (the Cap) and the implementing zoning ordinance did not bear a rational relationship to a valid municipal purpose and that the ordinances were confiscatory as applied to appellees' property. Our study of the briefs and record convinces us that there is substantial competent evidence to support the finding of an absence of a rational relationship regarding the charter amendment and zoning ordinance. That being the case, we need not reach the question of confiscation vel non because the finding that there is no compelling need justifying an exercise of the police power burdening private property is sufficient to warrant striking down the legislative act. As the Supreme Court of Florida [stated]:

> "The constitutional right of the owner of property to make legitimate use of his lands may not be curtailed by unreasonable restrictions under the guise of police power. The owner will not be required to sacrifice his rights absent a *substantial need for restrictions* in the interest of public health, morals, safety or welfare. If the zoning restriction *exceeds the bounds of necessity* for the public welfare, as, in our opinion, do the restrictions controverted here, they must be stricken as an unconstitutional invasion of property rights."

That is not to say there must be an absolute necessity requiring the enactment of certain zoning restrictions before they can be tolerated as a proper exercise of the police power. But, as here, an excessive restriction on the use of private property which does not contribute substantially to the public health, morals, safety and welfare is arbitrary and unreasonable and thus unconstitutional. The trial court found, and the record supports such finding, that the charter amendment and implementing ordinances bore no such rational relationship to the requisite purposes.

We would concede that most of the cases where judicial invalidation of zoning laws has been upheld have in some measure involved the issue of confiscation. Those cases hold that as applied to the property involved the zoning ordinance was unreasonable because it deprived a property owner of the beneficial use of his property. We suggest the reason that the confiscation issue is so pervasive in the case law on this subject is because someone's ox is getting gored. Who is going to institute litigation but the person who feels his property rights infringed upon by excessive restrictions upon the use thereof?

There are cases, however, which support the principle that zoning which unnecessarily restricts property, zoning which bears no rational relationship to the public health, safety, morals and welfare is unconstitutional without raising the confiscation issue. In *State v. DuBose*, the County owned property within the City of Vero Beach and applied for a permit to construct a jail thereon. The permit was denied because the zoning ordinance applicable to this property did not authorize construction of a jail on said property and thus the County sought a Writ of Mandamus. The City contended the reason for prohibiting construction of a jail on said property was that it would increase taxes, increase traffic near a school, and it would diminish the value of school property nearby. Mandamus was denied by the trial court, but on appeal the Supreme Court found there was no support for the City's reasons for denying the County's proposed use of the property. Without a sound rational basis upon which to bottom the refusal, the court found the ordinance to be arbitrary and unreasonable as applied to this property. In a nutshell, there just was not any public need to prevent construction of the jail on the particular property. The court make the point that:

> "The right of an owner to devote his land to any legitimate use is property within the terms of the Constitution, and the Legislature may not under the guise of the police power impose unnecessary or unreasonable restrictions upon such use.
>
> "The court is committed to the doctrine that courts should not set aside the determination of public officers relative to municipal zoning ordinances, unless it is clear that their action has no foundation in reason and is a mere arbitrary exercise of power without reference to public health, morals, safety, or welfare."

As far as one can tell from the opinion, no claim of confiscation was made. The property owner simply maintained the absence of any reasonable relationship to a permissible municipal purpose was sufficient to invalidate the law as it applied to the complainant's property.

In *City of Sherman v. Simms*, the City passed a comprehensive zoning ordinance which, among other things, excluded churches from dwelling and apartment districts. That provision was attacked by a church group which wanted to use a structure in a residential district for public worship. Their contention was that prohibiting the use of property is a residential zone for church purpose was arbitrary, discriminatory and violative of the Federal and State Constitutions, because the restriction had no real or tangible relation to the public health, safety, morals or general welfare. After examining various zoning authorities, the court adopted a quotation from another cited case to the effect that:

> "'* * *And we further conclude that the administrative act of respondents in refusing a permit to erect a church in the residential district, there being no adequate showing that this exclusion of the church was in furtherance of the public health, safety, morals or the public welfare, was arbitrary and unreasonable and in violation of relator's rights under the State and Federal Constitutions.'"
>
> "With this conclusion all the available authorities seem to agree. It must not be overlooked that the power to establish zones is a police power and its exercise cannot be extended beyond the accomplishment of purposes rightly within the scope of that power. To exclude churches from residential districts does not promote the health, the safety, the morals or the general welfare of the community, . . ."

Once again, the thrust of the attack upon the law was the absence of a reasonable relation to a legitimate municipal purpose; that absence being best demonstrated by the lack of any necessity for such restrictive provision.

In view of our conclusion that an otherwise valid attack may be made upon the charter amendment and implementing ordinances, we need not consider the trial judge's findings that the cap and implementing ordinances are so drastic and restrictive as to be confiscatory as applied to appellees' property.

We have not overlooked the rule that municipal legislative action is presumed to be constitutional. But, of course, the presumption is rebuttable and substantial competent evidence was adduced to prove invalidity of the legislative acts. The Supreme Court of Michigan, cited with approval the following:

> "Presumption of the existence of such relationship [the relationship between exercise of police power and the public health, safety, etc.], and hence of the validity of the ordinance is resorted to in the absence of proof on the subject, but not when there are proofs on whch a judicial determination thereof may be made as when the contrary is shown by competent evidence or appears on the face of the enactment."

The appellant also contends that the fairly debatable rule controls this case, but we disagree. In view of our decision to affirm the trial court's holding that the charter amendment and implementing ordinances bear no rational relationship to a valid municipal purpose, we do not reach the issue of confiscation. Thus, we have not found it necessary to consider the application of the various ordinances to specific parcels of property which would possibly bring the fairly debatable rule into play. The fairly debatable rule is a rule of procedure or application which can be simply stated as follows:

> "If the application of a zoning classification to a specific parcel of property is reasonably subject to disagreement, that is, if its application is fairly debatable, then the application of the ordinance by the zoning authority should not be disturbed by the courts. . . . The fairly debatable rule applies to the application of the ordinance and does not modify the requirement that the ordinance itself *and* the application thereof must have a reasonable relationship to the health, safety, morals or general welfare."

However, if it had become appropriate for us to consider the propriety of the trial court's action in the light of the fairly debatable rule, we would affirm the judgment because, as we mentioned earlier, even though there was expert testimony adduced in support to the City's case, that in and of itself does not mean the issue is fairly debatable. If it did, every zoning case would be fairly debatable and the City would prevail simply by submitting an expert who testified favorably to the City's position. Of course that is not the case. The trial judge still must determine the weight and credibility factors to be attributed to the experts. Here the final judgment shows that the judge did not assign much weight or credibility to the City's witnesses.

* * *

Accordingly, the final judgment under review is affirmed.

AFFIRMED.

---

b. *Timed Sequential Development*

As population grows, or shifts from one place to another, the need for **community infrastructure** grows or shifts with the population. Houses, streets, utilities, water supply, schools, recreational and other community facilities must be provided to meet the needs of the growing population. However, the need for infrastructure is a dynamic and changing need for which coordination is needed *over a period of time.* It becomes important to plan for and coordinate the **sequence of development** to maintain a balance between community needs and community services during the process of development to meet population growth over a period of time.

In *Golden v. Ramapo* set forth below, the New York Court of Appeals determined the validity of a system of land use regulation that permitted residential development to proceed only in accordance with a plan for **sequential development and timed growth**. The growth plan of the Town of Ramapo, New York was designed to achieve the following policies:

(*1*) To economize on the costs of municipal facilities and services in order to carefully phase residential development with efficient provision of public improvements

(*2*) To establish and maintain municipal control over the eventual character of development

(*3*) To establish and maintain a desirable degree of balance among the various uses of land

(*4*) To establish and maintain essential quality of community services and facilities. . . .

The land use regulations were based on a comprehensive plan for future growth and on a capital budget providing for the location and sequence of capital improvements for a period of 18 years. Residential development was permitted only after obtaining a special permit, the issuance of which is conditioned on the availability of five categories of facilities and services:

(*1*) Public sanitary sewers or approved substitutes

(*2*) Drainage facilities

(*3*) Improved public parks or recreation facilities, including schools

(*4*) State, county or town roads

(*5*) Firehouses

Special permits for development would be issued only when the services and facilities were available. A point system was created to assign values to each such facility and a permit would be issued only when 15 development points were applicable to the proposed development. A prospective developer could advance the date of development by agreeing to provide those improvements which would bring the proposed development within the number of development points required by the ordinance. Thus, residential development becomes a function of the availability of municipal improvements and may proceed in accordance with the overall program of orderly growth incorporated into the 18-year Capital Plan.

As you read the *Ramapo* decision, notice how the court responds to the issues raised by the complex problem involved in the conflict between (*1*) the constitutional protection of the right of people to travel and settle in places of their choice, (*2*) the constitutional protection of the right to use and develop private property and (*3*) the public interest in providing for a system of orderly growth and development.

GOLDEN et al.
v.
PLANNING BOARD OF the TOWN OF RAMAPO, et al.

30 N.Y. 2d 359, 334 N.Y.S.2d 138

285 N.E.2d 291 (1971)

SCILEPPI, Judge.

Both cases arise out of the 1969 amendments to the Town of Ramapo's Zoning ordinance* * *

Experiencing the pressures of an increase in population and the ancillary problem of providing municipal facilities and services, the Town of Ramapo, as early as 1964, made application for grant under section 801 of the Housing Act of 1964 to develop a master plan. The plan's preparation included a four-volume study of the existing land uses, public facilities, transportation, industry and commerce, housing needs and projected population trends. The proposals appearing in the studies were subsequently adopted pursuant to section 272-a of the Town Law, in July, 1966 and implemented by way of a master plan. The master plan was followed by the adoption of a comprehensive zoning ordinance. Additional sewage district and drainage studies were undertaken which culminated in the adoption of a capital budget, providing for the development of the improvements specified in the master plan within the next six years. Pursuant to section 271 of the Town Law, authorizing comprehensive planning, and as a supplement to the capital budget, the Town Board adopted a capital program which provides for the location and sequence of additional capital improvements for the 12 years following the life of the capital budget. The two plans, covering a period of 18 years, detail the capital improvements projected for maximum development and conform to the specifications set forth in the master plan, the official map and drainage plan.

Based upon these criteria, the Town subsequently adopted the subject amendments for the alleged purpose of eliminating premature subdivision and urban sprawl. Residential development is to proceed according to the provision of adequate municipal facilities and services, with the assurance that any concomitant restraint upon property use is to be of a "temporary" nature and that other private uses, including the constuction of individual housing, are authorized.

The Amendments did not rezone or reclassify any land into different residential or use districts, but, for the purposes of implementing the proposals appearing in the comprehensive plan, consist, in the main, of additions to the definitional sections of the ordinance, section 46–3, and the adoption of a new class of "Special Permit Uses," designated "Residential Development Use." "Residential Development Use" is defined as "The erection or construction of dwellings or any vacant plots, lots or parcels of land" (§ 46-3, as amd.); and, any person who acts so as to come within that definition, "shall be deemed to be engaged in residential development which shall be a separate use classification under this ordinance and subject to the requirement of obtaining a special permit from the Town Board" (§ 46-3, as amd.).

The standards for the issuance of special permits are framed in terms of the availability to the proposed subdivision plat of five essential facilities or services: specifically (1) public sanitary sewers or approved substitutes; (2) drainage facilities; (3) improved public parks or recreation facilities, including public schools; (4) State, county or town roads—major, secondary or collector; and, (5) firehouses. No special permit shall issue unless the proposed residential development has accumulated 15 development points, to be computed on a sliding scale of values assigned to the specified improvements under the statute. Subdivision is thus a function of immediate availability to the proposed plat of certain municipal improvements; the avowed purpose of the amendments being to phase residential development to the Town's ability to provide the above facilities or services.

Certain savings and remedial provisions are designed to relieve of potentially unreasonable restrictions. Thus, the board may issue special permits vesting a present right to proceed with residential development in such year as the development meets the required point minimum, but in no event later than the final year of the 18-year capital plan. The approved special use permit is fully assignable, and improvements scheduled for completion within one year from the date of an application are to be credited as though existing on the date of the application. A prospective developer may advance the date of subdivision approval by agreeing to provide those improvements which will bring the proposed plat within the number of development points required by the amendments. And applications are authorized to the "Development Easement Acquisition Commission" for a reduction of the assessed valuation. Finally, upon application to the Town Boad, the development point requirements may be varied should the board determine that such a variance or modification is consistent with the on-going development plan.

The undisputed effect of these integrated efforts in land use planning and development is to provide an over-all program of orderly growth and adequate facilities through a sequential development policy commensurate with progressing availability and capacity of public facilities. While its goals are clear and its purposes undisputed laudatory, serious questions are raised as to the manner in which these ends are to be effected, not the least of which relates to their legal viability under present zoning enabling legislation, particularly sections 261 and 263 of the Town Law. The owners of the subject premises argue, and the Appellate Division has sustained the proposition, that the primary purpose of the amending ordinance is to control or regulate population growth within the Town and as such is not within the authorized objectives of the zoning enabling legislation. We disagree.

In enacting the challenged amendments, the Town Board has sought to control subdivision in all residential districts, pending the provision (public or private) at some future date of various services and facilities. A reading of the relevant statutory provisions reveals that there is no specific authorization for the "sequential" and "timing" controls adopted here. That, of course, cannot be said to end the matter, for the additional inquiry remains as to whether the challenged amendments find their basis within the perimeters of the devices authorized and purposes sanctioned under current enabling legislation. Our concern is, as it should be, with the effects of the statutory scheme taken as a whole and its role in the propagation of a viable policy of land use and planning.

Towns, cities and villages lack the power to enact and enforce zoning or other land use regulations. The exercise of that power, to the extent that it is lawful, must be founded upon a legislative delegation to so proceed, and in the absence of such a grant will be held *ultra vires* and void. That delegation, set forth in section 261 of the Town Law, is not, however, coterminous with stated police power objectives and has been considered less inclusive traditionally. Hence, although the power to zone must be exercised under the aegis of the police power, indeed must inevitably find justification for its exercise in some aspect of the same, the recital of police power purposes in the grant, attests more to the drafters' attempts to specify a valid constitutional predicate than to detail authorized zoning purposes. The latter, "legitimate zoning purposes," are incorporated in accompanying section 263 and are designed to secure safety from various calamities, to avoid undue concentration of population and to facilitate "adequate provision of transportation, water, sewerage, schools, parks and other public requirements" (Town Law, § 263). In the end, zoning properly effects, and only in the manner prescribed, those purposes detailed under section 263 of the Town Law. It may not be invoked to further the general police powers of a municipality.

Even so, considering the activities enumerated by section 261 of the Town Law, and relating those powers to the authorized purposes detailed in section 263, the challenged amendments are proper zoning techniques, exercised for legitimate zoning purposes. The power to restrict and regulate conferred under section 261 includes within its grant, the way of necessary implication, the authority to direct the growth of population for the purposes indicated, within the confines of the township. It is the matrix of land use restrictions, common to each of the enumerated powers and sanctioned goals, a necessary concomitant to the municipalities' recognized authority to determine the lines along which local development shall proceed, though it may divert it from its natural course.

Undoubtedly, current zoning enabling legislation is burdened by the largely antiquated notion which deigns that the regulation of land use and development is uniquely a function of local government—that the public interest of the State is exhausted once its political subdivisions have been delegated the authority to zone. While such jurisdictional allocations may well have been consistent with formerly prevailing conditions and assumptions, questions of broader public interest have commonly been ignored.

Experience, over the last quarter century, however, with greater technological integration and drastic shifts in population distribution has pointed up serious defects and community autonomy in land use controls has come under increasing attack by legal commentators, and students of urban problems alike, because of its pronounced insularism and its correlative role in producing distortions in metropolitan growth patterns, and perhaps more importantly, in crippling efforts toward regional and Statewide problem solving, be it pollution, decent housing, or public transportation.

Recognition of communal and regional interdependence, in turn, has resulted in proposals for schemes of regional and State-wide planning, in the hope that decisions would then correspond roughly to their level of impact. Yet, as salutary as such proposals may be, the power to zone under current law is vested in local municipalities, and we are constrained to resolve the issues accordingly. What does become more apparent in treating with the problem, however, is that though the issues are framed in terms of the developer's due process rights, those rights cannot, realistically speaking, be viewed separately and apart from rights of others "'in search of a (more) comfortable place to live.'"

There is, then, something inherently suspect in a scheme which, apart from its professed purposes, effects a restriction upon the free mobility of a people until sometime in the future when projected facilities are available to meet increased demands. Although zoning must include schemes designed to allow municipalities to more effectively contend with the increased demands of evolving and growing communities, under its guise, townships have been wont to try their hand at an array of exclusionary devices in the hope of avoiding the very burden which growth must inevitably bring. Though the conflict engendered by such tactics is certainly real, and its implications vast, accumulated evidence, scientific and social, points circumspectly at the hazards of undirected growth and the naive, somewhat nostalgic imperative that egalitarianism is a function of growth.

Of course, these problems cannot be solved by Ramapo or any single municipality, but depend upon the accommodation of widely disparate interests for their ultimate resolution. To that end, State-wide or regional control of planning would insure that interests broader than that of the municipality underlie various land use policies. Nevertheless, that should not be the only context in which growth devices such as these, aimed at population assimilation, not exclusion, will be sustained; especially where, as here, we would have no alternative but to strike the provision down in the wistful hope that the efforts of the State Office of Planning Coordination and the American Law Institute will soon bear fruit.

Hence, unless we are to ignore the plain meaning of the statutory delegation, this much is clear: phase growth is well within the ambit of existing enabling legislation. And, of course, it is no answer to point to emergent problems to buttress the conclusion that such innovative schemes are beyond the perimeters of statutory authorization. These considerations, admittedly real, to the extent which they are relevant, bear solely upon the continued viability of "localism" in land use regulation; obviously, they can neither add nor detract from the initial grant of authority, obsolescent though it may be. The answer which Ramapo has posed can by no means be termed definitive; it is, however, a first practical step toward controlled growth achieved without forsaking broader social purposes.

The evolution of more sophisticated efforts to contend with the increasing complexities of urban and suburban growth has been met by a corresponding reluctance upon the part of the judiciary to substitute its judgment as to the plan's over-all effectiveness for the considered deliberations of its progenitors.

Implicit in such a philosophy of judicial self-restraint is the growing awareness that matters of land use and development are peculiarly within the expertise of students of city and suburban planning, and thus well within the legislative prerogative, not lightly to be impeded. To this same end, we have afforded such regulations, the usual presumption of validity attending the exercise of the police power, and have cast the burden of proving their invalidity upon the party challenging their enactment.

Deference in the matter of the regulations' over-all effectiveness, however, is not to be viewed as an abdication of judicial responsibility, and ours remains the function of defining the metes and bounds beyond which local regulations may not venture, regardless of their professedly beneficent purposes.

The subject ordinance is said to advance legitimate zoning purposes as it assures that each new home built in the township will have at least a minimum of public services in the categories regulated by the ordinance. The Town argues that various public facilities are presently being constructed but that for want of time and money it has been unable to provide such services and facilities at a pace commensurate with increased public need. It is urged that although the zoning power includes reasonable restrictions upon the private use of property, exacted in the hope of development according to well-laid plans, calculated to advance the public welfare of the community in the future[, t]he subject regulations go further and seek to avoid the increased responsibilities and economic burdens which time and growth must ultimately bring.

It is the nature of all land use and development regulations to circumscribe the course of growth within a particular town or district and to that extent such restrictions invariably impede the forces of natural growth. Where those restrictions upon the beneficial use and enjoyment of land are necessary to promote the ultimate good of the community and are within the bounds of reason, they have been sustained. "Zoning however is a means by which a governmental body can plan for the future—it may not be used as a means to deny the future." Its exercise assumes that development shall not stop at the community's threshold, but only that whatever growth there may be shall proceed along a predetermined course. It is inextricably bound to the dynamics of community life and its function is to guide, not to isolate or facilitate efforts at avoiding the ordinary incidents of growth. What segregates permissible from impermissible restrictions, depends in the final analysis upon the purpose of the restrictions and their impact in terms of both the community and general public interest. The line of delineation between the two is not a constant, but will be found to vary with prevailing circumstances and conditions.

What we will not countenance, then, under any guise, is community efforts at immunization or exclusion. But, far from being exclusionary, the present amendments merely seek, by the implementation of sequential development and timed growth, to provide a balanced cohesive community dedicated to the efficient utilization of land. The restrictions conform to the community's considered land use polices as expressed in its comprehensive plan and represent a bona fide effort to maximize population density consistent with orderly growth. True other alternatives, such as requiring off-site improvements as a prerequisite to subdivision, may be available, but the choice as how best to proceed, in view of the difficulties attending such exactions cannot be faulted.

Perhaps even more importantly, timed growth, unlike the minimum lot requirements recently struck down by the Pennsylvania Supreme Court as exclusionary, does not impose permanent restrictions upon land use. Its obvious purpose is to prevent premature subdivision absent essential municipal facilities and to insure continuous development commensurate with the Town's obligation to provide such facilities. They seek, not to freeze population at present levels but to maximize growth by the efficient use of land, and in so doing testify to this community's continuing role in population assimilation. In sum, Ramapo asks not that it be left alone, but only that it be allowed to prevent the kind of deterioration that has transformed well-ordered and thriving residential communities into blighted ghettos with attendant hazards to health, security and social stability—a danger not without substantial basis in fact.

We only require that communities confront the challenge of population growth with open doors. Where in grappling with that problem, the community undertakes, by imposing temporary restrictions upon development, to provide required municipal services in a rational manner, courts are rightfully reluctant to strike down such schemes. The timing controls challenged here parallel recent proposals put forth by various study groups and have their genesis in certain of the pronouncements of this and the courts of sister States. While these controls are typically proposed as an adjunct of regional planning, the preeminent protection against their abuse resides in the mandatory on-going planning and development requirement, present here, which attends their implementation and use.

We may assume, therefore, that the present amendments are the product of foresighted planning calculated to promote the welfare of the township. The Town has imposed temporary restrictions upon land use in residential areas while committing itself to a program of development. It has utilized its comprehensive plan to implement its timing controls and has coupled with these restrictions provisions for low and moderate income housing on a large scale. Considered as a whole, it represents both in its inception and implementation a reasonable attempt to provide for the sequential, orderly development of land in conjunction with the needs of the community, as well as individual parcels of land, while simultaneously obviating the blighted aftermath which the initial failure to provide needed facilities so often brings.

The proposed amendments have the effect of restricting development for onwards to 18 years in certain areas. Whether the subject parcels will be so restricted for the full term is not clear, for it is equally probable that the proposed facilities will be brought into these areas well before that time. Assuming, however, that the restrictions will remain outstanding for the life of the program, they still fall short of a confiscation within the meaning of the Constitution.

An ordinance which seeks to permanently restrict the use of property so that it may not be used for any reasonable purpose must be recognized as a taking: The only difference between the restriction and an outright taking in such a case "is that the restriction leaves the owner subject to the burden of payment of taxation, while outright confiscation would relieve him of that burden." An appreciably different situation obtains where the restriction constitutes a *temporary* restriction, promising that the property may be put to a profitable use within a reasonable time. The hardship of holding unproductive property for some time might be compensated for by the ultimate benefit inuring to the individual owner in the form of a substantial increase in valuation; or, for that matter, the landowner, might be compelled to chafe under the temporary restriction, without the benefit of such compensation, when that burden serves to promote the public good.

We are reminded, however, that these restrictions threaten to burden individual parcels for as long as a full generation and that such a restriction cannot, in any context, be viewed as a temporary expedient. The Town, on the other hand, contends that the landowner is not deprived of either the best use of his land or of numerous other appropriate uses, still permitted within various residential districts, including the construction of a single-family residence, and consequently, it cannot be deemed confiscatory. Although no proof has been submitted on reduction of value, the landowners point to obvious disparity between the value of the property, if limited in use by the subject amendments and its value for residential development purposes, and argue that the diminution is so considerable that for all intents and purposes the land cannot presently or in the near future be put to profitable or beneficial use, without violation of the restrictions.

Every restriction on the use of property entails hardships for some individual owners. Those difficulties are invariably the product of police regulation and the pecuniary profits of the individual must in the long run be subordinated to the needs of the community. The fact that the ordinance limits the use of, and may depreciate the value of the property will not render it unconstitutional, however, unless it can be shown that the measure is either unreasonable in terms of necessity or the diminution in value is such as to be tantamount to a confiscation. Diminution, in turn, is a relative factor and though its magnitude is an indicia of a taking, it does not of itself establish a confiscation.

Without a doubt restrictions upon the property in the present case are substantial in nature and duration. They are not, however, absolute. The amendments contemplate a definite term, as the development points are designed to operate for a maximum period of 18 years and during that period, the Town is committed to the construction and installation of capital improvements. The net result of the on-going development provision is that individual parcels may be committed to a residential development use prior to the expiration of the maximum period. Similarly, property owners under the terms of the amendments may elect to accelerate the date of development by installing, at their own expense, the necessary public services to bring the parcel within the required number of development points. While even the best of plans may not always be realized, in the absence of proof to the contrary, we must assume the Town will put its best effort forward in implementing the physical and fiscal timetable outlined under the plan. Should subsequent events prove this assumption unwarranted, or should the Town because of some unforeseen event fail in its primary obligation to these landowners, there will be amply opportunity to undo the restrictions upon default. For the present, at least, we are constrained to proceed upon the assumption that the program will be fully and timely implemented.

Thus, unlike the situation presented in Arverne Bay Constr. Co. v. Thatcher, the present amendments propose restrictions of a certain duration and founded upon estimate determined by fact. Prognostication on our part in upholding the ordinance proceeds upon the presently permissible inference that within a reasonable time the subject property will be put to the desired use at an appreciated value. In the interim assessed valuations for real estate tax purposes reflect the impact of the proposed restrictions. The proposed restraints, mitigated by the prospect of appreciated value and interim reductions in assessed value, and measured in terms of the nature and magnitude of the project undertaken, are within the limits of necessity.

In sum, where it is clear that the existing physical and financial resources of the community are inadequate to furnish the essential services and facilities which a substantial increase in population requires, there is a rational basis for "phased growth" and hence, the challenged ordinance is not violative of the Federal and State Constitutions. Accordingly, the order appealed from should be reversed and the actions remitted to Special Term for entry of a judgment declaring section 46—13.1 of the Town Ordinance constitutional.

For additional discussion of the *Ramapo* decision see, Note, *Time controls on Land Use: Prophylactic Law for Planners*, 57 CORNELL L. REV. 827 (1972); Finkler, *Nongrowth as a Planning Alternative: A Preliminary Examination of an Emerging Issue*, Report No. 283 (American Society of Planning Officials, September, 1972), p. 15; Comment, *Golden v. Town of Ramapo: Establishing a New Dimension in American Planning Law*, 4 THE URBAN LAWYER ix (Summer, 1972).

c. Population Growth Tied to Public Services

In many parts of the country, development of vacant land is not possible without water, sewer and other public facilities. Soil conditions and underground water resources may permit only limited development dependent on on-site well and septic tank sewage disposal. Under such conditions it would not be unreasonable for a local government to condition the growth of population on the adequacy of the public services.

The City of Livermore, California adopted such an ordinance in which the issuance of residential building permits was prohibited until the following standards were met:

(*1*) Educational Facilities. No double classrooms in the schools or overcrowded classrooms as determined by the California Educational Code.
(*2*) Sewage. The sewage treatment facilities and capacities must meet the standards set by the Regional Water Quality Control Board.
(*3*) Water Supply. No rationing of water with respect to human consumption or irrigation and adequate waste reserves for fire protection must exist.

In *Associated Home Builders v. Livermore*, below, the California Supreme Court held that the test of constitutional validity of the Livermore ordinance is whether it is reasonably related to the **welfare of the region** in addition to the welfare of the municipality. The court went even further and set up a three-step test to determine whether the zoning ordinance is "reasonably related" to the welfare of the region. The trial court was instructed to:

(*1*) *Forecast the probable effect and duration of the restriction*; i.e., how great is the need for municipal services; has the municipality undertaken to provide the facilities; when will they be completed?

(*2*) *Identify the competing interests*; e.g. environmentalists vs. housing proponents; residents who want to protect existing character and amenities vs. those seeking better housing and a place to live.

(*3*) *Determine whether the ordinance represents a reasonable accommodation of the competing interests*. The ordinance must have a real and substantial relation to the public welfare.

This decision by a state court should be compared with the decisions by the federal courts in *Petaluma*, above, and *Village of Belle Terre v. Boraas*, 416 U.S. 1 (1974), where those courts have held that there is no federal constitutional principle that requires a municipality to extend its services and facilities, or modify its zoning ordinances, to accommodate regional needs of population movement and growth.

The issue of public services is complicated by a principle of utility law that imposes an obligation on any entity that holds itself out as serving the public to provide that service to all members of the public that demand such service. A "public utility" may refuse to extend its service only for "utility-related reasons" such as insufficiency of water or power. This principle arose in *Robinson v. City of Boulder*, set forth below, where the City of Boulder operates the water and sewer services and refused to extend such services for a development that was inconsistent with the city comprehenisive plan.

ASSOCIATED HOME BUILDERS OF GREATER EASTBAY, INC. v. CITY OF LIVERMORE

18 Cal.3d 582, 135 Cal.Rptr. 41,
557 P.2d 473 (1976)

TOBRINER, Justice.

We face today the question of the validity of an initiative ordinance enacted by the voters of the City of Livermore which prohibits issuance of further residential building permits until local educational, sewage disposal, and water supply facilities comply with specified standards. Plaintiff, an association of contractors, subdividers, and other persons interested in residential construction in Livermore, brought this suit to enjoin enforcement of the ordinance. The superior court issued a permanent injunction, and the city appealed.

In *Hurst v. City of Burlingame* (1929) 207 Cal. 134, 277 P. 308, we held that statutes requiring notice and hearing to precede enactment of municipal zoning and land use ordiances applied to initiatives, a holding which effectvely denied voters of general law cities the power to enact such legislation by initiative. In accord with that precedent, the trial court here held that Livermore, as a general law city, lacked authority to enact the initiative ordinance at issue. We have concluded, however, that *Hurst* was incorrectly decided; the statutory notice and hearing provisions govern only ordinances enacted by city council action and do not limit the power of municipal electors, reserved to them by the state Constitution, to enact legislation by initiative. We therefore reverse the trial court holding on this issue.

We also reject the trial court's alternative holding that the ordinance is unconstitutionally vague. By interpreting the ordinance to incorporate standards established by the Livermore Valley Joint School District and the Regional Water Quality Control Board, we render its terms sufficiently specific to comply with constitutional requisites. The failure of the ordinance to designate the person or agency who determines when its standards have been fulfilled does not make it unconstitutionally vague; the duty to enforce the ordinance reposes in the city's building inspector, whose decisions are subject to judicial review by writ of mandamus.

Finally, we reject plaintiff's suggestion that we sustain the trial court's injunction on the grounds that the ordinance unconstitutionally attempts to bar immigration to Livermore. Plaintiff's contention symbolizes the growing conflict between the efforts of suburban communities to check disorderly development, with its concomitant problems of air and water pollution and inadeqate public facilities, and the increasing public need for adequate housing opportunities. We take this opportunity, therefore, to reaffirm and clarify the principles which govern validity of land use ordinances which substantially limit immigration into a community; we hold that such ordinances need not be sustained by a compelling state interest, but are constitutional if they are reasonably related to the welfare of the region affected by the ordinance. Since on the limited record before us plaintiff has not demonstrated that the Livermore ordinance lacks a reasonable relationship to the regional welfare, we cannot hold the ordinance unconstitutional under this standard.

1. *Summary of proceedings*

The initiative ordinance in question was enacted by a majority of the voters at the Livermore municipal election of April 11, 1972, and became effective on April 28, 1972. The ordinance, set out in full in the margin, states that it was enacted to further the health, safety, and welfare of the citizens of Livermore and to contribute to the solution of air pollution. Finding that excessive issuance of residential building permits has caused school overcrowding, sewage pollution, and water rationing, the ordinance prohibits issuance of further permits until three standards are met: "1. EDUCATIONAL FACILITIES—No double sessions in the schools nor overcrowded classrooms as determined by the California Education Code. 2. SEWAGE—The sewage treatment facilities and capacities meet the standards set by the Regional Water Quality Control Board. 3. WATER SUPPLY—No rationing of water with respect to human consumption or irrigation and adequate water reserves for fire protection exist."

Plaintiff association filed suit to enjoin enforcement of the ordinance and for declaratory relief. After the city filed its answer, all parties moved for judgment on the pleadings and stipulated that the court, upon the pleadings and other documents submitted, could determine the merits of the cause. On the basis of that stipulation the court rendered findings and entered judgment for plaintiff. The city appeals from that judgment.

2. *The enactment of the Livermore ordinance by initiative does not violate the state zoning law.*

The superior court found that the initiative ordinance was adopted "without complying with the statutes . . . governing general law cities," specifically Government Code sections 65853 through 65857. These sections provide that any ordinance which changes zoning or imposes a land use restriction listed in Government Code section 65850 can be enacted only after noticed hearing before the city's planning commission and legislative body. The superior court concluded that notice and hearing must precede enactment of any ordinance regulating land use. Since Livermore passed its ordinance pursuant to the procedures specified in the statutes governing municipal initiatives (Elec.Code, § 4000 et seq.), which do not provide for hearings before the city planning commission or council, the court held the ordinance invalid.

The amendment of the California Constitution in 1911 to provide for the initiative and referendum signifies one of the outstanding achievements of the progressive movement of the early 1900's. Drafted in light of the theory that all power of government ultimately resides in the people, the amendment speaks of the initiative and referendum, not as a right granted the people, but as a power reserved by them. Declaring it "the duty of the courts to jealously guard the right of the people"* * * the courts have described the initiative and referendum as articulating "one of the most precious rights of our democratic process."* * * "[I]t has long been our judicial policy to apply a liberal construction to this power wherever it is challenged in order that the right be not improperly annulled. If doubts can reasonably be resolved in favor of the use of this reserve power, courts will preserve it."

* * *

The 1911 amendment, in reserving the right of initiative to electors of counties and cities, authorized the Legislature to establish procedures to facilitate the exercise of that right. Accordingly the Legislature enacted statutes, now codified as sections 4000–4023 of the Election Code, providing for the circulation of petitions, the calling of elections, and other procedures required to enact an initiative measure.

The 1911 amendment was first applied to zoning matters in 1927 in *Dwyer v. City Council, supra*, 200 Cal. 505, 253 P. 932, in which the court mandated the Berkeley City Council to submit a zoning ordinance to referendum. The opinion reasoned that since the city council had the legislative authority to enact zoning ordinances, the people had the power to do so by initiative or referendum. Rejecting an argument that the referendum procedure denied affected persons the right, granted them by municipal ordinance, to appear before the city council and state their views on the ordinance, the court replied that "the matter has been removed from the forum of the Council to the forum of the electorate. The proponents and opponents are given all the privileges and rights to express themselves in an open election that a democracy or republican form of government can afford to its citizens. . . . It is clear that the constitutional right reserved by the people to submit legislative questions to a direct vote cannot be abridged by any procedural requirements. . . ." (200 Cal. at p. 516, 253 P. at p. 936.)

Two years later the court decided *Hurst v. City of Burlingame, supra*, 207 Cal. 134, 277 P. 308, the decision on which the trial court in the instant case based its ruling. The City of Burlingame had enacted by initiative a city-wide zoning ordinance which classified as residential the property where plaintiff had a retail store. Contending that he had been denied the right to a public hearing established in the Zoning Act of 1917 (Stats. 1917, p. 1419), plaintiff sued to enjoin enforcement of the ordinance. Beginning with the premise that "an ordinance proposed by the electors of a county or of a city in this state under the initiative law must constitute such legislation as the legislative body of such county or city has the power to enact . . ."

* * *

The *Hurst* court reasoned that since the board of trustees of the City of Burlingame could not lawfully enact a zoning ordinance without complying with the hearing requirement of the state law, the voters could not adopt such an ordinance by initiative.

Responding to the argument that the enactment of the ordinance complied with the state initiative law, the court stated that "The initiative law and the zoning law are hopelessly inconsistent and in conflict as to the manner of the preparation and adoption of a zoning ordinance. The Zoning Act is a special statute dealing with a particular subject and must be deemed to be controlling over the initiative, which is general in its scope." (P. 141, 277 P. at p. 311.) Finally, the court distinguished *Dwyer v. City Council, supra*, 200 Cal. 505, 253 P. 932, on the ground that *Dwyer* upheld a referendum, and thus persons affected by the referendum had already been granted a right to notice and hearing at the time of the original enactment of the ordinance. (See 207 Cal. p. 142, 277 P. 308.)

Although *Hurst* thus held the Burlingame initiative invalid for noncompliance with the state zoning law, the court added a constitutional dictum, asserting that "the statutory notice and hearing . . . becomes necessary in order to satisfy the requirements of due process. . . ." (P. 141, 277 P. at p. 311.) In later years this constitutional dictum overshadowed the statutory holding of *Hurst*. Courts and commentators alike questioned *Hurst*'s statutory holding, but reexamination of that holding seemed pointless if the landowner's right to notice and hearing derived from constitutional compulsion independent of statute.

Two years ago, however, in *San Diego Bldg. Contractors Assn. v. City Council** * *we expressly disapproved the constitutional dictim of *Hurst* and later decisions. We held that a city violates no constitutional prohibition in enacting a zoning ordinance without notice and hearing to landowners, and hence may do so by initiative.

* * *That decision clears the way for a long-needed reconsideration of the actual holding of *Hurst* that bars a general law city from enacting a zoning ordinance by initiative.

At first glance it becomes apparent that something must be wrong with the reasoning in *Hurst*. Starting from a premise of equality—that the voters possess only the same legislative authority as does the city council—*Hurst* arrived at the conclusion that only the council and not the voters had the authority to enact zoning measures. Thus in the name of equality *Hurst* decrees inequality. The errors which lead to this non-sequitur appear after further analysis.

First, *Hurst*, erroneously contriving a conflict between state zoning statutes and the initiative law, set out to resolve that presumed conflict. No conflict occurs, however; the Legislature never intended the notice and hearing requirements of the zoning law to apply to the enactment of zoning initiatives. * * * The Legislature plainly drafted the questioned provisions of the zoning law with a view to ordinances adopted by vote of the city council; the provisions merely add certain additional procedural requirements to those already specified in government Code section 36931–36937 for the enactment of ordinances in general. Procedural requirements which govern *council* action, however, generally do not apply to initiatives, any more than the provisions of the initiative law govern the enactment of ordinances in council. No one would contend, for example, that an initiative of the people failed because a quorum of councilmen had not voted upon it, any more than one would contend that an ordinary ordinance of a council failed because a majority of voters had not voted upon it.

In the second place, *Hurst*, in treating the case as one involving a conflict between two statutes of equal status—the zoning law and the initiative law—overlooked a crucial distinction: that although the procedures for exercise of the right of initiative are spelled out in the initiative law, the right itself is guaranteed by the Constitution. The 1911 constitutional amendment, in reserving the right of initiative on behalf of municipal voters, stated that "This section is self-executing, but legislation may be enacted to facilitate its operation, *but in no way limiting or restricting* either the provisions of this section or *the powers herein reserved.*" * * * Although the Legislature can specify the manner in which general law cities enact ordinances restricting land use, legislation which permits council action but effectively bars initiative action may run afoul of the 1911 amendment. * * * Thus the notice and hearing provisions of the state zoning law, if interpreted to bar initiative land use ordinances, would be of doubtful constitutionality; all such doubt dissolves in the light of an interpretation which limits those requirements to ordinances enacted by city councils.

The fact that the zoning law is a special statute will not support *Hurst*; special legislation is still subject to constitutional limitations. If, for example, a "special" statute were enacted prohibiting criticism of a named official, such as the Vice-President, it would not be deemed controlling over the First Amendment on the ground that the latter is "general in its scope." Indeed if the constitutional power reserved by the people can be abridged by special statutes, then by enacting a host of special statutes the Legislature could totally abrogate that power.

Finally, *Hurst* erred in distinguishing *Dwyer v. City Council, supra*, 200 Cal. 505, 253 P. 932, on the ground that *Dwyer* involved a referendum on a zoning ordinance; as *Dwyer* itself pointed out, "if the right of referendum can be invoked, the corollary right to initiate legislation must be conceded to exist." (200 Cal. at p. 511, 253 P. at p. 934.)

Thus both precedent and established principles of judicial construction dictate the conclusion that *Hurst* erred in holding the notice and hearing provisions of the Zoning Act of 1917 applied to zoning ordinances enacted by initiative. Resting upon the precepts that statutes which are apparently in conflict should, if reasonably possible, by reconciled * * * that a statute should be construed to "eliminate . . . doubts as to the provision's constitutionality" * * * that the initiative power must be broadly construed, resolving all doubts in favor of the reserved power * * *, we resolve that *Hurst v. Burlingame, supra*, 207 Cal. 134, 277 P. 308, was incorrectly decided and is therefore overruled.

The notice and hearing provisions of the present zoning law (Gov.Code, §§ 65853 65857), like the provisions of the 1911 law before the *Hurst* court, make no mention of zoning by initiative. The procedures they prescribe refer only to action by the city council, and are inconsistent with the regulations that the Legislature has established to govern enactment of initiatives. For the reasons stated in our discussion of *Hurst v. Burlingame, supra* we conclude that sections 65853–65857 do not apply to initiative action, and that the Livermore ordinance is not invalid for noncompliance with those sections.

3. *The Livermore ordinance is not void for vagueness.*

The trial court found the ordinance unconstitutionally vague on two grounds: (1) that the ordinance did not contain sufficient specific standards for the issuance or denial of building permits, and (2) that it did not specify what person or agency was empowered to determine if the ordinance's standards have been met. We disagree with both rationales and find the ordinance sufficiently specific to fulfill constitutional requirements.

The controversy concerning the specificity of the ordinance centers upon the standard as to education. The ordinance prohibits issuance of residential building permits until a "satisfactory solution" has been evolved to the problem of "Education Facilities"; it defines a satisfactory solution as one characterized by "No double sessions in the schools nor overcrowded classrooms as determined by the California Education Code."

The term "double sessions" is sufficiently specific; as stated by Professor Deutsch, it "can be defined by reference to common practice, since the term is frequently used to refer to a situation where different groups of students in the same grade are attending the same school at different times of the day because of a lack of space." (Deutsch, *op. cit., supra*, pp. 22–23.) The phrase "overcrowded classrooms as determined by the California Education Code," however, is less clear, since nowhere in the Education Code does there appear a definition of "overcrowded classrooms."

The City of Livermore, however, points out that the ordinance does not refer to a definition of "overcrowded classrooms" contained in the Education Code, but to a *determination* of that subject. The language, it contends—and plaintiff does not dispute the contention—was intended to refer to resolution 3220, adopted by the board of the Livermore Valley Joint School District on January 18, 1972, in which that board, pursuant to authority granted it by Education Code section 1052, established clear and specific standards for determining whether schools are overcrowded.

Rather than interpret the ordinance in a manner which would expose it to the charge of unconstitutional vagueness, we adopt the suggestion of the city and construe the ordinance's standard on education to incorporate the specific guidelines established in board resolution 3220. In so doing we conform to the rule that enactments should be interpreted when possible to uphold their validity * * *, and the corollary principle that courts should construe enactments to give specific content to terms that might otherwise be unconstitutionally vague.* * *

Our decision in *Braxton v. Municipal Court* * * *, illustrates the principle and provides a close analogy to the present case. In *Braxton*, we construed Penal Code section 626.4, which authorized a state college or university to bar from its campus anyone who had "disrupted" the orderly operation of the campus. Defendants argued that the term "disrupted" was unconstitutionally vague. We determined, however, that the Legislature had intended to authorize banishment only of persons who had violated other more specific criminal statutes. Although section 626.4 did not expressly refer to such other statutes, we interpreted section 626.4 to incorporate the specific standards set out in those statutes in order to uphold the constitutionality of the section.* * *

Following the course suggested by *Braxton*, we construe the Livermore ordinance to incorporate the standards for determining the overcrowded condition of schools contained in the school board resolution of January 18, 1972. So construed, the ordinance provides a clear and ascertainable educational standard to guide the issuance or denial of a building permit, and is not void for vagueness.

The ordinance's standards relating to sewage and water supply present no constitutional difficulties. The sewage provision incorporates the "standards set by the Regional Water Quality Control Board"; that agency has in fact established specific and detailed standards of water purification and sewage disposal. The water supply provision describes a "satisfactory solution" as one in which water is not rationed, and "adequate water reserves for fire protection exist." The existence of rationing is an objective fact which can be ascertained by inquiry to the agencies having authority to ration. Although individuals may differ as to the adequacy of reserves for fire protection, the considered judgment of the agencies responsible for fire protection would provide a reliable guide.

Although we have determined that the ordinance's standards meet constitutional requirements of certainty, plaintiff argues, and the trial court held, that the ordinance is void because it fails to designate what agency or person determines whether these standards have been achieved. We question plaintiff's underlying assumption that an ordinance or statute is void if it does not specify on its face the agency that is to adjudge disputes concerning its application; by such a test most of the civil and criminal laws of this state would be invalidated. In any event, we believe that the Livermore ordinance, read in the light of the structure of Livermore's city government and the applicable judicial decisions, does indicate the method by which disagreements concerning the ordinance's standards are resolved.

The Livermore ordinance establishes standards to govern the issuance or denial of residential building permits. These standards must be directed in the first instance to the city building inspector, the official charged with the duty of issuing or denying such permits. Since the duties of this official are ministerial in character, his decision can be reviewed by writ of mandamus.* * * Thus the ultimate decision as to compliance with the standards will be rendered by the courts.* * *

4. *On the limited record before us, plaintiff cannot demonstrate that the Livermore ordinance is not a constitutional exercise of the city's police power.*

Plaintiff urges that we affirm the trial court's injunction on a ground which it raised below, but upon which the trial court did not rely. Plaintiff contends that the ordinance proposes, and will cause, the prevention of nonresidents from migrating to Livermore, and that the ordinance therefore attempts an unconstitutional exercise of the police power, both because no compelling state interest justifies its infringement upon the migrant's constitutionally protected right to travel, and because it exceeds the police power of the municipality.

The ordinance on its face imposes no absolute prohibition or limitation upon population growth or residential construction. It does provide that no building permits will issue unless standards for educational facilities, water supply and sewage disposal have been met, but plaintiff presented no evidence to show that the ordinance's standards were unreasonable or unrelated to their apparent objectives of protecting the public health and welfare. Thus, we do not here confront the question of the constitutionality of an ordinance which limits or bars population growth either directly in express language or indirectly by the imposition of prohibitory standards; we adjudicate only the validity of an ordinance limiting building permits in accord with standards that reasonably measure the adequacy of public services.

As we shall explain, the limited record here prevents us from resolving that constitutional issue. We deal here with a case in which a land use ordinance is challenged solely on the ground that it assertedly exceeds the municipality's authority under the police power; the challenger eschews any claim that the ordinance discriminates on a basis of race or wealth. Under such circumstances, we view the past decisions of this court and the federal courts as establishing the following standard: the land use restriction withstands constitutional attack if it is fairly debatable that the restriction in fact bears a reasonable relation to the general welfare. For the guidance of the trial court we point out that if a restriction significantly affects residents of surrounding communities, the constitutionality of the restriction must be measured by its impact not only upon the welfare of the enacting community, but upon the welfare of the surrounding region. We explain the process by which the court can determine whether or not such a restriction reasonably relates to the regional welfare. Since the record in the present case is limited to the pleadings and stipulations, and is devoid of evidence concerning the probable impact and duration of the ordinance's restrictions, we conclude that we cannot now adjudicate the constitutionality of the ordinance. Thus we cannot sustain the trial court judgment on the ground that the ordinance exceeds the city's authority under the police power; that issue can be resolved only after trial.

We turn now to consider plaintiff's arguments in greater detail. Seeking to capitalize upon the absence of an evidentiary record, plaintiff contends that the challenged ordinance must be subjected to strict judicial scrutiny; that it can be sustained only upon a showing of a compelling interest, and that the city has failed to make that showing.

Many writers have contended that exclusionary land use ordinances tend primarily to exclude racial minorities and the poor, and on that account should be subject to strict judicial scrutiny.* * * These writers, however, are concerned primarily with ordinances which ban or limit less expensive forms of housing while permitting expensive single family residences on large lots. The Livermore ordinance is not made from the mold; it impartially bans all residential construction, expensive or inexpensive. Consequently plaintiff at bar has eschewed reliance upon any claim that the ordinance discriminates on a basis of race or wealth.

Plaintiff's contention that the Livermore ordinance must be tested by a standard of strict scrutiny, and can be sustained only upon a showing of a compelling state interest, thus rests solely on plaintiff's assertion that the ordinance abridges a constitutionally protected right to travel. As we shall explain, however, the indirect burden imposed on the right to travel by the ordinance does not warrant application of the plaintiff's asserted standard of "compelling interest."

In asserting that legislation which burdens a right to travel requires strict scrutiny, and can be sustained only upon proof of compelling need, plaintiff relies on recent decisions of this court* * *

The legislation held invalid by those decisions, however, directly burdened the right to travel by distinguishing between nonresidents or newly arrived residents on the one hand and established residents on the other, and imposing penalties or disabilities on the former group.

Both the United States Supreme Court and this court have refused to apply the strict constitutional test to legislation, such as the present ordinance, which does not penalize travel and resettlement but merely makes it more difficult for the outsider to establish his residence in the place of his choosing.* * * The only contrary authority, the decision of the federal district court in *Construction Ind. Ass'n, Sonoma Cty. v. City of Petaluma* (N.D.Cal.1974) 375 F.Supp. 574 holding that an ordinance limiting residential construction must be supported by a compelling state interest has now been reversed by the Court of Appeals for the Ninth Circuit.* * *Most zoning and land use ordinances affect population growth and density. * * * As commentators have observed, to insist that such zoning laws are invalid unless the interests supporting the exclusion are compelling in character, and cannot be achieved by an alternative method, would result in wholesale invalidation of land use controls and endanger the validity of city and regional planning.* * * "Were a court to . . . hold that an inferred right of any group to live wherever it chooses might not be abridged without some compelling state interest, the law of zoning would be literally turned upside down; presumptions of validity would become presumptions of invalidity and traditional police powers of a state would be severely circumscribed."* * *

We conclude that the indirect burden upon the right to travel imposed by the Livermore ordinance does not call for strict judicial scrutiny. The validity of the challenged ordinance must be measured by the more liberal standards that have traditionally tested the validity of land use restrictions enacted under the municipal police power.

This conclusion brings us to plaintiff's final contention: that the Livermore ordinance exceeds the authority conferred upon the city under the police power. The constitutional measure by which we judge the validity of land use ordinance that is assailed as exceeding municipal authority under the police power dates in California from the landmark decision in *Miller v. Board of Public Works* (1925) 195 Cal. 477, 234 P. 381. Upholding a Los Angeles ordinance which excluded commercial and apartment uses from certain residential zones, we declared that an ordinance restricting land use was valid if it had a "real or substantial relation to the public health, safety, morals or general welfare." (195 Cal. at p. 490, 234 P. at p. 385.) A year later the United States Supreme Court, in the landmark case of *Euclid v. Ambler Co.* (1926) 272 U.S. 365, 47 S.Ct. 114, 71 L.Ed. 303, adopted the same test, holding that before a zoning ordinance can be held unconstitutional, "it must be said . . . that [its] provisions are clearly arbitrary and unreasonable, having no substantial relation to the public health, safety, morals, or general welfare." (272 U.S. at p. 395, 47 S.Ct. at p. 121.) Later California decisions confirmed that a land use restriction lies within the public power if it has a "reasonable relation to the public welfare."* * *

In deciding whether a challenged ordinance reasonably relates to the public welfare, the courts recognize that such ordinances are presumed to be constitutional, and come before the court with every intendment in their favor. (*Lockard v. City of Los Angeles, supra*, 33 Cal.2d 453, 460, 202 P.2d 38.) "The courts may differ with the zoning authorities as to the 'necessity or propriety of a enactment,' but so long as it remains a 'question upon which reasonable minds might differ,' there will be no judical interference with the municipality's determination of policy."* * *

In short, as stated by the Supreme Court in *Euclid v. Ambler Co., supra*, "If the validity . . . be fairly debatable, the legislative judgment must be allowed to control."

Recent decisions of th United States Supreme Court and the Court of Appeals for the Ninth Circuit have applied this liberal standard and, deferring to legislative judgment, have upheld ordinances attacked as exclusionary. In *Village of Belle Terre v. Boraas, supra*, 416 U.S. 1, 94 S.Ct. 1536, 39 L.Ed.2d 797, the court sustained an ordinance which banned all multiple family housing. The majority opinion by Justice Douglas found a rational basis for the ordinance in the community's desire to preserve a pleasant environment; "[t]he police power," he asserted, "is not confined to the elimination of filth, stench, and unhealthy places. It is ample to lay out zones where family values, youth values, and the blessings of quiet seclusion and clean air make the area a sanctuary for people." (416 U.S. at p. 9, 94 S.Ct. at p. 1541.) In dissent, Justice Marshall argued that the village's exclusion of groups of three or more unrelated persons from living in a single residence violated protected rights of privacy and association. He agreed, however, that the village could properly enact ordinances to control population density and restrict uncontrolled growth so long as it did not abridge fundamental rights,and that in reviewing such ordinances the courts should defer to the legislative judgment.* * *

In *Construction Industry Ass'n, Sonoma Cty. v. City of Petaluma, supra*, 522 F.2d 897, the Ninth Circuit Court of Appeals upheld a city ordinance fixing a housing development growth rate of 500 units per year. Relying largely on *Belle Terre v. Boraas, supra*, 416 U.S. 1, 94 S.Ct. 1536, 39 L.Ed.2d 797, the court concluded that "the concept of public welfare is sufficiently broad to uphold Petaluma's desire to preserve its small town character, its open space and low density of population, and to grow at an orderly and deliberate pace." (522 F.2d at pp. 908–909.) The Supreme Court denied certiorari.

We conclude from these federal decisions that when an exclusionary ordinance is challenged under the federal due process clause, the standard of constitutional adjudication remains that set forth in *Euclid v. Ambler Co., supra*, 272 U.S. 365, 47 S.Ct. 114, 71 L.Ed. 303: if it is fairly debatable that the ordinance is reasonable related to the public welfare, the ordinance is constitutional. A number of recent decisions from courts of other states, however, have declined to accord the traditional deference to legislative judgment in the review of exclusionary ordinances, and ruled that communities lacked authority to adopt such ordinances. Plaintiff urges that we apply the standards of review employed in those decisions in passing upon the instant ordinance.

The cases cited by plaintiff, however, cannot serve as a guide to resolution of the present controversy. Not only do those decisions rest, for the most part, upon principles of state law inapplicable in California, but, unlike the present case, all involve ordinances which impede the ability of low or moderate income persons to immigrate to a community but permit largely unimpeded entry by wealthier persons.

We therefore reaffirm the established constitutional principle that a local land use ordinance falls within the authority of the police power if it is reasonably related to the public welfare. Most previous decisions applying this test, however, have involved ordinances without substantial effect beyond the municipal boundaries. The present ordinance, in contrast, significantly affects the interests of nonresidents who are not represented in the city legislative body and cannot vote on a city initiative. We therefore believe it desirable for the guidance of the trial court to clarify the application of the traditional police power test to an ordinance which significantly affects nonresidents of the municipality.

When we inquire whether an ordinance reasonably relates to the public welfare, inquiry should begin by asking *whose* welfare must the ordinance serve. In past cases, when discussing ordinances without significant effect beyond the municipal boundaries, we have been content to assume that the ordinance need only reasonably relate to the welfare of the enacting municipality and its residents. But municipalities are not isolated islands remote from the needs and problems of the area in which they are located; thus an ordinance, superficially reasonable from the limited viewpoint of the municipality, may be disclosed as unreasonable when viewed from a larger perspective.

These considerations impel us to the conclusion that the proper constitutional test is one which inquires whether the ordinance reasonably relates to the welfare of those whom it significantly affects. If its impact is limited to the city boundaries, the inquiry may be limited accordingly; if, as alleged here, the ordinance may strongly influence the supply and distribution of housing for an entire metropolitan region, judicial inquiry must consider the welfare of that region.

As far back as *Euclid v. Ambler Co.*, courts recognized "the possibility of cases where the general public interest would so far outweigh the interest of the municipality that the municipality would not be allowed to stand in the way." * * *Recently, * * * we stated that "To hold . . . that defendant city may zone the land within its border without any concern for [nonresidents] would indeed 'make a fetish out of invisible municipal boundary lines and a mockery of the principles of zoning.'" (P. 548, 99 Cal.Rptr. p. 749, 492 P.2d p. 1141.) The New Jersey Supreme Court summed up the principle and explained its doctrinal basis: "[I]t is fundamental and not to be forgotten that the zoning power is a police power of the state and the local authority is acting only as a delegate of that power and is restricted in the same manner as is the state. So, when regulation does have a substantial external impact, the welfare of the state's citizens beyond the borders of the particular municipality cannot be disregarded and must be recognized and served."

We explain the process by which a trial court may determine whether a challenged restriction reasonably relates to the regional welfare. The first step in that analysis is to forecast the probable effect and duration of the restriction. In the instant case the Livermore ordinance posits a total ban on residential construction, but one which terminates as soon as public facilities reach specified standards. Thus to evaluate the impact of the restriction, the court must ascertain the extent to which public facilities currently fall short of the specified standards, must inquire whether the city or appropriate regional agencies have undertaken to construct needed improvements, and must determine when the improvements are likely to be completed.

The second step is to identify the competing interests affected by the restriction. We touch in this area deep social antagonisms. We allude to the conflict between the environmental protectionist and the egalitarian humanists; a collision between the forces that would save the benefits of nature and those that would preserve the opportunity of people in general to settle. Suburban residents who seek to overcome problems of inadequate schools and public facilities to secure "the blessing of quiet seclusion and clear air" and to "make the area a sanctuary for people"* * * may assert a vital interest in limiting immigration in their community. Outsiders searching for a place to live in the face of a growing shortage of adequate housing, and hoping to share in the perceived benefits of suburban life, may present a countervailing interest opposing barriers and immigration.

Having identified and weighed the competing interests, the final step is to determine whether the ordinance, in light of its probable impact, represents a reasonable accommodation of the competing interests. We do not hold that a court in inquiring whether an ordinance reasonably relates to the regional welfare, cannot defer to the judgment of the municipality's legislative body. But judicial deference is not judicial abdication. The ordinance must have a *real and substantial* relation to the public welfare. (*Miller v. Board of Public Works, supra*, 195 Cal. 477, 490, 234, P. 381.) There must be a reasonable basis in fact, not in fancy, to support the legislative determination.* * * that the ordinance reasonably relates to the regional welfare, it cannot be assumed that a land use ordinance can *never* be invalidated as an enactment in excess of the police power.

The burden rests with the party challenging the constitutionality of an ordinance to present the evidence and documentation which the court will require in undertaking this constitutional analysis. Plaintiff in the present case has not yet attempted to shoulder that burden. Although plaintiff obtained a stipulation that as of the date of trial the ordinance's goals had not been fulfilled, it presented no evidence to show the likely duration or effect of the ordinance's restriction upon building permits. We must presume that the City of Livermore and appropriate regional agencies will attempt in good faith to provide that community with adequate schools, sewage disposal facilities, and a sufficient water supply; Plaintiff, however, has not presented evidence to show whether the city and such agencies have undertaken to construct the needed improvements or when such improvements will be completed. Consequently we cannot determine the impact upon either Livermore or the surrounding region of the ordinance's restriction on the issuance of building permit pending achievement of its goals.

With respect to the competing interests, plaintiff asserts the existence of an acute housing shortage in the San Francisco Bay Area, but presents no evidence to document that shortage or to relate it to the probable effect of the Livermore ordinance. Defendants maintain that Livermore has severe problems of air pollution and inadequate public facilities which make it reasonable to divert new housing, at least temporarily, to other communities but offer no evidence to support that claim. Without an evidentiary record to demonstrate the validity and significance of the asserted interests, we cannot determine whether the instant ordinance attempts a reasonable accommodation of those interests.

In short, we cannot determine on the pleadings and stipulations alone whether this ordinance reasonably relates to the general welfare of the region it affects. The ordinance carries the presumption of constitutionality; plaintiff cannot overcome that presumption on the limited record before us. Thus the judgment rendered on this limited record cannot be sustained on the ground that the initiative ordinance falls beyond the proper scope of the police power.

5. *Conclusion.*

For the reasons we have explained, the Livermore ordinance is neither invalid on the ground that it was enacted by initiative nor unconstitutional by reason of vagueness. The more difficult question whether the measure is one which reasonably relates to the welfare of the region affected by its exclusionary impact, and thus falls within the police power of the city, cannot be decided on the limited record here. That issue can only be resolved by a trial at which evidence is presented to document the probable impact of the ordinance open the municipality and the surrounding region.

The judgment of the superior court is reversed, and the cause remanded for further proceedings consistent with the views expressed herein.

MOSK, Justice (dissenting).

I dissent.

Limitations on growth may be justified in resort communities, beach and lake and mountain sites, and other rural and recreational areas; such restrictions are generally designed to preserve nature's environment for the benefit of all mankind. They fulfill our fiduciary obligation to posterity. As Thomas Jefferson wrote,the earth belongs to the living, but in usufruct.[1]

But there is a vast qualitative difference when a suburban community invokes an elitist concept to construct a mythical moat around its perimeter, not for the benefit of mankind but to exclude all but its fortunate current residents.

The procedural posture of the ordinance does not detain me; the majority is correct in overruling *Hurst v. Burlingame*. The Hurst doctrine has long outlived its usefulness; it should no longer hobble the initiative process. Where I part company with the majority is in its substantive holding that a total exclusion of new residents can be constitutionally accomplished under a city's police power.

The majority, somewhat desultorily, deny that the ordinance imposes an absolute prohibition upon population growth or residential construction. It is true that the measure prohibits the issuance of building permits for single-family residential, multiple residential and trailer residential units until designated public services meet specified standards. But to see such restriction in practicality as something short of total prohibition is to employ ostrich vision.

First of all, the ordinance provides no timetable or dates by which the public services are to be made adequate. Thus the moratorium on permits is likely to continue for decades, or at least until attrition ultimately reduces the present population. Second, it is obvious that no inducement exists for *present* residents to expend their resources to render facilities adequate for the purpose of accommodating *future* residents. It would seem more rational, if improved services are really contemplated for any time in the foreseeable future, to admit the new residents and compel them to make their proportionate contribution to the cost of the educational, sewage and water services. Thus it cannot seriously be argued that Livermore maintains anything other than total exclusion.

The trial court found, inter alia, that the ordinance prohibited the issuance of building permits for residential purposes until certain conditions are met, but the measure does not provide that any person or agency is required to expend or commence any efforts on behalf of the city to meet the requirements. Nor is the city itself obliged to act within any specified time to cure its own deficiencies. Thus, in these circumstances procrastination produces its own reward: continued exclusion of new residents.

The significant omissions, when noted in relation to the ordinance preamble, reveal that the underlying purpose of the measure is "to control residential building permits in the City of Livermore"—translation: to keep newcomers out of the city—and not to solve the purported inadequacies in municipal educational, sewage and water services. Livermore concedes no building permits are now being issued and it relates no current or prospective schedule designed to correct its defective municipal services.

[1]Jefferson called this principle "self-evident."

A municipal policy of preventing acquisition and development of property by nonresidents clearly violates article I, sections 1 and 7, subdivisions (a) and (b), of the Constitution of California.

Exclusion of unwanted outsiders, while a more frequent phenomenon recently, is not entirely innovative. The state of California made an abortive effort toward exclusivity back in the 1930s as part of a scheme to stem the influx of poor migrants from the dust bowl states of the southwest. The additional burden these indigent new residents placed on California services and facilities was severely aggravated by the great depression of that period. In *Edwards v. California* * * * the Supreme Court held, however, that the nature of the union established by the Constitution did not permit any one state to "isolate itself from the difficulties common to all of them by restraining the transportation of persons and property across its borders." The sanction against immigration of indigents was invalidated.

If California could not protect itself from the growth of problems of that era, may Livermore build a Chinese Wall to insulate itself from growth problems today? And if Livermore may do so, why not every municipality in Alameda County and in all other counties in Northern California? With a patchwork of enclaves the inevitable result will be creation of an aristocracy housed in exclusive suburbs while modest wage earners will be confined to declining neighborhoods, crowded into sterile, monotonous, multifamily projects, or assigned to pockets of marginal housing on the urban fringe. The overriding objective should be to minimize rather than exacerbate social and economic disparities, to lower barriers rather than raise them, to emphasize heterogeneity rather than homogeneity, to increase choice rather than limit it.

I am aware, of course, of the decision in *Village of Belle Terre v. Boraas* * * * in which the Supreme Court, speaking through Justice Douglas, rejected challenges to an ordinance restricting land use to one-family dwellings, with a very narrow definition of "family," excluding lodging houses, boarding houses, fraternity houses, or multiple-dwelling houses. The village sought to assure that it would never grow much larger than 700 persons living in 220 residences. Comparable, although some growth was permitted, was the ordinance approved in *Construction Ind. Assn., Sonoma Cty. v. City of Petaluma* * * * Also similar, although allowing phased growth, was *Golden v. Planning Board of Town of Ramapo*[2] * * *

In *Belle Terre*, Justice Douglas declared, "The police power is not confined to elimination of filth, stench, and unhealthy places. It is ample to lay out zones where family values, youth values, and the blessings of quiet seclusion and clean air make the area a sanctuary for people. . . . A quiet place where yards are wide, people few, and motor vehicles restricted are legitimate guidelines in a land-use project addressed to family needs."

This is a comforting environmentalist declaration with which few would disagree, although the result was to allow the village of Belle Terre to remain an affluent island. Nevertheless, "preservation of the character of the community" is a stirring slogan, at least where it is used for nothing more harmful than the exclusion of the six students who rented the large house in Belle Terre. Complications arise when ordinances are employed to exclude not merely student lodgers, but all outsiders. While the affluent may seek a congenial suburban atmosphere other than Belle Terre or Livermore, what are the alternatives for those in megalopolitan areas who cannot afford similar selectivity?

[2]There are other variations in traditional zoning that attempt to accommodate both orderly development and community concerns: flexible zoning, compensatory regulations, planned unit development, density zoning, contract zoning, floating zoning and time-phased zoning. Until now total prohibition of all building permits has never been included among acceptable zoning schemes.

The right of all persons to acquire housing is not a mere esoteric principle; it has commanded recognition in a wide spectrum of aspects. In *Shelley v. Kraemer* * * *, race restrictive covenants were declared to be constitutionally unenforceable. Chief Justice Vinson noted in his opinion that among the guarantees of the Fourteenth Amendment "are the rights to acquire, enjoy, own and dispose of property." In *Reitman v. Mulkey* * * *, the Supreme Court upheld our invalidation of a ballot proposition, declaring that "'Neither the State nor any subdivision or agency thereof shall deny, limit or abridge, directly or indirectly, the right of any person, who is willing or desires to sell, lease or rent any part or all of his real property, to decline to sell, lease or rent such property to such person or persons as he, in his absolute discretion, chooses.'" Justice Douglas, in a concurring opinion in *Reitman*, went even further to insist that "housing is clearly marked with the public interest."* * *

One thing emerges with clarity from the foregoing and from numerous related cases: access to housing is regarded by the Supreme Court as a matter of serious social and constitutional concern. While this interest has generally been manifest in the context of racial discrimination, there is no valid reason for not invoking the principle when persons of all races and of all economic groups are involved. There are no invariable racial or economic characteristics of the goodly numbers of families which seek social mobility, the opportunities for the good life available in a suburban atmosphere, and access to types of housing, education and employment differing from those indigenous to crowded urban centers.

There is a plethora of commentary on efforts, in a variety of contexts, of local communities to discourage the influx of outsiders. In virtually every instance, however, the cities limited availability of housing; until now it has never been seriously contemplated that a community would attempt total exclusion by refusing all building permits.* * *

The trend in the more perceptive jurisdictions is to prevent municipalities from selfishly donning blinders to obscure the problems of their neighbors. The Supreme Court of New Jersey has taken the lead in frowning upon creation of local exclusive enclaves and is insisting upon consideration of regional housing needs. In *Oakwood at Madison, Inc. v. Township of Madison* * * * the court held, "In pursuing the valid zoning purpose of a balanced community, a municipality must not ignore housing needs, that is, its fair proportion of the obligation to meet the housing needs of its own population *and of the region*. Housing needs are encompassed within the general welfare. *The general welfare does not stop at each municipal boundary.*" (Italics added.)

Again in the oft-cited *Mt. Laurel* case * * * the New Jersey Supreme Court required that municipalities afford the opportunity for housing, "at least to the extent of the municipality's fair share of the present and *prospective regional need* therefor." (Italics added.) * * *

Pennsylvania is another state that has forthrightly spoken out against ordinances "designed to be exclusive and exclusionary." In *National Land and Investment Company v. Kohn*, a case remarkably similar to the instant matter, the Easttown community refused to admit new residents "unless such admittance will not create any additional burdens upon governmental functions and services." Justice Roberts, for the Supreme Court, replied: "The question posed is whether the township can stand in the way of the natural forces which send our growing population into hitherto undeveloped areas in search of a comfortable place to live. We have concluded not. A zoning ordinance whose primary purpose is to prevent the entrance of newcomers in order to avoid future burdens, economic and otherwise, upon the administration of public services and facilities cannot be held valid."

In *Appeal of Girsh* the Pennsylvania Supreme Court again spoke from a broad perspective. The community involved there barred all apartment houses for the identical reasons advanced by Livermore here. Said the court with irrefutable logic:

"Appellee argues that apartment uses would cause a significant population increase with a resulting strain on available municipal services and roads, and would clash with the existing residential neighborhood. But we *explicitly* rejected both these claims in *National Land*, supra: 'Zoning is a tool in the hands of governmental bodies which enables them to more effectively meet the demands of evolving and growing communities. It must not and can not be used by those officials as an instrument by which they may shirk their responsibilities. Zoning is a means by which a governmental body can plan for the future—it may not be used as a means to deny the future. . . . Zoning provisions may not be used . . . to avoid the increased responsibilities and economic burdens which time and natural growth invariably bring.'

". . . Appellee here has simply made a decision that it is content with things as they are, and that the expense or change in character that would result from people moving in to find 'a comfortable place to live' are for someone else to worry about. That decision is unacceptable. Statistics indicate that people are attempting to move away from the urban core areas, relieving the grossly overcrowded conditions that exist in most of our major cities. . . . It follows then that formerly 'outlying', somewhat rural communities, are becoming logical areas for development and population growth—in a sense suburbs to the suburbs. With improvements in regional transportation systems, these areas also are now more accessible to the central city.

"In light of this, Nether Providence Township may not permissibly choose to only take as many people as can live in single-family housing, in effect freezing the population at near present levels. Obviously if every municipality took that view, population spread would be completely frustrated. Municipal services must be provided *somewhere*, and if Nether Providence is a logical place for development to take place, it should not be heard to say that it will not bear its rightful part of the burden."* * *

In *Girsh* the Pennsylvania court added: "Perhaps in an ideal world, planning and zoning would be done on a *regional* basis, so that a given community would have apartments, while an adjoining community would not. But as long as we allow zoning to be done community by community, it is intolerable to allow one municipality (or many municipalities) to close its doors at the expense of surrounding communities and the central city." * * *

Ordinances comparable to those invalidated in New Jersey and Pennsylvania have also been held invalid in Michigan * * *

In sum, I realize the easiest course is for this court to defer to the political judgment of the townspeople of Livermore, on a they-know-what's-best-for-them theory * * * But conceptually, when a locality adopts a comprehensive, articulated program to prevent any population growth over the foreseeable future, it places its public policy intentions visibly on the table for judicial scrutiny and constitutional analysis.

Communities adopt growth limits from a variety of motives. There may be conservationists genuinely motivated to preserve general or specific environments. There may be others whose motivation is social exclusionism, racial exclusion, racial discrimination, income segregation, fiscal protection, or just fear of any future change; each of these purposes is well served by growth prevention.

Whatever the motivation, total exclusion of people from a community is both immoral and illegal. * * * Courts have a duty to prevent such practices, while at the same time recognizing the validity of genuine conservationist efforts.

The problem is not insoluble, nor does it necessarily provoke extreme results. Indeed, the solution can be relatively simple if municipal agencies would consider the aspirations of society as a whole, rather than merely the effect upon their narrow constituency. * * * Accommodation between environmental preservation and satisfaction of housing needs can be reached through rational guidelines for land-use decision-making. Ours, of course, is not the legislative function. But two legal inhibitions must be the benchmark of any such guidelines. First, any absolute prohibition on housing development is presumptively invalid. And second, local regulations, based on parochialism, that limit population densities in growing suburban areas may be found invalid unless the community is absorbing a reasonable share of the region's population pressures.

Under the foregoing test, the Livermore ordinance is fatally flawed. I would affirm the judgment of the trial court.

ROBINSON
v.
The CITY OF BOULDER

547 P.2d 228, (1976)

DAY, Justice.

This is an appeal brought by appellant, City of Boulder (Boulder), seeking reversal of a trial court order mandating its extension of water and sewer service to appellees. We affirm.

Appellees (landowners) sought to subdivide approximately 79 acres of land in the Gunbarrel Hill area northeast of Boulder and outside of its city limits. The landowners proposed a residential development in conformity with its county rural residential (RR) zoning.

As a condition precedent to considering the question of development, the county required the landowners to secure water and sewer services; they were referred to the city for that purpose.

Boulder operates a water and sewer utility system. In the mid 1960's it defined an area beyond its corporate limits, including the subject property, for which it intended to be the only water and sewer servicing agency. The record reflects that this was accomplished in order to gain indirect control over the development of property located within the service area. Boulder contracted with and provided water and sewer service to the Boulder Valley Water and Sanitation District (the district), which is located within the service area. The subject property is immediately adjacent to the district. The contract between Boulder and the district vests in the former almost total control over water and sewer service within district boundaries. The latter functions in merely a nominal administrative capacity. For example, Boulder retains control over all engineering and construction aspect of the service as well as decision-making power over the district's authority to expand its boundaries. Pursuant to a city ordinance, the district cannot increase its service area without the approval of city council.

The landowners applied to the district for inclusion, and the application was accepted; however, Boulder disapproved the action on the grounds that the landowners' proposal was inconsistent with the Boulder Valley Comprehensive Plan and various aspects of the city's interim growth policy. The trial court found that:

> ". . . The City seeks to effect its growth rate regulation goals in the Gunbarrel Hill area by using its water and sewer utility as the means to accomplish its goals. . . ."

The decision was *not* based on Boulder's incapacity to supply the service or the property's remote location from existing facilities or any economic considerations.

The landowners then filed suit for declaratory relief, and the district court concluded that Boulder is operating in the capacity of a public utility in the Gunbarrel area. In terms of supplying water and sewer services, it must treat all members of the public within its franchise area alike—including these landowners. The court held that Boulder had unjustly discriminated against appellees by denying them service, while having previously approved service extensions to neighboring residential and industrial developments. The court concluded that Boulder can only refuse to extend its service to landowners for utility-related reasons. Growth control and land use planning considerations do not suffice. We agree.

I.

On appeal Boulder argues that its service program in Gunbarrel is not a public utility under the test which we enunciated in *City of Englewood v. Denver*, (1951):

> ". . . to fall into the class of public utility, a business or enterprise must be impressed with a public interest and that those engaged in the conduct thereof must hold themselves out as serving or ready to serve all members of the public, who may require it, to the extent of their capacity. The nature of the service must be such that all members of the public have an enforceable right to demand it. . ."

Boulder contends that it has never held itself out as being ready to serve all members of the public to the extent of its capacity. The trial court made findings to the contrary and the record amply supports them.* * *

Boulder relies on *City of Englewood, supra*, to support its position that it is not operating as a public utility within the area in question; that reliance is misplaced. The determination that Denver did not operate as a public utility is supplying Englewood with water was premised on an entirely different factual background. Denver's supplying of water to Englewood users was wholly incidental to the operation of its water system which was established for the purpose of supplying Denver inhabitants. Denver did not "stake out" a territory in Englewood and seek to become the sole supplier of water in the territory. Here, by agreements with other suppliers to the effect that the latter would not service the Gunbarrel area and by opposing other methods or sources of supply, Boulder has secured a monopoly over area water and sewer utilities. Further, as the trial court pointed out:

> ". . . The City of Boulder had dedicated its water and sewer service to public use to benefit both the inhabitants of Boulder and the residents of the Gunbarrel Hill area in the interest of controlling the growth of the area and to provide living qualities which the City deems desirable. . . ."

II.

Boulder argues that even if its program satisfies the test of a public utility in the Gunbarrel area that it may use public policy considerations in administering its service program. It contends that the rules which apply to private utilities should not apply to a governmental utility authorized to implement governmental objectives, one of which is the adoption of a master plan of development.

Section 31-23-106(1), C.R.S.1973, in relevant part, states:

> "*Master plan.* (1) It is the duty of the municipal planning commission to make and adopt a master plan for the physical development of the municipality, including any areas outside of its boundaries, *subject to the approval of the legislative or*

governing body having jurisdiction thereof, which in the commission's judgment, bear relation to the planning of such municipality. Such plan, with the accompanying maps, plats, charts, and descriptive matter, shall show the commission's recommendations for the development of said territory including, among other things:

"(b) The general location and extent of *public utilities* and terminals, whether publicly or privately owned or operated, *for water*, light, *sanitation*, transportation, communication, power, and other purposes;

"(c) The removal, relocation, widening, narrowing, vacating, abandonment, change of use, or extension of any of the ways, grounds, open spaces, buildings, property, *utility*, or terminals referred to in paragraphs (a) and (b) of this subsection (1); . . ." (Emphasis added.)

To this end, the city of Boulder and Boulder County jointly developed and adopted the Boulder Valley Comprehensive Plan, one of the purposes of which is to provide a basis for the discretionary land use decisions which it must make. Boulder also cites section 31-23-109, C.R.S.1973, which states in relevant part:

"*Legal status of official plan*. When the municipal planning commission has adopted the master plan of the municipality or one or more major sections or districts thereof, no street, square, park or other public way, ground or open space, or public building or structure, or *publicly* or privately *owned public utility* shall be constructed or authorized in the municipality or in such planned section and district until the location, character, and extent thereof has been submitted for approval by the commission. In case of disapproval, the commission shall communicate its reason to the council, which has the power to overrule such disapproval by a recorded vote of not less than two-thirds of its entire membership. If the public way, ground space, building, structure, or utility is one the authorization or financing of which does not, under the law or charter provisions governing the same, fall within the province of the municipal council, then the submission to the planning commission shall be by the board, commission, or body having jurisdiction, and the planning commission's disapproval may be overruled by said board, commission, or body by a vote of not less than two-thirds of its membership. The failure of the commission to act within sixty days from and after the date of official submission to it shall be deemed approval." (Emphasis added.)

Boulder argues that its decision to deny the extension of services to the landowners in this case was based on the proposed development's noncompliance with growth projections outlined in the comprehensive plan. In the event of an alleged conflict between Boulder's public utility and land use planning duties we are asked to rule that the latter are paramount.

A municipality is without jurisdiction over territory outside its municipal limits in the absence of legislation. *See Pueblo v. Flanders*, 122 Colo. 571, 225 P.2d 832 (1950). We find nothing in the above-cited statutes which indicates a legislative intent to broaden a city's authority in a case such as the one before us. In our view, section 31-23-106(1) and 31-23-109 place ultimate governmental authority in matters pertaining to land use in unincorporated areas in the county. In effect a city is given only an advisory role.

The record reflects that the proposed development would comply with county zoning regulations; and the county planning staff has indicated that it conforms with their interpretation of the comprehensive plan, though final consideration was put off pending a determination of whether the area would have adequate water and sewer facilities.

In view of the fact that it is the board of county commissioners—not Boulder—which must make the ultimate decision as to the approval or disapproval of the proposed development, we do not need to address the question of whether the Boulder Valley Comprehensive Plan relieves the City of Boulder of its duty to the public in its proprietary role as a public utility.

In conclusion, we hold that inasmuch as Boulder is the sole and exclusive provider of water and sewer services in the area surrounding the subject property, it is a public utility. As such, it holds itself out as ready and able to serve those in the territory who require the service. There is no utility related reason, such as insufficient water, preventing it from extending these services to the landowners. Unless such reasons exist, Boulder cannot refuse to serve the people in the subject area.

Judgment affirmed.

Index